Masonry Construction Manual

PFEIFER
RAMCKE
ACHTZIGER
ZILCH

BIRKHÄUSER – PUBLISHERS FOR ARCHITECTURE
BASEL · BOSTON · BERLIN

EDITION DETAIL
MÜNCHEN

The original German edition of this book was conceived and developed by
DETAIL, Review of Architecture

Authors:

Günter Pfeifer, Professor, freelance architect
Department of Design and Construction I, Darmstadt Technical University

Rolf Ramcke, Prof. Dipl.-Ing., architect
Department of Planning Theory and Building Technology, Humboldt University, Berlin

Joachim Achtziger, Dr.-Ing.
Forschungsinstitut für Wärmeschutz e.V. (Thermal Insulation Research Institute), Munich

Konrad Zilch, Prof. Dr.-Ing.
Martin Schätz, Dr.-Ing.
Chair of Monolithic Construction, Munich Technical University

Published by:
Institut für internationale Architektur-Dokumentation GmbH, Munich

Editorial services:
Andreas Gabriel, Dipl.-Ing.; Christian Schittich, Dipl.-Ing.;
Sabine Drey, Dipl.-Ing.; Cornelia Hilpert M.A.;
Johanna Reichel-Vossen, Dipl.-Ing.; Heike Werner, Dipl.-Ing.;
Drawings:
Marion Griese, Dipl.-Ing.; Kathrin Draeger, Dipl.-Ing.; Martin Hämmel, Dipl.-Ing.;
Oliver Katzauer, Dipl.-Ing.; Emese Köszegi, Dipl.-Ing.; Nicola Kollmann, Dipl.-Ing.;
Peter Lingenfelser, Dipl.-Ing.; Isabel Mayer

Translators (German/English):
Gerd Söffker, Philip Thrift, Hannover; Elizabeth Schwaiger, Toronto

A CIP catalogue record for this book is available from the Library of Congress,
Washington, D.C., USA

Deutsche Bibliothek – Cataloging-in-Publication Data

Masonry construction manual / [publ. by: Institut für Internationale Architektur-Dokumentation GmbH, Munich].
Joachim Achtziger ... [Transl. (German/Engl.): Gerd Söffker; Philip Thrift, Elizabeth Schwaiger]. –
Basel; Boston; Berlin: Birkhäuser; München: Ed. Detail, 2001
ISBN 3-7643-6543-9

This book is also available in a German language edition (ISBN 3-7643-6478-5).

© 2001 Birkhäuser – Publishers for Architecture, P.O. Box 133, CH-4010 Basel, Switzerland
Member of the BSpringer Publishing Group.

Printed on acid-free paper produced from chlorine-free pulp. TCF ∞

Printed in Germany

ISBN 3-7643-6543-9

9 8 7 6 5 4 3 2 1   http://www.birkhauser.ch

Contents

Preface

When it was first published more than 15 years ago, the *Masonry Construction Manual* immediately established itself as a standard work dealing with all the issues and problems of masonry construction. Its great success is evident in the fact that it became necessary to reissue the book a total of five times. Although each new issue had been adapted to take new technical developments into account, changes to the standards and regulations governing the building industry, likewise changing architectural fashions and aesthetic values, had assumed such dimensions over this long period of time that a completely new edition of the work had by now become essential. This new edition would allow the authors to present, demonstrate and assess the current state of the art in masonry construction.

There are many indications that masonry construction will, in future, be paid more attention in the building industry. Although masonry was just as popular as ever during the late 20th century, in terms of respect and significance it had taken a back seat behind elegant designs of metal, stone panels and glass. Today, we detect a need for a style of architecture that puts a personal imprint on a structure to contrast with the anonymously controlled production process. Masonry construction can achieve this.

The requirements of energy conservation, which play an ever increasing role in building, can be realized in masonry in a way that is compatible with our modern lives. In its infinite number of possibilities we see the spirit and charm of an ancient but never outdated trade. The revolutionary technical inventions of the 19th century, which made possible constructions of concrete, reinforced concrete, steel, glass and many other materials, also brought about fundamental changes in the production and use of masonry materials. Since then the very essence of building has had to be redefined and relearned at regular intervals. During this evolution, masonry construction, like all other forms of building, adapted to the technical conditions in a way appropriate to the material, thus proving its unique, fascinating character. However, realization and aesthetic accomplishment did not always correspond to these developments; shortcomings are evident which must be attributed to the designers and observers but not the masonry construction itself.

This new edition of the *Masonry Construction Manual* provides a fresh, apposite means of expression for the latest developments in this field. It acts as a textbook for planners, teachers and students, as a work of reference for all today's issues in masonry construction, and also as a source of inspiration for individual creations in masonry, a material which immediately inspires engineering faith, which quickly reveals the limits to its engineering and architectural strengths, and thereby exerts a unique incentive to draw artistic vigour from this dilemma. The simplicity of the masonry material allows the observer to experience the design process, as it were, including him in the creation – watching and supervising. This compulsion to establish clarity leads to a vitality which fascinates us again and again on buildings of masonry.

The Authors

Part 1 · Masonry in architecture

What is masonry?

Positions in history

Masonry materials · Clay brick masonry ·
The unifying force of building · The plastic
spirit in Greek and Roman architecture ·
Technical advances in Roman antiquity ·
Technical development in the Middle Ages ·
Geometry and system in the Middle Ages ·
The world as a representational system ·
The functional method · Technical developments in the 19th century · The technical
aesthetics of brick · Historicism and dogmatism · Jugendstil – a new path · The
United States in the 19th century · Action-
oriented building · The power of expression
in continuous space · System rationality
and structural analysis

Design

Basics · Manufacture · Formats · Colours
and surfaces · The bond · Natural stone ·
The joint · Division in masonry · Vaults ·
Openings and lintels · Columns and piers ·
Plinths and ramps · Terminations and junctions · Sills · Framework · Free-standing
walls

Masonry – today and tomorrow

Masonry in architecture

Rolf Ramcke

What is masonry?

We rarely see the simplicity of building – the layering and jointing – at work on modern construction sites. Today, the scene is dominated by "montage", assembly and prefabricated building components. "Montage", it would seem, has come to dominate our everyday lives. Robert Musil even likened a person's character, his nature, to a "montage". What we experience as nature is merely naturalized. On closer inspection, the fiction of untouched nature is rapidly debunked.

These internal and external conditions of daily life are rarely at the forefront of our thoughts. It takes images of catastrophic events – a car accident, a building after an explosion – to open a window and look behind the mask of stability. The main task of the mask is to provide a visual representation of stability without being stable itself.

If we are only too willing to accept the daily "montage" of architecture as an image, it is because we live in an image-driven world. Images have more clout than the objects they represent. Hence the importance of the observer and his perception. He must decipher the illusion and judge the veracity of the image in its deciphered state. In other words: the act of looking shapes the object that is looked upon. And the image formed by the act of looking is also changed. On closer inspection, the image of our highly artificial world is revealed as a web of relationships between its components.

Today, building is a deliberate and carefully planned intervention in this vast array of mutual dependencies, in an effort to render them accessible within the planning limitations and to subjugate them to our intention. Unintentional effects must be taken into consideration.

In this interpretation of building, material is but one interchangeable aspect of planning, dependent on supply. The formative and aesthetic power of the natural resistance inherent in a material is simply eliminated through substitution. This "virtual" approach to design makes building materials arbitrary in a synthesizing manner. Resistance is not tolerated. Layering and jointing, the simplicity of building

1.1.1

turns out to be antagonistic. Being simple is not the same as being accommodating. Simplicity tends to baffle and amaze because it contains what is basic and renders it visible.

Building a wall is an activity that obscures its own process. A wall is impenetrable, its core is inaccessible. Layering and jointing enable the surface to communicate this activity in extraordinary variety, as if the surface held out a promise to provide insight into the plan of the internal design. The observer is always in search of traces. Traces intentionally and unintentionally left behind on the surface of the wall are self-referential signs, the legacy of its mass. It has appropriately been referred to as mimesis, a play of gestures and expressions. The interpretation of the observer produces a different cipher for each age, thereby forming a new image of history. All surfaces – even those that are hermetic – are visible and hence open to interpretation.

The following sections explore a variety of positions against the background of the history of masonry. They are by no means intended as examples for contemporary building but allow us to draw conclusions with regard to our own perception. These conclusions, in turn, can alter our present perspectives, thereby making a contribution to current issues in designing masonry structures.

In each instance, we aim to answer the question: What is masonry?

The question of authenticity is a natural by-product of this investigation. Illusions, even forgeries can be legitimate means of design. The observer is deliberately addressed. The person shapes the perception. A phenomenology of perception would lead to the question of what is illusory in an illusion, what is forged in a forgery. The question of authenticity and verisimilitude is one of image interpretation and discovery.

Another question arises from the fact that the technical development in building and the perception of building have grown in opposite directions, with no parallels or converging lines. Thus far, there are few convincing answers that provide a clear differentiation – from the perspective of design – between the meaning of layering units as a half-brick curtain wall or as a bonded wall. Where does this deficit originate? Is it a poverty of theory?

And finally, there is yet another conflict to be addressed, one that has arisen only recently in the urban renewal of Berlin and in the current debate of tectonic versus geometric architectural interpretation. The morphological challenge that a building's character must express its function seems to contradict another challenge, namely that the facade must reflect the building's functions. In other words, the facade is understood as a mirror of internal relationships. Is the expression in masonry an extension of the building's character, directed at effect? Or should masonry be an informative reflection of internal processes relating to structure, building science and use? We've come full circle, back to our original question: What is masonry?

Positions in history

When people shifted from a nomadic to a settled lifestyle, they began to build walls to create solid, self-made security, enduring foundations for settlements, to differentiate between identity, beginning and end. Such concepts are only insufficiently explained by metaphors of establishing roots or by indigenous customs. However, giving form to that which is formless is a basic human need, as is the instinct to explain the exotic, to conquer fear, to oppose the overwhelming onslaught of nature with order, to transform the heterogeneous outside into a homogeneous inside. Transferred to the interior domain, the hidden materiality of masonry is expressed in how the mass of the wall, its weight, is designed. The history of masonry is the story of how this problem has been approached and newly interpreted in design across the ages.

If we were to present a material chronology of these history-making designs to derive and explain the current state of our culture, or yet, if we were to attempt to discover a causality between historic phenomena and ourselves, we would inadvertently fall into the trap of two questionable misconceptions. First, when we look at buildings from the past, our interpretation is always informed by contemporary knowledge, that is, we look at historic manifestations through the lens of modern contexts. And second, we are far from being distanced, uninvolved observers. Rather, we are participants who cannot escape our own history and – in that sense – we're always too late. Every age rediscovers history. History only exists through our own awareness of it. Hence, the history of building does not unfold in a continuity of meaning. It is a record of events that change what came before, interpreting it, creating new contexts, and, paradoxically, resulting in a reverse chronology. Events make or alter history.

What follows is therefore not a chronology or even a documentation of progress. Instead, we propose to illuminate specific positions in history and the changes in production and manufacturing techniques across the ages.

Masonry materials

With the building of walls came the manufacture of specialized building materials: mortar as binder and masonry units. Bitumen ("mineral pitch") as a binder for or additive in mortar can be traced back to prehistoric times in Mesopotamia. Hand-moulded clay bricks found in the lower layers of Nile deposits in Egypt date back as far as 14 000 BC, while the knowledge of preserving clay bricks by firing has been documented for circa 5000 BC. Natural stone

1.1.2

was already quarried and cut in the same era. With the discovery of bronze (circa 2500 BC), ashlar stones could be cut with great precision. By that time, fired brick had already undergone a long evolution. In the river basins of the Nile, the Euphrates, the Tigris and the Indus, archaeological traces have been discovered and researched of early civilizations that used both fired and unfired, i.e. sun-baked, brick. In Mesopotamia, bordered by the Euphrates and the Tigris rivers, builders employed bricks of different colours, and even glazed brick or tile, as early as 3000 BC. The Tomb of Menis, circa 3000 BC, was built with sun-baked clay bricks. The lower reaches of the Indus River were home to sophisticated cultures with major urban centres, e.g. Mohenjo-Daro and Harappa, where houses up to five storeys high were built with fired bricks. These structures offered an impressive degree of comfort. These cultures, among the earliest to be documented, and other building cultures in Asia and on the American continents, relied on natural stone as well as fired and unfired clay brick for building, and most continue to do so to this day. A large percentage of the world population still lives in buildings constructed of clay in a variety of processing methods.

Clay brick masonry

Loam is a mixture of clay and siliceous sand. The clay components consist of ultrafine platelets of broken-down primary rock, such as granite, gneiss or feldspar. The crystalline structure of the platelets binds the clay particles. When moisture is added, the water adheres to the platelets, surrounds them and causes the clay to expand and grow slick in consistency. Pure types of clay, which exist in all parts of the world in alluvial deposits, are unsuitable as building materials since they lack dimensional stability and tend to shrink and crack during the drying process that follows

moulding or shaping them with moisture. They must be blended with siliceous sand and other aggregates. Straw or chaff are common aggregates that have been used for the past 16 000 years. They improve the tensile strength of loam and dry out more evenly. The sandy fillers provide the supporting and loadbearing function. Loam prepared in this way can be worked in moist consistency. During the drying process, the clay particles form a solid envelope around the coarser sand grains, decreasing the degree of shrinkage and ensuring that it is evenly distributed, to produce a stable structure. Clay soil that is the product of wind erosion tends to more blended even in its natural state and not as "rich" (in clay content). In other words, clay does not set like hydraulic lime or cement, but simply hardens. This process is reversible. As soon as moisture penetrates into building components, they lose hardness and cohesion. This vulnerability to water, more specifically to rain, is countered in a variety of ways. We need only look to northern Germany to understand that all methods basically aimed at providing protection against wind erosion and rain washout. Here we find farmhouses in the northern plains which feature contained rammed earth screeds in their living areas and barns well into the 20th century. Coupled with a core of packed stone, these screeds are impervious to moisture rising from the ground, for clay can be waterproof when used in layers. Clearly, building with clay was (and is) not only common in arid, equatorial climate zones. The properties of the material and its workability, the excellent insulating and thermal storage characteristics of this monolithic construction method, and finally the low energy consumption in manufacture, were obviously equally appreciated in mountainous countries and in the lowlands of northern Europe. Nor does the list of advantageous properties end here; the high dead weight also provides good sound insulation, low natural resonance and fire resistance.

Clay has the ability to absorb, store and release air humidity. Although this is a positive characteristic in principle, it can also result in unhealthy living conditions in humid climate zones.

The plinth was usually built in natural stone, as protection against splashing rainwater and washout. Even the early cultures of Mesopotamia protected their walls with reed matting suspended in front of the external surfaces, with bitumen additives, or by facing solid clay brick walls with fired bricks on the outside. Material erosion is also minimized by the shape into which the clay mortar daub is formed, a softly rounded roof parapet covered with stones, or sharp points that offer little resistance to rainwater runoff, a solution whose only disadvantage is that it requires constant maintenance (fig. 1.1.4).

A simple means of rain protection is to build beneath a rocky overhang; this is common in the south-west of North America and in Mali in Africa (fig. 1.1.2).
It goes without saying that roofs with wide canti-levered projections also provide rain protection for clay walls.
Similar climatic conditions and building materials have obviously resulted in equally similar architectural forms in all areas of the world for millennia. However, this alone should not be understood as a cultural criterion: the urban clay structures in Yemen, for example, are distinctly different from those in Mali even though they are subject to identical external conditions (figs. 1.1.3 and 1.1.4).

In addition to hand-beading techniques and rammed earth technique with sliding formwork, masonry construction with clay brick has been the most common building technique world-wide from the beginning of recorded history. Wall thickness ranges between 400 and 650 mm. As we describe later on, there are a number of shell-like or rhomboid brick formats whose stability under load is improved with joggle jointing, in addition to orthogonal bricks with a nominal size of 100 x 200 x 400 mm. Clay brick construction is suitable for multistorey structures. The above-mentioned limitations in construction technology have produced architecture of stunning sculptural variety within the framework of these parameters. The material can be formed and worked by hand, and allows for a plasticity of design, which can be highly expressive.

The history of advanced civilizations abounds with examples of structures built with unfired brick, many of which have gone unnoticed as such. Even large sections of the Great Wall of China are built from clay that is still stable today. And in the age we generally associate with the monumental stone architecture of the pharaohs, most Egyptians lived in dwellings constructed of unfired clay bricks. Rome, too, evolved from being a city of clay to a city of marble (or, to be precise, marble facing).

1.1.3

1.1.1　Tunnel entrance to the stadium at Olympia, Greece, 300 BC
1.1.2　Pueblo in Mesa Verde, USA
1.1.3　Clay architecture in Yemen
1.1.4　Clay architecture in Mali

1.1.4

The unifying force of building

The urban Sumerian and Babylonian cultures were the first to develop baked and glazed brick successfully and to use coloured bricks in surface ornamentation. This achievement stood at the end of a long development beginning around 3500 BC. The most stunning example among excavated fragments from this period is the Ishtar Gate in Babylon (fig. 1.1.5). It was built under Nebuchadnezzar II around 600 BC. The complex at the Ishtar Gate was both processional roadway and defence fortification. The gate was ornamented with over 500 animal reliefs on the front and side walls, integrated into the faced wall as brick reliefs. The size, splendour and artistry of the individual figures of lions, bulls and mythical creatures in the masonry on either side of the processional roadway of the Ishtar Gate is a

masterful example of relief. Similar brick reliefs had appeared once before, on the great temple at Uruk, where perfectly preserved niche figures from circa 1400 BC have been excavated (fig.1.1.7).

The most significant structures of the Sumerian and Babylonian cultures were soaring temple buildings, called ziggurats, erected as stepped pyramids on whose uppermost platform stood a temple reached via one or several continuous stairways. The earliest ziggurats were constructed from unbaked bricks and presumably faced at a later period in baked brick. The best known are the Ziggurat at Ur (2300 BC; fig. 1.1.6) and the Tower of Babel, which was destroyed and reconstructed several times. The last, and largest, reconstruction of the tower had a 90-m-wide foundation and rose to an equal height. Calculations estimate that 85 million bricks were used in the construction. A monu-

mental stairway led to the top platform from which a two-storey temple rose into the sky. The tower was part of a temple complex on the shores of the Euphrates. Archaeological findings of inscribed clay tablets indicate that each section of the tower had a specific meaning. The same tablets also give us fairly good insight into the liturgical rites practised there. What is important in the context of this study is the fact that the building of the ziggurats was undertaken as an act of promoting culture and unification. "[...] let us build a city and a tower, whose top may reach unto heaven [..] lest we be scattered abroad upon the face of the whole earth." (Genesis, 10, 11: 4)

Babylonian culture declined only when the ziggurats ceased to be effective symbols of the unifying force of communal building after 1800 years of continuous building and reconstruction. European humanistic tradition has

1.1.5

frequently explored this symbol as a metaphor for the unifying force of language or the confusion that results from a Babylonian profusion of languages. In his short story *The Coat-of-Arms of the City*, Franz Kafka describes how building intended as a unifying activity in fact undermines unity, concluding that architectural perfection breeds a yearning for destruction.

Architecture owes one of its most significant inventions to the "Land Between Two Rivers": the vault. Excavations at Ur, on the lower reaches of the Euphrates, led to the discovery of Sumerian tombs of kings with brick vaults constructed circa 3500-3400 BC.

The shift in early Sumerian culture towards durable, baked brick, vaulting and the invention of cuneiform script mark a spiritual and intellectual liberation whose profundity is unique in human history. It was a victory over the force of gravity that seemed to emanate from unworked stone. In northern Europe, efforts to overcome this force during the same period were expressed by assembling huge boulders into dolmens or cromlechs on barrows (burial mounds) and by engraving the surfaces with symbols. Stones were regarded as sacred objects with magical powers. Working the stone created a sense of coming to terms with, or perhaps even taming, these powers, and appropriating stone as a building material and vehicle to express one's own ideas and perceptions.

Despite many highly inventive efforts, the transitory nature of buildings constructed from sun-baked clay bricks was demonstrated all too frequently in the erosion and subsequent oblivion of even the most monumental structures. There had been a prevailing sense that this was an inevitable fate. These two achievements in building technique responded to those fears and, in combination with the invention of cuneiform script, satisfied a need for permanence. Man's domination over the material world had begun.

Ever since we have become accustomed to building with other materials (iron, glass, concrete), the sense of the power of worked stone has increased. What seemed like a natural manner of building for millennia has become not only a symbol of life in the past or of a natural state of things, but also a key symbol of cultural evolution, of human activity.

The towering structure of the ziggurat is an expression of the superhuman effort to create order through a communal effort, of opposing the risk of being "scattered" and falling into obscurity by setting a monument, of linking heaven and earth with a stairway. In short, of

1.1.6

1.1.5   Ishtar Gate of Babylon, circa 570 BC
1.1.6   Ziggurat of Urnammu in Ur, circa 2100 BC
1.1.7   Detail of wall relief on Innin temple in Uruk,
         circa 1430 BC

1.1.7

reacting to life's uncertainties by creating permanence through self-determination. Taken to the extreme, this approach can lead to paradoxical solutions, as it did under the pharaohs in Egypt when quarried stone was manipulated to simulate sun-baked brick in a tribute to the emancipating value of man-made units.

The plastic spirit in Greek and Roman architecture

The architectural knowledge of Mesopotamia, Egypt and India reached Greece, regarded by many as the cradle of architectural development in Europe, by many different routes: trade, war and migration.

Masonry laid in courses of fired and unfired bricks and natural stone was the standard building material for most building tasks, even for major tasks such as the city wall of Athens (fig. 1.1.9), royal palaces and temple interiors. Vaulting techniques were also widely known. At its best, however, masonry from this period is sculpture built of finely worked ashlar stone. The plasticity in Greek temple structures stems from the mastery of representing the human form in sculpture and drama as a swelling body held in tension by pulsating liquids. This idea applies to the temples of the classic Hellenic era. Ashlar stones were subtly modified with carefully calculated minimal deviations in measurement (fig. 1.1.8).

This "animation" of the stone and of the structure would remain a secret for millennia. Entasis, the very slight curvature on columns and plinths, has been a familiar term only since the early 19th century. Schinkel referred to these optical illusions as "irrational tumescences". His buildings contain inclines, curvatures and banks that are so subtle that one has to look long and hard to discover them. And even the "unaware" observer cannot escape their effect.

1.1.8

of looking, objects are brought to life as drawings themselves. The term "vision" defines the principle of designing as an act of remembrance, awareness, and communicating knowledge, whose prerequisite is self-knowledge rather than knowledge of the world.

To recognize or determine knowledge of the world, origin, references and influences – these are what make Roman architecture so attractive to the educated observer. Fascinating though these aspects are, they do not help us to evaluate its achievement. To do proper justice to the grandiose technical and visual feats of engineering, we would do better to undertake a technological and historical inquiry into the science of building. In the first century AD, Vitruvius authored just such a treatise on building in 10 volumes. It is a systematic, scholarly

compendium that contains all that is necessary for building, from material selection to material manufacture, and from design to the execution of a variety of building tasks. Vitruvius engages in a polemic condemnation of "disfiguration" and the lack of expertise among certain architects and builders. He aimed to develop a unifying technical language of building. Two of his basic ideas have been revisited over the past two millennia. In analogy to proportion in human anatomy, Vitruvius demanded that the internal proportions of a building must similarly be derived from the building itself and to ensure that each building component relates to the others in scale. This is indeed a challenge worth supporting in our modern world of ubiquitous external standardization, where too much attention is paid to unifying scale and too little to the internal relationships within a building.

Hellenic buildings, especially their isodose ashlar masonry (fig. 1.1.10), demonstrate perfect technical mastery of the task of breathing life into each stone, each joint as an individual element, achieving buildings that are based on an intrinsic scale. Viollet-le-Duc gave us an antithetical definition of this design law of antiquity by noting that as the real scale of a (Greek) temple increases, man becomes smaller, while the soaring height of a medieval cathedral has no such influence. The building grows independently.

Viollet-le-Duc's remark indicates that the inherent laws of Hellenic architecture are linked to effect, much like an antique statue. The readability of its distinct character – which the observer can reconstruct in his own mind – is self-referential.

Outside is inside, and this inside reflects our own character. The object we are looking upon is shaped by our interest in looking. In the act

1.1.9

1.1.10

Technical advances in Roman antiquity

The basis for the development and outstanding quality of Roman engineering lay in the rationalization and commercialization of the building task. Construction materials and cladding materials were systematically separated, which led to tremendous advantages in organization. In the Augustan era (around the time of Christ's birth), Rome consisted largely of buildings constructed from unfired clay brick. They were rendered or faced with ceramic tiles.

Fired brick became a cost-efficient, industrially manufactured construction material that was, however, rarely in evidence in the form of facing brickwork. The brick industry had its own differentiated hierarchy: there were state-run brickworks and the legions in the provinces operated their own brickworks to satisfy public and private supply needs. In addition, there were private brick manufacturers, who usually set up field factories next to construction sites. We have fairly precise information about the manufacturing processes and the variety and quality of the products as a result of excavations of entire brickworks and manufacturing tools. One of the largest brick-firing kilns from the 3rd/4th century was discovered in Rehlingen near Trier in 1999. The kiln alone measures 8 x 13 m. The bricks used in buildings within the sphere of Roman culture measured between 200 and 800 mm in length and between 20 and 100 mm in thickness. They were rectangular, square or divided along the diagonal, that is triangular, to use the material as efficiently as possible and to achieve a better bond between shell and infill. They were often laid in header courses between natural stone masonry. The bed joints were up to 30 mm thick. Perpends were kept to a minimal dimension. The effect of this masonry, which came to light only as Roman buildings began to decay, is one of powerful stability with rigorous courses enhanced even further by the nearly imperceptible perpends. Vaults were easily built with this brick material as the wedge-shaped joints were never too widely spaced because of shallow prefabricated bricks. Wedge-shaped bricks (voussoirs) were also used and openings were often covered by several layers of arches (figs. 1.1.12 and 1.1.13).

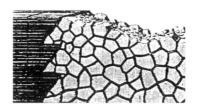
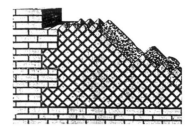

1.1.11

1.1.12

1.1.8   Poseidon Temple, Paestum, 460-450 BC
1.1.9   Athens city wall at Karameikos, in 1900,
         clay brick on natural stone base
1.1.10   Antique isodone ashlar masonry at the Temple
         of Nike, Athens, 421 BC
1.1.11   Roman masonry charts, after Rondelet
1.1.12   Imperial Baths, Trier, begun 293 AD, main apse

Masonry generally consisted of exterior leaves, clad and ornamented with precious materials or plaster. Coarse rubble was used to fill the space between these leaves. At times, the cavity was also filled with a mass of gravel and broken rubble bound with trass, reinforced at regular intervals with three to four layers of brick masonry (Vitruvius: Greek method) or simply filled without header courses (Vitruvius: Roman method). The filler mass (*opus caementitium*) corresponds to modern concrete. *Opus caementitium* was also used without masonry as a substructure in large buildings, such as amphitheatres, cast in formwork as walls or even in loadbearing vaults. The ring wall construction of the Pantheon (120-25 AD) is an example of this type of brick construction with *opus caementitium* filling. Roman architecture was highly sophisticated in the vaulting technique. It was evolved further and perfected

in the East Roman Empire. The cupola of the Hagia Sophia in Byzantium, for example, was built in 532-537 AD: spanning 35 m, it is one of the most impressive and famous masonry cupolas in the world.

With the fall of the Roman Empire, this knowledge was lost in the West for some time. We need only look at the Kaiserdom in Speyer, built some 1000 years after the Pantheon (span approx. 40 m) as the first, fully vaulted church space north of the Alps. It was to span barely 14 m, yet even this proved a daring feat at the time and it succeeded only after several failed attempts and structural modifications.

Another area in which Roman engineering excelled was aqueduct and bridge construction in stone. The aqueduct at Segovia, circa 100 AD, is part of a 17-km-long water conduit that bridges a valley and leads to the high town of Segovia in a succession of 119 arches, at

times in two storeys. What we see here is naked masonry of huge granite ashlar units, without mortar and joggle jointing (fig. 1.1.14). The adaptation of the Greek universe of gods, their philosophy, the copying and reproduction of Greek works of art and architectural form are universal characteristics of the Roman culture of antiquity. But Roman architecture is also distinct for the widespread use of facing and cladding elements. The organizational division of construction tasks into components with specific functions led to the development of architecture marked by a high degree of structural sophistication. Parallels with the schematic repetition that is quite frequent in today's architecture of cladding and sheeting are obvious and, perhaps, cause for concern.
In the sophisticated context of rational Roman architecture, the Tomb of Theoderich in Ravenna (first quarter of 6th century), topped by a

1.1.13

monolith of massive proportions, appears almost atavistic.

After the technical and organizational knowledge and traditional experience had disappeared almost completely in Europe after the fall of the Roman Empire, marginal influences of upper Italian, Byzantine and Arabian architecture reached the countries to the north of the Alps in the age of the Carolingians (800 AD onwards) and the Ottonians (950 AD onwards).

Technical development in the Middle Ages

We cannot describe here the full range of problems that arose in building tasks in the Middle Ages, such as the endless difficulties in transport and mortar production, or the quarrying and cutting of stone, and brick manufacture. The latter took several years from digging clay to storage, chilling in winter, forming, drying and firing to the final step of sorting out nearly 40% rejects. In contrast to construction with natural stone, building now became a matter of long-term planning and obtaining materials far in advance. Important advances occurred between the 10th and 11th centuries in natural stone masonry, all aimed at reducing the time required for construction and improving efficiency in manufacturing. This goal was achieved by means of rationalization and series production.

When stone was first quarried, the practice was to break off as large a block of stone as possible and cut it into ashlar stones, which were then made to fit into the masonry. The cutting, transport and laying of stone had to be carried out consecutively and this slowed the progress of construction quite considerably. Preparatory work in winter did not help to speed up the laying process and continuous bed joints were simply not possible.

The masonry in the west tower on the north side of St Cyril in Gernrode from the 10th century is an example of this working method (fig. 1.1.16), while the immediately adjacent masonry of the west choir from the 12th century reveals a more methodical, organized approach. Quarrying and cutting stone in advance meant that the masonry could be laid much more rapidly. The masonry bond in Chartres Cathedral (fig. 1.1.15) is horizontal with embedded joints. Wall and piers had to be built simultaneously. While preparation and storage had become possible, they were still cumbersome tasks. The nave of St Denis, on the other hand, shows piers that were manu-

1.1.14

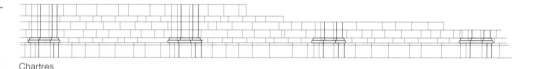

Chartres

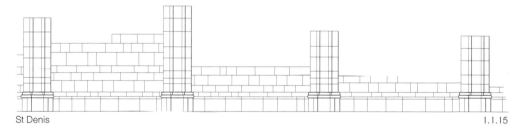

St Denis

1.1.15

1.1.13 Roman masonry, Imperial Baths, Trier
1.1.14 Roman aqueduct in Segovia, circa 100 AD
1.1.15 Masonry bonds of the cathedrals at Chartres and St Denis
1.1.16 Collegiate church St Cyril, Gernrode, 10th and 12th centuries

1.1.16

1.1.17

factured, laid and staggered independently of
the masonry. The masonry between the projections was constructed with a great quantity of
prefabricated pieces in frame construction.
By improving the arrangement of joints, the
moulded bricks were standardized and the
number of types reduced. The ultimate goal
was to develop ashlar forms that would minimize the need for pitting and reduce cutting
time, transport and waste.
Without this extraordinary development, the
speed with which church buildings were erected in the 13th century would not have been
possible. The sophistication in design is
matched by an equally sophisticated approach
to planning and labour organization.

Geometry and system in the Middle Ages

Early Romanesque churches express the
weight and strength of masonry and enclosed
spatial volume in an elemental, "cubic" manner. With the rise of the Cluniac order in France,
Burgundy became the centre for sacral architecture in Europe. The Jurassic limestone of
Burgundy was processed into rubble stone,
which marks the stunning simplicity of the capi-
tals at St Martin (fig. 1.1.17) at the transition
from the square cross section of the arched
vault to the column in pure geometric form. Its
brittle roughness gives the stone a particular
plasticity and supports the demi-columns, as if
this were completely natural. The Michael

Chapel at St Philibert shows the same capital
motif some 20 years earlier in a geometry that
is even more economic and elemental (fig.
1.1.18). The primeval, dense, heavy, almost
otherworldly power of the wall speaks directly
to the senses, without any need for intellectual
interpretation. Over the subsequent centuries,
a concept of masonry would develop out of the
elemental-geometric division of space and the
systematic organization of the plan, whose
main objective was to dematerialize the wall.
The architectural forms seem to negate their
own volume and weight, and draw our attention
away from their material self. Indeed, the massive material dimension is but a representation
of something greater. In other words, they do
not derive their right to exist solely from the
gaze of the observer. They demand no optical-
spatial comparison or visual perception, but
the viewer's identification with a speculative
construct of meanings presented as a wall that
aspires to an intellectual superstructure, an
allegoric interpretation. In complete contrast to
the sensuous-spatial presence of stone in St
Martin in Burgundy (fig. 1.1.17), the theme here
is to tame this primordial power of the stone, to
transpose and integrate it into a transcendent
hierarchy of meanings. The observer is chal-
lenged to grasp the meaning of the wall. This
presupposes that he already has an idea of the
meaning and is willing to subordinate himself
to its abstraction by reconstructing, as it were,
the "train of thought contained in the masonry".
This makes a high demand on the observer
indeed, triggered by the feeling of identifying
with the wall. During this period of the Gothic
age, masonry – especially in churches – is a
thoroughly systematic, cleverly calculated geometric game and a mathematical game, too, in
which the smallest part visualizes the whole. It
is a functional construct in the purest sense, in
which all parts reciprocally create, cause,
explain and derive from one another. Such
masonry systems do not create spaces.
Instead, they represent a wholly independent,
transcendental world of their own, inhabited by
flows of energy. Space is only manifest within
the diaphanous, translucently formed wall,

1.1.18

1.1.19

1.1.20

which creates its own boundary by means of its visual divisions. This idea of masonry is perfectly expressed in the triforium of Prague Cathedral (fig. 1.1.21). Peter Parler lets the triforium arcades swing into the attached colonnettes and back again. This movement is continued in the clerestory windows. The result is that the entire plane of the wall comes alive in a surge that leaps from the internal wall volume, which the wall creates by its own boundaries, to the adjacent borders, exposing the internal energy of the wall in an animated surface. Such artificial masonry concepts are not dependent on the design potentiality of the material. They are equally effective when applied to brick. The fenestration in the south tower of St Nikolai

Church (fig. 1.1.22) is a textbook example of Gothic masonry: the four-part recesses demonstrate the energy at work in the depth of the masonry. The rendered tracery panels – like the entire three-dimensional treatment – are images of the diaphanous nature of the interior space. The tracery that stretches like a membrane across the north and south gables of the St Catherine's Church in Brandenburg (fig. 1.1.23) is one of the richest and most precious facades of the Hanseatic Gothic. The north gable especially is realized in complete independence from the building task itself; it perfectly embodies the paradox of minimizing material by maximizing the effort put into working it, in order to express the spiritual, referential goal.

In later developments of Gothic masonry the forces represented in the masonry are resolved with Mannerist aloofness, until vault ribs traverse space freely and unencumbered and then return to the surface. In other examples, sharp-edged, sinewy profiles rise from surfaces soft as putty in an equally eloquent expression of internal energy. The resolution of forces in vault ribs sometimes misses the springing, landing next to it instead. With the advent of the more playful Mannerism in the 16th century, the immaterial-spiritual interpretation of masonry begins to wane.

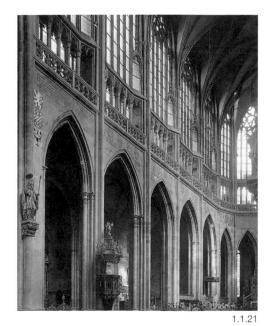

1.1.21

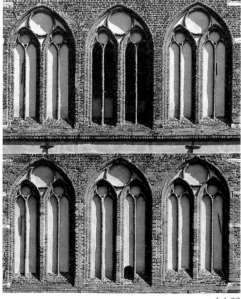

1.1.22

1.1.23

The world as a representational system

The Palazzo Pitti in Florence (1457), a structure built for defence like all Florentine palazzi of its day, features a plinth storey of barbaric, almost violent, rusticated ashlar stones of mammoth proportions. Stone with such rough surface treatment and an almost "natural" appearance was chiefly a building material for fortresses with little artistic value. It had no relationship to the elemental, pure cubism of Roman architecture. Its purpose was simply to be coarse so that one might tap into the violent force of the material as a design element – an interpretation of the natural power of stone that harks back to ancient beliefs in the material's magical powers in Norse barrows.

The reference here is not to the power of the spirit or yet the religious power of healing, but to political might and the power of wealth. The oversized dimensions had no practical purpose for defence, for it was no more than facing bonded to a masonry backing. Rustication, introduced here as a new motif in architecture, has recurred in the history of architecture in a variety of forms ever since, most recently in the form of citation.

Another feature worth noting in Renaissance architecture is the emphasis on the quoin. The corner, where two walls converge, was structurally reinforced in ashlar masonry by choosing larger formats with deeper bonds and in brickwork frequently by means of random bond or ashlar bonded with masonry. This reinforcement by projecting the corner stones from the wall or visually emphasizing them by means of a pier, indicates a new attitude born from looking back at the lessons of antiquity. It was a means of creating a clear contrast between buildings and surroundings, volume and space.

If the keystone was a metaphorical completion of the flush system of wall and vault in medieval Gothic architecture, (indeed, its meaning was so significant that it was placed beneath the vaulting crown in a detached, plastic manner in the Late Gothic) then the spatial boundary of volumes is now emphasized in a downward, lateral and upward direction. The spatial relationships – that is, top/bottom, right/left, and in front/behind – become the principal theme. This made it possible to create perspectival sequences. Gothic walls, on the other hand, had been designed to materialize energy set into a void and not to enclose space. Differentiation of planes – front, rear and lateral – engaged the mind of the observer, demanded the purifying, creative effect of looking. It also required specific constructional means. Perspective transforms the world into a new system of representation. It aims to condition the eye to recognize and comprehend clarity. Transposing the material character of unprocessed stone to a processed wall as if it were unprocessed, as seen on the Palazzo Pitti, is an idea that would become an enduring formative element for the development of architecture in the modern age. Palladio's application of the Greek temple front on the facades of his Venetian churches resulted in presentations of the facade as a series of images staggered in relief (fig. 1.1.24). By translating, modifying or multiplying the original figure of the temple, the architect transforms the facade into an image of the same.

Applied to material characteristics, this approach of mental and visual paraphrases creates architectonic quality. To reconstruct rough-hewn ashlar in rendered brick masonry is a deliberate deception undertaken to enrich the visual experience (fig. 1.1.26).

Plaster instead of stone, stucco vaulting instead of stone vaults, colour instead of relief – in short, illusion and revelation – contribute to the complexity of the observer's experience. When material is borrowed for artful purposes

1.1.24

for which it was not originally intended, when it is masked, when what is actually false is cleverly put right again, the observer is enchanted and the link with reality is multiplied and modified through the visual reality of the architecture. The question of what is masonry actually, is answered here with a proposal that takes us by surprise: it is an altered reality that is open to interpretation. All the world becomes a stage on which everything is a show. The Hofbibliothek in Vienna (fig. 1.1.27), whose elaborately designed rendered facade has in fact been achieved with only a few projections and recesses, can serve as a perfect example of plasticity in plaster design. The facade contains only a small number of natural stone components. A disciplined concept achieves this elaborate effect by resorting to the Baroque stylistic vehicle of crossover. Thus the plinth in the central projection rusticated with horizontal grooves and batter has a more powerful presence than the incline at the corner projections, which has been reduced to a delicate, angled edge projecting from the vertical surface. By continuing the rustication upwards into the surfaces between the projections, the plasticity is reversed: the window reveals retreat and the observer, seeking order, is confused.

The same can be said of the two-storey-high main windows in the projections. A string course, which runs along the surface between the first and second floor, and which seems to have been placed there as an afterthought, lies behind the projecting pilasters but in front of the rusticated surfaces and pulls the openings back into the facade relief. More confusion for the eye! In the vertical, the same visual ambivalence is achieved by repeating the arch above the main windows on the second floor in the tympanum of the lateral windows on the first floor. This puzzling articulation of depth in the facade is played out on planes that are

1.1.25

1.1.26

differentiated by no more than a few centimetres. Here is refinement of a rare beauty, executed in humble plaster. It is founded in the artistic challenge that we must borrow the properties of a different material to reveal the artful truth hidden within the illusion. An effect that can only succeed if the relationship between familiarity and alienation is explored independently each time and brought into harmony.

The concept that design is always a process of translating an idea into material form is the very foundation of the most powerful spatial inventions of the 18th century. An observer who surrenders to these relationships also becomes a calculated element in the drama. He must prove his "worth" through his own clever interpretations. This attitude heralds the idea of exploring the sequence of action itself. Or, to stay with the image of the world as a stage: the actors are aware of themselves as actors. This idea would become the dominant theme as the second half of the 18th century unfolded, and ultimately, the point of departure for the dissolution and revolution of all previously familiar laws of building.

The functional method

Conscious experience, that is, an awareness of one's own action as action, transforms origin and destination into a theme. Indeed, it is awareness of history in a dual sense: the studied recognition of something as historical simultaneously recognizes itself to be "historical". This thought process of the Enlightenment exploded all previously established contexts and moved on to the next logical step: dividing the history of building into distinct, readable periods. To begin with, the focus was on external features as criteria for this division. Later, the division, catalogued as a compendium of styles, gave rise to studies on the conditions of style and, by extension, to the need for establishing one's own stylistic position within this context of order, which in turn led to the challenge of defining "style in itself". This approach was soon revealed as too superficial. Building was divided into further categories: measurement, space, physics, structure and production.

As an extension to the catalogue of definitions, the individual elements of masonry become independent of their respective tasks: load-bearing, insulating, blocking and cladding. Immaterial tasks are not part of the equation in this analysis. This (pseudo-)scientific, or rather, functionalistic method of inquiry has been applied to building ever since, and changes have evolved and still evolve on the basis of ideas that raise the system of self-sufficiency to a new level, either by reflecting on one's own ideas or by an awakening to new ideas. Another direction evolved out of the 18th-century

1.1.27

principle which had inspired a critical study of the actions of living creatures, especially of humans. Actions, sequences of actions, the relationship between action and man (society), action and object (work) became determinants of building. The challenge that building forms should be made to satisfy the needs of human activity is a purpose-driven demand, which can only apply to the realization of buildings for individual uses. It must be differentiated from the aforementioned functionalistic method, although it is easily confused with it. Here, we are confronted by yet another influence that changes our understanding of what masonry is: it is an envelope, a skin stretched around actions. The distance, which the so-called architecture of the revolution had already put between itself and the past in the 18th century, is evident in the utopian drawing by architect Étienne Boullée (fig. 1.1.28). The doll-like, diminutive Greek temple appears like an eye

that looks straight at the viewer. The representational system has been overthrown!

The pyramid, built in masonry of alternating scale (one course corresponding to nearly one man-height) renders the temple abstract, that is it sets the temple apart, makes it self-sufficient. It is transformed into a historical set piece.

1.1.24 Il Redentore, Venice, begun 1577, architect: Andrea Palladio
1.1.25 Palazzo Pitti, Florence, begun 1540
1.1.26 Güstrow Castle, 16th century
1.1.27 Hofbibliothek, Vienna, 1721-26, architect: Johann Bernhard Fischer von Erlach
1.1.28 Étienne-Louis Boullée, design

1.1.28

Technical developments in the 19th century

Set in motion by the principles of the 18th century, a drastic change took hold of the process of building in the 19th century: the technical and machine development. The manufacture of masonry bricks was revolutionized by two inventions. In 1854, the Berlin manufacturer Carl Schlikeysen invented the extrusion press, which consisted of a worm-like ram and an interchangeable die through which premixed clay was extruded and cut into pieces with a wire. The process of brick manufacture could thus be transformed into one continuous operation from preparing the material to firing, whose every step could be controlled, regulated and automated. The same goal had been pursued for some time, and experiments had been undertaken in England since the beginning of the 17th century. Prior to Schlikeysen's invention, bricks were manufactured by hand in a variety of forming and moulding methods. This had been linked to a far greater risk of shrinkage and cracking, as well as greater energy requirements and longer production times. A few years later, in 1858, Friedrich Hoffmann, also from Berlin, invented the continuous ring kiln, in which brick could be fired more quickly, more economically and using less energy. Fixed-cycle operation for firing had already been introduced in England some time before. That is, two or three kilns were heated from the outside in alternating cycles. As soon as one load of bricks was fired and had cooled, it could be removed and the kiln reloaded.

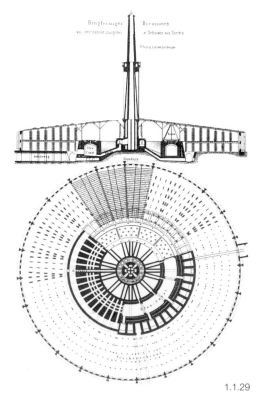

1.1.29

The novelty of Hoffmann's invention was that the fixed cycle was developed into a continuous process by arranging at least two firing chambers in a circle and by shifting the firing or heating process from the outside to the inside (fig. 1.1.29). The chambers are separated from each other with iron dampers. As soon as one chamber is loaded with "green" bricks, a stoking apparatus is lowered from the top through a shaft to add fuel. The bricks themselves serve as a heating grate. When the firing process is completed, the stoking apparatus is drawn up and the damper is opened in the direction of the next chamber, closed and so forth. Ring kilns can be operated continuously for decades. They were called "efficiency kilns" because the heating of one firing chamber also preheated the neighbouring chamber. This effect was even augmented by integrating fans to increase the performance despite existing savings in energy and fuel. The inventions multiplied the production capacity of a brickyard fivefold. One weak point in the process was the manual loading and unloading of the firing chambers. The invention of the tunnel kiln, which came into use only 10 years after Hoffmann's invention, albeit with some hesitation at first, made it possible to automate even this step in the process. Some ring kilns are still in use today. They achieve a livelier surface and distinct manufacturing traces by means of scale modifications. In the tunnel kiln, green bricks were transported through a 40-50 m long firing tunnel, heated from the sides and from above. By blowing the oxygen required for combustion into the tunnel from the far end, the fired bricks were automatically cooled down and reached the end of the tunnel ready for unloading. Today, tunnel kilns increase the productivity of a comparable brickyard twelve fold. Full automation has made heavy manual labour redundant. Berlin, of which Mark Twain wrote admiringly (in *The Innocents Abroad*) that it was built entirely of stone and immune to conflagrations, consumed 550 million bricks during its growth spurt in the Gründerzeit in 1871. The bricks were transported into the city from surrounding brickyards on barges. By 1905, the figure had risen to 1775 billion bricks. The ziggurat of Babylon consisted of 85 million bricks. The performance capacity of the new building industry increased through the production of prefabricated elements in the last quarter of the 19th century. Prefabricated steel structures such as Paxton's Crystal Palace or the Eiffel Tower are not the only examples worth mentioning in this context. In addition to construction "kits" for balcony balustrades, cast-iron fountains, zinc-sheet oriels and prefabricated stucco pieces for interior finishing, the catalogues of the day offered complete building kits for the ceramic elements of masonry: columns, lintels, consoles, crowns etc., which looked liked oversized stone building kits by Lilienthal and which were intended

to inspire a playful treatment of masonry and trims and, above all, sales.

At the same time as Schlickeysen's and Hoffmann's inventions revolutionized brick manufacturing, the first lever pumps were introduced for a material that had always been an essential component for building with masonry: mortar made of sand and lime. The Romans had already tried to manufacture building bricks from mortar, or to use it as filler in twin-leaf walls. However, two prerequisites had to be fulfilled to achieve the necessary compressive strength: the ability to press the material for greater density and solidity, and the ability to accelerate the setting process, which usually took two years. Thirty years would pass in experiments before an accelerated and practical setting process was discovered. In 1880 a patent application for a steam-hardening process was filed; the first automated, industrial cylinder press for the production of calcium silicate units was set up in Neumünster. From there, the building material soon spread throughout Europe. In structure, calcium silicate units are similar to natural stone and at first they were used in much the same manner. The inexpensive units were initially produced in field factories set up right at the construction site. The units were immediately used for private and public buildings, as well as for industrial building projects. This development was much helped by the fact that the manufacturers formed an association as early as 1900 and established quality standards in 1902 that would become the model for brick standardization. To demonstrate that the units were also suitable for facing masonry, buildings were erected shortly after the start of the 20th century in exposed calcium silicate masonry. However, calcium silicate units were only "discovered" on a large scale as facing bricks in the 1960s. The aesthetic appeal of the material lies in its blend of a severe, technical character and a natural grain that distinguishes it from all other stone building materials.

1.1.29   Hoffmann ring kiln, patented in 1858
1.1.30   St Matthew's, Berlin, 1844-46,
         architect: Friedrich August Stüler
1.1.31   Jugendstil window in Nancy

1.1.30

passionate as it was unremitting. Had sentiments and dogmatism of this nature existed in an earlier time, there would have been no Renaissance (no Bramante, Palladio, Alberti, Raphael, Michelangelo ...) in the era when antiquity was rediscovered. The buildings of the various schools of the 19th century certainly demonstrate great knowledge of history, but they are often unimaginative and "dry" despite the excellent detail in material treatment.

Jugendstil – a new path

Style had now been freed from the context of building and established itself as sufficient unto itself. As a result, style became the theme that defined the external character and was then reintegrated with the remaining components of building; in other words, following a path that was reversed, from the outside in. During a short phase of 20 years at the beginning of the 20th century, this path was successfully practised by a small group of architects in cities such as Vienna, Paris, Brussels and Glasgow. Artificial ornament and structure merged in a feverish and at times bombastic fusion that perfectly expressed the *fin-de-siècle* sensibility. The synthesis was characterized by the fact that architectural elements were deformed and warped less by the tectonic or spatial forces of architecture than by ornamentation (fig. 1.1.31). This style, which flourished briefly under various names and was called Jugendstil in German, was more or less a way station along the new path toward transition, for it demanded further exploration of the very conditions that make stylistic thought possible in the first place. In this sense, it was but the final, rebellious phase of historicism.

The technical aesthetics of brick

The first half of the 19th century saw a number of improvements in the quality of brick materials.
We should perhaps note Karl Friedrich Schinkel's efforts in this context. Impressed by the industrial brick buildings he had encountered on his journey to England in 1862, Schinkel began to pursue a style of building in which the character of the material determined the architecture. From the character of brick as "a single material", he developed a technical conception of building, whose theory he formulated in his "Treatise on Architecture" and whose influence was felt well into the 20th century. Several of his students continued to evolve this building style, in which the material set the tone for the design (fig. 1.1.30).
Even the silhouettes of buildings, whose stylistic revetment was basically laid onto the surface like a veneer, such as the Houses of Parliament in London (1836), are characterized by a severity and clarity that is comparable to a brick building by Schinkel.

Historicism and dogmatism

The naïve and superficial application of historical styles gradually evolved into a profound and structural penetration over the course of the century. Architectural competence was increasingly measured by historical knowledge, and theorists of architecture engaged in heated debates over style and concept. "Gothic" and "classic" schools developed. Proponents of dogmatism formed their own opinion in opposition to the emerging functionalism, although the intellectual premise was basically identical. Hard lines were drawn in the development of architecture in the second half of the 19th century. Indeed, opinions were so inflexible that historicizing schools of building were founded (the guilds) whose doctrines many architects adopted with fervour, while others were "converted" to them. Nine schools existed in the German-speaking countries alone: the Nuremberg, Cologne, Kassel, Hannover, Vienna, Aachen, Berlin, Munich and Karlsruhe schools. They proselytized a German-Christian Gothic revival with a fervour that was as

1.1.31

1.1.32

1.1.33

1.1.34

The United States in the 19th century

In the United States, architecture emancipated itself over the course of the 19th century, especially in the industrial centres.
A brick building such as the Monadnock Building in Chicago (1890-91) – executed with such rigorous restraint from using any facade ornamentation – would have been inconceivable in Europe for at least another 20 years.
Masonry was the standard material in the 1920s for the construction of skyscrapers in Chicago, New York and other major cities in the USA. It was reinforced with iron frames, a building method that found its way back to Europe. Many larger masonry structures of the 1920s, e.g. Chile House in Hamburg (Fritz Höger, 1923-24) and the warehouse of the Gute-Hoffnungs-Hütte in Oberhausen (Peter Behrens, 1921-25), were built around steel cores (fig. 1.1.33).
The best-known forerunner in the United States of building that rigorously realized the intellectual tradition of the 18th century was Robert Louis Sullivan. His famous statement "form follows function" is one of the most misunderstood and, owing to this misinterpretation, trivialized quotes of the day. What Sullivan meant was that individual functions seek expression in form. He explained it with the example of an oak tree in which each part – trunk, branch, leaf, flower, fruit – is pure oak and applied this image to the skyscraper: "It must be tall, every inch of it must be tall. It must express the power and violence of height [...]."
Function is an organic force of expression, not inane fulfilment of purpose.

Action-oriented building

As historicism was being rejected for the hypocrisy of its stylistic aspirations, a number of factors combined to give rise to a new view of architecture. These were chiefly the Arts and Crafts movement in England, and a new awareness of nature, of the social problems of living and working and of the building process itself. The principal focus of architecture shifted towards the simple act of manufacturing buildings and their uses. At the start of the 20th century, this movement gathered under the umbrella of the Werkbund. In Austria, the Wiener Werkstätten set the same goals. The Werkbund was as passionate in its moral demands on building as the guilds of the 19th century had been.
The Viennese architect Adolf Loos decided to dispense with ornamental trimmings altogether. This went so far that he wanted to build the windows on the upper floors of his commercial building on Michaelerplatz in Vienna without frames. He defended his position with furious energy and such high ethical demands on building that a public scandal ensued.
Meanwhile, in a small town in northern Germany, Walter Gropius succeeded at exactly the same time in a pioneering act of architectural perfection that has rarely been matched since: the Faguswerk shoe last factory (fig. 1.1.35). The harmonious scale of the facade is subtle and differentiated. (Gropius was originally commissioned exclusively for the facade design.) The corner areas of the glass facade are only a few centimetres wider than the glazed sections in the walls. By the same token, the upper windows are again a few centimetres taller than the windows on the lower floors. The structure is pure brickwork. The columns are recessed by one face length. The

number of courses of the masonry in the entrance projection, rusticated by recessed single courses, alternates between these recesses, which are harmonized with the glass facade. The design concept – incidentally, also a clever response to Behrens's AEG Turbine factory in Berlin – is geared towards creating a sense of fragility, both in its totality and in its details, down to the choice of brick and brick colour, of bond and brick quality. This fragility is the result of design characteristics that seem to contradict one another. The most prominent detail is the absence of a corner column in the glass wall as well as the ambiguous architectural response to the question whether the curtain wall supports or is supported by the brick cornice! In all this, the recessed columns are the least conspicuous and yet the most effective element in this aesthetic feat. This design marks the beginning of a new phase in the development of architecture and yet another answer to the question of what is masonry. Here, it is the exploration of support and load. Yet masonry isn't seen in relative terms.
It no longer defines supporting and being supported, outside and inside, but derives its tectonic and spatial expression from the potential of transposition.
In the evolution from the Palazzo Pitti to the Hofbibliothek and on to the Faguswerk, this shift is clearly legible in the rustication of the Faguswerk (which, in turn, is an interpretation of Behrens's rustication on the AEG Turbine factory).
Gropius's design is independent and convincing by comparison to the narrow, dogmatic Arts and Crafts ethic of truth, honesty, justice, sincerity, decency, clarity and loyalty. Once upon a time, these principles had been a polemic call to arms of the arts against the stultified orders of historicism. Faced with the

1.1.32   Monadnock Building, Chicago, 1890-91,
            architects: Burnham and Root
1.1.33   Hannover municipal library, 1929,
            architect: Karl Elkart, during construction
1.1.34   as in fig. 1.1.33, after completion
1.1.35   Faguswerk, Alfeld, 1911,
            architects: Walter Gropius and Adolf Meyer

vacuity that marked the pose of the latter, these principles made as much sense as did the moral revolt of the Impressionists against the pomposity of salon painting, which – much like architecture – had allowed itself to be (ab-)used as an ancillary art that expressed the interests of the state. These retrospective "declarations of war" expressed in the moral principles of building at the decline of the 19th century reverberate even today. Perhaps because they seem to offer ready and comfortable solutions without the need for an exhaustive, and exhausting, investigation of facts. Thus, they run the risk of becoming a cause for opposition themselves.

To Gropius, however, they were appeals worth taking to heart and he adopted them as the principles for the Bauhaus. But, like Mies van der Rohe, he was always conscious of the superiority and persuasiveness of the design.

The purifying intent of the Bauhaus is expressed in liberating architecture from its character of being a means, of giving rise to and directing feelings and moods. The Bauhaus seeks to establish immediacy by looking upon building as a social task directly linked to work and society, that is, the sphere of the human activity, certain that these tasks can be transmuted into building forms without styles that cloak the intent. In doing so, the movement unconsciously delves so deeply into aesthetic principles of the architecture that the final built products take on a common, unmistakable character. To stay with the metaphor: the intended "naked reality" unintentionally becomes a cloak, as if it were naked.

Ultimately, historicism was rejected out of the same spirit from which it had been born.

1.1.35

25

The power of expression in continuous space

Simultaneous with the rather bourgeois tone of the masons' guild and the Werkbund, there emerged a strong movement towards the spiritual creative forces of man. Embracing and reflecting primordial, natural elements, these tendencies met with widespread approval. But they came dangerously close to "cosmology" and exaggeratedly "earthy" evocations of the forces of the soil and the elements. Still, the combination of turning away from civilization and towards the mythology of nature and the enthusiasm for utopian, futuristic concepts released creative energies that encouraged an abandoned, violent and inspired development among artists.

Antonio Gaudí's buildings had none of the offensive, occasional character of the Faguswerk or the scandalous effect of Loos's architecture. They were immediately popular. Academically speaking, they were a blend of clear, precise, structural-constructive thinking and a baffling transposition of primeval power into masonry that reveals the basics of tectonics and is reminiscent of the equilibrated structure of tectonic plates (fig. 1.1.37).

From this perspective, the Bauhaus (with its outward focus on social relationships and work) and Expressionism (with its inward-looking focus) are but logical developments of the

functional method. The common interest in material-construction-production is subsumed in the pre-eminence of action and use: all building tasks and building goals are projected onto the human canvas. Another strong influence on the building concepts of the following decades was provided by the De Stijl movement in the Netherlands, whose founder. Theo van Doesburg, sought to gain a feeling of space, of floating, from the wall by translating time into pictorial movement. Gerrit Rietveld realized these ideas (fig. 1.1.36). Mies van der Rohe's interpretation of masonry was equally influenced by this movement in architecture. His residential buildings from the 1920s demonstrate an open flowing sense of space (fig. 1.1.38). Van der Rohe established the spatial movement of walls and openings as the principle theme of architecture in the 20th century. During the same period, the Amsterdam School, represented by Michel de Klerk, Piet Kramer and others, translated ideas borrowed from the visual arts into plastic masonry, whose curved or vertical bed joints and folded openings qualify its loadbearing property, yet by this very device also emphasize the original spatial quality (fig. 1.1.40).

Van Doesburg explored a duality that is a recurring topic in the history of masonry, namely that masonry is both mass and surface, by stressing colour as a two-dimensional, all-

1.1.36

encompassing design element, a determinant in addition to the elements of mass and space. Fritz Schumacher, who greatly influenced the development of masonry in the first three decades of the 20th century as both an architect and an author, referred to examples of *Backsteingotik* (the impressive and very simplified Gothic in northern Germany) to draw attention to the importance of the surface and the difficult relationship between colour and plasticity in the surface. These ideas on two-dimensionality, surprising as they may be at first, also identify the qualifying relationship between columns and loadbearing, outside and inside, that we encounter in Gropius's work as a new attitude.

Building mass is an image of building mass, uniting two-dimensionality and cubic form, a visualization of the spatial concepts of movement. The aesthetic influences of photography and, above all, film are evident here. The new laws of cinematography begin to show their impact, which would continue to grow stronger as the century advanced.

In contrast to German Expressionism, which was founded in the internal dynamic of spiritual-emotional forces, De Stijl and the Amsterdam School were more intellectual, but at the same time also more geometric-cosmic in orientation. Both were open to exploring the problems of industrial production and its impact on society. Housing shortages after World War I led to a building boom in the Netherlands and in Germany, which made it possible to translate the previously theoretical-speculative developments into practice.

Red bricks and engineering bricks were the building materials of choice. The latter are marked by a weather-resistant quality resulting from the sintering of clay and lend themselves to expressive wall articulations with projecting and recessed blocks and courses.

The effect of buildings by Fritz Schumacher and Fritz Höger differs from the Amsterdam School in that it is created by the rhythmic design of the masonry surfaces.

1.1.37

1.1.38

To Schumacher, brick as a material is a unique opportunity for discipline in design in the sense of concentrating on the building purpose as well as on the unity of material and form. In analogy with musical composition, the masonry bonds and unit projections were to emphasize and illustrate the functional relationship of the walls. Fritz Höger is a master of this art of illustration in engineering bricks. He transforms the exterior image of building through projections and recesses, dog-toothing and inventive variations on masonry bonds into a fabric that breathes rhythm.

To look upon the surface image exclusively in terms of its importance as a dynamic effect of functional internal references is simply the logical continuation of the fragmenting building analysis. New structural possibilities opened up with the bracing of masonry by means of a surrounding steel structure, which nevertheless maintained the massive character of the masonry.

1.1.36   Schröder House, 1924, architects:
         Gerrit Rietveld and Trus Schröder-Schrader
1.1.37   Chapel crypt Santa Coloma, 1898-1914,
         architect: Antonio Gaudí
1.1.38   Ludwig Mies van der Rohe, study for country
         house in brick construction, 1923
1.1.39   Sulphuric acid treatment plant in Luban,
         1911-12, architect: Hans Poelzig
1.1.40   De Dageraad housing complex, Amsterdam,
         1921-23, architect: Pieter Lodewijk Kramer

1.1.39

1.1.40

1.1.41   Indian Institute of Management, Ahmedabad,
         India, 1962-74, architect: Louis I. Kahn
1.1.42   "Morris Gift Shop", San Francisco, USA,
         1948-49, architect: Frank Lloyd Wright
1.1.43   St Peter's, Klippan, 1963-66,
         architect: Sigurd Lewerentz
1.1.44   Säynätsalo town hall, 1949-52,
         architect: Alvar Aalto

materials is the direct expression of a complex structural analysis. The buildings gain an abstract internal tension by means of the paradoxical manner in which the materiality is intensified and simultaneously dematerialized, reducing the masonry to its basic conditions.

The planning laws and building regulations of today are lasting symbols of the analytical autonomy of individual aspects of living. At the dawn of the 21st century a new autonomous component has been added, that of environ-

1.1.41

System rationality and structural analysis

Based on the aforementioned tenets of the Bauhaus and Expressionism, extraordinary new exponents of architecture were developed by the succeeding generations, although they remained true to the fundamental theories of the 18th century, which we have discussed in detail.

Its artistic variety notwithstanding, Frank Lloyd Wright's architecture is always firmly grounded in working with primary geometries. In one of his later works, the "Morris Gift Ship" in San Francisco (1948-49), a circular matrix and a linear, dynamic matrix overlap (fig. 1.1.42). The Roman brickwork, which Wright had already employed in Windsor House (1893) and Robie House (1909), supports the basic geometric-dynamic idea.

Alvar Aalto's buildings are a continuation of the formal canon of the Bauhaus (fig. 1.1.44). Here, the division of volume is more original than the expression of the plan, which once again traces the plot in the interior.

As architecture continued to evolve in the subsequent decades, it began to divide the city into individual sections for living, work, recreation and traffic. The mid-20th century saw the rise to prominence of an abstract, performance-oriented order that strove to address the purpose of building. The rational approach of exploring the function of each purpose and to create strategic alternatives as a self-referential system, now culminated in a structural analysis that would have an impact on the subsequent development of masonry.

The basic premise of the autonomy of each individual element became an independent system itself. In the work of Herman Hertzberger, for example, buildings answer to the requirements of use; but the latter are held captive in the structural scheme of the building.

The architectural language of Louis Kahn is characterized by a demonstrative play with the structural conditions of building, above all the compression and tensile forces. Kahn invites the viewer to experience the elemental forces of masonry. Two examples in particular illustrate this approach: the segmental arches at the Indian Institute for Management at Ahmedabad (fig. 1.1.41), where the shear is visibly absorbed between the springings with the help of a concrete tension anchor, and the circular walls cut open with spherical vaults in the government buildings in Dhaka, Bangladesh (fig. 1.1.116). Each of these examples is achieved independently of the relevant building task. Kahn views masonry as independent of history, discovering the truth of building in this basic premise.

This is a different kind of demand for truth than the retrospective moral imperative of the masons' guild and the Werkbund. It also incorporates the demand that traces of production should remain visible – and not hidden, as had been an unspoken rule in the history of building. In this regard, Kahn's structural approach is not unlike Le Corbusier's. Both architects show the simple and hence elemental conditions of building.

The late brick buildings by Lewerentz are designed with an archaic flavour (fig. 1.1.43). The seemingly simple combination of sparse

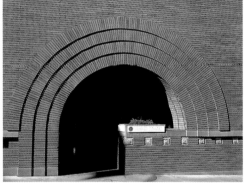

1.1.42

1.1.43

mental protection, opening up new design considerations in a planning approach that is increasingly characterized by fragmentation. In recent decades there has been no let-up in the development of a unifying building concept. Post-modernism and deconstruction, for example, are terms borrowed from literature and philosophy, to provide a theoretical underpinning for the new architecture. It is difficult to imagine, however, which kinds of architectural postulates could be derived from Paul de Man's textual concepts. The term architectural minimalism – borrowed from the visual arts in this instance – is simply a new name for design in the tradition of Mies van der Rohe. These attempts at theoretical adaptation by means of literary catchwords are still caught up in the tradition of historicism and do not reveal any traces of change in masonry. What remains today is the need to explore the ideas of the Werkbund, which have become stale and hackneyed, in more depth and with less obedience to the "bogged-down scheme" (Ernst Bloch), to confront them with the problem of modern incrustations. Only then can we answer the question of what is masonry in the full knowledge of our current situation.
We should remember that the functional method of rationalization has permeated all areas of human activity. New construction methods with materials such as steel and reinforced concrete, developed for increased performance, relegated masonry to the secondary role of facework and infill over the course of the 20th century. Moreover, the same developments in masonry itself meant that the wall structure was divided into individual functions to reduce material consumption and construction effort. With few exceptions, this development no longer allowed for the homogeneous treatment of masonry, which in turn has resulted in great uncertainty in design. The common reaction is to quote, with much bravado and little thought, the typical argument of the trade that masonry – which is usually a curtain wall today – should show what it is. Conventional arguments of honesty etc. are dragged out as justifications, a stance that is as phlegmatic as it is bigoted.

The situation hasn't changed, but the conditions have. However, this too is no novelty. Design doesn't end at this point; it's just beginning.

1.1.44

Design

Basics

Design has less and less to do with realizing ideas, sketching out concepts and defining details. The division between the abstract world of drawings, numbers, measurements and the subsequent implementation activities all the way to the construction site, has been lamented for some time.

By now, the division has become so great that the profession is at risk of being degraded to mere draughtsmanship. Some may regard this as an advantage, a lightening of the workload. But it has had a profound impact on the built results, making them less diverse, levelling out differences. Consequently, many feel a growing need to re-establish contact with the construction site, to return to the real, material problems of building in order to achieve authenticity in design and accountability in execution. The masonry unit – natural stone, concrete blocks, calcium silicate units and especially clay bricks – is an effective tool to achieve this goal.

The ease with which elements are substituted in today's progressive architecture, the relentless search for equivalencies in material and construction, leads us to remember the formative, real power of material resistance. To use the trade jargon: when you work with masonry, you've always got one foot on the construction site. Masonry makes us aware of the challenges of the material; we can feel its weight and design for it. Masonry is by its very nature equipped to age. This is expressed in the fact that when materiality and purpose grow apart, as they inevitably will, a kind of objectivity that is independent of purpose gradually evolves in the relationship between materiality and workability, which ultimately produces material waste.

The rigidity of masonry, the limited design range imposed by the units, course depths and spans, constantly force the designer into a tight corner. It is a struggle against the constraints of the material, its limited ability to fulfil the purposes of construction, use, manufacturing requirements and many other factors. Yet anyone who has noted these conditions has also praised the abundance of design options that arise from this difficulty. The creative secret lies in overcoming these constraints in an assured manner and in the lessons of simplicity to be learned from processing masonry materials. The limitations of the material are a defining aesthetic criterion. The success of masonry across the millennia is founded in its ability to offer stunningly simple solutions for a number of individual problems. It would be unjust to describe masonry units as prefabricated units. The workability of these

1.1.45

1.1.46

units and the abundance of applications go beyond such a simplistic definition. Like all simple devices or tools, the masonry unit is an ingenious element of everyday life. Its typology is deeply rooted inside us and has grown impervious to misuse.

Let us introduce another vital relationship that is particularly evident in masonry buildings: the link between design and observation. Observation, the act of looking, is always an act of deciphering, recognizing and interpreting contexts and connections. We are only able to look because we are taught to do so from birth and we practise this ability until it becomes a routine of which we are no longer even aware. Whenever we want to understand a building or architecture through looking, our mental repertoire of deciphering is automatically set in motion. By applying this knowledge "in the light of theory" as Karl Popper put it, we learn what lies behind the surface by looking at the surface: we know how to decipher the core by looking at the skin. Yet this is a highly complex process, in which looking and being looked upon merge into a single event. By covering and uncovering connections between outside and inside, exposing the invisible, the observed object is transformed into a mirror of the observer. The observer deciphers a building in much the same manner he applies to himself.

The design of the wall surface, which is difficult to grasp as matter, its structural, plastic, material, colour and tactile characteristics, each shed light on another relationship with the wall – the design relationship. The surface reflects these relationships in ever-new connections or is cleverly self-referential, a topic that has been explored in detail in the historical section. To design means to develop this relationship.

Design must re-create the link between designer and observer. Conversely, the observer, too, is called upon to "design" by looking, recognizing and drawing conclusions, and by his observation make the building what it is.

One example of extraordinary refinement in design is Jean Nouvel's idea of copying the image of the facade, itself an image, and transferring it back onto the facade, making, as it were, the copy into an image of the copy, which in turn is a copy of an image. In this instance, the tectonic is lost in itself.

When designing and building with masonry, this intellectual-aesthetic link is inescapable because it has come to define architecture, design and the fine arts. But not only that. Today, it also means exploring the idea that the surface, the exterior world of masonry, has its own interior world, whose fascinating qualities it communicates to the observer so that he may reconstruct the logic, tectonic, imagery and mimesis (the "as if") in his own mind. Unlike most building methods, masonry is suited to meet this demand not least of all because it has an inherent power that calls for simplicity.

Manufacture

The manufacture of masonry has changed fundamentally as a result of technical development. Nevertheless, it can still be carried out by hand at any time and without great effort (fig. 1.1.45-47). In the meantime, the entire process from digging clay or other materials to firing has become a fully automated process in all industrial countries, as we have already described.

1.1.47

Formats

Clay bricks come in a wide variety of formats and shapes. There are shell-shaped, irregular, compacted bricks made to fit into courses. They are always dimensioned to be gripped in one hand. The manufacture and processing of sun-dried clay or earth bricks is the most ancient building method still practised today. The problem of vulnerability to rain is addressed in a number of ways. In the early Mesopotamian cultures (4000-2000 BC) panels of woven reed, fabric or skins were suspended from fired ceramic rods in front of the wall, presumably as rain protection. Clay brick was also used as backing for exterior leaves built from fired brick. In northern Europe, clay or earth walls were erected beneath wide roof overhangs and protected with a neat lime wash that was renewed each year. This method was also common to Asia. In Africa (Mali) the structural timber members of floors and bracing were pushed through the wall like a scaffolding to facilitate any repairs in case of washout (see fig. 1.1.4). Until very recently, the rule of thumb that each masonry unit should be of a size and format that could be lifted and laid with one hand also applied to bricks, calcium silicate units and concrete units. One historical exception is Roman bricks, which, as we described in the historical chapter, were manufactured as flat elements and laid in alternating straight and diagonal courses.

In Catalonia, Roman bricks are used to this day. In addition to the Roman/Catalan bricks there may be other unique regional formats, which are, however, not fundamentally different and still comply with the aforementioned basic requirement of the "one-hand lift".
We are used to seeing a single format in one building. In the past, this was not necessarily

so. The buildings on the Place des Vosges in Paris, built in 1612, feature walls of large bricks of monumental appearance on the facades overlooking the square. The formats of the units in the cross-vaults in the colonnades surrounding the square are adapted to the scale of the space and the detail work in the spandrels.
Apart from units in large formats, which are unsuitable for facing masonry, the selection of standard formats is fairly limited today. On the other hand, the industry offers and uses a tremendous variety of moulded bricks. But it is a mistake to try and improve masonry with moulded bricks.

Colours and surfaces

In contrast to formats, the selection of colours and surface treatments is quite manageable. Brick colour is influenced by the composition of the clay and the firing method and temperature. Two colour scales are predominant: the red scale, from dark purple through all shades of red to orange; and the yellow scale, from dark leather brown to red-brown, yellow-brown, ochre, light yellow-pink, sienna, beige and yellow. But nearly all other colours are available as well: from black through all shades of grey, and from blue to white. The surface of the brick is the other important feature of appearance. There is the grainy surface of hand-moulded brick, the various horizontal and vertical grooves and notches created by the nozzle of the extrusion press, the sintering traces from the firing process and plastic characteristics from firing, slag marks, surfaces smooth as tile and sand coatings in a variety of hues. Inexpensive units are often treated with an imitation grain to simulate the fine surfaces of expensive units. A decisive factor in selecting

a unit is the combined effect of colour and surface texture with the colour, surface and design of the joints, a point we shall return to in more detail.

When it comes to evaluating the cubic, plastic and rhythmical disposition of the building components and the building volume, the quality of architectural design is evident without taking material into consideration. On the contrary, it would even impede our judgement. However, this is not true of brickwork buildings. In these buildings, the quality of the architectural design is inextricably linked to the material used to build them. It would be impossible to imagine the one without the other. Anyone designing with this material must be willing to get involved with it. The quality of the masonry is less distinctively expressed when the surface is treated with colour. A white or red coat of colour moderates the moulding without erasing it. To a lesser degree, the same rules apply to calcium silicate units, although the colour scale in these units is more or less limited to the natural colour of the material in a few variations of grey. The similarity with the various grey hues of concrete and the interaction with it can achieve a subtle iridescent effect that transforms the oft-maligned coldness of exposed concrete into a velvety warmth. This iridescence, a changing atmospheric veil, comes together in front of the observer's eye out of a series of elements: first, the unit surface – its colours created by fire, shine, cinder holes, blisters, tears and grooves; next, the joint – its width, colour, surface and relief; and finally the bond – its horizontal, vertical and diagonal relationships and interactions as visible reminders of invisible deeds.

1.1.45 Tomb model of brick production, Egyptian wood sculpture, circa 2000 BC, Berlin State Museums
1.1.46 Brick production in Pakistan, 1999
1.1.47 Building site in Mali, 1999

Header bond   1.1.48

English bond   1.1.49

English cross bond/St Andrew's bond   1.1.50

Gothic bond   1.1.51

Gothic bond – variation   1.1.52

Flying bond   1.1.53

The bond

In masonry, the bond is the most important means of design in two regards: first, it has no model in nature, but is entirely based on abstract calculation. It is a system of rules for the creation of a readable, but largely invisible composition, of which the observer is constantly reminded. And second, while its function today is to guarantee the stability of a wall, it is also a representation of a world order, a fetter, a constraint imposed by a system, as indeed the word "bond" intimates. Any keen observer of masonry that has been laid and jointed with expertise will experience this captivating tension. The unique beauty of Cistercian masonry is widely appreciated and has been the topic of much praise. The Cistercian Order was founded on a philosophy of fulfilling the promise of salvation in the Christian faith by serving the community in practical ways. Walls were raised, as they still are today, in accordance with a basic system, the bond. The profane, functional character is replaced by a metaphorical reference to the overriding logic in the geometric plan of the universe. Herein lies the core of the forces at work: exposing the invisible. The same forces are still felt today when knowledgeable observers stand in front of a building with an expert bond and make an effort to reconstruct this discriminating rapport, an effort that requires a great amount of systematic thought, spatial vision, concentration, imagination and experience. Yet the naturalness, simplicity and clarity are convincing in their own right, even without the aforementioned references. Small movements, projections and recesses of no more than 10 to 20 mm are sufficient to produce significant architectonic effects. This is because the eye measures the wall in units of bricks and since

this narrow range of expression – which we have called "resistance" – harbours an abundant reservoir of invention, which stirs receptivity in a most unusual manner.

In the following, we shall present and describe the most common bonds among the great variety of systems in use today. Each has its own unique effect, which is important for the quality of the design, since a carefully planned building will offer an attractive visual image from any distance. The scale seen from a distance should be harmoniously reflected and logically interpreted in each intermediate scale from distant to close-up, where the character of the material, the surface texture and the bond are in the foreground. A bond must always adhere to a distinct precision and yet appear perfectly natural and without artifice.

Header bond (fig. 1.1.48)
Header bond derives its name from the fact that it reveals only the headers or end faces of the units. Structurally, it is rather a poor solution because the load distribution is compromised in the longitudinal direction of the wall. It's adaptability is chiefly exploited in curved walls and arches. From the very beginning another common application of this bond has been to create patterns with polychrome or glazed bricks. Plain brickwork surfaces (see St Mary's in Stralsund, fig. 1.1.56) can be enriched with diamond patterns. The facing masonry has been integrated into the backing as an incrustation. Header bonds were widely used during the Gründerzeit at the end of the 19th century, an era of rapid industrial growth. The principal rationale was its efficiency. The visible external surface consisted of quarter and half bats, frequently even of quarter and face slips made of high-precision extruded elements, similar to today's split-faced units. With these elements, the effect of expensive, fine facing masonry could be simulated cheaply. The result, however, is a surface that is obtrusively perfect and without tension or interest.
The Faguswerk in Alfeld, Germany, on the other hand, designed and executed by Walter Gropius and Adolf Meyer beginning in 1911 and well into the 1920s (fig. 1.1.35), is a subtle play with contradictions. It is a brick masonry building, although the glass curtain facade would have us believe otherwise. It paraphrases the monumentality of Behrens's Turbine factory into a parody. As Julius Posener comments, Gropius contradicts the "natural" relationship between support and load. The result comes as a shock to the observer. The choice of header bond, known for its low loadbearing capacity as mentioned above, is another case in point. Used, for example, at the point of highest stress, the junction between the angled masonry column and the tympanum, it is a clever device to create an effect of extreme fragility. The cubist

1.1.54

residential block design by architects Kahlfeldt (see example 20 in part 4 "Details of built examples") is intended to provide a stark contrast to the frame structures in the courtyard. To achieve such cool neutrality, the half-brick masonry facing is executed in header bond. It comes alive above all through the firing marks on the bricks.

English bond (fig. 1.1.49)
English bond is the most sober and powerful masonry bond, which can, however, achieve remarkable effects in the hands of an expert precisely because of the simplicity of its arrangement. The extremely sparse and sober volume of the Catholic Church in Güstrow, designed by Paul Korff-Laage with masonry in English bond (fig. 1.1.57), is distinguished by its impressive lighting strategy. A large west window illuminates the church interior and two choir windows allow light to fall onto the altar from the north and south sides. Only a narrow slit between the column and the wall behind it illuminates the vestibule.
In the former provincial bank of Pomerania in Stralsund (fig. 1.1.54) shallow projections and recesses of no more than 10 mm between the stretcher and header courses give the volume an effortless, layered monumentality. The English bond on the Meyer warehouse building designed by Hans Poelzig (fig. 1.1.55) is structured by two narrow stepped projections, one in front of the other, whose vertical edges produce a four-course-high zigzag pattern set off from the regular bond. The windows diminish imperceptibly in width from storey to storey. Towards the cornice, the stepped reliefs grow increasingly dense. The reliefs frame the building at the top and yet maintain a measure of openness. A surface with a vibrating tension has been created on this building with efficient, deliberated discipline.

1.1.55

English cross bond (fig. 1.1.50)
The technical quality of English cross bond is only evident in masonry depths greater than 365 mm, because this thickness allows for both the longitudinal and the transverse bond to be staggered, which alternates the joint pattern on both external surfaces by one course each. By shifting the stretcher course by one half brick length, a diamond pattern develops on the external surface, more or less visible depending upon the angle of the light and the precision or clarity of the joints. Fritz Höger mastered this diagonal cross pattern with its changing, atmospheric moods – especially apparent when bricks of iridescent colours and a glossy surface are employed – with tremendous

variety (by projecting and recessing individual headers).

Gothic bond (figs. 1.1.51 and 1.1.52)
Gothic bond is often called Flemish bond (especially in North America and the UK). Both bonds illustrated above were used as early as the *German Backsteingotik*. Apart from flying bond, most monumental buildings of that time are executed in Gothic bond. The dogmatic severity we usually apply to bonds was still unknown then. It was not unusual to see flying bond alternate with Gothic bond in different components of the same building. This may be explained by the duration of the building phase, spanning several generations or even

1.1.54 Former provincial bank of Pomerania, Stralsund 1930, architect: Adolf Theßmacher
1.1.55 Meyer warehouse building, Hannover 1921-22, architect: Hans Poelzig
1.1.56 St Mary's, Stralsund, 15th century, west facade detail
1.1.57 Catholic Church, Güstrow 1929, architect: Paul Korff-Laage

1.1.56

1.1.57

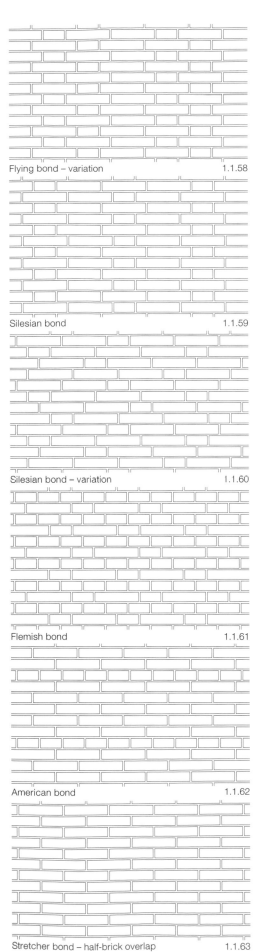

Flying bond – variation   1.1.58

Silesian bond   1.1.59

Silesian bond – variation   1.1.60

Flemish bond   1.1.61

American bond   1.1.62

Stretcher bond – half-brick overlap   1.1.63

1.1.64

centuries. Irregularities in the hand-moulded monastery brick format also imposed changes on bond design. Projections, recesses and perforations in a church courtyard wall in Prague perfectly illustrate the tremendous opportunities for variety in working with this bond (see fig. 1.1.115).

The large side wall to the nave of the Sacred Heart Church in Prague, designed by Josef Plečnik (fig. 1.1.64), is faced with bluish-purple engineering bricks in Gothic bond. The plasticity of projecting concrete bricks in the never-ending pattern register adds a second scale to the surface, which flares outward at the top, changing the value of the concrete units from bas-relief to spatial components – a highly unusual and inventive design. Mies van der Rohe preferred thin formats for his brick homes in the 1920s because of the precision in scale they offer. One of his most beautiful designs, Villa Wolf in Guben on the Neisse River, is realized with carefully proportioned, expansive brick masonry walls in Gothic bond (fig. 1.1.67). The captivating texture, terminating in soldier courses set into the bond, is almost painfully incised with openings without lintels, no doubt a horror to naïve purists of brickwork.

Flying bond (fig. 1.1.53 and 1.1.58)
Flying bond, also called monk's bond or York-shire bond, is an ancient bond like Gothic bond; these two bonds dominate the image of medieval buildings in northern Europe. The oldest brickwork church building, the Jerichow monastery church (1114 AD) is largely executed in flying bond. Influences from northern Italy in many details may also indicate that the bond originated in Lombardy. Flying bond does not have the same two-dimensional tension as Gothic bond. By doubling the stretcher component in each course, the tension is slightly

diminished, resulting in a rather stolid overall appearance.
Fritz Höger proves his mastery of working with facing bricks in the church on Hohenzollern-platz in Berlin (fig. 1.1.65). The gilded headers glow softly in the dark brown brick fabric of the nave. Despite the expressive sequential disposition of vertical wall components, the volume is characterized by a hermetic and disciplined cohesion.

Silesian bond (figs. 1.1.59 and 1.1.60)
An artful variation of the Silesian bond, also called Flemish garden wall bond, and similar to the Flemish bond in the diagonal cross pattern, features one header in each course alternating with three stretchers and a register of 12 courses.

Flemish bond (fig. 1.1.61)
Flemish bond is also called Dutch bond or English cross bond. It derives its lively character from a loose, seemingly random diagonal arrangement of five stepped headers per pattern segment. The result is a slightly hyperactive image that is shown to best advantage on large surfaces (fig. 1.1.66).

American bond (fig. 1.1.62)
American bond, also called English garden wall bond, is a modified English bond in which three or usually five courses of stretchers are laid in half-brick overlap between two header courses on the face of the wall. It is largely unknown in Europe. The classic brick architecture on the East Coast of the United States, in Boston, New York or Philadelphia for example, as well as Thomas Jefferson's famous estate at Monticello, Virginia, do not feature this system, but the bonds described above. Due to the high component of stretcher courses, this bond

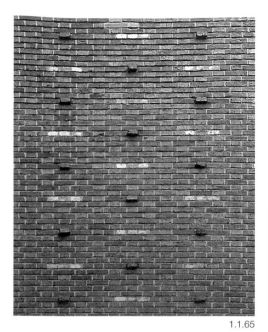

1.1.64   Church of the Sacred Heart, Prague, 1921-32,
         architect: Josef Plečnik
1.1.65   Church on Hohenzollernplatz, Berlin 1929,
         architect: Fritz Höger
1.1.66   Flemish bond on Deutsches Technikmuseum,
         Berlin, 2000, architects: Titz, Wolff, Breune
1.1.67   Villa Wolf, Guben 1925-26,
         architect: Ludwig Mies van der Rohe

1.1.65

1.1.66

offers little stability. The simplicity of the pattern, transparent even at a brief, casual glance, lacks the discriminating sophistication of the "European" bonds.

Stretcher bonds
In masonry, we always differentiate between an external, visible, weatherproof and attractive layer and the material behind it, consisting of backfilling (in hollow masonry), unfired bricks, backing clay bricks, natural stone, concrete, reinforced concrete, steel cores, etc. Until very recently, however, this facing masonry was integrated with the internal part of the wall or

through-bonded to form an indivisible whole: the masonry structure. Developments in building science and scientific studies on wall composition have separated these components into independent parts according to the task they need to fulfil. The principal tasks are load-bearing, insulating, blocking and cladding. Each is now represented in an independent wall layer. What may seem a simple and logical step had far-reaching consequences for the aesthetic of the whole. This may come as a surprise at first glance, since the basic theoretical problems of this new concept of wall composition have always been considered in many

different ways throughout the long history of architecture, as we have shown in the preceding section. In the functional context of building science in multilayered wall composition, masonry is simply "suspended", usually in half-brick, in front of the other layers for reasons of economy. Since the connection to the rear is achieved with the help of wall ties and storey-high brackets supporting, the technical task of this facing is reduced to one of integrating the longitudinal forces. And, as was explained at the beginning, it is a common and generally ignored misconception that the design task is simply limited to fulfilling this function.

1.1.67

Stretcher bond – half-brick overlap (fig. 1.1.63)
Stretcher bond with half-brick overlap (raking stretcher bond) as a curtain wall of clay or calcium silicate units is a very popular and widespread application. Owing to its even scale it is, however, quite banal and even boring, especially in surfaces that stretch across large areas. Justifying its use by referring to the honest, sober and functional quality of the bond merely reveals a poor understanding of the true quality in the design of a masonry surface. Honesty cannot be experienced as an abstract value; it must find concrete expression and is, moreover, too superficial a basis for aesthetic judgement. It does not reflect the complexity at work in the perception and evaluation of visual phenomena. This process of evaluation is always informed by the observer's own conscious and unconscious concepts, beside which morality can only play a secondary role. Moreover, truthfulness in design can also contradict the structural or engineering truth. And which "truth" would then be valid?
The claim to truthfulness can thus only be regarded as an attempt at justification. It can

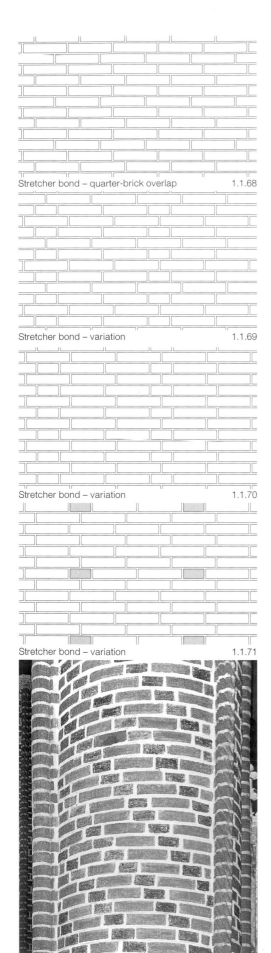

Stretcher bond – quarter-brick overlap   1.1.68

Stretcher bond – variation   1.1.69

Stretcher bond – variation   1.1.70

Stretcher bond – variation   1.1.71

1.1.72

1.1.73

never equal the elemental power of aesthetic conviction. Truth in design as an artful lie has always been stronger in the history of building than other forces. This is equally true for functional justifications, since functionality is an aesthetic term in origin; that is, it belongs to the same category.

Stretcher bond – quarter-brick overlap (fig. 1.1.68). The simple, quarter-brick stretcher bond (also known as raking stretcher bond) demonstrates a variety of compositions with ease, which create a rhythm in the vertical joint disposition that guides the eye (from one joint to another) and stimulates the visual imagination. It is reminiscent of a repetitive rhyming scheme – a tercet, for example – making the logic and wit of the scheme readily accessible. In a variation of this bond, the horizontal weight of the predominant stretcher courses is contrasted with a vertical course and diagonal "cross-knots" (fig. 1.1.69). The vertical pattern in the bond shown in fig. 1.1.70 has the rhythm of four-four time in music, with alternating accentuated and non-accentuated measures. The half-brick facing on a bridge abutment shown in fig. 1.1.71 is visually grounded by means of slightly darker headers. The continuous register of stretchers is transformed into a finite and defined surface through the contrapuntal grid of the headers. The aesthetic here

lies in the discreet colour difference between stretchers and headers. The observer is presented with a changing image hovering between confusion and clarity. A masterful tour de force!
In the trade, these bonds are now commonly, and erroneously, referred to as "ornamental bonds". To interpret bonds as ornament, as mere decoration, is in direct contradiction with the tectonic quality of these bonds. However, beyond tectonics, masonry has also found expression in a wealth of embellishments since the very beginning. One possibility of enriching the bond is to use coloured or colour-glazed brick patterns on the surface. The round choir columns of the main aisle in St Gotthard's in Brandenburg (fig. 1.1.72) feature green glazed headers staggered into a spiral in Gothic bond. Expressionist architecture of the 20th century favoured relief styles with projecting and recessed bonds in engineering bricks. Another possibility of treating masonry as an "ornamental bond" is to abandon the usual practice of laying bricks as headers and stretchers, but to place them on vertically and diagonally. This design form has been employed throughout history in endless variations. During the 19th century in particular to decorate verges and gables.
The dovecote in Varangeville-sur-Mer, Normandy (fig. 1.1.73), demonstrates the playful

abundance of materials, colours and relief in the horizontal bands of masonry whose plasticity increases as the colours grow more subtle towards the cornice. Here is an example of bond as ornament.

Natural stone

Magnificent buildings have been erected in natural stone by all advanced civilizations around the world. Today, this material is used chiefly for cladding and – with the exception of repairs to old buildings and historic reconstructions – it no longer plays an important role in building. Still, it is important to mention several design characteristics.

Three types of natural stone are used in building construction:

Primary rock (plutonic and igneous rock) such as granite, porphyry, diorite, diabase, basalt. They all have a random crystalline structure, are extremely hard with high compressive strength and are difficult to process.

Stratified rock (in flinty, limy or argillaceaous compositions) such as sandstone, calcite or limestone, shell lime, calcareous sediment, Jurassic limestone, marble, quartzite and slate. Owing to their geological origin in consolidated sediment they have a layered structure, subjected to additional geological pressure in some cases, e.g. in slate. The layered structure must be taken into consideration when processing stratified rock or using any of these rocks in walls.

Conglomerates such as calcareous tufa and nagelfluh. The structure of conglomerates is amorphous and random in character, making them suitable for many applications.

Natural stones must be processed and combined into masonry according to their origin.

Some examples follow to illustrate this principle. Crystalline plutonic rocks, such as granite, result in a block-like, stocky image in the masonry (fig. 1.1.74). A geological exception is the boulder (also called erratic block), a granite polished into a round shape by the movement of glaciers in the last great ice age and transported across vast distances in the process. In earlier times, boulders were used in their original shape for foundations and battlements, as in this example in Rheinsberg (fig. 1.1.75). It takes great skill to erect high walls with these rounded rocks. When boulders are split into natural shapes, they can be joined into powerful random rubble masonry with spauled joints (fig. 1.1.76). In contrast to random crystalline primary rock, slate – which can be split easily along its natural layers – should be used in masonry that shows these layers to the best effect. Owing to its natural horizontal supporting surfaces, slate can be used for dry walling that is stable even without mortar. It can also be set vertically without a batter (fig. 1.1.77). These highly different parameters for working with stone have evolved into rules on how to build walls, which have been followed in traditional masonry ever since Vitruvius's drawings and definitions from the 1st century AD. The unspoken rule in all these traditions is that the artistic quality in natural stone masonry is in direct proportion to erasing any traces of construction. This evaluation, beginning with coursed random rubble masonry, culminated in the polished surface without (visible) joints. Even when architecture began to focus on human activities in the 18th century, increasingly making them the topic of building, another 150 years would pass before the same principle was reflected in how buildings themselves were executed. Whenever possible, any trace of how a stone was lifted, laid and fastened was hidden in the finished wall.

1.1.74

1.1.68 Stretcher bond, quarter-brick overlap
1.1.69 Stretcher bond with interspersed flying bond I
1.1.70 Stretcher bond with interspersed flying bond II
1.1.71 Bond pattern in bridge abutment in Hannover, 1995-96, architect: Kai-Michael Koch
1.1.72 Choir pier, St Gotthard's, Brandenburg
1.1.73 Dovecote, Varangeville-sur-Mer, Normandy, Manoir d'Ango
1.1.74 Romanesque portal, St Gotthard's, Brandenburg, 12th century
1.1.75 Medieval city wall at Rheinsberg Castle
1.1.76 Monastery wall, Chorin, 1827
1.1.77 Dry walling with slate, Pyrenees

1.1.75

1.1.76

1.1.77

Le Corbusier was the first to draw the observer's eye deliberately to signs of the building process, the work itself. The manufacture of ashlar stone and processing the stone into the most challenging architectural components was and is a crowning cultural achievement. In all this, the disposition of the joints, the joint layout, is of prime importance. Bed joints must always be arranged perpendicular to the compressive load; perpends between ashlar stones must never occur in an angle, coving or corner of the volume, but always at inconspicuous orthogonal positions. This attitude towards joints is directed at reshaping tooled pieces and combining them artfully in the masonry (fig. 1.1.78). It is fundamentally different from the bonding rules of clay brickwork. Only terracotta relief is divided according to ashlar stone rules. One of the astonishing and alarming facts in the history of building is that the knowledge of working with ashlar stone has become nearly obsolete within just two generations after millennia of expertise and practice. Today, the upright joint in ashlar jambs is (*horribile dictu*) often set into the window sill slab. Depending upon hardness and composition, natural stone surfaces can be processed from the natural cleft (or quarry-faced) condition by sawing, bossage, pointing, bush hammering, charring, smoothing, grinding and polishing. Nearly all these processing steps can be machine-tooled today.

The joint

The joint characterizes the masonry, it is an enduring testament to the intelligent and artistic achievement of building, that is of "jointing", the wall. In Old High German the word "Fuge" (joint) signified both the place where two pieces were joined as well as the dexterity and skill in making the joint; originating as a term in this trade, it gradually took on a figurative meaning in many other areas of life. The joint reveals how the pieces are linked: it defines the bond. It has always sparked theoretical debate in architecture, e.g. the "joint dressing" metaphor in the Semperian theory of cladding. The treatment of joints is invariably an indicator of the architectonic stance. Hence, it plays an important role in the design.

1.1.79

1.1.78

In facing masonry with clay, calcium silicate and concrete bricks, the aesthetic and technical importance of the joint is often underestimated. It is even more important here than in natural stone masonry. The joints cover the surface like a dense mesh and give it scale. In the case of masonry units, the width of the joint is dependent on the format of the unit.

By accentuating or downplaying the importance of the joint, the designer can influence the tone, liveliness and character of the surface to a great degree, even so far as to reverse its effect completely. The colour repertoire ranges from pure black to dark blue, red, muted greys and yellow to pure white. One rule of thumb is that the colour of the stone is intensified the darker the colour is in the joint. A pure white joint tends to appear clumsy and bleaches colour from the units. It pushes itself into the foreground, becoming too dominant in the overall image and thereby violates another rule: namely, that the joint design must never become the primary feature, but always support the overall visual intention in as inconspicuous a manner as possible. Creative solutions such as tinting the mortar – for example, in order to emphasize the horizontal in the masonry by tinting the perpends in stone colours or moving them closer together, while executing the bed joints in the usual manner – were applied in many different ways in the 1920s. Today, these solutions have almost fallen into obscurity. Colour effects in joints are at their best when the difference in colour between joint and unit is imperceptible in the overall appearance of the surface and is only

discernible upon closer inspection.

A certain liveliness or, in the most successful cases, an iridescent tension is, however, not merely a product of attuning the differences in colour between unit and joint. The scale, which is defined by the network of joints, is just as important. It is also influenced by creating a harmony between the size of the unit and the width of the joint, and for this reason we must deviate briefly to the topic of format. The relationship between joint and unit is harmonious with the formats commonly used today, the standard format or the thin format. In facing masonry with 2 DF formats, the joints are already out of balance. This is one of the reasons why 2 DF masonry is never truly satisfactory from an aesthetic point of view. In the past there were a number of larger and smaller formats, always appropriate in size for manual handling. This was chiefly a result of the technology then available, but also because of the quality of the clay and other practical reasons. The medieval monumental buildings of the Hanseatic Gothic were constructed with bricks in monastery format with an approximate joint width of 15 mm. The decisive factor in these structures was the greater elasticity offered by pure lime mortar with coarse aggregates compared with brittle masonry units. At the same time, consideration was given to the lower loadbearing capacity of mortar. But the overall effect in colour and tectonics of these expansive walls, as well as the treatment of the joint network to scale, is also in harmony with the large formats. One basic rule is that the scale of the building and its subdivisions should establish a specific, deliberate relationship with the scale of the joints. Smaller formats, such as the Dutch or the Oldenburg format, can easily tempt one towards a more decorative treatment of joints with widths ranging from 15 to 20 mm – especially in the case of fine Dutch hand-moulded bricks. The tectonic context is lost. The units float in a mass of joints because the intention is not to integrate them into the overall context of the masonry but to highlight them as individual features.

The manner in which the joint surface is produced is important for both the durability and the (visual) effect of the joint. The joint material is always less durable than the adjoining masonry unit. The simplest and most cost-efficient manner of creating a durable joint is "flush pointing", that is filling the joints of brick-work or blockwork with wet mortar and striking excess mortar off flush with a trowel. Any subsequent working of the joint with jointers, or even better with a piece of hose or a sliver of wood, has the sole purpose of matching the roughness of the joint surface to that of the surrounding stone. In that case, the entire mass of joint mortar must be premixed in the desired joint colour.

The common method, however, is to rake out the joint to 10 to 20 mm depth during the bedding process and to fill in (point) the joints later, thus gaining more control over achieving the desired visual effect. This methods allows for colour differentiation in the joints, projecting or recessing the joints, plastic rendering of the joint, scoring the joint, embossing, pressing gravel, porcelain or similar materials into the joint. When joints between hard-fired units are recessed, the resulting shadow lines articulate the masonry surface in a particularly impressive manner.

Again, there are a number of rules to be considered. Thus, the roughness of the joint should match the degree of roughness of the unit's surface. The same is true of the hardness of the joint, which also should correspond to the hardness of the unit. A soft facing unit should be jointed with pure lime mortar and siliceous, gritty aggregates.

Fig. 1.1.79 shows a carefully executed battlement wall, which has already been subjected to weather abrasion.

1.1.80

1.1.81

The lime-bonded grit is especially easy to recognize. Catalan masonry of prefabricated brick elements, 200 x 420 x 40 mm, similar to Roman bricks, such as Antonio Gaudí used in his buildings in Barcelona, have been used. Sintered units required cement additives. The surface of the joint must never be "ironed out" with the jointer because this will concentrate the binding agent on the surface of the joint; this results in fine fissures whose capillary effect "draws" rainwater into the joint. The "clinker disease" (masonry saturated with moisture on the inside), dreaded in the 1920s, was partly due to such erroneous joint design. Irregular units, e.g. hand-moulded bricks, should have flush joints whenever possible. The following four historic examples illustrate different approaches and interpretations of working with joints:
The masonry of the Friedrichswerder Church (fig. 1.1.80) is stretched like a membrane. The joints project in pronounced half-rounds, like

veins on an anaemic, thin-skinned body. At the time of Ludwig I, the Munich school promoted a style of masonry in which the joints were elegantly and artfully reduced to a millimetre-thin minimum. This is achieved with facing bricks which diminish into wedges towards the interior of the wall or by creating an approx. 20-mm-wide bearing area for both the bed joint and the perpend, behind which the brick is reduced in width and height.

As in Friedrich Gärtner's saltworks administration building in Munich, the joints are often almost invisible in the buildings designed by his students (fig. 1.1.81). Specials were manufactured to achieve the interior angle at the projecting pilaster. The beauty of this solution lies in the enchanting interaction of colours on the planar, delicately stretched brick surfaces. The world-renowned curtain wall of the Fagus-werk is one example of a group of brickwork buildings in which fragility and extreme tension became the thematic focus of the design in a

1.1.78 Notre-Dame de l'Epine, Champagne,
        1400-1527 AD
1.1.79 Self-supporting battlement wall of a fortress,
        Collioure, Pyrenees, end of 17th century
1.1.80 Friedrichswerder Kirche, Berlin, 1824,
        architect: Friedrich Schinkel
1.1.81 Kunstmuseum Hannover, 1852-56,
        architect: Conrad Wilhelm Hase
1.1.82 Faguswerk, Alfeld, 1911,
        architects: Walter Gropius and Adolf Meyer
1.1.83 Madsack House, Hannover, 1972,
        architect: Fritz Höger

1.1.82

1.1.83

1.1.84

fascinating manner. The pure header course masonry in third grade bricks features careful jointing by means of undercutting at the brick edge and pencil-thin beads of mortar in a well-balanced, graceful harmony (fig. 1.1.82). Fritz Höger's masonry surfaces are designed with true virtuosity, both optically and aesthetically. In a private house, designed in a Cubist spirit, the angular projecting bed joints provide the sole optical division, carried throughout the wall with great consistency (fig. 1.1.83). The entire house has a reserved, solid presence achieved primarily by the simple expedient of the divisions created by the joint design.

The joint in natural stone masonry
The ashlar masonry of antiquity – especially in ancient Greece – is characterized by a degree of precision in the joint design that surpasses the mere necessity of scale and takes on a monumentality of its own. The aesthetic goal is to create a visible reference of the independent value of masonry as a designed volume – a piece of nature reassembled by human hands through the technical perfection in the visible trace of this "assembly", that is in the joints (fig. 1.1.84).
This philosophy sheds light on the contradiction that the tension in the appearance of the

masonry and the stone treatment increases proportionately to the delicacy and restraint in the joint design. There are few opportunities today to revel in the organizing power of stone in quite the same manner, since natural stone is rarely used as masonry, but most commonly as mere stone facing in panels with open slits. The material appeal of natural stone is lost. Without the importance of the joints, the stone is deprived of its authenticity, its true self. It can only deteriorate into a "natural" veneer.

Division in masonry

In the first third of the 20th century there was a heated argument about whether division in masonry should be flush or three-dimensional. Various schools of thought formed which defended their claim to representing the only valid dogma with arguments based on theory and examples drawn from the history of building. With the perspective of time, it is perhaps difficult to comprehend fully how passionate the disagreement was at that time, for convincing examples exist in support of both principles.

In northern Europe, where climate conditions are harsh, it was common to create smooth external masonry with flush window frames. The timber frame and the window casement are flush with the external surface. The casements open outwards, and the prevailing strong winds press them firmly into the rebate. The graceful appearance of Dutch or Danish homes in facing masonry is the product of a small-scale texture consistently combined with flush window frames. Even upscale bourgeois homes in Lübeck or Danzig (today Gdansk) were characterized by fairly discreet and sparse divisions.

Conversely, three-dimensional divisions in a cubist spirit can look back on a tradition that is just as long and continues to this day.
The west facade of the Chorin monastery (fig. 1.1.87) is the most compelling historic validation of the plastic spirit in masonry. Since the monastic rule forbade any excess, the spiritual power of the design is expressed precisely in its ascetic restraint.

Another dogma prescribes that masonry must always be divided in the vertical direction because the material allows only for limited span widths. Once again, there are convincing built examples that support this rule and equally convincing examples that argue against it.

Figures 1.1.85 and 1.1.86 demonstrate that the schools of thought we have discussed are both true and false. The first building is just as convincing and differentiated in its plastic division as the second is by means of its rigorous planar tension. What both buildings have in common is the rhythmic tripartite division and the additive facade development, bordered by very simple and sparse means on the left and right sides. In the Bewag base in Berlin, the narrow plinth and the five-storey-high half-brick muntins, which are flush with the face and projecting by one full brick, are brilliantly conceived.

Mies van der Rohe (fig. 1.1.88) shows that such doctrines invite contradiction, that design is more than the mere effort to satisfy a certain dogma, that good architecture cannot be restricted by such narrow, superficial rules. He demonstratively dispenses with window sills, negates that there might be any limitation to spans in masonry and offers a contrapuntal response to the narrow, theoretical attitude of purists "who would like to diminish all architecture to prose" (Goethe). He cuts masonry

1.1.84   Fortifications at Messéne, Greece,
         4th century BC
1.1.85   Höhere Webeschule (Weaving College), Berlin,
         1909-14, architect: Ludwig Hoffmann
1.1.86   Bewag base, Berlin-Neukölln, 1926-27,
         architect: Hans Heinrich Müller
1.1.87   West facade of Chorin monastery church,
         13th century, gable of south aisle

1.1.85

1.1.86

1.1.87

1.1.88

surfaces open to reveal the dynamic of the joint in a new light: the fluctuating ambivalence between outside and inside. This approach interprets structural analysis as a design component, which is optically enhanced, one might say, in order to develop a heightened spatial connection through the negation and to portray it as a contradiction.

Vaults

Masonry units can bridge openings horizontally, or nearly horizontally, but not areas. One simple form of creating the ceiling is the blind vault in which the bricks are corbelled by degrees and piled towards the apex. In southern Italy this method is still in use.
A more sophisticated solution is to arrange the

bricks into an arch in such a manner that they would fall were it not for the support provided by other, similarly arranged bricks. This dynamic is even echoed to some degree in the terminology used in the trade for the most important components of such a construction: the bearing point of the vault is called the "springing", the last and decisive brick, which produces the retaining thrust, is the keystone. The achievements in vaulting, which were discussed in detail in the historical section, are a testimony to breathtaking struggles against the force of gravity. One famous example is Balthasar Neumann's nearly horizontal vaulting in the staircase of the Bishop's Residence at Würzburg.
Volumes on the history of vaulting techniques fill entire bookshelves. Yet very few masonry vaults are constructed today, with the excep-

tion, naturally, of historic reconstructions. One highly efficient 19th-century vaulting technique, the "Prussian Cap", in which segmental arched sections are spanned between steel columns, is still used from time to time. Prussian caps generate enormous horizontal thrust in the direction of the vault, which must be resisted by horizontal edge masonry or by a buttress set in front of the wall or (as in the shallow tunnel vaults in Le Corbusier's Jaoul Houses, fig. 1.1.89) by means of ties. From the perspective of design, the demise of the vaulting technique is regrettable since it represents the highlight in the art of masonry.

Openings and lintels

Anyone who has read the account of how Rat Krespel built his house and went about creating the wall openings, will understand the planning challenge this procedure poses, E.T.A. Hoffmann's eccentric storytelling style notwithstanding. Throughout the history of building, the relation of wall to opening, the design of the wall penetration, has provided the answer to the question of what is a wall. It also reflects how the architect, and the era, view the relationship between outside and inside, separation and connection, corporeality and space, shelter and danger – ultimately, how they view the world.
A Baroque "œil de boeuf" speaks volumes on this issue when contrasted with a diaphanous tracery rosette.
The technical problems of how to span openings are identical to those encountered in vaulting. Small windows can be spanned with cantilevered stones, as the following four examples demonstrate.
Fig. 1.1.90 shows a window composed of monastery brick formats in a bond with bricks

1.1.89

placed on end as window reveals. This solution is stunningly simple and natural. The window in fig. 1.1.91 is set into the bond and is covered by two projecting stretcher faces, supporting one stretcher which serves as a keystone and is braced with chamfered joints, an idea that is as ingenious as it is convincing. The window in fig. 1.1.92 is set into the bond and features a semicircular arch of stretchers, continued as a vertical jamb, which in turn is interlaced with the bond. The lintel with stepped, cantilevered headers in the English cross bond wall in fig. 1.1.93 exudes a reserved naturalness. Such stepped solutions were used for windows twice the width of the example shown in this figure (approx. 750 mm).

For wider window openings, considerable spans can be achieved with the vaulting technique. For reasons of expediency, however, most masonry is simply used as facing over arches constructed from other loadbearing materials, although the lintel stones used for this purpose tend to part into wide gaps along the top of the vault. A good solution to this problem is to create two or more arches one above the other, a technique that was already used in Roman masonry (see also fig. 1.1.13).

During the last third of the 19th century, the aforementioned Gründerzeit in Germany, the rapid expansion in the number of building tasks led to the predominant use of the segmental arch since it offered the best loadbearing capacity.
When repeated in one and the same building, the segmental arch can appear uninteresting and undecided. The nearly horizontal, so-called cambered arch offered a solution to this problem. (figs. 1.1.55 and 1.1.94) As a building form, the cambered arch had been familiar for centuries and it was frequently used for lintels in bourgeois homes in northern Europe. In the past, it was constructed across spans of up to 2.5 m without any difficulties or technical aids. To achieve this construction, there are, however, several prerequisites. It should always be carefully bricked up with full joints. It should be formed with a barely visible rise of several millimetres. In the past, this rise was created by applying a fine layer of sand onto the centering. Moreover, it should not exceed a span of

1.1.88 Esters House and Lange House, Krefeld 1928-30, architect: Ludwig Mies van der Rohe
1.1.89 Brick vaulting in Jaoul Houses, Le Corbusier, Neuilly-sur-Seine, 1952-56
1.1.90 Chorin monastery, 13th century, sexpartite window in brewery
1.1.91 as in fig. 1.1.90, window in brewery
1.1.92 as in fig. 1.1.90, window in west facade
1.1.93 Barn window, Hannover, 19th century
1.1.94 Stables on estate in Neustrelitz, 1870, architect: Friedrich Wilhelm Buttel
1.1.95 Faguswerk, Alfeld, smithy, 1911-14 architects: Walter Gropius and Adolf Meyer

1.1.90

1.1.91

1.1.92

1.1.93

1.1.94

1.1.95

1.1.96

1.1.97

2 m – especially in half-brick leaves.
The cambered arches in the brilliantly conceived masonry of the smithy in the Faguswerk (fig. 1.1.95) were processed from extruded material and subsequently installed as individual moulded units, fitted into the lintel bond across five courses.
Even in the era dominated by the Werkbund spirit, which held that masonry should only be constructed with genuine masonry materials, leading architects such as Fritz Schumacher and Fritz Höger took the liberty of resorting to auxiliary means to solve the problems that arise in spanning openings.
The horizontal cambered arches composed of specials in the entrance pavilion to the Kunstgewerbeschule (fig. 1.1.96) are suspended from the steel beams of the loadbearing structure. This solution in no way diminishes the aesthetic quality of the arches because the observer perceives the entire band of masonry beneath the cupola as a loadbearing component. All the elements are effortlessly subordinated to the conviction of the design concept.

In the Hanseatic regions on the North and the Baltic Seas, frames set into the windows, so-called sash frames, were used to span larger wall openings, additionally braced with centre muntins and wooden transoms in openings with even greater dimensions. The sash frames did double duty as falsework. This continues to be a frequent method in building with masonry in the Netherlands.

The next two examples serve to illustrate specific problems in creating lintels with masonry. The Jurassic lime door jamb illustrated in fig. 1.1.98 features corbel bricks on the top of the opening on which one-third of the ashlar lintel rests on either side. The profiles in the corbel bricks are harmonized with the beam width to achieve a natural and attractive ornamental head to the opening.
The community hall is carefully executed with pebbled sandstone in regular courses. The design of the window in fig. 1.1.99 is a textbook example of correct ashlar treatment. The sandstone lintel beam bridging the opening is

relieved by a lintel stone set above it. The joint between lintel and beam is left open to avoid load transfer. The joint between the window sill slab and the ashlar stone beneath it is open for the same reason, to prevent the window sill from bending upwards and breaking as a result of the stress exerted by the weight of the reveals in the rigid vertical joints.

Columns and piers

Next to vaulting, erecting columns from masonry has always been a high art. This is where the architect demonstrated his expertise. One need only remember the monumental order by Claude Perrault on the east facade of the Louvre. These columns could only be loadbearing due to their iron cores, a sensational solution at the time. Since Vitruvius, ideas on proportion in the order of columns have filled the prototype books of nearly every generation of architects. The confusing, albeit structurally logical, design of Gothic multiple rib pillars was breath-

1.1.98

1.1.99

1.1.100

takingly artful in execution. In modern design practice, masonry columns no longer play a role. For free-standing masonry columns, we must consider that, for the context of the masonry in the whole building volume, 240 mm columns can only be constructed with a half-brick overlap. For 365 mm columns, the choice lies between half-brick overlap and quarter-brick bond, which requires a large number of cut units. Moreover, the scale in such a column can no longer be harmonized with brick-on-edge or soldier courses.

To achieve a continuous soldier course in the column surround shown in fig. 1.1.97, the remainder is recessed as a slit and emphasized with a fluorescent orange colour.

Plinths and ramps

Plinths have the practical function of protecting a wall from dampness, splashing water, moss and dirt. They mark the boundary between building and ground and emphasize the stability of the foundation. Until the 18th century, people believed that the ground was home to mysterious, terrifying forces, that harmful rays emanated from the soil and dangerous spirits dwelled in the earth. Accordingly, plinth walls were often engraved with symbols, presumably to repel such evil spirits.

To give the storeys rising above the base a more significant and refined air, fortresses, castles and palaces often featured storey-high plinths in rusticated masonry. Another method was to create emphasis by means of an inclined or angled wall, a ramp. It, too, had the task of underscoring the massiveness of the base in contrast to the living areas above. The motif of the ramp continued well into the 20th century. Peter Behrens employed it in several of his buildings.

1.1.96 Entrance to Kunstgewerbeschule Hamburg, 1911-13, architect: Fritz Schumacher
1.1.97 Anderten clubhouse, Hannover, 1991, architect: Rolf Ramcke
1.1.98 Stables at Château de Nieuil, Perigord, France, 17th/18th century
1.1.99 Buchau community hall, Upper Franconia, 1879
1.1.100 Transformer station, Berlin-Neukölln, 1927, architect: Hans Heinrich Müller
1.1.101 Rectifier substation, Berlin-Zehlendorf, 1928, architect: Hans Heinrich Müller

1.1.101

The monumental buildings of the Hanseatic Gothic show only a frugal use of the plinth motif. The granite plinths constructed of rough-hewn boulders were at most 300 to 500 mm high. Many large and smaller buildings rose straight from the ground without a plinth.

While rendered buildings require a waterproof plinth of at least 300 mm height for protection against splashing rainwater, faced brickwork buildings appear at their most natural without a plinth or only with a slight gesture in that direction, e.g. a brick-on-edge or soldier course, which is flush with the street front as shown in the industrial building in fig. 1.1.100. In this building, a brick-on-edge course projects by one half-course depth, sufficient to "carry" the five-storey building.

1.1.102

1.1.103

1.1.104

Terminations and junctions

Flat roof terminations
Owing to roofing guidelines, which stipulate that horizontal edges of the coping must have a min. 50 mm overlap, the proportional balance of facing masonry is considerably compromised because this is a dimension that does not fit into its natural scale.
Many older buildings are ruined by the clumsiness of the new termination when the roof edge is repaired. The argument that rainwater is driven behind the roof covering by wind and saturates the wall with moisture is erroneous. On the contrary, rainwater is virtually drawn up by the negative pressure that exists in the lee-side cavities within the sheet metal capping. A simple solution to this problem is to seal the upper wall areas with bitumen or PVC sheeting, which also makes it possible to minimize the overlap to the ideal optical dimension of 10 to 15 mm. If the surround is constructed from hard-fired units, calcium silicate or concrete units, roofing felt welded flush to the wall will suffice, the only prerequisite being that the joints are flush and that the entire horizontal area is carefully bonded.

Ornamentation and decorative profiles in the coping have become a thing of the past. The powerful cantilevers are reduced to minimum measures.

The sober facade of the industrial building in fig. 1.1.101 is realized in flying bond. The closed surfaces are divided by diagonal oriels, supported by stepped, cantilevered courses. The building terminates in stepped, projecting headers. This design achieves a powerful impact with a few simple means. The only area where the otherwise smooth wall surfaces take on a three-dimensional expression is in this

upper cornice. The slight increase in the projection of each course completes the masonry wall in a harmonious manner. This clever device more or less leads to a natural termination of the wall: it simply cannot go any further.

In the pumping station shown in fig. 1.1.102, the roof and parapet rest on cantilevered piers at the corner of the wraparound walls. Like the lintels in the bond, the soffits are integrated into the floor formwork. The soldier course beneath the window sill is continued as facing on the external wall.

The continuous dividing scheme with recessed courses on the Faguswerk (fig. 1.1.104) also provides the final motif at the top of the building. The only difference is that the brick-on-edge course is projected by the same dimension used for the recessed courses; this doubling enhances the shadow cast in this area. It should be noted, however, that this construction required the use of steel flats at the corners.

In all these examples, the zinc plate enclosure is rolled (a stable sheet metal edge, easily manufactured on a folding press).

The pavilion of the university canteen in Eichstätt (fig. 1.1.105) features a highly successful surround on the rendered parapet. The razor-sharp edge consists of galvanized sheet iron, bolted to the wall surface with a 20 mm projection. The butt joints have a sheet metal lining to the expansion joints.

Verges
The transition between roof and wall at the verge of a steep roof invariably inspires some interesting design solutions. Some may look to historic predecessors, such as traditional Black Forest houses or alpine styles for inspiration.

It is important to reiterate that the quality of masonry lies in simplicity.

Two examples demonstrate this admirably. In fig. 1.1.106, roof and wall are constructed from the same limestone. The roof slabs are pushed from below and from the sides underneath the cantilevered stones of the tower wall rising above. The verge unabashedly reveals the roof construction above the carefully executed courses of ashlar masonry.

The masonry in fig. 1.1.103 is expertly "tumbled-in" perpendicular to the roof slope. The roofing tiles are laid in mortar and project only slightly beyond the gable.

Steep roof junctions

One of the issues in creating junctions to steep roofs is the junction between chimney and roof. The rule that chimney and roof junctions must be equipped with zinc flashings remains widely unchallenged although it is false. Before sheet zinc ever existed, structures were built that were the technical equivalent of modern solutions and far superior in design. The chimney junction was usually realized by thrusting the roofing tile underneath the chimney base at the sides and at the bottom (see also "Construction details", fig. 3.10.2). The joint was filled with fibre-reinforced mortar. This type of junction is easy to execute and many examples built in this manner remain in immaculate condition after many decades.

1.1.105

1.1.106

1.1.102 Pumping station, Hannover, 1996-96,
architect: Rolf Ramcke
1.1.103 Közal estate, Cologne, 19th century
1.1.104 Faguswerk, Alfeld, 1911,
architects: Walter Gropius and Adolf Meyer
1.1.105 Eichstätt college canteen, 1988,
architect: Karljosef Schattner
1.1.106 Former priory church at Ougy, Burgundy,
first half of 12th century

1.1.107

1.1.108

Sills

Prior to the invention of zinc sheeting, one major problem was how to conduct water away from the facade, and handling this difficulty required great experience, know-how and imagination. Medieval buildings treated this problem in an almost playful manner. Gothic churches, especially, are often covered in winding gutters on flying buttresses with canal ducts through column projections, re-routed into sloping open and closed gutters through which water was conducted to the gargoyles from whose mouths it was spewed clear of the building. Sills serve to drain water away from windows, from the reveals and the external surfaces of window sills. They are a rather inconspicuous wall detail. Although one might presume that conducting water away from a build-

ing should pose few problems, many deficiencies in this area occur in building practice. The design of the sill is generally a good indicator of the quality of detail in the overall planning. The recently restored 19th century building in fig. 1.1.109 demontrates that rendered surfaces without sheet coverings can also be a sustainable solution. Upkeep and a new surface coat are necessary every two to three years, although this is a small price to pay in view of the clean profile of render without sheet coverings.

Calcium silicate units are hard and dirt-repellent. A drip detail is therefore not required, and the concrete sill can finish flush with the wall (fig. 1.1.110). If, as in this example, the sill has the same surface density and dimension as the adjacent masonry unit, it will fit inconspicuously into the surrounding surface. The lateral per-

pends are filled with mortar and do not normally crack across standard spans. The example in fig. 1.1.111 illustrates how the problem at the three critical junctions can be solved. The rendered reveal is undercut to prevent water from penetrating into the joint between reveal and sill. The sill consists of galvanized sheet metal and features a recessed drip edge finished with a riveted steel angle. The rear edge is slid beneath the window frame profile.

In masonry of fired bricks, the tried-and-tested method of forming the sill is to lay a brick-on-edge course which is pushed beneath the window frame and projects by 10 to 20 mm beyond the faced of the wall at a slight angle. Flush joints and carefully executed joints in the brick-on-edge course are essential. (See also "Construction details", pp. 224, 226.)

1.1.109

1.1.110

1.1.111

Framework

One of the many applications of versatile masonry units is to use them as infilling between other structures built with timber, steel and reinforced concrete. In this case, the unit is non-loadbearing.

One of the most widespread combinations in the past was the half-timbered framework with infill masonry panels (bricknogging). It was used nearly everywhere because it was such an economic building method. In these constructions the masonry unit demonstrates its property as an infill element in a variety of ornamental bonds, usually just a half-brick thick. As illustrated in the northern German 18th-century warehouse in fig. 1.1.107, the infill panels and windows are always flush with the exterior to offer a minimal corroding surface exposed to the effects of wind and weather.

The industrial buildings of the 20th century, especially in regions with heavy industries such as iron and coal, proved that masonry units can also be combined with steel framework construction, which gives them an entirely new, streamlined, "engineered" appearance. Early examples are the water tower in Posen designed by Poelzig, as well as the industrial buildings by Hertlein and Behrens. Large steel mills in Germany's industrial Ruhr region, such as the Zollverein Colliery (fig. 1.1.112), took advantage of this economic and structurally sound construction method, adding a new, sinewy character to the landscape. Today, this method is no longer used in industrial building due to the problems of insulation in the steel construction.

Mies van der Rohe's campus buildings at the Illinois Institute of Technology (fig. 1.1.108) are reduced to scale, number and proportion. Steel framework and English bond masonry infill express an elemental simplicity in which even the smallest part is significant and defining. This invests the image in its entirety with an inimitable universality.

1.1.107 Half-timbered wool warehouse, Güstrow,
         18th century
1.1.108 Illinois Institute of Technology, Chicago, 1952,
         architect: Ludwig Mies van der Rohe
1.1.109 Town house, Brandenburg,
         first quarter of 19th century
1.1.110 Kindergarten, Hannover, 1967,
         architect: Rolf Ramcke
1.1.111 Eichstätt college canteen, 1988,
         architect: Karljosef Schattner
1.1.112 Zollverein Colliery, Essen, south entrance 12/1/2,
         1928-32, architects: Fritz Schupp and
         Martin Kremmer

1.1.112

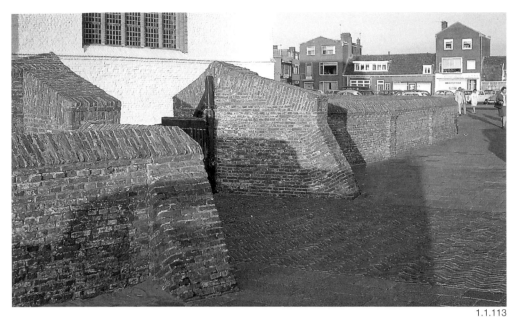

1.1.113

1.1.114

1.1.115

Free-standing walls

External walls follow their own building rules. Apart from their role as a boundary, they must also be impervious to decay. The walls can easily be protected from dampness rising from the ground, an aspect that must not be overlooked. Protection against frost and rain is more important, however. Frost protection is guaranteed primarily by selecting frost-resistant units. This is especially true for fired clay bricks. Calcium silicate and concrete units are inherently frost-proof. Joints fully filled with mortar are equally vital, for water penetrates more easily into cavities in the masonry of a free-standing wall, which leads to frost-induced cracks. Rendered walls require an overhanging coping with lateral drip edges. This requirement is often overdone for walls with facing masonry. What is necessary is to achieve a workmanlike joint surface, not completely "ironed out" or smooth.

The ancient and massive wall in fig. 1.1.113, which serves as a flood barrier for the church, is able to withstand the rough climate on the North Sea coast without any special coping.

Driving rain and gusty winds in the Pyrenees have eroded, but not destroyed, the masonry and joints of the wall coping in fig. 1.1.114. The perforated facing masonry, shown in fig. 1.1.115 in Gothic bond, remains without a coping, while the plaster pillars are protected by flared pagoda roofs.

The retaining wall in fig. 1.1.117 in the flood plain along the River Leine is constructed from Oldenburg bricks. The column and lintel at the end of the wall form an open window that frames the changing views of the river.

1.1.113 Churchyard wall in Katwijk, The Netherlands
1.1.114 Battlement parapet wall at Fort Collioure, France, 18th century
1.1.115 Church wall, Prague, 1920s
1.1.116 Parliamentarians building, Dhaka, Bangladesh, 1962-74, architect: Louis I. Kahn
1.1.117 Retaining wall on the bank of the River Leine, Hannover, 1993, architect: Rolf Ramcke

Masonry – today and tomorrow

When we look at the plastic treatment of walls across several millennia, we are astonished by the technical continuity in a building method that continues to express what building has always signified by means of simple layering and jointing. Manufactured units still fulfil their loadbearing and aesthetic task in much the same manner. Thus, the high thermal storage capacity of masonry is superior to other methods of thermal resistance. No insulating material, no matter how advanced, can equal the advantages of thermal storage. The concept of slowing thermal transmittance by means of insulation is not a sustainable method of energy conservation per se.

Since time immemorial, masonry as a building envelope has fulfilled a full range of tasks, both in terms of structure and building science. With a plaster finish it was shaped into panels and rough-hewn ashlar, or helped to create subtle, artistic effects such as in the Hofbibliothek in Vienna. If Erich Mendelssohn had used masonry for his Einstein Tower instead of a mix of materials with concrete, he would have been able to avoid building deficiencies. Regardless of the differences in how the internal structure of the wall is designed, natural stone or fired clay brick produce a surrounding shell. Thus, in the Oldenburg method it provided protection from wind and driving rain in the form of an external envelope set off from the actual wall by a cavity, long before such demands were made by the requirements of building science. We can only admire the variety and inventiveness with which masonry has adapted to new demands and resisted misuse without compromising its own intrinsic character over the course of the history of building. What has remained of this constancy in the contemporary debate on architecture?

1.1.116

1.1.117

Incrustations will develop into design elements in their own right; this is a simple fact in the history of building. It was, however, heatedly refuted towards the end of historicism, because incrustation had degenerated into routine decoration. What the debate ignored was the enclosing function, which had always existed, and whose aesthetic challenges had inspired specific solutions as an autonomous design task.

This is why we still use the metaphor of cladding, that is "a cloak" around the structure, for the skin, a term that originated with Gottfried Semper's cladding symbolism. Semper viewed the building as an unformed mass across which symbolic, referencing design characteristics are cast in the design process much like a cloak is thrown around a body. This view betrays its roots in historicism. While it is a step on the road towards considering external characteristics in relation to internal context, the symbolism limits the goal to one of meaning rather than function.
The action-related challenges of designing, which have become the dominant development in architecture since the beginning of the 20th century, cannot be addressed with the help of this theory.

The premise of this new focus in building is that envelope and core, skin and structure, are an integral and inseparable whole, which must also be treated as such from the perspective of design. Yet what we see beneath the skin, the surface, is not pure building, naked reality, as had been the desired aim of this new design philosophy, but simply another surface with all the familiar properties we had hoped to leave behind.

Moreover, the action-oriented attitude of building also results in a logical dilemma. Actions are but fleeting temporal sequences and can therefore not be transformed into a sustainable built substance. Purpose seems to offer the key to solving this dilemma. Purpose is to give permanence to the action. Even this approach is doomed to fail, however, for purposes are also subject to change. Hence, in the course of the 20th century purpose has been transposed into an enduring system rationale. Purpose is integrated with strategic equivalents of action by posing the question as to the function of each purpose.

Conversely, experience has shown that historic buildings, which do not adhere to a logical purpose rationale, retain a material "surplus" and are thus equipped to age. Such buildings can accommodate new purposes even when their framework no longer supports the original vision of the function/purpose relationship.

1.1.118

1.1.118 Museum of Roman Art, Merida, Spain, 1985,
architect: José Rafael Moneo

These buildings derive material resistance from the masonry quality. The perceived inaccessibility creates a sense of alienation, which can metamorphose into familiarity with new uses. Such buildings become "places to be".

Even masonry conceived as an envelope for reasons of rationalization has a specific relationship to the building, which is reflected in the design. This relationship must go beyond simulated symptoms of a fictitious building function or tectonic. The demand for honesty, for baring the purpose of the building, has seduced architects into decorating or enriching buildings with visual facade symbols of functions that do not exist inside the building. Thus, a multistorey apartment building can be made to appear like a shed-like structure by linking the window fronts across two or three storeys. We have to look closely to distinguish the divisions and to uncover the simulated function. It is even easier to simulate building tectonics. Buildings that feature an ornamental blend of functional and tectonic props have the noncommittal character of cinematic scenarios, made even more complete through the use of architectonic illusions.

Yet these approaches cannot fulfil the design tasks and the new problems they need to address; Novalis expressed it thus: "The exterior is elevated to become a secret expression of the interior." The open-minded observer who believes that he has long since grasped all the relationships and denies the existence of any secret, is taken aback and yet stimulated to tear himself away from everyday perceptions. The pictorial transformation of things – the interior transformed into secret expression on the exterior – is the aesthetic domain. Seen in this light, the contradiction between aesthetic effect and functional reflection, which we set forth at the outset, no longer exists. What we have instead is the outer world of the inner world. And this is a perfect illustration of the position which perception occupies in design.

Through the approach of alienation we are confronted with a manner of perception from the outside, from a type of perspective that compromises and destroys contexts that seemed familiar. This is the case, for example, when cultural developments are explained by economic conditions, unleashing a new perception of the same developments. The spirit

that has been trapped in the world of things is liberated, transformed and awakened to new life.

Since the beginning of the 20th century, inside and outside, load and loadbearing, and hence our interpretation of masonry, have undergone fundamental changes as a result of qualifying spatial relationships. Now, we are called upon to do justice to these changes with our perception. The analogy of the human body, which had been our unconscious emotional reference point, no longer applies. The definition of the skin, that is, to be a barrier between outside and inside, has ceased to be an appropriate metaphor for building.

The impending danger is that the image may no longer reflect reality, but become an autonomous entity itself without making reference to reality. Masonry is no longer presented as the impenetrable mass it is, but as an image of solidity assembled and presented with a noncommittal, superficial attitude. This undermines the need for authenticity, believability and reliability. It cannot be regained by resorting to building methods that clearly display a nostalgic yearning for the past, nor can it be bridged by a design philosophy whose building forms express an ironic distance.

In Gothic buildings we experience massive, suspended weight precisely because of their antithetical treatment of stone. In the Renaissance, the full force of the masonry in the palazzi is wrested from incompatible elements. In the Baroque, weight was the product of a cycle of meanings, investing the stone with more meaning than it had before in an immaterial manner.

All three examples prove that authenticity is not a problem of the material, the masonry material, but an intellectual and spiritual achievement of accepting the challenge of what we are given and transforming it. The chapter "Built examples in detail" presents a selection of current examples to explore this very same topic: namely that the "inner idea", the design stamped upon the mass of exterior matter, is the essence of masonry construction.

Part 2 · Fundamentals

Material

Masonry units
  Clay bricks · Calcium silicate units · Auto-claved aerated concrete units · Concrete and lightweight concrete units · Granulated slag aggregate units · The designation of masonry units · New types of masonry units · Testing the mechanical properties of masonry units
Natural stone units
Mortar for masonry
  Forms of production and supply · Types of mortar · The properties of mortar and the requirements it has to meet · Mortars for natural stone masonry· New types of mortar
Plasters
  Plastering mixes · Coating materials · Plasters and plastering systems – applications and requirements · The application of plaster

Masonry bonds

General
Formats and specials
  Historical formats · Standard formats · Large-format elements · Special formats, special units
The relationship between dimensional coordination and unit format
  Dimensional coordination in buildings · Modular coordination in buildings · Dimensional tolerances and permissible deviations
The rules of bonding
Masonry wall bonds
  Wall bonds · End bonds · Column bonds

Structural masonry

The loadbearing behaviour of masonry
  Compression · Tension and tensile bending · Shear stresses
The principles of masonry design
  The evolution of European and national standards · Method of analysis · Safety concept · Determining the cross-sections from the loads · Three-dimensional stability · Analysis of concentric and eccentric compression · Analysis of safety against buckling · Analysis of tension and bending tension · Analysis of shear
Deformation and crack formation
  Deformations in masonry · Cracks in masonry · Causes and prevention of cracks in masonry

Natural stone masonry
  Design · Consolidation of natural stone masonry
Reinforced masonry
  Materials for reinforced masonry· Protecting reinforcement against corrosion · Structural reinforced masonry · Non-structural reinforcement · Shallow lintels · Prestressed masonry
Prefabricated masonry elements
  Materials · Production · Design · Safety during transport and erection
Masonry in earthquake zones

Masonry details

External walls
  Single-leaf external walls · Twin-leaf external walls · Non-loadbearing external walls · Gable walls
Internal walls
  Loadbearing internal walls · Non-loadbearing internal walls
Columns and free-standing masonry walls
  Columns · Free-standing masonry walls
Party walls
External basement walls
  Stability of external masonry basement walls · Waterproofing
Natural stone masonry
Openings in walls
  Arching action over openings · Beam-type lintels · Shallow lintels with masonry above · Masonry lintels and arches
Vaulting and arch floors
  Vaults · Masonry arch floors between beams
Point loads
Connections
  Connecting walls to floors and roof frames · Ring beams and capping beams

The building of masonry

Mixing and using mortar on site
  Mixing mortar · Using mortar
Protecting masonry against moisture
Laying during cold weather
Suitability and quality tests
  Quality control of prescribed masonry (RM) · Quality control of masonry according to suitability test (EM)
Perpends and bed joints
  Laying with mortar to the perpends · Laying without mortar to the perpends

Junctions with intersecting walls
  Bonded junctions · Butt-jointed junctions
Chases and recesses
Building and cleaning facing masonry
  Construction principles · Cleaning facing masonry
Jointing
  Flush and "bucket handle" joints · Pointing
Joint design
  Types of joints · The sealing of joints · The spacing and width of joints
Gauged brickwork
Mechanical fixings in masonry
  Anchors · Nail anchors
Rationalization measures
  Building to save space and costs · Rational laying techniques · Rational working with large-format masonry units · Modular masonry

Building science

Thermal insulation
  Heat transfer, thermal insulation parameters, terms · Thermal conductivity of building materials · Thermal insulation provided by layers of air · Determination of design values for thermal conductivity · Thermal performance of external walls · Windows · Translucent thermal insulation (TI) · Solar gains of opaque external walls · Heat storage · Thermal bridges · Airtightness · Requirements for thermal insulation · Energy-savings Act · Method of calculation · Thermal comfort · Thermal insulation in summer
Climate-related moisture control
  Humidity · Hygroscopic moisture · Capillarity · Water vapour diffusion · Calculating the quantity of condensation within components · Moisture behaviour of masonry · Water vapour convection · Protection against driving rain
Sound insulation
  Terms and definitions · Requirements · Sound insulation against internal noise · Sound insulation against external noise · Single-leaf walls · Twin-leaf party walls · Flanking components · External walls
Fire protection
  Building material classes · Fire resistance classes · Types and functions of walls · Requirements · Fire walls · Complex party walls · Classification of proven components · External walls with thermal insulation
Units and symbols for building science

Material

Konrad Zilch, Martin Schätz

Masonry should be considered as a composite building material consisting of masonry units and mortar. The minimum requirements regarding mechanical properties, quality and quality control of the units and the mortar are covered by numerous standards. Quality control is divided into the manufacturer's own measures during production and those of outside centres. In the factory, quality control is carried out by the manufacturer of the material independently at specified intervals. Monitoring of the production by acknowledged test and certification centres is carried out unannounced at regular intervals. Products for walls that owing to their technological innovation are not yet in general use and not fully proven in practice, or cannot be standardized because of their particular properties, are covered by temporary general building authority certificates. Such certificates are issued by the Deutsche Institut für Bautechnik (DIBt – German Building Technology Institute) in Berlin. The quality control of these materials is again guaranteed by the manufacturer's own measures during production, backed up by those of independent centres.

Masonry units

Masonry units are divided into man-made units and natural stone units. The man-made units are in turn divided into clay, calcium silicate, autoclaved aerated concrete, normal-weight concrete, lightweight concrete and granulated slag aggregate units, depending on their raw materials. The natural stone units, which these days are primarily used for the repair of stone masonry and rarely for new building work, include all naturally found types of rock that exhibit adequate minimum compressive strength without structural and weather-induced damage. While the natural stone units are all covered by the German masonry design code DIN 1053 part 1, the man-made masonry units are dealt with in various standards according to their raw materials.

In terms of geometry, the man-made masonry units are distinguished both by their dimensions and also by the percentage and arrangement of any perforations (circular, rectangular, cellular, slotted). Furthermore, there are differences in strengths, deformation behaviour, building science properties and surface finishes. The different properties are the result of the various raw materials used or the method of production. In geometric terms, the man-made masonry units are divided into bricks, blocks and elements. In terms of perforations, they are classified as solid (max. 15% perforations) or perforated (hollow block, horizontally perforated, vertically perforated). The perforations are introduced either to provide a better grip for the bricklayer or to improve the building science properties. And finally, man-made bricks can be distinguished by the type of mortar bedding (thin-, medium- or thick-bed masonry) and the form of the perpends (with or without mortar). Units for thin-bed masonry are described as precision or gauged units; these differ from standard units in that they are subject to tighter tolerances regarding their height and length. The header faces of units can be arranged in such a way that during construction either the complete perpend or only part of it is provided with mortar (thin- or thick-bed) or that the units are simply butted together. This type of perpend is increasingly used to satisfy building science requirements and for rationalization.

In masonry the choice of unit is primarily dependent on the structural and building science specifications for the particular wall to be built. The criterion for the structural requirement is the strength of the masonry units; the building science aspect is influenced by the dry gross density. Masonry units with high strengths exhibit a high dry gross density and hence good sound insulation characteristics as well. On the other hand, masonry units with good thermal insulation properties have a low dry gross density and usually a low compressive strength. Further aspects to be considered when choosing a type of masonry unit are resistance to freeze-thaw cycles and water absorption, as well as economic issues such as cost of materials and rational workability. The resistance to freeze-thaw cycles and water absorption are decisive factors in the choice of materials for facing work subjected to frost and driving rain.

Thermal conductivity values for the most important masonry materials are specified in EN 1745 in relation to the gross density. The values given in the tables are statistical evaluations of large numbers of test results from several European countries. As an example of the various masonry materials, fig. 2.1.1 shows the results of 446 separate tests on aerated concrete samples with their mean value and upper and lower tolerances. The figures specify the thermal conductivity values for the dry state as mean value and upper tolerance with 90% certainty for a 90% confidence coefficient. These values serve as the basis for calculating the thermal conductivity of a masonry construction. For building work in Germany the thermal conductivity design value for calculating the thermal insulation of a construction is based on moisture content equilibrium at 23°C and 80% relative humidity.

Clay bricks

There is verifiable evidence that fired clay bricks have been used for about 5000 years. In Mohenjo-Daro on the River Indus, part of present-day Pakistan, great quantities of these were used in walls, floors and canal building instead of the air-dried bricks used hitherto [59]. Therefore, clay bricks are the oldest and best-known man-made masonry units. They are produced from the natural materials clay and loam, or mixtures of the two. Preparing the materials for production involves passing them through a feeding unit, which achieves the best consistency of the mixture. In doing so, additives such as sawdust or polystyrene beads are frequently introduced; these are completely destroyed during the firing process to leave behind innumerable tiny pores. The pores reduce the gross density and hence the weight of the brick. This in turn decreases the thermal conductivity of the brick, which results in better thermal insulation properties. Preparation of the raw material includes passing the mixture through a mill, where it is both crushed and

2.1.1 Thermal conductivity of aerated concrete in relation to gross density

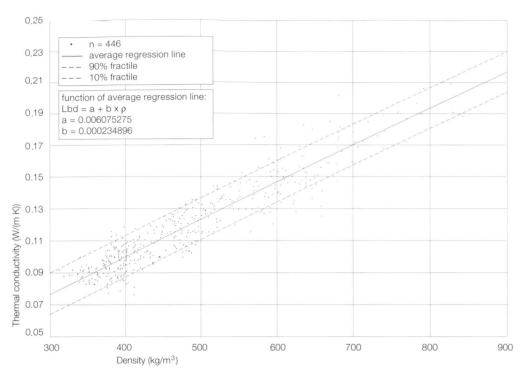

torn apart. This is necessary because the raw materials often include impurities of stone, slate or wood, whose influence is eliminated by the crushing process. Apart from that, this brings about a homogenization of the mixture. An ageing process concludes the preparation of the raw materials. This involves adding water to improve both the plasticity and the bonding power, and hence the overall quality of the clay. The prepared clay is fed to a worm extruder fitted with interchangeable dies. The mixture (evacuated and heated by steam to 30-40°C) is forced through the die at a pressure of about 13 bar. This produces a continuous ribbon, which is then cut by means of tightly stretched steel wires into individual "green" bricks. These stable units are dried at temperatures of up to about 100°C to remove the mixing water used in preparing the clay. This process is necessary to prevent the formation of steam during the firing process, which would otherwise burst the clay. Following the drying phase, which lasts between 90 minutes and 190 hours, the "green" bricks are fired at temperatures of between 900 and 1100°C. In doing so, the fine raw material particles are irreversibly fused to form a stable unit. In addition, the clay loses the chemically bonded water. After 10 to 48 hours the fired clay brick leaves the kiln. It now possesses its final properties and can be used immediately after cooling down (see fig. 2.1.3). The colour of the clay brick mainly depends on the percentage of metal oxides in the raw materials, as well as on the air surrounding the "green" brick during the firing process. Red bricks owe their colour to a certain iron oxide content and to an oxygen-rich kiln atmosphere. A lower iron oxide content leads to a yellow colouring of the brick, and an oxygen-starved kiln atmosphere results in a darker colour [39, 71, 207, 216].

The standard types of clay brick are given in table 2.1.4. These bricks, with the exception of moulded and hand-moulded varieties, must have a cuboid shape. The header faces of bricks with formats ≥ 8 DF may be provided with mortar keys. To improve the adhesion of plasters, grooves or similar keys are permissible on the stretcher faces. In the case of lightweight horizontally perforated bricks and bricks for use in prefabricated brick elements, additional recesses may be provided on the bed faces to permit the introduction of

2.1.2 Compressive strength classes, gross density classes and formats available

Type of clay brick	Abbreviation	Gross density class	Strength class	Formats
Vertically perforated brick DIN 105, part 1	HLzA HLzB	1.2–1.6	4–28	NF–16 DF
Vertically perforated facing brick, DIN 105, part 1	VHLzA VHLzB	1.4–1.6	12–28	NF–3 DF
Solid brick Solid facing brick DIN 105, part 1	Mz VMz	1.6–2.0 (2.2)	12–28	NF–5 DF
Vertically perforated engineering brick DIN 105, part 1	KHLzA KHLzB	≥ 1.9	28	NF–3 DF
Solid engineering brick DIN 105, part 1	KMz	≥ 1.9	28	NF, DF
Lightweight vertically perforated brick DIN 105, part 2	HLzA HLzB HLzW	0.7–1.0	4–12	2 DF–16 DF
Brick element DIN 105, part 2	HLzT	0.8–1.0	6–28	8 DF–24 DF
Solid brick Vertically perforated brick Solid engineering brick Vertically perforated engineering brick DIN 105, part 3	Mz / VMz HLz / VHLz KMz KHLz	1.2–2.2	36–60	NF–5 DF
Solid engineering brick Vertically perforated high-strength engineering brick DIN 105, part 4	KK KHK	1.6–2.2	60	NF–2 DF

reinforcement. Non-standard clay bricks are described in the section "New types of masonry units" [81].

Solid bricks
may exhibit max. 15% perforations perpendicular to the bed face.

Vertically perforated and lightweight vertically perforated bricks
are bricks provided with holes perpendicular to the bed face. According to DIN 105 parts 1 and 2, the total cross-sectional area of the holes may be between 15 and 50% of the area of the bed face. For vertically perforated bricks to DIN 105 part 3, the cross-sectional area of the holes is restricted to max. 35% of the area of the bed face. Vertically perforated bricks according to parts 1 and 3 should have a gross density exceeding 1000 kg/m³, lightweight vertically perforated bricks according to part 2 must exhibit a bulk density < 1000 kg/m³. These bricks are characterized by better thermal insulation properties and are therefore particularly suitable for the building of external walls.

Brick elements and lightweight brick elements
are large-format vertically perforated units with hole arrangements that form continuous vertical ducts after being laid. Reinforcement is passed through these ducts and grouted in with mortar. These are used for producing prefabricated brickwork elements to DIN 1053 part 4.

Solid, vertically perforated and lightweight vertically perforated facing bricks
are bricks characterized by good frost resistance. This is verified according to DIN 52252 part 1. The surfaces of these bricks may have a textured finish.

Solid and vertically perforated engineering bricks
are frost-resistant bricks whose surfaces have been vitrified and whose mean gross density is at least 1900 kg/m³. Water absorption is max. 7% by weight. The surfaces of these bricks may have a textured finish. Engineering bricks to DIN 105 part 1 must achieve at least compressive strength class 28, those to DIN 105 part 3 at least class 36. Owing to their high compressive strength, these bricks are particularly suitable for heavily loaded masonry.

Solid and vertically perforated high-strength engineering bricks
are bricks manufactured from high-quality, densely burning clays. They are frost-resistant and exhibit a water absorption of max. 6%. Solid high-strength engineering bricks may have max. 15% perforations perpendicular to the bed face, vertically perforated high-strength engineering bricks max. 35% perforations. High-strength engineering bricks must have a

mean gross density of at least 2000 kg/m³ and must reach at least compressive strength class 60. The abrasion hardness of the surface must be at least 5 according to the Mohs scale, and these bricks must be resistant to hydrofluoric acid. Owing to these requirements, high-strength engineering bricks are primarily used in facades as well as wherever high resistance to aggressive substances and mechanical damage is required.

Lightweight horizontally perforated bricks and prefabricated brick elements
are mainly used in the construction of internal walls. When used in this way, lightweight horizontally perforated bricks may be used for both loadbearing and non-loadbearing masonry, but lightweight horizontally perforated prefabricated brick elements only for non-loadbearing walls. The holes in this type of brick run parallel to the bed face. The bulk density is limited to max. 1000 kg/m³.

Moulded bricks and hand-moulded bricks
are bricks with an irregular surface whose shape may deviate slightly from the prismatic form.

The formats available as well as the gross densities and compressive strength classes are listed in table 2.1.2 for each type of brick. The thermal conductivity of the brick material is given in relation to the gross density in table 2.1.5. These are average values, 90% fractiles and design values based on the 90% fractiles and moisture content equilibrium at 23°C and 90% relative humidity. The splitting tensile strength β_{SZ} of clay bricks lies between 2 and 9% of the compressive strength, the tensile strength β_Z along the brick in the case of a solid brick is between 1 and 8%, for vertically perforated bricks between 1 and 4%, and for lightweight vertically perforated bricks between 0.2 and 1% of the compressive strength [189]. Clay bricks can swell up to 0.3‰ and shrink up to 0.2‰. The final creep figure φ_∞ reaches values between 0.5 and 1.5 [57, 180, 182, 185].

Calcium silicate units
Calcium silicate units are currently covered by DIN 106. The non-fired, binding agent-bonded units are produced according to a method developed in Germany by Michaelis and patented in 1880. This method involves curing a mixture of naturally moist lime and sand under high pressure in a saturated steam atmosphere, which results in a very hardwearing material strong in compression. The sand used should comply with DIN 4226 parts 1 or 2; generally, silica sand with particle sizes 0-4 mm should be used. Colouring agents and other additives may be introduced provided that the properties of the units are not impaired. The binding agent used in the production of

2.1.3 The production of clay bricks

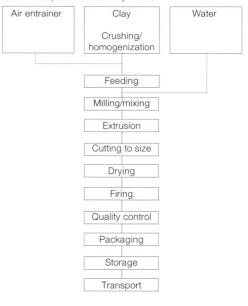

2.1.4 Standard types of clay brick

DIN 105, part 1	Mz	Solid brick
	HLz	Vertically perforated brick
	HLzT	Brick element
	VMz	Solid facing brick
	VHLz	Vertically perf. facing brick
	KMz	Solid engineering brick
	KHLz	Vertically perf. engineering brick
		Moulded brick
		Hand-moulded brick
DIN 105, part 2	HLz	Ltwt vertically perforated brick
	HLzT	Lightweight brick element
	VHLz	Lightweight vertically perforated facing brick
		Lightweight moulded brick
DIN 105, part 3	Mz	Solid brick
	HLz	Vertically perforated brick
	HLzT	Brick element
	VMz	Solid facing brick
	VHLz	Vertically perf. facing brick
	KMz	Solid engineering brick
	KHLz	Vertically perf. eng. brick
		Moulded brick
DIN 105, part 4	KK	Solid high-strength eng. brick
	KHK	Vertically perforated high-strength engineering brick
		Moulded high-strength engineering brick
DIN 105, part 5	LLz	Lightweight horiz. perf. brick
	LLp	Lightweight horizontally perforated prefab. brick element

2.1.5 Thermal conductivity of clay units in relation to their gross density. Dry values for 50% and 90% fractiles as well as design values for ambient conditions $y_{23,80}$ and 90% fractiles.

Moisture content $\Psi_{23,80} = 0,012$
Moisture correction factor $f_\Psi = 10$

Gross density kg/m³	Thermal conductivity λ (W/mK)		
	dry		moist $\Psi_{23,80}$
	p = 50%	p = 90%	p = 90%
1000	0.184	0.254	0.287
1200	0.260	0.329	0.371
1400	0.336	0.405	0.456
1600	0.412	0.481	0.542
1800	0.488	0.557	1.628
2000	0.564	1.634	1.715

2.1.6   The production of calcium silicate units

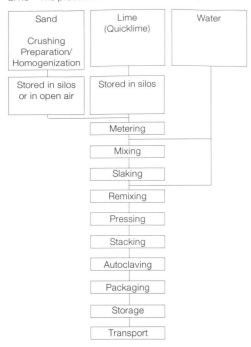

2.1.7   Standard calcium silicate units

DIN 106, part 1	KS	Solid brick/block
	KS L	Perforated/hollow block
	KS (P), KS L (P)	Gauged brick
	KS-R, KS L-R KS-R (P) KS L-R (P)	Tongue and groove system for solid brick/block, perforated/ hollow block, gauged brick
	KS P	Prefabricated brick element
DIN 106, part 2	KS Vm	Facing brick, solid brick
	KS Vm L	Facing brick, perforated brick
	KS Vb	Facing brick, solid brick
	KS Vb L	Facing brick, perforated brick

2.1.8   Thermal conductivity of calcium silicate units in relation to their gross density. Dry values for 50% and 90% fractiles as well as design values for ambient conditions $\Psi_{23,80}$ and 90% fractiles.

Moisture content $\Psi_{23,80} = 0.024$
Moisture correction factor $f_\Psi = 10$

Gross density kg/m³	Thermal conductivity λ [W/mK]		
	dry		moist
			$\Psi_{23,80}$
	p = 50%	p = 90%	p = 90%
1000	0.237	0.299	0.380
1200	0.297	0.359	0.456
1400	0.402	0.565	0.590
1600	0.551	0.613	0.779
1800	0.745	0.805	1.024
2000	0.983	1.045	1.328

2.1.9   Gross density and strength classes for calcium silicate units

Type of unit	Gross density class	Strength class
KS, KS (P) KS-R, KS-R (P)	1.6–2.2	4–60
KS L, KS L (P) KS L-R, KS L-R (P)	0.6–1.6	4–60
KS Vm, KS Vm L	1.0–2.2	12–60
KS Vb, KS Vb L	1.0–2.2	20–60

calcium silicate bricks is usually quicklime with a calcium oxide content exceeding 90%; this is obtained by firing limestone at about 900°C. Afterwards, the quicklime is ground to form fine white lime. Before adding water, the quicklime is thoroughly mixed 1:12 with the sand. The naturally moist mixture is buffered in reaction vessels. Here, the quicklime slakes to form the actual hydrated lime binding agent in an exothermic process.

The standard calcium silicate units currently available are listed in 2.1.7. Non-standard calcium silicate units are described in the section "New types of masonry units" [81].

Solid calcium silicate bricks
are masonry units with a height ≤ 113 mm whose cross-section through the perforations perpendicular to the bed face may be reduced by up to 15%.

Perforated calcium silicate bricks
are masonry units with a height ≤ 113 mm closed on five sides – apart from continuous grip openings – whose reduction in cross-section through the perforations perpendicular to the bed face may exceed 15%.

Calcium silicate blocks
are masonry units with a height > 113 mm closed on five sides – apart from continuous grip openings – whose cross-section through the perforations perpendicular to the bed face may be reduced by up to 15%.

Hollow calcium silicate blocks
are masonry units with a height > 113 mm closed on five sides – apart from continuous grip openings – whose reduction in cross-section through the perforations perpendicular to the bed face may exceed 15%.

Calcium silicate gauged bricks
are solid, perforated and hollow bricks and blocks designed for laying in thin-bed mortar. Consequently, the height tolerances of the masonry units are subject to more stringent requirements.

Calcium silicate R-units
are bricks and blocks with a tongue and groove system as well as grip openings. These have been designed according to ergonomic criteria and hence simplify the handling of the bricks during bricklaying. The perpends are not provided with mortar. Calcium silicate R-units are available as solid, perforated and hollow bricks and blocks as well as gauged bricks.

Calcium silicate prefabricated brick elements
are solid elements for non-loadbearing masonry with a thickness < 115 mm. Prefabricated brick elements have a peripheral tongue and

groove system and are laid in thin-bed mortar. The perpends are always provided with mortar.

Calcium silicate facing bricks
are intended for facing brickwork exposed to the weather. They are used for both load-bearing and non-loadbearing masonry. Their surface may be plain or have a textured finish. These are frost-resistant units (25 freeze-thaw cycles) of strength class ≥ 12 but are also available in a better quality (50 freeze-thaw cycles) of strength class ≥ 20. In addition to these requirements, these calcium silicate units are subject to stricter dimensional tolerances and must be supplied free from detrimental influences or substances which might later lead to spalling, microstructure defects, efflorescence or discoloration [25, 91, 143].

Calcium silicate solid and perforated bricks and calcium silicate facing bricks are produced in the NF and DF (up to 6 DF) formats, calcium silicate gauged bricks in the customary 4 DF to 20 DF formats. The calcium silicate R-units are available in formats 4 DF to 12 DF. Calcium silicate prefabricated brick elements with a wall thickness of 70 mm are designated KS-P7 elements (see "Masonry bonds"). Table 2.1.8 shows the thermal conductivity values in relation to the gross density for various statistical confidence coefficients and moisture contents of the calcium silicate. Calcium silicate masonry units are divided into compressive strength classes from 4 to 60 and gross density classes from 0.6 to 2.2. Solid bricks and blocks are allocated to gross density classes ≥ 1.6, perforated and hollow units to bulk density classes ≤ 1.6. Compressive strength classes 12, 20 and 28 are the ones most frequently used in practice (see 2.1.9). For calcium silicate facing bricks to be classed as frost-resistant, they must withstand the prescribed number of freeze-thaw cycles without damage but also suffer no more than a 20% reduction in their compressive strength compared to their original strength. The splitting tensile strength β_{SZ} of calcium silicate units lies between 3 and 10% of the compressive strength, the longitudinal tensile strength β_Z between 3 and 8% of the compressive strength [189]. The shrinkage $\varepsilon_{\eta\infty}$ of calcium silicate units lies in the range -0.1‰ to -0.3‰, the final creep figure φ_∞ reaches values between 1.0 and 2.0 [57, 180, 182, 185].

Autoclaved aerated concrete units
Autoclaved aerated concrete units are covered by the standards DIN 4165 and 4166. The development of aerated concrete stems from Hoffmann's patent of 1889, which describes the reaction of diluted hydrochloric acid with limestone dust in order to produce cement and gypsum mortars with air pores. In 1914 Aylsworth and Dyer developed a method involving

a reaction between lime, water and a metal powder (aluminium or zinc). This reaction liberates the hydrogen gas, which then makes the mortar rise. The first aerated concrete was produced by Eriksson between 1924 and 1927 by combining the Aylsworth/Dyer method with curing in an autoclave. A mixture of silica sand and lime is made to rise with the addition of a metal powder. After it has set it is cured in steam at high pressure. A method for the mass production of aerated concrete units was invented in 1945; this involves cutting the stable material by means of tightly stretched steel wires prior to autoclaving.

The raw materials for the production of autoclaved aerated concrete units these days are sand containing silica, binding agent, expanding agent, water and, if necessary, additives. The sand must be essentially free from impurities and comply with the requirements of DIN 4226 parts 1 or 2.

Pulverized fuel ash (PFA) may be used instead of sand containing silica. The sand is ground in large mills to form a fine powder or slurry. Quicklime (see "Calcium silicate units") and/or cement is used as the binding agent. In addition, small amounts of gypsum or anhydrite can be mixed in. Aluminium in the form of powder or finely grained paste is employed as the expanding agent. The composition of the mix depends on the desired properties of the aerated concrete and the method of production. The raw materials are metered in and mixed to form an aqueous suspension. Besides the primary raw materials, the mix also contains aerated concrete recycled from the production process, and sorted, finely ground recycled material. After filling the moulds with the raw material mixture, the water slakes the lime under the action of heat. The aluminium reacts with the calcium hydroxide, liberating the hydrogen. This forms the pores and immediately afterwards escapes completely from the expanded aerated concrete. The macropores reach a diameter of about 0.5 to 1.5 mm. The stable "green" unit after expansion is cut both horizontally and vertically to form bricks/blocks prior to autoclaving. In the autoclave the units are subjected to a saturated steam atmosphere (190°C and 12 bar) for about 6-12 hours. During this time the silicon oxide of the ground silica sand reacts with the help of calcium hydroxide and water. Autoclaved aerated concrete with a high compressive strength is formed from the hydrated calcium silicate, corresponding to the natural mineral tobermorite. After cooling, the aerated concrete bricks possess their final properties (see fig. 2.1.10) [27, 75].

The standard and currently available aerated concrete units are listed in table 2.1.11. Non-standard aerated concrete units are dealt with in the section "New types of masonry units" [81].

Autoclaved aerated concrete blocks and gauged bricks
are large-format, cuboid solid units. The header faces of these units may either have a mortar key or tongue and groove system. Blocks are laid in normal-weight or lightweight mortar; the height tolerance of the block may be max. ±3.0 mm in this case. Gauged bricks, on the other hand, are laid in thin-bed mortar; the height tolerance in this case is only ±1.0 mm.

Autoclaved aerated concrete prefabricated brick elements and gauged bricks
are used for non-loadbearing walls and to improve thermal insulation. They are either laid in normal-weight or lightweight mortar (prefabricated brick elements) or in thin-bed mortar (gauged bricks). The header faces may be plain, or be provided with a mortar key or tongue and groove system. The bed faces may also be tongued and grooved. The dimensional accuracy requirements are identical to those for aerated concrete blocks and gauged bricks. As these units are only used for non-loadbearing walls, they are not divided into strength classes.

Sizes of autoclaved aerated concrete units and prefabricated brick elements are specified by their length, width and height. The maximum common dimensions are currently 615 x 365 x 240 mm for autoclaved aerated concrete units, and 615 x 150 x 240 mm for gauged bricks. The gross density of autoclaved aerated concrete units lies between 300 and 1000 kg/m³; the corresponding subdivision into gross density classes ranges from 0.35 to 0.70 in steps of 0.05, and from 0.70 to 1.00 in steps of 0.10. The gross density, which depends on the volume of pores and the solids content, is controlled during production by the careful addition of expanding and binding agents. For example, autoclaved aerated concrete with a gross density of 500 kg/m³ requires a solids content of 20% and pore volume of 80%. Table 2.1.12 shows the thermal conductivity in relation to the gross density. The format is irrelevant here.

Autoclaved aerated concrete units to DIN 4165 are divided into compressive strength classes 2 to 8. Autoclaved aerated concrete prefabricated brick elements to DIN 4166 are not divided into strength classes because they are only used for non-loadbearing walls (see fig. 2.1.13) [211]. The splitting tensile strength β_{SZ} of autoclaved aerated concrete units lies between 5 and 14% of the compressive strength [189], the tensile bending strength β_{BZ} of prefabricated brick elements reaches values between 0.5 and 2.0 N/mm². The modulus of elasticity of autoclaved aerated concrete units depends on the respective gross density and lies between 1200 and 2500 N/mm².

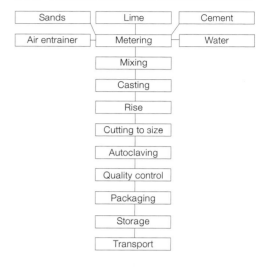

2.1.10   Production of autoclaved aerated concrete units

2.1.11   Standard autoclaved aerated concrete units

DIN 4165	PB	Block
	PP	Gauged brick
DIN 4166	Ppl	Prefabricated brick element
	PPpl	Prefabricated gauged brick panel

2.1.12   Thermal conductivity of autoclaved aerated concrete units in relation to their gross density. Dry values for 50% and 90% fractiles as well as design values for ambient conditions $u_{23,80}$ and 90% fractiles.

Moisture content $u_{23,80}$ = 0.045
Moisture correction factor f_u = 4

Gross density kg/m³	Thermal conductivity λ (W/mK)		
	dry value		design value
			u = 0.045
	p = 50%	p = 90%	p = 90%
300	0.077	0.089	0.11
400	0.100	0.113	0.14
500	0.124	0.136	0.16
600	0.147	0.160	0.19
700	0.171	0.183	0.22
800	0.194	0.207	0.25
900	0.218	0.230	0.28

2.1.13 Gross density and strength classes for aerated concrete units

Type of unit	Gross density class	Strength class
PB, PP	0.35–0.50	2
	0.50–0.80	4
	0.65–0.80	6
	0.80–1.00	8
Ppl, PPpl	0.35–1.00	–

2.1.14 Standard concrete and lightweight concrete units

DIN 18148	Hpl	Hollow wall elements of lightweight concrete
DIN 18151	Hbl	Hollow blocks of lightweight concrete
DIN 18152	V	Solid bricks of lightweight concrete
	Vbl	Solid blocks of lightweight concrete
	Vbl S	Solid blocks of lightweight concrete with slots
	Vbl S-W	Solid blocks of lightweight concrete with slots and special thermal insulation properties
DIN 18153	Hbn	Hollow concrete blocks
	Vbn	Solid concrete blocks
	Vn	Solid concrete bricks
	Tbn	Hollow blocks
	Vm	Concrete facing bricks
	Vmb	Concrete facing blocksn
DIN 18162	Wpl	Wall elements of lightweight concrete, non-reinforced

2.1.15 Thermal conductivity of pumice concrete units in relation to their gross density. Dry values for 50% and 90% fractiles as well as design values for ambient conditions $\Psi_{23,80}$ and 90% fractiles.

Moisture content $\Psi_{23,80}$ = 0.035
Moisture correction factor f_Ψ = 4

Gross density kg/m³	Thermal conductivity λ [W/mK]		
	dry value		design value
			Ψ = 0.035
	p = 50%	p = 90%	p = 90%
500	0.114	0.138	0.16
600	0.135	0.158	0.18
700	0.160	0.183	0.21
800	0.190	0.212	0.24
900	0.223	0.245	0.28
1000	0.260	0.282	0.33

2.1.16 Thermal conductivity of gas concrete units in relation to their gross density. Dry values for 50% and 90% fractiles as well as design values for ambient conditions $\Psi_{23,80}$ and 90% fractiles.

Moisture content $\Psi_{23,80}$ = 0.03
Moisture correction factor f_Ψ = 2.6

Gross density kg/m³	Thermal conductivity λ [W/mK]		
	dry value		design value
			u = 0.03
	p = 50%	p = 90%	p = 90%
400	0.099	0.117	0.13
500	0.137	0.155	0.17
600	0.176	0.193	0.21
700	0.214	0.231	0.25
800	0.252	0.269	0.30
900	0.290	0.308	0.35
1000	0.328	0.346	0.39

The moisture movement $\varepsilon_{\eta\infty}$ fluctuates between 0.1‰ (swelling) and -0.3‰ (shrinkage). The final creep φ_∞ lies between 1.0 and 2.5 and hence reaches similar figures to calcium silicate units [180].

Concrete and lightweight concrete units
The requirements for (normal-weight) concrete units are covered by DIN 18153, those for lightweight concrete units by DIN 18151 and 18152, and wall elements of lightweight concrete by DIN 18148 and 18162. While concrete units of dense normal-weight concrete employ mineral aggregates to DIN 4226 part 1 or 2, and binding agents, e.g. cement, to DIN 1164 or pulverized fuel ash to DIN EN 450, the production of lightweight concrete units may employ only lightweight aggregates with a porous microstructure to DIN 4226 part 2 (pumice, foamed slag, foamed lava, tuff, expanded clay, expanded shale, sintered pulverized fuel ash or brick chippings) besides the hydraulic binding agents. The addition of aggregates with a dense microstructure to DIN 4226 part 1 are permitted up to a volume of max. 15% of the compacted concrete. However, this rule is not very important in practice. Solid blocks of lightweight concrete with slots and special thermal properties may make use of just pumice or expanded clay, or a mixture of the two, in order to achieve the required thermal insulation. The only additives which may be used are building lime to DIN 1060 part 1, stone dust to DIN 4226 part 1, trass to DIN 51043 and concrete additives to DIN 1045. The same principle is applied for the production of both concrete and lightweight concrete units. The measured raw materials (binding agent, aggregates, water) are thoroughly mixed. The shaping of the concrete and lightweight concrete units is carried out on modern casting beds. Here, the mixture is poured into vibratory casting machines. The vibration and application of a surcharge causes the mixture to be compacted such that after striking the moulds, the fresh, "green" units are stable. After brushing to remove loose particles and burrs, they are pre-cured by storing them in racks protected from the weather. During the warm months of the year the ambient heat serves to pre-cure the units, during colder periods the heat of hydration of the cement. No additional heating is required. Following the pre-curing process, which can take between 24 hours and three days depending on the weather, the units are turned and stacked with their voids downwards. Therefore, the units are already in the correct position for bricklaying on site. The final curing to reach the necessary nominal strength takes place in the open air [8, 19]. The various standard types of concrete and lightweight concrete masonry units are shown in table 2.1.14. Non-standard concrete and lightweight concrete units are dealt with in the section

"New types of masonry units" [81].

Hollow wall elements and wall elements of lightweight concrete
are suitable for building non-loadbearing walls according to DIN 4103. The header and bed faces are either plain or provided with grooves or a tongue and groove system. The gross density of the elements lies between 800 and 1400 kg/m³. Wall elements must have an average tensile bending strength of at least 1.0 N/mm²; hollow wall elements must exhibit an average minimum compressive strength of 2.5 N/mm² after 28 days.

Hollow blocks of lightweight concrete
are large-format masonry units with cells perpendicular to the bed face. They are used for loadbearing and non-loadbearing masonry to DIN 1053. Block formats 8 DF to 24 DF for wall thicknesses from 175 to 490 mm are available with one to six cells. The length and width of the blocks is limited to 490 mm, the height to 238 mm.

Solid bricks and blocks, solid S and S-W blocks of lightweight concrete
are masonry units for loadbearing and non-loadbearing masonry to DIN 1053 using lightweight aggregates to DIN 4226 part 2. Solid S-W blocks may employ only aggregates of pumice or expanded clay, or a mixture of the two. Solid bricks are units without cells with a maximum brick height of 115 mm; solid blocks, on the other hand, may be up to 238 mm high. Solid S blocks have slots and solid S-W blocks have special thermal insulation properties in addition to the slots. The slots of solid S-W blocks must always be closed off. Solid bricks and blocks may have grip openings. The preferred formats of solid bricks range from DF to 10 DF, with the intermediate formats 1.7 DF, 3.1 DF and 6.8 DF also being widely used. The large-format solid blocks are produced in the preferred formats of 8 DF to 24 DF for wall thicknesses from 175 to 490 mm. The length and width of the blocks is limited to 490 mm, the height to 238 mm. The thermal conductivity of lightweight concrete units is influenced by the type of aggregate. As 2.1.15 and 2.1.16 show, pumice aggregates achieve slightly better values than expanded clay aggregates.

Masonry units of normal-weight concrete
are used for loadbearing and non-loadbearing masonry to DIN 1053. Hollow blocks are large-format masonry units (8 DF to 20 DF) with cells perpendicular to the bed face and a height of, preferably, 238 mm. Solid blocks are masonry units without voids measuring 175 or 238 mm high and with a maximum length and width of 490 mm. The cross-sectional area may be reduced by up to 15% by grip openings. They are produced in formats from 8 DF to 24 DF for wall thicknesses from 175 to 490 mm. Solid

bricks are similar to solid blocks but their height is limited to 115 mm. These are manufactured in the preferred formats of DF to 10 DF. Facing blocks are masonry units with the cells closed off at the top and smooth or "split" finish exposed faces. The height of such units lies between 175 and 238 mm. Facing bricks are masonry units with smooth, "split" or rugged finish exposed faces. The bricks are formed without cells but with grip openings, and are between 52 and 238 mm high. Facing bricks and blocks are intended for masonry exposed to the weather.

The header faces of hollow blocks, solid blocks and solid bricks of lightweight concrete as well as masonry units of normal-weight concrete may be smooth, provided with a groove on one or both header faces, or have a tongue and groove system. The division of lightweight concrete and normal-weight concrete units into the customary gross density and strength classes is summarised in 2.1.17. The splitting tensile strength β_{SZ} of concrete and lightweight concrete units lies between 7 and 18% of the compressive strength, the longitudinal tensile strength β_Z between 4 and 21% of the compressive strength. Lightweight concrete units shrink between 0.2 and 0.5‰ , normal-weight concrete units between 0.1 and 0.3‰ . The creep behaviour of concrete and lightweight concrete units is similar to that of aerated concrete units, with the final creep value φ_∞ lying between 1.5 and 2.5 [57, 180, 182].

Granulated slag aggregate units
Granulated slag aggregate units are covered by DIN 398. They are manufactured from artificially recovered aggregates, mostly granulated blast furnace slag, and hydraulic binding agents like cement or lime. After metering the raw materials and mixing with water, the units are formed in steel moulds and compacted by pressing or vibrating. After striking the moulds, the stable "green" units are cured in air, in steam, or in gases containing carbonic acid. Standard granulated slag aggregate units to DIN 398 are listed in 2.1.18.

Solid granulated slag aggregate bricks
are masonry units whose cross-section may be reduced by up to 25% by holes perpendicular to the bed face. Formats up to 2 DF may be provided with grip openings and those above this size must be provided with such openings. Solid granulated slag aggregate bricks are usually manufactured in the formats DF to 5 DF.

Perforated granulated slag aggregate bricks
are masonry units closed on five sides with perforations perpendicular to the bed face

exceeding 25%. The holes must be evenly distributed over the bed face in at least three rows. The arrangement of grip openings is the same as that for solid granulated slag aggregate bricks. At present, the formats 2 DF to 5 DF are generally available.

Hollow granulated slag aggregate blocks
are large-format masonry units closed on five sides with voids perpendicular to the bed face. The voids for blocks 300 mm wide are in at least five rows, those of 240 mm blocks at least four, and those of 175 mm blocks at least three, in each case evenly distributed over the length and the width. Owing to the size of these hollow blocks, grip openings should be included. The dimensions of the large-format blocks are specified by the wall thickness 30 (= 300 mm), 24 (= 240 mm), 17.5 (= 175 mm) and the height (a = 238 mm, b = 175 mm). This results in the formats 30 a, 30 b, 24 a, 24 b and 17.5.

Granulated slag aggregate units are divided into gross density classes 1.0 to 2.0 in steps of 0.2 as well as strength classes 6, 12, 20 and 28. In order to use granulated slag aggregate units for facing work, they must reach at least strength class 12 (see table 2.1.19). Owing to a lack of statistical data for the thermal conductivity, no mean values and 90% fractiles can be given here. The thermal conductivity values given in 2.1.20 should be understood as values "on the safe side" applicable for all types of aggregates.

The designation of masonry units
Clay, calcium silicate, lightweight concrete and normal-weight concrete units are designated with a system which employs DIN standard number, abbreviation, compressive strength class, gross density class and format code, e.g.:

DIN 105	Mz 12–1.8–2 DF
DIN 106	KS 12–1.6–2 DF
DIN 18 151	3 K Hbl 2–0.7–20 DF
DIN 18 152	V 6–1.2–2 DF
DIN 18 153	Vn 12–1.8–6 DF

If different unit widths are possible within the same format code, then the width of the unit is given in millimetres following the format code, e.g.:

| DIN 105 | HLzW 6–0.7–10 DF (300) |
| DIN 18 152 | Vbl S 2–0.7–16 DF (240) |

Granulated slag aggregate units are designated with abbreviation, gross density, compressive strength class, format code and

2.1.17 Gross density and strength classes for normal-weight and lightweight concrete units

Type of unit	Gross density class	Strength class
Hbl	0.5–1.4	2–8
V, Vbl, Vbl S	0.5–2.0	2–12
Vbl S-W	0.5–0.8	2–12
Hbn	0.9–2.0	2–12
Vbn, Vn	1.4–2.4	4–28
Vm, Vmb	1.6–2.4	6–48

2.1.18 Standard granulated slag aggregate units

DIN 398	HSV	Solid granulated slag aggregate bricks
	HSL	Perforated granulated slag aggregate bricks
	HHbl	Hollow granulated slag aggregate blocks

2.1.19 Gross density and strength classes for granulated slag aggregate units

Type of unit	Bulk density class	Strength class
HSV	1.6–2.0	12–28
HSL	1.2–1.6	6–12
HHbl	1.0–1.6	6–12

2.1.20 Thermal conductivity of concrete units with any type of aggregate in relation to their gross density

Moisture content $\Psi_{23,80} = 0.05$
Moisture correction factor $f_\Psi = 4$

Gross density kg/m³	Thermal conductivity λ [W/mK]	
	dry value	design value $\Psi = 0.05$
500	0.24	0.29
600	0.27	0.33
700	0.30	0.37
800	0.33	0.40
900	0.37	0.45
1000	0.41	0.50
1200	0.52	0.63
1400	0.66	0.81
1600	0.83	1.01

2.1.21   Shape factor for compressive strength classification of bricks

Height of brick

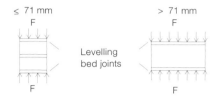

≤ 71 mm   > 71 mm

Levelling
bed joints

$\beta_{st} = \beta_{PR} \times f$
β_{PR} : Test result
f : Shape factor

$h < 175$ mm -> $f = 1.0$
175 mm $\leq$ $h < 238$ mm -> $f = 1.1$
$h \geq 238$ mm -> $f = 1.2$
for brick strength class 2 -> $f = 1.0$

2.1.22   Relationship between longitudinal tensile
strength β_Z and compressive strength β_{ST} [3]

Type of brick	β_Z N/mm²
Calcium silicate	$0.051\beta_{ST}$
Clay	$0.026\,\beta_{ST}$
Lightweight concrete	$0.086\,\beta_{ST}$
Aerated concrete:	
strength class 2	$0.182\,\beta_{ST}$
strength classes 4, 6, 8	$0.092\,\beta_{ST}$

DIN standard number, e.g.:

HSL 1.6–15–2 DF DIN 398.

Aerated concrete units are designated with
DIN standard number, abbreviation, compressive strength class, bulk density class and
dimensions in millimetres (length x width x
height), e.g.:

DIN 4165 PP 2–0.4–499 x 300 x 249

New types of masonry units
New types of units are those which are not
covered by corresponding standards. General
building authority certificates, as issued by the
Deutsche Institut für Bautechnik, are required
for these units. These masonry units deviate
from the standard requirements for the following reasons:
• Dimensions and shapes deviating from those
  laid down in the standards are being continu-
  ally developed by the masonry industry. The
  reasons for this lie in the desire to develop
  units offering optimized thermal properties
  (e.g. units with integral thermal insulation,
  small frogs or tongue and groove interlocks
  on the header faces) as well as improved
  methods of manufacture and new methods of
  construction (e.g. clay gauged bricks in thin-
  bed mortar, dry masonry, filled units).
• Dimensions deviating from the standards may
  also be necessary to meet the needs of more
  rational construction and the larger-format
  units which need to be manufactured for this
  (e.g. calcium silicate and aerated concrete
  precision elements).
• Other strengths are achieved in addition to
  the standard strength classes. This is frequently associated with different gross densities.
• Finally, the certificates also deal with units
  available on a regional basis which, for
  example, traditionally have different dimensions and hence lead to wall thicknesses
  which differ from those laid down in DIN 1053
  (units employing the decimetre system).
According to the type of construction, the new
types of units with their associated certificates
are allocated to thin-, medium- or thick-bed
masonry, to grouted masonry, to prefabricated
wall elements and to dry masonry of man-
made units. The certificates are grouped
according to materials within these types of
construction. A summary of the certificates currently valid is given in [79] and [84].

Testing the mechanical properties of masonry units
The testing of the mechanical properties is
crucial for the classification and identification
of masonry units. Apart from that, it forms the
basis for designing masonry, for analysing
cases of damage and for carrying out research

into and further development of the loadbearing behaviour of masonry.
A distinction should be made between the testing necessary within the scope of standards
and certificates or for an individual situation,
and additional tests outside the standards.
For such tests there is usually no uniform
method of testing. The main standard and non-
standard tests to establish properties are
explained in the following.

Compressive strength β_{ST}
The testing of compressive strength is an intrinsic part of the various standards covering
masonry units.
Six test samples are generally required.
Masonry units of low height (DF, NF) are cut
halfway along the stretcher face and put together for testing. For all other heights, a single
masonry unit serves as the test sample. These
test samples with their bed faces levelled up
using cement mortar or gypsum are loaded to
failure perpendicular to the bed face. The test
value β_{PR} determined from the maximum load
and the area of the bed face is multiplied by
the shape factor f (see fig. 2.1.21). Therefore,
the influence of the platen through which the
test load is applied and which hinders lateral
movement is taken into account in relation to
the height of the unit.
For the compressive strength of the masonry
unit to be allocated to a strength class, the test
results must comply with the requirements for
mean value and lowest individual result as laid
down in the appropriate standard. The nominal
strength (compressive strength class) corresponds to the 5% fractile of the compressive
strength of the units. This is equivalent to the
lowest permissible individual value.
The current scatter regarding raw materials,
production processes etc. means that the 5%
fractile is about 20% lower than the mean
value.

Unit gross density, dry gross density ρ_{ST}
The standardized unit gross density test is
generally carried out on six test samples. For
this, the dry mass md of the dried masonry
units is to be determined at 105°C up to constant mass. The unit gross density is calculated
by dividing the dry mass by the volume of the
unit including any voids, grip openings and
frogs present. To be allocated to a unit gross
density class, the mean value of the test results
must lie between the limits stipulated in the
respective standard. Individual results may not
lie more than 100 kg/m³ above or below the
class limits.

Net density ρ_{sch}
This requirement applies to clay bricks to DIN
105 parts 1 to 4 and to thermally insulating
lightweight concrete units for verifying the thermal conductivity. Again, the test is carried out
on six samples. The net density is calculated

from the quotients of the dry mass determined at 105°C and the volume. The volume of the unit is made up of the overall volume minus volumes of voids, frogs and grip openings. This should be measured underwater and in the case of solid engineering bricks without voids by subtracting the volume of the perforations. The requirement is that the mean net density as well as the lowest individual results of the test must be higher than the lower threshold.

Frost resistance
This test is critical for facing masonry units and engineering bricks. The frost resistance test is carried out on units soaked in water, which are then subjected to multiple freeze-thaw cycles. Units are said to be frost-resistant when, following these freeze-thaw cycles, they exhibit no significant damage, e.g. bulging of the stretcher faces, larger cavities and spalling or a clear reduction in the stability of the arris.

Content of expanding particles and efflorescent salts
The requirements here only apply to clay bricks. These must be free from damaging, expanding particles, e.g. lime, which could impair the usability of the unit. This is checked using the steam test, which should result in no damage to the microstructure or only a limited amount of spalling. Furthermore, clay bricks must be free from damaging salts which likewise could lead to damage to the microstructure of the unit or the plaster. Facing and engineering bricks must also be free from salts which lead to a efflorescence and hence permanently impair the appearance of exposed masonry. In the test for damaging salts, the proportion of magnesium sulphate in clay bricks should not exceed 0.12% by weight, and for facing or engineering bricks the proportion of sodium sulphate, potassium sulphate and magnesium sulphate determined at the same time may not exceed 0.08% by weight in each case.

Longitudinal $\beta_{D,l}$ and lateral $\beta_{D,b}$ compressive strength
Knowledge of the longitudinal and lateral compressive strength is necessary above all when certain areas are loaded perpendicular to the plane of the wall, for horizontal thrust in the plane of the wall and for cases of bending and cambering. Testing methods and available results are given in [58, 190, 191].

Tensile strength β_Z
The tensile strength – both longitudinal and lateral – of masonry units is, as a rule, the decisive parameter for the compressive strength of the member being designed in the case of the compressive loading of masonry perpendicular to the bed joints. Furthermore, it is also important for the tension-, flexural tension- and shear-carrying capacity of masonry. However, as the testing of tensile strength is relatively complicated and the results difficult to reproduce (and hence not so reliable), tests for tensile strength have not been incorporated in a testing standard up to now. The approximate relationship between tensile strength along the unit and compressive strength perpendicular to the bed face is shown in 2.1.22 [189].

Lateral secant modulus E_q
The lateral secant modulus is determined from the quotients of one third of the compressive strength of the unit perpendicular to the bed face and the appropriate longitudinal $e_{q,l}$ or lateral $e_{q,b}$ strain. The lateral secant modulus, both that of the masonry unit and that of the mortar, influences the compressive strength of the masonry as a whole. It is helpful if the lateral secant modulus of the unit is equal to, larger or slightly less than that of the mortar. The value is determined from a masonry unit bonded on its bed face. The method of testing is at present not standardized; guidance figures for the lateral secant modulus of masonry units can be found in [180].

Testing the thermal insulation properties
When using the generally recognized design values for thermal conductivity (from tables), no tests of actual performance are necessary. Different, better design values for standard masonry units or units covered by building authority certificates can be determined by measuring the unit itself or by measurement of the material of the unit and subsequent calculation, taking into account the voids [3]. Tests are carried out using a plate apparatus according to DIN EN 12664, with conversion to reference and design conditions being carried out to DIN EN ISO 10456.

Natural stone units

Natural stone units include igneous (volcanic) rocks, sedimentation rocks and metamorphic rocks. The igneous rocks can be subdivided into plutonite, effusive rock and gangue material (e.g. granite, diorite, gabbro, basalt and tuff). The sedimentation rocks are subdivided into fragmental sediments, the rocks of chemical precipitation and biogenetic sediments (e.g. sandstone, graywacke, limestone, dolomite and flinty slate). The metamorphic rocks are classified according to the pressure and temperature during their formation; examples are crystalline slate, gneiss and marble. In order to be able to use natural stone as masonry units, it must be prepared either by hand or by machine. The ease of workability – from easy to difficult – allows us to subdivide the types of stone further into light hard rocks (e.g. granite, gneiss, rhyolite), dark hard rocks (e.g. diorite, gabbro, lamprophyre) and soft rocks (e.g. sandstone, limestone, tuff). The stages of working the stone range from the lightly worked rubble stone without a regular geometric form to the square rubble stone with natural surface finish right up to the carefully worked ashlar stone with high-quality surface finish. The masonry bonds which can be produced using such stones are described in "Masonry details". Only good-quality stones without structural or weather damage may be used for natural stone masonry. When required for exposed work, they must be sufficiently resistant to the influences of the weather, e.g. freeze-thaw cycles, changes in temperature, changes in humidity. Slate is ideal for this because of its durability, high frost resistance and low water absorption. The length of natural stone units should be at least equal to their height but not more than four to five times the height.

Natural stone units should exhibit a certain minimum compressive strength depending on the type of stone in order to be used in natural stone masonry to DIN 1053 part 1. The compressive strength β_D is determined according to DIN EN 1926.

External walls of natural stone have only low thermal insulation values and will usually need additional thermal insulation. The thermal conductivity values of natural stone (see 2.1.24) are of only minor importance.

2.1.23 Material parameters of natural stone types [3]

Natural stone	β_D N/mm²	β_{BZ} N/mm²	$E_D \times 10^3$ N/mm²	$\varepsilon_s, \varepsilon_q$
Granite, syenite	160–240	10–20	40–60	0–0.2
Diorite, gabbro	170–300	10–22	100–120	0–0.2
Porphyres	180–300	15–20	20–160	0–0.2
Basalt	250–400	15–25	50–100	0.4
Basaltic lava	80–150	8–12	–	0.4
Diabase	180–250	15–25	60–120	0–0.2
Quarzite, graywacke	150–300	13–25	50–80	0–0.1
Quartzitic sandstone	120–200	12–20	20–70	0.3–0.7
Other sandstones	30–180	3–15	5–30	0.3–0.7
Dolomites, dense lime-stones, marble	80–180	6–15	60–90	–
Other limestones	20–90	5–8	40–70	0.1–0.2
Travertine	20–60	4–10	20–60	–
Volcanic tuffaceous rock	5–25	1–4	4–10	0.2–0.6
Gneisses, granulite	160–280	13–25	30–80	–
Serpentine	140–250	25–35	–	0.1–0.2

2.1.24 Thermal conductivity of natural stone types

Material	Gross density kg/m³	Thermal conductivity W/mK
Basalt	2700–3000	3.5
Gneiss	2400–2700	3.5
Granite	2500–2700	2.8
Marble	2800	3.5
Slate	2000–2800	2.2
Sandstone	2600	2.3
Limestone	1600	0.85
	1800	1.1
	2000	1.4
	2200	1.7
	2600	2.3

Mortar for masonry

Mortar is a mixture of sand, binding agent(s) and water, plus admixtures and additives if required. For the sand, the largest particle size should be 4 mm, for a thin-bed mortar 1 mm. Only mortar conforming to the stipulations of appendix A of DIN 1053 part 1 may be used for masonry to DIN 1053. The sand used must comply with DIN 4226, consisting of natural or artificial, dense or porous mineral substances in crushed or uncrushed form. It should exhibit a range of particle sizes and must not contain any constituents, e.g. large amounts of settle-able solids of clay or other organic materials, which could damage the mortar or the mason-ry. The binding agent is usually lime to DIN 1060 part 1, cement to DIN 1164 part 1 and/or plaster and masonry cement to DIN 4211; other binding agents require a building author-ity certificate. The lime used may be hydraulic, semi- or non-hydraulic, or Roman lime; the cement used should be ordinary portland, port-land granulated slag, portland blastfurnace or portland pozzolanic.

Admixtures are finally distributed additions which have a favourable influence on the prop-erties of the mortar (adhesion to the masonry unit, workability, frost resistance) and are added in larger quantities. The only admixtures that may be used are building limes to DIN 1060 part 1, stone dust to DIN 4226 part 1, trass to DIN 51043, and certified concrete additives and pigments. Examples of additives are air entrainers, plasticizers, waterproofers, accelerators, retarders and adhesion agents. These change the properties of the mortar by way of chemical and physical processes and may only be added in small amounts. Further, they must not lead to damage to the mortar or the masonry or accelerate corrosion of rein-forcement or fixings. The effects of additives must always be established by way of tests prior to their use. Mortars for masonry can be categorized according to their strength, the admixtures used and the resulting building science properties as well as with respect to their applications in masonry and their methods of production and supply.

Forms of production and supply

Mortar can be produced both on the building site (site-mixed mortar) and in a special factory (premixed mortar). The raw materials for site-mixed mortar must be stored in dry conditions protected from the weather. Site-mixed mortar is mixed either by hand or by machine. Machine mixing is based on proportions by weight or by volume; mixing by hand is sens-ible only in exceptional circumstances when very small amounts of mortar are required. The raw materials are mixed until a workable consistency has been reached, which can be easily used by the bricklayer. As a rule, only

"prescribed mixes" can be produced on site; the mixing ratios given in 2.1.25 should be adhered to. In the case of "prescribed mixes" without quality control, it is assumed that the mortar will satisfy the necessary requirements. Consequently, deviations from the mix (e.g. different mixing ratios or the addition of ad-mixtures/additives) require tests to be carried out to determine the suitability of the on-site mix.

Mortars produced in the factory or under factory-like conditions will have a composition and consistency much more accurate than is possible with site mixing. Furthermore, factory-produced mortars must be constantly mon-itored to DIN 18557 during production, which guarantees constant properties and monitored optimization of the mortar for the respective application. The result of this is that over 90% of the mortars used today are of the premixed variety. On site the premixed mortar only needs to be mixed with the required amount of water – or in the case of "coarse stuff" the necessary amount of cement as well – but no aggregates or additives/admixtures. Premixed mortar can be supplied in the following forms [3]:

Premixed dry mortar
is a finished mixture of the raw materials sup-plied from a silo or in plastic-lined sacks. The mixture must be prepared on the building site in a mixer by adding water in order to achieve a workable consistency.

Ready-mixed mortar
is supplied ready to use in a workable consis-tency ("trowel-ready" mortar). The use of a retarder means that it generally remains work-able for 36 hours; longer or shorter periods must be specified on the delivery note.

Coarse stuff
is widely used in northern Germany in particu-lar and consists of a mixture of sand and lime as well as other additives/admixtures if neces-sary. The mortar is prepared in a mixer by adding cement and water.

Multi-chamber silo mortar
describes a mortar whose raw materials are stored in separate chambers in one silo. They are measured out and mixed with water so that a ready-to-use mortar is available at the outlet of the mixer attached to the silo. Multi-chamber silo mortar must be supplied with a preprogrammed mixing ratio which cannot be altered on site.

Types of mortar

Mortars for masonry are subdivided as follows according to the thickness of the mortar joint, the threshold value of the dry gross density and the associated building science properties as well as with respect to the raw materials used:

Normal-weight mortars

are mixed on site or in a factory using aggregates with a dense microstructure according to DIN 4226 part 1 and a dry gross density $\rho_D \geq 1500$ kg/m^3. Using sand as the aggregate, normal-weight mortar can be produced as a "prescribed mix" (without admixtures/additives) according to table 2.1.25. Owing to the considerable experience with this "prescribed mix" mortar, fewer requirements need to be tested. Normal-weight mortars are divided into groups I, II, IIa, III and IIIa according to ascending minimum compressive strength. Only cement may be used as the binding agent for groups III and IIIa. The necessary strength for group IIIa mortars is achieved by using suitable sands.

The thickness of the bed joint is 12 mm for normal-weight mortar. This permits a height-of-unit tolerance of ±5 mm for clay bricks and ±4 mm for all other types of masonry unit. The recommended applications as well as limits for normal-weight mortar according to DIN 1053 part 1 are given in table 2.1.26.

Lightweight mortars

are factory-mixed dry or factory-produced ready-mixed mortars which exhibit a dry bulk density $\rho_D < 1500$ kg/m^3. This is usually achieved by using lightweight aggregates (e.g. expanded clay, expanded shale, pumice, perlite, foamed glass, bottom ash). The composition of the mix is determined by means of tests. Lightweight mortar is classified according to its calculated thermal conductivity λ_R as belonging to group LM 21 ($\lambda_R = 0.21$ W/mK) or group LM 36 ($\lambda_R = 0.36$ W/mK). The two groups are further distinguished by the dry bulk density ($\rho_D \leq 700$ kg/m^3 and $\rho_D \leq 1.0$ kg/dm^3 respectively) and lateral secant modulus ($E_q > 7500$ N/mm^2 and $E_q > 15\,000$ N/mm^2 respectively). The requirements concerning the necessary thickness of the bed joint as well as the permissible height tolerance of the masonry units are identical to those for normal-weight mortar. The recommended applications as well as limits are given in table 2.1.26.

2.1.25 Prescribed mixes for (normal-weight) mortar, mixing ratios by volume

Mortar group MG	Non-hydrated lime		Hydraulic lime (HL2)	Hyd. lime (HL5), plaster binder and masonry cement (MC5)	Cement	Sand from natural rock
	Lime putty	Hydrated lime				
I	1	–	–	–	–	4
	–	1	–	–	–	3
	–	–	1	–	–	3
	–	–	–	1	–	4.5
II	1.5	–	–	–	1	8
	–	2	–	–	1	8
	–	–	2	–	1	8
	–	–	–	1	–	3
IIa	–	1	–	–	1	6
	–	–	–	2	1	8
III	–	–	–	–	1	4
IIIa	–	–	–	–	1	4

2.1.26 Recommended and non-permissible applications of mortars for masonry

Component			Normal-wt mortar MG I	II / IIa	III / IIIa	Lightweight mortar	Thin-bed mortar
External walls	single-leaf	without weather protection (facing brickwork)		+		–	0
		with weather protection (e.g. rendering)		- to +		0 to +	0 to +
	twin-leaf (cavity)	outer leaf (facing brickwork)		+		–	0
		inner leaf	+	+	+	– to +	0 to +
Internal walls	acoustic insulation		+	+	+	0	+
	thermal insulation			0 to –		+	+
	high strength				+	–	+
Vaulting			N[3]			N	N
Basement masonry			N[3]				
> 2 full storeys			N				
Wall thickness > 240 mm[1]			N				
Non-loadbearing outer leaf of twin-leaf external walls • facing brickwork • rendered facing bricks			N N	N[2] N[2]		N	
Facing brickwork, with flush joints externally			N			N	
Unfavourable weather conditions (precipitation, low temperatures)			N				
Masonry units with height tolerance ≥ 1.0 mm							N
Masonry after test to assess suitability			N				

[1] In the case of twin-leaf walls with or without continuous air cavity: wall thickness = thickness of inner leaf.
[2] Apart from subsequent pointing and for areas of reinforced masonry.
[3] Application permitted for the repair of natural stone masonry using MG I.
+ recommended, 0 possible, - not recommended, N not permitted

2.1.27 Requirements for mortar (excluding prescribed mixes[1]) according to DIN 1053 part 1, tested at 28 days

Test parameter / Test standard	Abbreviation	Test to assess grade	Normal-weight mortar					Lightweight mortar		Thin-bed mortar
			I	II	IIa	III	IIIa	LM 21	LM 36	
Mortar mix	–	EP	compulsory							
Comp. strength DIN 18 555 part 3	β_D N/mm²	EP	–	≥ 3.5[2]	≥ 7[2]	≥ 14[2]	≥ 25[2]	≥ 7[2]	≥ 7[2]	≥ 14[2]
		GP	–	≥ 2.5	≥ 5	≥ 10	≥ 20	≥ 5	≥ 5	≥ 10
Comp. strength, joint Draft guidelines[3]	β_{DF} N/mm²	EP	–	≥ 1.25	≥ 2.5	≥ 5.0	≥ 10.0	≥ 2.5	≥ 2.5	–
		EP	–	≥ 2.5	≥ 5.0	≥ 10.0	≥ 20.0	≥ 5.0	≥ 5.0	–
Comp. strength humid storage conditions (DIN 18 555 part 3)	β_{Df} N/mm²	EP	–	–	–	–	–	–	–	≥ 70% from actual value β_D
		GP								
Adhesive shear strength DIN 18 555 part 5	β_{HS}	EP	–	≥ 0.10	≥ 0.20	≥ 0.25	≥ 0.30	≥ 0.20	≥ 0.20	≥ 0.5
Dry gross density DIN 18 555 part 3	ρ_d kg/dm³	EP	≥ 1.5	≥ 1.5	≥ 1.5	≥ 1.5	≥ 1.5	≤ 0.7	≤ 1.0	–
		GP	–					max. deviation + 10% from actual value		–
Lateral secant modulus DIN 18 555 part 4	E_q N/mm²	EP	–	–	–	–	–	> 7500	> 15000	–
		GP	–	–	–	–	–	[4]	[4]	–
Long. secant modulus DIN 18 555 part 4	E_l N/mm²	EP	–	–	–	–	–	> 2000	> 3000	–
		GP	–	–	–	–	–	–	–	–
Thermal conductivity DIN 18 555 part 1	$\lambda_{10,tr}$ W/mK	EP	–	–	–	–	–	≤ 0.18[5]	≤ 0.27[5]	–
Workability time DIN 18 555 part 8	t_v h	EP	–	–	–	–	–	–	–	≥ 4
Correction time DIN 18 555 part 8	t_k min	EP	–	–	–	–	–	–	–	≥ 7

[1] The requirements are deemed to be met for these.
[2] Guide value for premixed mortar.
[3] Requirements for cube compressive strength (upper line) and plate loading test (lower line); one of the two tests may be chosen.
[4] Dry bulk density as substitute test.
[5] Deemed to be satisfied when maintaining the threshold for ρ_d in GP.

2.1.28 Tests required for mortar to assess suitability

Test to assess suitability is necessary for:	Mortar		
	NM	LM	DM
determining mortar mix, apart from prescribed mortars	×	×	×
normal-weight mortar of group IIIa, also prescribed mortars	×		
verification of usability of aggregate	×	×	×
use of > 15% by vol. admixtures, related to sand component	×		
use of admixtures and additives	×	×	×
structures with > 6 full storeys of masonry	×	×	×
significant change of mortar raw materials or mortar mix	×	×	×

2.1.29 Recommended mortar mixes for natural stone masonry

Application	Mortar group	Trass cement	Hydrated lime	Trass lime, hydrated lime	Aggregate [mm]
Natural stone masonry (random coursing)	II	–	–	–	–
	II	1	2	3	8 (0/4)
	IIa	–	–	–	–
	IIa	1	1	–	6 (0/4)
Natural stone masonry (regular coursing)	II	–	–	–	–
	II	–	1	3	8 (0/4)
	IIa	–	–	–	–
	IIa	1	2	–	8 (0/4)
	III	1	–	–	4 (0/4)
Pointing of nat. stone masonry	IIa	–	–	1	2.5 (0/4)

Thin-bed mortars

are premixed dry mortars consisting of aggregates with a dense microstructure according to DIN 4226 part 1, standard cement and additives/admixtures. The composition is based on suitable tests. Thin-bed mortars are used for gauged bricks with a permissible height tolerance of ±1 mm (see "Masonry bonds"). Owing to the bed joint thickness of 1-3 mm, the maximum particle size of the aggregate is limited to 1.0 mm. The dry gross density ρ_D usually exceeds 1500 kg/m³. Thin-bed mortars are allocated to group III; their applications are summarised in 2.1.26.

Medium-bed mortars

are currently not covered by DIN 1053 but a number of building authority certificates have already been issued. The medium-bed mortars approved so far correspond to the composition of normal-weight and lightweight mortars. They are generally produced as premixed dry mortars with the addition of fibres and must comply with the requirements regarding volume stability, compressive strength ($\beta_D \geq 5$ N/mm²), dry gross density ($\rho_D \leq 1000$ kg/m³) and adhesive shear strength ($\beta_{HS} \geq 0.20$ N/mm²). The difference between these and the normal-weight and lightweight mortars lies in the thickness of the bed joints, which at 5-7 mm are considerably thinner than those of normal-weight and lightweight mortars. However, there are no medium-sized perpends and, as a result, a change in the longitudinal dimensions of the masonry units. The construction of walls using the medium-bed method presupposes unit dimensions with a height tolerance of ±2 mm in order to avoid the occurrence of tension peaks and the considerable reduction in loadbearing capacity associated with this. The background to the current development of medium-bed mortar is that a reduction in the thickness of the bed joints with units having a low transverse tensile strength increases the compressive strength of the masonry. This applies, above all, to vertically perforated bricks, which require expensive and elaborate means (e.g. grinding) in order to achieve the necessary even surfaces and dimensional accuracy for thin-bed masonry. In order to minimize this work and the costs, but at the same time increase the compressive strength of the masonry, a compromise – medium-bed mortar – is currently undergoing development. The reliable construction of medium-bed horizontal joints requires the use of special equipment and techniques [3, 89].

Mortar for facing work

This term is not included in DIN 1053. As this type of mortar is used in conjunction with facing bricks and blocks, it is referred to as mortar for facing work by mortar manufacturers. It is specially formulated to meet the requirements of facing work with regard to weather resistance and appearance. Mortar for facing work is always supplied premixed. For facing work it meets the requirements of mortar groups II or IIa, for single-leaf facing work the requirements of mortar groups II to IIIa, and as a pointing mortar for subsequent work on joints the requirements of mortar groups III and IIIa (see "The building of masonry").

The properties of mortar and the requirements it has to meet

Mortar parameters and specifications for mortars for masonry are contained in DIN 1053 part 1 appendix A. Quality control makes use of DIN 18555 and 18557 in addition. The most important parameters for mortar used in masonry are its compressive strength β_D, adhesive shear strength β_{HS}, dry gross density ρ_D, lateral secant modulus E_q longitudinal secant modulus E_l, and in the case of thin-bed mortar the workability time t_v and correction time t_k. The requirements for these are given in table 2.1.27, the requirements for testing mortar in table 2.1.28.

The compressive strength β_D of mortar is a critical parameter for the compressive strength of the masonry. Besides the compressive strength, in the case of normal-weight and lightweight mortar the joint compressive strength $\beta_{D,F}$ of the bed joints is to be determined according to DIN 18555 part 9. A calcium silicate reference brick, which is classed as particularly poor owing to its absorption behaviour and surface properties, is used for the test to determine the compressive strength of the mortar; this is intended to show the influence of the unit-mortar interface and take into account the water absorption behaviour of the masonry unit.

The adhesive shear strength β_{HS} has to be determined for normal-weight mortar – with the exception of prescribed mixes – as well as for lightweight and thin-bed mortars. To produce a composite panel, all masonry units of formats DF, NF and 2 DF may be used. However, as calcium silicate units deliver the most unfavourable test results, the test for adhesive shear strength is usually carried out on a calcium silicate reference unit (DIN 106 – KS 12-2.0-NF). The adhesive shear strength is critical for the tensile, tensile bending and shear strength as well as the durability (watertightness against driving rain) of the masonry. The dry gross density ρ_D is required for lightweight mortar. This serves to distinguish normal-weight mortars from lightweight mortars and to determine to which category – LM 21 or LM 36 – the mortar belongs. The dry gross density is necessary in order to assess the building science properties and self-weight of the masonry. As lightweight mortars in masonry deform relatively severely in the transverse direction upon application of a load owing to the lightweight aggregates and hence have a

decisive influence on the compressive strength of the masonry, the lateral secant modulus E_q must be determined. This is the secant modulus obtained at one third of the mortar strength and the associated lateral strain determined from mortar prisms measuring 100 x 100 mm or 95 x 95 mm in plan and 200 mm high. The longitudinal secant modulus E_l is also determined during this test. The smaller the E_q value, the larger is the transverse deformability of the lightweight mortar and the lower is the compressive strength of the masonry. The workability time tv and the correction time t_k only need to be determined for thin-bed mortars. A workability time of min. 4 h is necessary because the quantity of mortar usually mixed can only be used very slowly owing to the thin bed joints. A correction time of min. 7 min is necessary in order to be able to adjust the position of a masonry unit already laid.

Mortars for natural stone masonry

As a rule, normal-weight mortars of groups II and IIa to DIN 1053 part 1 appendix A or lime mortar containing trass or trass-cement-lime mortar are to be recommended. However, it may also be necessary to develop special mortar mixes for natural stone masonry [105]. In particular, certain types of marble may be sensitive to discoloration by lime. In such cases lime must be never be added to the mortar, and special trass and rapid-hardening cement should be used. Table 2.1.29 shows the recommended mortar mixes for natural stone masonry.

New types of mortar

New types of mortar are currently undergoing development for the medium-bed and lightweight categories. In both cases the aim is to optimize the thermal insulation behaviour through the use of particularly lightweight aggregates. The newly developed lightweight mortars are currently still subject to building authority certification because non-standard requirements (mix, instructions for mixing with other aggregates, safety issues concerning residues) have been placed on the special lightweight aggregates in order to be able to classify them as lightweight mortars to DIN 1053 part 1. The lightweight aggregates requiring certificates include expanded mica, expanded perlite, pulverized fuel ash, foamed glass and polystyrene beads. The newly developed lightweight mortars are dealt with in [79].

Plasters

Plaster is a surface finish that achieves its final properties only after being applied to a building element. It is applied to walls and soffits in one or more coats of a certain thickness. Terminology and requirements are covered by DIN 18550 parts 1 to 4 (see table 2.1.30). The tasks of plasters can be divided into their use as a surface finish and their use to help attain required building science properties. As a surface finish, plasters create a flat and accurately aligned surface, which can remain exposed (e.g. textured, coloured) or serve as the base for paint, wallpaper or other finishes. Their building science tasks include protection against the weather and moisture (rain) by use of water-resistant and water-repellent plasters, thermal insulation by the use of lightweight or thermally insulating plasters, improvement to sound insulation and fire protection (plaster as a fire protection cladding) as well as the creation of a temporary means of storage for excessive internal moisture (interior wall and ceiling plasters in kitchens, bathrooms etc.). In addition, plasters can satisfy requirements for mechanical strength or abrasion resistance (plaster to plinths and basement walls) and increased absorption of radiation.

A distinction must be made between plasters containing mineral binding agents, which make use of plastering mixes, and those with organic binding agents (artificial resin plasters), which are produced from coating materials.

Plastering mixes

A plastering mix is a mixture of one or more binding agents, aggregate with the particle size mainly lying between 0.25 and 4 mm, and water as well as additives if necessary. In special cases plastering mixes for finish coats may contain a large proportion of particles exceeding 4 mm. The aggregate may be omitted from plastering mixes made from calcined gypsum and anhydrite binders. Plastering mixes are divided into groups P I to P V. Besides lime and cement, gypsum and anhydrite may be used as a binding agent. Plastering mix groups P I to P III correspond, in terms of composition, to mortar groups MG I to MG III. When plastering mixes are produced according to the mixing ratios in DIN 18550 part 2 table 3, then they can be treated like prescribed mortar mixes. These generally fulfil the requirements of DIN 18550 part 2 table 2 (see 2.1.31) and can therefore be used for the plastering systems given in tables 3 to 6 of DIN 18550 part 1. Tests to assess suitability must be carried out in the case of a mix which deviates from the prescribed ratio. Plastering mixes are further classified as "green" or hardened depending on their state and according to their production either on site or in the factory.

2.1.30 Basic terminology for plasters

Term	Explanation
Plastering system	The coats of plaster which, in their entirety and in conjunction with the background, fulfil the requirements placed on the plaster. Even a single-coat plaster can be called a plastering system.
Coat	A layer of plaster which is applied in one operation. Lower coats are called "undercoats", the uppermost coat "final coat" or "finish coat". A coat of plaster can also be applied in several "plies", wet on wet and generally per lift of scaffolding.
Undercoat	The bottom coat(s) of a multi-coat plastering system.
Finish/final coat	The uppermost coat of a multi-coat plastering system.
Second plaster undercoat	A coat of plaster applied to a first plaster undercoat and necessary for certain thin finish coats.
Water-resistant plastering system	Plastering systems are classed as water-resistant when the water absorption coefficient is < 2.0 kg/(m² · h$^{0.5}$).
Water-repellent plastering system	Plastering systems are classed as water-repellent when the water absorption coefficient is ≤ 1.0 kg/(m²h$^{0.5}$) after 28 days.

2.1.31 Mortar groups for plastering mixes and coating materials

Plastering mix group, type of coating material		Type of binding agent or type of mortar	$\beta_{D, mean}$ after 28 d [N/mm²]
P I	a	Non-hydraulic limes	no requirement
	b	Semi-hydraulic limes	no requirement
	c	Hydraulic limes	1.0
P II	a	Hydraulic limes, plasters and masonry cement	2.5
	b	Lime-cement	2.5
P III	a	Cement and hydrated lime admixture	10.0
	b	Cement	10.0
P IV	a	Gypsum mortar	2.0
	b	Gypsum-sand mortar	2.0
	c	Gypsum-lime mortar	2.0
	d	Lime-gypsum mortar	no requirement
P V	a	Anhydrite mortar	2.0
	b	Anhydrite-lime mortar	2.0
P Org 1		Coating materials with organic binding agents for rendering and internal plasters	no requirement
P Org 2		Coating materials with organic binding agents for internal plasters	no requirement

2.1.32 Examples of rendering systems to DIN 18550 part 1

	Requirement or rendering application	Plastering mix group or coating material for	
		undercoat	finish coat
1	Water-resistant	P I	P I
2		–	P I c
3		–	P II
4		P II	P I
5		P II	P II
6	Water-repellent	P I c	P I
7		P II	P I
8		–	P I c
9		–	P II
10		P II	P II
11	Enhanced strength	–	P II
12		P II	P II
13		P II	P Org 1
14	Basement wall rendering	–	P III
15	Rendering near ground level	–	P III
16	(water-repellent)	P III	P III
17		P III	P Org 1

Coating materials

Coating materials consist of organic binding agents in the form of dispersions or solutions and fillers/aggregates with the majority of particles > 0.25 mm. Coating materials fall into two groups: P Org 1 and P Org 2 (see 2.1.31).

Plasters and plastering systems – applications and requirements

The various types of plaster are primarily classified according to their place of use on the structure and the associated conditions to which they will be subjected. Plastering systems are frequently used to achieve the requirements placed on the plaster. These comprise several coats, sometimes of different plastering mix groups and/or coating materials.

Rendering

is a form of plaster applied to the external surfaces of structures. It is divided into different types according to degree of exposure and use above, near or below ground level for walls and soffits. As the main task of rendering is to permanently protect the structure from the weather and other environmental influences, it is an important component in the external wall construction. The rendering should resist the effects of moisture, better still the effects of rainwater or driving rain and the associated saturation of the rendering, in order to prevent impairment of the building science properties of the complete wall. To do this, the rendering must possess water-resistant or even water-repellent properties. On the other hand, the rendering must exhibit good water vapour permeability in order to prevent a build-up of moisture in the wall through interstitial condensation. The rendering is also responsible for the visual appearance of the facade (textured, coloured) and for improving the thermal insulation. In this case the rendering is of the thermal insulation variety or is provided as part of a thermal insulation composite system. Rendering which serves as a background for organic coatings or which is subjected to severe mechanical loads (compression, abrasion) must have a minimum compressive strength of 2.5 N/mm². Apart from that, the mechanical compatibility (strength, stiffness) with the substrate must be taken into account. The outside faces of basement walls below ground level may be rendered before applying the waterproof tanking. This rendering should be made from mortars with hydraulic binding agents. They must reach a minimum compressive strength of 10 N/mm², which is guaranteed by using rendering of group P III. However, for masonry made from units of compressive strength class 6 and less, it is advisable not to exceed a strength of 10 N/mm² too much owing to the compatibility between rendering and substrate. Rendering suitable for the external faces of

plinths must extend at least 300 mm above ground level. Such rendering must be sufficiently firm, should exhibit low water absorption and be resistant to the effects of moisture (splashing water and snow) as well as frost. When using mixes with mineral binding agents, the minimum compressive strength must be 10 N/mm². For a substrate of masonry units of compressive strength class 6 and less, water-repellent mortar with hydraulic binding agents and a minimum compressive strength of 5 N/mm² may also be used.
Possible systems that satisfy the respective requirements for rendering are given in table 2.1.32.

Internal plasters
are those applied to the internal surfaces of structures. They are divided into different types according to their uses on walls or ceilings in rooms of normal or high humidity. Internal plasters serve both to produce flat, accurately aligned surfaces, and also to act as a temporary means of storage for excessive internal moisture. Internal plasters also contribute to improving sound insulation and fire protection. When internal plasters are used as a base for paint and wallpaper, and hence must transfer additional stresses to these, the plastering mixes employed must exhibit a minimum compressive strength of 1.0 N/mm².
Plasters with increased abrasion resistance are necessary for internal wall surfaces which are subject to mechanical loads (e.g. adjacent stairs and in the corridors of public buildings and schools). The requirements for the abrasion resistance of the finish coat are satisfied by plastering mixes of groups P II to P V. Plasters containing calcined gypsum and/or anhydrite as the binding agents may not be used for internal walls and ceilings which must resist the long-term effects of moisture (e.g. commercial or public sanitary facilities and kitchens). Plasters which are intended to act as a base for ceramic finishes (tiles) must exhibit a minimum compressive strength of 2.5 N/mm² and may not be worked with a trowel or sponge. Plastering systems for internal applications are given in table 2.1.33.

Lightweight plasters
are, in terms of their strength and deformation characteristics, suited to masonry with high thermal insulation properties and low strength. In contrast to other types plastering mixes both upper (≤ 5.0 N/mm²) and lower (≥ 2.5 N/mm²) limits for the strength of lightweight plaster have been defined. Lightweight plasters exhibit a particularly high "degree of decoupling", i.e. they "decouple" the finish coat from the undercoat and hence make a decisive contribution to the prevention of cracks. They may be used for both finish coat and undercoat. Lightweight plastering mixes for use as a finish coat may not contain any organic aggregates. Systems

for lightweight rendering must be water-repellent [3].

Thermal insulation plasters and thermal insulation plastering systems
are employed to improve the thermal insulation properties of single-leaf external walls on new buildings and in the refurbishment of existing buildings. Owing to the low requirements placed on the substrate, they are also used to even out larger irregularities in the external walls as well as for less stable substrates such as lightweight masonry. Thermal insulation plasters are produced from premixed mortars with aggregates of low bulk density. They are designated as such when the calculated thermal conductivity $\lambda_R \leq 0.2$ W/mK. This is generally achieved with a dry bulk density of the hardened mortar $\rho_{tr} \leq 0.6$ kg/dm³.
Thermal insulation plastering systems consist of a 20-100 mm thick thermal insulation plaster undercoat with an expanded polystyrene aggregate plus a compatible 8-15 mm thick water-repellent finish coat consisting of mineral binding agents and mineral aggregate. Thin finish coats should only be applied to a levelling coat of plaster at least 6 mm thick. After completing the thermal insulation undercoat, a period of at least seven days should elapse before the finish coat is applied; with thicker undercoats the minimum waiting period should be one day per 10 mm thickness. The waiting times should be increased in the case of adverse weather (high humidity and low temperatures). Besides the standard plastering systems with polystyrene aggregates as specified in DIN 18550 part 3, there are also thermal insulation plastering systems based on inorganic lightweight aggregates and covered by building authority serviceability certificates. Owing to their low strength, thermal insulation plastering systems are not suitable for either lightly or heavily loaded external wall plinth areas. They are divided into thermal conductivity groups 060, 070, 080, 090 and 100, with group 070 being the one most frequently used (070 means that the calculated thermal conductivity $\lambda_R = 0.070$ W/mK).

Thermal insulation composite systems
consist primarily of three layers: bonding mortar, thermal insulation (hard polystyrene foam or mineral wool) and plaster (composed of reinforcing and finish coats). Depending on their composition and the underlying construction, the systems can be attached by means of bonding, dowelling or rails. The mortars used (bonding mortar, reinforcing and finish coats) may be dispersion-, silicate- or also cement-bound varieties. These systems are currently still regulated by building authority certificates. Thermal insulation composite systems are used for new buildings with single-leaf masonry but also for improving the thermal insulation properties of existing masonry.

Renovation plasters
are used to plaster over damp masonry and/or masonry containing salts. Efflorescence is avoided by capturing the damaging salts in the plaster and hence keeping them away from the surface of the plaster. A plaster with a high water vapour permeability at the same time helps to allow the masonry to dry out. Renovation plasters make use of plastering mixes which in the hardened state exhibit high porosity and water vapour permeability with, at the same time, considerably reduced capillary action. Renovation plasters are mainly employed when refurbishing old buildings and historic monuments. At present they are not covered by a standard but are dealt with in great detail in [165].

The application of plaster
Substrate, background, reinforcement
The substrate must guarantee a stable and permanent bond for the plaster. Therefore, the properties of the substrate are critical for the properties of the plaster itself. If the substrate is sufficiently stable, consistent, even, not too smooth, not too absorbent, clean, dry and free from frost, then treatment prior to applying the plaster is not necessary; the first coat of plaster can be applied directly to the substrate. However, if the requirements on the substrate are not fulfilled, then this must be treated first. This includes prewetting of the substrate, a complete or partial "splatterdash" covering to provide a key, bonding agents and primers based on organic binding agents as well as making good irregularities in the masonry.
Highly absorbent substrates should be prewetted or given a complete splatterdash covering. Substrates consisting of different materials should also be given a complete splattedash covering. This mixture consists of a mortar with coarse aggregate thrown on to form a thick coat which completely covers the substrate. A partial splatterdash covering improves adhesion of the plaster in the case of substrates with low absorption. In this case, the mortar (with coarse aggregate) is only applied in a thin layer so that the substrate is still visible through it. With both full and partial coverings, the splatterdash is not treated any further. Making good irregularities in the masonry is mainly necessary in the case of perpends without mortar where the open joints are more than 5 mm wide, and to close off chases for pipes and cables. Such irregularities should be flushed up. This also applies to tongue and groove faces or mortar keys exposed at corners and jambs as well as to holes for securing scaffolding and missing fragments of clay bricks. These irregularities must be made good at least four weeks prior to plastering. As a rule, lightweight mortar is used [164].
A background is attached to cover the surface and also to improve the bond between the

plaster and the substrate. A background is employed as a substitute substrate in cases where this is inadequate or discontinuous (e.g. timber or steel frames). This essentially means a decoupling of the plaster from the supporting construction. If individual elements – unsuitable for use as a plaster substrate – are bridged over with a background, then this must overlap the surrounding (suitable) substrate by at least 100 mm on all sides and be fixed to this. Backgrounds can be made from metal, plasterboard, lightweight wood wallboards, multi-ply lightweight boards, wire mesh and cane mats. Backgrounds must be able to transfer the loads acting on the plaster skin (self-weight, wind pressure/suction) to the loadbearing construction. Reinforcement of metal, mineral fibres and synthetic fibres are integrated in the plaster in order to improve adhesion and minimize cracking in tension zones. However, this assumes that the stiffness and strength of the reinforcement are compatible with the properties of the plaster and that the reinforcement is incorporated properly. This includes minimizing contact between the plaster reinforcement and the substrate in order to avoid transferring unnecessary stresses from the substrate to the reinforcement. The reinforcement must overlap by at least 100 mm (see table 2.1.35).

Compatible plastering systems
Plasters can be applied in one or more coats. A coat of plaster is the application of a mortar or coating material to form one layer in one operation. Splatterdash applied to prepare the substrate is not classed as a coat of plaster. The total number of coats of plaster, which as a whole together with the substrate fulfil the requirements placed on the plaster, is termed the plastering system. As such, even a single coat of plaster could be termed a plastering system. The bottom layers of a plastering system are called undercoats, the uppermost layer the finish or final coat. Thermal stresses in an external wall decrease from the outside to the inside. Consequently, the finish coat is subjected to the greatest temperature-induced deformations and so must exhibit great elasticity. Accordingly, the coats of plaster should increase in elasticity from the inside to the outside, expressed by the plasterer's rule "soft on hard". The plastering systems listed in DIN 18550 part 1 are based on this rule. However, in order to guarantee the thermal insulation advantages and properties for the thermal insulation plasters and thermal insulation composite systems, the plasterer's rule must be reversed for such systems. Soft undercoats or soft thermal insulation materials are given a hard, water-repellent finish coat. However, this makes it necessary to decouple the coats by introducing an intermediate layer in order to minimize the risk of cracks [218]. The case is similar with lightweight plaster, where once again the finish coat is decoupled from the

undercoat by an intermediate layer as soft as possible. The reason for this is the thermal insulation properties of the masonry units, which can be achieved only by reducing the dry gross density and thereby increasing the deformability of the units. To achieve a compatible plastering system these units need an elastic undercoat in order to reduce cracking.

Thickness of plaster
Plaster thicknesses depend on the type of mortar and the purpose of the plaster, as defined in DIN 18550 part 2 (see table 2.1.34). In order to satisfy the general requirements, the average plaster thickness must be 20 mm for external work and 15 mm internally; 10 mm is sufficient for one-coat internal plasters made from premixed dry mortar. The permissible minimum thickness at individual places must not be less than 5 mm. "Thin-coat plasters", sometimes used for internal applications, do not comply with the requirements of DIN 18550.

Surface finishes
The finish coat may be worked in various ways to provide different appearances and textures. A plaster is finished with a sponge or metal trowel to produce the desired surface finish. The action of finely rubbing, felting or smoothing the plaster may enrich the concentration of binding agents at the surface, which then promotes the formation of shrinkage cracks and, in the case of non-hydraulic lime, hinders the setting of the undercoat(s).
Plaster with a float finish is known by many names according to the tool used (i.e. wooden float).
Plaster thrown on from a float is given its texture by the action of throwing the mortar. Generally, a coarse aggregate of up to about 10 mm is used.
Trowelled plaster is applied by means of a trowel or float to create panels or scales.
Sprayed plaster is produced by spraying on two or more coats of a fine-grain, fluid mortar from a special machine.
A scraped finish is achieved with combs, saw blades, cabinet scrapers or similar tools. This removes the binding agents and, as a result, the highly stressed surface of the finish coat. The projecting aggregate gives the plaster its characteristic texture. The right timing for the scraping depends on the progress of the setting of the plaster. The time is right when the aggregate springs out upon scraping but does not become attached to the scraping tool.
A scraped finish should not be classed as inadequate when individual pieces of aggregate become detached when rubbing the surface with the hand.
Scrubbed plaster is given its texture by washing the surface to remove the binding agent slurry which has not yet hardened. It requires selected coarse aggregates as well as an undercoat corresponding to mortar group III.

Application, subsequent treatment
In order to avoid flaws in the plaster (cracks, detached finish coat etc.), the influences of the weather should be considered when plastering. During frosty weather, rendering may only be applied when the area to be rendered is completely protected from the influence of the outside temperature and this covered area is heated until the plaster is sufficiently hard. Further, areas of rendering should be protected against rain as well as accelerated drying caused by strong sunshine, wind or draughts. Internal plastering may only carried out at internal temperatures of +5°C or higher. In the case of multi-coat plastering systems, an adequate waiting time must be allowed between applying the individual coats of plaster. A subsequent coat may be applied only when the preceding coat is stable, sufficiently dry and provides an adequate bond. Adequate drying time is necessary to guarantee that the inevitable shrinkage of the preceding coat has stopped. Applying a subsequent coat before shrinkage of the preceding coat has stopped leads to excessive stresses and cracks in the subsequent coat. This has resulted in the plasterer's rule of "one day waiting time per millimetre of undercoat" for normal plasters and "one day waiting time per 10 mm of undercoat, but at least seven days" for thermal insulation plastering systems. The first coat of plaster applied over splatterdash may only be applied after the mortar has hardened sufficiently, but at the earliest after 12 hours. Before applying the subsequent coat, the preceding coat must be roughened to form a key and prewetted if necessary.
Subsequent treatment of plasters should be carried out above all for groups P I, P II and P III. In doing so, the plasters should be protected to prevent them drying out too quickly and, if necessary, should be kept moist.

Controlling cracking

Plaster, and rendering in particular, shrinks by losing water. After the plaster has reached an adequate initial strength, this shrinkage is hindered by the substrate, which generally does not suffer from problems of shrinkage or at least not to the same extent. When the tensile stresses which ensue in the plaster exceed the low tensile strength of the plaster, then cracks appear. Further expansion of the masonry (e.g. due to temperature, chemical sources in clay bricks) and simultaneous shrinkage of the plaster increases the risk of cracks. However, the formation of cracks in plaster may be due to flaws in the substrate (inconsistent substrate with changes of material, weak points in the substrate, varying deformation behaviour of the substrate) or inadequate workmanship (insufficient pretreatment and post-treatment, time between coats too short, individual coats applied too thick, incompatible plastering system, varying thickness of plaster). Basically, a surface without any cracks is not possible, or at least requires a great deal of effort. Therefore, the aim is to achieve a compatible plastering system (observe plasterer's rules) applied correctly to prevent the formation of wider cracks at large spacings because otherwise moisture can penetrate the plaster and from there possibly penetrate the substrate, which in turn leads to damage (spalling caused by frost, impairment of the building science properties of the masonry). A limited number of finely distributed, hairline cracks up to about 0.2 mm wide are not regarded as a problem because they do not impair the function of the plaster. Although these cracks might allow more water to be absorbed under certain circumstances, this water quickly and easily evaporates again. The finely distributed hairline cracks in the finish coat of thermal insulation composite systems have no influence on the moisture content of the insulation, or on the thermal insulation properties of the system, because the insulation materials normally used (hard polystyrene and mineral wool) are neither hygroscopic nor have active capillaries.

2.1.33 Examples of internal plastering systems to DIN 18550 part 1

	Requirement or plaster application	Plastering mix group or coating material for undercoat	finish coat
1	Only light loads	P I a, b	P I a, b
2		P II	P I a, b; P IV d
3		P IV	P I a, b; P IV d
4	Normal loads	P I c	P I c
5	(including light loads)	–	P II
6		P II	P I c; P II; P IV a, b, c; P V; P Org 1; P Org 2
7		–	P III
8		P III	P I c; P II; P III; P Org 1; P Org 2
9		–	P IV a, b, c
10		P IV a, b, c	P IV a, b, c; P Org 1; P Org 2
11		P V	P V; P Org 1; P Org 2
12		–	P Org 1; P Org 2
13	Damp conditions	P I	P I
14	(not including domestic kitchens	–	P II
15	and bathrooms)	P II	P I; P II; P Org 1
16		–	P III
17		P III	P II; P III; P Org 1
18		–	P Org 1

2.1.34 Plaster thicknesses required

Plastering system		Average plaster thickness
Rendering (undercoat(s) + finish coat for multi-coat rendering)		≥ 20 mm
Single-coat water-repellent premixed rendering		≥ 15 mm
Internal plaster (undercoat(s) + finish coat for multi-coat internal plaster)		≥ 15 mm
Single-coat dry premixed internal plaster		≥ 10 mm
Thermal insulation plastering system	undercoat	≥ 20 mm, ≤ 100 mm
	second plaster undercoat (if required)	~ 10 mm ≥ 6 mm

2.1.35 Flaws in substrates and remedial measures

Flaw	Remedial measure
Substrate with areas of low strength, stability	Background, reinforcement, with adequate overlaps
Large cracks	Make good cracks or bridge over with background/ reinforcement
Wide joints > 5 mm	Fill joints with mortar to DIN 1053 part 1
Uneven substrate, depressions, projections	Dubbing out plaster coat
Changes of material	Splatterdash, background
Inconsistent, low surface roughness	Splatterdash
Inconsistent absorption	Prewetting
Soiled substrate, dust, loose sections	Clean substrate, remove loose sections, apply dubbing out plaster coat locally
Saturated, frozen substrate	Dry out, protect plastering surface from influences of weather, heat enclosed area
Substrate subjected to shrinkage, swelling, creep	Leave substrate for long time before plastering
Unacceptable reaction between substrate and plaster	Choose plastering mix to suit reactive materials

Masonry Bonds

Konrad Zilch, Martin Schätz with Christina Radlbeck

2.2.1 Historical formats

Designation	Length l [mm]	Width b [mm]	Height h [mm]
Imperial	250	120	65
Modified imperial	250	115	65
Oldenburg	220	105	52
Dutch	200	100	40
	215	105	40
Hamburg	220	105	55
	220	105	65
Waal	215	105	54
Vecht	215	105	42
Old Bavarian	295	145	65
	320	155	70
	340	165	70
	320	120	50

2.2.2 Dimensions of standard formats DF to 20 DF

Format designation	Length l [mm]	Width b [mm]	Height h [mm]
DF	240	115	52
NF	240	115	71
2 DF = 1.5 NF	240	115	113
3 DF = 2.5 NF	240	175	113
3.20 DF	145	300	113
3.75 DF	300 (308)	175	113
4 DF	240 (248)	115	238 (249)
4 DF	240 (248)	240	113 (124)
5 DF	300 (308)	115	238 (249)
5 DF	300 (308)	240	113 (124)
6 DF	365 (373)	115	238 (249)
6 DF	365 (373)	240	113 (124)
6 DF	490 (498)	175	113 (124)
7.5 DF	300 (308)	175	238 (249)
8 DF	240 (248)	240	238 (249)
8 DF	490 (498)	115	238 (249)
8 DF	490 (498)	240	113 (124)
9 DF	365 (373)	175	238 (249)
10 DF	240 (248)	300	238 (249)
12 DF	365 (373)	240	238 (249)
12 DF	490 (498)	175	238 (249)
14 DF	240 (248)	425	238 (249)
15 DF	365 (373)	300	238 (249)
16 DF	490 (498)	240	238 (249)
20 DF	490 (498)	300	238 (249)

General

A bond is the regular interlocking arrangement of masonry units in courses to form a wall construction.

The task of a bond is to enhance the strength of the masonry construction as well as its resistance to the formation of cracks and the influences of the weather. In addition, the bond distributes the loads and forces evenly within the masonry. The tasks of the mortar are to distribute the loads uniformly and to compensate for varying dimensions.

Formats and specials

Historical formats

The introduction of a useful standard size of masonry unit was originally influenced by the "one-hand hold", which allows a brick to be comfortably handled with one hand. This span is on average 120 mm and determines the width of a masonry unit. In 1852 the German Customs Authority defined the "imperial" format – 250 mm long and 120 mm wide. The height of 65 mm resulted from the fact that a round figure of 400 bricks, including the inevitable wastage, produced exactly 1 m³ of brickwork. However, the disadvantage of this brick size is that two courses plus one joint do not equal the width of a brick on edge. Therefore, the final brick always had to be cut lengthwise, a time-consuming and difficult process. The size of the header face also represented an aesthetic problem. The dimension of 130 mm (width of brick + joint) is difficult to incorporate in the decimal system and results in awkward multiples. For facing masonry (i.e. units left exposed), the imperial format appeared too long for its height and so could not be used for decorative areas of masonry. With the "Baden" format of 270 x 130 x 65 mm and the Bavarian "royal brick", measuring 290 x 140 x 65 mm, the height is calculated from (brick width - 1 x bed joint) ÷ 2.

If one joint of 10 mm is added to each of the brick dimensions (280 x 140 x 70 mm and 300 x 150 x 75 mm), then the resulting length to width to height ratio of 4:2:1 makes possible the wide use of bricks. Other historical brick formats are listed in table 2.2.1. Today, the historical formats are only produced for special purposes.

Standard formats

The various dimensions of the masonry units used in Germany are today almost exclusively determined by the "octametric" system of dimensional coordination according to DIN 4172 (see "The relationship between dimensional coordination and unit format"). Based on the dimension 1/8 m = 125 mm, the thin format DF (240 x 115 x 52 mm) and the normal format NF (240 x 115 x 71 mm) form the basic modules for brick and block dimensions. These two formats are also known as small formats. All larger formats are made up of these basic modules taking into account the joint thickness. It should be noted that depending on the combination of

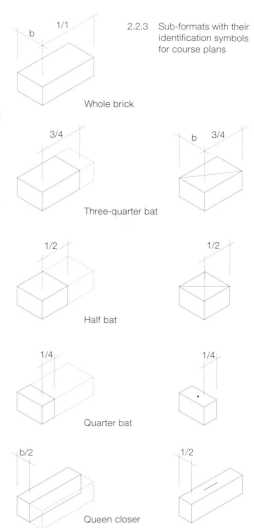

2.2.3 Sub-formats with their identification symbols for course plans

Whole brick

Three-quarter bat

Half bat

Quarter bat

Queen closer

basic modules, various masonry unit dimensions – length, width and height – can be described with one format designation (see fig. 2.2.4). The possible masonry unit dimensions for the formats DF to 20 DF are shown in table 2.2.2. The lengths in brackets apply to masonry units without mortar to the perpends (brick to brick), or those with interlocking header faces (tongue and groove system); the heights in brackets apply to gauged units for building masonry with thin-bed mortar. The formats 2 DF and 3 DF are called medium formats, those from 3.2 DF to 20 DF large formats.

Besides defining the unit dimensions from the multitude of thin and normal formats, there are also subformats resulting from the division of a whole brick into three-quarter bat, half bat, quarter bat or queen closer (see fig. 2.2.3). These units complement the standard formats and enable the masonry to be better adapted to particular building dimensions, thus avoiding costly on-site cutting of the units.

Large-format elements
Owing to the need to produce masonry inexpensively and rationally, larger formats have been in use for a number of years (see also "Rationalization measures").
The use of large-format elements results in the faster erection of masonry than when using small- and medium-format units. Above all, the calcium silicate and aerated concrete industries have promoted the development of large-format elements.
In combination with masonry materials with good thermal insulation properties, the mortar joint – even when using lightweight mortars – represents a zone of higher thermal transmission. Compared to standard formats, the use of large-format elements achieves a better result in terms of thermal insulation.

The calcium silicate "quadro" system
consists of solid units laid with mechanical fixings on a 125 mm module. The units are produced in wall thicknesses from 115 to 365 mm, in lengths from 248 to 498 mm, and in heights of 498 or 623 mm.

Calcium silicate gauged elements
were developed as complete wall building kits. The wall thickness is 100 mm for non-load-bearing internal walls, otherwise 115-300 mm. With a length of 998 mm and heights of 498 or 623 mm, these elements also fit into the "octa-metric" system of dimensional coordination.

Autoclaved aerated concrete units or gauged units and autoclaved aerated concrete pre-fabricated brick elements or gauged brick elements
have thicknesses ranging from 175 to 365 mm (units) or 50 to 150 mm (panels) and a maximum length x height of 615 (624) x 240 (249) mm. The figures in brackets apply to gauged bricks and panels.

2.2.4   Unit formats (cm) resulting from multiples of thin formats according to [83]

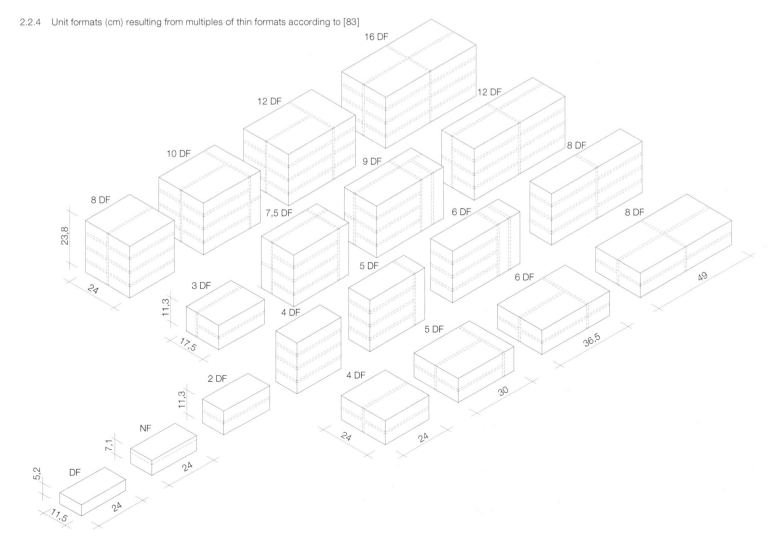

2.2.5   Special formats and special components

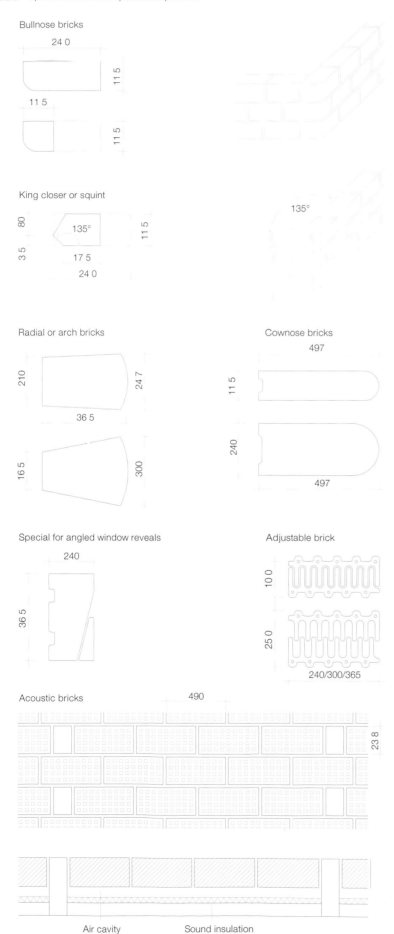

Bullnose bricks
24 0
11 5
11 5
11 5
11 5

King closer or squint
80
135°
11 5
3 5
17 5
24 0

135°

Radial or arch bricks
210
24 7
36 5
16 5
300

Cownose bricks
497
11 5
240
497

Special for angled window reveals
240
36 5

Adjustable brick
10 0
25 0
240/300/365

Acoustic bricks
490
23 8

Air cavity   Sound insulation

Autoclaved aerated concrete gauged elements are available with a maximum length x width x height of 999 x 365 x 623 mm, similar to the calcium silicate gauged elements.

Hollow wall and wall elements of lightweight concrete are produced in the sizes (length x width x height) 490 x 95 or 100 x 240 mm and 990 x 50 to 70 x 320 mm.

The only large-format units produced in clay are the *brick elements and lightweight brick elements*. The maximum format available here is 24 DF (497 x 365 x 238 mm). This format is also the largest common format for *hollow and solid blocks of lightweight concrete* as well as *solid (normal-weight) concrete blocks*.

Special formats, special units
Special formats and special units are produced in all standard types of masonry material. These complement the standard formats and units to produce a complete wall system. This helps rationalize the masonry construction operation and enables both consistent building science properties and a consistent substrate for plastering.

Specials
are units that deviate from the standard cuboid geometry and were developed to simplify the construction of certain masonry details. Cownose bricks, radial and arch bricks to DIN 1057 part 1 and bullnose bricks were developed for round masonry details. King closers or squints are used to simplify the corners of projecting bays. Dog-leg bricks with an angled stretcher face are used for window reveals, stop bricks (with or without angled faces) are used to simplify the incorporation of window and door openings. The dimensions of specials mainly correspond to the "octametric" system of dimensional coordination and so are readily incorporated in a masonry bond (see figs. 2.2.5 and 2.2.6).

Adjustable bricks
are two-part units whose length along the wall can be adjusted between about 100 and 250 mm through a system of telescoping internal webs. These avoid the need for supplementary formats or the need to cut large-format units on site. Adjustable bricks can be employed in the length of a wall, at corners and adjacent openings (see fig. 2.2.5). Adjustable bricks may only be used in masonry of vertically perforated units or lightweight vertically perforated units to DIN 105 part 1 or 2, or in accordance with a building authority certificate.
The wall value applies as the design value for thermal conductivity. The actual thermal conductivity of the adjustable brick does not need

to be taken into account. However, these adjustable units may only be used in walls with $\lambda_R > 0.18$ W/mK.

Brick slips

are primarily used for cladding spandrel panels and reinforced concrete elements, e.g. floor beams. This creates a uniform substrate for plastering across the whole wall. The lengths of the slips are based on the 1/8 m module, the height and thickness on the element to be clad.

Acoustic bricks

are employed to absorb noise both in external applications, e.g. noise barriers adjacent to busy roads, and internal applications, e.g. railway stations, machine shops, sports facilities. Acoustic bricks are provided with continuous horizontal or downward-sloping perforations perpendicular to the plane of the wall. Their dimensions are based on the "octametric" system of dimensional coordination and they are available in widths from 52 to 140 mm. Noise-absorbing acoustic walls are built like walls of facing masonry. Improved noise absorption is achieved by incorporating acoustic insulation and an air cavity (see fig. 2.2.5).

Hollow blocks for grouting

are large-format clay or lightweight concrete units with large voids which, after laying, are filled with mortar, grout or in-situ concrete either course by course or storey by storey. Therefore, these blocks act as permanent formwork. The filling makes these blocks particularly suitable for producing noise barriers. They are available in widths from 115 to 365 mm up to a maximum length of 1000 mm (see fig. 2.2.6).
For external walls systems are available in which these hollow blocks are delivered to site with an integral layer of thermal insulation. This insulation is placed within the outer skin of the block. Therefore, the unit with integral insulation does not present any problems with regard to the build-up of condensation caused by diffusion of water vapour.

Channel or lintel blocks

are used as permanent formwork for the production of horizontally reinforced masonry, beams, window and door lintels as well as vertical slots, columns etc. Their dimensions are based on the "octametric" system of dimensional coordination; maximum wall thicknesses of 365 mm are possible. Clay channel blocks over 300 mm wide are also produced with an integral hard foam core to improve the thermal insulation.
Channel blocks are used for plastered masonry and for facing work – in which case they have the same colour and texture as the facing or engineering bricks used for the rest of the wall.

Shallow lintel units

are prefabricated elements which – with steel tension reinforcement – normally act as the tension flange of a construction to span over door and window openings as well as recesses for radiators. Channel-shaped units made from the same material as the surrounding masonry are employed as permanent formwork. This creates a uniform substrate for plastering. Shallow lintel units achieve their loadbearing capacity by acting in conjunction with the compression zone comprising of the overlying brickwork or concrete of a beam or floor slab. They are based on a module of 250 mm and are available in lengths up to 3 m. Lintel widths of 115-175 mm mean that openings in walls up to 490 mm thick can be accommodated. Lintel depths are 71 or 113 mm so that they can be incorporated in the 1/8 m wall module (see fig. 2.2.6).

L-units

simplify the cladding of slabs and hence speed up progress on site. The dimensions of the units are the same as those for channel blocks. With a bottom leg of 60 to 80 mm, slab depths of up to 180 mm can be clad with these units. An integral hard foam core improves the thermal insulation properties of masonry in the region of the support (see fig.2.2.6).

Service duct and pre-chased units

in the customary "octametric" dimensions simplify the construction of vertical and horizontal ducts and chases for building services. When incorporated into bonded masonry, the service duct units enable vertical shafts up to 145 mm diameter to be formed without having to build the masonry around the shaft. Besides being suitable for building services, the ducts formed in this way can also incorporate steel reinforcement for reinforced masonry. The pre-chased units mean that subsequent cutting of slots for cables and pockets for junction boxes and switches is no longer necessary (see fig. 2.2.6).

Roller-blind boxes of clay, concrete or lightweight concrete

are self-supporting or structural prefabricated elements with integral components for roller-blind operation as well as, in some cases, integral thermal insulation. Roller-blind boxes are manufactured in widths from 300 to 490 mm and lengths up to 6.5 m based on a module of 250 mm. Besides the standard shapes, corner boxes with up to four corners and curved boxes are also possible. The use of roller-blind boxes made from the same material as the surrounding masonry creates a uniform substrate for plastering. An accessory available is the standard-size roller-blind belt winder which is built into the masonry bond. Therefore, the belt winder is incorporated without the need to cut any additional chases.

2.2.6 Special formats and special components

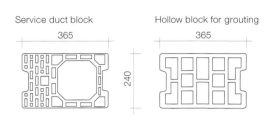

Service duct block

Hollow block for grouting

Channel or lintel blocks

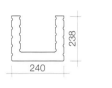

Shallow lintel units

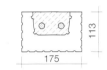

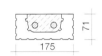

L-units

Roller-blind box

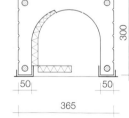

Door and window stop bricks

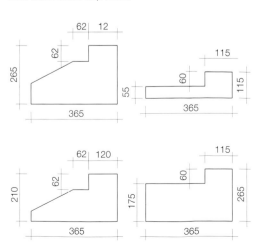

2.2.7 Relationship between nominal measurements and reference sizes

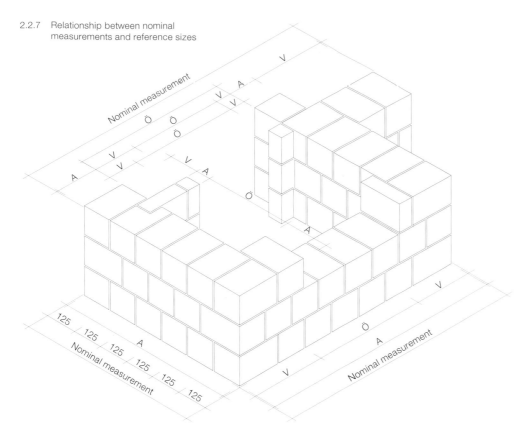

Adequate thermal insulation at roller-blind boxes is verified either experimentally in laboratory tests or by calculation according to the stipulations of the building code. Special attention should be given to ensuring air tightness on the inside (see fig. 2.2.6).

The relationship between dimensional coordination and unit format

A system of dimensional coordination is employed to simplify the design and construction of masonry. Within this system, the sizes of components are specified based on a basic dimension as well as multiples of that dimension. Adhering to this system of dimensional coordination ensures that components such as walls, projections, doors, windows etc. all match in terms of their dimensions. This system makes it unnecessary to adjust the length of a wall to account for the progressive assembly of small masonry units and simplifies the inclusion of prefabricated items, e.g. doors and windows, which are also manufactured according to this system of dimensional coordination. In addition, adhering to the system means that the products and building systems of various manufacturers are interchangeable and compatible, which in turn leads to economy thanks to mass production, and a reduction in the number of products. At present there are two different systems in use in Germany: DIN 4172 "Modular coordination in building construction" and DIN 18000 "Modular coordination in building".

Dimensional coordination in buildings

DIN 4172 was introduced in 1955. The basic dimension for all masonry work is based on the "octametric" system of 1/8 m = 125 mm. This basic module serves for the geometric determination of nominal measurements, which in the first place – as theoretical measurements – are even multiples of this module. Therefore, as grid or centre line dimensions, the nominal measurements form the basis for the coordinating sizes that occur in practice.
The reference size is the dimension with which the components and elements must comply, and is the dimension stated on the drawings (work size). It is made up of the nominal measurements taking into account the appropriate number of joints. With regard to the work size, we must distinguish between the external dimension (with joints subtracted from the nominal measurement), the opening size (with joints added to the nominal measurement) and the projection dimension (in which joints are not considered) (see fig. 2.2.7). The heights of components are also coordinated within the "octametric" system (see fig. 2.2.8).
In traditional masonry bonds with a perpend thickness of 10 mm and bed joint thickness of

2.2.8 Vertical nominal measurements and heights of units

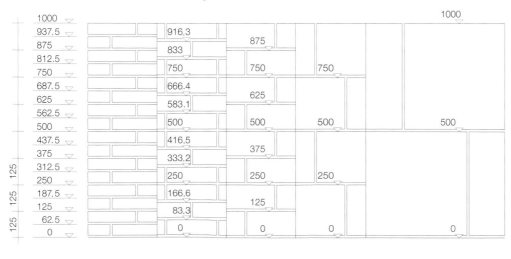

	NM	NM	NM	DM	NM	DM	DM
Height of unit (mm)	52	71	113	123	238	248	499
Thickness of bed joint (mm)	10.5	12.3	12	1–3	12	1–3	1–3
Height of course (mm)	62.5	83.3	125	125	250	250	500
Example of format	DF	NF	1.5 NF	= 2DF	4 DF	gauged unit	

NM = normal mortar   DM = thin-bed mortar

12 mm, the basic modules are therefore 115 + 10 mm for the length and 113 + 12 mm for the height. Accordingly, the relationship between nominal measurement and reference size is as follows:

Work size	Nominal measurement	Reference size
Ext. dimension (A)	x · 12.5	x · 12.5 – 1
Opening (Ö)	x · 12.5	x · 12.5 + 1
Projection (V)	x · 12.5	x · 12.5
Height (H)	x · 12.5	x · 12.5 –1.2

As the "octametric" system of dimensional coordination has remained unchanged despite recent developments in masonry construction, improved types of joint have given rise to new unit dimensions rather than new work sizes. For example, the omission of mortar in the perpends for gauged or tongue and groove units has led to masonry units increasing in length from 240 mm to, for example, 247 mm, and the bedding of units in thin-bed mortar has resulted in units increasing in height from 238 to 249 mm.

The desire for rationalization means that the preferred sizes of openings for doors in DIN 18100 being matched to the dimensional coordination requirements. The following tolerances are assumed:

width   ± 10 mm
height + 10/-5 mm

These measurements are illustrated in fig. 2.2.9. The reference sizes are related to the level FFL (finished floor level), which must be taking into account by the designer on the working drawings and in the tender documents.

Modular coordination in buildings

It is mainly in other countries that basic length units for components and structures are based on metric dimensions. DIN 18000 was introduced in order to incorporate these international agreements. The basic dimension, as the smallest planning dimension in this "decimetric" system of modular coordination, is the basic module M = 100 mm. Other basic dimensions in this system are the multimodules 3 M = 300 mm, 6 M = 600 mm and 12 M = 1200 mm, the preferred multiples of the basic module, and the submodules (whole-number divisions of the basic module) plus the complementary dimensions 25, 50 and 75 mm, which are smaller than the basic module but are combined to form modular dimensions. In practice on the building site, e.g. during the construction of masonry, it is the preferred sizes and multimodules which are most relevant, and these too are components in the dimensional coordination to DIN 4172, e.g. 5 x 3 M = 15 M = 1500 mm = 12 x 125 mm and consequently 15 M, 30 M, 45 M on plan, and 5 M, 10 M, 15 M etc. in elevation.

However, as the "octametric" system is the best one for the materials used, "decimetric" modular coordination has not become established for masonry.

Dimensional tolerances and permissible deviations

Inaccuracies during production and erection inevitably lead to components and structures with lengths, heights and angles that deviate from those laid down on the drawings. This is particularly true for masonry construction, which in contrast to automated production in a factory, is erected on site by manual labour. The deviations here are primarily length and planar discrepancies, out-of-plumb and out-of-line problems. Dimensional inaccuracies are frequently simply accepted because more stringent requirements are normally associated with considerably more technical input and hence also higher production costs [141].
The permissible values for deviations (tolerances) from the intended dimension are specified in DIN 18201 and 18202. The terms relating to dimensional tolerances are defined in DIN 18201 (see fig. 2.2.10):
The *reference size* is a dimension which is specified to designate the size, arrangement and position of a component or structure and is entered on the drawings.
The *actual size* is a dimension established by measurement.
The *actual deviation* is the difference between reference size and actual size.
The *maximum size* is the largest permissible dimension and the *minimum size* the smallest permissible dimension.
The *limit deviation* is the difference between maximum size and reference size or between minimum size and reference size.
The *tolerance* is the difference between the maximum and minimum sizes.
The *flatness tolerance* is the range for determining the permissible deviation of a surface from a plane.
DIN 18202 defines the permissible tolerances for buildings (limit deviations, angular and planar tolerances). The limit deviations apply to lengths, widths and heights as well as to grid and centre line dimensions, and openings (see table 2.2.11). They represent the accuracy achievable within the scope of normal working practices. Higher demands on accuracy must be specially agreed in the specifications and contractual documents.
The permissible tolerances are maintained in masonry by limiting the material-related dimensional deviations of the units. These values are specified in the individual standards covering different types of units (see tables 2.2.13 and 2.2.14). Furthermore, in traditional masonry bonds the mortar joints permit adjustments in the order of 2-3 mm; this means about 10 mm adjustment for every 1 m of wall length. In terms of visual appearance, it is advisable to

2.2.9   Reference points for nominal measurements for wall openings

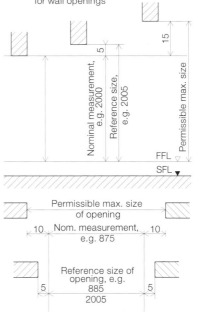

2.2.10   Definitions of terms for dimensional coordination

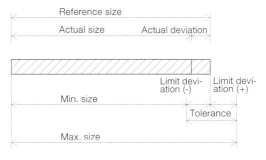

2.2.11   Permissible tolerances to DIN 18202

Reference	Limit deviations in mm for reference sizes in m				
	≤ 3	3 < x ≤ 6	6 < x ≤ 15	15 < x ≤ 30	> 30
Dimensions on plan, e.g. lengths, widths, centre and grid lines	± 12	± 16	± 20	± 24	± 30
Dimensions in elevation, e.g. storey heights, landing levels, distances from contact faces and corbels	± 16	± 16	± 20	± 30	± 30
Clear dimensions on plan, e.g. dimensions between columns and piers	± 16	± 20	± 24	± 30	–
Clear dimensions in elevation, e.g. beneath slabs and beams	± 20	± 20	± 30	–	–
Openings, e.g. for windows, doors and built-in elements	± 12	± 16	–	–	–
Openings as above but with finished reveals	± 10	± 12	–	–	–

2.2.12 Applying the bonding rule along the length of a wall

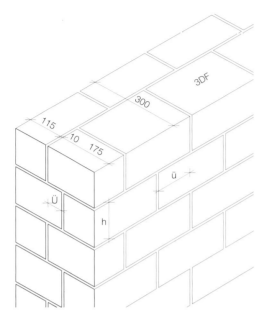

"compress" the perpends but they should not be less than 8 mm thick in order to remain impervious.

The task of a masonry bond is to distribute the loads acting on the masonry uniformly within the masonry. To do this, the perpends (vertical joints) and bed joints of adjacent courses in the plane of the wall must be offset by the bonding dimension ü. According to DIN 1053 part 1 clause 9.3, ü ≥ 0.4 x h ≥ 45 mm, where h = height of unit (work size). This requirement applies to the masonry bond both along the length of the wall and across the thickness of the wall (see fig. 2.2.12).

With medium- or thin-bed masonry as well as perpends without mortar and dry walling, this adjustment by means of the joints is no longer possible, or at best limited. This is why tighter tolerances are stipulated in the appropriate standards covering the masonry units.

The rules of bonding

A masonry bond is the regular assembly of masonry units in vertical and horizontal alignment in order to form a masonry construction. For loadbearing masonry, units may be laid in stretcher courses (side faces in the plane of the wall); header courses (end faces in the plane of the wall); brick-on-edge courses (end faces in the plane of the wall but turned through 90°); or soldier courses (side faces in the plane of the wall but turned through 90°). "Dog-toothing" (projecting and recessed) involves laying header and brick-on-edge courses at an angle; "leaning" soldier courses are also possible (see 2.2.15).

Maintaining the minimum bonding dimension prevents the masonry bond from being easily disrupted and, as a result, prevents a reduction in the tensile and shear strength of the masonry. Therefore, to improve the bonding effect, maximum, i.e. centric, bonding is desirable.

2.2.13 Permissible deviations from intended dimensions (work sizes) for calcium silicate, aerated concrete, concrete, lightweight concrete and granulated slag aggregate units [mm]

Designation of type of unit	Calcium silicate units								Aerated concrete units		Concrete, lightweight concrete units				Gran. slag agg. units	
	KS KS L		KS (P) KS L (P)		KS Vm		KS Vb	gauged units	PB Ppl	PP PPpl	Hbl, Hbn Vbl, Vbn VbL S, Tbn	V, Vn Vmb	Vm		HSV HSL	HHbl
Format	≤ NF	> NF			≤ NF	> NF							≤ NF	> NF	≤ NF	> NF
Length, width															L[1]	
• individ. value	± 3	± 3	± 3	± 3	± 3	± 2	± 3	± 3	± 1.5	± 3	± 3	± 3	± 3		± 4	± 4
• mean value	± 2	± 2	± 2	± 3	± 3	± 1	± 2								± 3	± 3
Height															B, H[2]	
• individ. value	± 3	± 4	± 1	± 3	± 4	± 2	± 1	± 3	± 1	± 4	± 3	± 2	± 3		± 3	± 4
~ average value	± 2	± 3		± 2	± 3	± 1	± 1								± 2	± 3

[1] L = length of granulated slag aggregate units ≤ NF   [2] B = width of granulated slag aggregate units ≤ NF, H = height of granulated slag aggregate units ≤ NF

2.2.14 Permissible deviations and dimensional spreads[1] for clay bricks

Reference size [mm]	DIN 105, part 1 DIN 105, part 2			DIN 105, part 3			DIN 105, part 4			DIN 105, part 5 Lightwt horiz. perf. units			DIN 105, part 6		
	min. dim. [mm]	max dim. [mm]	dim. spread [mm]	min. dim. [mm]	max. dim. [mm]	dim. spread [mm]	min. dim. [mm]	max. dim. [mm]	dim. spread [mm]	min. dim. [mm]	max. dim. [mm]	dim. spread [mm]	min. dim. [mm]	max. dim. [mm]	dim. spread [mm]
Length, width															
90	85	95	5	–	–	–	112	118	4	–	–	–	85	95	5
115	110	120	6	112	118	5	112	118	4	110	120	6	110	120	6
145	139	148	7	141	148	6	–	–	–	–	–	–	139	148	7
150	–	–	–	–	–	–	–	–	–	–	–	–	145	155	7
175	168	178	8	170	178	7	–	–	–	168	178	8	168	178	8
240	230	245	10	233	245	10	235	245	8	230	245	10	230	245	10
247[2]	–	–	–	–	–	–				–	–	–	237	252	10
300	290	308	12	293	308	12				290	308	12	290	308	12
307[2]	–	–	–							–	–	–	297	315	12
365	355	373	12							355	373	12	355	373	12
372[2]	–	–	–							–	–	–	362	380	12
425	415	434	12							–	–	–	415	434	12
432[2]	–	–	–							–	–	–	422	441	12
490	480	498	12							480	498	15	480	498	12
497[2]													487	505	12
Height															
52 / 66[3]	50	54	3	50	54	3	50	54	2	–	–	–	65	67	2
71 / 82[3]	68	74	4	69	73	3	69	73	3	68	74	4	81	83	2
113 / 123[3]	108	118	4	110	116	4	110	116	4	108	118	4	122	125	2
155 / 166[3]	150	160	5	–	–	–				–	–	–	165	167	2
175	170	180	5	–	–	–				–	–	–	174	176	2
198[3]	–	–	–	–	–	–				–	–	–	197	200	2
238 / 248[3]	233	243	6	233	243	6				233	243	6	247	250	2

[1] Dimensional spread is the permissible difference between the size of the largest and smallest brick within a delivery to a building site.
[2] Reference length for gauged bricks to DIN 105 part 6
[3] Reference height for gauged bricks to DIN 105 part 6

The bonding dimension also specifies the distance between the perpends of intersecting walls and internal corners. Only one perpend in every course may be set out from an internal corner, i.e. the perpends of adjacent courses must be offset (see 2.2.16).

The following bonding rules should also be observed:

- The units in a course should have the same height in order to prevent the wall exhibiting varying deformation behaviour as result of a varying number of bed joints, and – consequently – to prevent areas of the wall with a greater number of bed joints shedding any load placed on them as result of their increased deformability. However, an additional bed joint is permissible in alternate courses at the ends of walls and beneath lintels in order to adjust height and length when the contact area of the units is min. 115 mm long and units and mortar exhibit a strength at least equal to that of the surrounding masonry (see fig. 2.2.17).
- If within a course, several units are laid adjacent each other in order to create a wall with the desired thickness, the bonding rule also applies across the thickness of the wall and the height of a unit may not be greater than its width. This also applies accordingly to piers and short walls. This ensures adequate bonding in the transverse direction and prevents the wall splitting apart as a result of splitting tensile forces caused by yielding of the bed joints under load. An exception to this rule is units with a contact area min. 115 mm wide. In this case the height of the units may be max. 240 mm (see fig. 2.2.18).
- When laying units of different heights simultaneously in a continuous and stiffening wall, the heights of the courses must be maintained exactly in order to ensure that the units are properly bonded in.

The masonry bonds commonly taught and used in practice all satisfy the requirements with respect to the bonding rule. When using these bonds, which in a consistent arrangement achieve a more attractive pattern of joints in the wall than walls produced using the minimum bonding rule, the following supplementary bonding rules should also be observed [32, 141, 161]:

- Every course must be horizontal and penetrate the complete masonry construction.
- Single-leaf external walls employing facing bricks/blocks must consist of at least two courses.
- In header courses only the header faces are visible. At the ends of walls each stretcher course should begin with as many three-quarter bats as there are header faces in the thickness of the construction (special formats must be used in the case of blocks).

- At corners, wall intersections and abutting walls, the stretcher courses always pass through, while the header courses abut.
- As many whole units as possible should be used to minimize the proportion of joints and hence increase the bonding dimension and compressive strength of the masonry.
- Parallel walls should be constructed with the same sequences of courses.

Masonry wall bonds

We distinguish between wall bonds, end bonds and column bonds depending on the masonry element under construction.

Wall bonds

This type of bond is used between two corners or junctions. Four types are taught and generally used, characterized by a defined alternation between stretcher and header courses.

Stretcher bond
All the courses consist exclusively of stretchers, with each course being offset by half the length of a unit (centric bonding) or by one third to one quarter of the length of a unit (raking stretcher bond). Owing to the generous bonding dimension, employing this bond results in masonry with good compressive and tensile strength. Stretcher bond is used for walls just half a brick thick, e.g. thin internal walls, the outer (facing) leaf of twin-leaf walls, chimneys. It is also used for large-format masonry units in order to rationalize the construction. In these cases the thickness of the wall is equal to the width of the unit. Therefore, large-format units in stretcher bond can be employed to construct one-brick walls in the thicknesses 240, 300, 365 and 490 mm.

Header bond
This bond is only suitable for walls one brick thick where all the courses consist exclusively of headers, with each course offset by half the width of a unit. Compared to stretcher bond, header bond has a reduced loadbearing capacity owing to the shorter bonding dimension. As this fact is not considered when designing masonry, this type of bond should be avoided with heavily loaded walls. Apart from that, owing to the steep racking back of one quarter of the length of a unit, header bond tends to develop diagonal cracks.
Header bond is used for single-leaf facing work, for curved masonry with a tight radius and for large-format units when constructing one-brick walls in the thicknesses 240-490 mm.

English bond
This bond consists of alternate courses of stretchers and headers. The overlap is one quarter of the length of a unit, but the perpends

2.2.15 Course of bricks/blocks for use in masonry bonds

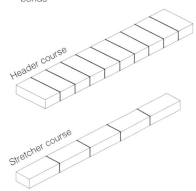

Header course

Stretcher course

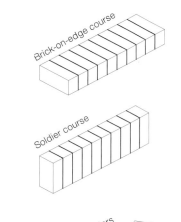

Brick-on-edge course

Soldier course

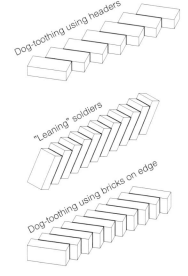

Dog-toothing using headers

"Leaning" soldiers

Dog-toothing using bricks on edge

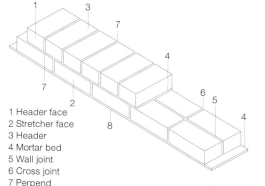

1 Header face
2 Stretcher face
3 Header
4 Mortar bed
5 Wall joint
6 Cross joint
7 Perpend
8 Bed joint

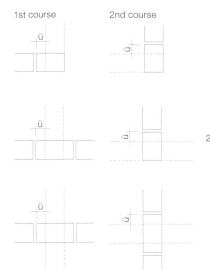

2.2.16 Bonding dimensions at corners and intersections (plan views)

1st course   2nd course

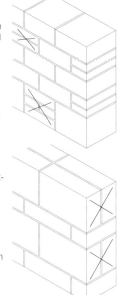

2.2.17 Inefficient bonding owing to different numbers of bed joints within a course. Not permitted because it leads to severe compression at concentrations of bed joints. Additional bed joints at ends of walls and beneath lintels are permissible in alternate courses.

2.2.18 Non-permissible bonding owing to unit height-to-width ratio > 1. Joint cannot be fully closed with mortar. Splitting tension effect due to yielding of joint; h > b not permitted (exception: b ≥ 115 mm and h ≤ 240 mm).

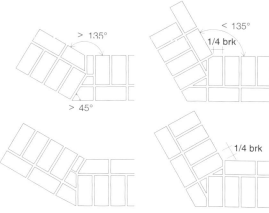

2.2.19 Detail of bonding at obtuse corners of masonry walls

Spacing of joints in header courses set out from outer corner (no cut faces left exposed).

Spacing of joints in header courses set out from inner corner (some cut faces left exposed, otherwise specials required).

of all stretcher and all header courses are aligned vertically. Owing to the shallow racking back, i.e. alternating between one quarter and three quarters of the length of a unit, this produces a particularly good longitudinal bond. This type of bond is used for wall thicknesses > 240 mm.

English cross bond (St Andrew's bond)
In this bond there is a regular alternation between stretcher and header courses. However, they are offset in such a way that they repeat only every four courses. The first and second courses are laid like English bond, and the third course like the first one. In the fourth course (stretchers) the first unit (three-quarter bat) is followed by a header before laying the first stretcher. Therefore the perpends in the header courses are aligned vertically but those of the stretcher courses are offset by half the length of a unit. This results in the characteristic pattern of English cross bond. Racking back is at one quarter the length of a unit. This bond is vulnerable to diagonal cracks. On the other hand, the risk of longitudinal cracks is relatively low thanks to the good toothing.
In both English bond and English cross bond we speak of bonded masonry as opposed to one-brick masonry because several units are laid adjacent each other in every course or every second course.

End bonds
are formed at the ends of walls, at corners, at junctions and intersections with other walls and at projections and recesses. It is recommended to establish the arrangement of intersections, corners etc. before starting construction. This guarantees proper bonding and

avoids having to cut units to be able to fit them into the wall. This is important when using medium- and large-format units in particular because as the units get larger so the adaptation options decrease.

Acute corners in masonry
are built by building the outer row of stretchers in one wall right up to the corner. The other wall is then built up to this row of stretchers as a header course. The three-quarter bat at the apex must be cut in such a way that its outer stretcher face is longer than the diagonal narrow side by one quarter brick.

Obtuse corners in masonry
are bonded according to the size of the corner angle. For angles > 135° the joints in the header course are set out from the outer corner. This avoids cut surfaces being left exposed. For angles ≤ 135° the joints in the header course are set out from the inner corner. This means that cut surfaces are left exposed in some courses (see fig. 2.2.19) [141].

Masonry piers
are projections which serve to stiffen continuous walls or support larger concentrated loads from beams etc. In piers the headers cantilever out, while the stretchers are laid parallel with the plane of the wall.

Recesses and slots in masonry
As these decrease the thickness of the wall, they must be taken into account when designing loadbearing masonry. Recesses may not be cut into a loadbearing wall. They must be constructed in a proper bond and are usually required to accommodate radiators, built-in cupboards etc. The cutting of chases is

allowed when the dimensions are small, e.g. for pipes and cables. In the case of recesses and slots, the remaining continuous wall must be at least half a brick thick.

Column bonds
Square columns employ the same bond in each course but with each course offset by 90°. Square, one-brick-thick columns consist entirely of whole units. Each course of a square, 1$\frac{1}{2}$-brick column consists of six three-quarter bats. To observe the bonding rules, there is much wastage with 2- and 3-brick square columns because of the large number of three-quarter bats required.
The two narrow sides of rectangular columns are treated like the ends of a wall. These contain as many three-quarter bats as the narrow side has headers, with the remaining intermediate space being filled with whole or half bricks.

English bond

Bonding at end of wall   External corner   Bonding-in of return wall

Through-bonding · Obtuse external corner · Acute external corner

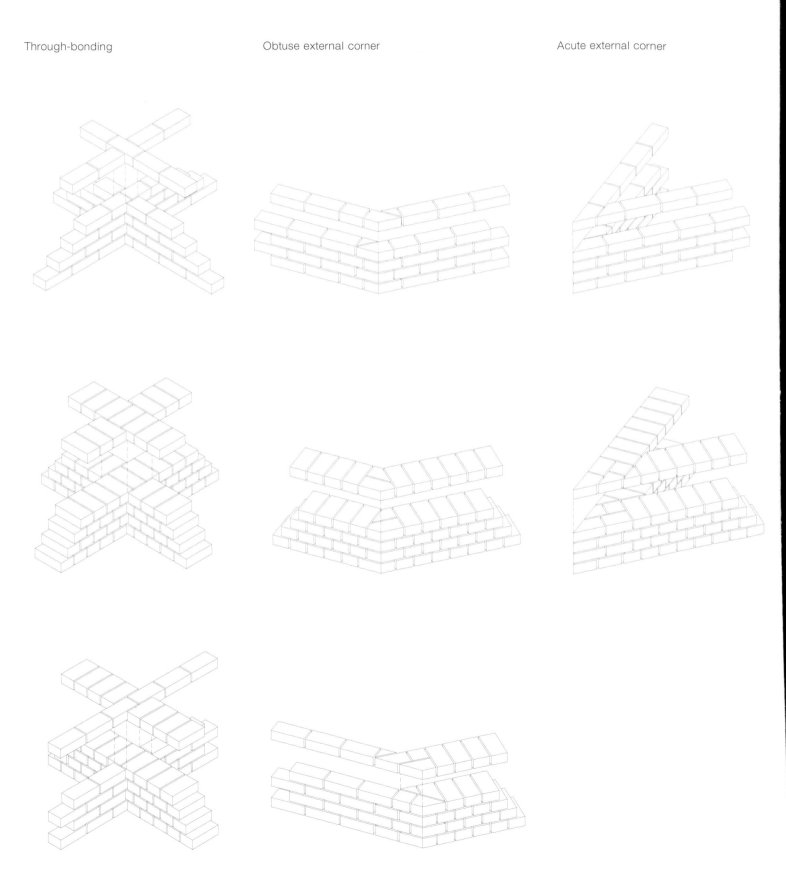

Types of bonds

External corner

Bonding-in of return wall

Stretcher bond
Wall thickness (½ brick)
115 mm

Header bond
Wall thickness (1 brick)
240 mm

Junction between
stretcher and header bonds

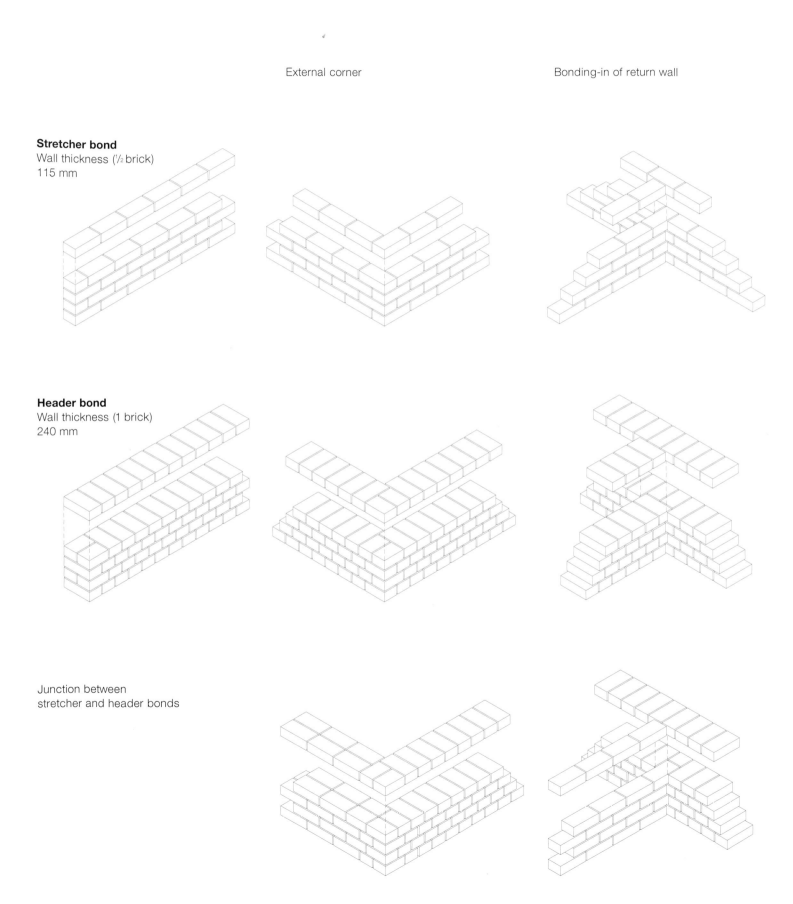

Through-bonding

Obtuse external corner

Acute external corner

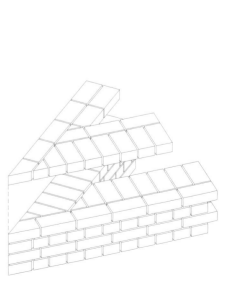

Piers

(shown here for English cross bond – English bond similar)

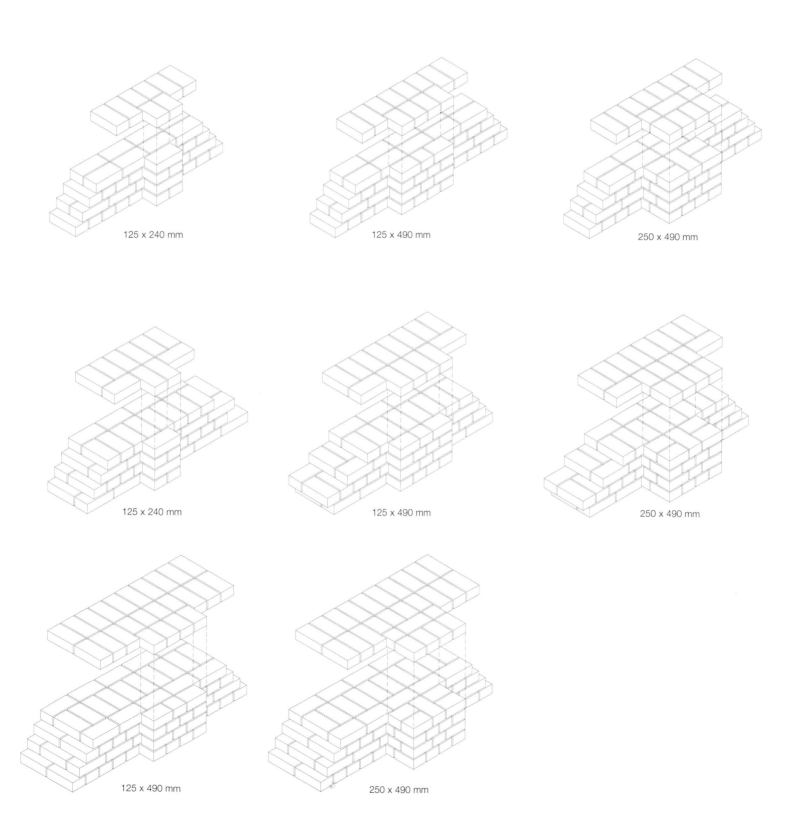

125 x 240 mm

125 x 490 mm

250 x 490 mm

125 x 240 mm

125 x 490 mm

250 x 490 mm

125 x 490 mm

250 x 490 mm

English cross bond

Bonding at end of wall

External corner

Bonding-in of return wall

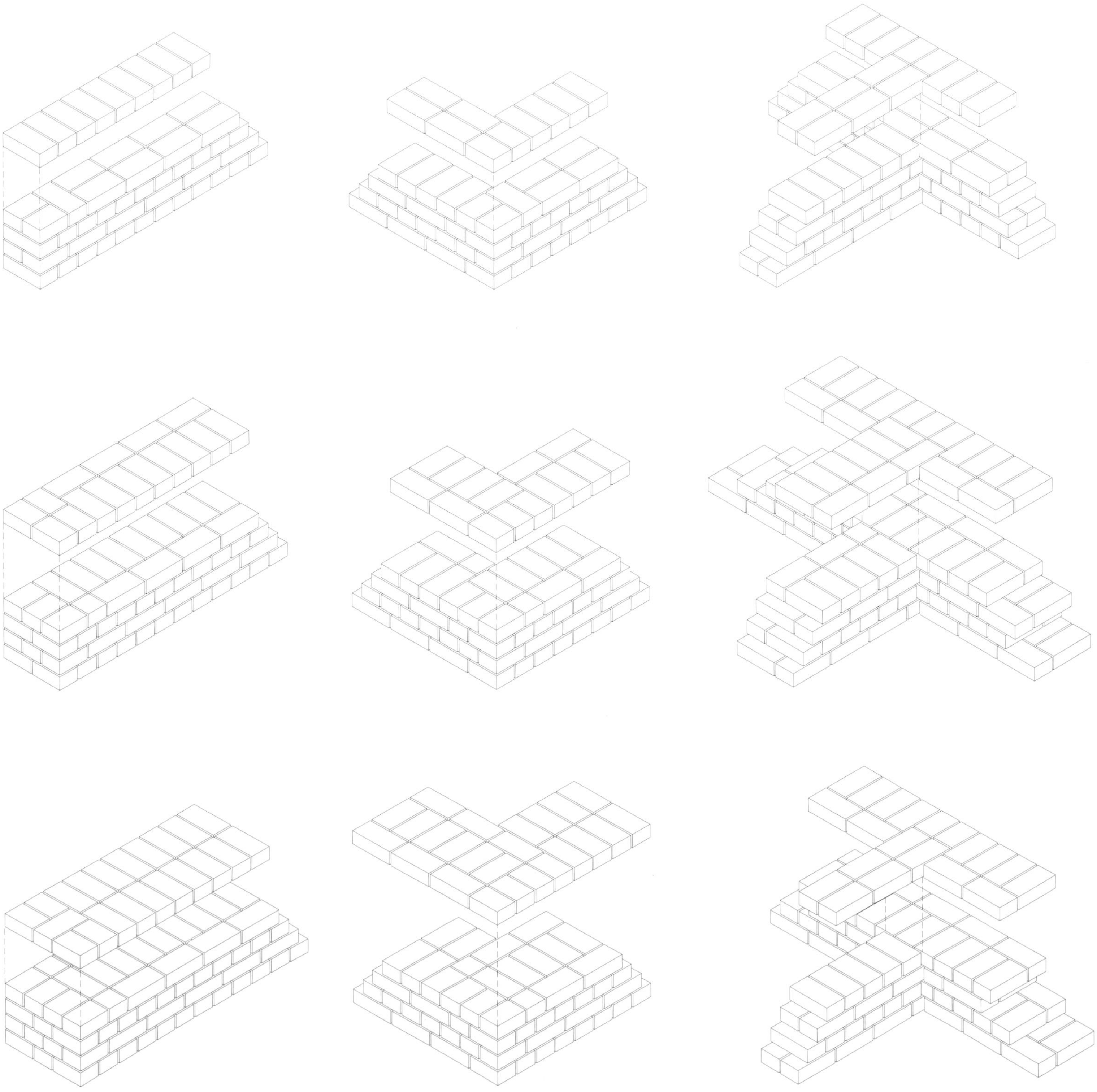

Large-format masonry unit

Bonding at end of wall

External corner
walls of same thickness

External corner
walls of different thicknesses

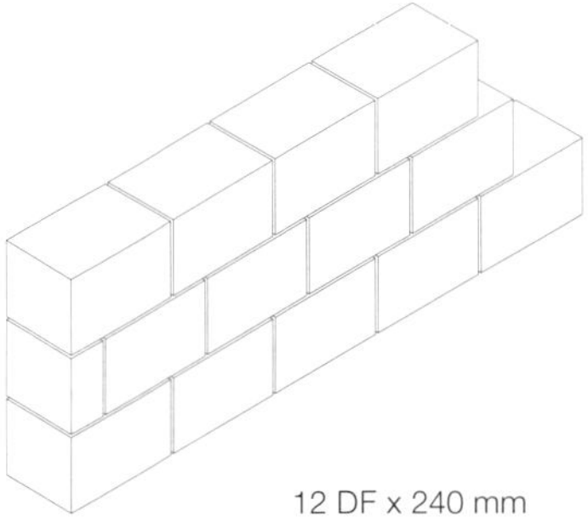

12 DF x 240 mm

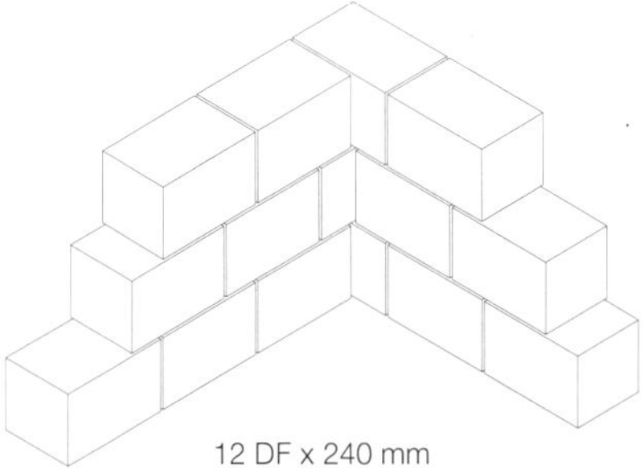

12 DF x 240 mm

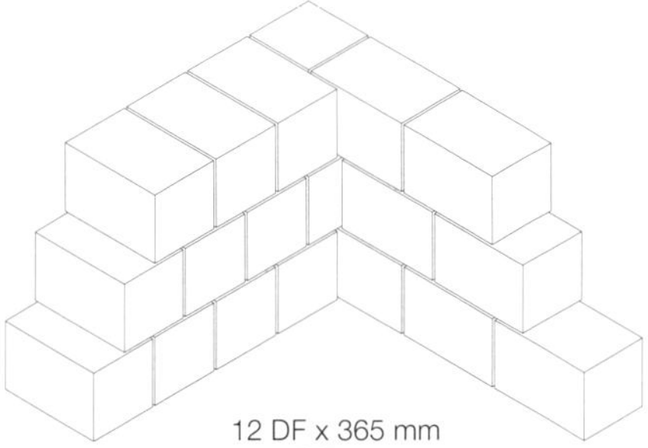

12 DF x 365 mm
and 12 DF x 240 mm

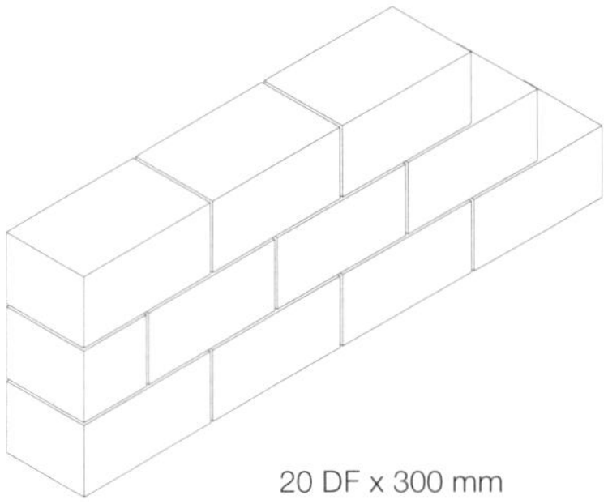

20 DF x 300 mm

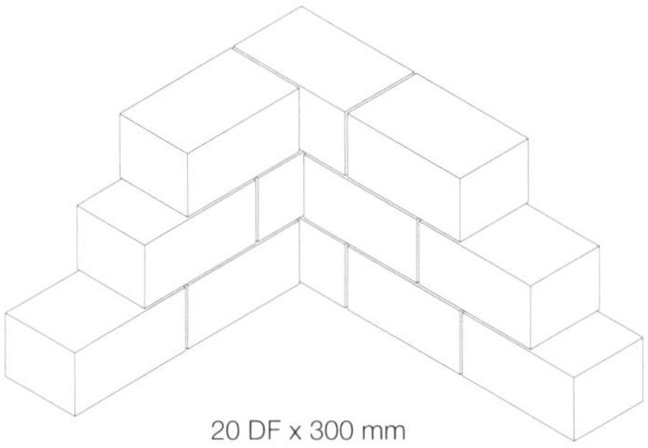

20 DF x 300 mm

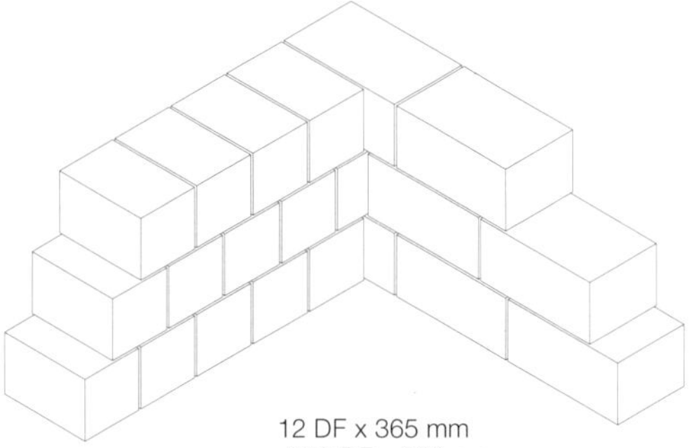

12 DF x 365 mm
and 20 DF x 300 mm

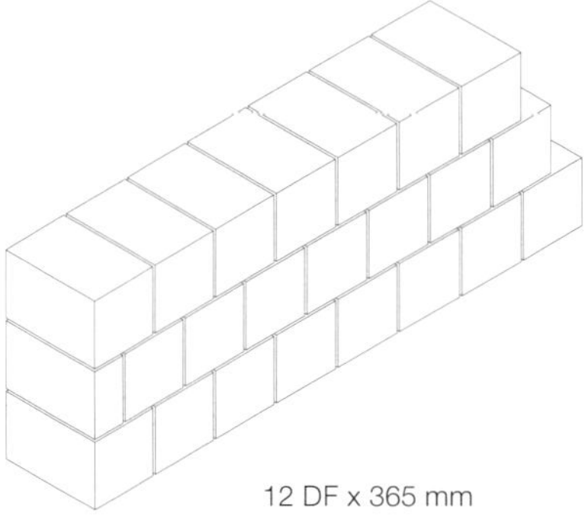

12 DF x 365 mm

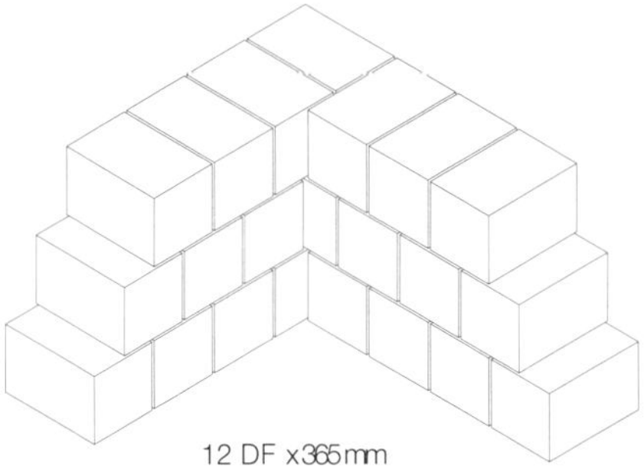

12 DF x 365 mm

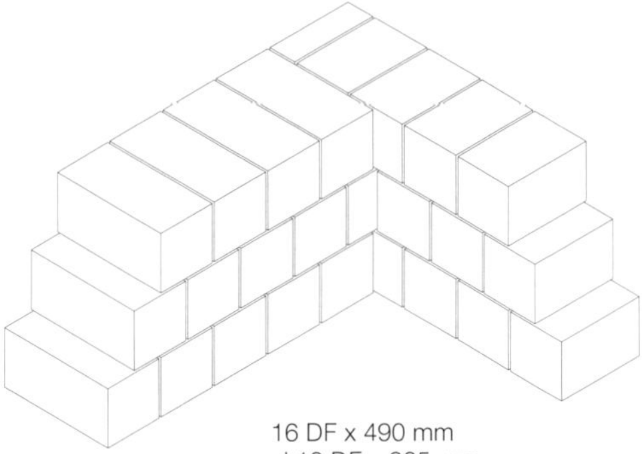

16 DF x 490 mm
and 12 DF x 365 mm

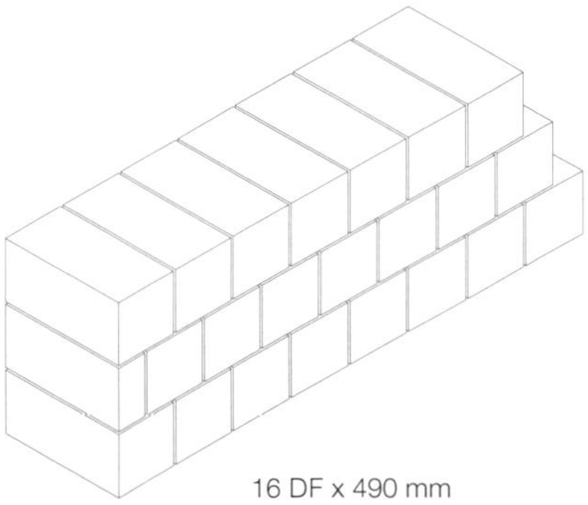

16 DF x 490 mm

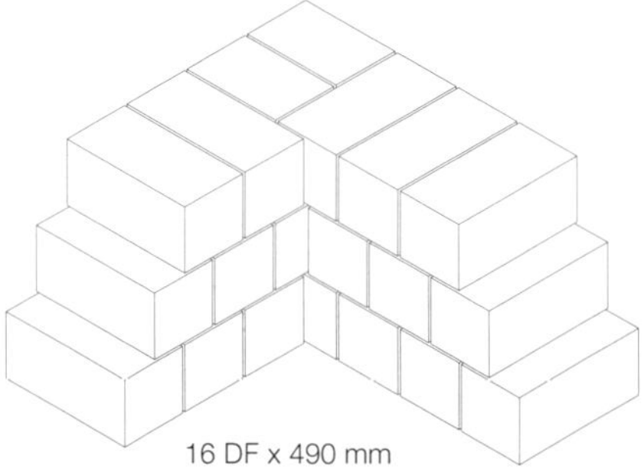

16 DF x 490 mm

Recesses

(shown here for English cross bond – English bond similar)

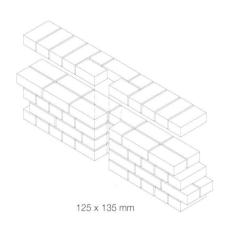

125 x 135 mm

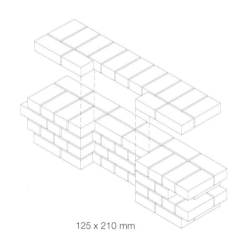

125 x 210 mm

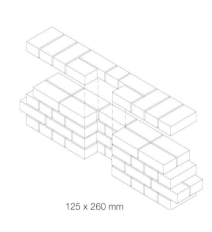

125 x 260 mm

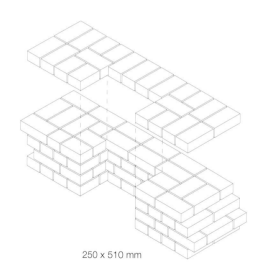

250 x 510 mm

Column bonds

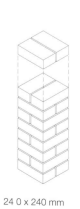

24 0 x 240 mm

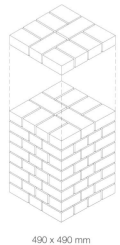

365 x 365 mm

490 x 490 mm

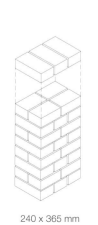

240 x 365 mm

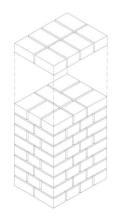

365 x 490 mm

490 x 615 mm

Through-bonding

Obtuse external corner

Acute external corner

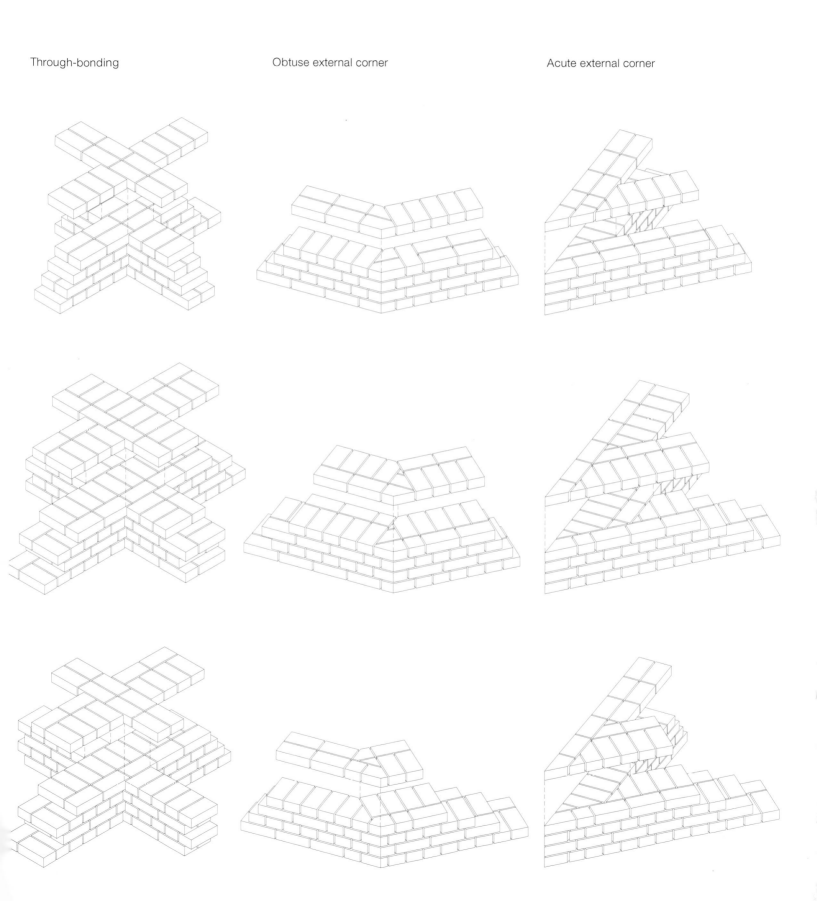

Bonding-in of return wall,
240 mm thick

Bonding-in of return wall,
300 mm thick

Bonding-in of return wall,
365 mm thick

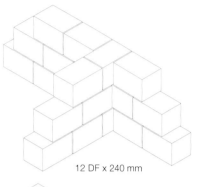

12 DF x 240 mm

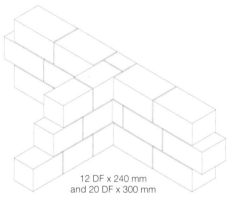

12 DF x 240 mm
and 20 DF x 300 mm

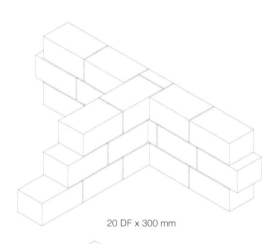

20 DF x 300 mm

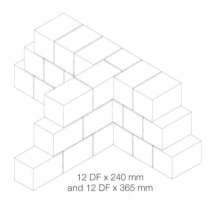

12 DF x 240 mm
and 12 DF x 365 mm

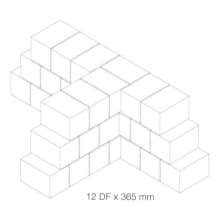

20 DF x 300 mm
and 12 DF x 365 mm

12 DF x 365 mm

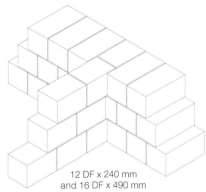

12 DF x 240 mm
and 16 DF x 490 mm

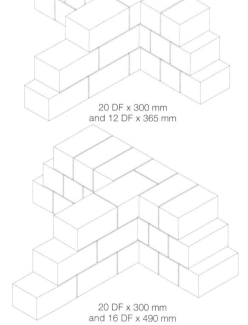

20 DF x 300 mm
and 16 DF x 490 mm

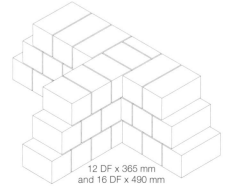

12 DF x 365 mm
and 16 DF x 490 mm

Through-bonding
walls of same thickness

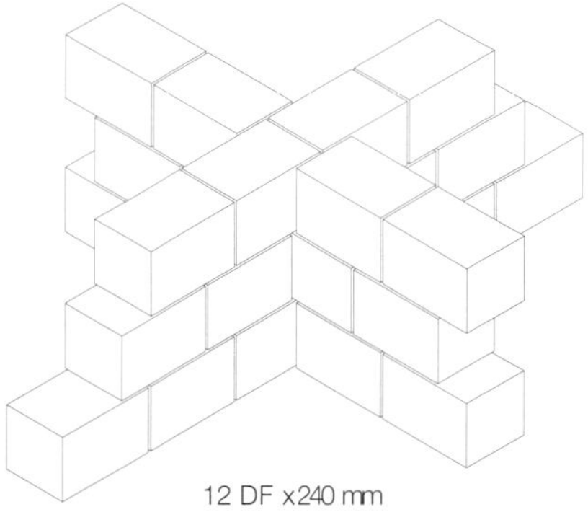

Through-bonding
walls of different thicknesses

Through-bonding
walls of different thicknesses

12 DF x240 mm

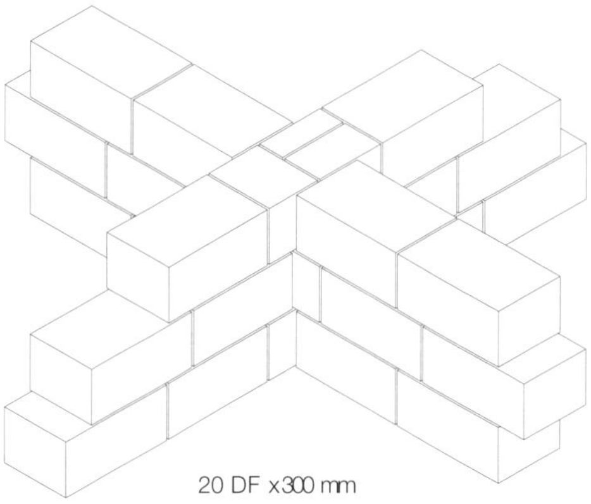

20 DF x300 mm

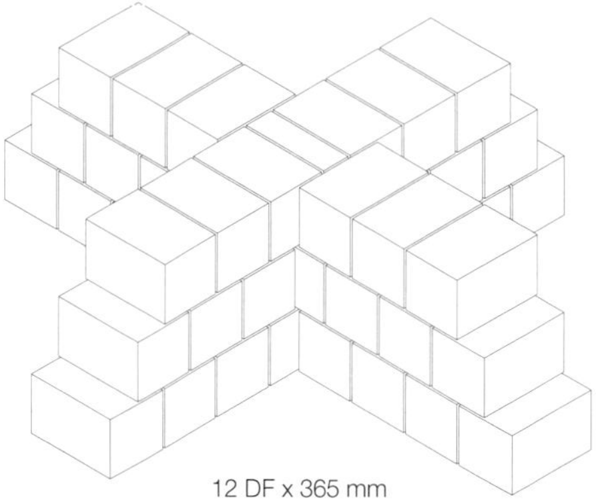

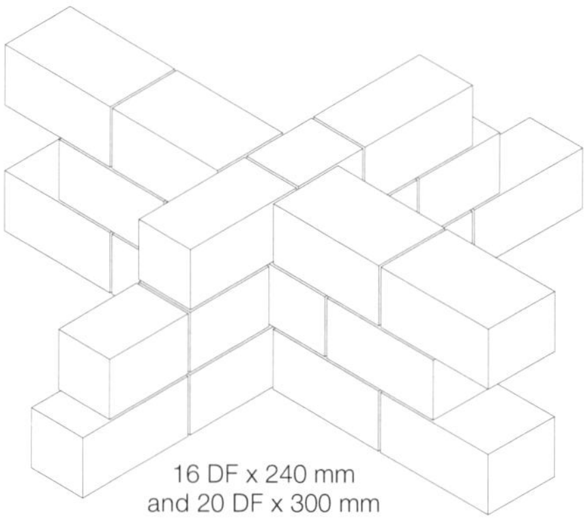

16 DF x 240 mm
and 20 DF x 300 mm

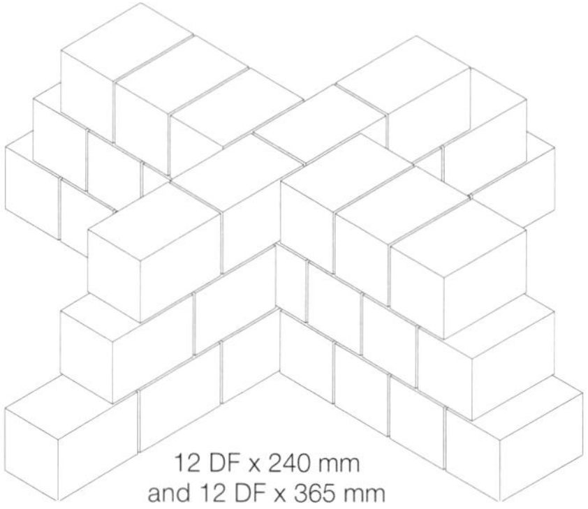

12 DF x 365 mm

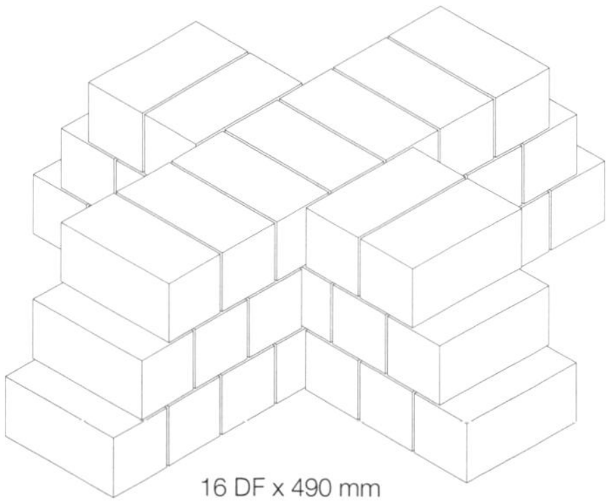

12 DF x 240 mm
and 12 DF x 365 mm

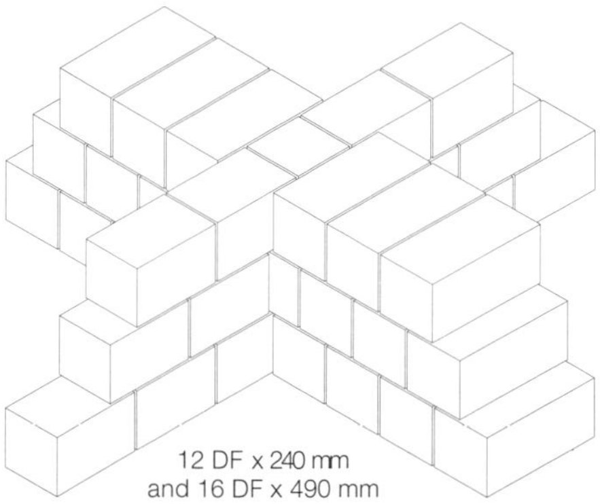

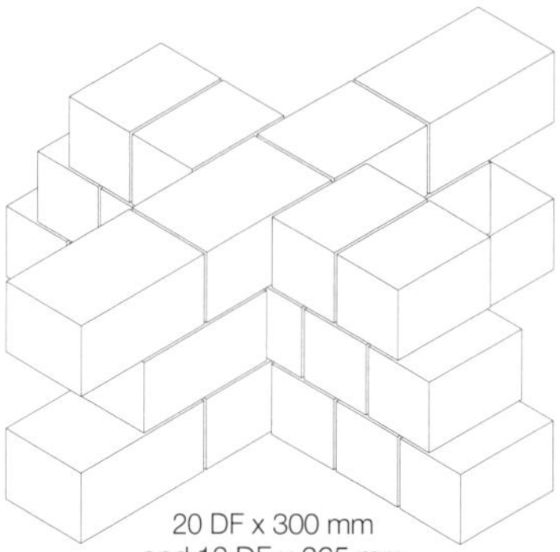

20 DF x 300 mm
and 12 DF x 365 mm

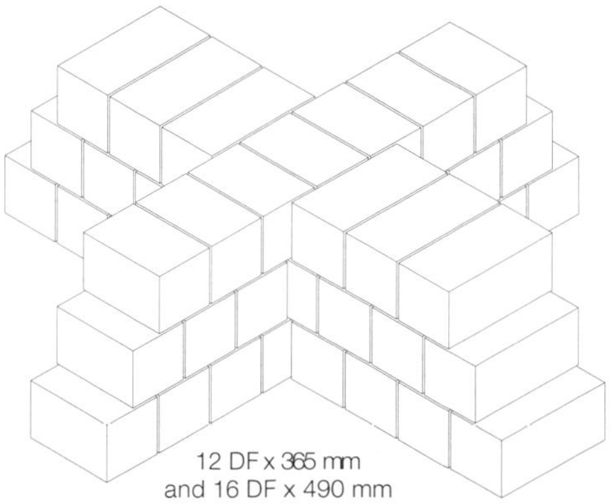

16 DF x 490 mm

12 DF x 240 mm
and 16 DF x 490 mm

12 DF x 365 mm
and 16 DF x 490 mm

Structural masonry

Konrad Zilch, Martin Schätz

2.3.1 Stress condition of masonry subjected to compression

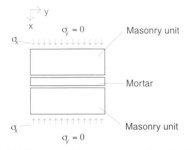

Uniaxial compression on masonry unit and mortar

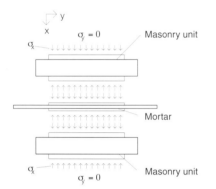

Unrestrained transverse deformation of masonry unit and mortar with a slip plane

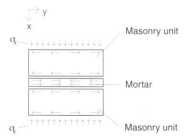

Stress condition of composite body as a result of hindering differential transverse deformation between masonry unit and mortar by way of bonding

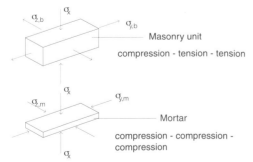

Isometric presentation of triaxial stress condition in masonry unit and mortar

The loadbearing behaviour of masonry

Masonry walls are subjected to loads in the plane of the wall (as plates) and perpendicular to the plane of the wall (as slabs). Loads in the plane of the wall may be vertical loads, e.g. self-weight or imposed loads, and horizontal loads, e.g. out-of-plumb problems or wind loads in the case of shear walls. As a slab, a masonry wall may be subjected to loads perpendicular to the plane of the wall, e.g. wind loads or earth pressures on external walls. As a result, the masonry is subjected to compression, shear, tension or bending stresses and combinations of these. As the compressive strength of masonry is considerably higher than its tensile or tensile bending strength, it is primarily used for components subjected to compression.

Owing to the different geometries and material properties of masonry units and mortars (shape of unit, dimensions of unit, perforations, ratio of unit height to bed joint thickness, strengths and moduli of elasticity of raw materials etc.), masonry is an anisotropic composite material. Therefore, when describing the loadbearing behaviour of masonry we must always take into account the interaction of masonry unit and mortar. This composite action of masonry is made possible through the masonry bond. The bond helps to ensure that horizontal forces between unit and mortar are transferred by means of adhesion and/or friction, and that vertical forces are transferred uniformly over the height of the component. The uniform distribution of the loads is also assisted by the mortar in the bed joints because this compensates for deviations in the sizes of the masonry units and hence prevents stress concentrations. In principle, the modes of failure in masonry construction are: failure of the masonry unit, failure of the mortar and failure of the bond between unit and mortar.

The strength of masonry is determined by the properties of both the units and the mortar. The strength, geometry, dimensional accuracy, proportion and arrangement of perforations, as well as suction rate and moisture content of the units are just as crucial as the strength, joint thickness and type, water retention and plasticity of the mortar. Other parameters influencing the strength of masonry are type of loading and rate of application, bond, quality of production and standard of workmanship [10].

Compression

Stress conditions, failure mechanism and influences on the compressive strength of masonry

In a masonry element loaded in compression perpendicular to the bed joints, compressive stresses build up in the direction of the load. As with the customary combinations of masonry units and mortar, the mortar exhibits a greater transverse deformability than the masonry units, and tries to deform more in the transverse direction than do the units. This differential transverse deformation is hindered by the bond between masonry unit and mortar, which sets up transverse tensile stresses in the masonry units and transverse compressive stresses in the mortar. A triaxial stress condition arises in the units and the mortar. A further increase in the vertical load leads to the transverse tensile strength of the units being exceeded and the appearance of vertical cracks in the units. Increasing the load still further finally leads to failure of the masonry element. Incomplete bed joints give rise to stress concentrations which can lead to failure of the masonry under relatively light loads (see fig. 2.3.1) [77]. Therefore, the main criterion for the compressive strength of masonry is the transverse tensile strength of the masonry units and the decrease in the vertical compressive strength of the units brought about by transverse tensile stresses. The low compressive strength of the mortar is not critical because it is increased by the triaxial stress condition. However, as the transverse tensile strength of the units is very difficult to determine and reproduce in tests, the compressive strengths of units and mortars are used as the characteristic parameters for describing the compressive strength of masonry. As the compressive strength of a masonry unit increases, so does the compressive strength of a masonry construction, but at a shallower gradient. As the compressive strength of the mortar increases, so the compressive strength of a masonry construction increases at a similar rate. The gradient is steeper for high-strength units than for those with a lower compressive strength. The type of joint affects the compressive strength of the masonry because the transverse deformability of the mortar is a major influencing factor, and so a thicker joint leads to a lower compressive strength for the masonry. Consequently, considerably higher compressive strengths have been achieved with medium-bed mortar (joint thickness 5-7 mm) and thin-bed mortar (joint thickness 1-3 mm) than with thick-bed mortar (normal mortar with a joint thickness of approx. 12 mm). With thin-bed mortar, which in terms of compressive strength is comparable to normal mortar of mortar group III, the masonry compressive strengths possible are assisted by the high dimensional accuracy of the units and the high adhesion between units and mortar.

In contrast, lightweight mortars reduce the compressive strength of masonry. Compared to normal mortars with the same compressive strength, the lightweight aggregates used lead to a higher transverse deformability and therefore increase the transverse tension on the units. This adverse effect which lightweight mortar has on the compressive strength of the masonry worsens as the compressive strength of the units increases because then the differential transverse deformation between mortar and units increases. Therefore, it is necessary to harmonize the deformation characteristics of masonry unit and mortar in order to achieve the maximum and most economical loadbearing capacity for the masonry. Combinations of high-strength units with low-grade mortars or low-strength units with high-grade mortars are not recommended.

The suction rate and moisture content of the masonry units during laying can have a considerable influence on the compressive strength of the finished masonry. Units with a high suction rate absorb water (needed for the hydration process) from the mortar and hence reduce the compressive strength of the mortar and the adhesion between units and mortar. Both lead to a reduction in the compressive strength of the masonry. On the other hand, units with a high moisture content cause too much water to remain in the mortar, which again reduces the compressive strength of the mortar and, as result, that of the masonry too. For clay bricks, maximum masonry compressive strength is achieved when the bricks are used as dry walling (i.e. without mortar), and when used with mortar by wetting the units just prior to laying [133].

The compressive strength of masonry is lower for long-term compressive loads than for short-term loads. This is due to the formation of micro-cracks in the composite microstructure of the mortar as a result of creep under long-term loading; these reduce the strength of the mortar. The strength under long-term loading is about 80-90% of the short-term strength.

Cyclic compressive loads on masonry also lead to a reduction in the compressive strength. This is attributed to the fact that with repeated application and removal of the loads the transverse tensile stresses in the units caused by the transverse deformation of the mortar do not decay completely and so accumulate over time. This process finally leads to premature

failure of the masonry.

Tension and tensile bending
The tensile loading of masonry perpendicular and parallel to the bed joints is primarily important for elements without any significant vertical load. In such cases, hindering deformation (shrinkage, cooling) can lead to tensile stresses which are not "neutralized" because of the lack of vertical load. Cracks are the result of the tensile strength of the masonry being exceeded. Tensile bending stresses are mainly due to horizontal loads, e.g. earth pressures on basement walls, infill panels, cladding, free-standing walls.

Tensile and tensile bending stresses perpendicular to the bed joints
Masonry can accommodate only very low tensile and tensile bending stresses perpendicular to the bed joints. This is mainly influenced by the adhesive tensile strength between unit and mortar. In most cases, failure takes place at the interface between unit and mortar. Tensile failure of the unit itself only takes place in the case of a high adhesive tensile strength (e.g. thin-bed mortar) in conjunction with a low tensile strength in the unit (in the height direction) (see fig. 2.3.2).

The adhesive tensile strength, which is subject to very severe scatter, is influenced both by the properties of the unit (e.g. surface roughness, suction rate, moisture content) and those of the mortar (e.g. mix, proportion of sand, moisture content, water retention capacity), as well as by the construction of the masonry itself (e.g. vibration during the during process, subsequent treatment).

Tensile stresses parallel to the bed joints
With masonry stressed in tension parallel to the bed joints, the tensile stresses are not transferred from unit to unit via the perpends but rather by means of shear resistance via the bed joints (see fig. 2.3.3).

The reason for this is that the perpends cannot transfer any, at best only very low, tension, which is afflicted by a very large scatter. This is, above all, the case for perpends without mortar (tongue and groove system) or perpends not completely filled with mortar (brick to brick with grooves filled with mortar). However, even using perpends with a complete filling of normal or lightweight mortar we can assume that inadequate workmanship combined with shrinkage of the mortar and the associated separation of the mortar from the unit means that the adhesive tensile strength in the perpends is so low that tensile forces cannot be transferred. Only in the case of thin-bed mortar and filled perpends can we assume a certain adhesive tensile strength in the perpends.

The nature of the flow of forces means that the masonry can fail because the shear strength in

2.3.2 Stress condition and failure cases for tension perpendicular to bed joints

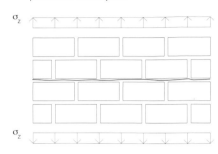

Failure of contact between masonry units and mortar

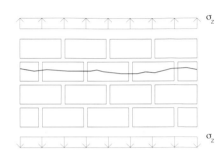

Tension failure of masonry units

2.3.3 Flow of forces in masonry subjected to tension parallel to bed joints

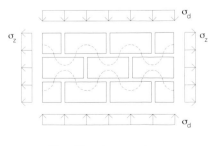

----- Flow of forces

2.3.4　Stress condition and failure cases for tension parallel to bed joints

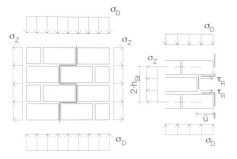

Failure of bed joint: $2\,\tau_R\,\ddot{u} = 2\,h_{St}\,\sigma_z$

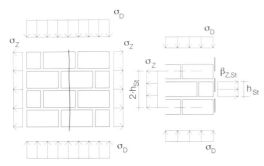

Tension failure of masonry units: $h_{St}\,\beta_{Z,St} = 2\,h_{St}\,\sigma_z$

2.3.5　Transition from failure of joints to failure of masonry units in relation to vertical loading

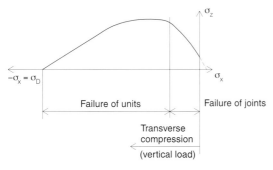

2.3.6　Failure modes of masonry wall subjected to biaxial plate loading

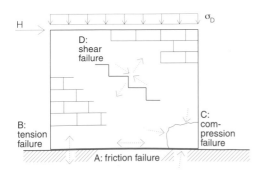

the bed joints between units and mortar or the tensile strength of the unit parallel to the bed joint is exceeded (see fig. 2.3.4).

Failure of the bed joint corresponds to a sliding of the bed joint in which the masonry bond breaks down owing to a zigzag fracture through perpends and bed joints.

The shear strength between unit and bed joint is determined by the adhesion between unit and mortar or the cohesion within the mortar and the degree of friction in relation to the compressive stress perpendicular to the bed joint.

Adhesion plus cohesion is designated adhesive shear strength. Like adhesive tensile strength, this too is subject to parameters affected by the materials and the production (e.g. surface roughness, arrangement of perforations, mortar mix, workmanship, subsequent treatment of the masonry), with the interface between unit and mortar playing a critical role. Generally, the adhesive shear strength rises as the compressive strength of the mortar increases, although the different surface finishes of different types of masonry unit give rise to differences in the adhesion properties.

Owing to their good adhesion, vertically perforated clay bricks exhibit excellent adhesive shear strength values, whereas the values for calcium silicate and aerated concrete units are rather lower [47].

The friction component in the shear strength depends not only on the coefficient of friction but, above all, on the vertical loading perpendicular to the bed joints. The friction increases in proportion to the load. If the load is sufficient to prevent the friction resistance being exceeded in the bed joints and if the units themselves have a low tensile strength, failure is characterized by a vertical tearing of the units (see figs. 2.3.4 and 2.3.5), whereby the adhesive tensile strength in the perpends is neglected. Failure occurs when the tensile stress σ_z from two courses exceeds the tensile strength of a unit. The transition from one type of failure to another is also influenced by the masonry bond employed and by the ratio of bonding dimension to height of unit. The tensile strengths of the individual types of masonry units vary considerably depending on the proportion and arrangement of perforations as well as the tensile strength of the material of the unit itself.

Tensile bending stresses parallel to the bed joints

Both tensile and compressive stresses in the direction of the bed joint are present in bending stresses parallel to the bed joint. Masonry with no mortar or incomplete mortar in the perpends can accommodate neither tension nor compression via the perpends. The stresses must be transferred like pure tensile stresses via the available shear stresses in the bed joint. Perpends with a complete mortar filling can transfer compressive bending stresses via the

perpends. Upon failure of the bond, the bending moment causes twisting of the unit, which activates both the adhesive shear strength of the bed joint and the shear resistance in the perpend. If the bed joints do not fail, a compression zone can develop over the full height of the component, while the tensile stress is accommodated only in every second course. Owing to the distribution of stresses according to the geometry of a T-beam, there is a theoretical increase in the bending strength of the masonry element compared to one with perpends without mortar [122]. The magnitude of the tensile bending strength depends on the shear strength between unit and mortar, but mainly on the tensile bending strength of the unit and the longitudinal compressive strength of the unit. The longitudinal compressive strength of, in particular, blocks with a high percentage of perforations can be so low that in these cases failure of the unit is the main factor determining the tensile bending strength of the masonry.

Shear stresses

Masonry walls can be loaded by horizontal loads, e.g. wind, earth pressure and earthquakes, both in the plane of the wall (as a plate) and perpendicular to the plane of the wall (as a slab). The plate shear resistance of masonry walls is mainly utilized to aid the lateral stability of a structure (shear walls).

Stress conditions and modes of failure for shear stresses in the plane of the wall

In this condition the masonry wall is subjected to the aforementioned horizontal loads and, in addition, vertical loads in the plane of the wall. This biaxial plate effect is simplified for design purposes by assuming a vertical loading uniformly distributed along the length of the wall and a resultant horizontal load acting at the top of the wall. The following modes of failure may then occur: friction failure with horizontal shearing along one bed joint; tension failure in the bottom bed joint caused by a moment; compression failure of the masonry at the base of the wall as a result of the transverse tensile strength of the unit being exceeded (see "Compression"); and shear failure (see fig. 2.3.6). In the case of shear failure, the combination of primary compressive and tensile forces leads to diagonal cracks in the wall. This mode of failure can be divided into failure of the bed joint and tension failure of the unit. With a low vertical load and low adhesive shear strength, diagonal cracks form along the perpends and bed joints (stair cracks). With a high vertical load and units of low tensile strength, the diagonal cracks pass through the units and along the perpends. This latter mode can also be called brittle failure and brings about a marked reduction in the stiffness of the masonry. On the other hand, failure of the joint is a ductile failure because even after the stair cracks have formed, horizontal forces can still be accommodated by way of friction. This property is exploited in the seismic design of masonry walls [47].

Shear failure theory after Mann/Müller for shear in the plane of the wall
The failure theory devised by Mann/Müller for masonry stressed in the plane of the wall assumes that no, or at best negligible, shear stresses are transferred by the perpends. The main cause of this is that owing to the lack of horizontal compressive stresses, no shear stresses in the perpends can be activated by friction. In addition, perpends which should be completely filled with mortar are often not properly filled in practice, which can lead to the edges of the mortar becoming detached from the masonry units as the mortar shrinks. This means the bond strength between unit and mortar is so severely reduced that no significant shear stresses can be transferred. This relationship is aggravated when the perpends are designed without mortar or with partial mortar (tongue and groove system). The transfer of shear stresses is even reduced completely to zero when the units are laid brick to brick or without any contact at all. The lack of a path for the shear stresses across the perpends means that a unit, in order to achieve equilibrium within the masonry element, has to accommodate the shear stresses from two courses in the vertical direction (see fig. 2.3.7). Furthermore, the shear stresses acting in the bed joints create a torsion moment acting on the individual unit. To achieve equilibrium of moments, the axial stress is distributed around the upper and lower sides of the unit. The distribution of compressive stress, represented (simplified) by a stair-like progression in the model, was verified by tests [127, 136] (see fig. 2.3.7). Using this model, Mann/Müller developed a failure envelope (see fig. 2.3.8) for the allowable shear stresses in relation to the size of the vertical axial stress. Failure takes place above this curve. The four associated modes of failure are as follows (fig. 2.3.9):

1. Adhesive tensile failure between masonry unit and bed joint mortar
If the compressive stresses perpendicular to the bed joint are very small because of the low loading, then the smaller axial stress in the region of an individual unit becomes a tensile stress. If the adhesive tensile strength β_{HZ} is exceeded, then the bed joint splits apart.

2. Joint failure
Friction failure in the bed joint happens when the shear strength – as the sum of adhesive shear strength β_{HS} and friction resistance $\mu \times \sigma_2$ – is exceeded in the region of the less heavily loaded half of the unit. This type of failure occurs with a low load σ_x and with units having

good tensile strength. It leads to a stair-like diagonal crack along the perpends and bed joints.

3. Unit tension failure
This type of failure takes place with a larger vertical load and units with lower tensile strength. Here, the shear strength in the bed joint is increased owing to the better friction resistance. The units must transfer shear forces from two courses because it is not possible to transfer vertical shear stresses in the perpends. Together with the perpendicular compressive stresses, this leads to diagonal primary tensile stresses in the unit. If the tensile strength of the unit is exceeded, then shallow diagonal cracks appear in the units and continue through the perpends.

4. Compressive failure of masonry
Very high vertical loads cause the masonry to fail as a result of diagonal primary compressive stresses when the larger axial stress acting on the individual unit exceeds the compressive strength β_{MW} of the masonry.

Accordingly, the shear strength of masonry acting as a plate depends, above all, on the magnitude of the vertical load, the shear strength that can be assumed in the bed joints (adhesive shear strength and friction component), the tensile strength of the units and the compressive strength of the masonry. In addition, the standard of workmanship and type of bond have to be considered. The model developed by Mann/Müller was based on stretcher bond with the bonding dimension approximately equal to half the length of a unit.
The model is only approximate for bonds with a lower shear area (e.g. English bond) [126, 127, 187].

Stress conditions for shear stresses perpendicular to the plane of the wall
Shear stresses also occur when a masonry wall acts as a slab, e.g. due to earth pressure or wind loads perpendicular to the plane of the wall. However, the shear stresses in this case do not assume tearing of the units but rather only a friction failure in the bed joints when the shear strength – made up of adhesive shear strength and friction resistance components like for shear stresses in the plane of the wall – is exceeded. In this case the splitting zone of the bed joint may not be used because here the adhesive shear strength drops to zero.

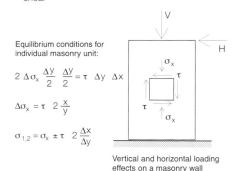

2.3.7   Stress distribution after Mann/Müller for plate shear

Equilibrium conditions for individual masonry unit:

$$2\,\Delta\sigma_x\,\frac{\Delta y}{2}\,\frac{\Delta y}{2} = \tau\;\Delta y\;\Delta x$$

$$\Delta\sigma_x = \tau\;2\,\frac{x}{y}$$

$$\sigma_{1,2} = \sigma_x \pm \tau\;2\,\frac{\Delta x}{\Delta y}$$

Vertical and horizontal loading effects on a masonry wall

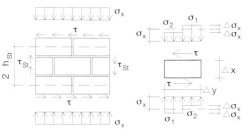

Equilibrium at element   Equilibrium at individual masonry unit

2.3.8   Failure envelope with failure cases after Mann/Müller

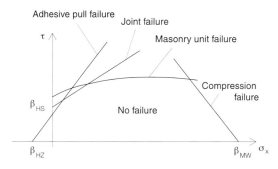

2.3.9   Failure modes for masonry subjected to plate shear

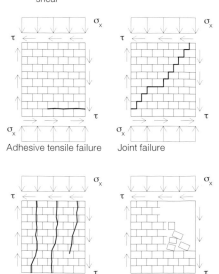

Adhesive tensile failure   Joint failure

Masonry unit failure   Compression failure of masonry

The principles of masonry design

The evolution of European and national standards

The development of standards for masonry construction is being pursued in two directions by German engineers. On the one hand, the Eurocode for masonry (EC 6) is being updated and revised, while on the other, the national standard DIN 1053 continues to be developed. EC 6 part 1-1 "General rules for buildings – rules for reinforced and unreinforced masonry" was adopted in June 1994.

Following editorial work, translation and the drafting of the National Application Document (NAD), EC 6 was introduced for a trial period with building authorities in a number of federal states in Germany as draft standard DIN V 1996 part 1-1, December 1996 edition. Since then, masonry in those federal states may be built to DIN 1053 part 1 or DIN V 1996 part 1-1 supplemented by the NAD. This rule applies as long as the trial period for EC 6 continues. Following surveys in 1997 and 1998 in the member states concerning how to proceed with the European draft standards, the majority of the member states decided in favour of updating EC 6 with a view to introducing this as the definitive European standard. This means that after the introduction of EC 6, the national standard would be withdrawn after a certain period, whereupon only EC 6 would then be valid.

As design according to EC 6 part 1-1 appears very complicated, a simplified method of analysis – EC 6 part 3 "Simplified structural design" – is currently being drawn up. Basically, this method of analysis uses the simplified method of DIN 1053 part 1. Although EC 6 part 1-1 should the adopted as the European standard by 2002 and, together with part 3, as the German version of the European standard by 2004, this timetable should be seen rather as an aspiration than as a realistic target. The work on the European standards is taking such a long time that in recent years a certain resignation has been evident. The outcome is that at present we cannot predict when the European codes might replace the national standards. This never-ending development of the Eurocode programme has the effect that at national level important sections of DIN 1053 are revised at regular intervals and adapted to meet new findings. The last revision of DIN 1053 parts 1 and 2 took place in November 1996 and resulted in a better breakdown of tasks between the individual standards. Up until then, the more accurate method of analysis was contained in DIN 1053 part 2, although it was also applicable to prescribed masonry designs. The misunderstandings which occurred in practice have been rectified by the new edition as follows:

DIN 1053 part 1 is the basic standard for the design and construction of masonry. It applies to both prescribed masonry designs (RM) as well as those assessed by suitability tests (EM) and contains both the simplified and the more accurate methods of analysis.

DIN 1053 part 2 merely regulates the classification of masonry into strength classes based on suitability tests and is hence purely a testing standard without information on design and construction.

Originally, this state of development should have been maintained until DIN 1053 was replaced by EC 6. Fundamental new concepts like the new safety concepts with partial safety factors, the incorporation of parabolic or rectangular-parabolic stress distributions instead of linear stress distributions or a more accurate analysis to check buckling stability would have first appeared with the introduction of EC 6. However, as the construction industry could no longer wait for the introduction of the Eurocode programme, above all for reinforced concrete, it was decided to develop a new generation of standards – the DIN 100 series. These are currently being drawn up on the basis of the principles of the existing editions of the Eurocodes and are intended to bridge over the period before introduction of the Eurocodes, or even to replace them. This decision forces the masonry industry to adapt DIN 1053 to suit the fundamental changes in the draft European standards because it does not appear sensible to design the individual elements of a structure according to different safety concepts and methods of analysis.

At the moment only a draft copy of the new DIN 1053 part 100 is available; this will very soon be developed into a masonry standard [24, 88, 101, 120, 121, 123].

Plain (i.e. unreinforced) masonry in Germany is currently covered by DIN 1053 parts 1 and 2 (November 1996 editions) and so only these two standards are referred to in the following sections.

Method of analysis

Simplified method of analysis

In certain situations masonry components may be designed according to the simplified method of analysis (DIN 1053 part 1 section 6). Simplified in this case means that the assumptions and the design itself is more straightforward than the more accurate method. This is made possible through a simpler treatment of the design equations in which the margin of safety is not explicitly expressed but instead is already incorporated in the permissible stresses. In addition, certain complicated forces acting on the masonry, e.g. bending moments from built-in floor slabs, unintended eccentricities when checking buckling, or wind loads on external walls, do not have to be taken into account during the design because they are already allowed for in the margin of safety, by reducing the permissible stresses or

by applying limits and rules appertaining to the construction. However, the use of the simplified method is subject to certain restrictions which guarantee that the result of the design is always on the safe side but, at the same time, not too uneconomical and not too different from the result of a more accurate examination (see table 2.3.10).

More accurate method of analysis

If the application falls outside the limits for the simplified method of analysis or if the stability of a whole structure, individual storeys or components is to be verified more accurately, then the more accurate method of analysis according to DIN 1053 part 1 section 7 should be used. When using this method to analyse an individual component or storey, other components may still be designed by means of the simplified and hence shorter method, provided they comply with the requirements for that method.

Basically, the more accurate method of analysis is necessary in order to derive the rules for the simplified method and to guarantee that the safety of the components checked using the simplified method is not less than that which would result from using an accurate method.

Safety concept

Analysis of stability

According to DIN 1053, stability is analysed by way of permissible stresses for the serviceability state or for the ultimate load at failure. In the new generation of standards, EC 6 and DIN 1053 part 100, analysis is carried out by way of partial safety factors.

The simplified method of analysis according to DIN 1053 part 1 makes use of the condition

$$\text{exist } \sigma \leq \text{perm } \sigma$$

for verifying stability. Here, the existing stresses have to be determined for the serviceability state. The permissible stresses defined in DIN 1053 part 1 already contain the necessary margin of safety with regard to loading capacity. The more accurate method of analysis uses the condition

$$\gamma \times S \leq R_k (f_k)$$

in order to prove that g x serviceability loads can be carried by the characteristic strength values at failure.

In the future generation of standards, partial safety factors for loading and loading capacity will be introduced in order to be able to assess the circumstances more accurately. In doing so, the condition to be verified

$$S_d (\gamma_f \times S) \leq R_d (f_k / \gamma_M)$$

will be used to increase the serviceability loads by way of partial safety factors to a design value S_d for loading effects, and to reduce the loading capacity by the partial safety factor γ_M covering material properties to the design value R_d for material strength. Therefore, the level of analysis lies between the loading and loading capacity sides (see fig. 2.3.11).

Safety factors
The safety factors for the more accurate method of analysis are based on a defined and proven margin of safety of approx. 3.0 between the characteristic value β_R and the average value for the masonry's compressive strength determined in short-term laboratory tests. The characteristic value β_R is defined here as the 5% fractile value and also takes into account the influence of the long-term strength (85% of the short-term strength). The ratio between fractile value and average value of approx. 0.80 is hence used to determine the safety factor for walls under long-term loading:

$$\gamma_W = 3.0 \times 0.85 \times 0.80 = 2.04 \approx 2.0$$

Besides walls with a cross-sectional area > 1000 cm², this safety factor also applies to "short walls", or columns with a cross-sectional area < 1000 cm² consisting of either one or several whole units or non-whole units with a proportion of perforations < 35% and without any recesses or chases. For all other "short walls" or columns of non-whole units with a proportion of perforations > 35% or consisting of cross-sections with chases or recesses, the higher safety factor $\gamma_P = 2.5$ should be used. Differentiating the safety factors for walls and "short walls" or columns depending on the cross-sectional area was decided upon because irregularities have a greater effect on smaller cross-sections (e.g. half bats, the lack of a strengthened edge zone in non-whole units with a high proportion of perforations, chases etc.) than they do on larger cross-sections and hence lead to a greater risk of failure. This is taken into account by the higher safety factor γ_P.
In the simplified method of analysis the margin of safety is not explicitly expressed by a safety factor but rather implicitly included in the permissible stresses (see "Analysis for concentric and eccentric compression").

2.3.10 Conditions for the application of the simplified method of analysis

	Component	Wall thickness d [cm]	Clear storey height h_s [m]	Imposed load on floor $p^{3)}$ [kN/m²]	No. of storeys/ Height of building [m]	Spacing of stiffening transverse walls e_q [m]
1	Internal walls	≥ 11.5 < 24.0	≤ 2.75	≤ 5.0	≤ 20[1]	not required
2		≥ 24.0	no limit			
3	Single-leaf external walls	≥ 11.5 < 17.5	≤ 2.75		[2]	
4		≥ 17.5 < 24.0			≤ 20[1]	
5		≥ 24.0	≤12 x d			
6	Loadbearing leaves of twin-leaf external walls and twin-leaf	≥ 11.5 < 17.5	≤ 2.75	≤ 3.0 including party wall surcharge	≤ 2 full storeys + attic storey	e_η ≤ 4.5 Edge distance from an opening e ≤ 2.0
7	party walls	≥ 17.5 < 24.0		≤ 5.0	≤ 20[1]	not required
8		≥ 24.0	≤ 12 x d			

[1] For pitched roofs: halfway between level of eaves and level of ridge.
[2] Only for single-storey garages and similar structures not permanently occupied by persons.
[3] Floor span l ≤ 6.0 m, provided the bending moments from the angular rotation of the floor are not limited by non-structural means (e.g. centering bearing). For two-way-spanning floors l is the shorter of the two spans.

2.3.11 Safety concepts according to DIN 1053 and EC 6

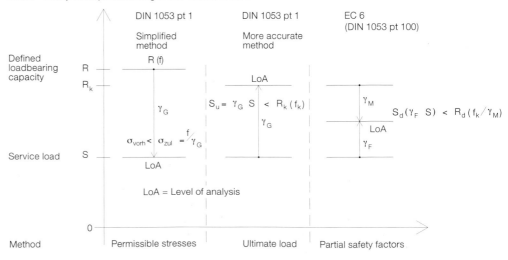

LoA = Level of analysis

Determining the cross-sections from the loads

A wall can be loaded by vertical loads made up of self-weight, floor loads and roof loads. The horizontal loads on a wall result from the action of the wind, the inclination of the structure, earth pressures and other, sometimes extraordinary, loads like earthquakes or impacts. All the loads have to be transferred via the masonry element to the storeys or the subsoil below. The special features of masonry construction are explained in the following with regard to the cross-sections resulting from the loads.

Support reactions from floors and roofs

The support reactions for continuous, one-way-spanning floors and beams supported on walls are to be determined as follows:
• End support reactions ignoring the effects of continuity.
• Support reactions at the first internal wall/column adjacent the end support always taking into account the effects of continuity.
• Support reactions at the remaining internal walls/columns only allowing for the continuity effect when the ratio of neighbouring spans is < 0.7.

Otherwise the support reactions may be calculated without taking the effects of continuity into account but assuming that the beam/floor is simply supported on internal supports and free to rotate at all of them.

For loadbearing walls below one-way-spanning floors which run parallel to the direction of the span of the floor, the design loads are taken to be those from a strip of floor of appropriate width in order to take account of possible load transfer from the floor in the transverse direction. As a rule, we assume that the wall is affected by a strip of the floor one metre wide. The support reactions from two-way-spanning floors and roofs are determined from the influencing areas of the slab. These depend on the type of support (unsupported, pinned, fixed) and are illustrated in DIN 1045 fig. 46.

Moments from wall-slab junctions

The junction points between walls and slabs form rigid corners due to the loads from walls above and so normally represent a statically indeterminate framework with a high degree of indeterminacy. An accurate analysis of this framework is only justified in exceptional cases owing to the great effort this requires. In addition, the great number of mechanical and material inaccuracies in the system mean that excessively accurate calculations do not produce a significantly more exact outcome. The inaccuracies are primarily caused by including the stiffness of slab in the transition from condition I to condition II, by determining the stiffness of the wall in relation to the scatter of moduli of elasticity of the wall and by cracked zones in the wall, the influence of transverse walls on the stiffness of the wall as well as the

creep behaviour of the wall and the slab, which can only be described very approximately by the creep coefficients. In the simplified method of analysis the fixity of the slab and the bending moments resulting from this to do not need to be explicitly calculated because their influence is taken into account in factor k_3 by limiting the spans and by reducing the permissible stress (see "Analysis for concentric and eccentric compression").

In contrast, the more accurate method of analysis takes account of the influence of the slab-support angle of rotation on the eccentric transfer of the load into the walls. For slab imposed loads $p \leq 5.0$ kN/m^2 this can be calculated by using a simplified equation for the moment at this node, otherwise by treating it as a frame.

The simplified method for calculating the node moment reduces the amount of design effort required by replacing the slab restraint moment by an eccentric application of the support reaction A for the slab. For roof slabs the restraint moment $A_D \times e_D$ is transferred completely to the top of the wall. For intermediate floors the restraint moment $A_Z \times e_Z$ is distributed roughly equally between the top of the wall and the base of the wall, with the axial forces N_o from the storeys above being applied concentrically. The eccentricities e_D and e_Z can be taken as 5% of the difference between adjacent floor spans for internal walls and 5% of the adjacent floor span for external walls. Two-way-spanning slabs with span ratios up to 1:2 may use two thirds of the shorter side as the span for determining the eccentricity e_D or e_Z. The node moment may be determined by way of a frame analysis using a subsystem around the node under consideration, with an estimate of the points of contraflexure in the rising walls, normally at half the story height. The rigidity of the walls and slabs may be simplified by assuming an uncracked section and determined using elastic theory. The modulus of elasticity of masonry may be assumed to be $E_{mw} = 3000 \times \sigma_0$ in this case. As the node moments are usually not necessary for the equilibrium of the supporting elements and hence are only restraint moments, it would appear sensible not to assume the most unfavourable arrangement of imposed loads in each bay when calculating these but rather to replace this by half the imposed load as a permanent load. Apart from that, in cases in which the calculated node moment is not called upon to relieve the adjoining bays of the slab, may be reduced to two thirds of its value upon analysing the wall. The reason for this is that the node failure does not represent a rigid restraint owing to the formation of cracks in the masonry, so the frame analysis based on a rigid node supplies restraint moments which are too large [121]. Irrespective of the method of analysis for the node moment, a (possibly) theoretical eccentricity at the top or base of the

wall e > d/3 from the resultant load of the slab and storeys above should be limited to one third of the thickness of the wall. In this case, non-structural measures (e.g. joints, centering bearing, edge groove etc.) are necessary in order to prevent cracks in the masonry and plaster.

Wind loads

Wind loads at right angles to the plane of the wall may be neglected in the simplified method of analysis, provided they have sufficient horizontal support in the form of, for example, slabs acting as plates or structural capping beams. When using the more accurate method, wind loads at right angles to the plane of the wall are generally neglected up to height of 20 m above the ground, provided wall thicknesses d ≥ 240 mm and clear storey heights h_S ≤ 3.0 m.

Both methods of analysis should ensure that wind loads in the plane of the wall can be accommodated by way of the three-dimensional stability of the building.

Three-dimensional stability

Bracing the building

The reason for bracing the building is to ensure that horizontal forces (e.g. wind, horizontal eccentricity, earth pressures, seismic loads, vibration etc.) can be accommodated and transferred to the subsoil; and to limit horizontal deformations. To do this, both the stability of the entire building and the stability of individual masonry walls must be guaranteed. Structures which consist of several parts separated by joints must be designed in such a way that each part is stable and braced in itself. This also applies, for example, to houses in the middle of a terrace, which must be designed to remain stable should they ever find themselves standing alone with wind loads perpendicular to their gables! Overall stability is crucial and must be checked and guaranteed at the start of designing a structure. A braced construction is accomplished with two elements: horizontal plates to accommodate horizontal loads, vertical plates to support the horizontal ones and hence transfer both horizontal and vertical forces to the subsoil.

Horizontal plates are provided in the form of floors, horizontal frameworks or – for short spans between vertical plates – by capping beams designed for bending and shear. The floors may consist of, for example, reinforced concrete slabs with continuous reinforcement or precast floors with shear connectors between the precast components and peripheral ring anchors. Even timber joist floors can be turned into horizontal plates by including diagonal bracing nailed on or floorboards providing a rigid floor in conjunction with peripheral ring anchors.

2.3.12 Arrangement of vertical shear walls

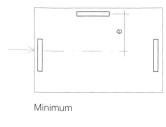

Minimum

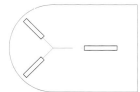

Unstable – system lines intersect

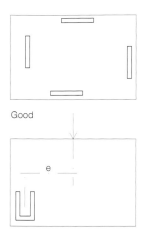

Good

Very poor

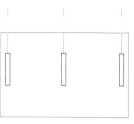

Unstable – system lines intersect
at infinity

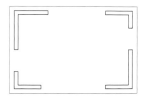

Not recommended

2.3.13 Determination of effective plate forces resulting from horizontal loads

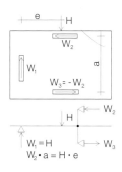

$W_1 = H$
$W_2 \cdot a = H \cdot e$

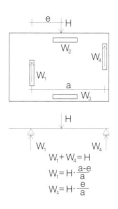

$W_1 + W_4 = H$
$W_1 = H \cdot \frac{a-e}{a}$
$W_4 = H \cdot \frac{e}{a}$

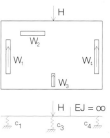

Distribution corresponding
to stiffnesses

Vertical plates are provided in the form of frameworks, portal frame constructions or, better, by way of solid walls of reinforced concrete or masonry. If in exceptional cases it is not possible to carry the full strength of the plates into the subsoil (e.g. because of openings), transfer structures are necessary. However, care must be taken with such structures to ensure a clear flow of forces, a consistent transfer of bending moments and shear forces, and adequate stiffness.

A compression-, tension- and shear-resistant connection between the horizontal and vertical plates is essential for the effectiveness of the bracing. A minimum of three wall plates together with one floor plate in an appropriate arrangement are necessary to create a stable three-dimensional cell and hence stable equilibrium. The lines of action of the wall plates should not intersect at a single point because otherwise there is no equilibrium against rotation about this point. The lever arm between the plates should be as large as possible in order to minimize the forces for accommodating torsion moments. In addition, the wall plates should be distributed as evenly as possible and placed symmetrically because an

eccentric layout leads to unnecessarily large moments – and hence rotations – generated by the horizontal forces. An unrestrained arrangement of the vertical plates means that shrinkage and thermal movements of the floors are not hindered and cracks in the walls which result from such restraint are avoided (see fig. 2.3.12).

The horizontal forces acting on the individual vertical plates are determined from the equilibrium of forces and moments. If there is only one plate in the direction of loading, the two plates in the other loading direction must establish equilibrium against rotation. Two plates in the direction of loading means that the plate forces can be calculated from the equilibrium conditions of a statically determinate system. More than two vertical plates in one loading direction gives us a statically indeterminate system in which the plates act like springs. The spring stiffness c for tall, non-rigid plates is calculated from the bending stiffness EI, for stocky plates from the shear stiffness GA. Plates made from the same material – with the same moduli of elasticity and rigidity – distribute the loads in the first case in proportion to the moments of inertia, in the second case in

proportion to the cross-sections of the plates, whereby equilibrium against rotation must also be considered. It is assumed here that the floor plate is infinitely stiff and all bracing elements and the structure itself undergo the same deformation (see fig. 2.3.13). According to DIN 1053 part 1 an analysis of stability is not compulsory for either method of analysis, provided that the floors are constructed as stiff plates and there is an adequate number of sufficiently long shear walls both along and across the building which continue to the foundations without being weakened (e.g. by openings, recesses) and without changes in geometry. If the three-dimensional stability of a structure is not readily apparent, horizontal forces from a skewed position of the building also must be taken into account in an appropriate analysis.

2.3.14   Requirements to be met by return walls

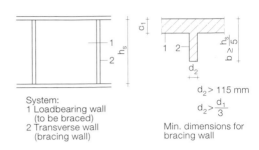

System:
1 Loadbearing wall
   (to be braced)
2 Transverse wall
   (bracing wall)

$d_2 > 115$ mm
$d_2 > \dfrac{d_1}{3}$

Min. dimensions for
bracing wall

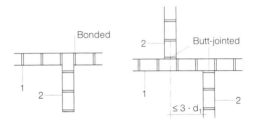

Bonded

Butt-jointed

$\leq 3 \cdot d_1$

Support to loadbearing wall
provided by bonding in
transverse wall on one side

Support provided by transverse walls butt-jointed on
both sides

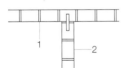

Support provided by tensic
and compression-resistant
fixings between loadbearin
and transverse walls

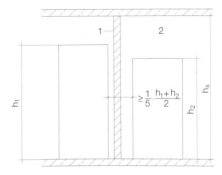

$\geq \dfrac{1}{5} \cdot \dfrac{h_1 + h_2}{2}$

Min. length of bracing wall
interrupted by openings

Lateral restraint to walls

A wall is very thin in comparison to its length and height and so must be considered as a two-dimensional element susceptible to lateral overturning. In order to prevent this and also guarantee the necessary stability of the building in conjunction with the floors, it is necessary to stabilize the wall, i.e. provide lateral restraint. This can be provided by the horizontal plates (e.g. slabs, beams), and by including return walls or piers.

In order to be able to consider walls as bracing elements, they must exhibit adequate stiffness and fix the position of the wall to be restrained at right angles. Adequate stiffness is guaranteed when the necessary length of the wall is equal to at least 1/5 of the clear storey height hs and the required wall thickness is 1/3 of the thickness of the wall to be restrained, however, at least 115 mm.

If the return wall is interrupted by openings, the necessary wall length is to be at least 1/5 of the average clear height of the openings. The restraint provided by the return wall can be achieved by building the walls simultaneously using a suitable bond, by providing return walls to both sides butt-jointed to the face of the wall, or by means of connections using steel flats, masonry anchors or similar fixings to provide a tension- and compression-resistant connection. When building the walls simultaneously using a suitable bond, return walls on one side only can be assumed to provide adequate support only if approximately equal deformation of the two wall materials, in particular similar shrinkage, is to be expected. The purpose of this is to prevent the walls becoming detached because the shear strength of the connection is exceeded as a result of different longitudinal deformations. Walls placed on both sides may be considered as through-walls when they are offset by no more than three times the thickness of the wall to be braced (see fig. 2.3.14).

Stiffening piers can be included in long loadbearing walls when no stiffening return walls are possible. These can be built from vertically reinforced masonry employing specials (e.g. channel blocks), reinforced concrete columns or steel sections. When employing such piers, it must be ensured that the bending strength of the stiffening pier is at least equal to that for a return wall of minimum dimensions. Furthermore, it should be noted that a stiffening pier can only ever be a substitute for a return wall, and can lead to substantial problems in certain circumstances with regard to the building of the wall (e.g. interruption of wall construction, connection between wall and pier, subsequent grouting of the connection), as well as affect the mechanical and building science properties (different deformation and crack behaviour under load, thermal and acoustic bridges).

Support to walls

We distinguish between walls with their edges held immovably at right angles to the plane of the wall on two, three and four sides as well as free-standing walls.

Free-standing walls supported only at their base are reserved for less critical situations (e.g. garden walls) because their buckling length is too large and there is a risk of overturning due to horizontal wind or impact loads. In most situations a wall is supported on two sides by horizontal plates top and bottom. The loads are then carried uniaxially in the vertical direction.

If the loadbearing wall is additionally restrained laterally by means of return walls or piers, we speak of walls supported on three or four sides. This can result in loads being carried biaxially. This effect is lost if the return walls exceed a certain spacing. We must also consider that the horizontal loads generate transverse bending moments, which unreinforced masonry can accommodate only to a certain extent. In order to take these conditions into account in the design, in DIN 1053 part 1 the distance b between return walls for support on four sides is limited to $b \leq 30d$ and for support on three sides to $b \leq 15d$, where d = thickness of wall to be stiffened. If these limits are exceeded, the walls should be considered as supported on only two sides. Openings in the wall to be stiffened can also impair the biaxial loadbearing capacity. Such walls are divided into sections supported on two and three sides (see fig. 2.3.15).

Buckling lengths of walls

The type of support to the wall to be designed is taken into account when checking the compressive strength by way of a reduction in the buckling length of the wall. Walls supported on one side are free-standing and must be fully fixed at their base conforming to Euler case I. For the boundary condition $N_o = 0$ (e.g. garden wall), $h_k = 1.15 h_s$. However, owing to the large buckling length, such "soft" systems should be avoided whenever possible.

Walls supported on two sides can always be considered simply as Euler case II, using the clear storey height h_s as the buckling length. This buckling length is primarily encountered with timber joist floors owing to the lack of fixity they provide. In-situ and precast concrete floors with an adequate bearing on the wall reduce the buckling length to $h_k = \beta \times h_s$ thanks to the favourable elastic fixity effect of the wall-floor node. The buckling length lies between the limits of Euler case II (b = 1.0) and IV (b = 0.5) depending on the ratio of the bending strengths of floor and wall. With normal forms of construction, assuming a buckling length of $h_k = 0.75 \times h_s$ is on the safe side. Walls supported on three and four sides may take into account the favourable influence of the restraint by again reducing the buckling length to $h_k = \beta \times h_s$ (see 2.3.16).

Analysis of concentric and eccentric compression
According to DIN 1053 part 1, it is assumed that concentric compression brings about an even stress distribution within the cross-section. In the case of eccentric compression, a linear stress distribution – with no tension – is assumed. This stress distribution is based on the assumption that the cross-section remains plane (Bernoulli hypothesis) and that stress and strain are in direct proportion to each other (Hooke's law). Hence, cracks in joints appear above an eccentricity $e > d/6$. In order to guarantee a factor of safety against overturning of 1.5 in this case as well, the permissible eccentricity is restricted to $e = d/3$, which corresponds to a permissible cracked joint reaching to the middle of the wall. When calculating the stress, assuming a linear distribution results in two sections having to be considered:

the uncracked cross-section for $0 \leq e \leq d/6$ and the cracked cross-section for $d/6 \leq e \leq d/3$.

The equations for determining the stresses in the extreme fibres are illustrated in 2.3.17. In the simplified method of analysis, the compressive stresses for the serviceability state are calculated using

$$\sigma_{const} = N/A \leq perm\ \sigma_D = k \times \sigma_0.$$

The assumption of a constant distribution of stresses over the cross-section is generally possible because in the simplified method linear stress distributions as a result of intended eccentricities arising from, for example, floor restraint moments or wind on external walls, or those caused by unintended eccentricities do not need to be taken into account when checking buckling. These aspects are already included in the margin of safety on which the permissible stresses are based using the reduction factors k_i, or by design rules and limits.
The basic value σ_0 [MN/m²] for permissible compressive stress as a characteristic parameter for masonry can be found from tables for prescribed masonry or from the results of suitability tests (see "Characteristic strength of masonry"). The reduction factor k is calculated from $k = k_1 \times k_2$ for walls acting as intermediate supports and from $k = k_1 \times k_2$ or $k_1 \times k_3$ for walls acting as one-sided end supports, with the smaller value being used. The factor k_1 takes into account the different safety factors for walls and "short walls". $k_1 = 1.0$ applies to walls and "short walls" or columns with a cross-sectional area < 1000 cm², constructed from either one or several whole units or divided units with a proportion of perforations < 35%

and no recesses or slots. For all other "short walls" or columns $k_1 = 0.8$. Masonry cross-sections with an area < 400 cm² may not be used as loadbearing components.

Factor k_2 takes into account the reduction in loadbearing capacity because of the risk of buckling.
Factor k_3 takes into account the reduction in loadbearing capacity brought about by the angle of rotation of the floor at end supports. For intermediate floors we assume

$k_3 = 1.0$ for $l \leq 4.20$ m
$k_3 = 1.7$ to $l/6$ for 4.20 m $< l \leq 6.00$ m

where l = floor span [m].
For floors above the ground floor storey $k_3 = 0.5$ for all values of l.

If the reduction in loadbearing capacity as a result of the angle of rotation of the floor is prevented by constructional measures (e.g. centering bearing), then $k_3 = 1.0$.

When checking the stresses according to the more accurate method of analysis, at failure the average compressive stress

$$\gamma \times \sigma_{const} = \gamma \times N/A \leq \beta_R$$

and the compressive stress in the extreme fibres

$$\gamma \times \sigma_{max} = \gamma \times \sigma_{edge} \leq 1.33 \times \beta_R$$

may not be exceeded. The value β_R [MN/m²] for the characteristic strength of the masonry can in this case be determined either by converting the basic values σ_0 in the table for prescribed masonry, or from the results of a suitability test (see "Characteristic strength of masonry").

Prescribed masonry (RM)
Prescribed masonry is masonry whose basic values for permissible compressive stress σ_0 are determined depending on strength classes for masonry units, type of mortar and mortar groups, and are tabulated accordingly (see 2.3.19). Inadvisable unit/mortar combinations (see "Stress conditions, failure mechanism and influences on the compressive strength of masonry") are not taken into account in these and the maximum permissible basic stress is restricted to 5.0 MN/m².
The σ_0 values are determined based on the simultaneous inclusion of all standard masonry units without distinguishing them according to type, grade and arrangement of perforations. This omission is only possible when the most unfavourable unit/mortar combination is used to define an individual σ_0 value in each case. The outcome of this is that for some unit/mortar combinations, high reserves of compressive strength remain unused.

2.3.15   Providing support to walls

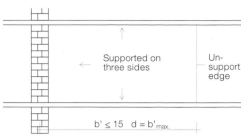

$b' \leq 15\ \ d = b'_{max.}$
Wall supported on three sides

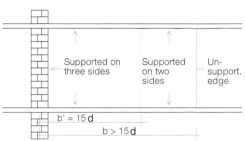

$b' = 15\ d$
$b > 15\ d$
Wall with three supported and one unsupported edge

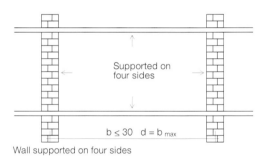

$b \leq 30\ \ d = b_{max}$
Wall supported on four sides

$b' = 15\ d$ $b' = 15\ d$
$b > 30\ d$
Wall with four supported edges

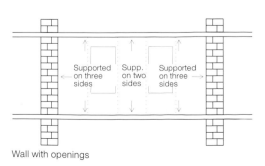

Wall with openings

2.3.16 Buckling lengths of walls in relation to type of support

Cantilever (free-standing) wall

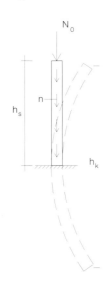

$$1.15 \, h_s \leq h_K \leq 2 \, h_s$$

$$h_K = 2 \, h_s \sqrt{\frac{1 + N_o / N_u}{3}}$$

N_o = Axial force at top of wall
N_u = Axial force at base of wall

Wall supported on two sides

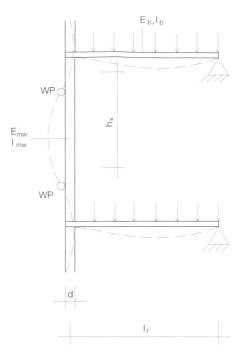

$h_K = h_S$ (in general)
$h_K = \beta \times h_S$ (more acurate method of analysis)

with:
$$\beta = 1 - 0.15 \times \frac{E_b I_b}{E_{mw} I_{mw}} \times h_s \times \frac{1}{l_1} + \frac{1}{l_2} \geq 0.75$$

E_{mw}, E_b = Modulus of elasticity of masonry or concrete
I_{mw}, I_b = 2nd moment of area of masonry wall or concrete floor
l_1, l_2 = Spans of adjoining floor bays; for external walls use
$$\frac{1}{l_2} = 0$$

Wall supported on three sides

$$h_K = \frac{1}{1 + \left(\frac{\beta \times h_s}{3b}\right)} \times \beta \times h_s \geq 0.3 \times h_s$$

Wall supported on four sides

for $h_S \leq b$:
$$h_K = \frac{1}{1 + \left(\frac{\beta \times h_s}{b}\right)} \times \beta \times h_s$$

for $h_S > b$:
$$h_K = \frac{b}{2}$$

b = Distance of unsupported edge from centre of return wall or centre-to-centre spacing of return walls
β = As for walls supported on two sides

Masonry according to suitability test (EM)
Here, the compressive strength of the masonry for a certain unit/mortar combination is determined by way of tests according to DIN 1053 part 2 from which the basic value σ_0 for the permissible compressive stress or the characteristic value β_R for compressive strength is derived via a conversion factor. As the suitability test reveals any potential high reserves of compressive strength over and above the σ_0 value for prescribed masonry (which can be exploited in the design), the use of masonry according to the suitability test is particularly interesting in economic terms for those unit/mortar combinations for which experience has shown that higher σ_0 values are to be expected than for prescribed masonry (see table 2.3.18).

Characteristic strength of masonry
Having obtained the basic value σ_0 as the characteristic strength for the masonry, design according to the simplified method is now carried out. The σ_0 value the relates to a masonry slenderness ratio $\lambda = 10$ as well as the service loads. The basic value σ_0 for prescribed masonry is taken from table 2.3.19.

For masonry according to a suitability test, the basic value σ_0 is determined based on the nominal strength of the masonry β_M [MN/m²] to DIN 1053 part 2 as follows:

$\sigma_0 = 0.35 \times \beta_M$ for $1.0 \leq \beta_M \leq 9.0$
$\sigma_0 = 0.32 \times \beta_M$ for $11.0 \leq \beta_M \leq 13.0$
$\sigma_0 = 0.30 \times \beta_M$ for $16.0 \leq \beta_M \leq 25.0$

It should be noted that the classification may only be up to 50% higher than it would be for corresponding prescribed masonry to DIN 1053 part 1.
If the design is carried out according to the more accurate method, the characteristic value β_R should be used for the compressive strength. This relates to the theoretical slenderness ration 0 for masonry and the failure condition. The characteristic value can be determined either from the σ_0 values by using the equation

$$\beta_R = 2.0 \times 1.333 \times \sigma_0 = 2.67 \times \sigma_0$$

or from the nominal strength β_M of the masonry according to a suitability test. When establishing the σ_0 values, the factor 1.333 corresponds to the buckling reduction as a result of the slenderness ratio $\lambda = h/d = 10$ applicable for σ_0 compared to the theoretical slenderness ratio 0 for β_R; the factor 2.0 is the safety factor γ_W for walls and hence represents an adjustment of the margin of safety between serviceability and failure conditions.
When determining β_R from the nominal strength β_M, the influence of long-term loads compared to the short-term test is taken into account with the factor 0.85; furthermore, conversion of the

slenderness from the Rilem body to the theoretical slenderness ratio 0 is allowed for by using the factor 1.1. For masonry with strengths $\beta_M \geq 11.0$ MN/m² , an additional safety factor of 10-15% should be included because of the lack of experience with such strengths. Therefore, the characteristic value β_R determined from the suitability test is [121]:

$\beta_R = 0.93 \times \beta_M$ for $1.0 \leq \beta_M \leq 9.0$ N/mm²
$\beta_R = 0.85 \times \beta_M$ for $11.0 \leq \beta_M \leq 13.0$ N/mm²
$\beta_R = 0.80 \times \beta_M$ for $16.0 \leq \beta_M \leq 25.0$ N/mm²

Analysis of safety against buckling

In the simplified method of analysis, checking buckling as a result of unintended eccentricity and deformation according to second order theory is taken into account in the permissible compressive stresses σ_D via the reduction factor k_2, i.e. an explicit analysis does not need to be carried out. It is assumed that at half storey height the only bending moments that occur are those from node moments at the top and bottom of the wall, plus those from wind load. In the case of larger horizontal loads, an analysis of buckling, and hence of the compressive stresses, should be carried out according to the more accurate method of analysis. As the basic values σ_0 are related to a slenderness ratio $h_k/d = 10$, this reduction is necessary only for larger slenderness ratios. A slenderness ratio $h_k/d = 25$ is the maximum permitted for buckling using the k_2 factor.

In the more accurate method of analysis the eccentricities f_1 from imperfections in the construction of the wall and f_2 from second order theory are established separately and added to the intended load-related eccentricity e = moment/axial force at half storey height. The value for e results from the bending moments at half storey height caused by wind, earth pressure and floor restraint. As possible cracked joints and hence changing cross-sectional stiffnesses complicate the determination of additional eccentricities, the simplified equation

$$f = f_1 + f_2 = h_k/d \times (1 + m)/1800 \times h_k$$

may be employed for the additional eccentricity. Here, h_k is the buckling length of the wall and m = 6(e/d) is the related intended eccentricity at half storey height. Slenderness ratios $h_k/d > 25$ are not permitted. This simplification allows for the unintended eccentricity caused by construction imperfections $f_1 = h_k/300$ and an allowance for the effects of creep. The total eccentricity at half storey height is calculated from the intended eccentricity e and the additional eccentricity f to give

$$e_m = e + f.$$

The linear stress distribution across the thickness of the wall at half storey height is

2.3.17 Stress distribution resulting from concentric and eccentric axial force

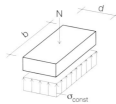 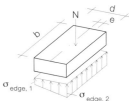

Concentric axial force

e = 0

$$\sigma_{const} = \frac{N}{A} = \frac{N}{b \cdot d} = const$$

Eccentric axial force

$$e = \frac{d}{6}$$

$$\sigma_{edge,1} = \frac{N}{b \cdot d} \cdot (1 - \frac{6 \cdot e}{d})$$

$$\sigma_{edge,2} = \frac{N}{b \cdot d} \cdot (1 + \frac{6 \cdot e}{d}) = \sigma_{max}$$

Eccentric axial force

$$\frac{d}{6} < e < \frac{d}{3}$$

$$\sigma_{edge} = \frac{2 \cdot N}{3 \cdot c \cdot b} = \sigma_{max}$$

where: $C = \frac{d}{2} - e$

2.3.18 Classification of masonry according to suitability test (EM) to DIN 1053 part 2

Masonry strength class M	Nominal strength of masonry β_M[1] N/mm²	Min. compressive strength Lowest individual value β_{MN} N/mm²	Min. compressive strength Average value β_{MS} N/mm²
1	1.0	1.0	1.2
1.2	1.2	1.2	1.4
1.4	1.4	1.4	1.6
1.7	1.7	1.7	2.0
2	2.0	2.0	2.4
2.5	2.5	2.5	2.9
3	3.0	3.0	3.5
3.5	3.5	3.5	4.1
4	4.0	4.0	4.7
4.5	4.5	4.5	5.3
5	5.0	5.0	5.9
5.5	5.5	5.5	6.5
6	6.0	6.0	7.0
7	7.0	7.0	8.2
9	9.0	9.0	10.6
11	11.0	11.0	12.9
13	13.0	13.0	15.3
16	16.0	16.0	18.8
20	20.0	20.0	23.5
25	25.0	25.0	29.4

[1] The nominal strength is based on the 5% percentile of the populations

2.3.19 Basic values s_0 for permissible compressive stress for masonry to DIN 1053 part 1

Masonry unit strength class	Normal mortar Mortar group					Thin-bed mortar[2]	Lightweight mortar	
	I	II	IIa	III	IIIa	LM 21	LM 36	
	MN/m²	MN/m²	MN/m²	MN/m²	MN/m²	MN/m²	MN/m²	MN/m²
2	0.3	0.5	0.5[1]	–	–	0.6	0.5[3]	0.5[3][5]
4	0.4	0.7	0.8	0.9	–	1.1	0.7[4]	0.8[6]
6	0.5	0.9	1.0	1.2	–	1.5	0.7	0.9
8	0.6	1.0	1.2	1.4	–	2.0	0.8	1.0
12	0.8	1.2	1.6	1.8	1.9	2.2	0.9	1.1
20	1.0	1.6	1.9	2.4	3.0	3.2	0.9	1.1
28	–	1.8	2.3	3.0	3.5	3.7	0.9	1.1
36	–	–	–	3.5	4.0	–	–	–
48	–	–	–	4.0	4.5	–	–	–
60	–	–	–	4.5	5.0	–	–	–

[1] $s_0 = 0.6$ MN/m² for external walls with thickness ≥ 300 mm. However, this increase does not apply to the analysis for bearing at supports.

[2] Only use for aerated concrete gauged units to DIN 4165 and for calcium silicate gauged units. The values for the other types of masonry are covered by the respective general building authority certificates. The values apply to solid units. For perforated calcium silicate units and hollow calcium silicate blocks to DIN 106 part 1 use the corresponding values for normal mortars of mortar group III up to masonry unit strength class 20.

[3] $s_0 = 0.4$ MN/m² for masonry using clay bricks to DIN 105 parts 1-4.

[4] $s_0 = 0.5$ MN/m² for calcium silicate units to DIN 106 part 1 of bulk density class ≥ 0.9 and for clay bricks to DIN 105 parts 1-4.

[5] $s_0 = 0.6$ MN/m² for external walls with thickness ≥ 300 mm. However, this increase does not apply to the case given in footnote 3) nor to the analysis for bearing at supports.

[6] $s_0 = 0.7$ MN/m² for masonry using the masonry units stated in footnote [4].

2.3.20   Distribution of shear stresses in masonry plates

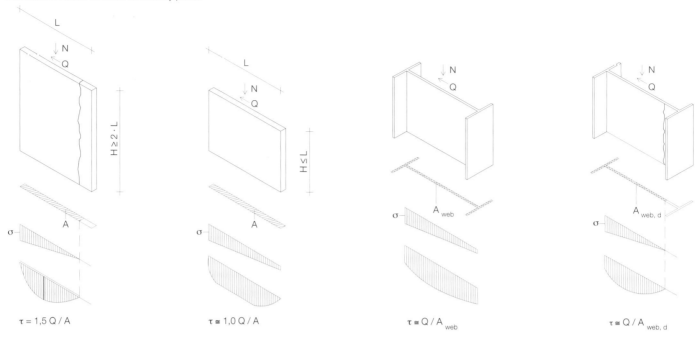

$$\tau = 1{,}5\,Q/A \qquad \tau \cong 1{,}0\,Q/A \qquad \tau \cong Q/A_{web} \qquad \tau \cong Q/A_{web,\,d}$$

determined from the total eccentricity e_m and the vertical load N, and the analysis of concentric or eccentric compression according to the more accurate method of analysis.

Analysis of tension and bending tension

Check perpendicular to the bed joints
The tensile strength of the masonry perpendicular to the bed joints may not be used when assessing the stability of loadbearing walls. It is very low and, in particular, is subject to very severe scatter. Although laboratory tests have proved a certain tensile strength in the bed joints, this cannot be transferred to site conditions (quality of workmanship, subsequent treatment of the masonry, moisture content of the units etc.). On the other hand, infill panels that carry only wind loads but no vertical loads can make use of design rules which assume a certain tensile strength in the bed joints (see "Non-loadbearing walls"). The reason for this is that in contrast to loadbearing walls, failure of these walls does not lead to the complete structure collapsing or becoming totally unstable.

Check parallel to the bed joints
We can assume a low tensile strength parallel to the bed joints so that in a horizontal direction tensile or tensile bending stresses can be accommodated by the masonry. The distribution of stresses is assumed to be linear according to simple bending theory. Both the simplified and the more accurate method of analysis should use the equation

exist $\sigma = N/A + M/W \le$ perm σ_z

to check this for the serviceability condition. The tensile strength parallel to the bed joints which may be assumed is given in DIN 1053 part 1 and is based on the adhesive shear strength, the friction component (from load and friction coefficient), the ratio of bonding dimension to height of unit and the characteristic value for the tensile strength of the units.

Analysis of shear
An analysis of shear stresses is usually only necessary when three-dimensional stiffness is not available (see "Three-dimensional stiffness"). This is mainly the case with tall structures and structures with only a few shear walls. The distribution of shear stress is determined according to simple bending theory or plate theory. In doing so, it should be noted that cracked cross-sectional areas resulting in cracked joints may not be used because shear stresses cannot be transferred across a crack (see fig. 2.3.20).
The equation for rectangular cross-sections (not compound cross-sections) is

exist $\tau = c \times Q/A$

where A = uncracked cross-sectional area, and c = factor to allow for distribution of shear stress over the cross-section.

In tall, beam-like walls with $H \ge 2L$ the distribution of shear stress over the cross-section is

parabolic with c = 1.5; in approximately square walls with $H \le L$ the shear stress is almost constant and c = 1.0. Linear interpolation may be employed between these two figures.
In the case of slab shear, owing to the low wall thickness we once again assume a beam-like component with c = 1.5.
Both methods of analysis should use the equation

exist $\tau \le$ perm τ

to check for shear in the serviceability state. The shear strength of masonry also depends on the axial stress s acting at the same time but not usually constant over the cross-section and so several positions within the cross-section should be analysed in order to determine the worst case. However, for rectangular cross-sections only the position of maximum shear stress needs to be checked because this is sufficiently accurate.
In compound cross-sections (e.g. T-, I-sections) an analysis of the shear should also be carried out at the junctions between the different parts of the compound section in order to guarantee the distribution of stress in the flanges.
We distinguish between plate shear and slab shear when determining the theoretical shear strength τ.

Characteristic strength for plate shear
DIN 1053 part 1 requires two checks to be carried out in both the simplified and the more accurate method of analysis.

The first relates to failure of the bed joints, the second to tensile failure of the units.
An adhesive tensile strength failure between masonry unit and bed joint mortar as a result of low vertical loading is taken into account by assessing the shear strength (joint failure). Compressive failure of the masonry is generally accounted for in the analysis of concentric or eccentric compression.
This approach is based on the fact that this type of failure is only critical in exceptional cases because the maximum values from shear and vertical stresses cannot normally occur for the same loading case and not at the same position.
When checking for joint failure, a reduced friction coefficient $\bar{\mu}$ is defined to simplify the calculation of the constant compressive stress s due to imposed loads occurring simultaneously. The average friction stress $\bar{\mu} \times \sigma$ in the bed joints is taken into account in the Mann/Müller model by assuming that the simultaneous compressive stress has a stepped progression within the individual units.
In the simplified method of analysis the check for tensile failure of the units is made simpler (compared to the more accurate method) by just assuming a constant value max. t for the tensile failure mechanism of the units. This is certainly on the safe side. This characteristic value is determined similarly to the tensile strength of the unit β_{RZ} depending on the compressive strength of the unit β_{Nst} and the arrangement of perforations (see fig. 2.3.21).

Characteristic strength for slab shear
Only failure of the joints has to be taken into account when checking slab shear, and so in DIN 1053 part 1 the characteristic strength for the more accurate method of analysis is defined as

perm $\tau \leq 1/\gamma \times (\beta_{RHS} + \mu\sigma)$

and for the simplified method of analysis as

perm $\tau \leq \sigma_{0HS} + 0.3 \, \sigma_{Dm}$.

Deformation and crack formation

Owing to the constant advancements in masonry construction with regard to method of construction (compound construction using materials with different deformation behaviour), the reduction in size of components (slimmer walls to increase usable floor space) and the more accurate modelling of the loadbearing behaviour of masonry (good use of material), design work must increasingly take account of material deformations and the risk of cracking under service loads and not just examine load-bearing capacity. Ignoring the different deformation behaviour of materials or components can lead to cracks if the material strengths are exceeded. Such cracks do not normally impair the stability of the structure but can influence its serviceability (thermal and acoustic insulation, moisture control, appearance). Cracks can be avoided if the deformation behaviour of the materials and components is taken into account during the planning phase and the appropriate consequences derived from this work for the design.
Suitable approximate methods and the wealth of knowledge about the deformation parameters are available to assess the deformation behaviour and hence also the risk of cracking [184].

Deformations in masonry
Masonry is similar to concrete in terms of forms of deformation. In addition, clay bricks can also be affected by irreversible chemical swelling. An overview of the possible deformations in masonry is shown in fig. 2.3.22.

Load-related deformations
occur as a result of self-weight, other permanent loads and imposed loads. The strains that these cause can be divided into those resulting from short-term loading effects and those from long-term loading effects.
The strain brought about by short-term loading is called elastic strain e_{el}. The elastic strain is calculated from the stress s and the modulus of elasticity of the masonry E_{mw}:

ε_{el} = exist σ/E_{mw} [mm/m or ‰]

The modulus of elasticity E_{mw} is defined as the secant modulus at 1/3 of the maximum compressive stress with associated total elongation tote from a single application of the load:

E_{mw} = max $\sigma/(3 \text{ tot } \varepsilon)$ (see 2.3.23)

Owing to the single application of the load, the modulus of elasticity E_{mw} includes a small component of permanent elongation and is therefore slightly smaller than the modulus of elasticity resulting from purely elastic strain. The modulus of elasticity depends on the

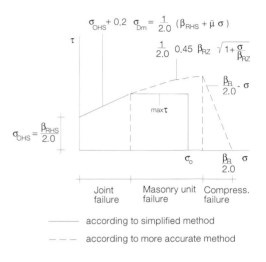

2.3.21 σ-τ diagram as multi-part envelope of shear capacity to DIN 1053 part 1 for the simplified and more accurate methods of analysis

——— according to simplified method

– – – according to more accurate method

2.3.22 Deformation of masonry

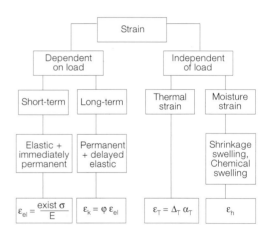

2.3.23 Definition of modulus of elasticity for masonry

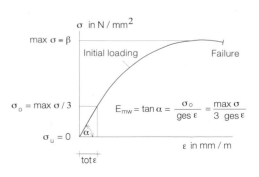

2.3.24 Crack formation due to shrinkage at the edge of masonry units and mortar

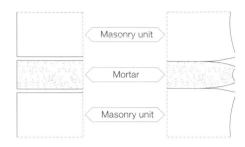

2.3.25 Relationship between shrinkage strain ε_s and moisture content h_v (sketch of principle)

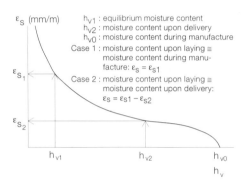

2.3.26 Relationship between E_{mw} and β_{mw} or β_{St} [18, 19, 21, 22]

Masonry unit	Mortar	Equation	Scatter
Calcium silicate	Normal mortar Thin-bed mortar	$E_{mw} = 600 \beta_{mw}$	± 50%
Ltwt concrete	Ltwt mortar Normal mortar	$E_{mw} = 1240 \beta_{mw}^{0.77}$ $E_{mw} = 1040 \beta_{mw}$	± 20% ± 20%
Autoclaved aerated concrete	Normal mortar Thin-bed mortar	$E_{mw} = 520 \beta_{mw}$ $E_{mw} = 570 \beta_{St}^{0.69}$ $E_{mw} = 540 \beta_{mw}$ $E_{mw} = 320 \beta_{St}$	± 50% ± 50% ± 20% ± 20%
Ltwt vertically perforated	Ltwt mortar Normal mortar Thin-bed mortar	$E_{mw} = 1480 \beta_{mw}$ $E_{mw} = 1200 \beta_{mw}$ $E_{mw} = 1330 \beta_{mw}$ $E_{mw} = 420 \beta_{St}$	± 50% ± 50% ± 50% ± 50%

2.3.27 Modulus of elasticity E_{mw} to DIN 1053 part1

Masonry unit	Characteristic value	Range of values
Clay	$3500 \sigma_0$	$3000–4000 \sigma_0$
Calcium silicate	$3000 \sigma_0$	$2500–4000 \sigma_0$
Lightweight concrete	$5000 \sigma_0$	$4000–5500 \sigma_0$
Concrete	$7500 \sigma_0$	$6500–8500 \sigma_0$
Aerated concrete	$2500 \sigma_0$	$2000–3000 \sigma_0$

compressive strength of the units and the mortar, on the type and grade of unit, and the type of mortar. As a rule, it is determined by tests on a Rilem body according to DIN 18554 part 1. For approximate calculations

$$E_{mw} = 1000 \beta_{mw}$$

can be assumed, although fluctuations

$$500 \beta_{mw} \leq E_{mw} \leq 1500 \beta_{mw}$$

must be taken into account. β_{mw} is the compressive strength of the masonry determined from suitability tests according to DIN 1053 part 2.
Alternatively, DIN 1053 part 1 table 2 specifies values for the modulus of elasticity for individual types of masonry unit depending on the basic value τ_0 for permissible compressive stress (see "Deformation values").
The elastic strain ε_{el} is not very significant for the assessment of safety against cracking of masonry because ε_{el} is comparatively small and occurs during construction without causing cracks. ε_{el} is normally ignored when assessing the risk of cracking. Shortening in the direction of the load as a result of long-term loading effects is called creep. Creep strain is defined as

$$\varepsilon_{k,t} = \varphi_t \times \varepsilon_{el} \text{ [mm/m or ‰]}.$$

The creep coefficient φ is approximately constant for the range of service stresses and hence not related to stress. Creep strains are predominantly irreversible, but their severity gradually decreases. The final creep strain $\varepsilon_{k\infty}$ or final creep coefficient φ_∞ are determined from experimental creep strain tests by way of mathematical extrapolation. Under roughly constant ambient conditions, creep comes to a halt after about 3-5 years. The main influences on the progression and final value of creep are the type of masonry, the initial moisture content of the component, the size of the component, the creep stress (if higher than the service stress) and the proportion of masonry units to mortar. The duration of the load plays only a minor role because the masonry's properties generally change only very slightly after application of the load. Characteristic values for the final creep coefficient φ_∞ of masonry are listed in DIN 1053 part 1 table 2 (see "Deformation values"). They are only specified in relation to masonry units because test results up to now have not shown type and strength of mortar to have a significant and quantifiable influence.
Generally, creep is significant for the cracking of masonry. However, it can either increase or reduce the stress.

Deformations not related to load
are divided into thermal strain ε_T and moisture strain ε_h. Moisture strain is a term that includes

the effects of all deformations resulting from chemical and physical processes.
Thermal strain ε_T is the change in length resulting from the influence of heat or temperature changes. It is determined from the temperature change Δ_T and the coefficient of thermal expansion α_T specific to the material:

$$\varepsilon_T = \Delta_T \times \alpha_T \text{ [mm/m or ‰]}.$$

The coefficient α_T must be determined from tests; it can be assumed to be constant for the temperature range -20 to +80°C. The value of α_T depends on the type of masonry unit and the mortar as well as the moisture content of the masonry element. α_T increases as the moisture content rises. The range of values and the characteristic value for the coefficient of thermal expansion are given in DIN 1053 part 1 table 2 related to type of masonry unit (see "Deformation values").
The generally high level of thermal insulation to wall components means that thermal strain plays only a minor role when assessing possible cracking of masonry.
The possible moisture strains resulting from physical processes are called shrinkage and swelling. Shrinkage is a contraction caused by loss of moisture or drying out; swelling is an expansion caused by moisture absorption. Both processes are reversible to some extent. The final values for shrinkage $\varepsilon_{s\infty}$ and swelling $\varepsilon_{q\infty}$ are determined from the results of tests by mathematical extrapolation. An adequate approximation is to check the masonry units without taking into account the mortar.

The magnitude of the shrinkage is influenced by the type of unit, to a certain extent also by the type of mortar, by the extent of preparatory work carried out on the units prior to laying and hence their moisture content upon laying, and by the drying conditions (relative humidity, movement of the air) and hence the final moisture content of the component. Shrinkage increases with increasing initial and decreasing final moisture content as well as with decreasing relative humidity. The time span of the shrinkage process is accelerated by units drying out rapidly, lower relative humidity, stronger movements of the air and thin components. A drying-out process which is too rapid and just involves the surface at the unit/joint interface can lead to cracks between masonry unit and mortar (tearing of the joint) in extreme cases (see fig. 2.3.24). In roughly constant ambient conditions shrinkage is essentially complete after about 3-5 years.

Preventing shrinkage leads to tensile stresses. These bring with them a high risk of cracking owing to the low tensile strength of masonry materials. Therefore, shrinkage is considerably more important than swelling in terms of crack formation, particularly as the compressive stresses caused by preventing swelling can generally be accommodated without cracking owing to the high compressive strength of masonry. The relationship between shrinkage and moisture content is useful in assessing the risk of cracking due to shrinkage (see fig. 2.3.25). Shrinkage strains for various initial and equilibrium moisture contents can be determined from this. In addition, consequences for reducing shrinkage can be deduced, e.g. lowering the moisture content of masonry units during manufacture or avoiding excessive saturation of the masonry units prior to laying.

Chemical swelling ε_{cq} is the increase in volume as a result of molecular water bonding (chemisorption). This can occur in clay bricks and begins immediately after completion of the firing process. This process can only be reversed at very high temperatures (approx. 650°C). The magnitude of chemical swelling depends on the constituents of the clay brick and the proportion of clay bricks to mortar in the masonry. A higher lime content can have a positive influence on chemical swelling in terms of speeding up the process and reducing the final value. Likewise, chemical swelling of the masonry can be reduced by increasing the proportion of mortar and hence the degree of mortar shrinkage. The swelling process can take place very rapidly but also very slowly over a period of several years, and the firing conditions of the clay bricks can either accelerate or slow down the process. If chemical swelling takes place very quickly and is soon over, then this type of moisture strain is insignificant in practical terms because subsequent swelling of the clay brick within the masonry construction is unlikely or, at worst, only very low. Chemical swelling becomes critical and dangerous when it continues after the wall has been built. In conjunction with contracting components in particular, it can promote the formation of cracks.

DIN 1053 part 1 table 2 lists characteristic values and ranges of values for shrinkage and chemical swelling related to type of masonry unit (see "Deformation values").

Deformation values

In Germany deformation values for masonry are updated each year in the *Mauerwerk-Kalender* ("Masonry Yearbook") [181]. This lists final values, characteristic values and ranges of values, and includes minimum and maximum values as well as statistical parameters (average values, percentile values, numbers of tests etc.) in tables. An overview of the values for compressive modulus of elasticity E_{mw}, final creep coefficient φ_{∞}, coefficient of thermal expansion α_T and moisture strain ε_h is given in the following.

The modulus of elasticity values E_{mw} for masonry made from normal, lightweight and thin-bed mortar based on the latest findings are given in table 2.3.28.

2.3.28 Modulus of elasticity E_{mw} of masonry [x 10^3 N/mm²] for compression perpendicular to the bed joints [19-22]

Masonry unit		Strength class	Mortar Normal mortar, group				Lightweight mortar	Thin-bed mortar
Type of unit	DIN		II	IIa	III	IIIa		
HLz	105	4	–	–	–	–	2.5	4.0
		6	–	–	–	–	4.0	4.5
		8	–	–	–	–	5.0	5.5
		12	3.5	5.0	6.0	8.0	6.5	–
		20	5.0	6.5	8.5	11.0	–	–
		28	6.5	8.5	10.5	13.5	–	–
		36	–	–	12.5	16.0	–	–
		48	–	–	15.0	19.0	–	–
		60	–	–	18.0	22.5	–	–
Lightweight vertically perforated	105 pt 2 and certificate	4	2.0	2.5	3.0	4.5	3.0	3.5
		6	2.5	3.5	4.5	6.0	4.0	4.5
		8	3.0	4.0	5.5	7.5	5.0	5.5
		12	4.5	6.0	8.0	10	6.5	7.5
		20	7.0	9.0	12.0	15	9.0	–
KS	106	4	1.9	2.2	2.5	2.9	–	–
		6	2.6	3.0	3.4	4	–	–
		8	3.2	3.7	4.2	4.9	–	–
		12	4.3	5.0	5.7	6.6	–	8.0
		20	6.3	7.2	8.4	9.7	–	10.0
		28	8.1	9.3	10.7	12.4	–	–
		36	9.7	11.2	12.9	15	–	–
		48	12.0	13.9	16.0	18.5	–	–
		60	14.2	16.4	18.9	21.8	–	–
KS L	106	12	3.2	3.7	4.2	4.9	–	–
		20	5.0	5.8	6.6	7.7	–	–
		28	6.1	7.0	8.0	9.3	–	–
Hbl	18 151	2	2.2	2.2	2.3	–	2.2	2.0
		4	3.5	3.6	3.8	–	3.0	–
		6	4.6	4.8	5.0	–	3.6	–
		8	5.6	5.9	6.1	–	4.1	–
V, Vbl	18 152	2	2.2	2.4	2.5	–	2.0	2.0
		4	3.7	3.9	4.1	–	3.0	3.5
		6	4.9	5.2	5.6	–	3.7	5.0
		8	6.0	6.4	6.8	–	4.3	–
Hbn	18 153	4	4.5	5.8	7.6	–	–	–
		6	5.8	7.5	9.8	–	–	–
		8	6.9	9.0	11.7	15.2	–	–
		12	8.8	11.5	15.0	19.5	–	–
PB, PP	4165	2	–	–	1.1	–	–	1.0
		4	–	–	1.8	–	–	1.8
		6	–	–	2.4	–	–	2.5
		8	–	–	3.0	–	–	3.1

2.3.29 Final values for moisture strain $\varepsilon_{h\infty}$, final creep coefficient φ_{∞}, coefficient of thermal expansion α_T [18, 23-25]

Masonry unit	DIN	$\varepsilon_{h\infty}$ [1] Char. value mm/m	Range of values [2] mm/m	φ_{∞} Char. value mm/m	Range of values mm/m	α_T Char. value 10^{-6}/K	Range values 10^{-6}/K
Clay	105	0	+ 0.3 to – 0.2 [3]	1.0	0.5 to 1.5	6	5 to 7
Calcium silicate	106	– 0.2	– 0.1 to – 0.3	1.5	1.0 to 2.0	8	7 to 9
Lightweight concrete	18 151 18 152	– 0.4	– 0.2 to – 0.5	2.0	1.5 to 2.5	10; 8 [4]	8 to 12
Concrete	18 153	– 0.2	– 0.1 to – 0.3	1.0	–	10	8 to 12
Aerated concrete	4165	– 0.2	+ 0.1 to – 0.3	1.5	1.0 to 2.5	8	7 to 9

[1] minus sign = shrinkage; plus sign = swelling; swelling for clay = chemical swelling
[2] Range of customary values
[3] For masonry of small-format units ((≤ 2 DF), otherwise -0.1.
[4] For lightweight concrete units with mainly expanded clay as aggregate.

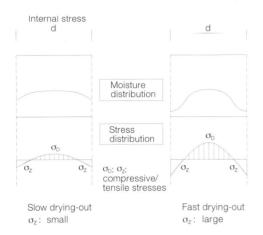

2.3.30 Internal stresses across wall thickness resulting from differential drying; restraint stresses [17]

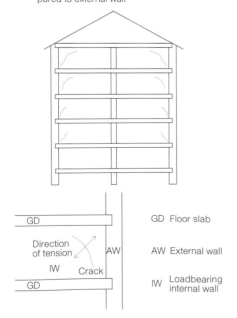

2.3.31 Diagonal cracks in internal walls due to more pronounced shortening of internal wall compared to external wall

GD Floor slab

AW External wall

IW Loadbearing internal wall

The relationship between modulus of elasticity Emw and compressive strength of the masonry β_{mw} according to suitability test or compressive strength of the unit β_{St} as given by these findings are shown in table 2.3.26.

The modulus of elasticity values E_{mw} depending on the basic value σ_0 of permissible compressive stress are given in table 2.3.27. These values correspond to those of DIN 1053 part 1 table 2.

The mathematical final values for moisture strain $\varepsilon_{h\infty}$ (shrinkage, swelling, chemical swelling) and creep φ_∞ as well as the coefficient of thermal expansion α_T are specified as characteristic values in 2.3.29. These are representative "average" values. The ranges of values also listed indicate possible limits. The characteristic values and ranges of values have also been included in DIN 1053 part 1 table 2. They apply to masonry constructed using normal mortar but are approximately correct for masonry using lightweight and thin-bed mortar as well as for masonry with approved units (e.g. large-format units). The $\varepsilon_{h\infty}$ and α_T values can be used both perpendicular and parallel to the bed joints. On the other hand, the φ_∞ values apply only to compression perpendicular to the bed joints.

Cracks in masonry

Deformations which are allowed to take place without being restrained do not cause any stresses. A homogenous body supported without friction and subjected to uniform strain can deform completely free from stress. In practice, however, a masonry component is not usually free to deform without restraint because it is joined to neighbouring components. If the two connected components deform differently as a result of, for example, deformations of different magnitudes or at different times, stresses ensue. If the deformations are prevented by external forces (restraint), then the stresses thereby caused are designated external or restraint stresses.

However, stresses in a component can also ensue without the need for external forces, e.g. if different parts of a component are heated differently or if it dries out unevenly (the outside more than the inside). The stresses thereby caused are then termed internal or residual stresses. In masonry this occurs when, for example, units laid with a high moisture content subsequently dry out. The uneven drying over the cross-section causes internal stresses: tensile in the outer, drier zones and compressive towards the middle of the unit (see fig. 2.3.30).

The magnitude of the stresses that arise is essentially influenced by the magnitude of the deformations, the degree of restraint and fixity, the ratios of the stiffnesses of the connected components and the magnitude of the relaxation – the decrease in the initial stress over

time at constant strain. This decrease in stress is mainly due to slow deformation processes (shrinkage, long-term temperature changes, creep). Cracks occur when the stresses exceed the strength or the strains exceed the failure strain. Tension and shear stresses are critical and particularly liable to cause cracks because the tensile and shear strengths of masonry are comparatively low [184].

Vertical, horizontal and diagonal cracks are the basic forms that can occur in masonry. Vertical cracks either pass alternately through the bed joints and the masonry units or zigzag along the perpends and bed joints. Horizontal cracks mainly occur in the bed joints owing to the low adhesive pull strength between masonry unit and mortar. Only in the case of thin-bed mortar in conjunction with units whose vertical tensile strength is lower than the adhesive tensile strength do the horizontal cracks pass through the masonry units. Diagonal cracks usually take the form of steps along the perpends and bed joints. However, with units of low tensile strength combined with good shear strength between unit and mortar, cracks can also run along the perpends and pass through the masonry units (see fig. 2.3.32).

The significance of cracks

In many cases avoiding cracks at all costs is simply not economic. It is also not necessary, provided they do not cause any damage to the structure or component. Therefore, the significance of cracks is related to their affect on the stability, serviceability and appearance of the individual component, and is influenced by the position, width, depth and length of the individual cracks as well as the extent of cracking. While larger cracks can seriously impair the building science properties of external components (thermal and acoustic insulation, moisture control) and internal components (acoustic insulation), individual hairline cracks up to 0.2 mm wide are not detrimental to either the function of the component nor its appearance. The degree to which the building science properties are impaired depends on the size and number of cracks as well as their effect on the component (position, depth, location of component). The aesthetic effect of cracks is determined by their size and extent as well as the surface finish and the distance of the observer from the wall. For instance, relatively small cracks in internal walls of facing brickwork can represent a flaw in aesthetic terms, while the same cracks in heavily textured, inaccessible external wall surfaces will probably not be noticeable.

Consequently, the significance of cracks is always to be considered in relation to the component and their effect. However, cracks which have a significant adverse effect on serviceability should always be avoided [184].

Causes and prevention of cracks in masonry

As at present many of the critical variables which influence the formation of cracks cannot be measured sufficiently accurately, any analysis of the risk of cracking or factor of safety against cracking in masonry is very limited and only approximate. However, with a certain understanding of the relationships in crack formation, the frequent occurrence of damaging cracks in individual masonry constructions can be avoided.

Cracks in facing work as a result of shrinkage and, possibly, cooling

These vertical non-loadbearing (or notionally non-loadbearing) components try to shorten as a result of shrinkage and/or falling temperatures. Their deformation is hindered by their connections to other components. This gives rise to tensile stresses which cannot be "neutralized" by compressive stresses owing to the lack of vertical imposed load. The cracks run vertically the full height of the wall owing to the virtually horizontal tensile stresses.

Cracks can be avoided by reducing the deformation of the masonry (masonry units with more favourable shrinkage strain, good conditions while constructing the walls), by providing less resistance to deformation at the supports (intermediate pads of card or foil), and by including movement joints and non-structural bed joint reinforcement to distribute the cracks or limit their width [186] (see fig. 2.3.34).

Cracks in spandrel panels

are caused by excessive horizontal tensile stresses at the upper edge of the panel as a result of a "spreading" of the vertical compression trajectories below the opening as well as lintel support reactions introduced eccentrically. In addition, higher shrinkage tension often occurs in spandrel panels owing to the reduced cross-section and this amplifies the risk of cracking in this area. Cracks can be

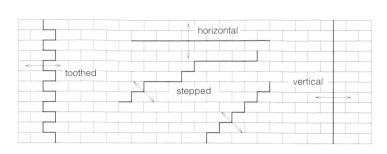

2.3.32 Fundamental forms of cracking in masonry walls

2.3.33 Cracks adjacent to openings

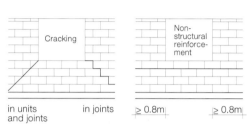

in units and joints | in joints | ≥ 0.8m | ≥ 0.8m | Compression trajectories in masonry plate | Deformation pattern (qualitative) resulting from lintel support loads introduced eccentrically

2.3.34 Cracks in facing masonry as a result of shrinkage

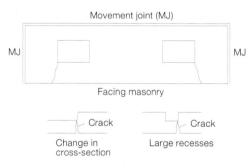

2.3.35 Horizontal cracks in external walls due to more pronounced shortening of external wall compared to internal wall

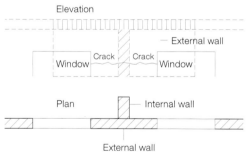

2.3.36   Cracks in external masonry walls below concrete floor/roof slabs

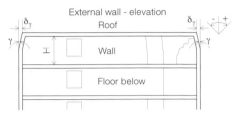
External wall - elevation

Roof

Wall

Floor below

Shortening of roof slab compared to floor below

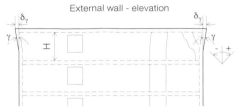
External wall - elevation

Lengthening of roof slab compared to floor below

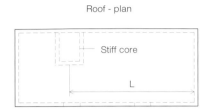
Roof - plan

Stiff core

L

avoided by providing movement joints on one or both sides to separate the spandrel panel from the rest of the wall or adjacent piers. And bed joint reinforcement included in the top of the spandrel panel helps to distribute the cracks more evenly and limit their width (fig. 2.3.33).

Diagonal cracks in an internal wall connected to an external wall
Differential vertical deformation can ensue between interconnected internal and external walls as a result of different loads or the different deformation properties of the respective masonry. As a rule, however, independent and unrestricted deformation is not possible owing to the connection between the two walls. Restricting the deformation between internal and external walls leads to tensile and shear stresses in the wall which wishes to shorten with respect to the other wall. Internal walls exhibiting severe shrinkage and creep, as well as external walls which shrink little or indeed swell, exhibit little creep and probably expand as the temperature rises lead to differential deformation between internal and external wall and hence to cracks in the internal wall. These run diagonally upwards from the external wall. The largest cracks appear in the internal walls of the topmost storey, while the lower storeys exhibit fewer and fewer cracks as the load increases (see fig. 2.3.31).
External walls of lightweight clay bricks and internal walls of calcium silicate or lightweight concrete units represent an increased risk of cracking. The cracking can be reduced by using masonry materials better able to

accommodate deformation, by employing a favourable stiffness ratio between the walls (stiff internal wall, soft external wall), by adding more load to the wall at risk of cracking and by butt-jointing (i.e. not bonding) the walls together. This last technique in particular is a good way of considerably easing the restriction to deformation – and hence the stresses – between external and internal walls.

Horizontal cracks in an external wall connected to an internal wall
For a connection that resists deformation between internal and external walls it is now the internal wall which barely shrinks (or possibly even swells) and exhibits little creep. The external wall on the other hand is severely affected by shrinkage, and contracts as a result of cooling. The severe shortening of the external wall leads to a transfer of load to the internal wall.
The external wall "hangs" on the internal wall. If in the external wall the adhesive pull strength in the bed joints between units and mortar or the tensile strength of the masonry units is exceeded, horizontal cracks occur. These are finally distributed around the junction with the internal wall; as we move further away from the internal wall the number of cracks decreases but at the same time their width increases. They tend to occur at places where the cross-section is weakened, often near openings (see fig. 2.3.35).
External walls of lightweight or autoclaved aerated concrete units and internal walls of clay bricks increase the risk of cracking. The cracking can be reduced by using masonry

materials better able to accommodate deformation, by employing a favourable stiffness ratio between the walls (soft internal wall, stiff external wall), by adding more load to the external wall vulnerable to cracking or by butt-jointing the walls together.

Cracks in external masonry walls below concrete roof slabs
Differential deformation between roof slabs and the masonry walls or floor slabs below gives rise to restraint stresses which can cause cracks in the masonry walls. Differential deformation arises mainly through the shrinkage of the concrete slab, possibly through additional swelling of the masonry, and through differential thermal expansion. However, the very well thermally insulated roof slabs common these days mean that larger temperature differences are only to be expected during construction before the thermal insulation is installed. If the roof slab shortens with respect to the external masonry walls as a result of shrinkage, then horizontal forces occur where the roof slab is supported on the top of the masonry wall. These cause shear stresses in the masonry and lead to horizontal cracks. With a good connection between roof slab and masonry, these cracks usually first appear in the second or third bed joint below the roof slab.
If the roof slab expands with respect to the external wall as a result of rising temperature, diagonal primary tensile stresses build up in the masonry, meaning a high risk of cracking owing to the low tensile strength of the masonry. This risk must be taken into account, above all during construction (see fig. 2.3.36).

2.3.37   Cracks in external masonry walls between concrete floor slabs

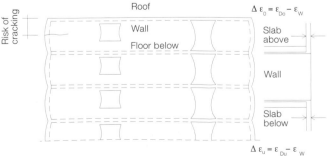
Risk of cracking

Roof

Wall

Floor below

$\Delta \varepsilon_o = \varepsilon_{Do} - \varepsilon_W$

Slab above

Wall

Slab below

$\Delta \varepsilon_u = \varepsilon_{Du} - \varepsilon_W$

Shortening of slabs compared to wall

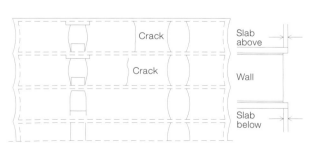
Crack

Crack

Slab above

Wall

Slab below

Shortening of wall compared to slabs

The risk of temperature-related deformation in this area can be avoided by providing good thermal insulation to the roof slab and by introducing a sliding bearing between roof slab and wall [151, 152].

Cracks in external masonry walls between concrete floor slabs
Large differences in the horizontal deformations between concrete slabs all deforming equally and the walls in between lead to cracks in the masonry because the deformation is restricted at the top and bottom of the wall.If the floor slabs shorten with respect to the wall as a result of shrinkage and, possibly, the wall simultaneously expanding as a result of a temperature rise or chemical swelling, horizontal cracks appear at half storey height in the external wall at the corners of the building, starting at the corner and running along both sides of the building, gradually tapering to zero. Such cracks can be avoided either by separating the masonry from the floor slabs at the corners by way of joints (which can subsequently be masked) or by employing reinforced concrete tie columns to link the floor slabs together at the corners of the building. If the wall shortens with respect to the floor slabs, vertical cracks form over the full height of the storey. These can be avoided by introducing vertical movement joints in the wall at a spacing of approximately twice the height of the wall (see fig. 2.3.37).

Horizontal cracks in external masonry walls as a result of floor slab deflection
Vertical loads cause the deflection of cement-bound concrete slabs as well as shrinkage and creep. A correspondingly large deflection can cause the slab to lift and twist, thereby loading the masonry eccentrically. If the vertical tensile strength of the masonry is exceeded at the same time as the vertical load on the wall is relieved, horizontal cracks in the outer face of the wall occur immediately below the floor slab, or perhaps first in the courses of masonry below this, according to the connection between slab and masonry. Owing to the lower load, this risk of cracking is prevalent beneath roof slabs and the floor slabs of the uppermost floors. At the corners of a building this pattern of horizontal cracks can also occur as a result of the lifting effect of torsionally stiff slabs. The width of the cracks decreases towards the middle of each wall. Cracks can be avoided by reducing the deflection of the slabs (limiting the slenderness ratio, cutting shrinkage and creep); increasing the depth of support for the slab on the wall; developing a better detail for the slab support (by centering the load transfer; or by separating the slab from the masonry), or by anchoring the slab to the slab below via a vertical tie (see fig.2.3.38).

Cracks in external masonry walls as a result of shrinkage of ring beams
Cracks in masonry caused by ring beam deformations are more likely to be caused by greater shrinkage of the beam compared to the masonry below than by temperature changes in today's well-insulated buildings. The deformations brought about by shrinkage of the ring beam lead to shear stresses in the masonry and, if the low shear strength of the masonry is exceeded, to horizontal cracks, which usually start in the corners of the wall owing to the shortening of the beam on two sides. However, as the cross-section of the capping beam is smaller than that of a reinforced concrete slab, the effects are usually less apparent.

Cracks in lightweight partitions
Cracks in lightweight partitions can be caused by shrinkage of the masonry in the horizontal direction or by floor slab deflection. Excessive deflection of a floor slab below a stiff partition leads to cracking as the wall tries to adapt to the changing boundary conditions: horizontal cracks at the base between wall and slab (separation), vertical and diagonal cracks in the body of the masonry wall. The cracking can be reduced by minimizing the deflection of the slab (limiting the slenderness, cutting shrinkage and creep); separating the base of the wall from the slab to force and fix the horizontal separation; providing adequate deformation opportunities at the top of the wall in order to avoid the wall being unintentionally loaded by the floor above; or by providing bed joint reinforcement, primarily at the bottom of the wall (see fig. 2.3.39).

Diagonal cracks in infill panels
The infill masonry panels within a reinforced concrete frame can exhibit diagonal cracking if there is a fixed connection between frame and masonry. This is caused by differential deformation of the components (shrinkage, chemical swelling of the masonry, heating and cooling of the frame). Separating the masonry from the reinforced concrete provides adequate opportunities for both to deform independently, and thus avoids cracking.

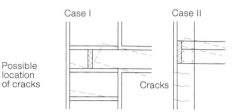

2.3.38   Horizontal cracks in external masonry walls due to deflection of floor/roof

Case I   Case II

Possible location of cracks

Cracks

Floor slab lifting off bearing on external wall as a result of deflection and lack of vertical load

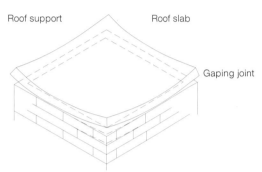

Roof support   Roof slab

Gaping joint

Roof slab lifting at corners as a result of torsional stiffness and lack of vertical load

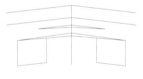

Cracking at corners

2.3.39   Formation of cracks in lightweight partitions due to deflection of floor slab

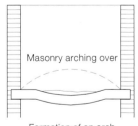

Masonry arching over

Formation of an arch

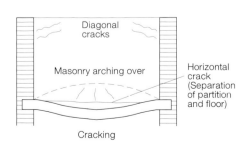

Diagonal cracks

Masonry arching over

Horizontal crack (Separation of partition and floor)

Cracking

2.3.40 Requirements to be met by perpends and bed joints in natural stone masonry

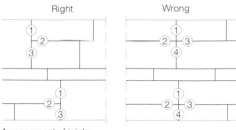

Right — Wrong

Arrangement of joints

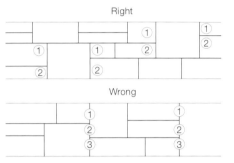

Right

Wrong

Layout of wall and cross joints within one course

2.3.41 Geometric parameters for describing the standard of workmanship of natural stone masonry

Elevation

Bed joint

Horizontal section

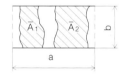

α = Inclination of bed joint
a b = Cross-sectional area of wall
$\bar{A}_1, \bar{A}_2$ = Stress transfer areas (overlap of stones)

$$\eta = \frac{\Sigma \bar{A}_i}{a \; b}$$

2.3.42 Reference values for classifying natural stone masonry (based on 2.3.41)

Class	Description	Joint height/ Stone length h/l	Inclination of bed joint tan α	Transfer factor η
N1	Uncoursed random	≤ 0.25	≤ 0.30	≥ 0.5
N2	Hammer-dressed	≤ 0.20	≤ 0.15	≥ 0.65
N3	Coursed - square	≤ 0.13	≤ 0.10	≥ 0.75
N4	Ashlar masonry	≤ 0.07	≤ 0.05	≥ 0.85

Natural stone masonry

In designing natural stone masonry we make a fundamental distinction between new building work and the repair or analysis of existing natural stone masonry. When analysing existing natural stone masonry we often find that the components cannot be verified according to today's standards. The reason for this is that our knowledge of the loadbearing and failure behaviour of natural stone masonry is still not very extensive, which results in information relating to permissible design variables lying well on the safe side. One example of this is the restriction placed on the slenderness of natural stone masonry: $h_k/d \leq 20$ according to DIN 1053 part 1. However, numerous late Gothic churches were erected with slenderness ratios up to $h_k/d = 34$! This means that when analysing the safety of existing natural stone structures we have to go well beyond the design codes and employ engineering intuition with respect to the structural systems and loadbearing behaviour of the existing constructions and the reserves of strength that may be activated.

Design
The design of natural stone masonry is currently regulated by DIN 1053 part 1 section 12. According to this, only "healthy" stone may be used for natural stone masonry. Masonry exposed to the elements without protection must be weather-resistant. Courses of natural stone are to be incorporated in the structure in such a way that this corresponds to their natural stratification, with the direction of force always at right angles to the stratification. The length of a stone should not be less than its height but not exceed 4-5 times its height. Only normal mortars of mortar groups I, II, IIa and III may be used. The minimum wall thickness for loadbearing walls is 240 mm, the minimum cross-sectional area is 1000 cm².

Bonding rules
The various types of natural stone masonry (e.g. dry walling, rubble, squared rubble, ashlar) are described in detail in "Masonry details". The following rules apply to all types of natural stone masonry in order to ensure a workable bond:

• No more than three joints should coincide on the front and rear faces.
• A perpend may not pass through more than two courses (see fig. 2.3.40).
• There should be at least one header for every two stretchers, or header and stretcher courses should alternate.
• The thickness (depth) of a header must be about 1.5 times the height of the course but at least 300 mm; the thickness (depth) of a stretcher is roughly equal to the height of the course.

• The bonding dimension (overlap) for perpends must be at least 100 mm for coursed masonry, at least 150 mm for ashlar masonry.
• The largest stones – if necessary two courses high – should be incorporated at the corners.

If voids within the masonry cannot be avoided, then these should be filled with pieces of stone surrounded by mortar. If the mortar joints are not finished flush, facing work should be pointed afterwards. Such pointed joints in faces exposed to the weather must be complete and the depth of the joint should be at least equal to the thickness of the joint. However, a depth of twice the thickness but not less than 20 mm is recommended.

Classification
Apart from the compressive strength of the units themselves, the compressive strength of the masonry depends essentially on the thickness of the joint in relation to the height of the unit, the inclination of the bed joint and the stress transfer faces between two natural stones bonded one above the other. These geometric parameters describe the standard of workmanship for natural stone masonry (see fig. 2.3.41).
DIN 1053 part 1 table 13 (see table 2.3.42) specifies reference values as average values for the geometric parameters. These allow natural stone masonry to be classified in classes N1 to N4. As a rule, the types of natural stone masonry given in table 2.3.42 correspond to the classes N1 to N4. Classifying natural stone masonry in this way is the basis for determining the basic values σ_0 for the permissible stresses.

Compressive strength of natural stones
However, stone for masonry of class N4 need only have a minimum compressive strength of 5 or 10 N/mm². Tests according to DIN EN 1926 are used to determine the compressive strengths β_{St} of units. "Healthy" natural stones can also be used without being tested for compressive strength if they can be clearly assigned to the types of rock listed in DIN 1053 part 1 table 12 (see table 2.3.45). In that case the empirical values for minimum compressive strength given in table 2.3.45 should be used for the compressive strength β_{St} of units.

Consolidation of natural stone masonry

The aim of consolidation is the re-establishment or safeguarding of the loadbearing capacity and durability of natural stone masonry. This assumes a very careful procedure in conjunction with the appropriate specialists [29, 30, 35]. Besides the partial replacement or rebuilding of components, consolidation mainly involves the following measures:

Pointing of natural stone masonry
is carried out in order to ensure the load transfer or loadbearing capacity of the masonry and to prevent water penetrating the masonry. The strength of the pointing mortar used should not be significantly higher than that of the existing mortar in order to prevent load concentrations. Furthermore, a low-shrinkage mortar should be used, which adheres well to the natural stone and exhibits similar deformation properties (modulus of elasticity, coefficient of thermal expansion α_T) to those of the stone used. The pointing mortar should not exhibit efflorescence during alternating cycles of wetting and drying, and must also have a good resistance to frost. The pointing should not create a waterproof shell because this traps water in the wall and causes the build-up of hydrostatic pressure.

Needling of natural stone masonry
Needles are incorporated as transverse reinforcement, particularly in rubble-filled masonry walls in order to create a loadbearing connection between the two skins of masonry (see fig. 2.3.43). This enables the transfer of tension and shear. The needles used are made from reinforcing bars, prestressing rods or stainless steel rods, normally 12-16 mm diameter with a rough surface to achieve a good key and hence transfer of forces. The needles are inserted into drilled holes. Grout is injected afterwards to fill any cavities within the wall.

Tying natural stone masonry with anchors
The tying of masonry by means of anchors is carried out to accommodate unbalanced horizontal forces (e.g. from vaulting) and hence to avoid large deformations and crack formation. Only high-quality prestressing or stainless steel rods are suitable for accommodating the necessary tensile forces. These are then anchored in the masonry using reinforced concrete or needling with anchor plates to spread the load and avoid a concentrated transfer of load into the natural stone masonry and hence damage to the microstructure in the area of the anchorage (see fig. 2.3.44). Care should be taken to ensure that the tension anchors are positioned not only so that the anchorage is acceptable, but also so that the anchors have adequate protection against corrosion. Ties should be either concealed, e.g. above suspended ceilings, or, if left exposed, given appropriate architectural treatment.

Grouting of voids in natural stone masonry
The injection of grout into voids within the cross-section of the wall is carried out to increase the loadbearing capacity of the natural stone masonry. When doing this it should be ensured that the strength of the grout is not significantly higher than the surrounding masonry in order to avoid unfavourable load concentrations. The grouts used are either synthetic resin (epoxy resin) or a cement suspension with fine sand. The high cost of synthetic resin means that it is economic only when the voids are small. The cement suspension is a thoroughly blended water-cement mix (mixed by propeller), which is much easier to pump and inject than normal cement mortar. In addition, it hardly mixes with water. In masonry containing gypsum the risk of swelling phenomena is avoided by using cement with a high sulphate resistance.

Reinforced masonry

Like concrete, masonry can accommodate high compressive forces but little tension. However, the tensile strength can be increased by incorporating reinforcing bars. Therefore, reinforced masonry is a form of construction which combines conventional, traditional masonry with vertical or horizontal reinforcement. Besides its use to control cracking in masonry, reinforcement is also included to provide a structurally effective means of increasing the bending strength of masonry. In doing so, the reinforcement resists the tension and the masonry the compression. For example, horizontal bed joint reinforcement is suitable for resisting loads perpendicular to the plane of the wall as a result of wind or earth pressures, even in the case of little or no vertical load (e.g. a basement wall subject to earth pressure below an outdoor terrace). Ring beams may also be provided by way of bed joint reinforcement. Instead of bed joint reinforcement, vertical reinforcement can accommodate tensile stresses perpendicular to the bed joints. However, vertical reinforcement requires the use of specials with voids to enable the reinforcement to be inserted. The inclusion of reinforcement also improves the ductility of the masonry, and hence its resistance to cracking, by increasing the deformation capacity of the component. This means that cracks appear later but are then more finely distributed and narrower. And finally, reinforcement improves the damping capacity of the masonry; this gives it a higher resistance to surge-like, horizontal loads, e.g. seismic loads. This leads to a considerable increase in the margin of safety for masonry constructions subjected to extraordinary loading effects. However, it should be pointed out that reinforced masonry alone is not sufficient to guarantee the stability of a structure during an earthquake. A series of non-structural

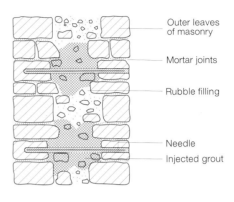

2.3.43   Needling of rubble-filled masonry wall

Outer leaves of masonry

Mortar joints

Rubble filling

Needle

Injected grout

2.3.44   Diagram of tie rod with tie plates to both ends

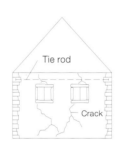

Tie rod

Crack

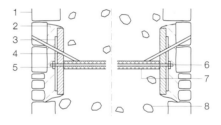

1   Facing masonry
2   Concrete filling
3   Tie plate
4   Grout injection tube
5   Clamping nut
6   Tie rod
7   Injected grout
8   Filling between masonry

2.3.45   Empirical values for the minimum compressive strength of rock types

Type of rock	Min. compressive strength MN/m²
Limestone, travertine, volcanic tuffaceous rock	20
Soft sandstones (with argillaceous material) and similar	30
Dense (firm) limestones and dolomites (including marble), basaltic lava and similar	50
Quartzitic sandstones (with siliceous material), graywacke and similar	80
Granite, syenite, diorite, quartz porphyry, melaphyre, diabase and similar	120

2.3.46 Reinforcement systems for structurally reinforced masonry to DIN 1053 part 3 [32]

System (schematic)	Designation	Applications according to certificate[1]
	Murfor reinforcing element with duplex coating	Reinforcement according to structural analysis
	Murfor stainless steel reinforcing element	Reinforcement according to structural analysis
	ELMCO-Ripp reinforcing system	Lintels in facing masonry
	MOSO perforated strip	Lintels in facing masonry

[1] See also provisions of certificate

2.3.47 Reinforcement systems without building
authority certificate [32]

Product	Description
Brictec	Ladder-type, plain stainless steel bars. Longitudinal bars d_s = 3.65 mm, element width 28 mm. Intended for use in lintel zones of facing masonry in conjunction with special supporting section. Certificate applied for.
FIXOVER	Ladder-type, reinforcing system of flattened plain stainless steel bars, cross-section of longitudinal bars corresponds to d_s = 4.0 mm. Element length 2700 mm, available in various widths. Can be used according to product information – as structural reinforcement[1] as well as non-structural widths.
GRIPPRIPP	Reinforcing fabric of aramide fibres with a mesh size of 15 x 15 mm, available in various widths. Can be used – according to product information – as structural reinforcement1) as well as non-structural reinforcement.
Murinox	Reinforcing system comprising two longitudinal bars with projecting studs, connected by diagonal wires. Various cross-sections and widths available. Intended for use as structural reinforcement as well as non-structural reinforcement. Certificate applied for.

[1] Not permitted without appropriate building authority certificate!

boundary conditions must be maintained. In regions of major seismic activity (Southern Europe, America, Japan), the use of reinforced masonry is much more widespread than in Germany, where its use is mainly limited to controlling cracking. Nevertheless, a separate code – DIN 1053 part 3 "Reinforced masonry" – was introduced in February 1990 to cover this form of construction. This standard applies to loadbearing components made from reinforced masonry and areas of masonry that include reinforcement. Individual sections of a building or component that require reinforcement for structural reasons may employ this form of construction without the remaining areas of masonry having to be designed and constructed according to DIN 1053 part 3. The use of reinforcement to distribute cracking or limit the size of cracks is not reinforced masonry in the sense of DIN 1053 part 3 because the reinforcement is not taken into account in the structural analysis. However, even for such "non-structural" reinforcement, following the requirements of the standard, in particular with regard to protecting the reinforcement against corrosion, is to be recommended. One special case is the design and construction of lintels made from reinforced masonry. After many years of positive experience with the guidelines for designing and using shallow lintels [35], both these guidelines and the provisions of DIN 1053 part 3 may be used. This is possible because the guidelines more or less agree with the provisions of DIN 1053 part 3. However, the difference between the two methods lies in the actual construction of the lintel. While the shallow lintel guidelines make use of a prefabricated tension flange – the shallow lintel itself – which acts in conjunction with a compression zone of masonry and/or concrete, according to DIN 1053 part 3 the tension flange is built from masonry units (e.g. hollow blocks for grouting), reinforcement and mortar or concrete in situ; prefabrication is not intended here.

Materials for reinforced masonry
Masonry units
Only standard units or standard specials with a percentage of perforations ≤ 35% may be used. The webs between non-round perforations along the length of the wall may not be offset with respect to each other. In addition, approved vertically perforated clay bricks with up to 50% perforations may be used provided the webs in these bricks are not offset along the length of the wall and provided the bricks exhibit a minimum compressive strength of $\beta_{DI,St} \geq 3.5$ N/mm² parallel to the bed joint. These requirements are necessary to guarantee adequate compressive strength in the direction of the axis of the wall. However, these requirements do not apply to ring anchors since the element acts as a tension member.

Apart from shape and weight, the properties of specials must conform to the standards for masonry units. Specials used in conjunction with vertical reinforcement are divided into those with "small" and those with "large" openings. Small openings must measure at least 60 mm in every direction, large openings at least 135 mm. In specials for horizontal reinforcement the height of the opening may be reduced to 45 mm owing to the addition of the bed joint mortar.
In Germany masonry units suitable for reinforced masonry must be identified on the delivery slip using the designation BM.

Mortar
Only normal mortar of mortar groups III and IIIa, i.e. cement mortar with aggregates having a dense microstructure, may be used for the mortar surrounding the reinforcement. The reason for this restriction is to ensure an adequate anchorage for the reinforcement and not to guarantee adequate protection against corrosion. The use of normal mortar of mortar group IIa and lightweight mortar LM 36 is technically possible but at present still requires a building authority certificate. The sections of masonry which do not contain any reinforcement may make use any of the mortars in DIN 1053 part 1 except normal mortar of mortar group I.

Concrete for filling openings and voids
If the openings and voids provided for the reinforcement are to be filled with concrete, the concrete used must be at least class B 15 to DIN 1045, provided that the level of corrosion protection required does not demand a higher strength class. The largest aggregates used should be retained by an 8 mm sieve.

Reinforcement, reinforcement systems
According to DIN 1053 part 3 only ribbed reinforcing bars to DIN 488 part 1 may be used to obtain adequate anchorage and control crack widths. Plain and profiled bars must always include end hooks; their use requires a building authority certificate.
The minimum diameter for individual bars is d_s = 6 mm. Bars with a smaller diameter may only be used in reinforcement systems, and then only as approved by the building authority. The maximum bar diameter depends on the application and must be chosen to ensure that there is sufficient mortar or concrete cover to the bar (see "Structural reinforced masonry"). Reinforcement systems are prefabricated reinforcing elements that differ from the ribbed individual bars of DIN 488 part 1 (e.g. smaller diameter, plain or profiled surface, mat- or lattice-like arrangements, materials other than steel). Such reinforcement systems must be covered by a building authority certificate if they are to be used for loadbearing reinforced masonry. However, when used merely to control cracking, a certificate is not required

because at present there are no regulations covering this type of use and so, in principle, any type of reinforcement may be employed. The reinforcement systems covered by building authority certificates are shown in fig. 2.3.46, those without certificates in table 2.3.47. For detailed descriptions of the systems, please refer to [60].

Protecting reinforcement against corrosion
Studies of masonry components have established that the mortar carbonates considerably faster than concrete. The causes of this are to be found in the larger pore volume brought about by the higher water/cement ratio (w/c ratio), which increases the permeability; the fact that mortar is not compacted as thoroughly as concrete; and the lack of subsequent treatment. All this gives the mortar a porous structure. The high w/c ratio is a consequence of the plastic to soft or fluid consistency of the mortar necessary for bricklaying. Carbonation means the loss of the mortar's alkali protection for the reinforcement. The reinforcement will then corrode in the presence of moisture and oxygen.

For this reason, unprotected reinforcement may be included only in the mortar joints of components permanently subjected to a dry atmosphere, e.g. internal walls of houses. In all other cases the steel must either be embedded in concrete – in which case the rules for corrosion protection in reinforced concrete structures must be adhered to – or must be protected by some other suitable measure. This might be the use of galvanized reinforcement and/or protective organic coatings. Electrogalvanizing or hot-dip galvanizing may be employed, the latter being more common for reinforcing bars. However, this produces a very brittle layer of iron-zinc alloy which can flake off when the bar is bent; so galvanized reinforcement may not be bent after galvanizing and must be protected against damage prior to being built in. And as hot-dip galvanized reinforcement is not resistant to sulphates and chlorides, the mortars and masonry units used should include only limited amounts of these constituents, which attack zinc. If sulphates and chlorides are expected in the ambient atmosphere of the masonry, hot-dip galvanized reinforcement is not permitted.

The protective organic coatings employed are mainly epoxy resin-bound systems. Reinforcement with duplex systems is also available in which the corrosion protection is achieved by galvanizing the steel and subsequently applying an epoxy resin coating. Such systems require a building authority certificate. The advantage of properly applied epoxy resin coatings compared to galvanizing is the permanent corrosion protection that they offer, even in the presence of aggressive ions. Alternatively, resistance to corrosion can be achieved by using reinforcement made from stainless steel or other materials, e.g. glass, carbon and aramide fibres. Stainless steel is very expensive – about three times the cost of galvanized reinforcement. However, it provides guaranteed protection against corrosion, even in aggressive environments. Fibres are usually used as a composite material, i.e. embedded in a matrix. Up until failure they exhibit a particularly linear load deformation behaviour and their strength is clearly superior to that of steel. The moduli of elasticity of glass and aramide fibres reach about 40% that of steel, while carbon fibres have a modulus of elasticity comparable to that of steel. Their use is, however, still at the development stage and, in particular, their long-term behaviour in conjunction with concrete and mortar must be investigated.

Structural reinforced masonry
Position of reinforcement and design
The design and construction of reinforced masonry must follow very closely the techniques for erecting conventional masonry in order to achieve adequate economy for this type of construction. First, we must consider how the reinforcement is to be placed. According to DIN 1053 part 3, horizontal reinforcement may be laid in the bed joint, in specials or in trough-shaped specials; vertical reinforcement may be inserted into specials with large or small openings and into cavities or voids enclosed by masonry. Continuous cavities require the leaves of masonry to be tied together with wall ties or similar. Possible reinforcement arrangements are shown in fig. 2.3.48. These illustrations also contain details of the mortar, concrete and reinforcement used.
To ease erection, masonry units with recesses in the sides are preferred because they can be placed around the reinforcement. Voids within the masonry unit mean that the units have to be threaded onto the vertical reinforcement. Long reinforcing bars slow down the erection of masonry. The size of the void or cavity has an effect on the filling with concrete or mortar. With small openings having side lengths between 60 and 135 mm, the filling and compacting must be carried out for every course, while larger openings must be filled after every 1 m of wall height.The design and construction of reinforced masonry should also take into account the following points:

- Walls for reinforced masonry must be ≥ 115 mm thick.
- Bed joints must always be filled completely with mortar. Likewise perpends when the wall and the reinforcement spans horizontally. Brick to brick and perpends without mortar are permitted when the wall and the reinforcement spans vertically.
- Bed joints containing reinforcement may be up to 20 mm thick in order to achieve good

2.3.48 Positioning of reinforcement with min. dimensions in millimetres according to DIN 1053 part 3

Horizontal reinforcement

a) Bed joint

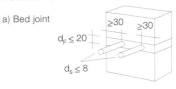

NM III, NM IIIa

b) Specials

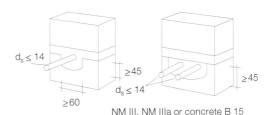

NM III, NM IIIa or concrete B 15

Cover
Mortar: ≥ 2d_s to all sides
≥ 30 mm to face of wall
Concrete: to DIN 1045

Vertical reinforcement

a) Small openings, specials

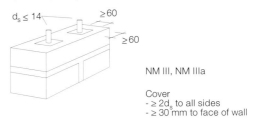

NM III, NM IIIa

Cover
- ≥ 2d_s to all sides
- ≥ 30 mm to face of wall

b) Large openings, specials

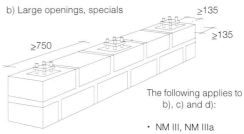

The following applies to b), c) and d):

- NM III, NM IIIa or concrete ≥ B 15
- Cover
  - Mortar: ≥ 2d_s to all sides
  - ≥ 30 mm to face of wall
  - Concrete: to DIN 1045
- Max. bar diameter:
  - Mortar: 14 mm
  - Concrete: to DIN 488 part 1

c) Void enclosed by masonry

d) Continuous cavity

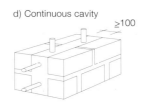

2.3.49 Requirements for and restrictions on reinforced masonry to DIN 1053 part 3

	Horizontal reinforcement			Vertical reinforcement		
	in bed joints	in specials		in specials with small openings	in specials with large openings or in voids/cavities between masonry	
Filling material	Mortars of groups III or IIIa	Mortars of groups III or IIIa	Concrete ≥ B 15	Mortars of groups III or IIIa	Mortars of groups III or IIIa	Concrete ≥ B 15
Filling to vertical openings	–			in every course	at least after every 1 m of wall height	
Max. bar diameter	8	14	14	14	14	to DIN 488 pt 1
Cover	≥ 30 mm to face of wall	≥ 2d_s to all sides ≥ 30 mm to face of wall	to DIN 1045	≥ 2d_s to all sides ≥ 30 mm to face of wall		to DIN 1045
Corrosion protection — in permanently dry conditions	No special requirements			No special requirements		
Corrosion protection — in all other conditions	Hot-dip galvanizing or other permanent measures[1]		to DIN 1045	Hot-dip galvanizing or other permanent measures[1]		to DIN 1045
Min. thickness of reinforced masonry [mm]	115					

[1] Serviceability is to be verified by, for example, a general building authority certificate.

embedment of the reinforcement. As a guideline, bed joint thickness should be twice the bar diameter.
• Bars up to 8 mm diameter may be laid in bed joints, up to 14 mm diameter in recesses and voids. This restriction is determined by the possible anchorage effect within the mortar. Diameters > 14 mm are permitted only in voids and recesses filled with concrete.
• The concrete cover to unprotected reinforcement in voids and recesses filled with concrete should be at least equal to that recommended for reinforced concrete construction.
• The distance between the surface of a reinforcing bar and the face of the wall must be > 30 mm in order to guarantee adequate anchorage.
• The mortar cover to reinforcement in specials must be twice the diameter of the bar on all sides.
• Reinforcement to a bay is to be laid over the full span and not staggered.
• Reinforcement that crosses may only be max. 5 mm diameter, otherwise special measures (e.g. specials) are necessary.
• Walls reinforced horizontally require at least four reinforcing bars per metre of wall height with at least every second bed joint being reinforced.
The requirements and restrictions concerning reinforced masonry are outlined in table 2.3.49.

The design of reinforced masonry to DIN 1053 part 3
The design of reinforced masonry to resist bending, and bending combined with axial forces is similar to the design of reinforced concrete to DIN 1045. The reinforcement placed in the tension zone resists the tensile stresses, which are in equilibrium with the compressive stresses in the compression zone. The stress distribution in the compression zone is assumed to be parabolic-rectangular – any tensile strength available in the masonry is ignored. In contrast to reinforced concrete design, the maximum compressive strain of the masonry is $|\varepsilon_{mw}| \leq 2.0‰$, and maximum strain in the reinforcement $\varepsilon_s \leq 5.0‰$.
The slenderness ratio l/d of members subjected to bending may not be greater than 20 in order to limit deflection. In the case of wall-like (i.e. deep) beams, the useful structural height must be $h \leq 0.5l$, where l = span, otherwise it must be designed as a plate.
The cross-section for design is the loadbearing masonry including voids and recesses filled with mortar or concrete. The characteristic value β_R for determining the compressive bending force that can be carried by the reinforced masonry is to be determined according to DIN 1053 part 1 or 2. β_R is used in the direction of the perforations, but reduced by 50% perpendicular to the perforations (along the length of the wall) for perforated solid units and other perforated units to allow for the anisotropy and hence the considerably lower compressive strength in this direction.

However, β_R is not reduced for solid units. In the case of filled voids and recesses, the smallest characteristic value – β_R of masonry or filling – is to be used for the entire cross-section:

- filling of MG III: $\beta_R = 4.5$ N/mm²
- filling of MG IIIa: $\beta_R = 10.5$ N/mm²
- filling of concrete: β_R to DIN 1045

Concrete above the masonry may also be incorporated but the smaller β_R value must always be applied in the analysis. On the other hand, masonry on top of concrete may not be used to help resist the compression.
Aids for designing reinforced masonry to resist bending, taking into account the requirements outlined here, are given in [40] and [128]. The anchorage of the reinforcement is to be checked according to DIN 1045. However, the permissible basic values for bond stress perm τ_1 given in 2.3.50 apply to reinforcing bars laid in mortar.
When designing reinforced masonry to resist shear forces, we must distinguish between loads in the plane of the wall (plate shear) and those perpendicular to the plane of the wall (slab shear). The existing shear stress is determined from

$$\text{exist } t = Q_s / (b \times z)$$

where Q_s = critical shear force applied at 0.5 x h (useful height of beam) from edge of support, and z = inner lever arm.

For plate shear on a compressed cross-section it is sufficient to examine the position of maximum shear stress, but for cracked cross-sections an analysis must be carried out at the height of the neutral axis in condition II. In both cases it must be ensured that the existing shear stress exist t ≤ perm t.
The value for perm τ is determined according to the more accurate method of analysis in DIN 1053 part 1. The calculated axial stress σ in the bed joints may be estimated from the support reaction F_A, the width of the cross-section b and the span l of the deep beam from

$$\sigma = F_A / (b \times l)$$

This is certainly on the safe side.
For slab shear the analysis is similar to that for reinforced concrete but here only shear zone 1 is permitted. Accordingly, it has to be proved that

$$\text{exist } \tau \le \tau_{011} = 0.015 \, \beta_R$$

The effect of shear reinforcement may not be taken into account. The β_R value is determined according to DIN 1053 part 1 or 2 and may also be applied to perforated solid units and other perforated units – irrespective of the

direction of the stress – over the full height. An analysis of buckling only has to be carried out in the case of compression members. The slenderness ratio $\lambda = h_K/d$ is determined according to the simplified or more accurate method of analysis in DIN 1053 part 1.
The buckling analysis does not need to be carried out for stocky members with slenderness ratios $\lambda \le 5.75$. An analysis of the stress is carried out in the middle third of the buckling length without taking into account additional eccentricity.
Compression members with moderate slenderness ratios ($5.75 < \lambda \le 20$) must take into account the risk of buckling due to unintentional eccentricity and deflection according to second order theory using the additional eccentricity $f = h_K/46 - d/6$ when analysing the stress in the middle third of the buckling length. Buckling must be checked according to DIN 1045 for compression members with large slenderness ratios ($20 < \lambda \le 25$). Slenderness ratios $\lambda > 25$ are not permitted.

Minimum reinforcement
To avoid wide cracks, minimum amounts of reinforcement are necessary. The required minimum amounts of reinforcement – related to the total cross-section – purely for loading are given in table 2.3.51.

Non-structural reinforcement
Reinforcement may be used in masonry construction purely to control crack widths. In contrast to reinforced concrete construction, this reinforcement does not play a loadbearing or structural role. Therefore, DIN 1053 part 3 does not deal with this type of reinforcement. It is important to point out that freedom from cracks in masonry is achieved only by including suitably designed and adequately spaced movement joints. Non-structural reinforcement does not prevent the formation of cracks in masonry. Its task is to distribute the inevitable restraint deformations over several cracks and hence limit the widths of those cracks. This is not necessary for stability but rather to guarantee, in particular, the serviceability (e.g. thermal and acoustic insulation, moisture control, frost resistance) and aesthetics of the masonry element.
The influence of cracks on corrosion of the reinforcement can be ignored because of the necessary measures taken to prevent corrosion. The durability of external masonry elements with respect to moisture protection and thermal insulation is generally not adversely affected by crack widths w ≤ 0.20 mm, although driving rain can penetrate the facade even with crack widths w < 0.1 mm. However, limiting cracks to this very small width is hardly possible under practical conditions, but is hardly necessary because the water does not damage the facade [183].

2.3.50 Permissible basic values for bond stress perm τ_1 for ribbed reinforcing bars to DIN 488 part 1

Mortar group	Basic value of τ_1 in bed joint	in specials and openings
	MN/m²	MN/m²
III	0.35	1.0
III a	0.70	1.4

2.3.51 Minimum reinforcement to DIN 1053 part 3 for pure loading and reinforcing steels BSt 420 S and BSt 500 S

Position of main reinforcement	Min. reinforcement, related to total cross-section	
	main bars min μ_H	transverse bars min μ_Q
Horizontal, in bed joints or openings	at least 4 No. 6 mm dia. bars per m	–
Vertical, in openings of specials and in voids within masonry	0.1%	if $\mu_H < 0.5\%$ then $\mu_Q = 0$ Interpolate intermediate values if $\mu_H > 0.6\%$ then $\mu_Q = 0.2 \, \mu_H$
In continuous cavities between masonry	0.1%	0.2 μ_H

2.3.52 Examples of applications for non-structural reinforcement in masonry

Cracking without reinforcement	Position of reinforcement to suit possible cracking

Door opening

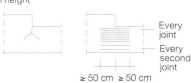
Every joint
Every second joint
≥ 80 cm

Window opening

Every joint
≥ 80 cm

Change in height

Every joint
Every second joint
≥ 50 cm ≥ 50 cm

Under concentrated load

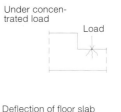
Load

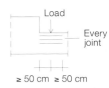
Load
Every joint

≥ 50 cm ≥ 50 cm

Deflection of floor slab

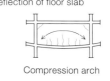

Soft joint

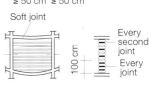
Every second joint
Every joint
100 cm

Compression arch

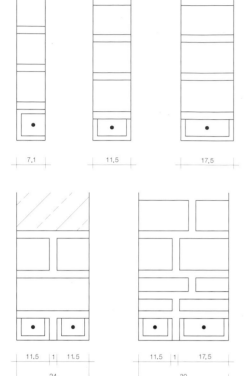

2.3.53   Sections through shallow lintels with tension
flanges of trough-shaped masonry units;
structural behaviour of shallow lintel.

7.1   11.5   17.5

11.5 | 11.5   11.5 | 17.5
24   30

Compression
zone

Tension
flange

17.5   17.5
36.5

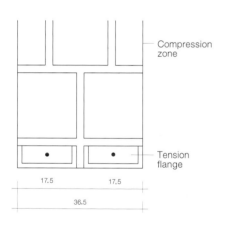

P   P   Frame
                     (in compression)

Tension flange

a

$\frac{\text{max } M}{z}$

z

$\frac{\text{max } M}{z}$

A = max Q

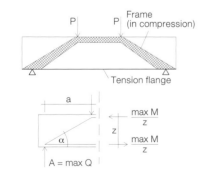

D

α H = $\frac{\text{max } M}{z}$

max Q

D   max Q
α

H = $\frac{\text{max } M}{z}$

Specifying a maximum crack width in masonry
elements that is acceptable from an aesthetic
point of view is very difficult because this crack
width depends to a large extent on the subjec-
tive opinion of the observer and also on the
distance of the observer from the cracked element.
Non-structural reinforcement should limit the
average crack width w_m in readily accessible
reinforced masonry elements to about 0.1-
0.3 mm to comply with aesthetic considerations. However, it is important to establish right
from the very start just what demands are to be
placed on the appearance of individual components (e.g. facing brickwork or exhibition
surfaces) and whether hairline cracks – above
all in relation to the surface finish – can be
accepted [60].

*The possible applications of masonry with non-
structural reinforcement*
Limiting the widths of cracks as a result of
restraint stresses (shrinkage, thermal, floor slab
deflection, differential settlement etc.) is really
only possible by including reinforcement in the
bed joints of the masonry. This reinforcement
resists mainly horizontal but also slightly
inclined restraint stresses.
The inclusion of bed joint reinforcement
appears to be advisable wherever cracks can
occur but cannot reliably be predicted. Thus,
possible damage and expensive repairs can
be avoided from the very start. Furthermore,
the appearance is not unnecessarily impaired
by an excessive number of movement joints.
Typical applications are the corners around
door and window openings, as well as at
changes in height, beneath concentrated loads
and non-loadbearing partitions in conjunction
with slab deflections (see "Cracks in lightweight partitions"). The causes of cracks at
corners are, above all, diverted vertical compressive stresses, increased shrinkage stresses as a result of the reduction in cross-section
adjacent openings, changes in height and
stress concentrations in the corners [177]. The
areas below concentrated loads are subjected
to increased transverse tensile stresses parallel to the bed joints which must be resisted by
non-structural reinforcement (see 2.3.52).
Another possible application for non-structural
bed joint reinforcement is in facing work and
infill panels. This helps to avoid cracks caused
by restraint to the differential deformation
between leaves of facing masonry or infill panels and loadbearing members caused by
shrinkage and/or temperature differences as
well as possible additional lateral support or
adhesion at the base of the wall.

*Minimum non-structural reinforcement to resist
restraint stresses*
The minimum amount of reinforcement in
masonry must be chosen in such a way that
when a crack occurs, the tensile stresses can

be accommodated by the reinforcement without its yield stress being reached. This avoids
wide cracks in masonry and also limits the
crack width to a dimension acceptable in terms
of both serviceability and appearance.
In the case of restraint stresses with a risk of
very wide cracks, DIN 1053 part 3 recom-
mends reinforcement equal to at least 0.2% of
the total cross-section in the direction of the
restraint.
Based on newer findings, Meyer [135] recom-
mends the following guidelines for minimum
reinforcement to limit crack width:

• central restraint:
$$\mu_{s,min} = 0.25\%$$

• bending restraint, perpends filled with mortar:
$$\mu_{s,min} = 0.15\%$$

• bending restraint, perpends not filled with
mortar:
$$\mu_{s,min} = 0.10\%$$

The amount of reinforcement specified is related to the total cross-section in the direction of
the restraint and takes into account most
unfavourable unit/mortar combinations. So in
some cases these figures are on the safe side.
More accurate approaches to assessing the
amount of reinforcement are given in [135].

Shallow lintels
Shallow lintels are bending members spanning
over openings for doors and windows. They
may be designed and constructed according
to DIN 1053 part 3 or the guidelines covering
shallow lintels [35].
Shallow lintels consist of a prefabricated or in-
situ reinforced tension flange. They achieve
their loadbearing capacity by acting in conjunction with the compression zone of masonry
or concrete (or both) above the lintel.
The prefabricated tension flange can be made
from trough-shaped masonry units (specials)
matching the material of the surrounding
masonry and containing tension reinforcement
embedded in concrete, or from normal-weight
or lightweight reinforced concrete. The in-situ
tension flange is usually made from a soldier
course with reinforcement fed through the perforations in the units. In practice, however, the
prefabricated shallow lintel employing specials
has become established, mainly owing to its
building science and operational advantages
(e.g. the avoidance of thermal bridges thanks
to the use of uniform wall materials, faster construction thanks to prefabrication and simple
erection, uniform substrate for plastering) (see
fig. 2.3.53).
The reinforcement in the tension flange is not
normally prestressed but may be if required.
The structural action of a shallow lintel corresponds to that of a tied frame, i.e. the tension

forces in the lintel are transferred to the tension flange (tie), while the compression zone (frame) is formed by the masonry above the lintel. A compression zone consisting of masonry and concrete above that may not call upon any further masonry above the concrete to assist in resisting the compression. In transferring the load to the supports, the "struts" place shear loads on the masonry supports. Depending on the angle of the struts, failure of the bed joints or failure of the units is possible. Aids for designing and constructing shallow lintels are given in [128] and [145].

Prestressed masonry

A further development of reinforced masonry is prestressed masonry. The possible applications include the prestressing of existing masonry as well as the prestressing of new structural masonry. In the former, prestressing (i.e. post-tensioning) is used to repair cracks when injection and needling are not adequate (see "Consolidation of natural stone masonry"). Vertical or diagonal cracks are repaired by using horizontal prestressing tendons. Gaping bed joints caused by eccentric loading can be closed again by installing vertical prestressing tendons. With new structural masonry the prestressing is introduced as the wall is erected (i.e. pretensioning). To do this, the prestressing tendons are integrated in vertical ducts in the wall at a spacing of 1.0-2.5 m. Special masonry units or hollow blocks are necessary to form the ducts. The ducts can be left open or subsequently filled with grout.

When the ducts are left open, the prestressing tendon remains accessible for checking, further stressing and replacement. Protection against corrosion is ensured by a coating of grease in conjunction with a polyethylene sheath. In ducts that are not left open, corrosion protection is ensured by the grout injected into the ducts. This creates a shear-resistant connection between masonry and prestressing tendon and ensures the uniform transfer of the prestressing force into the masonry to prevent sudden failure of the end anchorage.

Structural masonry is often prestressed when masonry carries only light vertical loads, but at the same time can be subjected to horizontal loads in and perpendicular to the plane of the wall, e.g. earth pressure, wind or seismic loads. The prestressing compensates for the lack of vertical load and hence considerably increases the bending and shear strength of the wall as well as providing better insurance against cracking. This method of construction can be used for shear and gable walls, for infill panels in frames and for basement walls. Prestressed masonry contributes to increasing the stiffness of masonry construction in structures located in regions of seismic activity. By using prefabricated masonry elements, this form of construction can be employed to facilitate transport and erection as well as the use of dry walling.

Prestressed masonry has been used in the UK since about 1960; design is covered by BS 5628 part 2. In the meantime, the Swiss have also had experience of this type of construction, reflected in their standard SIA V 177 "Masonry". Prestressed masonry can also be designed according to Eurocode EC 6. The provisions are based on BS 5628 part 2 and on Eurocode EC 2. The corresponding sections for prestressed masonry have not been included in the German document covering the application of EC 6 (NAD). Likewise, the German masonry standards do not contain any design rules for prestressed masonry. Therefore, in Germany there is no acknowledged set of engineering rules for the design and construction of prestressed masonry.

Furthermore, there is currently no general building authority certificate to regulate the use of this type of construction. The reason is lack of experience, both experimental and practical, in dealing with prestressed masonry [56, 65, 158].

Prefabricated masonry elements

The production of prefabricated masonry elements under factory conditions is an elaborate technique, which has undergone major development in recent years so that traditional masonry construction can continue to compete with other forms of construction. Prefabricated masonry elements can be employed wherever conventional masonry would otherwise be used. The main reason for using prefabricated masonry are the economic advantages. These include rational and inexpensive factory production, shorter on-site times as a result of exact scheduling of prefabrication, delivery and erection, thus speeding up progress on site, less extensive site facilities, a shorter period of noise and dirt on site, wall construction unaffected by weather conditions, and finally the guarantee of a fixed price. Factory production also results in a high-quality product with fewer flaws, and means that the masonry delivered to site is normally already dry and so no longer needs time to dry out later. However, there are also disadvantages to prefabricated construction, such as the need for precise advance planning or heavy lifting equipment for erection, and problems in accommodating subsequent alterations. On the whole, construction using prefabricated masonry elements is to be recommended only when it leads to better quality at a lower price than masonry erected conventionally on the building site.

This calls for improved products and – in the light of high wages – better productivity in the factory. In practice this means the increasing use of partial or fall automation.

Prefabricated masonry elements are covered by DIN 1053 part 4. This standard mainly applies to storey-height, bay-wide prefabricated panels and the structures erected from these. Besides design guidance it also contains methods for assessing stability during transport, erection and in the final condition, as well as detailed requirements concerning transport and erection of such components to prevent damage and ensure safety.

Prefabricated masonry elements can be produced as brickwork panels, cast panels and composite panels. Brickwork panels are made from masonry units and mortar manufactured vertically as a one-brick-thick wall. Cast panels are made from clay bricks to DIN 4159 and concrete cast on horizontal formwork. Reinforcing bars are included to accommodate tensile stresses. These are placed in ribs or recesses in the bricks and embedded in concrete. Cast panels can be made as vertically perforated panels, with bricks whose perpends are filled with mortar, or as ribbed panels, with bricks whose perpends are partly filled. Composite panels are manufactured horizontally from hollow bricks to DIN 278 with profiled outer walls connected by vertical, reinforced concrete ribs and plates (fig. 2.3.54) [18].

Materials
Masonry units
Any of the masonry units in DIN 1053 part 1 may be used for constructing brickwork panels. Cast panels make use of clay bricks for prefabricated wall panels according to DIN 4159. A distinction must be made here between clay bricks with full mortar joints and partial mortar joints. The difference between the two types lies in the perpend recesses along the length of the brick. This establishes the theoretically usable cross-section when assessing the stability of cast panels (see "Design of cast panels").

Profiled hollow bricks to DIN 278 should be used for composite panels.

2.3.54   Brickwork panel, cast panel (vertically perforated panel) and composite panel

Bay-wide brickwork panel with minimum reinforcement

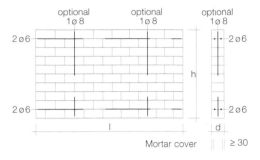

Vertically perforated panel with clay bricks for full mortar vertical joints

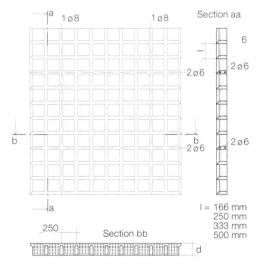

Composite panel with hollow clay bricks and minimum reinforcement

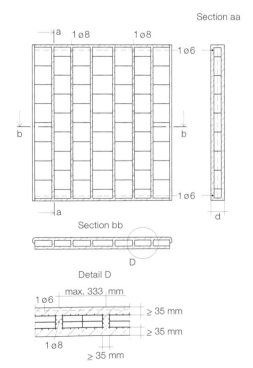

Concrete and mortar
Normal-weight or lightweight concrete should be used for cast and composite panels. Mortars according to DIN 1053 part 1, apart from normal mortars of mortar groups I and II, may be used for producing brickwork panels and for the vertical joints between individual brickwork panels.

Production
Cast and composite panels are manufactured horizontally, sometimes in moulds.
Vertical production is prescribed for brickwork panels. The requirements of DIN 1053 part 1 are to be observed here.
The production of prefabricated elements must take place under cover and the ambient temperature must be at least +5°C. During storage, until the prefabricated elements have hardened adequately, the conditions must be such that neither the adhesion between mortar or concrete and masonry units nor the microstructure of the mortar is adversely affected or disrupted. The production and transport conditions must be adhered to in order to guarantee not only the loadbearing capacity but also adequate safety during transport and erection of the components.

Design
The design of brickwork panels and cast panels is based on DIN 1053 part 1 with the additional provisions of DIN 1053 part 4. Composite panels are designed like reinforced concrete elements to DIN 1045.

Basis for design
Prefabricated masonry elements are predominantly storey-height units, which must be held in position top and bottom by beams or other equivalent structural measures, e.g. stiffening floor plates. The minimum width of the component must be 1.25 m. For brickwork panels and cast panels the minimum component, and hence wall, thickness is 115 mm; the requirements of DIN 1045 apply to composite panels. The provisions of DIN 1053 part 1 apply with respect to determining the cross-section based on loading (support reactions from floors, node and wall moments), the influence of restraints, the assessment of three-dimensional stability, determination of the buckling length of walls and allowing for openings in walls. This is also valid for the assumptions applying to shear walls. In addition, it should be remembered that return walls on one side may be assumed to constitute an immovable lateral support only when there is a tension- and compression-resistant connection between the wall requiring support and the wall acting as the support. Walls supported on three or four sides are only those walls formed by bay-wide prefabricated components. In this case the vertical ends

must have a shear-resistant connection, which must be verified. Walls comprising several brickwork panels assembled to form a wall the width of the bay are always considered to be supported on just two sides.

Design of brickwork panels
The analysis of brickwork panels for compression and shear is carried out according to DIN 1053 part 1. To assess the interaction of several adjacent brickwork panels in one plane, an additional analysis of the shear in the vertical joints between the individual panels must be carried out. The permissible shear stresses perm τ_v in the vertical joints may be taken as 0.09 MN/m² for mortars MG IIa, LM 21 and LM 36, and as 0.11 MN/m² for MG III, MG IIIa and DM. The shear area is the cross-section of panel height and width of mortar joint, i.e. the thickness of the wall for a fully filled joint. The permissible shear stress in the vertical panel joint may not be higher than the permissible shear stress in the panel itself.
For brickwork panels loaded at right-angles to the plane of the wall, the tensile bending strength of walls comprising several panels assembled to form a wall the width of the bay may not be taken into account. For such a loading case, only the loadbearing capacity at right angles to the bed joints and excluding the tensile bending strength (vertical compression arch with cracked joints) may be assumed. Only the tensile bending strength parallel to the bed joint according to DIN 1053 part 1 may be used for bay-wide brickwork panels. The requirements of DIN 1053 part 3 should be followed when designing and constructing prefabricated panels of reinforced brickwork.

Design of cast panels
The design of masonry made from cast panels depends on the magnitude of the eccentricity of the axial force.
Low eccentricities (e/d ≤ 0.33) may be designed for compression according to DIN 1053 part 1 using the basic value σ_o for permissible compressive stress given in table 2.3.55 in relation to masonry unit and concrete strength classes. The design cross-section for vertically perforated panels is the full cross-section, for ribbed panels the mortar-filled compression zone of the concrete ribs plus the adjacent brickwork up to a width of 12.5 mm on both sides (see fig. 2.3.56).

High eccentricities (e/d > 0.33) require an analysis of compression and shear according to DIN 1045. The tensile stresses occurring in the cross-section are to be resisted by reinforcement laid parallel to the direction of the perforations. The panels should be considered as one-way spanning. Only clay bricks of strength classes 18 and 24 in conjunction with concrete grades according to 2.3.55 may be used. Slenderness ratios $s_k/d > 20$ are not

2.3.55 Basic values σ_0 for permissible compressive stresses in cast panels

Strength class of		Basic value σ_0 for permissible compressive stress on calculated cross-section MN/m^2
concrete	clay brick	
Lightweight concrete LB 10	6	1.2
	8 1.4	
	12	1.7
Normal-weight B 15/B 25	6	1.2/1.2
	8	1.6/1.7
	12	2.0/2.2
	18	3.0/3.3
	24	3.5/4.4
Normal-weight B 35	30	4.7
	36	5.0

2.3.56 Calculated cross-section (shaded area) for cast panels

Vertically perforated panels with clay bricks for full mortar joints

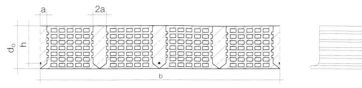

Ribbed panels with clay bricks for partial mortar joints

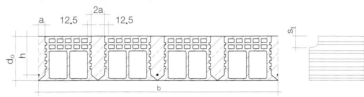

permitted. When analysing shear, the permissible shear stress perm $\tau = 0.005\,\beta_{NSt}$ may be used irrespective of the concrete strength class. β_{NSt} is in this case the strength class of the clay bricks. The value for permissible shear stress is also valid for the vertical joints between individual cast panels. In cases of pure bending, the regulations for clay hollow pot floors to
DIN 1045 or DIN 1045 part 100 are applicable.

Design of composite panels
The design and construction of composite panels is carried out according to DIN 1045. Only the cross-section of the concrete may be considered in the design.

Seismic design
As buildings made from prefabricated masonry elements are not covered by DIN 4149 part 1, seismic considerations are dealt with in DIN 1053 part 4. The requirements of DIN 4149 part 1 apply to brickwork panels as well as composite and cast panels in earthquake zones 1-4. In addition, an analysis is always required for cast panels, which are sensitive to shear loads, when used in earthquake zones 3 and 4.

Safety during transport and erection
Prefabricated masonry elements must be manufactured in such a way that no damage is likely when they are transported and erected properly. The requirements for the transport and erection loading cases are satisfied when the prefabricated components are manufactured according to DIN 1053 part 4, the rules appertaining to safety and health risks when building with prefabricated masonry elements [48] are observed, and the components are moved using the proper lifting and transport devices. These can take the form of reinforcing bars in grouted vertical channels, loadbearing bolts or slings. In all cases the loadbearing capacity of the lifting arrangement and the distribution of the lifting loads within the component must be verified.
Temporary erection conditions must be catered for by including at least two supports in the upper third of the component to prevent it from falling over.

Masonry in earthquake zones

The behaviour of masonry walls under seismic loads is of fundamental importance for construction work in earthquake zones. Besides carrying vertical loads, in most structures masonry walls also stabilize the entire structure. Therefore, during an earthquake their stability determines whether a building collapses or remains standing. In Germany the design of masonry subjected to seismic loads is currently covered by DIN 4149 part 1 in conjunction with DIN 1053 parts 1-4. In future this will be replaced by Eurocode EC 8 in conjunction with the associated National Application Document DIN 4149 part 1 [45]. Besides designing the walls to cope with horizontal seismic loads, it is essential that the building is planned according to seismic principles. The most important fundamental rule for such design is the minimization of the weight of the building to reduce the horizontal forces induced by acceleration. Furthermore, the floor slabs and foundations must form plates without changes in height if possible so that the horizontal forces are distributed evenly to the shear walls, and so that the walls are adequately held top and bottom. It is important here to ensure that the floors are properly built into the masonry and correctly supported. If it is not possible to construct horizontal plates, rigid ring beams must be provided to support the walls at top and bottom. The masonry shear walls must be evenly distributed so that the centre of gravity of the mass of the building is as close as possible to the centre of gravity of the shear walls in order to prevent additional loads being introduced into the

walls through torsion. Finally, the masonry plates must be carried down to the foundations in a consistent manner. Transfer structures and large openings cause the flow of forces to be diverted and can create "soft" storeys which are particularly vulnerable to dynamic loading. The use of reinforced masonry increases the ductile deformation capacity of masonry and is to be recommended. In particular, wall junctions and openings benefit from the inclusion of horizontally and vertically reinforced masonry, and this makes a major contribution to stabilizing the construction.
In the case of infill masonry panels, we must distinguish between partially loadbearing and non-loadbearing. The fixings of partially loadbearing panels must guarantee to transfer horizontal loads even after several loading cycles. The wall must be sized according to the effective compression and shear stresses. For the non-loadbearing panels the stability perpendicular to the plane of the wall, as well as the unrestricted deformability of the loadbearing framework, must be guaranteed. For a more detailed discussion of the design and construction of masonry subjected to seismic loads, please refer to [69, 125, 159, 220].

Masonry details

Konrad Zilch, Martin Schätz

Walls are not only enclosing, decorative elements. They also have major structural and building science functions to perform. In terms of structure, we distinguish between loadbearing, stiffening and non-loadbearing walls. Loadbearing walls carry vertical and horizontal loads and transfer these to the subsoil. Stiffening walls in the form of shear walls guarantee the load-carrying capacity of the building, and in the form of crosswalls or return walls provide lateral support to prevent the buckling of loadbearing walls. Therefore, they are always considered as loadbearing walls.

Non-loadbearing walls generally only carry their own weight and have merely an enclosing function. They are not called upon to assist in stabilizing the building or to provide support to other loadbearing walls. However, non-loadbearing walls must be able to transfer horizontal loads perpendicular to the face of the wall to loadbearing members.

The building science functions of the wall are thermal (insulation and heat storage), sound insulation, fire protection and protection against driving rain. Special requirements that may need to be fulfilled by a wall are protection against water (both pressurized and non-pressurized), e.g. basement walls, and security functions (external walls of certain buildings), e.g. banks, military establishments. The many demands placed on walls can lead to conflicts of interest, which can be solved only through careful detailing and selection of materials. Basically, the following criteria apply when choosing the type of masonry:

For facing work the decisive factors are the surface finish and the strength of the units or their frost resistance and resistance to mechanical damage and saturation. External walls, on the other hand, are primarily chosen depending on thermal requirements, while for internal walls it is sound insulation and load-carrying capacity that influence our choice. When selecting the type of wall and type of material, other aspects such as weight, opportunities for rationalization on site and the costs of materials and construction have to be considered [32, 71, 91, 41, 161].

External walls

External walls must be designed and built so that they withstand driving rain. This requirement is mandatory for all buildings occupied more or less permanently by people. External walls are divided into single- and twin-leaf walls. The single-leaf wall consists of just one wall of masonry, whereas the twin-leaf wall consists of two parallel walls up to 150 mm apart, joined together with wall ties. As a rule, only the inner leaf is loadbearing. From a thermal point of view, external walls are divided into single- and double- or multi-layer wall constructions. The masonry of a single-layer wall is like that of a single-leaf wall, but apart from carrying the loads also fulfils the necessary thermal requirements. The double- or multi-layer wall is a loadbearing construction but the masonry fulfils only part of the thermal requirements. The other layers are made from materials that generally only contribute to the thermal insulation, e.g. single-leaf external wall with thermal insulation plastering system.

Single-leaf external walls

The design of single-leaf external walls is these days determined mainly by thermal requirements. According to DIN 1053 part 1, the minimum thickness for a single-leaf external wall is 115 mm. The wall constructions commonly in use are illustrated in fig. 2.4.1. The regulations on thermal insulation have led to the development of different solutions to comply with those regulations. So the single-leaf monolithic external wall with ever better thermal insulation values for the masonry and mortar will continue to be favoured for certain applications. And the use of insulating plasters will also help to secure the use of monolithic masonry. Adding a layer of insulation to the loadbearing masonry allows external walls to satisfy practically all demands. Only in the case of curtain wall facades do we have to consider the additional heat losses via the wall ties between wall and facade.

Plastered single-leaf external walls
are built without additional layers of thermal insulation and are provided with a coat of plaster on the inside and water-repellent rendering on the outside. The rendering prevents moisture from penetrating the masonry and subsequently freezing, and permits the use of non-frost-resistant masonry units. In order to comply with the strict thermal insulation requirements and, at the same time, avoid unjustifiably thick walls, which although satisfying building science demands are usually too expensive in terms of construction and consumption of valuable space. Such walls only use masonry units with very good thermal insulation properties (e.g. aerated lightweight clay, autoclaved aerated concrete, lightweight hollow concrete blocks, the formation of voids, cells and slots, masonry without mortar to the perpends) in conjunction with thermal insulation plasters or plastering systems.

Table 2.4.2 shows the thermal transmittance values that can be achieved for masonry 300 and 365 mm thick, and how the thermal insulation can be improved by using a thermal insulation plaster.

The use of thin-bed and lightweight mortars instead of normal mortar together with large-format masonry units and laying without mortar to the perpends further reduces the thermal bridging effect of the mortar joints.

The diagrams in fig. 2.4.3 show the influence of length of unit and type of perpend as well as thickness of bed joint for normal, LM 36 and LM 21 mortars. A medium-bed joint of LM 36 is practically identical with the thin-bed joint. The use of lightweight or thin-bed mortar represents a marked improvement in thermal insulation irrespective of the thermal conductivity of the masonry units.

In walls with normal mortar, the thickness of the bed joint and the length of the unit with mortar to the perpends has a noticeable effect on the thermal conductivity of the masonry. Differences within lightweight and thin-bed mortars merely amount to the order of magnitude of the range of one thermal conductivity class. However, this can be important if, when deter-

2.4.1 Forms of single-leaf external walls

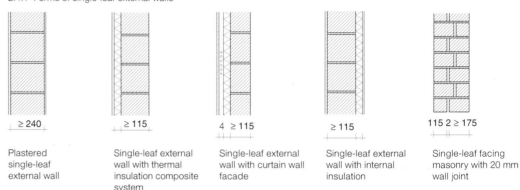

≥ 240	≥ 115	4 ≥ 115	≥ 115	115 2 ≥ 175
Plastered single-leaf external wall	Single-leaf external wall with thermal insulation composite system	Single-leaf external wall with curtain wall facade	Single-leaf external wall with internal insulation	Single-leaf facing masonry with 20 mm wall joint

mining characteristic values, the measured or calculated result for the masonry being evaluated lies on the threshold of a class [A.1, p. 116].

Single-leaf external walls with thermal insulation composite systems
are constructed from masonry units performing structural and other functions but exhibiting relatively poor thermal insulation properties in conjunction with a thermally insulating coating applied to the external wall surface. This wall system is employed for new building work, as well as for subsequently improving the thermal insulation of existing masonry. The coating consists of three layers: bonding coat, thermal insulation (hard polystyrene foam or mineral fibre batts) and a two-coat plaster finish comprising reinforcing and final coats.
Rail systems or dowels create an additional fixing to the substrate. The heat losses caused by the thermal bridges formed by such mechanical fixings are taken into account by increasing the thermal transmittance values. However, this effect can be ignored when using thermally optimized dowels.
As the thermal insulation composite system is fully responsible for the thermal insulation function, this type of wall is often referred to as a "thermoskin" and is used with masonry with relatively low thermal insulation but high compressive strength (e.g. calcium silicate masonry). This system results in relatively thin walls, which greatly benefits the total amount of internal space available.
In principle, this type of wall is an improvement on the thermal insulation plastering system because layers of thermal insulation with better insulation values are used instead of the plaster.
As the thermal insulation composite system does not satisfy the requirement for decreasing strength of the layers from the inside to the outside, the materials used in the three layers must be compatible in order to avoid the negative consequences (see "Plasters"). This is guaranteed by using complete systems. Nevertheless, it should be noted that this type of wall

2.4.2   Thermal transmittance values for single-leaf masonry

Wall thickness [mm]	Type of plaster	Rendering	Design value for thermal conductivity of masonry [W/mK]						
			0.1	0.11	0.12	0.13	0.14	0.16	0.18
300	LP	2	0.31	0.34	0.36	0.39	0.41	0.47	0.52
	WDP	4	0.27	0.29	0.31	0.33	0.34	0.38	0.41
366	LP	2	0.26	0.28	0.3	0.33	0.35	0.39	0.44
	WDP	4	0.23	0.24	0.26	0.28	0.3	0.33	0.36

External: 20 mm lightweight plaster (LP) or 40 mm thermal insulation plaster (WDP)
Internal: 10 mm lime-gypsum plaster

2.4.3   Thermal conductivity of masonry in relation to thermal conductivity of masonry unit, type of mortar, thickness of bed joint and length of unit

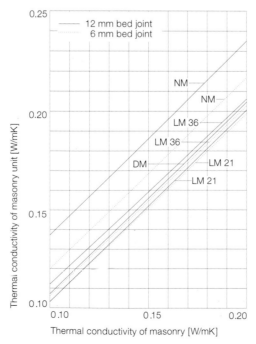

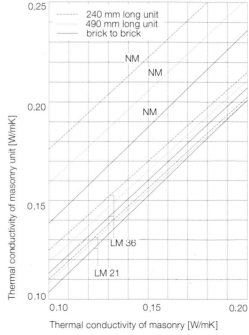

2 4.4 Section through 375 mm single-leaf faced wall (sketch showing principle)

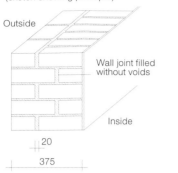

Outside

Wall joint filled without voids

Inside

20
375

2.4.5 Forms of twin-leaf external walls

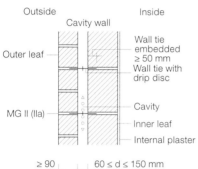

Outside   Inside
Cavity wall

Outer leaf

MG II (IIa)

Wall tie embedded ≥ 50 mm
Wall tie with drip disc
Cavity
Inner leaf
Internal plaster

≥ 90   60 ≤ d ≤ 150 mm

Partial-fill cavity wall

Facing masonry

MG II

Thermal insulation

Loadbearing leaf
Air space ≥ 40 mm
Internal plaster
Wall tie with drip disc

≥ 90   ≤ 150 mm
≥ 40

Full-fill cavity wall

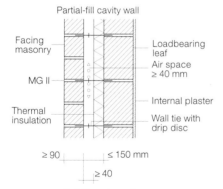

Facing masonry

MG II (IIa)

Loadbearing leaf
Internal plaster
MG II

≥ 150   ≤ 150

Plaster-filled collar-jointed wall

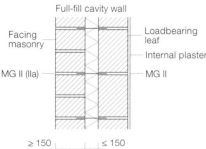

Facing masonry

Minimal air space
Plaster
Inner leaf
Wall tie

≥ 90

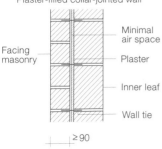

is vulnerable to mechanical damage. Apart from that, additional soft skins have an unfavourable effect on the sound insulation properties of the masonry.

Fire protection requirements must be observed when using flammable or not readily flammable thermal insulation materials.

Single-leaf external walls with curtain wall facade
If external walls made from non-frost-resistant masonry units are not rendered, the external wall can be protected against the weather and damage by adding a weatherproof cladding to the outside. This curtain wall can be attached either directly to the external wall or to external insulation, which is then protected by the ventilated curtain wall facade.

The mechanical fixings for the curtain wall result in additional heat losses which can be quite considerable.

Single-leaf external walls with internal insulation
The thermal insulation effect of a single-leaf external wall can also be improved by attaching insulation made from hard polystyrene foam or mineral fibre batts to the inside face. This type of wall is particularly suitable for the refurbishment of existing buildings with facades worthy of preservation, and for those rooms in new building work which are not permanently heated (e.g. assembly halls). Owing to the loss of the heat storage effect of the external walls, rooms insulated internally are quickly heated and store less thermal energy after the heating is switched off. Condensation problems within the wall construction can be a problem with absorbent masonry, particularly at junctions between floors and partitions. Likewise, the sound insulation of adjacent rooms can be impaired through flanking transmissions caused by unsuitable internal insulation systems.

Single-leaf external walls without rendering (single-leaf faced wall)
The decision to omit the rendering from an external wall, i.e. the facade masonry remains exposed (facing brickwork etc.), depends on the desired appearance as well as local traditions and experience. The main advantage of facing masonry – in single- or twin-leaf walls – is the low cost of maintenance.

A single-leaf faced wall consists of an outer skin of frost-resistant, usually small-format, facing or engineering bricks or calcium silicate facing bricks and a backing of, usually, non-frost-resistant masonry units. The use of different masonry materials for the backing and the facing work should be avoided because of the possible differential deformation and the associated risk of cracking. Facing and backing are bonded together and together form the loadbearing cross-section. The permissible stress which may be used in the design is governed

by the lowest unit strength class used in the wall. Saturation and attack by frost is assumed to only affect the outer masonry units in single-leaf faced walls. To avoid saturation of the backing masonry in regions with severe weather, every course of masonry should include at least two rows of units of equal height separated by a 20 mm wide wall joint (offset in each course to follow the bond) over the full height of the wall. This must be filled without voids using waterproof mortar or, better still, run in liquid waterproof mortar course by course. By increasing the thickness of the wall joint from 10 mm to 20 mm, guaranteed by the full mortar filling, the minimum wall thickness becomes 310 mm. This is due to the fact that a 240 mm thick wall would mean that the wall joint could only be formed in every second course and a continuous moisture barrier the full height of the wall would not be possible (see fig. 2.4.4.). Thicknesses of 375 and 500 mm are also feasible.

The joints in the exposed face – if flush pointing is not carried out – should be raked out to a depth of 15 mm and properly pointed. Subsequent pointing has the advantage that pigments can be added to the pointing mortar to vary the appearance of the joints (see "Pointing"). It is very difficult to fulfil the thermal insulation requirements with single-leaf facing masonry. Therefore, these days facing masonry is almost exclusively built as part of a twin-leaf masonry wall.

Twin-leaf external walls
Twin-leaf masonry is increasingly being used for external walls to achieve the necessary thermal insulation. The various functions of a wall are separated in this type of construction and allocated to the individual leaves. The inner leaf (backing masonry) provides a solid enclosure to the interior and carries the vertical and horizontal loads. The outer leaf (facing masonry or rendered outer leaf) determines the visual appearance and serves as protection against the weather and mechanical damage. Any thermal insulation required is fixed against the whole of the outside face of the inner leaf. The outer skin uses non-efflorescent, frost-resistant solid masonry units. Perforated units are less suitable because they can become severely saturated, which can be aggravated by possible lack of care during pointing.

We distinguish between cavity, partial-fill cavity, full-fill cavity and plaster-filled collar-jointed (see fig. 2.4.5).

Only the thickness of the inner leaf (min. 115 mm) may be considered in the structural analysis. When analysing the inner leaf according to the simplified method of analysis, the thickness of 115 mm is only suitable for buildings of no more of than two full storeys plus an attic; in addition, crosswalls must be provided for stability. The minimum thickness of the outer leaf should be 90 mm for reasons of stability during construction.

Supporting the outer leaf

The weight of the outer leaf must be supported on the loadbearing leaf. The complete outer leaf should be supported over its full length (e.g. on nibs projecting from the floors, on steel sections bolted on or cast in). If the support is non-continuous (e.g. separate brackets), every masonry unit must be supported at both ends at the support level.

Using a metal angle as a support creates a continuous thermal bridge which, in the arrangement shown in fig. 2.4.6, means an additional heat flow to the outside of 0.15 W/mK [A.2] along the length of the angle. For support over two storeys this means an increase in heat losses of $\Delta U = 0.025$ W/m²K compared to a wall without such supports. The influence of the support can be neglected for an outer leaf 12 m high. Support details which can no longer be inspected after being built in must be permanently protected against corrosion.

Outer leaves 115 mm thick have proved to be worthwhile in practice. Owing to their good stability, these need to be supported only every 12 m in height. When supported at every second floor, a 115 mm outer leaf can project beyond its support by up to one third of its thickness. Outer leaves less than 115 mm thick must be supported every 6 m in height and may not be built more than 20 m above ground level owing to their limited resistance to wind loads. Buildings comprising no more than two full storeys may include a triangular gable up to 4 m high without any additional support. If a 115 mm leaf is not provided with flush pointing, weakening due to subsequent raking out of the joints must be taken into account.

Anchoring the outer leaf

The outer leaf is to be anchored to the loadbearing inner leaf by means of wall ties to prevent it from overturning, buckling and bulging as a result of unequal temperature changes. In addition, this anchoring serves to transfer the wind loads. As the wind generates both pressure and suction forces, the anchors must be able to resist tension and compression. Wall ties must be of stainless steel to DIN 17440. Their shape and dimensions must be as given in fig. 2.4.7.

When the bonding of the loadbearing leaf and the outer leaf coincide, then Z-shape ties may be used. Otherwise the L-shape is more suitable because this can be bent to suit. If the bed joints of the two leaves are not in the same plane or if the outer leaf is built at a later date, ties for subsequent fixing into the inner leaf of masonry are necessary.

The use of such anchors is also recommended when attaching an additional layer of thermal insulation in order to ensure that the insulation

is pressed tightly against the outside face of the inner leaf.

Wall ties should be spaced at max. 500 m vertically, max. 750 mm horizontally. In addition to the requirements outlined in table 2.4.8, three ties per metre of edge length are required around openings and at the corners of the building as well as along movement joints and at the tops of outer leaves.

The type, number and arrangement of ties in curved masonry or masonry with projections should be specified, taking into account the deformation due to, for example, wind and/or temperature changes.

Table 2.4.10 shows the influence of wall ties on heat transmission for a number of typical types of wall. In cavity walls the ties are practically ineffective as thermal bridges.

The use of additional layers of insulation in the cavity increases the heat transmission by up to 5% for optimum 150 mm thick cavity insulation and 5 mm thick wall ties; these influences can be ignored. Therefore, to comply with DIN 4108 part 2, no analysis of the thermal bridge effect has to be carried out for minimum thermal insulation when using conventional forms of fixing, e.g. wire ties. When using lightweight mortar, LM 36 is always required when wall ties are to be built in. Other types of tie are permissible when they can accommodate min. 1.0 kN tension and compression at 1.0 mm slip per tie. The number of ties must be increased if this value cannot be guaranteed. Other types of ties (e.g. flat steel) and dowelled fixings in the masonry are permissible when their serviceability is verified by a building authority certificate.

Wall ties should be built in so that they cannot convey moisture from the outer to the inner leaf. This is achieved by positioning the ties horizontally and by fitting a plastic disc (drip disc). The drip disc ensures that water penetrating the outer leaf does not reach the thermal insulation or the loadbearing leaf, but is intercepted.

Additional requirements

A damp proof course (dpc) should be included at the bottom of the cavity between the leaves in order to protect the inner leaf and the floor from moisture which penetrates the outer leaf and collects at the base of the cavity. The damp proof course must be laid with a fall to the outside within the cavity and horizontal under the outer leaf. The outer leaf must be supported in such a way that it cannot slip. To do this, place the first row of ties as low as possible and ensure that the waterproofing complies with DIN 18195 part 4. The damp proof course should extend as far as the front edge of the outer leaf and should continue min. 150 mm up the inner leaf on a firring piece and be fixed to this leaf (see 2.4.9).

Openings for doors, windows etc. in the outer leaf are formed as transfer structures

2.4.6 Outer leaf support details

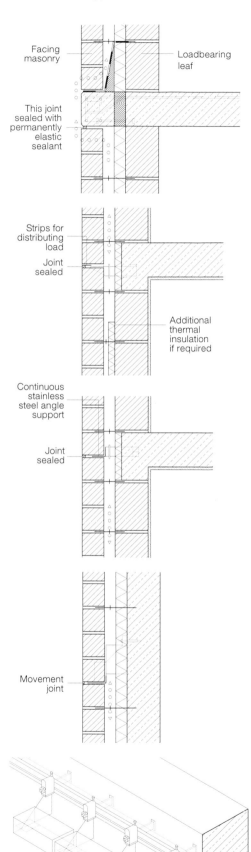

Facing masonry

Loadbearing leaf

This joint sealed with permanently elastic sealant

Strips for distributing load

Joint sealed

Additional thermal insulation if required

Continuous stainless steel angle support

Joint sealed

Movement joint

2.4.7 Wall ties for twin-leaf external masonry

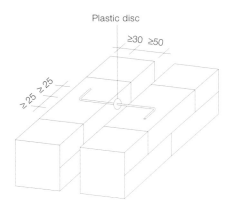

Plastic disc

≥30 ≥50

≥25 ≥25

2.4.8 Minimum number and diameter of wall ties per m²
       of wall area

	Wall ties: min. No.	diameter [mm]
Minimum, provided neither of the following two lines apply	5	3
Wall sections > 12 m above ground level, or	5	4
distance between masonry leaves 70-120 mm	7 or 5	4 5

A wall tie diameter of 3 mm is adequate for a plaster-filled collar-jointed wall.

2.4.9 Detail at base of twin-leaf facing masonry

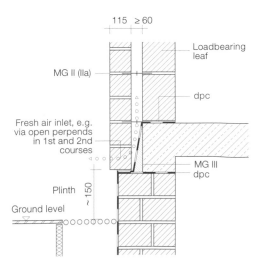

115 ≥60

Loadbearing leaf

MG II (IIa)

dpc

Fresh air inlet, e.g. via open perpends in 1st and 2nd courses

MG III dpc

Plinth

~150

Ground level

(e.g. individual brackets or steel sections), as reinforced masonry or as lintels. The latter may be constructed using specials or in the form of cambered or semicircular arches.
Refer to "Joint design" for details of the arrangement of movement joints.

Cavity walls
In contrast to the curtain wall facade, in this type of wall, the cavity between the masonry leaves may be included in calculations to determine the thermal insulation because the open vertical joints in the outer leaf are not provided for ventilation. Rainwater or condensation in the cavity can drain away or evaporate without causing problems and without the inner leaf becoming saturated. In addition, the cavity helps the outer leaf to dry out faster. The thermal insulation is mainly determined by the inner leaf, although this is usually only economical in conjunction with inner leaves with very high insulation values.
The cavity should be at least 60 mm wide. This minimum distance is based on the fact that adequate circulation of the air cannot be expected if the gap is too small. However, the width of the cavity may be reduced to 40 mm if the mortar is struck off flush on at least one side of the cavity, thus preventing mortar bridges from interrupting the cavity. The maximum distance between the two leaves is determined by the load-carrying capacity of the wall ties under compression and should be no more than 150 mm. Ventilation openings (e.g. open perpends) should be included at the top and bottom of the cavity and at any intermediate supports to guarantee circulation of the air. Openings at the bottom also serve to drain the cavity (weep holes). This also applies to spandrel panels. A total of 7500 mm² of ventilation openings should be provided for every 20 m² of wall area (including doors and windows). This figure means that for a single-storey building and an outer leaf of thin-format units approximately every second perpend at the base and below the roof or the underside of supports in the outer leaf must be left open. The damp proof course must be positioned exactly in order to prevent the masonry below the open perpends becoming saturated at the base of the wall. As water may collect in certain areas at the base, the inner leaf is to be protected against rising damp by extending the damp proof course up the face of the inner leaf. Openings must be at least 100 mm above ground level.

Partial-fill cavity walls
In this type of wall the functions of the individual layers are clearly demarcated under optimum building science conditions. A layer of thermal insulation is attached to the outside face of the inner, loadbearing leaf but a ventilated gap remains between this and the outer leaf. This cavity means that condensation and

driving rain penetrating to the inside face of the outer leaf can drain without saturating the thermal insulation. Consequently, the outer leaf protects the layer of thermal insulation against the direct effects of the weather and impact or other damage. If a vapour-permeable material is used for the thermal insulation, then the circulating air not only dries out the outer leaf but also keeps the insulation dry, causing any condensation to evaporate.
The maximum distance between inner and outer leaves is 150 mm (see "Cavity walls"). This does not need to be fully exploited if the inner leaf has good insulation properties. But it is important when the inner leaf makes use of masonry types that exhibit high compressive strength but low thermal insulation. In that case, the thermal properties of the wall are provided solely by the layer of insulation. This can partly compensate for the disadvantage of the total thickness of the wall construction necessary to accommodate thermal insulation plus cavity. A further disadvantage is the high cost of constructing such walls.
The minimum width of the air space is 40 mm. If we use the maximum width of 150 mm between the two leaves, we are left with 110 mm which may be filled with insulation. However, owing to the unevenness of the surfaces of the two leaves, it is advisable to include a reasonable tolerance in our planning. Insulating batts are recommended; these are butt jointed together and fixed by suitable means (e.g. clamping discs on wall ties or wall anchors etc.). Blankets, on the other hand, tend to swell or expand and hence reduce the width of the air space. Therefore, they should not be used for this type of wall.
The details at the top and bottom of the wall regarding openings and waterproofing correspond to those for cavity walls.

Full-fill cavity walls
These are external walls in which the cavity between the leaves is filled completely with insulation material in order to increase the thermal insulation value, or the cavity is omitted in order to reduce the overall thickness of the wall. The outer leaf should consist of frost-resistant masonry units at least 115 mm thick to increase the resistance to driving rain. The clear distance to the face of the loadbearing inner leaf should not exceed 150 mm. Glazed units or units with surface coatings must exhibit enhanced frost resistance. The thermal insulation is installed between the leaves without any air space. The insulation materials used may be in the form of batts, blankets, granulates and loose materials which are permanently water-repellent (hydrophobic) as well as injected cellular foams (e.g. hard polystyrene or polyurethane), mineral wool, loose expanded perlite or polyurethane or urea formaldehyde resin injected cellular foams. Up to now, the serviceability of these materials has had to be

verified by a general building authority certificate. In future the requirements these insulation materials have to meet will be covered by corresponding standards.

In practical terms, it is virtually impossible to build the outer leaf without a gap for the bricklayer's fingers when using batts and blankets (not loose materials or injected cellular foams). However, this has the advantage that any water which does penetrate can drain away unhindered.

When used as full-fill cavity insulation, waterproof or water-repellent materials do not need to be treated any differently to their use elsewhere with respect to their thermal conductivity. However, full-fill cavity insulation can function effectively only when the amount of water penetrating the insulation is not excessive and, above all, does not accumulate at certain positions. This is guaranteed by ensuring that the outer leaf is built to a high standard of workmanship – which means erecting the masonry with fully filled joints capable of transmitting stresses. Lime-cement mortars of group II or IIa with a good sticky consistency are preferred. In addition, proper bricklaying techniques appropriate to the material of the outer leaf are essential (e.g. prewetting high absorbency units, reducing the plasticity of the mortar for low absorbency units). Furthermore, openings in the outer leaf totalling at least 5000 mm² per 20 m² of wall area (including doors and windows) must be included at the base of the wall so that any moisture that does become trapped in the cavity insulation – despite careful construction – can drain to the base of the wall and escape to the outside.

Mineral fibre insulation materials in the form of batts and blankets, or sheets of foamed plastic and foamed glass are to be fixed to the inner leaf by, for example, plastic discs fitted to the wall ties, in such a way that the thickness of the insulation remains constant. Blankets of insulating materials are butt jointed together but the stiffer batts require joints to be formed (e.g. rebate, tongue and groove) or fixed with layers offset so that water cannot penetrate the joints. Missing sections of hard foam materials (e.g. where wall ties penetrate) must be made good with a suitable sealing compound.

When using loose thermal insulating materials (e.g. mineral fibre granulate, polystyrene foam beads, expanded perlite), it must be ensured that the insulating material completely fills the cavity between the leaves with a consistent packing density and also that the drainage openings at the base of wall remain unobstructed by using, for example, a stainless steel mesh. An inconsistent, incomplete filling to the cavity impairs the thermal insulation value. This is particularly so at the top of the wall if the material settles shortly after filling or over the course of time. However, voids and irregularities in fillings of loose insulating materials and injected foams are particularly

2.4.10   Influence of wall ties on thermal transmittance values of twin-leaf masonry

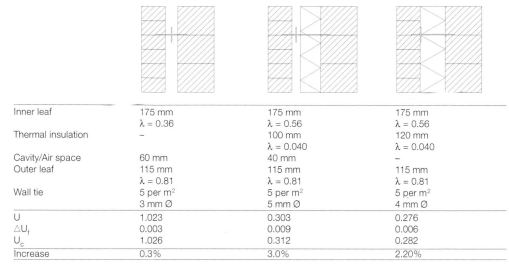

Inner leaf	175 mm	175 mm	175 mm
	λ = 0.36	λ = 0.56	λ = 0.56
Thermal insulation	–	100 mm	120 mm
		λ = 0.040	λ = 0.040
Cavity/Air space	60 mm	40 mm	–
Outer leaf	115 mm	115 mm	115 mm
	λ = 0.81	λ = 0.81	λ = 0.81
Wall tie	5 per m²	5 per m²	5 per m²
	3 mm Ø	5 mm Ø	4 mm Ø
U	1.023	0.303	0.276
$\triangle U_f$	0.003	0.009	0.006
U_c	1.026	0.312	0.282
Increase	0.3%	3.0%	2.20%

2.4.11   Max. permissible sizes of infill panels in non-loadbearing external walls without mathematical analysis

Wall thickness	Permissible max. size of infill panel for a height above ground level of:					
	0 to 8 m		8 to 20 m		20 to 100 m	
	ε = 1.0	ε ≥ 2.0[1]	ε = 1.0	ε ≥ 2.0[1]	ε = 1.0	ε ≥ 2.0[1]
mm	m²	m²	m²	m²	m²	m²
115	12.0	8.0	8.0	5.0	6.0	4.0
115[2]	16.0	10.6	10.6	6.7	8.0	5.3
175	20.0	14.0	13.0	9.0	9.0	6.0
240	36.0	25.0	23.0	16.0	16.0	12.0
≥ 300	50.0	33.0	35.0	23.0	25.0	17.0

where e = ratio of longer to shorter side of infill panel
Max. permissible sizes for side ratios 1.0 < e < 2.0 may be interpolated linearly.
[1] The sizes may be doubled for masonry units of strength classes ≥ 20 and ratios h/l ≥ 2.0 (where h = height of infill panel, l = length of infill panel).
[2] Permissible for masonry unit compressive strength classes ≥ 12

2.4.12 Sliding and elastic joints at sides of infill panels

Joint masked by channel or angle section

Wall recessed into groove

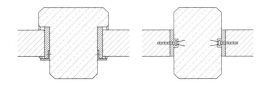

Anchor in slot, e.g. of stainless steel

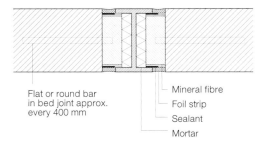

Sliding joint at steel column

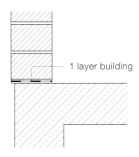

Flat or round bar in bed joint approx. every 400 mm

Mineral fibre
Foil strip
Sealant
Mortar

2.4.13 Detail at base of infill panel

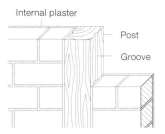

1 layer building

2.4.14 Junction between infill panel and timber post

Internal plaster

Post
Groove

Mortar group II or self-adhesive sealing strips

Stainless steel flat anchor bent to form angle

Galvanized clout nails

critical as these allow moisture to penetrate unchecked right up to the inner leaf. The only way to avoid this is to use proven equipment and techniques in the hands of experienced personnel.

Plaster-filled collar-jointed external walls
This type of twin-leaf construction makes use of a continuous layer of plaster applied to the outside face of the inner leaf. Like the cavity wall, the inner leaf in this case consists of masonry units with good thermal insulation properties. This type of construction prevents water from reaching the inner leaf and provides protection against driving rain. The outer leaf (facing masonry) is erected as close as possible to the plaster (gap for bricklayer's fingers) with joints fully filled with mortar. In terms of construction and function, this wall is an improvement on the single-leaf faced wall with its continuous 20 mm wall joint. In contrast to the single-leaf external wall, which often suffers from damage attributable to lack of care when casting the wall joint, plastering the outside face of the inner leaf and hence the standard of workmanship and function of the continuous coat of plaster can be easily inspected before the outer leaf is built. However, the disadvantage of the twin-leaf wall compared to the single-leaf faced wall is that the vertical loads must be carried solely by the inner leaf. Compared to the cavity wall, this type of wall is thinner overall.
If a rendered outer leaf is preferred to facing masonry, then the plaster coat on the outside face of the loadbearing, inner leaf may be omitted. Frost-resistant facing bricks are not necessary with such a rendered outer leaf.
Drainage openings (e.g. weep holes) are required only at the base of the wall to allow water which has penetrated the outer leaf and drained down to escape. Openings at the top of wall are not necessary because ventilation in the narrow gap between inner and outer leaves cannot be expected. Wall ties just 3 mm thick are adequate to connect the two leaves.

Non-loadbearing external walls

Non-loadbearing external masonry walls are slab-like components which, apart from their own weight, have to carry loads acting perpendicular to their face (e.g. wind loads) and transfer these to adjoining, loadbearing components, e.g. shear walls, floor plates. In the structural analysis they may not be taken into account when assessing the stability of the building or as lateral restraint to loadbearing walls. These walls are popular for the infill panels of frame or cellular structures of reinforced concrete, steel or timber. Such panels can be built in single- or multi-leaf form, with or without plaster, with additional thermal insulation and/or curtain wall facade. Single-leaf, rendered walls must be min. 115 mm thick, single-leaf facing masonry min. 310 mm. In a twin-leaf wall the outer leaf must be at least 90 mm and the inner leaf at least 115 mm thick.

Basis for design

According to DIN 1053 part 1, the infill panels of frame or cellular structures need not be assessed structurally when the panels are supported on four sides (e.g. by bonding, tongue and groove joints or anchors), normal mortar of at least mortar group IIa or lightweight mortar LM 36 or thin-bed mortar is used and the conditions of DIN 1053 part 1 table 9 (see table 2.4.11) are maintained. The dimensions of the infill panel are to be taken as the clear dimensions between the supporting construction. The heights above ground level refer to the top edge of the respective infill panel. To classify twin-leaf masonry, it is recommended to use the thickness of the inner leaf plus half the thickness of the outer leaf as the design wall thickness. In contrast to loadbearing masonry, the conditions of table 2.4.11 take into account the low tensile strength perpendicular to the bed joints. This is possible because failure of a panel does not lead to collapse of the entire structure. If the above conditions are not met or openings are provided in non-loadbearing external walls (e.g. windows, doors) which impair the load-carrying ability, a structural analysis is required.

Connections to loadbearing components

Infill panels achieve their stability by being fixed to adjoining components. The connections must be able to transfer loads acting on the infill panels to the loadbearing construction and also accommodate deformations in the adjoining construction. They may be rigid or sliding and elastic. However, a rigid connection, e.g. steel inserts, anchors, mortar joints, bonding, should only be used when excessive restraint and deformation is not expected from the masonry and the surrounding loadbearing construction. The use of sliding connections means there is no opportunity to span the infill walls between the adjoining components. The infill panel is generally built into a groove, or

between overlapping fittings or attached by way of stainless steel anchors in slots (see fig. 2.4.12) in order to achieve the sliding and elastic connection. Strips of resilient, elastic, rotproof material (e.g. mineral fibre or bitumen felt) are placed between infill panel and adjoining component, outer and inner joints sealed with elastoplastic material or prefabricated joint fillers. The sides of panels are easily connected to steel columns when the overall dimensions of the sections are selected to suit the thickness of the infill panel (see fig. 2.4.12). Strips of foil are placed between steel flange and mortar to achieve a sliding joint. Mineral fibre pads between the mortar and the web of the steel section help to improve sound insulation and fire protection. The transfer of forces between masonry and column is ensured by completely filling the void between steel section and panel with mortar. At the top of the panel a 20 mm tolerance is generally sufficient. The gap is filled with a soft, rotproof material. This prevents the loadbearing adjoining component unintentionally transferring loads to the non-loadbearing panel by way of deformation and subsequent deflection. At the base of the wall the horizontal forces from, for example, wind loads, are transferred from the non-loadbearing external wall to the loadbearing component by friction. A layer of roofing felt can be included between the wall and the loadbearing component (fig. 2.4.13).

Infill panels to a timber frame should always be completed with a mortar joint 10-20 mm wide between timber and masonry. This compensates for tolerances and deformations in the timber construction. A secure connection to the timber is provided by way of triangular fillets to all sides fixed with stainless steel nails. This presupposes reliable adhesion between mortar and masonry units (e.g. provided by suitable pretreatment, the use of low-shrinkage mortar etc.). Alternatively, stainless steel flat anchors bent to form an angle can be specified as a mechanical fixing, particularly with large panels.

Gable walls

Gable walls without vertical load

Masonry gable walls are necessary on buildings with pitched roofs. With steep roof slopes, such walls can constitute considerable areas of masonry. Couple and collar roofs do not transfer any load to the gable wall, which therefore only carries its own weight and wind loads. These should be considered as non-loadbearing external walls. They may be analysed structurally or by comparison with the permissible values for infill panels according to DIN 1053 part 1 table 9, provided the gable wall is supported at the edges or by crosswalls or integral piers. At the base the wall is held in position by the reinforced concrete floor either by means of tension anchors or via adhesion and friction, at the top by a ring beam or the roof construction. To do this, the roof construction must be braced (e.g. timber or metal diagonal bracing). The better solution in structural terms is the formation of a ring beam, whose ends at least must be connected to the roof construction by way of steel anchors. The simpler solution is to support the gable wall at roof level via a connection rigid in the horizontal direction. This is usually achieved by way of masonry anchors.

Gable walls with vertical load

If purlins span onto the gable wall, then a loadbearing masonry pier can be assumed beneath the bearing for the purlin as a result of the vertical load. Apart from carrying the roof load, this also stiffens the gable wall. Therefore, the gable wall is divided into loadbearing and non-loadbearing areas. The loadbearing sections (masonry piers) beneath the purlins have to be examined according to the more accurate method of analysis. In doing so, the clear height of the pier should be used as the buckling length. The distribution of load below the purlins may be assumed to be 60°. The roof construction must accommodate the horizontal support reactions, e.g. by way of diagonal bracing in the plane of the roof, arising from the provision of support to the pier. The non-loadbearing sections adjacent to the masonry piers should be analysed as gable walls without vertical load.

Internal walls

Loadbearing internal walls

In the latest edition of DIN 1053 part 1, the minimum thickness for a loadbearing internal wall has been reduced from 240 mm to 115 mm. This reduction in thickness has resulted in a useful gain in floor space, particularly for single- and two-storey buildings in which the loads are only minimal. This is particularly evident when it can be guaranteed that the cross-sections of such thin walls are not reduced by chases and recesses. Reducing the minimum

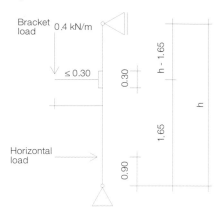

2.4.15 Structural loading scheme according to DIN 4103 part 1 for non-loadbearing internal partitions

Bracket load 0.4 kN/m

≤ 0.30

0.30

h - 1.65

h

1.65

Horizontal load

0.90

Location 1: p_1 = 0.5 kN/m
Location 2: p_2 = 1.0 kN/m

wall thickness to 115 mm has also allowed internal walls, previously classed as non-loadbearing on account of their thickness, to now be included as loadbearing elements. As a result, stiffening to the building is improved, floor spans are shortened, connection problems for non-loadbearing walls are minimized etc. In some circumstances, design and construction of the building is, on the whole, made easier.

Non-loadbearing internal walls
When built from masonry, non-loadbearing internal walls – or non-loadbearing internal partitions – are usually built as lightweight partitions in the sense of DIN 1055 part 3. Non-loadbearing internal partitions are only subjected to considerable wind loads in exceptional cases, e.g. in shed-type buildings with large door openings where the pressure can build up inside the building. In such cases they are to be treated as non-loadbearing external walls. Otherwise, non-loadbearing internal partitions not subjected to wind loads are covered by the provisions of DIN 4103. The requirements and analyses of DIN 4103 part 1 are not related to material. Construction guidelines for masonry partitions are stipulated in DIN 4103 part 3. At present this standard only exists in the form of an unpublished draft. Details given here are based on the current state of knowledge with respect to non-loadbearing masonry partitions based on the information sheet published by Deutsche Gesellschaft für Mauerwerksbau (German Masonry Association) [97, 172].
Non-loadbearing internal partitions are walls between interior spaces that do not fulfil any structural function for the overall structure, i.e. they are not called upon to stabilize the building not to carry vertical loads. Consequently, they may be removed without adversely affecting the stability of the building.

Requirements
Apart from self-weight plus plaster and/or cladding, these walls must be able to carry light loads from brackets and horizontal impacts from people or hard objects and transfer these loads to adjoining, loadbearing components. They gain their stability from being connected to adjoining components.
DIN 4103 part 1 distinguishes between the following locations for partitions with their associated loads:

Location 1:
Locations with low numbers of people, e.g. housing, hotels, offices, hospital patient accommodation and interiors with similar functions (including corridors):
horizontal line load
p_1 = 0.5 kN/m at a height of 900 mm above the base of wall.

Location 2:
Locations with large numbers of people, e.g. larger assembly buildings and schools, lecture theatres, exhibition halls, retail premises and similar facilities:
horizontal line load
p_2 = 1.0 kN/m at a height of 900 mm above the base of wall.
Irrespective of location, a bracket load of 0.4 kN/m wall length (see 2.4.15) and an impact load with a force of E_{basic} = 100 kNm acting at an unfavourable position must also be allowed for. The impact load can be caused by a person (soft impact) or a hard object (hard impact).
According to DIN 1055 part 3, the structural analysis of a loadbearing floor supporting such partitions may assume – instead of a more accurate calculation – a uniformly distributed additional imposed load of 0.75 kN/m² for wall weights (including plaster) < 1.0 kN/m² wall area and 1.25 kN/m² for wall weights (including plaster) 1.0-1.5 kN/m² wall area.
For wall weights > 1.5 kN/m² wall area – or > 1.0 kN/m² wall area for floors without adequate transverse distribution of the loads – the position and magnitude of the wall load is to be taken into account accurately when analysing the floor.

Materials for non-loadbearing internal masonry partitions
Only materials covered by DIN standards or building authority certificates may be used for building partitions. Partitions of masonry units or wall elements may use only mortar of mortar groups II, IIa or III to DIN 1053 part 1. The mortar should not be unnecessarily firm in order to preserve sufficient elasticity in the masonry to accommodate deformation. Thin-bed mortar covered by building authority certificate may be used for wall elements and gauged units.

Structural analysis
An assessment of the ability to carry horizontal loads according to DIN 4103 part 1 (see fig.2.4.15) may be carried out mathematically or by means of tests. However, a mathematical analysis is difficult because tensile stresses perpendicular to the bed joint may not be taken into account even though they are present to a limited extent.
Maximum dimensions that satisfy the requirements of DIN 4103 part 1 have been determined experimentally[97].
These maximum dimensions (taken from [97]) are given in table 2.4.16 for various types of masonry and support conditions according to location, thickness and height. Designers adhering to these dimensions do not need to carry out a (less favourable) mathematical analysis. If these maximum dimensions are exceeded, additional support in the form of steel, reinforced concrete or reinforced masonry columns must be provided.

The type of junction between a partition and the floor above determines whether any load is transferred from the floor to that partition. Therefore, we distinguish between partitions with and without vertical loading. Reinforced concrete floors with high slenderness ratios require us to assume partitions with vertical loading. The minimum thickness of 50 mm in the tables is based on practical considerations. The maximum wall length is restricted to 12 m in order to limit cracking. Load transfer on three sides may be assumed up to a height/length ratio of $h/l \leq 0.66$. Smaller ratios mean that the partition is supported only top and bottom. In this case there must be a mortar joint between top of wall and underside of floor slab.

Design and construction rules
Following the recommendations below will help ensure good quality non-loadbearing internal partitions:

- Max. final floor slab deflection $l_i/500$ (l_i = equivalent span depending on structural system).
- Reduce the floor slab deflection due to creep and shrinkage by adhering to striking times and subsequently treating the concrete.
- Build non-loadbearing internal partitions after completion of the primary structure whenever possible so that the majority of deformations resulting from shrinkage and creep of the loadbearing construction are already completed. At the very least, the topmost course of masonry units and the plastering should be carried out as late as possible in order to minimize the risk of cracks.
- Erect non-loadbearing partitions in such a way that floor slab deformation due to the weight of such partitions does not introduce any additional loads into non-loadbearing partitions in the storey below (if possible, start in the topmost storey and work down).

Up to an equivalent floor span of $l_i = 7.00$ m, a non-loadbearing partition can carry a load by way of arching action without damage, providing the recommendations are followed and it is guaranteed that the horizontal thrust can be carried by the supports at the ends of the wall. Larger spans require additional measures to be taken, e.g. separating the base of wall from the floor slab by means of sanded building paper or reinforcing the areas of wall at risk of cracking.

2.4.16 Max. dimensions for non-loadbearing internal partitions of man-made masonry units

Supported on 4 sides

Supported on 3 sides with 1 unsupported vertical edge

Supported on 3 sides with unsupported top edge

Max. dimensions for walls supported on 4 sides[1] **without** vertical load[2]

d [mm]	Max. wall length [m] for wall height [m] for location 1 (upper value) and location 2 (lower value)				
h [m]	2.5	3.0	3.5	4.0	4.5
50	3.0	3.5	4.0	–	–
	1.5	2.0	2.5	–	–
60	4.0	4.5	5.0	5.5	–
	2.5	3.0	3.5	–	–
70	5.0	5.5	6.0	6.5	7.0
	3.0	3.5	4.0	4.5	5.0
90	6.0	6.5	7.0	7.5	8.0
	3.5	4.0	4.5	5.0	5.5
100	7.0	7.5	8.0	8.5	9.0
	5.0	5.5	6.0	6.5	7.0
115	10.0	10.0	10.0	10.0	10.0
	6.0	6.5	7.0	7.5	8.0
120	12.0	12.0	12.0	12.0	12.0
	6.0	6.5	7.0	7.5	8.0
175	no restriction on length				
	12.0	12.0	12.0	12.0	12.0

[1] The max. wall lengths are to be halved for walls supported on 3 sides (1 unsupported vertical edge).
[2] The values given here apply to calcium silicate and autoclaved aerated concrete units when using MG III or thin-bed mortar. For wall thicknesses < 175 mm and MG II or IIa, the values are to be halved when using these types of masonry units.

Max. dimensions for walls supported on 4 sides[1] **with** vertical load[2]

d [mm]	Max. wall length [m] for wall height [m] for location 1 (upper value) and location 2 (lower value)				
h [m]	2.5	3.0	3.5	4.0	4.5
50	5.5	6.0	6.5	–	–
	2.5	3.0	3.5	–	–
60	6.0	6.5	7.0	–	–
	4.0	4.5	5.0	–	–
70	8.0	8.5	9.0	9.5	–
	5.5	6.0	6.5	7.0	7.5
90	12.0	12.0	12.0	12.0	12.0
	7.0	7.5	8.0	8.5	9.0
100	12.0	12.0	12.0	12.0	12.0
	8.0	8.5	9.0	9.5	10.0
115	no restriction on length				
	12.0	12.0	12.0	12.0	
120	no restriction on length				
	–	–	12.0	12.0	
175	no restriction on length				

[1] The max. wall lengths are to be halved for walls supported on 3 sides (1 unsupported vertical edge).
[2] The values given here apply to calcium silicate and autoclaved aerated concrete units when using MG III or thin-bed mortar, and also for MG II or IIa with wall thicknesses > 100 mm. For wall thicknesses ≤ 100 mm and MG II or IIa, the values are to be halved when using these types of masonry units.

Max. dimensions for walls supported on 3 sides **without** vertical load[1] (top edge unsupported)

d [mm]	Max. wall length [m] for wall height [m] for location 1 (upper value) and location 2 (lower value)						
h [m]	2.0	2.25	2.5	3.0	3.5	4.0	4.5
50	3.0	3.5	4	5	6	–	–
	1.5	2.0	2.5	–	–	–	–
60	5.0	5.5	6.0	7.0	8.0	9.0	–
	2.5	2.5	3.0	3.5	4.0	–	–
70	7.0	7.5	8.0	9.0	10.0	10.0	10.0
	3.5	3.5	4.0	4.5	5.0	6.0	7.0
90	8.0	8.5	9.0	10.0	10.0	12.0	12.0
	4.0	4.0	5.0	6.0	7.0	8.0	9.0
100	10.0	10.0	10.0	12.0	12.0	12.0	12.0
	5.0	5.0	6.0	7.0	8.0	9.0	10.0
115	11.5	8.0	9.0	10.0	10.0	12.0	12.0
	6.0	6.0	7.0	8.0	9.0	10.0	10.0
120	8.0	9.0	10.0	12.0	12.0	12.0	12.0
	6.0	6.0	7.0	8.0	9.0	10.0	10.0
175	no restriction on length						
	8.0	9.0	10.0	12.0	12.0	12.0	12.0

[1] The max. lengths given here apply to masonry units of clay or lightweight concrete with normal mortar as well as autoclaved aerated concrete blocks or calcium silicate units with thin-bed mortar or mortars of mortar group III. When using units of autoclaved aerated concrete and calcium silicate with normal mortar, reduce the max. wall lengths as follows: a) for walls 56 and 70 mm thick reduce to 40%; b) for walls 90 and 100 mm thick reduce to 50%; c) for walls 115 and 120 mm thick in location 2 reduce to 50% (no reduction for location 1). The units should be prewetted when using mortar group III.

2.4.17 Sliding joint details

Sliding joints between walls

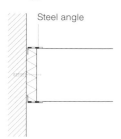

Steel angle

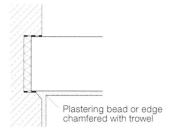

Plastering bead or edge
chamfered with trowel

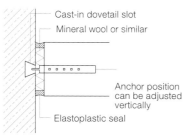

Cast-in dovetail slot
Mineral wool or similar

Anchor position
can be adjusted
vertically

Elastoplastic seal

Sliding joint at underside of floor

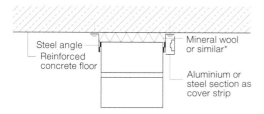

Steel angle
Reinforced
concrete floor

Mineral wool
or similar*

Aluminium or
steel section as
cover strip

* Incombustible material if required to comply with fire
protection regulations

Sliding joint at intermediate column

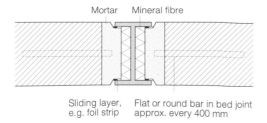

Mortar   Mineral fibre

Sliding layer,   Flat or round bar in bed joint
e.g. foil strip   approx. every 400 mm

*Junctions with adjoining, loadbearing
components*

Connections must take account of the possible
influence that deformations in adjoining components may have on the internal partition.
According to DIN 4103 part 1, the serviceability of junctions must be guaranteed.
The junction details shown in figs. 2.4.17 and
2.4.18 do not normally require further assessment.
Rigid junctions are those which are fully bonded, filled with mortar or employ similar measures (anchors, dowels or steel inserts). Such
details are used for walls where no or very low
restraint forces from the adjoining members
are expected to act on the wall.
Rigid lateral connections are usually limited to
housebuilding (wall length l ≤ 5.0 m). A rigid
junction between top of wall and underside of
floor slab can be achieved by filling the joint
with mortar. Introducing a strip of hard foam
reduces the influence of the deformation of the
adjoining loadbearing construction, but guarantees the transfer of horizontal forces due to
the hard foam strip being compressed as the
floor slab deflects.
Sliding junctions are particularly suitable for
applications where it is necessary to reduce
the risk of cracking due to unintentional forces
being introduced into the non-loadbearing
internal partition as a result of the deformation
of adjoining components.
Sliding connections are achieved by using profiles, grooves and stainless steel anchors in
slots, maybe with the addition of foil to create a
sliding bearing.
The joint should be filled with mineral wool in
order to improve fire protection and sound
insulation (see "Non-loadbearing external
walls").

Columns and free-standing masonry walls

Columns

Columns are elements with a cross-sectional
area < 0.01 m². To act as a loadbearing element, a column must have a minimum cross-
section of 0.004 m². Hence, the minimum
dimensions of a loadbearing column are 115 x
365 mm or 175 x 240 mm. Columns have a low
moment of area and therefore a low stiffness
EI. Their help in distributing horizontal loads is
negligible, and so they are not called upon to
carry horizontal loads in the structural analysis.
So columns carry only vertical axial loads. They
may be analysed for concentric or eccentric
compression using either the simplified or
more accurate method of analysis. The simplified method makes use of the reduction factor
k_1 = 1.0, and the more accurate method uses
the safety factor γ_W = 2.0. In this case the
column should consist of one or more whole
masonry units or divided units with < 35% perforations and should not weakened by chases

or recesses. In all other cases, the safety factor
is increased to γ_P = 2.5.
The reduction factor is consequently defined
as k_1 = 2.0/2.5 = 0.8. The use of divided
masonry units or divided units with ≥ 35% perforations makes the columns more vulnerable
to irregularities and flaws in the construction.
Unlike walls, these cannot be compensated for
by neighbouring parts of the cross-section and
so this high risk of structural failure has to be
taken into account by way of an increased
safety factor.

Free-standing masonry walls

The problem of the free-standing masonry wall
is that it is supported only at its base, and so
the system must span vertically. The exception
to this rule is when suitable measures, e.g.
reinforced concrete columns, masonry piers or
crosswalls at close spacing, are introduced to
ensure that the wall spans horizontally by way
of arching action or by employing reinforced
masonry. Without such measures, the permissible height of the wall is very limited owing to
the fact that the cross-section may only crack
as far as the centre of the wall.
Masonry units for free-standing walls must be
frost resistant if they are not rendered. Free-
standing masonry walls are always built with a
proper bond and with all joints filled.
The foundation should be taken down to a level
where it is not affected by frost. A horizontal
damp proof course of water-repellent mortar or
waterproof paint should be included above
ground level in order to protect the wall against
rising damp and splashing water. Vertical
faces of masonry in contact with the ground
should also be protected against ingress of
moisture from the soil. The length of an individual segment of masonry should not exceed
6-8 m; longer lengths should include movement joints. They are a number of ways in
which long walls may be segmented attractively (see fig. 2.4.19). The top of the wall must
be covered in such a way that water cannot
penetrate, indeed that it drains away clear of
the face of the wall. If used as a coping, a
brick-on-edge course must consist of whole
bricks and be carefully jointed. The joint below
a brick-on-edge coping must be waterproof.
Owing to the many joints, this type of coping is
limited in its applications. Other types of coping include clay roof tiles, corrugated roofing
units of fibre-reinforced cement or specially
designed coping units. Also suitable are precast concrete units with permanently plastic
joints laid in water-repellent mortar or on a
damp proof course, or metal cappings of
galvanized steel, copper or aluminium either
nailed or screwed on.

Party walls

For reasons of sound insulation, party walls between adjoining residential buildings (terraced houses, semi-detached houses) should be built as twin-leaf walls with a continuous separating joint (cavity) from foundation to roof. If twin-leaf external walls are used, the separating joint must be taken through the outer leaf as well in order to avoid an acoustic bridge. According to DIN 1053 part 1, the minimum thickness of each leaf should be 115 mm. If the weight of the party wall exceeds 100 kg/m² wall area (including plaster), the width of the joint must be at least 50 mm; if over 150 kg/m², then 30 mm is permissible but 50 mm is still recommended. To comply with the sound insulation requirements of DIN 4109, the cavity must be completely filled with mineral fibre batts to DIN 18165 part 2. Closed-cell hard foam sheets or wood-fibre boards are unsuitable for sound insulation. The insulation must always extend above the leaf built last in order to prevent mortar and debris falling into the cavity and possibly forming acoustic bridges between the leaves. Installing the insulation in two layers with their joints offset is recommended for improving the sound insulation. As the separating joint also passes through the floors, the insulation should extend above the thickness of the floor during casting, be protected by suitable means and supported against the pressure of concrete on one side. If the weight of a single leaf exceeds 200 kg/m² wall area, the separating joint may remain open. Special care must be taken here to ensure that mortar or debris does not drop into the cavity and form acoustic bridges. This is less of a problem when using thin-bed mortar if the mortar is applied by way of mortar sledges. Otherwise, mortar – or concrete when casting the floors – can be prevented from falling into the cavity by using suspended battens raised as the work proceeds or joint forms, which have to be removed subsequently.

External basement walls

Basements are no longer restricted to subordinate roles such as the storage of food or fuel, but provide space for diverse activities, e.g. washing, hobbies, workshop, playroom, guest room, study etc. They represent a relatively inexpensive way of extending the useful floor space available. At the same time, they correspond to the concept of dense, space-saving construction [8].
Basement rooms normally heated require additional thermal insulation if that of the masonry alone is not sufficient. External thermal insulation is recommended. This should consist of materials covered by a standard but with extra functions regarding resistance to water, frost and earth pressure covered by a general build-

ing authority certificate or by the provisions of DIN 4108 part 4. Products suitable for external insulation include extruded polystyrene sheets, foamed glass sheets and polystyrene bead foam sheets with a minimum bulk density of 30 kg/m³.

External basement walls are subjected to vertical loads in the plane of the wall and horizontal loads resulting from, for example, earth pressure, perpendicular to the plane of the wall. Earth pressure loads are assumed to be mainly active earth pressures, provided the walls are not substantially thicker than the structural analysis requires, and the backfill material is only compacted to medium density. If the backfill material is highly compacted, an increased earth pressure, e.g. earth pressure at rest, must be assumed. The earth pressure generates bending moments in the wall which are usually the deciding factor in the design of the wall.

Stability of external masonry basement walls
Vertical uniaxial loadbearing action
If the basement wall is supported top and bottom, we can assume that the wall acts as a vertical loadbearing member spanning in one direction between two supports with a cracked section of no more than half the wall thickness. The tensile stresses perpendicular to the bed joints may not be taken into account (see "Analysis of tension and bending tension"). They are "neutralized" by vertical loads.
DIN 1053 part 1 includes two methods which may be applied in order to avoid the need to analyse the wall for earth pressure. The following conditions have to be satisfied for both methods (see fig. 2.4.20):

- Clear height of basement wall $h_s \leq 2.60$ m, thickness of wall $d \geq 240$ mm.
- The roof to the basement must act as a plate and be able to accommodate the forces generated by the earth pressure.
- The imposed load on the ground over the area in which the earth pressure influences the basement wall may not exceed 5 kN/m². At the same time, the surface of the ground should not slope upwards from the wall and the depth of fill h_e must be less than the clear height of the basement wall h_s.

In the first method the decisive criterion is the permanent load N_0 at the top of the basement wall below the basement roof, which must lie within the following limits:

$$\text{max } N_0 \geq N_0 \geq \text{min } N_0$$

Compliance with the permissible edge pressure is checked using the equation

$$\text{max } N_0 = 0,45 \, d \, \sigma_0$$

2.4.18 Rigid joint details

Rigid joints between walls

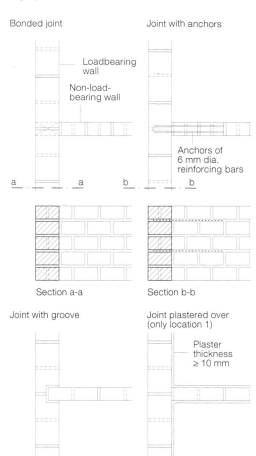

Bonded joint   Joint with anchors

Loadbearing wall
Non-load-bearing wall
Anchors of 6 mm dia. reinforcing bars

Section a-a   Section b-b

Joint with groove   Joint plastered over (only location 1)

Plaster thickness ≥ 10 mm

Rigid joint at base of wall

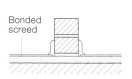 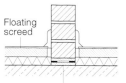

Wall built on bonded screed   Wall built on loadbearing floor

Bonded screed   Floating screed

Mortar joint

2.4.19 Segmentation of free-standing masonry walls (plan views)

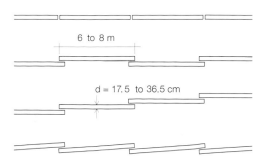

6 to 8 m

d = 17.5 to 36.5 cm

2.4.20 Loading assumptions for basement walls without mathematical analysis

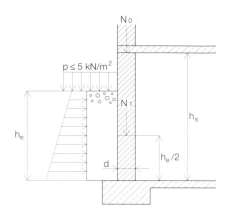

2.4.21 Min. N_0 for basements walls without mathematical analysis

Wall thickness d mm	min N_0 in kN/m for depth of backfill h_e of			
	1.0 m	1.5 m	2.0 m	2.5 m
240	6	20	45	75
300	3	15	30	50
365	0	10	25	40
490	0	5	15	30
Intermediate values may be obtained by linear interpolation				

2.4.22 Waterproofing of basement walls for the "non-hydrostatic pressure" loading case

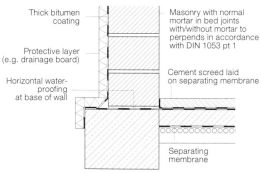

2.4.23 Waterproofing of basement walls for the "temporary build-up of seepage water" loading case

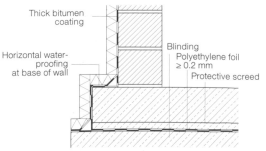

where d = wall thickness and σ_0 = basic value of permissible compressive stress.

The minimum loads min. N_0 are listed in DIN 1053 part 1 table 8 (see table 2.4.21). These ensure compliance with the permissible eccentricity of the basement wall as a result of axial force and bending moment due to earth pressure.
The second method is based on the findings of Mann/Bernhardt [9] and enables the wall to be analysed with slightly less vertical load. The axial force N_1 resulting from permanent loading at half the depth of fill must lie within the following limits:

$$d \times \beta_R / (3\,\gamma) \geq N_1 \geq \min N$$

where
min $N = (\rho_e \times h_{sx} \times h_e{}^2) / (20\,d)$
β_R characteristic compressive strength of masonry
γ safety factor
ρ_e bulk density of fill [kN/m³]

If the vertical loads N_0 and N_1 do not lie within the given limits, the basement wall must be designed according to the more accurate method of analysis taking the earth pressure into account. This involves analysing the compressive stresses as well as the slab shear resulting from the shear force generated by the earth pressure. Alternatively, the permissible upper and lower limits may be adjusted by increasing the thickness of the wall, reducing the height of the wall by forming the base in reinforced concrete, or choosing a unit/mortar combination with a higher compressive strength. This is also necessary if the design according to the more accurate method of analysis taking earth pressure into account is not possible. Finally, the load-carrying capacity of the basement wall can be increased by using reinforced masonry or by considering it to span in two directions or horizontally [154].

Biaxial loadbearing action
Stability can be checked by assuming that the external basement wall subjected to earth pressure spans in two directions when crosswalls or structural components, e.g. piers or stiffening columns of reinforced, concrete-filled channel blocks, support the wall at a clear spacing $b \leq 2\,h_s$. The necessary vertical loads may then be reduced as follows according to DIN 1053 part 1 (intermediate values may be obtained through linear interpolation):

• for $b \leq h_s$:
     $N_0 \geq 0.5 \min N_{0\ \text{uniaxial}}$
     $N_1 \geq 0.5 \min N_{\text{uniaxial}}$

• for $b \geq 2\,h_s$:
     $N_0 \geq \min N_{0\ \text{uniaxial}}$
     $N_1 \geq \min N_{\text{uniaxial}}$

Horizontal loadbearing action
If supports are closely spaced, then it is possible to carry the horizontal load of earth pressure to the supports by way of tensile bending stresses parallel to the bed joints. Owing to the low tensile bending strength of masonry parallel to the bed joints, this form of horizontal loadbearing action is, however, very limited, particularly with walls which need to be thin in order to maximize the usable interior space. If the vertical loads are very low owing to, for example, large window openings or floor slabs spanning parallel to the basement wall, or if there are segments of wall with unsupported top edges, e.g. spandrel panels beneath large basement windows, the structural system can be taken to be a horizontal arch. However, the external basement wall must be supported by the transverse elements and at a close spacing to guarantee that the arch is formed and the horizontal thrust accommodated. At an intermediate support between two arches with roughly equal spans and loads, the arch thrusts in the plane of the wall cancel each other out and only the component perpendicular to wall has to be resisted by the support. But at an end support, resistance to horizontal shear has to be proved. The type of construction which usually fulfils the requirements of such an analysis is reinforced masonry using reinforced, concrete-filled specials. The basement wall must be as thick as possible in order to achieve an adequate "rise" to ensure arching action. In addition, a cracked section up to half the thickness of the wall may be assumed at the centre of the arch in the calculations. The perpends must be fully filled with mortar in order to transfer the compression. The characteristic value that may be used for the strength of the masonry in the basement wall perpendicular to the perpends is – based on DIN 1053 part 3 – the characteristic value β_R for solid units and half the characteristic value β_R for compressive strength perpendicular to the bed joint for perforated solid units and other perforated units.

Reinforced masonry

Reinforced external basement walls are useful when the vertical loads are so low that a cracked section larger than half the thickness occurs under vertical or biaxial loadbearing action, or when carrying the loads horizontally via tensile bending stresses parallel to the bed joints or via horizontal arching action leads to uneconomically thick walls. Generally, the reinforcement is placed horizontally in the bed joints. However, vertical reinforcement is possible in conjunction with specials. Please refer to "Reinforced masonry" for details of the design and construction of reinforced external basement walls.

Waterproofing

As they are constantly in contact with the soil, external basement walls are permanently subjected to especially arduous conditions. If the basement is an extension to the living or ancillary space of a building, then the external walls must be permanently protected against the ingress of moisture.

Together with the customary waterproofing systems, masonry basements, without elaborate treatment, satisfy the requirements for design and construction to meet the loading cases "ground damp" to DIN 18195 part 4, "non-hydrostatic pressure" to DIN 18195 part 5 and "hydrostatic pressure" to DIN 18195 part 6 with "low load" (temporary build-up of seepage water). Most basement walls designed for the loading case "hydrostatic pressure" with "high load" (groundwater) will continue to be constructed in concrete to ensure adequate waterproofing (external tanking). The most popular waterproofing systems for external basement walls are bitumen and polymer bitumen sheeting; cold-application self-adhesive bitumen sheeting; and modified synthetic bitumen thick coatings. The latter are used for the majority of waterproofing tasks in housebuilding and represent the most economic solution [93].

Horizontal waterproofing

Horizontal waterproofing in the form of a complete sealing membrane is applied to the ground slab for the loading cases "ground damp" and "non-hydrostatic pressure". It is extended to the outside at the base of the external walls beneath the first course of masonry units to overlap with the vertical waterproofing. The ground slab must project sufficiently beyond the external wall to ensure an adequate connection between horizontal and vertical waterproofing. Placing the waterproofing beneath the first course of masonry units means that the entire floor construction, e.g. floating screed, is carried out in the dry. No further horizontal waterproofing is required. Sheets of waterproofing material are usually used because these are more robust than coatings with regard to mechanical damage

during the subsequent construction of the floor (see fig. 2.4.22).
The loading case "temporary build-up of seepage water" requires a layer of blinding to be laid first which is then covered with a min. 0.2 mm thick polyethylene foil as a separating membrane and then a screed to protect this against mechanical damage. The ground slab is then cast on this (internal tanking) (see fig. 2.4.23).

Vertical waterproofing

Waterproof sheeting bonded to the wall or sealing compounds worked cold (modified synthetic bitumen thick coatings) spread or sprayed on are suitable for the vertical waterproofing. The number of layers of waterproof sheeting depend on the type of sheeting selected. Thick coatings may be one- or two-component sealing systems and are always applied in two operations.
Special care must be exercised at the junction with the horizontal waterproofing. The foundation/wall transition should be rounded off with a concave fillet (min. radius 40 mm). The overlap should be at least 100 mm and be formed as an overlapped water check joint.

Protective layer

This protects the vertical waterproofing to the basement walls against mechanical damage during backfilling and subsequent compaction of the excavation. Suitable materials are, for example, textured plastic sheeting, thermal insulation batts or drainage boards of no-fines bitumen-bound polystyrene. This protective layer guarantees that the vertical waterproofing system remains fully functional.

Separating membrane

The inclusion of a non-woven fabric as a separating or sliding membrane between waterproofing and protective layer prevents loads due to settlement of the backfill from being transferred to the waterproofing, causing this to become detached.

Service penetrations

Building services (e.g. waste water, fresh water, electricity etc.) must be routed in such a way that the waterproofing is not impaired. In addition, service penetrations must be able to accommodate settlement of the structure without damage.

Construction joints

The waterproofing must safely bridge over construction joints. Any waterstops that are included must be permanently connected to the waterproofing.

Transition to superstructure, plinth

It is undesirable – both from a visual and a technical point of view – to continue the vertical waterproofing above ground level at the base

of the superstructure. A plinth must be water-proofed and protected against splashing water to a height of about 200 mm above ground level. Therefore, waterproof paint or suitable rendering is applied to exposed surfaces and this must overlap the vertical waterproofing by at least 100 mm. In twin-leaf masonry the waterproofing is placed on the outside face of the inner leaf.

Natural stone masonry

Natural stone masonry can be classed as dry walling, rubble masonry, various forms of coursed masonry, ashlar masonry or faced masonry depending on the degree to which the natural stones are worked and their resulting geometry.

Dry walling

is made from rubble stone without mortar. The stones should be laid with minimal dressing in a proper bond so that joints and voids are as small as possible. Smaller stones are to be wedged into the voids to create tension between the main stones. This helps the wall to keep its shape and remain stable. Dry walling is used for gravity retaining walls. In assessing stability, the density used should be taken as half the bulk density of the natural stone. When building gravity retaining walls, the natural stones are allowed to pile up against the soil to be retained in order to improve the stability of the wall. The largest and most regular (rectangular) stones are used to frame the wall at the corners and ends, and for the base (see fig. 2.4.24).

Uncoursed random rubble masonry

is made from unworked stones as they occur in nature. The round form of the stones results in a highly irregular appearance.
The finished wall is highly susceptible to sliding and does not exhibit any noteworthy compressive strength despite the hard rock used.
To secure the masonry bond, the joints must be carefully filled with mortar and small pieces of stone. In addition, the corners are built using stones with a more regular shape and the courses held together with headers (through-stones) trued up horizontally every approx. 1.0 m of wall height (see fig. 2.4.25).

Coursed random rubble masonry

The bed faces of these stones (150-300 mm high) obtained from quarries undergo only minimal working. Natural stones of various sizes are laid in mortar in approximate courses. Coursed random rubble masonry is trued up horizontally across its complete thickness (≥ 500 mm) every max. 1.5 m of wall height. The same applies to the inclusion of a damp proof course, which should be built in approx. 150 mm above ground level. Large stones

2.4.24   Dry walling

2.4.26   Coursed random rubble masonry

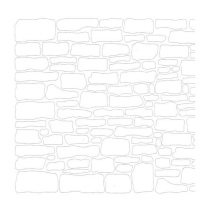

2.4.28   Irregular coursed masonry

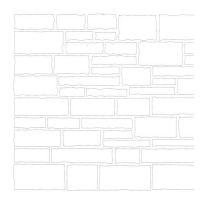

2.4.30   Ashlar masonry

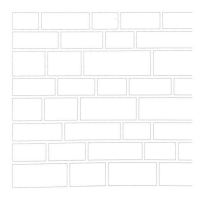

2.4.25   Uncoursed random rubble masonry

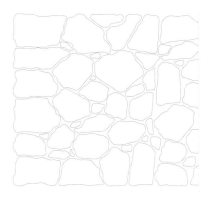

2.4.27   Hammer-dressed masonry

2.4.29   Regular coursed masonry

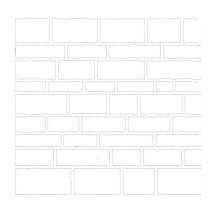

2.4.31   Stone facing with backing of man-made masonry units or concrete

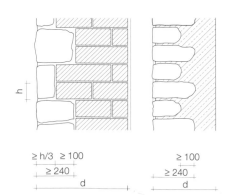

should be used at the base and at corners in order to secure the masonry bond. Normal mortar of group II or IIa is used depending on the type of rock.

These days, coursed random rubble masonry is only used for less important basement walls, free-standing boundary walls and for retaining walls in vineyards (see fig. 2.4.26).

Hammer-dressed masonry
The bed joints and perpends of the stones in exposed faces are worked to a depth of at least 120 mm. However, the natural stones beyond this depth of wall are either not worked at all or only very little. Vertical and horizontal joints are approximately at right-angles.
The height of a course may change within a course and between courses; however, the masonry is to be trued up horizontally across its complete thickness every max. 1.5 m of wall height. For information on mortars and horizontal damp proof courses, refer to "Coursed random rubble masonry" above (see fig. 2.4.27).

Irregular coursed masonry
The bed joints and perpends of the stones in exposed faces are worked to a depth of at least 150 mm. Vertical and horizontal joints are approximately perpendicular to each other and to the surface.
Perpends and bed joints may not be thicker than 30 mm. The height of a course may change within a course and between courses, but not excessively; however, the masonry is to be trued up horizontally across its complete thickness every max. 1.50 m of wall height (see fig. 2.4.28).

Regular coursed masonry

The stones should be worked as for irregular coursed masonry. However, the height of stones may not change within a course. In addition, the height of every course is to be trued up (see fig. 2.4.29).

When used for vaulting, domes and similar constructions, the bed joints must pass through the complete thickness of the curved element. Therefore, the bed joints should be worked over the full depth, while perpends need only be worked to a depth of 150 mm.

Ashlar masonry

The stones for ashlar masonry should be worked accurately to the specified dimensions and all perpends and bed joints worked to the full depth. The principles for bonding ashlar masonry are basically the same as for masonry using man-made units; all the different types of bonds using stretchers and headers can be produced. The joint thickness can be 4-30 mm; mortar is difficult to apply to joints thinner than 4 mm. Dry ashlar masonry requires the bed faces to be ground and is hardly used these days (see fig. 2.4.30).

Stone-faced masonry

consists of a skin of regular coursed or ashlar masonry on a backing of man-made units or concrete (see fig. 2.4.31).

The stone facing may be considered as part of the loadbearing cross-section when

- the stone facing is built at the same time as the backing and is bonded to it,
- the stone facing is bonded to the backing by at least 30% headers,
- the headers of the stone facing are at least 240 mm deep and are bonded at least 100 mm into the backing,
- the thickness of the stone facing is ≥ 1/3 its height or min. 115 mm,
- with backings of man-made units, at least every third course of natural stone consists entirely of headers.

The thickness of the total wall construction should be as determined by the structural analysis, but this is seldom less than 500 mm for practical reasons. The conditions described above apply similarly when the backing is made from concrete. Here, the concrete is poured and compacted after every course of facing stonework to prevent voids being formed beneath the header stones. The permissible stress for the complete wall construction is governed by the material with the lowest permissible stress. Stone facings that do not comply with the conditions outlined above may not be included as part of the loadbearing cross-section. Coursed stones may be laid against their stratification only when they exhibit a minimum compressive strength of 20 MN/m² parallel to their stratification. A non-loadbearing stone facing should be anchored and supported as for a non-loadbearing outer leaf of a twin-leaf wall. Cladding panels may not be included as part of the loadbearing cross-section of a column.

Openings in walls

Openings in walls for windows, doors and larger items, e.g. ventilation ducts and light wells, are bridged over by way of lintels or arches (masonry "lintels").

Arching action over openings

When designing a lintel or arch, we can assume an arching action in the masonry above the opening in the wall, provided there are no openings adjacent to and above the lintel or arch and the associated load triangle, and that the arch thrust (horizontal support reactions) can be resisted at the sides of the opening. Therefore, the lintel or arch carries the load only below the assumed arch (see fig. 2.4.32).

This is taken into account by the (equilateral) load triangle of masonry above the lintel or arch.

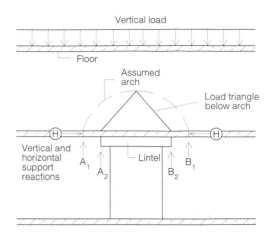

2.4.32 Arch action over opening in wall

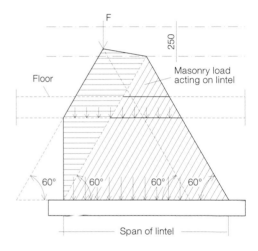

2.4.33 Effective loads over opening in wall with arch action

2.4.34   Reinforced concrete lintel details

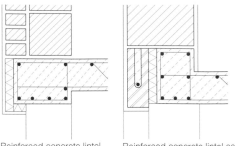

Reinforced concrete lintel with cast-in thermal insulation (only suitable for certain applications)

Reinforced concrete lintel as upstand beam with channel blocks as permanent formwork to outside face

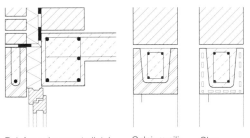

Reinforced concrete lintel masked by channel blocks for facing masonry

Calcium silicate channel blocks

Clay channel blocks

2.4.35   Shallow lintel details

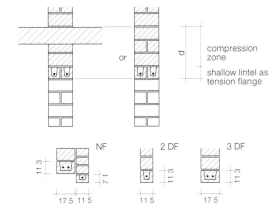

compression zone

shallow lintel as tension flange

NF   2 DF   3 DF

2.4.36   Supporting a soldier course "fake" lintel

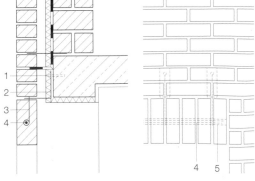

1   Bolt
2   Angle bracket
3   6 mm dia. V4A steel anchor
4   Continuous bar carrying soldiers (10 dia. V4A steel)
5   Continuous hole

Uniformly distributed floor loads above the load triangle are not taken into account when designing the construction over the opening in the wall. For floor loads that act within the load triangle as a uniformly distributed load on the masonry (e.g. floor slabs and joist floors with joist spacing ≤ 1.25 m), only the section which lies within the triangle is assumed to transfer load onto the lintel. Point loads, e.g. from beams, which lie within or near the load triangle are assumed to distribute their loads at 60°. If point loads occur outside the load triangle, they need be taken into account only if they lie within the span of the lintel or arch and below a horizontal line 250 mm above the apex of the load triangle. In this case the self-weight of the wall below the point load also has to be taken into account (see fig. 2.4.33).
If arching action cannot be established in the masonry above the load triangle over the opening in the wall, the lintel or arch must be assumed to carry the entire load above the opening.

Beam-type lintels

Beams of, for example, timber, steel or reinforced concrete transfer the loads acting on them to their supports at each end by way of bending. Therefore, the beams must be designed to resist bending and shear forces. Owing to their excellent material properties, steel sections can be generally quite small, but for reasons of fire protection have to be encased in concrete and to comply with building science requirements must be provided with thermal insulation.
Reinforced concrete lintels are usually chosen when the lintel can be combined with a reinforced concrete floor or in certain loading situations. They may be precast units or cast in situ with the reinforced concrete floor. A reinforced concrete lintel must always be provided with insulation to meet thermal insulation requirements. The problem with this is that the effective cross-section of the lintel must be reduced in order to accommodate the insulation and this creates a substrate for plastering which is different to the surrounding wall.
Despite the provision of a plaster backing spanning across the thermal insulation, this type of detail often leads to cracks in the rendering and staining of the finish.
One solution to this problem is to provide channel blocks in the respective type of masonry as permanent formwork instead of the reinforced concrete. The reinforced concrete lintel (precast or in situ) is then integrated into this. This can also be used in conjunction with a reinforced concrete lintel cast together with the floor slab. In this detail a prefabricated lintel unit made from channel blocks (with integral insulation) forms one side of the formwork for the reinforced concrete lintel. As the structurally effective width of this lintel is only very small,

it may need to be formed as an upstand beam. There are channel blocks available to match the respective formats and course heights of facing masonry and these may be used to form prefabricated lintels and employed as formwork to the side of a reinforced concrete lintel cast in situ (see fig. 2.4.34).

Shallow lintels with masonry above

Shallow lintels consist of a prefabricated, reinforced tension flange and only achieve their full load-carrying capacity in conjunction with a compression zone of masonry or concrete or both (e.g. masonry and floor or capping beam) above. The tension flange may be prefabricated from concrete or from channel blocks of clay, lightweight concrete, calcium silicate etc., filled with concrete in which the reinforcement (prestressed if required) is placed. In contrast to beam-type lintels, shallow lintels carry the loads acting on them in conjunction with the wall above like a tied frame (a closed system). The shallow lintel (tie) resists the tensile forces from the arch (frame) in compression and therefore replaces the end supports which would otherwise be necessary to accommodate the horizontal thrust.
The advantage of shallow lintels is that they can easily be made from the same material as the surrounding wall. This avoids cracks in and damage to the plaster. By matching the dimensions of the shallow lintel to the modular sizes of the surrounding wall, this type of construction can be integrated into the masonry without having to adapt or cut the masonry units adjacent the opening in the wall. This leads to more economic and more rational site operations. For further information, see "Reinforced masonry" and [35] (see fig. 2.4.35).

Masonry lintels and arches

Prefabricated or in-situ lintels of horizontally reinforced masonry may be used for facing work. The loadbearing behaviour corresponds to the tied frame model of the shallow lintel with wall above. The horizontal reinforcement is placed either in trough-shaped specials or horizontal channel blocks or perforated units with a continuous hole to suit the bond of the facing masonry. Design and construction should be in accordance with DIN 1053 part 3. Please also refer to "Reinforced masonry". In twin-leaf facing masonry the outer leaf above the opening in the wall can be carried by nibs on the side of the floor slab or by supports bolted to or cast into the floor slab (e.g. steel angles or brackets). To satisfy architectural requirements we can also provide a horizontal lintel in the form of a soldier course in conjunction with brackets and bars passing through the masonry units. The shear- and tension-resistant connection to a reinforced concrete beam behind means that this is only a "fake"

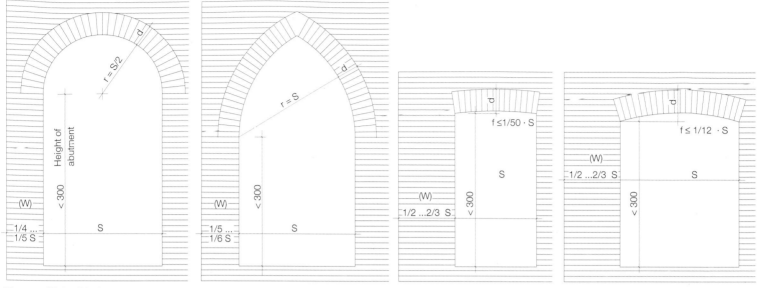

2.4.37 Semicircular and pointed arches according to [162]   2.4.38 Cambered and gauged arches according to [162]

The span (S) feasible depends on type of arch, compression in arch and vertical loads. The width (W) of the abutment depends on the span; the values given here apply to abutment widths essentially without vertical load. All values are guidelines which may be exceeded in an accurate analysis. Cambered arches in non-loadbearing facing work can be built for spans up to approx. 1.75 m without the need for a structural analysis.

lintel with no loadbearing function (see fig. 2.4.36).

Masonry lintels in the form of arches are primarily used in the refurbishment of older buildings, but are also being rediscovered as a modern design option in conjunction with facing masonry. Owing to the high labour input, these arches are often produced as prefabricated elements, which are then lifted into place on prepared abutments. With a favourable rise/span ratio and predominantly permanent loads, i.e. dead loads considerably higher than imposed loads, the arch may be designed according to the line of thrust method. This means that the construction is subjected only to axial compression and no shear or bending moments when the axis of the arch coincides with the line of thrust. However, this ideal case is hardly possible in practice because changing loads, and hence different loading cases, mean that various lines of thrust have to be considered when designing the arch. Nevertheless, to ensure that exclusively compressive stresses without a cracked section occur in the cross-section of the arch, the geometry of the arch should be such that, if possible, the lines of thrust for all possible loading cases lie in the middle third of the cross-section. Lines of thrust can thus be used independently of the loads in order to design a suitable, economic arch for masonry which, in theory, cannot accommodate any tension. In doing so, we assume that the structural system is based on determining the lines of thrust for a three-pin arch in which the pins are positioned at the springing points and at the crown of the arch. Arches with longer spans and more pronounced changes of loading have to be designed according to elastic theory. Providing resis-

tance to the arch thrust at the supports also has to be taken into account when designing an arch. Shallow arches with a low rise generate a greater horizontal thrust than arches with a smaller radius and larger rise. The horizontal thrust must be resisted without displacement at the supports irrespective of the curvature of the arch because the arch itself undergoes a severe increase in stresses due to the reduction in the rise even with only minimal displacement of the supports.

Semicircular and pointed arches
The radius of a semicircular arch is equal to half the width of the opening, and for a pointed arch equal to the full width of the opening, with the centres of the radii being the respective opposite springing points. The abutments for semicircular and pointed arches are generally positioned horizontally at the level of the springing points. The arches are normally constructed with tapering bed joints. The thickness of the joints at the underside of the arch (intrados) should not be less than 5 mm, at the outer ring of the arch (extrados) not greater than 20 mm. Special tapering units (voussoirs) may be necessary for small radii. When using small-format units, the size of the bed joints at the extrados of the arch increase as the arch becomes thicker. Therefore, thick arches are also built in individual rings, one above the other. Arches are always constructed using an odd number of units so that there is never a joint at the crown but rather always a keystone. The bed joints must be arranged perpendicular to the line of thrust and must run the full depth of the arch. The bond for masonry arches is to be produced according to the bonding rules for masonry piers [32, 141, 161] (fig. 2.4.37).

Cambered and gauged arches
have inclined (skewback) abutments aligned with the centre of the arch. The bed joints also point to the centre of the arch. The rise of a cambered arch is max. 1/50 of the width of the opening, that of a gauged arch max. 1/12. A cambered arch without any rise may also act as an arch in compression if the soldier course deviates slightly from the vertical and is wedged into abutments built at a very slight angle.

The arch lintel is produced from an odd number of courses, which can make it necessary to inset the abutments by half the width of a course on the masonry at the sides. The extrados should always end in a bed joint of the masonry above in order to avoid large compensating courses above the arch or unattractive gussets above the abutments. The requirements regarding joint thicknesses and bonding correspond to those for semicircular and pointed arches (see fig. 2.4.38).

Vaulting and arch floors

Vaults
These are roof-like, one-way-spanning, or also bidirectional arch-like or spherical curved roof constructions of masonry. The various types of vaulting are based on the two fundamental types: barrel vaults with cylindrical curvature, and domes with spherical curvature. Besides the barrel vault, other cylindrical forms include the Prussian cap vault; the cloistered vault; the trough vault; the cov; and the groined vault. The dome is a spherical form of vaulting whose surfaces generally form part of the surface of a sphere (see fig. 2.4.39).

2.4.39   Types of masonry vaulting

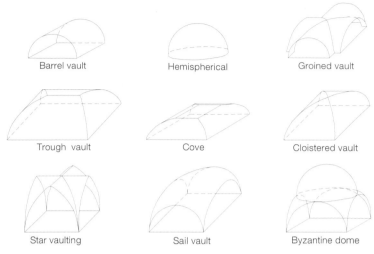

Barrel vault   Hemispherical   Groined vault

Trough vault   Cove   Cloistered vault

Star vaulting   Sail vault   Byzantine dome

2.4.40   Design requirements for masonry arch floors

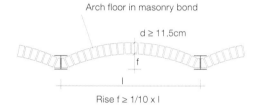

Arch floor in masonry bond

$d \geq 11.5$ cm

f

l

Rise $f \geq 1/10 \times l$

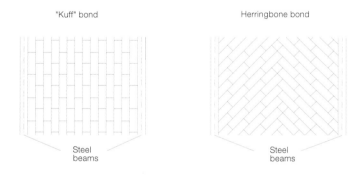

"Kuff" bond   Herringbone bond

Steel beams   Steel beams

2.4.41   Assumptions for arch thrust for multi-bay arch floor

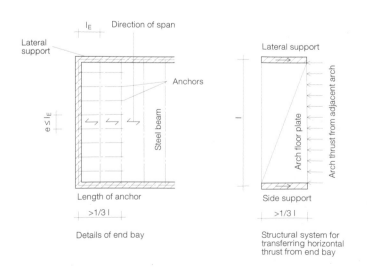

l_E Direction of span

Lateral support

Anchors

Steel beam

$e \leq l_E$

Length of anchor

>1/3 l

Details of end bay

Lateral support

Arch floor plate

Arch thrust from adjacent arch

Side support

>1/3 l

Structural system for transferring horizontal thrust from end bay

Vaults with smaller spans, a favourable span/ rise ratio (f/l > 1/10) and essentially permanent loading can be designed according to the line of thrust method. They are built from tapered masonry units that support each other and are supported on immovable abutments in such a way that they are only subjected to compression. The arch thrust can also be resisted by ties (in tension) instead of abutments.

Vaults with large spans and pronounced changes of loading are designed according to elastic theory.

Masonry arch floors between beams

These are the upper part of an arch built between steel beams as vertical supports (see fig. 2.4.40). The structural system employed for determining the vertical and horizontal support reactions for arch floors is a three-pin arch with the centre pin at the crown. With an essentially stationary imposed load according to DIN 1055 part 3, arch floors with a thickness based on empirical rules and with beams spaced at max. approx. 2.50 m do not need to be analysed structurally. In this case, the minimum thickness must be 115 mm, they must be built using "Kuff" bond or herringbone bond, and the ratio of rise to span must be at least 1/10. Centering for parallel arches should, like the bricklaying itself, be carried out simultaneously in order to limit the horizontal thrust caused by the arches at the end bays of multi-bay floors. Ties can be integrated to transfer the horizontal thrust from the end bays of multi-bay floors to the side walls. These must be included in the end bays parallel to the direction of span of the floor at the ends of the beams and at a spacing equal to the span of the end bay but at least at third-points. In order to consider the end plate formed by ties as an adequate abutment (rigid horizontal plate) able to transfer the horizontal thrust to the sides, the width of the end plate must be equal to one third of its length. The ties used must be longer than the minimum width of the plate. In the case of narrow end bays it is sometimes necessary to extend the ties over several bays (see fig. 2.4.41).

The end bays must be provided with supports at the sides which are in the position to accept the horizontal thrust of the middle bays even when the end bays are not loaded. The supports may be secured by means of masonry, permanent vertical load, anchors or other suitable measures. In the basements of buildings with an essentially stationary imposed load of max. 2.0 kN/m² we can assume, without a structural analysis, that the horizontal thrust from arch floors up to 1.3 m span can be accommodated by means of 2 m long, 240 mm thick crosswalls at a spacing of max. 6.0 m. The crosswalls must be built simultaneously with and fully bonded to the end bay support walls or – in the case of toothing – via a non-mechanical connection (see fig. 2.4.42).

Point loads

Masonry can be subjected to point (concentrated) loads from beams (e.g. window lintels); joists (e.g. joist floors); or columns (e.g. window mullions, roof posts). These generate vertical concentrations of stress on the bearing surfaces and horizontal spitting tensile forces in the load dispersion zone. The spitting tensile forces can be accommodated by the tensile strength of the masonry bond, by reinforcement or by reinforced concrete elements. A padstone or similar is always integrated into the masonry to distribute the load from heavy point loads. This is usually of reinforced concrete but may be of steel. The reinforced concrete ring beam or the support/floor strip is often used. It may also comprise masonry units of higher strength incorporated in the masonry bond below the point load. In both cases the designer must take account of possible cracking in the masonry as a result of restraints caused by the change in material (see fig. 2.4.43). A load distribution of 60° may be assumed within a section of wall strengthened with units of higher strength. The strength required for this masonry is determined by the bearing stresses beneath the point load. The height over which the wall must be strengthened is determined by the fact that the normal masonry of the wall (of lower strength) must be able to carry the load beneath the 60° load dispersion.

The permissible stresses for masonry below point loads are greater than for the rest of the wall because the inclined "struts" created by the 60° load dispersion generate a biaxial compression condition at the point of action of the point load which increases the load-carrying capacity of the masonry locally. However, the inclined struts mean that there are also horizontal "ties" in the lower courses of the wall, the tension in which has to be resisted by horizontal reinforcement or by the floor slab acting as a tie. Point loads that act at the end of a wall create an inclined strut, which is balanced by a horizontal tension at the top of the wall. This tension leads to vertical cracks, to tearing of the masonry bearing, if it cannot be accommodated by the masonry bond, the reinforced concrete floor slab or ring beam acting as a tie or by horizontal reinforcement in the masonry. When analysing the point load and the dispersion of the load according to DIN 1053 part 1, the position of the point load is taken into account through the dimensions of the point of action of the load (see fig. 2.4.43). Point loads perpendicular to the plane of the wall, e.g. from horizontal impacts, should not exceed $0.5\beta_R$ according to the more accurate method of analysis in DIN 1053 part 1 and $0.5 \times 2.67\,\sigma_0 = 1.33\,\sigma_0$ according to the simplified method of analysis. In addition, the shear stresses in the bed joints of the individual masonry units under load must be analysed for

horizontal point loads perpendicular to the plane of the wall where $F \geq 3$ kN. Perforated and cellular units require a plate or similar to be incorporated underneath so that the horizontal load is transferred to at least two webs in order to avoid overloading the webs of individual masonry units.

Connections

Walls must be connected to floors and roof frames in order to guarantee transfer of forces and provision of horizontal support for load-bearing and stiffening walls. This can be achieved either by anchors or through adhesion and friction.
In order to also achieve three-dimensional stability for the building, ring beams must be placed in all external and crosswalls which act as vertical plates for carrying horizontal loads (e.g. wind). This presupposes that the floors act as horizontal plates. Floors that do not act as plates (e.g. timber joist floors), or those which are supported on the walls via sliding bearings in order that deformations are not restrained (e.g. roof slabs) require that the walls, and hence the building, gain horizontal restraint by way of capping beams or other equivalent structural measures.

Connecting walls to floors and roof frames
In principle, all walls – including internal walls or party walls separating buildings – must be connected to floors such that forces can be transferred, provided the floors are intended to provide lateral support to the walls.

Connection using anchors
Anchors (with vertical straps in the case of timber joist floors) must always be included in loadbearing areas of walls and never in non-loadbearing spandrel panels. Only by providing vertical load is the wall in a position to accommodate the anchor forces and guarantee the transfer of forces to the floor. A lack of vertical load might dictate the use of a ring beam. Generally, the spacing between anchors should not exceed 2.0 m in order to limit the forces placed on them. However, the spacing may be increased to max. 4.0 m in exceptional circumstances if the particular construction does not permit any other solution.
Walls parallel to the direction of span of the floor require straps which extend at least 1.0 m into the floor and are fixed to at least two floor ribs or two beams (three joists in the case of timber floors). This distribution of load over several ribs or beams/joists is necessary because otherwise the restraint forces subject the floor members to lateral bending (see fig. 2.4.46). Beams spliced over internal walls and tied to the perimeter walls must have a tension-resistant splice connection. This is necessary

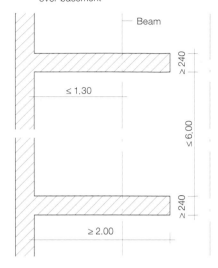

2.4.42 Accommodating the arch thrust without structural analysis for a multi-bay arch floor over basement

2.4.43 Load dispersion below point load

Masonry of higher strength

σ_1 from point load (beam, column, joist)

$\alpha = 60°$

σ_2

Masonry of lower strength

σ_1 : to be carried by masonry of higher strength
σ_2 : to be carried by masonry of lower strength

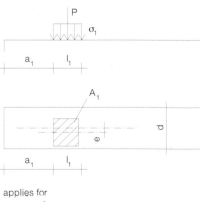

applies for
$A_1 = 2\,d^2$
and
$e \leq d/6$

$$\sigma_1 \leq \frac{\beta_R}{\gamma}\left(1 + 0.1\,\frac{a_1}{l_1}\right) \leq 1.5\,\frac{\beta_R}{\gamma}$$

Permissible bearing stress to DIN 1053 pt 1

141

2.4.44 Support options for gable walls

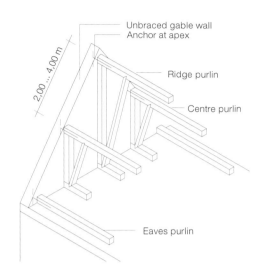

Unbraced gable wall
Anchor at apex
2,00 ... 4,00 m
Ridge purlin
Centre purlin
Eaves purlin

Support via braced roof frame

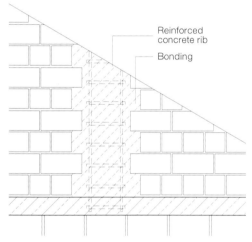

Reinforced
concrete rib
Bonding

Support via integral column

2.4.45 Load distribution of a ring beam for building
stiffened by floor plates

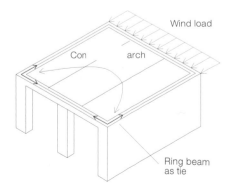

Wind load
Con   arch
Ring beam
as tie

in order to link opposing external walls together and ensure an effective connection between external walls and floors.

Gable walls can be connected via anchors to a braced roof frame. Alternatively, they gain their stability by way of crosswalls or other measures (e.g. reinforced concrete columns restrained by the floor slab, masonry piers) (see fig. 2.4.44).

Connection using adhesion and friction
Secure support for walls by way of adhesion and friction is provided by concrete floors when the depth of bearing of the slab on the wall is at least 100 mm; anchors are then unnecessary. An adhesion/friction connection assumes that a connection capable of transferring forces is generated by the adhesion alone, and is only reinforced by the friction arising from vertical loads if necessary; however, the presence of friction is not absolutely essential. We can also assume this situation at the junction between a wall and a capping beam.

Ring beams and capping beams
These are horizontal straight members in the plane of the wall. Ring beams accommodate tension within the wall plate, which ensues as a result of external loads or differential deformation, and hence increases the stability of the walls and that of the whole structure.
Capping beams also serve as ring beams when they form a complete ring around the whole building. Furthermore, their reinforcement arrangement allows them to accommodate loads perpendicular to the plane of the wall by way of bending.

Ring beams
act as ties to hold the structure together. They are required in buildings with more than two full storeys, or those longer than 18 m at wall elements provided for stabilizing the structure (external walls, twin-leaf party walls, crosswalls etc.) at or immediately below every floor level. Ring beams may be interrupted only when their effectiveness is guaranteed by other components, e.g. window lintels or landings in the case of continuous windows to a staircase.
It is also necessary to hold the structure together by way of ring beams in the case of walls with many or particularly large openings; this is especially the case when the sum of the widths of the openings exceed 60% of the length of the wall or 40% in the case of windows greater than 2/3 of the storey height.
Other functions of ring beams are to act as a tie for the compression arch in a horizontal floor plate; to act as a tie for the vertical masonry plate; and to accommodate tensile stresses in the masonry as a result of differential deformation caused by temperature fluctuations, shrinkage or differential settlement of the subsoil [54] (see fig. 2.4.45).

Ring beams may be made from timber, steel, reinforced masonry or reinforced concrete. They are to be designed for a tensile force of 30 kN under service loads. This figure corresponds to the forces to be expected in buildings of normal dimensions. The beams should be designed for greater tensile forces when a structural analysis of the wall plate, floor plate or differential deformation results in larger figures. Ring beams of reinforced masonry must comply with the corrosion protection, reinforcement arrangement and mortar or concrete cover requirements of DIN 1053 part 3. Ring beams of reinforced concrete must have at least two continuous 10 mm reinforcing bars to DIN 1045. The reinforcement laps should be in accordance with DIN 1045, and staggered if possible.
The reinforcement required for ring beams of reinforced masonry or reinforced concrete may include the full cross-section of continuous reinforcement not fully utilized in floor slabs or window lintels no more than 500 mm from the centreline of the wall or floor parallel to the beam (see fig. 2.4.47). The use of different materials for the masonry and the ring beam can lead to damage to masonry. Above all, severe temperature deformations in ring beams generally as well as the shrinkage of reinforced concrete ring beams in particular can lead to cracks in the masonry. Temperature deformations can be minimized by including adequate thermal insulation, shrinkage reduced by late striking of the formwork and by subsequently treating the concrete. To minimize cracking in rendering, a reinforced concrete ring beam should make use of fabric reinforcement or, alternatively, should be fabricated from channel blocks to match the surrounding wall and hence provide a consistent substrate for the rendering. This or the use of reinforced masonry as a ring beam means that the disadvantages of changing the material are, on the whole, avoided.

Capping beams
are subjected not only to tensile forces but also to bending moments from horizontal loads.
Capping beams are necessary when floors do not act as plates, e.g. timber joist floors, or are provided with sliding bearings where they are supported on the walls and so do not provide lateral restraint at floor level. The ring beam becomes a capping beam and takes on a stabilizing task. As a rigid horizontal beam it transfers the horizontal loads from wind, reversal of forces, earthquakes etc. to the shear walls (see fig. 2.4.48).
The capping beam and its connections to the shear walls should be designed for a horizontal load equal to 1/100 of the vertical load of the walls and for a proportion of the wind loads. In addition, capping beams beneath sliding bearings must take account of tensile forces from the residual friction forces of the floors.

Shear walls must be analysed to ensure they can accommodate the support reactions of capping beams, and that they adequately transfer the forces to the foundations.

If a capping beam does not fulfil ring beam functions at the same time, it needs only to extend as far as necessary to transfer its support reactions to another element. Capping beams may be made of timber, steel or reinforced concrete. They must be rigid enough to prevent any cracks in the masonry due to deformations. This requirement means that the feasible span of such a beam is sometimes limited. Reinforced concrete capping beams must have shear links and at least one longitudinal reinforcing bar in each corner of the link. Capping beams should be treated like ring beams with regard to the problem of the risk of cracks in masonry caused by a change of material between wall and beam. This also applies to the use of channel blocks to achieve a consistent plaster substrate.

2.4.46 Fixing tension anchors in masonry

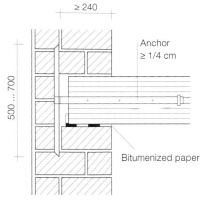

Fixing to masonry in direction of span of floor

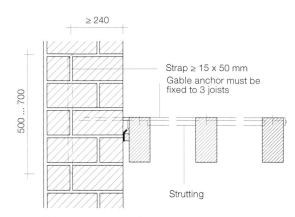

Fixing to masonry at right-angles to span of floor

2.4.47 Details of ring beams taking into account parallel reinforcement

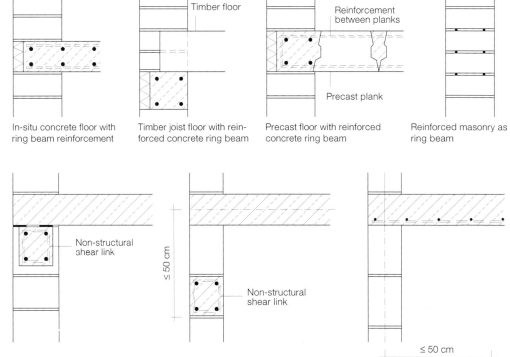

In-situ concrete floor with ring beam reinforcement

Timber joist floor with reinforced concrete ring beam

Precast floor with reinforced concrete ring beam

Reinforced masonry as ring beam

Ring beam made from prefabricated channel blocks

Max. spacing of parallel reinforcement which may be considered

2.4.48 Capping beam action

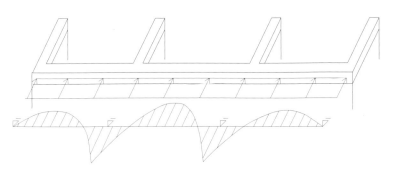

The building of masonry

Konrad Zilch, Martin Schätz

The standard of workmanship is a critical factor that determines the load-carrying capacity and serviceability of masonry especially because, in contrast to reinforced concrete, timber or steel, all the important structural and building science tasks are in this case fulfilled by one single building material.

Therefore, DIN 1053 part 1 includes a separate section devoted to the building of masonry. The aim of this section is not only to guarantee that the aforementioned tasks are fulfilled, but also that the appearance and aesthetics of masonry constructions comply with certain standards. In addition, these practical considerations are intended to resist the undermining of quality standards as a result of the growing pressure on costs and time, as well as the decline in standards of training evident on site. Consequently, the parameters for careful planning and building of masonry ensure that the practical realization is as free from flaws as possible.

In the end, rationalization measures such as building with large-format units, without mortar or with kit-type elements and so on, can lead to more economic masonry only if special requirements are placed on the standard of workmanship of the wall.

Mixing and using mortar on site

Mixing mortar

If mortar is to be mixed on site, the cement, admixtures and additives must be stored in a dry place protected from the weather. Aggregates must be stored under clean conditions so that they cannot be contaminated by salts, loam, organic substances or large stones. Gauging the quantities of mortar ingredients must be carried out using scales or suitable containers, e.g. buckets or gauge boxes with volumetric gradations, but never with shovels, in order to guarantee a consistent mortar mix. For small amounts, mixing is carried out manually in a tub with a sand shovel or – particularly with thin-bed mortars – with a mixing blade attached to an electric drill. As a rule, however, a suitably sized electric tilt or non-tilt drum

mixer is employed. Mixing instructions should be attached to the machine in a place where they are clearly visible. The raw materials should be mixed until the mortar has an even consistency that is suitable for the intended job. Premixed mortars are becoming increasingly popular as an aid to rationalization and for ensuring constant mortar quality in terms of consistency, workability, strength etc. According to the form of supply, we distinguish between premixed dry mortar, premixed "coarse stuff" and ready-mixed mortar (including multi-chamber silo mortar). On site, only the required amount of water needs to be added to premixed dry mortar or multi-chamber silo mortar, or the required amount of water plus cement to premixed "coarse stuff". No aggregates, additives or admixtures may be mixed into premixed mortars. Premixed dry mortar and premixed "coarse stuff" are prepared on site in a mixer, but ready-mixed mortar is delivered ready to use in a workable consistency (see "Mortars for masonry").

Different types and groups of mortars may only be prepared and used together on site if mistakes in identification can be ruled out. This is particularly so in the case of normal mortars of mortar groups II and IIa because they look very similar.

Mortar normally contains cement as the binding agent, which undergoes an alkaline reaction in the presence of water or moisture. Therefore, protect skin and eyes. Upon contact with the skin, rinse with water, upon contact with the eyes, consult a doctor without delay.

Using mortar

The trowel is still the best tool for laying small- and medium-format masonry units. The triangular trowel has a favourable centre of gravity and puts less strain on the bricklayer's wrist than the square trowel. The advantage of the latter is, however, that it is easier to lay and spread larger amounts of mortar evenly. The masonry and mortar industries have developed the so-called mortar sledge for economic construction with large-format masonry units as well as for one-brick-thick walls. This

tool matches the width of the wall and is pulled along the bed joint, thereby depositing a constant amount of mortar onto the bed joint through a slit. This makes it possible to apply a bed joint of constant thickness up to 10 m long across the full width of the wall in one operation.

Thin-bed mortars require the use of toothed trowels or mortar rollers, which guarantee a consistent application of the mortar just 1 mm thick. The masonry unit is frequently merely dipped in the mortar and then laid. A comparatively large amount of water is extracted from the "green" mortar in the case of high absorbency masonry units, which means that the hardening process of the mortar may not be completed because this requires a certain minimum amount of water. The mortar dries out and the result is poor adhesion between masonry unit and mortar. This can be prevented by adequate prewetting of high absorbency masonry units or by mixing an additive into the mortar to increase the water retention capacity. The recommendations of the mortar supplier should be followed in the case of premixed mortars.

Another advantage of prewetting or using water-retention additives is that leaching of water-soluble salts from the cement in the mortar is reduced or prevented. As the water evaporates, the salts cause efflorescence on the surface of the masonry units which, although harmless, is unattractive and therefore must be removed by repeated brushing (see "Building and cleaning facing masonry"). As mortar hardens it loses water and so is subjected to ever more severe conditions by the masonry units. Therefore, every type of pretreatment and subsequent treatment of the masonry, e.g. prewetting the masonry units, protecting the newly built masonry against rain, strong sunlight and premature drying-out by covering it with plastic sheeting, or spraying the new masonry with water, benefits the quality of the mortar and hence the masonry. This is particularly true in the first 3-4 days after laying [164].

2.5.1 Arrangement of perpends

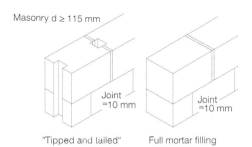

Masonry d ≥ 115 mm

Joint ≈10 mm — "Tipped and tailed"

Joint ≈10 mm — Full mortar filling

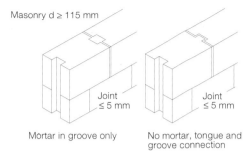

Masonry d ≥ 115 mm

Joint ≤ 5 mm — Mortar in groove only

Joint ≤ 5 mm — No mortar, tongue and groove connection

Protecting masonry against moisture

Masonry units are usually delivered wrapped in plastic sheeting on pallets and hence are protected against saturation up to the time of laying. As saturated masonry units do not develop adequate adhesion to the mortar and, furthermore, increase the energy required for drying out the primary structure, bricks and blocks awaiting laying, as well as the unprotected tops and sides of individual elements such as walls, spandrel panels and openings, must be protected against prolonged rainfall by means of tarpaulins or plastic sheeting. These should be secured against uplift by way of battens nailed down or by heavy materials. In addition, temporary drainage measures should be taken beneath roof gutters if the rainwater downpipes have not yet been connected in order to prevent local saturation of the masonry. Following these recommendations will ensure that there is no damage to the masonry in the form of, for example, shrinkage cracks, efflorescence or reduced strength [175].

Laying during cold weather

Masonry may be built during frosty conditions only if certain protective measures are carried out. These include covering the aggregate for the mortar with insulating blankets for the temperature range from 0 to +5°C; covering the masonry units waiting to be laid with insulating blankets for the temperature range from -5 to 0°C; heating the mixing water and the aggregate and working in tents or protective shelters. As the temperature drops still further, development of the mortar strength slows down and practically comes to a halt at about -10°C. Whenever possible, masonry should not be built at such low temperatures.

Frozen building materials may not be used at any temperature. Furthermore, newly built masonry, delicate elements and columns in particular, should be protected against frost and precipitation by a covering of insulating blankets. If such measures are not carried out, no further masonry units may be laid on masonry already frozen. Sections of masonry damaged by frost must be removed before work continues. On no account use antifreeze agents or de-icing salts because this can lead to efflorescence (e.g. salt deposits) appearing

on the masonry and to damage (e.g. spalling caused by the formation of salt crystals) [54, 164, 214].

Suitability and quality tests

According to DIN 1053, the properties of the building materials must be verified. This requirement is fulfilled by suitability and quality tests. The suitability test stipulates whether the types and quantities of certain raw materials are suitable for the production of a building material with defined properties, e.g. strength, gross density etc. This test is carried out before the actual production of the building material or the building of the masonry. The quality test is carried out on random samples of the building material produced for use on the building site and simultaneously with the actual construction, in order to verify that the intended material properties have been achieved. The quality control of masonry units is carried out within the scope of the manufacturer's own quality control measures, and those of outside centres, at regular intervals. The requirements for this are stipulated in the individual standards covering the different types of masonry units. The manufacturer's own quality control during production include constant monitoring of the production process to guarantee that the masonry units produced comply with the critical technical parameters. Monitoring by approved outside centres takes the form of checking the manufacturer's quality control measures during production and ensuring that the personnel and equipment used meet the required standards.

In the case of mortars, a suitability test according to DIN 1053 part 1 appendix A.5 is necessary only if the serviceability of the aggregate has to be verified or if admixtures and additives are to be used.

Furthermore, the suitability test needs to be carried out as a preliminary test for premixed mortars, including lightweight and thin-bed mortars only for structures with more than six full masonry storeys (see 2.1.28).

The building contractor is responsible for carrying out on-site quality tests for mortar within the scope of checking and assessing the quality of prescribed masonry (RM) or masonry according to suitability test (EM).

Quality control of prescribed masonry (RM)

Suitability and quality tests are not required for prescribed masonry because this type of masonry is based on many years of experience of using a "prescribed" combination of standard masonry units and standard mortar. The building contractor must check that the details on the delivery slip or the packaging of masonry units for prescribed masonry match those on the building authority documentation. Mortar mixed on site for prescribed masonry must be checked regularly during construction against table A.1 of DIN 1053 part 1 (see table 2.1.25) or using a suitability test to ensure that the mixing ratio is being maintained. For premixed mortars, the details of the type of mortar and mortar group on the delivery slip or packaging must be compared with the technical documentation, and the grade number and the supplying works compared with the order. Mortars of group IIIa must undergo a compressive strength test according to DIN 18555 part 3 carried out on three prisms from three different mix batches per storey, but at least every 10 m³ of mortar, and be checked against the requirements of DIN 1053 part 1 table A.2. Buildings with more than six full masonry storeys require a quality test to be carried out per storey, but at least for every 20 m³ of mortar, even for normal mortars of groups II, IIa and III as well as for lightweight and thin-bed mortars. This takes account of the higher requirements placed on the load-carrying capacity of such masonry and hence on the required consistency of the mortar properties in the lower storeys. As the increased requirements do not apply to the top three storeys, this extra quality test is unnecessary for those storeys.

Quality control of masonry according to suitability test (EM)

Suitability tests according to DIN 1053 part 2 are required to establish the strength class of masonry according to suitability test. This involves allocating the masonry to a strength class by way of a compressive strength test carried out on test samples according to DIN 18554 part 1 and the subsequent issue of a classification certificate. This must be provided to the building site prior to commencing construction work with such masonry. The suitability test must be carried out by an approved

2.5.2 Butt joint

materials testing laboratory. It must be repeated if masonry units with a different arrangement of perforations are to be used for the masonry or if changes to the combination of raw materials or the method of production of the masonry units could influence the strength of the masonry. Masonry according to suitability test does not need to undergo a quality test. In order to check the raw materials on site, every delivery of masonry units must include a document which includes details of the DIN designation of the masonry unit, EM designation, compressive strength (classification certificate), type of mortar and mortar group, masonry strength class, classification certificate number and testing centre. The delivery slip or packaging is to be checked to ensure that it matches the technical documentation. Mortar mixed on site should be checked at regular intervals during construction to ensure that it continues to comply with the mixing ratio on the classification certificate. In the case of premixed mortars, the details on the delivery slip regarding type of mortar and mortar group, the supplying works and the grade number must be checked to ensure they comply with the details on the classification certificate. As with the quality control of prescribed masonry, the compressive strength of the mortar must be determined according to DIN 18555 part 3 and compared with the requirements of DIN 1053 part 1 tables A.2, A.3 and A.4. These quality control measures must be carried out for every 10 m³ of mortar, but at least for every storey.

Perpends and bed joints

The principal tasks of the joints in masonry are to ensure that the masonry units are uniformly loaded and to guarantee the transfer of forces from unit to unit. Furthermore, they compensate for the (permissible) deviations in the sizes of the masonry units and play a major role with

respect to building science properties and the resistance of any rendering to driving rain and cracking.

Mortar should always be applied over the full bed joint because this joint has an important structural function for the loadbearing behaviour of masonry, i.e. the uniform transfer of vertical compressive stresses as well as tensile and shear stresses by way of adhesion and friction. Voids in the bed joints and varying joint thicknesses lead to stress concentrations which in turn reduce the load-carrying capacity and increase the risk of cracking.

The thickness of the bed joint influences the transverse tensile stress in the masonry units through the lateral strain behaviour and is therefore partly responsible for the compressive strength of the masonry. Therefore, thick bed joints are structurally less favourable, but on the other hand a minimum thickness is necessary to compensate for the (permissible) deviations in the sizes of the masonry units and to allow for practical building considerations. The thickness of the bed joint is about 12 mm for normal and lightweight mortars, between 5 and 7 mm for medium-bed mortars, and between 1 and 3 mm for thin-bed mortars in conjunction with gauged brickwork.

The perpends are much less relevant than the bed joints in terms of structural function because they do not help to accommodate tensile and shear stresses. Therefore, it is permissible to either fill perpends completely with mortar, only partly with mortar ("tipped and tailed"), or leave them without any mortar. However, it should be noted that resistance to cracking decreases noticeably when the perpends are only filled partly with mortar or left without mortar because the masonry units can no longer support each other as is the case when the perpends are completely filled with mortar (see fig. 2.5.1).

Laying with mortar to the perpends
It is necessary to provide mortar in the perpends when building reinforced masonry, single-leaf unplastered masonry which has to be sealed against wind and driving rain, in the compression zone above shallow lintels and in external basement walls (but depending on the loadbearing system). The perpends are classed as fully filled with mortar when at least half the wall thickness is provided with mortar.

The arrangement of mortar to the perpends depends on the type of masonry units used. A full mortar filling to the perpend is principally carried out with small- and medium-format masonry units. The thickness of the perpends should be 10 mm for normal and lightweight mortars, and 1-3 mm for thin-bed mortars.

Masonry units with mortar grooves in their end faces either have mortar applied to the faces either side of the groove to produce visible perpends with thicknesses corresponding to a

full mortar filling, or the units are laid brick to brick and the grooves filled later. In the brick-to-brick method, the units are laid as close together as the unevenness of the end faces – due to the manufacturing process – will allow. Generally, the gap between the units should not be more than 5 mm. If this dimension is exceeded, then the joints should be filled with mortar on both sides of the wall in order to guarantee an even substrate for plaster.

Laying without mortar to the perpends
The perpend without mortar is gaining in popularity because it speeds up construction and requires less mortar. However, certain measures must be taken to ensure that the requirements to be met by the component regarding protection against driving rain (e.g. rendering, cladding); thermal insulation (e.g. adequate wall thickness, additional layers of thermal insulation); sound insulation (weight per m² by way of heavy masonry units); and fire protection are still maintained. Masonry without mortar to the perpends is constructed either with the bricks simply butt-jointed together or by using masonry units with an integral tongue and groove system. This laying technique achieves a masonry construction with optimum homogeneity.

Perpends wider than 5 mm must be filled with mortar on both sides of the wall in order to guarantee an even substrate for plaster. In terms of the structural analysis of masonry without mortar to the perpends, it should be noted that when analysing shear the permissible reduced adhesive shear strength σ_{0HS} must be halved and that in the case of basement walls the earth pressure may only be carried uniaxially in the vertical direction.

Junctions with intersecting walls

During construction, the contractor must make sure that immovable supports for a wall (supported on two, three or four sides) as assumed in the structural analysis are actually realized on site. An immovable support to a shear wall, for example, is only guaranteed when the supporting wall and the shear wall are both constructed of materials with approximately equal deformation behaviour, the connection between the walls can resist tension and compression, and when separation of the walls as a result of severe differential deformation is not expected (see "Lateral restraint to walls").

A tension- and compression-resistant connection can be achieved by building both walls simultaneously and fully bonded together but also via a butt joint.

Bonded junctions

A fully bonded junction – also valid as such during construction – is guaranteed with racking or toothed arrangements only where the length of the return is at least one fifth the height of the wall (see fig. 2.5.3).

Both types of junction consume valuable space on the building site and this is often not desirable due to operational reasons, e.g. for easier erection of scaffolds, to maintain unobstructed access routes etc.

Therefore, to aid building operations the structurally equivalent toothing or reverse toothing may be used (see fig. 2.5.3). In this type of bonded junction, the walls are not built simultaneously – support and bracing to the wall are achieved at a later date. The tension- and compression-resistant connection is created through the transfer of compression via the masonry bond and tension with the aid of reinforcement. This should be built into the bed joints with sufficient embedment length and protected against corrosion. If tensile forces do not need to be transferred, these two forms of bonded junction are only considered to accommodate compression.

Butt-jointed junctions

The butt joint technique enables the junctions to be simplified. In this method the walls are butt-jointed without taking account of the bonding rules. Consequently, they may be offset laterally (see fig. 2.5.2). A tension-resistant connection is achieved by anchors (for which a structural analysis is required) placed in the bed joints. If the walls are not built simultaneously, then the anchors are left projecting and bent aside until required in order to prevent injuries (see fig. 2.5.4).

The butt joint technique may be used only for internal walls; external corners should always be formed as fully bonded junctions. Butt joints are fully filled with mortar in every course to ensure adequate transfer of compression and continuity of the acoustic insulation properties of the wall. The anchors are to be designed according to DIN 1045 section 19.8.3 in such a way that 1/100 of the vertical load of the load-bearing wall can be transferred at each of the third-points of the wall height. Under such conditions, the supported wall can be analysed as being supported on three or four sides. The anchors may be distributed over the height of the storey to avoid an accumulation at third-points, e.g. in all or alternate bed joints.

It is recommended that walls supported on only two sides be connected to intersecting walls with non-structural anchors.

In the structural analysis of the walls, only rectangular and not compound cross-sections may be used despite the inclusion of anchors.

The best anchors have proved to be perforated flat bars of stainless steel measuring 300 x 22 x 0.75 mm or pairs of V4A steel wire ties (as used for twin-leaf walls).

2.5.3 Arrangement of wall intersections

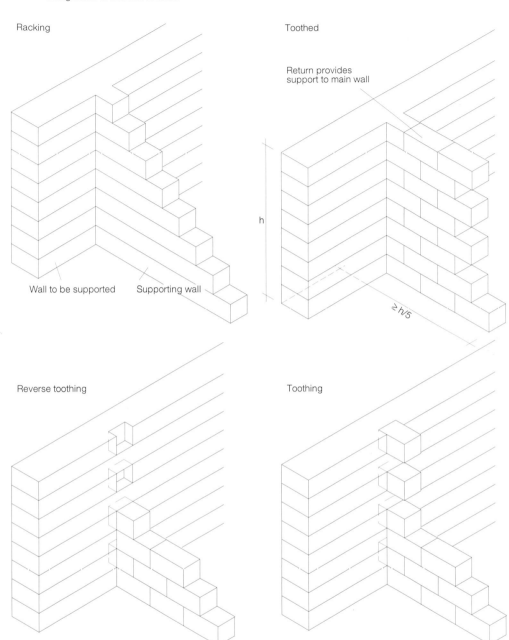

Racking

Toothed

Return provides support to main wall

h

≥ h/5

Wall to be supported   Supporting wall

Reverse toothing

Toothing

2.5.4 Butt-jointed junction with various types of anchors

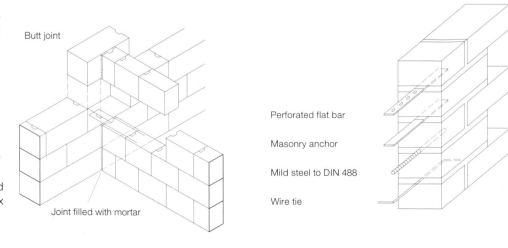

Butt joint

Joint filled with mortar

Perforated flat bar

Masonry anchor

Mild steel to DIN 488

Wire tie

2.5.5 Chases and recesses permissible in loadbearing walls without structural analysis (dimensions in mm)

1	2	3	4	5	6	7	8	9	10
Wall thickness	Horizontal and inclined chases[1] cut subsequently		Vertical chases and recesses cut subsequently			Vertical chases and recesses built in masonry bond			
	Length of chase unlimited Depth[3]	≤ 1.25 m long[2] Depth	Depth[4]	Width of single chase[5]	Distance of chases and recesses from openings	Width[5]	Remaining wall thickness	Min. distance of chases and recesses from openings	Min. spacing of chases and recesses
≥ 115	–	–	≤ 10	≤ 100	≥ 115	–	–	≥ 2 x width of chase or ≥ 240	≥ width of chase
≥ 175	0	≤ 25	≤ 30	≤ 100	≥ 115	≤ 260	≥ 115		
≥ 240	≤ 15	≤ 25	≤ 30	≤ 150	≥ 115	≤ 385	≥ 115		
≥ 300	≤ 20	≤ 30	≤ 30	≤ 200	≥ 115	≤ 385	≥ 175		
≥ 365	≤ 20	≤ 30	≤ 30	≤ 200	≥ 115	≤ 385	≥ 240		

[1] Horizontal and inclined chases are permissible only in an area < 0.4 m above or below the structural floor/roof slab, and only on one side of a wall. They are not permissible in horizontally perforated clay bricks.

[2] Min. distance from openings in longitudinal direction ≥ 490 mm, from next horizontal chase 2 x length of chase.

[3] The depth may be increased by 10 mm when using tools where the depth can be accurately maintained, e.g. masonry millers, masonry slot saws, etc. When using such tools, chases 10 mm deep on both sides may be cut in walls ≥ 240 mm thick.

[4] Chases that extend max. 1 m above floor level may be cut up to 80 mm deep and 120 mm wide in walls ≥ 240 mm thick.

[5] The total width of chases according to column 5 and column 7 per 2 m of wall length may not exceed the dimension given in column 7. For walls less than 2 m long, the values in column 7 should be reduced in proportion to the length of the wall.

The use of the butt joint technique has several important advantages for on-site operations and the later behaviour of the walls:

• The walls can be built separately without inconvenient toothing in one operation. The omission of toothing speeds up operations quite considerably. In addition, the flush wall surfaces and avoidance of short returns eases the erection and movement of working platforms and scaffolds.
• The flush wall connection means that fewer make-up units are required and there are no bonding problems at intersections.
• The two intersecting walls can be built with different course heights without bonding problems, i.e. its is easy to combine walls of units with different heights and formats (but still complying with the "octametric" system).
• The butt joint technique avoids the creation of thermal bridges at junctions between internal walls with high bulk density and external walls with a lower bulk density.
• The use of different types of masonry units in the two walls means that the effects of long-term deformations are less critical because the anchors preserve a certain vertical deformation capability while at the same time providing a tension- and compression-resistant connection between the walls [71, 211, 214].

Chases and recesses

Chases and recesses are required for all types of building services, e.g. heating, water and waste water pipes, electric cables, ventilation ducts. Owing to their significance for the stability of a wall, drawings showing the sizes and positions of chases and recesses should be provided at an early stage so that they can be taken into account in the structural analysis of

the masonry. At the very least, the arrangement of chases and recesses should be checked for their structural implications prior to construction. Planned chases and recesses formed within the masonry bond, or provided in the form of channel blocks, or service duct or pre-chased units (see "Special formats, special units"), should be taken into account on the working drawings. As a rule, these are more accurate and less time-consuming and costly than chases cut subsequently. When cutting chases, it must be ensured that the intended dimensions are not exceeded. Chases and recesses can considerably lower the load-carrying capacity of a wall because besides reducing the cross-section they also decrease, in particular, the bending strength of the wall and alter the eccentricity in the remainder of the wall. Vertical chases in walls spanning in one direction only reduce the cross-sectional area; their influence on the load-carrying capacity of the wall is hence of only minor importance. On the other hand, vertical chases in walls spanning in two directions, whose increase in load-carrying capacity is due to lateral restraint and hence is reliant on horizontal bending moments, can have a severe effect on the horizontal span. Therefore, their influence is taken into account when determining whether a wall is supported on three or four sides by using only the residual wall thickness in the design of the section adjacent to a vertical chase, or by assuming an unsupported edge at this position. We also assume an unsupported edge if the residual wall thickness is less than half the total wall thickness or < 115 mm.
Horizontal chases should be avoided if possible because they reduce the cross-sectional area, and hence the bending strength, along their full length. At the same time, they have an unfavourable effect on the eccentricity in the rest of the wall.

To simplify structural analysis, DIN 1053 part 1 table 10 specifies maximum dimensions for chases and recesses. If these dimensions are not exceeded, the effect of such chases and recesses on the load-carrying capacity of a wall is so minor that they can be ignored when designing the masonry (see table 2.5.5 and fig. 2.5.6). In addition, an analysis is not necessary for vertical chases and recesses if the reduction in the cross-section – per m of wall length – is no more than 6% and the wall is not assumed to be supported on three or four sides. In this case, a residual wall thickness according to DIN 1053 part 1 table 10 column 8 and a minimum spacing according to column 9 must be maintained (see table 2.5.5). If the dimensions of the chases and recesses differ from the values given in the tables or from the extra requirement for vertical chases, they must be taken into account in the design of the masonry. As the requirements of table 10 appear very complicated for the practically minded despite the graphic presentation in fig. 2.5.6, the following recommendations should be adhered to during construction:

• Chases and recesses should be positioned well clear of heavily loaded sections of masonry, e.g. bearings beneath lintels, openings. They should not be positioned in piers and chimney jambs.
• The depth of a chase or recess should be as small as possible, max. 30 mm, in order not to weaken the cross-section more than necessary.
• Horizontal chases should only be positioned immediately below floor/roof soffits or immediately above floor level because in these zones such chases have very little influence on the loadbearing behaviour of the wall (stability against buckling).
• Walls < 175 mm thick should not be chased if at all possible.

• As chases and recesses are detrimental to the acoustic and thermal insulation properties of a wall as well as its loadbearing behaviour, "false wall" installations are to be preferred wherever possible, i.e. all services are installed on the face of the wall or in service shafts. During the interior works, the services are concealed behind masonry or some other form of cladding.

Building and cleaning facing masonry

Certain rules have to be followed when planning and constructing facing masonry and faced walls in order to guarantee the appearance, serviceability and durability of the masonry. This is especially the case for external walls of facing masonry which are frequently exposed to driving rain. In particular, the risk of saturation due to inadequate workmanship or the wrong choice of material is frequently underestimated. The damage caused to the facing masonry is often extensive and necessitates major repairs.

Construction principles

Facing masonry and faced walls should only be built from free-standing scaffold, because putlog or other scaffold fixing holes are difficult to make good subsequently. The top course of masonry should be covered during longer interruptions in the work and during rain. If possible, masonry units should not be laid in the rain, and in cold weather should not be laid below certain temperatures (see "Laying during cold weather").

Facing masonry must be built very carefully because even very small irregularities, e.g. misaligned perpends above and below a header, are disagreeable to the observer – and it is often viewed from close quarters. Perpends or headers, which according to the bond should be aligned vertically, must be plumbed, because deviations of just a few millimetres can add up to considerable discrepancies over the full height of the wall. All the facing masonry units required for a certain section of the construction should be ordered from one supplier and intermixed between several pallets in order to avoid colour variations in the finished work. If necessary, a reference panel for assessing material (consistency of colour and dimensional accuracy), bond, jointing etc. should be produced on site.

Facing masonry units must be carefully transported and stacked on pallets, in packaging or in containers in order to avoid damaging corners and edges. Furthermore, they are to be protected against the weather, soiling and mechanical damage. Damaged units should be rejected or used in such a way that the damaged section is not visible in the finished wall. One important condition for building durable

facing masonry is that the units should be laid and worked in a way appropriate to the material. The different suction rates of different materials must be taken into account. Absorbent units must be prewetted before laying so that they do not extract too much mixing water from the mortar. The maximum rate for this is $1.5 \text{ kg/m}^2\text{/min}$. Prewetting is not necessary at lower suction rates. If prewetting is not carried out when required, shrinkage cracks between units and mortar or dehydrated adhesion zones in the mortar can form and help driving rain to penetrate the facing masonry. Less absorbent masonry units, however, must be laid dry. In some circumstances the plasticity of the mortar must be reduced in order to prevent such units from "floating" on the mortar due to their low suction rate.

Complete joints without voids are produced by applying the mortar to the end of the masonry unit and then pressing it against its neighbour, thereby squeezing out surplus mortar. Wall joints remain open at first and are filled with grout upon completion of each course of masonry [162].

Fresh joints must be cured for at least 3-5 days (see "Mixing and using mortar on site"). Please refer to "Jointing" below for further details of joints.

Cleaning facing masonry

First of all, for effective cleaning we must distinguish between the different types of soiling. The most frequent type of soiling, but the easiest to remove, is that caused by mortar and cement during construction. Second, efflorescence and lime staining can occur upon completion of the facing masonry. Finally, atmospheric pollution can spoil the appearance of facing masonry over time.

The soiling of facing masonry during construction is most easily dealt with by removing mortar droppings and cement splashes immediately as the work proceeds or when building the next section. Water, brushes and sponges are adequate for such cleaning.

The avoidance of soiling is also important in this context: adequate clearance between tubs of mortar and facade, newly built masonry covered with plastic sheeting to protect against mortar droppings and cement splashes or against splashes of concrete and plaster.

Efflorescence often occurs when larger quantities of water (e.g. mixing water from the mortar, poorly designed/built eaves details, leaking copings etc.) penetrate the masonry and wash out efflorescent substances, e.g. calcium hydroxide, sodium and magnesium sulphate, chlorides and nitrates, from the mortar and masonry units. The absorbency of the units allows the dissolved substances to be transported to the surface, where they are deposited at a point where the water can readily evaporate, e.g. at projecting piers and at the

2.5.6   Diagram of chases and recesses permissible in loadbearing walls without structural analysis (dimensions in mm)

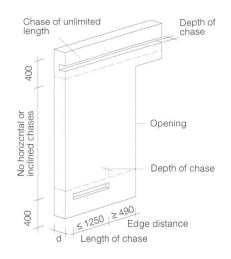

Horizontal and inclined chases cut subsequently

Wall thickness	Length of chase unlimited	≤ 1.25 m long[2]
d	Depth[3]	Depth[3]
≥ 115	–	–
≥ 175	0	≤ 25
≥ 240	≤ 15	≤ 25
≥ 300	≤ 20	≤ 30
≥ 365	≤ 20	≤ 30

[2] Min. distance from openings in longitudinal direction ≥ 490 mm, from next horizontal chase 2 x length of chase.

[3] The depth may be increased by 10 mm when using tools where the depth can be accurately maintained, e.g. masonry millers, slot saws etc. When using such tools, chases 10 mm deep on both sides may be cut in walls ≥ 240 mm thick.

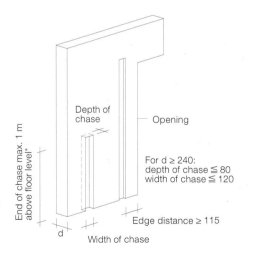

Vertical chases and recesses cut subsequently

Wall thickness d	Depth[4]	Width of single chase	Distance of chases and recesses from openings
≥ 115	≤ 10	≤ 100	≥ 115
≥ 175	≤ 30	≤ 100	≥ 115
≥ 240	≤ 30	≤ 150	≥ 115
≥ 300	≤ 30	≤ 200	≥ 115
≥ 365	≤ 30	≤ 200	≥ 115

[4] Chases that extend max. 1 m above floor level may be cut up to 80 mm deep and 120 mm wide in walls ≥ 240 mm thick.

2.5.7 Forming flush and
"bucket handle"
joints

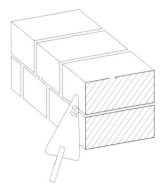  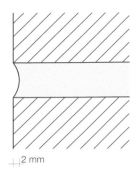

2 mm

corners of buildings, where higher wind speeds occur.
Efflorescence, which occurs during construction by the dissolving of efflorescent substances in the mortar (calcium carbonate), can be avoided by prewetting and hence reducing the absorbency of the masonry units. Most efflorescence disappears after a relatively short period of exposure to the weather. Otherwise, the most effective method for removal is cleaning the masonry dry with spatulas, suitable small wooden boards and bristle brushes. Sandblasting may be employed in certain cases, although this may place severe stresses on the facing masonry; or cleaning wet with a cleaning agent. In this case the masonry must be prewetted starting at the bottom before the cleaning agent is applied in concentrated or diluted form in accordance with the manufacturer's instructions. These methods are often employed for old lime staining and leaching of, for example, calcium carbonate. Very effective cleaning agents for clay brickwork have proved to be those based on hydrochloric, phosphoric or formic acid. The masonry should be rinsed thoroughly with water after cleaning to make sure that all impurities are removed. It also prevents the masonry from reabsorbing the solution again as it dries.
Masonry soiled by many years of atmospheric pollution should only be cleaned by specialist contractors. It is essential to carry out a cleaning test first in such cases to establish the most suitable method of cleaning – so that the masonry remains clean and does not suffer any significant damage.
High-pressure jets of cold and hot water, jets of water with additives, compressed-air water jets with additives and chemical cleaning processes involving the application of wetting agents, acidic or alkali cleaners and subsequent rinsing have all proved to be suitable methods of cleaning. When choosing a method, the effectiveness of safety requirements and disposal of the cleaning water must also be taken into account [52, 175]. One common problem these days is graffiti smeared over facades.

They can generally be removed by water jets with additives but softer surfaces will suffer under this treatment. Special graffiti cleaners based on γ-butyrolactone have proved to be a good alternative to mechanical cleaning.
This special plastic-dissolving product with a pH value between 5.5 and 6.0 is applied to the facing masonry and washed off afterwards with cold water without damaging the surface.

Jointing

Jointing plays a special role in facing masonry and faced walls: it seals the masonry against driving rain, and lends it the desired appearance. The composition of the mortar, the set-back, consistency and position of the joint surfaces, and the way they are made are crucial to the weather-tightness of facing masonry exposed to driving rain. Therefore, to be effective, joints should be water-repellent and finished flush with the surface of the masonry whenever possible. The joints form a fine lattice over the whole surface of the wall and so their appearance has a decisive influence on the character and overall colour of exposed masonry. Jointing can be carried out during construction, before the mortar has fully hardened (e.g. flush, "bucket handle"), or later, after raking out the joints (pointing) [162, 164].

Flush and "bucket handle" joints
The flush joint requires the visible joints of the masonry to be filled completely with mortar. Surplus mortar is trimmed off with the trowel. The "bucket handle" joint is formed after the mortar has started to harden by "ironing in" to a depth of 2 mm, compacting and smoothing with a sliver of wood, jointing iron or piece of plastic hose (diameter approx. 1.5 to 2 times the width of the joint). The smoothing must always be carried out at exactly the right time and starting from the first joint formed to ensure a consistent joint colour (see 2.5.7).
The advantage of these joints is that they are carried out immediately after building the masonry and so provide homogeneous, well-compacted joints formed "from one mould", so to speak, throughout their depth.
However, this type of jointing can be carried out properly only when bed joints and perpends are completely filled with mortar, to avoid having to make good when smoothing the joints. This presupposes careful bricklaying.
The disadvantage, that the facing masonry must be kept clean during construction

2.5.8 Pointing

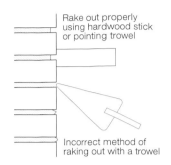

Rake out properly using hardwood stick or pointing trowel

Incorrect method of raking out with a trowel

15...20 mm

because subsequent cleaning of the facade could lead to cement being washed out of the joints, can be avoided by using a mortar with good cohesion and water-retention properties. This prevents the mortar running down the face of the masonry when it inevitably squeezes out of the joints.

Pointing
This requires the joints of exposed surfaces to be raked out to depth of 15-20 mm – but not as far as the first row of any perforations in the units – immediately after construction by using a slightly tapered strip of hardwood.
Attempting to construct facing masonry with the mortar left back from the edge to save raking out the joints later is not a proper way of preparing the outer joint substrate, and is therefore not permitted. It is also considered poor workmanship to rake out the mortar V-shaped, half-round or bevelled in the middle of a joint, because then the pointing mortar does not achieve a proper bond with the units and the mortar of the joints, and consequently does not protect the masonry against driving rain.
After raking out, any loose pieces of mortar should be removed from the facade surfaces and the joints by brushing and rinsing with water, possibly with the addition of a cleaning agent. Prior to pointing, the facade should be saturated with water starting at the bottom. The pointing mortar (mixed by machine to a "plastic" consistency) is then pressed into the joints and well compacted in two operations, and excess mortar removed.
In the first operation the perpends are first compacted and then the bed joint; in the second operation the bed joints first and then the perpends (see fig. 2.5.8).
Suitable measures, e.g. spraying with water, covering with plastic sheeting, should be taken to protect the fresh pointing against premature drying-out caused by draughts, sunshine etc. The composition of the pointing mortar should correspond more or less with that of the mortar of the joints, and should be preferably of mor-

tar group IIa, III or IIIa.
The disadvantages of pointing are that it encourages the production of masonry without fully filled joints, and that jointing and pointing mortars with different mixes, or pointing mortar which is too dry, leads to diminished adhesion between pointing and mortar or masonry unit. Both these disadvantages weaken the driving-rain resistance of the facing masonry and, as a result, impair the durability of the wall construction. Therefore, pointing should be used only when a particular effect (e.g. colour) is desired, or when the surface of the masonry unit is unsuited to a flush joint.

Joint design

The components of a building are subjected to stresses and strains such as those caused by temperature, creep and shrinkage deformations. Preventing such deformations causes restraint stresses, which can lead to cracks appearing in the structure. Therefore, the designer should include movement joints as a preventive measure to avoid cracking. Besides accommodating deformation, joints must compensate for manufacturing and assembly tolerances, and at the same time comply with building science requirements (thermal and sound insulation, weather and fire protection). To do this, they must be wide enough and be filled with suitable materials.
As joints affect the appearance of masonry, they should be considered as architectural elements in the planning. However, they should be included only where absolutely necessary, because their construction and maintenance are costly and involved. Joints should be straight and positioned logically, otherwise they become complicated and may not be fully effective.

Types of joints
Joints are divided into movement joints, rigid joints and dummy joints.
Movement joints include settlement and expansion joints. Settlement joints (e.g. between buildings) are called for when significant differential settlement is expected between two or more sections of a building. They extend over the full height of the building and also pass through the foundations. In such situations it must be ensured that the separate parts of the building each have an independent three-dimensional bracing system. The risk of differential settlement arises when different sections of the building impose different ground pressures on a subsoil susceptible to settlement or when the type of subsoil changes beneath the building. Expansion joints (e.g. vertical and horizontal joints in facing work) are required in

2.5.9 Feasible movement joint detail

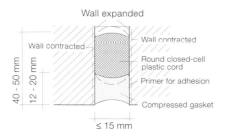

Compressed gasket

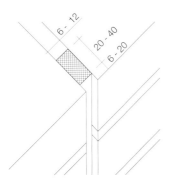

Self-adhesive side

Backing strip

Cover strips

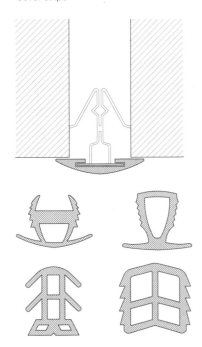

large components that undergo deformation as a result of shrinkage and temperature fluctuations. As a rule, vertical expansion joints continue down as far as the top of the foundations. This type of deformation is less damaging to foundations and undivided foundations tend to compensate for settlement. Rigid joints (e.g. assembly joints, construction joints, joints between prefabricated elements) arise as a result of the type of construction or building operations. Such joints can also act as movement joints, in which case they should be formed and sealed as for such joints. Dummy joints are produced only for appearance and have no functions regarding the accommodation of deformations or tolerances.

The sealing of joints
Sealing compounds, preformed sealing gaskets and cover strips are used to seal joints (see fig. 2.5.9) [9].

Sealing compounds
Here, the joint is sealed by permanently elastic and permanently elastoplastic one- and two-part compounds, e.g. polysulphide, silicone rubber, polyurethane or acrylic dispersions. These materials are permanently elastic but deform plastically under the influence of long-term loading and hence reduce stresses within the joint. They are available in various colours and can be expected to last 15-20 years. Sealing compounds must be applied in dry conditions at temperatures above +5°C. The masonry joints on both sides of the movement joint should be fully filled with mortar, and the opening for the joint itself must be free from dust, mortar droppings, oil and grease in order to achieve optimum adhesion between sealing compound and masonry and to avoid cracks in the long term.
A round backing strip of flexible foamed material is inserted into the opening before the sealing compound so as to be able to inject the compound with sufficient pressure and at the same time give it a suitable form. This so-called backing cord must have a diameter of about 1.5 times the width of the joint, must be compatible with the sealing compound and must not absorb any water. After injecting the sealing compound using a hand-operated or compressed-air gun, the joint is generally subsequently given a slightly concave profile.

Preformed sealing gaskets
Joints may be filled with preformed sealing gaskets made from open-cell plastic foam impregnated with a special bitumen or poly-acrylate. Therefore, the gaskets remain permanently elastic, do not crack or become brittle, and are resistant to ultraviolet radiation and alkaline solutions. The preformed gasket is squeezed together before being inserted, and

aligned with the joint. As it attempts to regain its original size and shape, it presses against the sides of the joint with sufficient adhesion to seal it immediately. In doing so, the gasket also compensates for the unevenness of the sides of the joint. Preformed gaskets compressed to one third their original size are adequate to create a dust-tight and airtight joint; a gasket compressed to one fifth its original size creates a watertight joint.

Cover strips
A cover strip can be clamped or glued into the joint to seal it. The contact pressure of cover strips clamped into place must be adequate to prevent the strip dropping out if the gap widens as a result of, for example, a drop in temperature.
The adhesion of the glue to the substrate is decisive for glued strips. To improve the adhesion, the sides of the joint may be carefully painted or, in the case of a highly absorbent material, sealed with an epoxy resin solution.

Drained joints
Vertical movement joints in facing masonry can be designed as drained, i.e. open, joints in buildings located in regions where less driving rain is to be expected, provided the backing masonry and any insulation are permanently protected against moisture, e.g. an airspace, plaster or plastic sheeting. Such joints are restricted to a maximum width of 15 mm and require an outer leaf thickness of at least 90 mm.

The spacing and width of joints
The design of the joints, i.e. establishing the widths of the joints and the distances between them, is carried out by the structural engineer and depends on numerous variables: the structural concept of the respective structure; the dimensions of the structure; the stiffness of the construction with respect to changes in length; the arrangement of stiffening elements; temperature changes; the insulation to the external walls; the shrinkage and creep behaviour of the walls and floors; the settlement anticipated etc.
Outer leaves of masonry undergo greater changes in length than inner leaves because they are subjected to greater temperature changes. Added to this we have the differential deformation of the leaves caused by different material properties and different loads on the inner and outer leaves. The advice below should be followed when designing movement joints in outer leaves of masonry:

• Vertical movement joints are required at the corners of buildings and also in long walls at a spacing of max. 6.0 m for lightweight concrete units, max. 8.0 m for calcium silicate units, and 10-16 m for clay brickwork. These different figures do not represent different standards but are the result of the different deformation properties of these facing materials. If a facade is taken around the corner of the building without a joint, the return should not be longer than 5.0 m. In the case of lintels over large window and door openings, movement joints are positioned in line with the window and door reveals above and below the openings.

- Horizontal movement joints are required beneath parapets and roof overhangs, below balcony floors and beams, below joists and purlins, beneath windows and thresholds, and below supports for outer leaves when they are more than 6.0 m high with an outer leaf < 115 mm thick, and when they are more than 12.0 m high with an outer leaf ≥ 115 mm thick.

The width of the joint depends on the anticipated deformation of the components and the deformability of the material to be used to seal the joint. The width is usually five to seven times the change in length to be accommodated by the joint. Joint widths of 15-25 mm are normally chosen and the joints spaced to suit this width. Wider joints are difficult to seal properly.

Gauged brickwork

When building with normal or lightweight mortar, the different positions and heights of the units can be compensated for to a certain extent by adjusting the thicknesses of the bed joints. However, gauged brickwork and thin-bed mortar (with joint thicknesses of 1-3 mm) permit only minimal adjustment of position and height. The result of this is that the base course must be laid with extreme care because it also serves as the course for adjusting the height as well as the longitudinal and transverse planarity.

The base course is laid on a bed of normal mortar of group III and then aligned horizontally. Small- and medium-format units or levelling units – 50-125 mm high and up to 500 mm long – are often used in the base course in conjunction with the actual gauged bricks.

Once the base course has hardened, the gauged bricks with their associated thin-bed mortar are used, starting from the second course. The bed faces of the gauged bricks should be brushed before the thin-bed mortar is applied in order to ensure a clean, smooth bed face, which helps to guarantee the adhesion between unit and mortar. The thin-bed mortar is applied to the bed joint either by dipping the gauged bricks approx.

5 mm into the mortar or by spreading the mortar directly onto the bed joint using a special trowel, roller or mortar sledge, which applies a constant layer of mortar to the joint. The width

of the trowel or roller or sledge should match the thickness of the wall. When using a trowel, the thin-bed mortar is only applied to the bed joint two or three bricks ahead of the brick being laid, but when using a roller or sledge, rationalization measures dictate that the mortar be applied to the whole length of wall. The roller can also be used to place a glass fibre mat between two layers of thin-bed mortar each approx. 1 mm thick. The high tearing resistance of the mat increases the compressive strength of the masonry and the adhesive shear strength between gauged bricks and mortar.

After the gauged brick is laid, the faces and edges are aligned accurately before tapping it into place with a rubber hammer. Any thin-bed mortar that squeezes out is trimmed off with a metal spatula once it has started to harden. At the same time, any flaws, e.g. unfilled perpends or bed joints or damaged edges, are made good.

From time to time, after a brick is laid it should be removed again immediately in order to check whether a complete bed of mortar is being achieved with the respective method of application.

Mechanical fixings in masonry

Very many different types of neighbouring constructions, components and fittings have to be fixed to masonry using anchors, drive screws and nails. These are subjected to tension, compression, shear, inclined tension and bending.

Neither standards nor guidelines are available for assessing such connections. Therefore, load-bearing fixings may only use anchors covered by a building authority certificate.

Other types of fixing (anchors and nails without certificates) may be used for minor applications. However, these may not be used for fixing constructions in the tension zones of roof and floor slabs and also not for attaching curtain wall facades and thermal insulation composite systems [43, 49, 78, 109, 110].

Anchors

Anchors are fixings inserted and secured into holes drilled into solid materials. Their main purpose is to permit the attachment of a whole range of minor items but they may also be used to anchor loadbearing components. Regardless of the type of application, they should always be properly planned and sized. Anchors can be classified according to various criteria. One common method is to distinguish between the type of anchorage in the drilled hole – undercut, mechanical expansion, friction, grouting, adhesion – and the material of the anchor. Up to now, only plastic expansion anchors and injected grout anchors have been

2.5.10 Examples of plastic and injection anchors covered by building authority certificates [15]

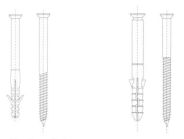

Plastic wall plugs

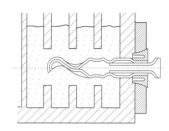

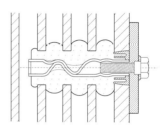

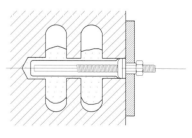

Injection wall plugs

2.5.11   Method of functioning
         of anchors [13]

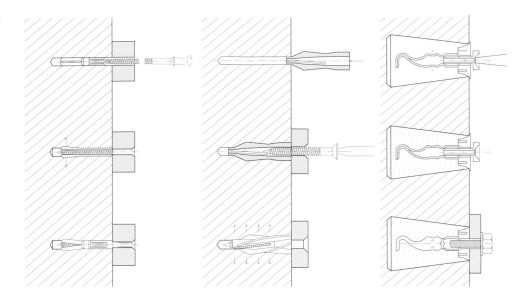

approved for fixings in masonry (see fig. 2.5.10).
There are also special anchors for fixing thermal insulation composite systems and for
anchoring wall ties for twin-leaf masonry and
facing masonry. These anchor systems are in
turn based on the plastic expansion anchors
and the injection anchors. Finally, there are
special wall plugs for autoclaved aerated concrete, which permit components to be attached
to this very soft material.

Plastic anchors
can be used for fixings in concrete as well as
in masonry of solid and perforated units. They
are normally inserted through the item to be
fixed and into the wall. The anchors consist of
a plastic sleeve, designed not to turn in the
hole, and an associated screw or nail. The
minimum depth of anchorage is marked on
the plastic sleeve. A collar at the outer end of
the sleeve prevents the anchor being pushed
too far into the hole during assembly.
The geometry and length of the screw or nail
are matched to the internal geometry and
length of the sleeve so that the anchor is properly expanded once the screw or nail is in
place. However, expanding plastic anchors
with nails may only be used for fixing facades
in concrete and solid masonry units.
Plastic anchors may not be used for pure axial
tension, but only for inclined tension at an
angle of at least 10°. In solid materials the tension is transferred by friction. The expanded
part of the anchor is pressed against the side
of the drilled hole and hence activates the friction. In hollow masonry units the tension is also
transferred by the interlock between the anchor

geometry and the shape of the substrate (see
fig. 2.5.11).

Injection anchors
are inserted into the wall before offering up the
item to be attached and up to now have only
been approved for fixings in hollow masonry
units.
They work by way of the bond between the
anchor or anchor sleeve and the substrate. The
bond is achieved by way of an injected grout
based on rapid-hardening cement or artificial
resin. However, injection anchors fitted in voids
also transfer the tension via the mechanical
interlock of the injected grout forced into the
void (see fig. 2.5.11).
When using rapid-hardening cement, the mortar is mixed with a prescribed amount of water
before being forced into the void by a hand-
operated pump. The result is that the void in
the masonry is more or less filled. The amount
of mortar required is minimized by using
anchors surrounded by a polyamide mesh.
Injection anchors based on artificial resin consist of a mesh sleeve and a threaded bar with
nut and centering ring, or a metal sleeve with
internal thread, plus the artificial resin mortar.
The separate components, resin and hardener,
are forced through a mixing tube and injected
– thoroughly mixed – into the mesh sleeve. The
threaded bar or the sleeve with internal thread
is subsequently pushed into the mesh sleeve.
Anchoring the wall plug in the web of a masonry unit requires the drilled hole to be carefully
cleaned by brushing and compressed air in
order to guarantee an adequate bond to transfer the tension.

Anchors for autoclaved aerated concrete
Plastic expansion and injection anchors with a
cylindrical drilled hole are not suitable for autoclaved aerated concrete because this material
is very soft, is damaged by the expansion
forces and also cannot accommodate any
significant bonding forces. Therefore, special
anchors have been developed for fixings in
autoclaved aerated concrete. They are
anchored by way of conical drilled undercuts
virtually without any compression due to
expansion, or injection, or a special arrangement which allows low expansion forces to be
transferred, thanks to a suitable surface design
and partial compaction of the autoclaved aerated concrete (see fig. 2.5.12). The fixing of
components subjected to heavy or dynamic
loads may require the use of bolts passed
through the aerated concrete wall.
In this case the wall is drilled right through to
match the diameter of the bolt and a wider
pocket formed on the rear face. The item to be
fixed is fitted over the bolt, which passes
through the wall and is secured on the rear
face, and pressed up against the autoclaved
aerated concrete. Large washers or anchor
plates are fitted to the bolt on both sides of the
wall to distribute the load.

Installing anchors
Anchors require the hole to be carefully drilled;
lack of care when drilling can lead to an over-
size hole, which results in a rapid decrease in
the pull-out strength of the fixing. Holes for
anchors in masonry can be drilled with a normal rotary drill, a percussion drill (rotation plus
rapid percussion action) or a hammer drill

(rotation plus slower but more powerful percussion action). Percussion and hammer drills may be used in solid units with a dense microstructure, but only rotary drills may be used in perforated, autoclaved aerated concrete and low-strength units so that the hole remains the proper size and the webs and walls of perforated units are not damaged by the percussive action. It is recommended to grind normal carbide drills, which are designed for rotation plus percussion action, sharp in the direction of rotation, similar to a steel drill, to achieve optimum progress when drilling a hole purely by rotation.

With few exceptions, the hole must be drilled at least 10 mm deeper than the depth of anchorage. This leaves room for any dust or for the point of the screw to protrude through the end of the wall plug, and hence guarantees the correct functioning of the anchor.

In solid cross-sections, dust resulting from the drilling should be removed from the hole during and after drilling in order to avoid diminished friction and bond effects, and to guarantee the load-carrying capacity of the anchor. There are various ways of fixing the actual neighbouring construction, component etc. The holes can be drilled (after having first used the fixing holes in the component to establish the positions of the holes in the wall) and the anchors inserted before positioning the component against the wall and screwing it into place. In this case the anchor usually finishes flush with the surface of the wall and the diameter of the hole in the wall is larger than that of the hole in the component. Alternatively, the holes in the wall can be drilled using the fixing holes in the component as a template (which guarantees accuracy) and the anchors inserted into the wall through the component. In this case the diameter of the hole in the component is at least as large as that of the hole in the wall. This procedure is particularly suitable when each component requires more than two anchors and for large numbers of fixings. It is also possible to attach a component at a certain distance from the wall. A tension- and compression-resistant fixing is achieved by using an injection anchor having a metric internal thread into which a screw, bolt or threaded bar with locknuts is fitted.

Modes of failure of anchors
Anchors can fail as a result of overloaded anchorage points, incorrect installation or the inadequate load-carrying capacity of the substrate. Plastic anchors can fail by being pulled out of the substrate, although this does not seriously damage. A pull-out failure means that an excessive load has overcome the friction or bond in the hole; a ruptured fixing means that the strength of the screw material was not adequate for the load.

Fracture of the masonry material itself is the normal mode of failure for an injection anchor.

This happens when the tension loads are too high, the masonry is not strong enough or the depth of anchorage is inadequate. A wall can fracture if it is not large enough to carry the loads or if the edge distances or spacings of fixings are too small for the expansion forces introduced.

Nail anchors
Nails and drive screws are employed only for minor constructions with low anchorage loads, and primarily in aerated concrete masonry. Lightweight items, e.g. battens for wooden panelling, are fixed in place by driving the nails or drive screws directly into the autoclaved aerated concrete.

The best nails for this are tapered, galvanized square nails 60-180 mm long with a rough surface finish. They should be hammered home from alternate angles. Other types of nails include twisted nails and special nail anchors and hammered plugs for autoclaved aerated concrete. The twisted nail gains its anchorage by way of friction and expansion, the other two forms by way of a mechanical interlock (see fig. 2.5.13).

Rationalization measures

Building to save space and costs
The rising cost of building means that the optimization of costs and space in the housing market is becoming increasingly important. The potential for optimizing the use of the available space is to be found principally in exploiting the options for optimizing the loadbearing structure as contained in standards and regulations. These options must be taken into account early in the planning stage of a building project.

One fundamental optimization option for the loadbearing structure is the regular arrangement of shear walls. A regular arrangement provides excellent stability and minimizes wall thicknesses. In addition, the spans of the floors can be made equal, which in turn minimizes slab depths and the amount of reinforcement required.

Another measure for saving money and space is to reduce the thicknesses of loadbearing walls to the minimum dimension necessary to satisfy structural and building science requirements by employing the more accurate method of analysis. According to DIN 1053 part 1, the minimum thickness for loadbearing internal and external walls, as well as the loadbearing leaf of twin-leaf external walls, is 115 mm. However, a minimum wall thickness of 175 mm is recommended for single-leaf external walls with a thermal insulation system in order to comply with thermal and sound insulation requirements. Internal partitions ≥ 115 mm may

2.5.12 Examples of anchors for autoclaved aerated concrete

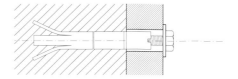

Expansion wall plug with compaction

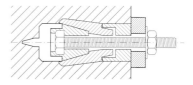

Wall plug expands when expanding shell is forced over cone.

Through-fixing for particularly heavy or dynamic loads

2.5.13 Nail anchors for autoclaved aerated concrete masonry

Square nail

Twisted nail

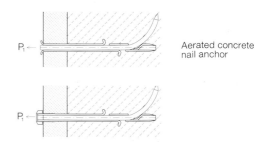

Aerated concrete nail anchor

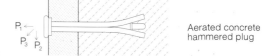

Aerated concrete hammered plug

2.5.14   Working hours guidance figures [h/m³]

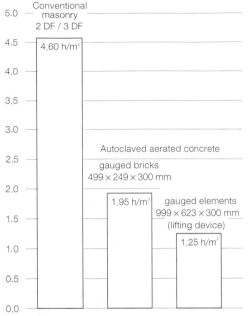

Rational laying techniques

The aim of rational bricklaying is to minimize the number of operations to be carried out by the bricklayer when building a wall, and at the same time to adapt the ergonomics of the work to meet the needs of the bricklayer better.

The handling of the masonry units themselves is crucial to manual bricklaying. Therefore, for example, the calcium silicate industry has developed grip aids with grip bar and thumb-hole especially for their heavy blocks for bricklayers to be able to handle the blocks easily. The bricklayer no longer has to rely on the friction between his fingers and the surface of the masonry unit to grip it. Apart from that, there are also blocks with grip aids at the bottom for when the bricklayer has to work on sections more than 1 m high.

Above a certain weight, handling devices are used to reduce the physical strain of lifting such heavy masonry units. At the same time, productivity is improved (see "Large-format elements"). Further rationalization measures for bricklaying are the use of masonry without mortar to the perpends (see "Laying without mortar to the perpends"), the use of thin-bed masonry and the omission of bonded intersections between walls (see "Butt-jointed junctions"). Building walls without mortar to the perpends involves using masonry units with an integral tongue and groove system, which can then be interlocked without using mortar. Tilted bricks are avoided by guiding each tongue and groove together, which helps produce a plane wall surface. The construction of masonry with conventional 10-12 mm perpends and bed joints means that 55% of the bricklayer's time is spent with the mortar. The use of the thin-bed technique in conjunction with tongue and groove masonry units cuts the consumption of

be considered as loadbearing. The gain in floor area when using masonry walls with these minimum thicknesses is approx. 5-7% compared to the common wall thicknesses of 240-365 mm. In addition, fewer masonry units and less mortar are required. Furthermore, thin masonry is more flexible and therefore less liable to crack than thicker masonry, in which the structural stresses are lower. The use of a skim coat instead of 15-20 mm "normal plaster" can also achieve an additional gain in floor area amounting to approx. 2% depending on the size of the room. However, masonry walls with large slenderness ratios call for the use of masonry units with high strength and high gross density, as well as high-quality mortar (MG III, MG IIIa, DM). The actual building of masonry at an optimized cost is less a question of optimizing the loadbearing structure than a matter for rationalized building operations, the use of large-format masonry units and special building methods (e.g. prefabricated construction) [139, 140].

mortar from 50 l/m³ for a thick joint to 5 l/m³ for a thin joint. Moreover, the application of a constant bed of mortar using a mortar sledge or special trowel, and the resulting laying of a row of masonry units, achieves a time saving of up to 25%. The bricklayers work in pairs, one spreading the thin-bed mortar along the wall with the mortar sledge or special trowel, and the other laying rows of masonry units in the prepared mortar bed [75].

Further rationalization in masonry construction can be achieved by using the various special units and special components produced by the masonry industry (see "Special formats, special units"). The aim here, in particular, is to integrate other materials – steel and concrete – required for structural reasons into an essentially homogeneous masonry construction, while reducing the work required to integrate such materials.

The quantities of materials and number of working hours required
can be determined theoretically but are subject to considerable fluctuationin practice. Organization on the building site is critical for this. To calculate the number of units required, it is important, for example, to know whether the units will be cut on site with a hammer or with a saw. The amount of mortar required is, for example, approx. 25-30% lower for masonry without mortar to the perpends than for masonry with mortar to the perpends. In Germany, comprehensive guidance figures for working hours have been published by the Federal Committee for Performance-linked Pay. These include ancillary work such as instruction, mixing mortar, moving scaffolds, setting out and building openings, cleaning the workplace etc. The figures clearly reveal the influences of the size of the masonry unit; whether bricklaying is carried out by hand or with a handling device; the use of thin-bed mortar and the omission of mortar to the perpends (see fig. 2.5.14). The speeding-up of operations when using large-format instead of small-format units can be attributed to the size of the units but also the technique of laying rows of units in thin-bed mortar. The economic advantage grows with the manufacturing accuracy of the masonry units because as deviations diminish so the mortar bed can be reduced to a minimum; savings in time and materials are the result. At the same time, the wall becomes more homogeneous – with all the advantages this implies in terms of structure and building science.

Organizing the building site and building operations
Rational construction of masonry also means careful planning of site and operations in order to avoid framework conditions that make it unnecessarily difficult. This includes the right use of personnel; choice of materials; timely

organization and suitable location of stored materials; preparations for optimum use of materials (the use of premixed mortar, pretreatment of masonry units etc.); and the right use of resources for bricklaying operations (e.g. handling devices, working platforms, mortar sledge etc.). Disruptions to on-site operations have a greater effect on the degree of rationalization when using large-format masonry units, which result in fewer working hours per m² of wall, than when working with small-format units. The correct provision of masonry units and mortar at the right time, in sufficient quantities and at the right place is especially important if the bricklayer is to avoid unnecessary walking and movements when working. This is also true when using handling devices. To achieve optimum handling times, it must be ensured that each delivery of masonry units is stacked at the place of work in a row without any gaps. This guarantees that the optimum number of units is laid per handling routine with the preset handling parameters. However, too many materials stored within the building can also be a disadvantage because this can hamper the movement of scaffolds or handling devices. The distance between bricklayers should be about 2.5-3.0 m in order to achieve a regular working rhythm. One bricklayer per 3.0 m of wall length brings about a 25% increase in performance over one bricklayer per 2.0 m because there are less interruptions to the working rhythm.
The use of a mortar sledge means that the distance between bricklayers and to the tub of mortar can be increased still further because, with one filling, longer lengths of wall can be provided with a constant bed of mortar than is the case when using a trowel. The bricklayer has to walk and move less and so the working rhythm is again made more consistent.

Scaffolds
The height of the work is critical to the performance, fatigue and health of the bricklayer, particularly when laying large-format masonry units. The time and effort required to lay a unit is lowest for working heights between 600 and 800 mm. Scaffold heights should be variable so that this optimum working height can be maintained for the entire wall. Modern steel scaffolds are useful here because they permit scaffold boards to be placed every 500 mm in height. In addition, extension brackets can be suspended 500 mm below each working level on the wall side to avoid unnecessary bending. Trestles and scaffolds on screw supports with infinite height adjustment mean that the working height can be adjusted to suit the bricklayer, and so improves the ergonomics of the work.
In contrast to scaffolds on adjustable supports, the bricklayer's platform with or without integral hoist provides a larger working area enabling the building of walls up to 4.0 m long. Such platforms also have their own wheels and so can be readily moved to a new location, or easily lifted by crane – representing a major economic advantage. With an integral hoist, even larger masonry formats can be laid quickly, accurately and without fatigue.

Templates
The building of corners or window and door reveals are particularly complicated operations because of the amount of plumbing and measuring work involved. Reusable corner and opening templates, which indicate the vertical and horizontal positions of courses and units, can make such work much easier. Building the corners first with the associated racking back is no longer necessary. When laying the base course, in which any unevenness in the floor has to be compensated for and so establishes the basis for the accuracy of subsequent courses, a noticeable rationalization effect is achieved when using a template, above all in the next course. An increase in productivity is particularly evident when doors and windows, or at least their frames, are incorporated as prefabricated elements and simply built around in one operation.

Rational working with large-format masonry units
Large-format masonry units and elements are those with lengths of 498-998 mm and heights of 373-623 mm. The length and height result from the use of thin-bed mortar with bed joint and perpend thicknesses of 1-3 mm. To reduce costs still further, the perpends are frequently tongue and groove units butted together without mortar (see "Large-format elements").
The high laying rates with handling devices and two-man teams, the use of thin-bed mortar and the reduction in subsequent work owing to the simple and accurate laying of the units are the rationalization possibilities which can be expected from the use of large-format masonry units. The rational laying process means that a length of up to 1.25 m of masonry in course heights of 375-750 mm can be constructed in one operation. This corresponds to rates of up to approx. 0.94 m² of finished masonry per operation. This is especially worthwhile for large uninterrupted areas of wall, but in other situations the rationalization effect can still be guaranteed by using supplementary formats, make-up pieces or specials.
The two-man team rationalizes bricklaying activities because one man operates the handling device and is only responsible for preparatory work (supplying masonry units and mortar, picking up units and transporting them to the place where they are to be laid), while the other man carries out the actual bricklaying, i.e. spreading the layer of mortar with a mortar sledge or similar tool, laying and aligning the units. Consequently, working rates of approx. 0.33 h/m² for uninterrupted flat walls and 0.42 h/m² for other walls can be achieved. In order to limit the physical strain on the bricklayer, the use of large-format masonry units has led to the introduction of a maximum per-

2.5.15   Installation drawings for modular masonry

Calcium silicate gauged element wall with few interruptions

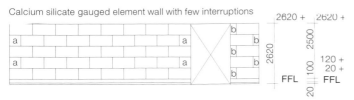

Gable wall

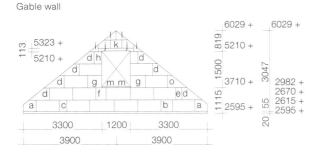

2.5.16   Prefabricated system walls

missible weight – including levels of moisture common on site – for masonry units when laying by hand. The maximum weight limits are mandatory and are stipulated in an information sheet published by the *Bau-Berufsgenossenschaften* (Building Employers' Liability Insurance Associations) [132], and are based on extensive ergonomic studies. The information sheet distinguishes between the one-hand and the two-hand lift.

The one-hand lift means that the masonry unit can be picked up with one hand and laid without unnecessary physical strain. The maximum permissible weight of a unit is 7.5 kg for a grip width of up to 70 mm, and 6.0 kg for a grip width of up to 115 mm.

The two-hand lift means that the masonry unit exceeds the maximum values for the one-hand lift. The maximum weight of a unit is 25 kg. Such units must be provided with grip aids or be designed in such a way that they can be gripped in both hands using suitable tools and laid manually. Heavy units should be lifted and laid by means of a handling device.

Masonry unit handling devices
The use of lifting equipment or handling devices is necessary for masonry unit formats larger than 16 DF for 240 mm thick walls and 10 DF for 365 mm thick walls or for masonry units weighing more than 25 kg. Travelling mini-cranes with a load-carrying capacity of up to 300 kg situated on the respective floor are increasingly being employed for this work. Depending on the size of the units, up to five large-format units can be gripped and laid side by side in one lift, i.e. approx. 1 m² of wall area can be produced in two lifts. Handling devices are normally used in conjunction with the two-man teams described above. They considerably relieve the physical strain on the individual

bricklayer despite the fact that improved productivity is expected from a smaller number of bricklayers. The use of a handling device in a two-man team only contributes to more rational masonry construction when the perpends make use of the tongue and groove system without mortar (because several units are gripped simultaneously), when the team is fully familiar with this system and each other, and when a continuous transport chain from production to placement is guaranteed. Therefore, the groups of masonry units should be aligned in rows with the tongue and groove end faces interlocking so that they can be readily lifted into place by the handling device. The fastest working times are achieved when the groups of masonry units are stacked between the handling device and the bricklayer. However, it should be noted that a concentrated arrangement of masonry units and handling device places a heavy load on the floor which may need to be carried by temporary additional supports beneath the floor. Adequate circulation zones are necessary in order to be able to move the handling device from place to place. This is helped by using butt-jointed wall intersections, which avoid the need for projecting racking or toothed returns, so that crosswalls can be built at a later date.

The cutting of large-format masonry units
The production of proper masonry bonds, as well as the need to construct given wall and column sizes, makes it necessary to divide, cut and bevel large-format units. While small-format units can be cut with a brick or scutch hammer, this is not a suitable method for large-format units because it would create too much unnecessary wastage. Moreover, cutting with a hammer or similar tool is inaccurate. In masonry of large-format units this leads to incorrect

bonding because the lower number of perpends (and frequently the use of perpends without mortar) means fewer opportunities for compensation along the length of the wall. This limits the load-carrying capacity of the masonry.

Consequently, large-format units must be divided with a bolster chisel or a mason's hammer or better still – especially for thin-bed masonry – by accurate sawing. Handsaws with a hardened blade, diamond cutting discs, bandsaws or chainsaws may be used. Clean edges can be produced with the aid of guides and templates. Cutting discs generally last longer than bandsaws or chainsaws.

Modular masonry
The idea of modular masonry was developed by the calcium silicate and autoclaved aerated concrete industries. The benefit that modular masonry brings to rationalization is that the large-format masonry units for each wall are delivered to site as factory-made wall "kits", including all make-up and complementary units, together with computer-produced installation drawings for a fixed price (see 2.5.15). In addition, the manufacturer of the masonry units provides the thin-bed mortar, handling devices and accessories.

The design of the walls (dimensions, layout and sizes of openings) must be coordinated with the building system or the large-format units in order to minimize the number of precut make-up and complementary units and hence the cost of materials. Flat panels of masonry without interruptions in cellular construction are advantageous.

The installation drawings and instructions simplify and accelerate the erection of masonry units delivered as kits. This leads to a

2.5.17 Gable in the form of a clay brickwork panel

2.5.18 Clay facade elements (Schätz-Preton system)

considerable reduction in labour costs, also helped by the complementary units supplied. In addition, cutting the units on site and the costly disposal of waste are avoided. The simple installation of wall kits can also be carried out by the unskilled in a "do-it-yourself" type of construction, which again saves labour costs.

Dry walling
is built by laying masonry units in a bond but without any mortar to the perpends or the bed joints. To achieve this, the masonry units must exhibit a very high standard of quality with regard to deviations from the intended height dimensions and in terms of the flatness and parallelism of bed faces. Laying the units without mortar to perpends or bed joints achieves further rationalization in the construction of masonry because the operations for supplying the mortar, applying it and removing surplus mortar after laying the units are all eliminated. This improves the ergonomics of bricklaying (number of bending and turning movements) and hence makes the working rhythm of the bricklayer more uniform. This leads to less time being required to construct each square metre of wall. In addition, the omission of thin-bed mortar saves not only labour costs but material costs as well.
As so far there is very little experience of dry walling in practice, its use is currently regulated by way of general building authority certificates. These restrict the use of dry walling to buildings with up to three storeys or a height above ground level of max. 10 m, to clear storey heights of max. 2.75 m, and to floor spans of max. 6.0 m. Apart from that, dry walling may not be used for reinforced masonry, vaulting, arches, brick arch floors or chimneys.
Dry walling must be loaded by floors along its

entire length, whereby the depth of bearing for walls with floor loads to one side only must be at least half the thickness of the wall or 120 mm. The floors (also roofs) are to be formed as rigid plates – equivalent measures (e.g. structurally designed capping beams) are not permitted. The stability of dry walling should be verified by way of various component tests as well as special structural analyses with regard to buckling lengths, bonds etc. [79].

Prefabricated construction
The advantages and economic effectiveness of prefabricated construction lie in the rational prefabrication of wall elements under optimum, industrial conditions in the factory, the fast erection using cranes and the subsequent simple structural connection of elements on site to thus form a homogeneous wall or structure. The elements are manufactured in the factory as brickwork panels, cast panels or composite panels (see "Prefabricated masonry elements") to match the respective storey heights and incorporate all necessary openings and service ducts. They are reinforced horizontally and vertically for transport and erection. Industrial prefabrication renders possible the use of computer-assisted machinery (e.g. masonry robots) to achieve a high daily output with a consistently high standard of quality but at the same time low labour costs.
Delivering the elements to the building site "just in time" and their rapid and economic erection speeds up progress on site and requires only a few personnel. Smooth erection on site demands good preparations (instruction of personnel, specification of erection procedure, preparation of crane hardstanding and temporary supports etc.) and usually the use of a mobile crane. Above basement level, this method of construction allows the primary structure of a

detached house to be completed in just 3-5 days. Only minimal site facilities are required and at the same time the environmental pollution due to noise and dirt from the building site is minimized. Another cost-saving results from the fact that factory prefabrication means the components are essentially dry when delivered, which means that less energy is required for drying out the building (see figs. 2.5.16 and 2.5.17).
Besides their use for loadbearing, single-leaf masonry, prefabricated elements are increasingly being used for curtain wall masonry facades. Such facade elements – up to 8.0 m long and 3.6 m high – are produced rationally and unaffected by the weather in the factory according to the guidelines for reinforced masonry with frost-resistant facing or engineering bricks. Factory production ensures a consistent and high-quality outer leaf with respect to joint pattern, colour of units and mortar, full joints without voids, even jointing etc. In addition, blinds, lintels and arches as well as special textures can be incorporated (see fig. 2.5.18).

Building science

Joachim Achtziger

2.6.1	Surface resistances in m²K/W		
	Direction of heat flow		
	Upwards	Horizontal	Downwards
R_{si}	0.10	0.13	0.17
R_{se}	0,04	0.04	0.04

Thermal insulation

The thermal insulation of a building is intended to contribute towards a hygienic and comfortable internal climate, which is not detrimental to the health of the occupants and users of the building, and at the same time protects the structure against the climate-related effects of moisture and their consequences. The energy required for heating in the winter and measures to provide an acceptable internal climate in the summer without the use of air conditioning for cooling must be optimized in conjunction with the necessary thermal insulation and energy-saving measures. These days, thermal insulation to a building is not just a means of saving energy but an important element in an environmental protection programme. Therefore, reducing emissions of pollutants from building heating systems is an important aspect. Besides saving heating costs for the user, an increasingly important factor, ever more precious energy and fuel resources are also spared.

The Construction Products Directive [13], the most important element in the creation of a European Single Market for the construction industry, acknowledges the importance of thermal insulation and defines the area of "Energy economy and heat retention" as one of six essential requirements. On the whole, the costs and adaptation problems of European standardization are outweighed by the benefits. The effects of these are to:
• harmonize the markets,
• create uniform framework conditions within the EU,
• attain European supply conditions,
• set uniform evaluation and testing standards,
• set uniform standards of quality recognized throughout Europe; different standards in different countries can be assessed according to a system of graded performance classes.

The objective of the principal document "Energy economy and heat retention" is, taking into account the location, to keep down the consumption of energy related to the use of a building and its technical systems, and to guarantee an adequate of standard of thermal comfort for the occupants. This encompasses and standardizes the following main factors:

• location, orientation and form of the structure,
• physical properties of materials and components used for the structure,
• the design of systems for the technical services,
• performance features for the components of these systems, and
• the behaviour of the users of the building.

The combination of planning and design standards, standards with generally acknowledged design data, standards for the measurement of components and materials as well as those covering products is shown in a very much simplified and generalized form in fig. 2.6.2. The quality of a building in energy terms is calculated according to a design standard. Further rules are necessary for assessing the thermal performance of parts of a building, such as rooms adjacent the soil, rooms in the roof space or parts of the building with lower temperatures, as well as standards for specifying the thermal performance of components and their non-constant behaviour upon heating and cooling. Tables of values or measurements of components prepared according to established rules serve for the calculation of transmission heat losses from a building envelope and given heat gains. Further, components can be assessed according to their constituents, based on the properties of the materials employed. Therefore, a complete, coordinated standardized concept from the product properties to final energy requirement is available for describing the performance of a building. In Germany, DIN 4108 remains as the National Application Document and the publication describing national requirements. The first national measures for saving energy in the heating of buildings were established within the scope of the Energy-savings Act of 1976, which led to the 1977 Thermal Insulation Act and its subsequent revisions in 1982 and 1995. The new Energy-savings Act of 2001 has the potential to achieve a further 30% saving in energy in the heating of buildings. A complete energy planning concept is available for the design of buildings, taking into account heating systems and an assessment of the energy carrier.

Heat transfer, thermal insulation parameters, terms

Heat transfer can take place in the form of conduction in solid, liquid and gaseous media, and in the form of radiation in transparent materials and vacuum. In building materials, heat transfer is expressed by the property of *thermal conductivity*. Thermal conductivity λ specifies the heat flow in W passing through 1 m² of a 1 m thick layer in 1 h when the temperature gradient in the direction of the heat flow is 1 K. The lower the thermal conductivity, the better is the thermal insulation for a given thickness of material. The thermal insulation capacity of a component is characterized by the *thermal resistance* R. It is determined by dividing the thickness of the layer concerned (in m) by the material's thermal conductivity λ (in W/mK). Multi-layer components require the value of each layer to be calculated separately according to this method. The total of the individual values gives the thermal resistance R for the complete component. The higher the thermal resistance, the better is the thermal insulation.

To determine the thermal transmittance through a component, we also need to know the internal and external *surface resistance* R_{si} and R_{se}. The surface resistance is the resistance of the boundary layer of air to the transfer of heat from the internal air to the component and from this to the external air. The surface resistances are generally standardized according to the orientation of the component (vertical, horizontal) and the external air circulation (unrestricted, ventilated, not ventilated) as given in table 2.6.1. They have been determined for a degree of emissions from the surface of $\varepsilon = 0.9$ and a wind speed n = 4 m/s at the external surface. The total of all resistances – those of the layers of the component and the surface resistances of the boundary layers of air – is the *total thermal resistance* R_T which the complete component applies to resist the flow of heat. The reciprocal of this value is the *thermal transmittance* U – the characteristic variable for the thermal insulation of a building component. The U-value is fundamental for calculating the heating requirement of a building. The smaller the U-value, the better is the thermal insulation. The calculation of the thermal resistance of single- and multi-layer components as well as the U-value is shown schematically in 2.6.3. The calculation of the U-value for components made from several neighbouring sections with different thermal conductivities is dealt with in the section entitled "Thermal bridges". The mathematical assessment of heat transfer and temperature gradients in components is a relatively difficult problem depending on time and geometry. Therefore, to simplify the work we assume stationary, i.e. constant, temperatures on both sides of the component as well as a one-dimensional heat flow across the thickness of

2.6.2   Diagram of relationship between materials, components and design standards for assessing buildings in terms of energy performance

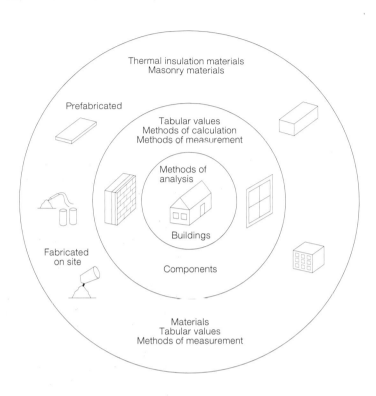

2.6.3   Calculation of thermal resistance and thermal transmittance values for single- and multi-layer masonry components

Construction	Sketch of principle	Equation
Thermal resistance Single-layer component		$R = \dfrac{d}{\lambda_H}$
Thermal resistance Multi-layer component		$R = \dfrac{d_1}{\lambda_{R1}} + \dfrac{d_2}{\lambda_{R2}} + ... + \dfrac{d_n}{\lambda_{Rn}}$
Thermal transmittance Single- or multi-layer component		$U = \dfrac{1}{R_{si} + R + R_{se}}$

2.6.4 Thermal conductivity of dry expanded clay and expanded shale concrete samples with and without various quartz sand additions by volume of total aggregate content (%) in relation to gross density (average temperature 10°C), after W. Schüle, Giesecke and Reichardt [195]

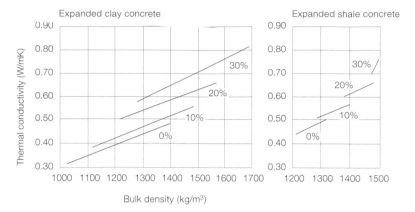

Bulk density (kg/m³)

the component. This approach is generally sufficiently adequate for winter conditions with permanently heated interiors and constant low temperatures outside, as well as for calculating a mean heat loss over a longer period of time. At equilibrium, the heat flow

$$\Phi = U \times A \, (\vartheta_i - \vartheta_e)$$

passes through an external component with an area A on one side of which there is internal air at a temperature ϑ_i and on the other, there is external air at a temperature ϑ_e. Therefore, the thermal transmittance U is critical for the transmission heat loss through the component. However, the graphic representation of the U-value in fig. 2.6.8 reveals that only slight improvements are possible beyond a certain thickness of component. This non-linear behaviour leads to the situation of increasing costs for more and more insulation having ever smaller energy-saving effects. The variables, symbols and units necessary for assessing the thermal performance of the building envelope are given in table 2.6.6. Further details are contained in DIN EN ISO 7345 and the respective parts of DIN 4108.

Thermal conductivity of building materials

With the exception of very dense stone, building materials are porous to some extent. They contain air-filled voids of various sizes in various arrangements, and these can have a significant effect on the transfer of heat. The thermal conductivity of masonry depends on:
- the thermal conductivity of the solid constituents,
- the porosity or gross/bulk density,
- the nature, size and arrangement of the pores,
- the radiation properties of the boundary walls of the voids,
- temperature, and
- the water or moisture content.

As the thermal conductivity of the material under observation depends on the temperature within its range of application, for building purposes all thermal conductivity values are related to a mean temperature of 10°C so that unequivocal comparisons can be made. For the same reason, material parameters are specified for the dry state of the material, initially without taking into account the fact that moisture increases the thermal conductivity. Table 2.6.5 provides an overview of the order of magnitude of the thermal conductivities of solid materials used to manufacture building and thermal insulation materials. Materials with mainly crystalline components exhibit a higher thermal conductivity than those with vitreous or lime-based components. For instance, the addition of quartz sand to concrete or mortar has a noticeably detrimental effect on the thermal conductivity. Measurements of concrete

2.6.5 Order of magnitude of thermal conductivity (W/mK) of solid constituents of building and thermal insulation materials, after J.S. Cammerer [29]

Inorganic building materials	
Crystalline	
perpendicular to crystal axis	4.7 to 7.0
parallel to crystal axis	to 14
Quartzite	6
Limestone, marble, granite	1.6 to 4.0
Basalt, feldspar, sandstone	
Amorphous solidified melts such as	
blast furnace slag and glasses	0.7 to 1.2
Natural organic substances	0.3 to 0.4
Plastics	0.16 to 0.35

2.6.6 Variables, symbols and units used in thermal performance

Physical variable	Symbol	Unit
Temperature	ϑ	°C
Thermal conductivity	λ	W/mK
Thermal resistance	R	m²K/W
Internal surface resistance	R_{si}	m²K/W
External surface resistance	R_{se}	m²K/W
Total thermal resistance (air-to-air resistance)	R_T	m²K/W
Thermal transmittance	U	W/m²K
Heat flow	ϕ	W
Heat flow rate	q	W/m²
Specific heat capacity	c	J/kgK
Gross/bulk density	ρ	kg/m³
Thickness	d	m
Area	A	m²
Volume	V	m³
Mass	m	kg

2.6.7 Thermal conductivity of building materials

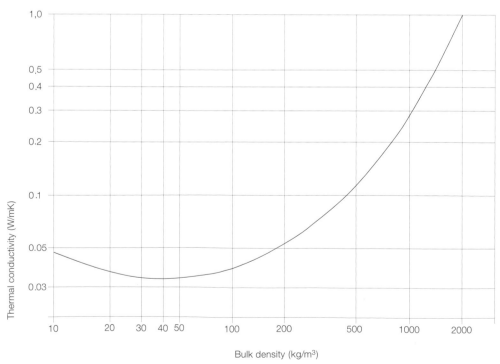

Bulk density (kg/m³)

with different quartz contents are shown in fig. 2.6.4. Generally speaking, the use of aggregates containing quartz can be assumed to reduce the insulating effect of the concrete by 20%. However, the characteristic variable influencing the thermal conductivity of building and insulation materials is the gross density. This relationship is shown in fig. 2.6.7 – the evaluation of more than 1000 measurements in a European research project. After being incorporated into a structure, especially in external components, building materials exhibit a greater or lesser water content. Owing to the generally relatively small proportion, this is known as moisture content. Depending on the porous structure and the magnitude of the moisture content, the water may partly or completely fill larger and smaller pores or just adhere to the sides of the pores or in corners of the pores. Damp building materials exhibit a higher thermal conductivity compared to the dry state, and this depends on the moisture content, which in turn is related to the type of material.

Figure 2.6.9 shows the thermal conductivity of various building materials as a function of the moisture content; this can be expressed related to either the volume or the mass. If the thermal conductivity in the dry state and the moisture content of the building material is known, the thermal conductivity in the moist state can be calculated according to DIN EN ISO 10456 using the equation

$$\lambda_{u,\psi} = \lambda_{10,tr} \times F_m$$

$$F_m = e^{f_u(u_2 - u_1)}$$

$$F_m = e^{f_\psi(\psi_2 - \psi_1)}$$

where:
f_u and f_ψ = conversion factor for mass- and volume-related moisture content respectively
u_1 and f_ψ = moisture content 0 of dry material
u_2 and ψ_2 = mass- and volume-related moisture content respectively.

The moisture contents u and y common in practice, as well as conversion factors for the moisture content, are given in DIN EN 12524 corresponding to table 2.6.10. The standardized moisture contents u (mass-related) and y (volume-related) are related to the moisture content equilibrium of the corresponding material at 23°C and 50% relative humidity, or 23°C and 80% relative humidity. The moisture contents in the desired reference ambient conditions and the conversion factors for the influence of the moisture content on the thermal conductivity can also be determined individually for certain materials by way of experiment, with the aim of achieving more favourable thermal conductivity values for real situations. The term "nominal value" was introduced to achieve a uniform specification for the properties of

building materials being marketed internationally. The nominal value for thermal conductivity is the value to be expected for the thermal insulation property of a building material or product, assessed by way of measurements taken at a reference temperature and humidity according to table 2.6.11, specified for defined percentiles and confidence ranges and corresponding to an expected service life under normal conditions. The term "service life" also includes the ageing behaviour of products, such as thermal insulation materials with high-molecular propellants, which over time undergo an exchange of gas with the surrounding air, or the settlement behaviour of loose thermal insulation materials in voids. Only the material scatter and the influence of moisture are relevant for masonry products.

The *design value for thermal conductivity* is the value of a thermal property of a building material or product under certain external and internal conditions, which can be regarded as typical behaviour of the material or product in its form as a constituent of a component. The design values are determined by the user/ planner, building authorities or national standards corresponding to the intended application of the product, the environmental or climatic conditions as well as the purpose of the calculation, e.g.:

• energy consumption
• design of heating and cooling plants
• surface temperature
• compliance with national building codes
• investigations of non-constant thermal conditions in buildings

Thermal insulation design values can be derived from the nominal values by means of the conversion factors given in DIN EN ISO 10456. This is customary for thermal insulation materials. Design values for masonry materials are derived from the thermal conductivity in the dry state.

Thermal insulation provided by layers of air
Layers of air in components transfer heat by conduction, convection and radiation. The various heat transport mechanisms have the effect that, unlike with solid materials, for air the thermal resistance R does not rise with increasing thickness but instead reaches a maximum value and then remains constant. Thermal resistances of layers of air according to table 2.6.12 are specified in DIN EN ISO 6946 and may be taken into account only when analysing thermal performance if they are isolated from the outside air. Such layers of air also include the cavities in twin-leaf masonry walls to DIN 1053 because the openings in the outer leaf are too small to bring about an exchange of air with the outside air. The extent to which a layer of air with small openings to the outside air can still be regarded as a

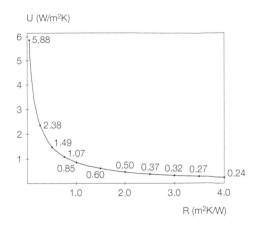

2.6.8 Thermal transmittance U in relation to thermal resistance R

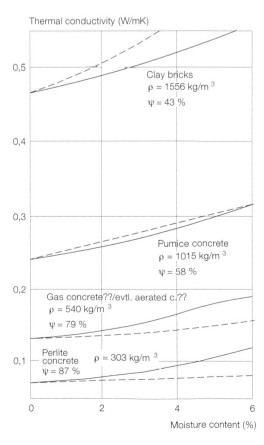

2.6.9 Thermal conductivity of building materials in relation to moisture content (volume- and mass-related)
——— volume-related
– – – – mass-related

2.6.10 Moisture-related properties of masonry materials

Material	Gross density	Moisture content at 23 °C, 50% re		Moisture content at 23 °C, 80% rh		Conversion factor for moisture content	
	ρ kg/m^3	u kg/kg	ψ m^3/m^3	u kg/kg	ψ m^3/m^3	f_u –	f_ψ –
Solid bricks (fired clay)	1000–2400		0.007		0.012		10
Calcium silicate	900–2200		0.012		0.024		10
Pumice concrete	500–1300		0.02		0.035		4
Normal-weight concrete	1600–2400		0.025		0.04		4
Concrete bricks							
Polystyrene concrete	500–800		0.015		0.025		5
Expanded clay concrete	400–700	0.02		0.03		2.6	
Concrete with predominantly expanded clay aggregate	800–1700	0.02		0.03		4	
Concrete with blast-furnace slag aggregate	1100–1700	0.02		0.04		4	
Autoclaved aerated concrete	300–1000	0.026		0.045		4	
Concrete with other lightweight aggregates			0.03		0.05		4
Mortar (masonry mortar and plastering mixes)	250–2000		0.04		0.06		4

2.6.11 Reference conditions according to DIN EN ISO 10456

Property	Boundary condition			
	I (10 °C)		II (23 °C)	
	a	b	c	d
Reference temperature	10 °C	10 °C	23 °C	23 °C
Moisture	u_{dry}	$u_{23,50}$	u_{dry}	$u_{23,50}$
Ageing	aged	aged	aged	aged

u_{dry} is a low moisture content attained after drying.
$u_{23,50}$ is a moisture content which becomes established in equilibrium at 23°C air temperature and 50% relative humidity.

2.6.12 Thermal resistance R of stationary air layers – surfaces with high degree of emissions

Thickness of air layer mm	Direction of heat flow R in m^{2}K/W		
	Upwards	Horizontal	Downwards
0	0.00	0.00	0.00
5	0.11	0.11	0.11
7	0.13	0.13	0.13
10	0.15	0.15	0.15
15	0.16	0.17	0.17
25	0.16	0.18	0.19
50	0.16	0.18	0.21
100	0.16	0.18	0.22
300	0.16	0.18	0.23

Note: Intermediate values may be obtained by linear interpolation.

2.6.13 Thermal resistances of stationary, poorly ventilated and well ventilated air layers according to DIN EN ISO 6946

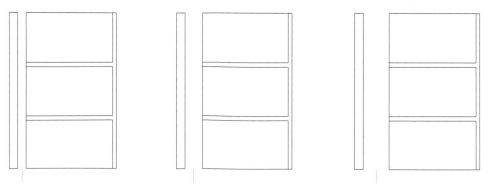

Opening ≤ 500mm^2 per 1 m length

Stationary air layer

Opening > 500 mm^2 per 1 m length
≤ 1500 mm^2 per 1 m length

Poorly ventilated air layer
R = half the value of the stationary air layer but max. 0.15 m^{2}K/W

Opening > 1500 mm^2 per 1 m length

Well ventilated air layer

$R_{se} = R_{si} = 0.13$ m^{2}K/W

stationary layer, or to which insulating values poorly or well ventilated layers of air can be given are shown schematically in fig. 2.6.13. Small or divided air spaces corresponding to fig. 2.6.14, as occur in perforated masonry units, horizontally perforated clay bricks and grip aids, require special consideration. In these cases, the geometry of the perforations – the gap width-to-thickness ratio – has an influence on the equivalent thermal conductivity of the void. The thermal resistances of air spaces with any dimensions can be calculated according to DIN EN ISO 6946. The thermal resistance of an air cell is found using the equation:

$$R_g = \frac{1}{(h_a + 1/2\ Eh_{ro}\ (1+d^2/b^2 - d/b))}$$

where:
R_g = thermal resistance of air space
d = thickness of air space
b = width of air space
E = degree of exchange through radiation
h_{ro} = external surface resistance due to radiation for a black body

h_a is as follows:
- for a horizontal heat flow:
  h_a = 1.25 W/m^{2}K or 0.025/d W/m^{2}K, whichever is the greater
- for an upward heat flow:
  h_a = 1.95 W/m^{2}K or 0.025/d W/m^{2}K, whichever is the greater
- for a downward heat flow:
  h_a = 0.12d$^{-0.44}$ W/m^{2}K or 0.025/d W/m^{2}K, whichever is the greater

where d = thickness of air space in direction of heat flow.

The thermal optimization of perforated masonry units depends on the distribution of perforations and their cross-section. In comparing different patterns of perforations, the proportion of perforations and the thermal conductivity of the solid material must be kept constant. Figure 2.6.15 illustrates the thermal insulation qualities for various arrangements of perforations in clay bricks with 40% perforations [46]. The 18 samples are arranged in order of descending thermal conductivity.
In lightweight concrete units the thermal conductivity – for the same gross density – depends quite crucially on the proportion of perforations and the arrangement of cells. Figure 2.6.16 shows thermal conductivities of masonry made from three- and four-cell hollow blocks, as well as a slotted unit calculated according to EN 1745 assuming a gross density of 600 kg/m^3. The values given apply to units made from expanded clay concrete and lightweight mortar LM 36.

Determination of design values for thermal conductivity

The design value for thermal conductivity for use in calculating the thermal insulation of buildings is defined for Germany on the basis of the practical moisture content or the moisture content equilibrium at 23°C and 80% relative humidity. To do this, the practical moisture content or the reference moisture content of the building material must be known. Practical moisture content is understood to be a quantity of water in the building material which becomes established in an adequately dry structure over the course of time. This is caused by water being absorbed from the air (hygroscopicity) and the formation of condensation on surfaces and within components. Therefore, practical moisture content excludes moisture due to building processes which has not yet fully disappeared and saturation resulting from precipitation, rising damp and damage to the building. The practical moisture content is defined by the relative cumulative frequency of a multitude of investigations on as many structures as possible. Figure 2.6.17 shows the typical progression for a building material. The results of measurements of autoclaved aerated concrete walls and roofs (see fig. 2.6.21) can serve as an example for the drying gradient of external components [104]. External walls with adequate rain protection and permitting evaporation on both sides dry out faster. The drying period lasts about two years under different conditions. As the drying gradient is considerably influenced by the weather, the occupation of the building, the standard of construction and the orientation of the walls, and determining the moisture by removing cores of material is expensive and complicated, a new method of determining the moisture characteristic of a building material by way of its hygroscopic moisture content equilibrium in a defined climate is now being used (fig. 2.6.18). Moisture absorption at 23°C and 80% relative humidity has proved equivalent to the field investigations. We speak then of the reference moisture content, a parameter which has also become established in European standards (see table 2.6.10, columns 5 and 6). The water content of a building material is specified either as the quantity of water contained in a mass unit of the material, related to the dry mass as the "mass-related water content" u in kg/kg, or as the volume of water contained in a volume unit of the material, related to the material volume as the "volume-related water content" ψ in m³/m³.

The mass-related moisture content is recommended for building materials because it remains constant over the entire gross density range. As an example, figure 2.6.19 shows the results of tests to measure the sorptive moisture of aerated concrete at an ambient temperature of 23°C and 80% relative humidity, and

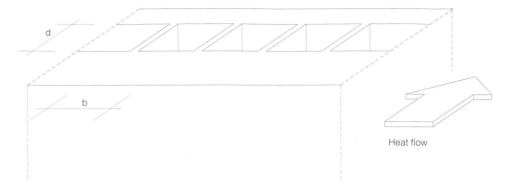

2.6.14   Small or divided non-ventilated voids (air spaces)

d

b

Heat flow

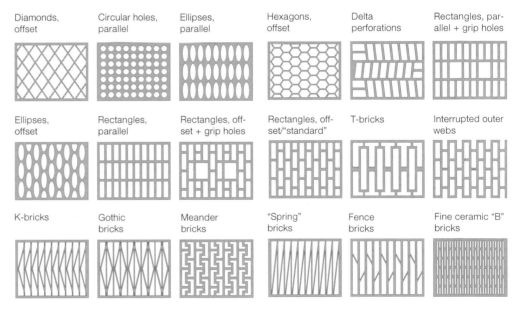

2.6.15   Variations in clay brick cross-sections for a constant proportion of perforations and constant total web thickness (heat flow horizontal) [2]

Diamonds, offset

Circular holes, parallel

Ellipses, parallel

Hexagons, offset

Delta perforations

Rectangles, parallel + grip holes

Ellipses, offset

Rectangles, parallel

Rectangles, offset + grip holes

Rectangles, offset/"standard"

T-bricks

Interrupted outer webs

K-bricks

Gothic bricks

Meander bricks

"Spring" bricks

Fence bricks

Fine ceramic "B" bricks

2.6.16   The influence of perforations on the thermal conductivity of lightweight concrete units with gross density 600 kg/m³

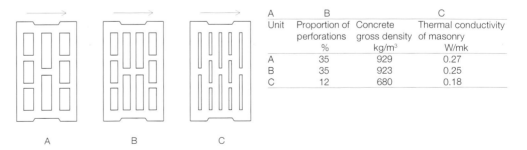

A   B   C

A Unit	B Proportion of perforations %	Concrete gross density kg/m³	C Thermal conductivity of masonry W/mk
A	35	929	0.27
B	35	923	0.25
C	12	680	0.18

2.6.17 Cumulative frequency of moisture content of pumice building materials in external walls determined in 88 samples

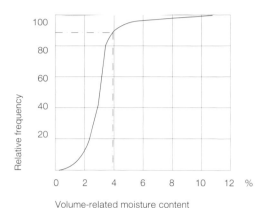

Volume-related moisture content

2.6.18 Volume-related moisture content in relation to relative humidity for absorption and desorption of a calcium silicate unit with gross density 1720 kg/m³, after Künzel

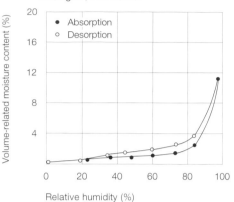

Relative humidity (%)

2.6.19 Sorbed moisture (equilibrium moisture content) of autoclaved aerated concrete at 20°C and 80% rh in relation to the volume (y) or the mass (u) of the material depending on gross density

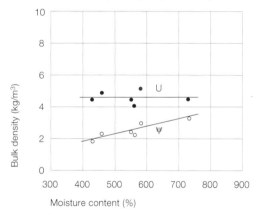

Moisture content (%)

2.6.20 Percentage increase in thermal conductivity of autoclaved aerated concrete depending on $\lambda_{10,tr}$, in relation to % by vol. or 1 mass %, after [6]

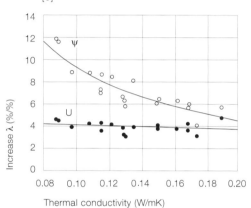

Thermal conductivity (W/mK)

2.6.21 Drying-out of autoclaved aerated concrete external components (walls and flat roofs) plotted against time [3]

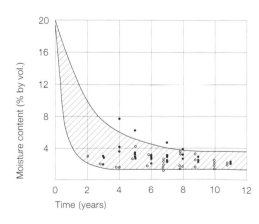

Time (years)

The initial progression of the given range stems from measurements on external walls at the Fraunhofer Institute's open-air site (lower limit: external wall, evaporation possible on both sides; upper limit: outer face sealed, evaporation only possible via inner face).
● external walls
o flat roofs
represent measurements of actual buildings.

2.6.22 Ventilated natural stone facades and lightweight curtain walls; increase in thermal transmittance of wall in relation to number of fixings and fixing material

ΔU (W/m²K)

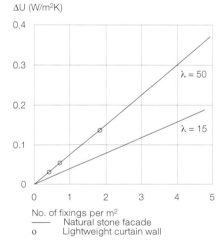

No. of fixings per m²
— Natural stone facade
o Lightweight curtain wall

fig. 2.6.20 shows the relationship between thermal conductivity and moisture content derived from this. Taking the mass-related moisture content as our reference point allows the use of a surcharge to cover the influence of the moisture on the thermal conductivity, which is independent of the material bulk density and the thermal conductivity. To carry out a thermal insulation analysis, the user requires a thermal conductivity design value for the particular type of masonry construction. This takes account of the type, form and gross density of the masonry unit as well as the type of mortar. The thermal insulation properties of different types of masonry can be determined from tables according to EN 1745 or by measuring samples of wall or by calculation based on the material parameters [3]. To take into account the influence of moisture on the thermal conductivity, the reference moisture contents and moisture correction values F_m given in table 2.6.23 apply in Germany. More favourable values not contained in the table may be verified experimentally.

Thermal performance of external walls
The thermal resistance R of single-leaf plastered external walls, single-leaf external walls with internal or external thermal insulation, or twin-leaf walls with or without additional insulation is calculated by simply adding together the R-values of the individual layers. As an example, figure 2.6.24 shows a plastered single-leaf wall with a thermal insulation composite system. If the insulation is attached with mechanical fixings, additional heat losses occur depending on the type of fixing. Based on experiments and numerical parameter studies [6, 205], the heat transfer for a component (including the thermal bridge effect) can be represented in a simplified estimation method as follows:
• by adding the increase ΔU to the thermal transmittance value U for the undisturbed section

$$U_c = U + \Delta U$$

• by a percentage increase in the thermal transmittance value U

$$U_c = U\left(1 + \frac{Z}{100}\right)$$

• by adding the increase in the conductance of a component by means of the discrete thermal transmittance χ

$$L = \Sigma U_i A_i + \Sigma \chi_j$$

The first method with a surcharge ΔU was first used in the European standard EN 6946. The correction values given in table 2.6.25 apply to the various types of anchors used for fixing thermal insulation composite systems. A masonry substrate behaves slightly better than a concrete one. The type of rendering has practically no influence on the outcome. The thermal conductivity of the insulation material and its thickness have no effect on the additional heat loss when adding ΔU. The ΔU-values given per anchor can be simply added together for the particular application, since in the most unfavourable situation the anchor only has an effect within a radius of max. 250 mm about its axis. Influences of ΔU < 0.002 can be ignored because the additional heat loss lies below 3%.

At just 1% the influence of the thermal bridges can be neglected for mechanical fixing systems using plastic rails. However, if the plastic rails are replaced by aluminium ones, this results in a considerable surcharge of ΔU = 0.05 W/m²K for horizontal rails fixed to the load-bearing substrate at 500 mm centres.

In the case of a thermally insulated wall with a ventilated external cladding made from any one of a number of different materials, the cladding fixings in the wall act as thermal bridges. Their effect depends on the following influences:

• material of the fixings
• number of fixings per unit surface area
• type of wall material.

Timber supporting constructions with vertical and horizontal battens for carrying the thermal insulation and the cladding have only a relatively small effect on the heat transfer. The thermal insulation of such constructions can be calculated according to DIN EN ISO 6946. One particularly unfavourable case with a high number of fixings is the ventilated facade with a cladding of natural stone. The natural stone slabs are usually fixed to the wall by means of supporting and retaining anchors. The absolute increase in the thermal transmittance caused by the anchors does not depend on the thickness of the insulation and the type of stone basically has no influence on the heat transfer. On the other hand, replacing a concrete loadbearing wall with one of masonry reduces the influence of the anchors by 40%. There is a linear correlation between the absolute increase in the heat transfer and the number of anchors per unit surface area (see fig. 2.6.22). The influence of the thermal bridges is cut by half when stainless steel anchors are used. If the natural stone facade is replaced by a lightweight ventilated cladding with other types of fixing to the loadbearing wall, surprisingly, the influence of the anchors remains the same. The use of a plastic underlay ("Thermostop") between bracket and masonry brings about a clear reduction in the thermal bridge effect, but a thermal break attached to the cold side of the bracket hardly has any effect.

An important planning instrument these days is the "Determination of the thermal influences of thermal bridges for curtain wall ventilated facades" [163]. The discrete thermal bridge

2.6.23 Moisture contents and conversion factors for moisture content according to draft standard EN 12524 table 2, and moisture correction factor F_m according to draft standard EN 10456

Material	Moisture content at 23 °C, 80% rh		Conversion factor for moisture content		Moisture correction factor F_m
	kg/kg	m³/m³	f_u	f_Ψ	
Autoclaved aerated concrete	0.045	-	4	-	1.2
Lightweight concrete with pumice	-	0.035	-	4	1.15
Lightweight concrete with expanded clay	0.03	-	2.6	-	1.08
Clay	-	0.012	-	10	1.13
Calcium silicate	-	0.024	-	10	1.27
Mortar	-	0.06	-	4	1.27

2.6.24 Example of calculation for external wall of plastered single-leaf masonry

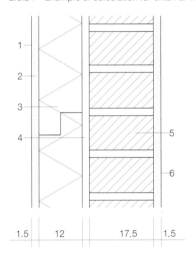

Layer		Thickness of layer in m	λ_R W/mK	R m²K/W
Internal plaster	6	0.015	0.35	0.04
Calcium silicate masonry	5	0.175	0.99	0.18
Bonding compound	4	–	–	–
Rigid expanded polystyrene foam	3	0.120	0.040	3.00
Textured rendering	1	–	–	–
Thermal resistance R = Σ d/λ_R = 3.22				
Thermal transmittance U = 1/(0.13 + 3.22 + 0.04) = 0.30 W/m²K				

2.6.25 Heat losses via various types of anchors

Type of anchor	Dia. of anchors mm	Δk per anchor W/m²K
Facade anchor with disc and steel screw with unprotected head	8	0.006
	10	0.008
Facade anchor with electrogalvanized steel screw with plastic coating	8	0.004
Facade anchor with V4A stainless steel screw with plastic coating	8	0.002
Facade anchor with thermal break	6.5	0.002

2.6.26 Recommended values for total energy transmittance of transparent components to DIN 4108 part 6

Transparent component	Total energy transmittance $g_\perp$
Single glazing	0.87
Double glazing	0.76
Heat-absorbing double glazing with selective coating	0.50 to 0.70
Triple glazing, standard	0.60 to 0.70
Triple glazing with 2-fold selective coating	0.35 to 0.50
Solar-control glass	0.20 to 0.50
Translucent thermal insulation	g_{TI}
Translucent thermal insulation Thermal insulation, 100-120 mm; 0.8 W/m²K ≤ U_e ≤ 0.9 W/m²K	0.35 to 0.60
Absorbent opaque thermal insulation with single layer glass cover, 100 mm	approx. 0.10

167

2.6.27 Ranges of standard thermal transmittance U for various external masonry walls

System	U-value W/m²K
	0.30 – 0.50
	0.30 – 0.45
	0.20 – 0.40
	0.25 – 0.40
	0.30 – 0.50
	0.40 – 0.50

loss value c in W/K or the thermal bridge surcharge ΔU in W/m²K is specified depending on the construction of the support system and the thermal resistance of the loadbearing construction (influence of transverse conduction). The effect of a thermal break is shown in fig. 2.6.28, a thermally advantageous supporting construction in fig. 2.6.29. Figure 2.6.27 is an overview of the thermal transmittance values for a number of different wall constructions.

Windows

The window as the "thermal hole" in the building envelope is now a thing of the past. Technological developments in insulating glazing systems have set standards in the energy assessments of heated buildings. The reduction in transmission heat losses and maintenance of a sufficient total energy transmittance for the passive use of solar energy mean that windows contribute to the heat gain during the heating season. However, the areas of glazing do have their limits in terms of thermal insulation during the summer, when they can lead to uncomfortably high interior temperatures. The thermal transmittance U_W of a window depends on:
• the distance between the panes
• the number of panes
• the emissivity of the glass surfaces towards the cavity
• the gas filling in the cavity between the panes
• the hermetic edge seal of insulating glazing
• the material of the frame.

The thermal transmittance U_W can be taken from tables according to DIN EN ISO 10077 part 1 (table 2.6.30) for constant frame proportions of 20 or 30%, depending on the glazing (U_g) and the type and design of the frame (U_F), or determined by a simple area-based assessment of the U-values for glazing and frame including a surcharge for the glass seal around the perimeter. Timber and plastic frames provide good thermal insulation; the inside and outside surfaces of metal frames must be carefully separated (thermal break). Widening the cavity between the panes only improves the U_g-value up to a certain width depending on the type of glass (for air about 20 mm). If this width is exceeded, then the improvement to the thermal insulation properties is counteracted by convection. By employing noble gases (argon, krypton, xenon), we can exploit their lower thermal conductivity (compared to air). The heat transport by way of radiation characterized by the emission behaviour of the glass surfaces can be drastically reduced by using low-E coatings. The development of low-E glazing began with sputtered, later pyrolytic coatings and an air filling to the cavity; this brought U_g-values of 1.8 W/m²K. Today, double glazing with magnetron coatings and noble gas fillings reach Ug-values of 1.1 W/m²K. And modern triple glazing systems based on silver

coatings and noble gas fillings have already reached peak values between 0.7 and 0.4 W/m²K.

The permeability of the window for solar radiation is expressed by the total energy transmittance g. This corresponds to the percentage proportion of incident radiation that passes through the glazing into the interior of the building. As the glazed surfaces are generally not positioned perpendicular to the solar radiation and so part of the solar energy is lost through reflection at the pane, the total energy transmittance is reduced by 15%. Furthermore, permanent shade, from parts of the building, trees, neighbouring buildings, window frames etc., as well as the degree to which the solar energy supplied is used must be taken into account when calculating solar heat gains. If no individual figures based on measurements are available for the total energy transmittance, the design values given in fig. 2.6.26 may be used. These values cover the lower, i.e. less favourable, range of permeability of insulating glazing with respect to the solar gains in the heating season. Figure 2.6.31 shows the thermal balance of two windows with double and triple glazing during the heating season in a reference environment (10°C heating threshold temperature, degree days factor 2900) compared to the heat losses of a well-insulated external wall. The U_g-values are achieved by using coated glasses and gas fillings to the cavity. It can be seen that double glazing with a combination of higher U_g-value but less favourable total energy transmittance has advantages on the southern side but for other orientations exhibits slight disadvantages compared to the triple glazing. The latter is not used so widely because of the considerably higher weight of the glass. In the search for solutions with even lower thermal transmittance values, countersash and coupled windows offer good alternatives in certain circumstances. The much better insulated external walls of modern buildings render it necessary to pay special attention to the detail at the junction between the window and the wall, or the position of the window in the wall. Poor design or workmanship can have a considerable effect on the heat losses. Various window arrangements in monolithic masonry walls with external, cavity and internal insulation have been investigated with respect to their heat losses via the window reveals and masonry [45]. Figure 2.6.32 shows the best positions for windows in different masonry wall constructions.
DIN 4108 supplement 2 contains window sill, reveal and head details for monolithic masonry or masonry with external or cavity insulation. An extract showing details for a wall with cavity insulation is shown in fig. 2.6.33.

Translucent thermal insulation (TI)

In contrast to normal opaque thermal insulation attached to the outside, TI allows the incident solar radiation to pass through the insulation material. The radiation is then absorbed and converted into heat at the loadbearing wall. As TI functions as thermal insulation, the heat loss to the outside is considerably impeded and the majority of the solar energy is conveyed as heat to the interior behind the TI wall. As fig. 2.6.34 shows, conventional, opaque thermal insulation converts the incident solar radiation into heat at the external surface and then radiates the majority of it back to the external environment. Only a negligible proportion of the absorbed incident solar radiation is transmitted through the wall to the interior. But the welcome passive use of solar energy during the winter can lead to undesirable heat gains during the warmer months of the year. The lower the thermal conductivity and storage capacity of the absorbent surface of a TI wall, the hotter it becomes upon the incidence of solar radiation. This means that the absorbent surface behind a TI wall can reach peak temperatures of 100°C and more with very lightweight masonry compared to maximum temperatures of 70°C for very heavy masonry. The translucent thermal insulation must be provided with sunshading for such situations. The more intensively the sun can shine on the facade, the higher the heat gains of a TI wall are. This means that the energy gains are greatest for a south orientation, the lowest for a north orientation. The heat losses during the heating season outweigh the benefits in the case of a north orientation. TI surfaces facing east and west exhibit an even energy balance. Clear gains have been recorded for south-facing TI surfaces during the heating season. The thickness of the masonry has no significant effect on the energy gains of a TI wall. Nevertheless, when planning a TI building it is important to consider the thickness of the masonry behind the translucent thermal insulation as this influences the delay between maximum incidence of solar radiation and the heat being passed on to the interior. This delay is about 4 hours for walls 175 mm thick, about 6 hours for walls 240 mm thick and about 8 hours for walls 300 mm thick, virtually irrespective of the type of wall material. Consequently, the time at which the heat is passed on to the interior is decisive for the comfort of the user. The thermal and energy effects and the influence of climate, material parameters and construction details have been investigated in a project sponsored by Germany's Federal Ministry for Research and Technology [63].

As the use of translucent thermal insulation frequently leads to excessive heat which cannot be used, the cost-benefit ratio can be considerably influenced in individual cases by providing only a partial covering of translucent thermal insulation. The area of translucent

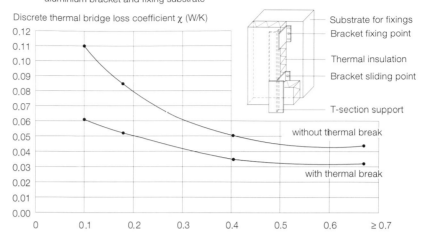

2.6.28　Thermal bridges in ventilated curtain wall facades; influence of thermal break between aluminium bracket and fixing substrate

Discrete thermal bridge loss coefficient χ (W/K)

Thermal resistance R of fixing substrate (m²K/W)

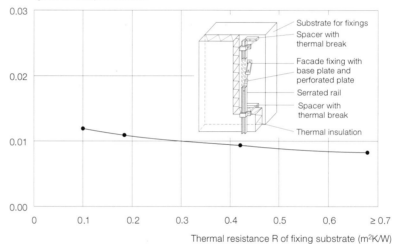

2.6.29　Thermal bridges in ventilated curtain wall facades; rail systems of chromium-nickel steel with good thermal performance

Thermal resistance R of fixing substrate (m²K/W)

2.6.30　Thermal transmittance of windows to DIN EN ISO 10077 part 1

Type of glazing	U_g W/m²K	U_f W/m²K								
		Proportion of frame area 30%								
		1.0	1.4	1.8	2.2	2.6	3.0	3.4	3.8	7.0
Single glazing	5.7	4.3	4.5	4.5	4.6	4.8	4.9	5	5.1	6.1
Double glazing	3.3	2.7	2.8	2.9	3.1	3.2	3.4	3.5	3.6	4.4
	3.1	2.6	2.7	2.8	2.9	3.1	3.2	3.3	3.5	4.3
	2.9	2.4	2.5	2.7	2.8	3.0	3.1	3.2	3.3	4.1
	2.7	2.3	2.4	2.5	2.6	2.8	2.9	3.1	3.2	4.0
	2.5	2.2	2.3	2.4	2.6	2.7	2.8	3.0	3.1	3.9
	2.3	2.1	2.2	2.3	2.4	2.6	2.7	2.8	2.9	3.8
	2.1	1.9	2	2.2	2.3	2.4	2.6	2.7	2.8	3.6
	1.9	1.8	1.9	2.0	2.1	2.3	2.4	2.5	2.7	3.5
	1.7	1.6	1.8	1.9	2.0	2.2	2.3	2.4	2.5	3.3
	1.5	1.5	1.6	1.7	1.9	2.0	2.1	2.3	2.4	3.2
	1.3	1.4	1.5	1.6	1.7	1.9	2.0	2.1	2.2	3.1
	1.1	1.2	1.3	1.5	1.6	1.7	1.9	2.0	2.1	2.9
Triple glazing	2.3	2.0	2.1	2.2	2.4	2.5	2.7	2.8	2.9	3.7
	2.1	1.9	2.0	2.1	2.2	2.4	2.5	2.6	2.8	3.6
	1.9	1.7	1.8	2.0	2.1	2.3	2.4	2.5	2.6	3.4
	1.7	1.6	1.7	1.8	1.9	2.1	2.2	2.4	2.5	3.3
	1.5	1.5	1.6	1.7	1.9	2.0	2.1	2.3	2.4	3.2
	1.3	1.4	1.5	1.6	1.7	1.9	2.0	2.1	2.2	3.1
	1.1	1.2	1.3	1.5	1.6	1.7	1.9	2.0	2.1	2.9
	0.9	1.1	1.2	1.3	1.4	1.6	1.7	1.8	2.0	2.8
	0.7	0.9	1.1	1.2	1.3	1.5	1.6	1.7	1.8	2.6
	0.5	0.8	0.9	1.0	1.2	1.3	1.4	1.6	1.7	2.5

Note: Calculated using ψ-values from appendix E. Values for windows whose frame proportion ≠ 30% should be determined using the equations in the main part of this standard.

2.6.31 Thermal balance of windows over a heating season for a reference location in Germany

KWh/HP m^2

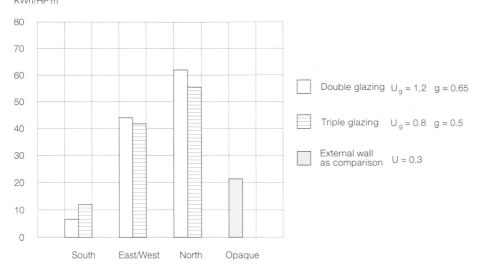

Double glazing $U_g = 1.2$ $g = 0.65$

Triple glazing $U_g = 0.8$ $g = 0.5$

External wall as comparison $U = 0.3$

2.6.32 Position of window in wall for different types of walls
+ small heat flow via window reveal
- large heat flow via window reveal

Position of window in wall	Type of external wall according to table 1			
	Monolithic	External insulation	Cavity insulation	Internal insulation
Outside	−	+	−	−
Central	+	−	+	−
Inside	−	−	−	+

thermal insulation is typically between 10 and 30% of the total area of insulation. In choosing which areas to cover, architectural aspects, the orientation of the facade, the planned use of the interior and the amount of space available on the facade all play a role. A solar energy system consisting of a translucent layer of polycarbonate with a capillary structure and a final coating of translucent plaster has proved to be an especially practicable option [204]. One important advantage of the system is that in summer a large part of the incident solar radiation is reflected at the surface of the translucent plaster, and so expensive and troublesome shading systems are generally unnecessary.

Solar gains of opaque external walls
External components absorb direct or diffuse incident solar radiation. Thus, the outer layers of the component heat up first and the heat is conducted to the inside of the component. This process reduces the heat transfer through the external component. The heat gain due to radiation depends on the available solar radiation and hence on the orientation and colour of the component's surfaces, any shading to those surfaces and the external surface resistance. The reduction in transmission heat losses which can be achieved due to the absorption of radiation by an opaque external wall is proportional to the U-value of the external wall. Whether the construction has one or more layers is virtually irrelevant; likewise, the sequence of layers in a multi-layer construction.
The annual solar net heat gains from opaque sections of the building envelope without translucent thermal insulation constitute only a fraction of the total solar heat gains and are partly offset by the radiation heat losses from the building to a cloudless sky. Therefore, they can usually be ignored. Table 2.6.35 contains solar gain factors for common external walls. The thermal transmittance of an external wall is only reduced by 2-12% by the radiation influence for average climatic relationships. The Fraunhofer Institute for Building Physics has reached similar conclusions in a computer-assisted experimental study on buildings with monolithic and multi-layer external walls [198].

Heat storage

The interior heats up and cools down, the sun shines on the outside and rapid changes to the air temperature take place on both sides of components. These effects lead to temperature changes and changes to the heat flows which cannot be taken into account by the thermal resistance R or the thermal transmittance U. In these cases the heat storage capacity of the materials and components in conjunction with the time play a decisive role.

For a mathematical analysis with numerical methods we require variables derived from the specific heat capacity, the thermal conductivity, the gross density and the thickness of the materials concerned. The heat storage capacity Q_s, i.e. the amount of thermal energy in J/m^2K stored in 1 m^2 of a slab-like component of thickness d in m made from a material with density r in kg/m^3 for a 1 K temperature rise, in a homogeneous construction is given by

$$Q_s = c \times \rho \times d$$

The propagation of a temperature zone in a material is described by its thermal diffusivity a in m^2/s. As the a-value increases, so the temperature change in a material spreads faster. The thermal diffusivity is derived from the thermal conductivity λ, the specific heat capacity c and the density ρ of the material concerned:

$$a = \frac{\lambda}{\rho \times c}$$

The thermal diffusivity of building materials lies in the range 0.4 to 1 x 10^{-6} m^2/s depending on bulk density (timber = approx. 0.2×10^{-6} m^2/s, steel = approx. 2.0×10^{-6} m^2/s). The heat penetration coefficient of the material concerned is the governing variable when assessing the behaviour of materials subjected to brief heat flow processes such as the heating and cooling of walls. The heat penetration coefficient b is derived from the thermal conductivity λ, the specific heat capacity c and the density ρ of the material concerned:

$$b = \sqrt{\lambda \times \rho \times c}$$

The b-values of some building materials are given in table 2.6.36. Figure 2.6.37 shows the heating and cooling behaviour for a change in interior air temperature of 15 K for two different wall constructions with approximately equal thermal resistance. Rapid heating-up of the walls is desirable from the point of view of comfort – with the heating operated briefly. However, the lighter component cools down quicker after switching off the heating. Practical investigations of the influence of the heat storage capacity all lead to the same result – that the influence of the heat storage capacity, especially that of external walls, on the energy consumption for the heating of a building is

relatively small. Theoretical studies have produced the same result [74]. Therefore, the question of whether the heat storage capacity or the thermal insulation of external components is more important from the point of view of saving energy can be answered: it definitely depends on thermal insulation. The importance of the thermal transmittance as the basis for calculating transmission heat losses through external walls is undisputed. Studies of buildings with the most diverse external masonry walls have revealed that despite severely fluctuating external climatic conditions quasi stationary heat flows become established after, at most, one week and the U-value adequately describes the heat losses through the opaque external surfaces of a building [2]. However, heavy components, which are thus suited to storing heat, do have a positive effect on the internal climate because they cool down slower when ventilating the interior or after switching off the heating and hence maintain the interior air temperature at a comfortable level for a longer period. The amount of heat lost through ventilation and transmission remains, however, the same as for the lighter type of construction.

We must distinguish between two opposing phenomena with regard to the effect of the heat storage capacity on the annual heating requirement. The heat gains due to internal heat sources and incident solar radiation can be better used by the heavy construction than the lightweight construction because overheating of the interior is considerably lower in the former. This effect is rewarded with a better use of the heat gains. In contrast, the behaviour of the lightweight construction is more favourable than the heavy construction in the case of a night-time temperature reduction because the internal air temperatures can fall more rapidly and hence the heat losses are smaller. It is not possible to make generalized statements as to which type of construction is better in terms of heating energy consumption because of the opposing effects of a night-time temperature reduction and overheating. During the warmer months of the year the heat storage capacity of the internal components of a building exerts a compensating influence on the internal air temperature gradient. If the heat from the sun is stored in the components before being radiated to the internal air, in summer we enjoy a pleasant, balanced internal climate even when cooler temperatures already prevail outside. DIN EN 13786 stipulates characteristic values related to the dynamic thermal behaviour of complete components and specifies methods for their calculation.

The characteristic values defined in the standard can be used as product specifications for components or for calculating
• the internal temperature in a room,
• the daily peak performance and the energy

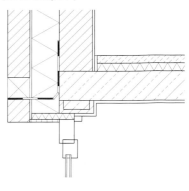

2.6.33   Favourable window position to DIN 4108 supplement 2 to reduce thermal bridge effect (full-fill cavity wall)

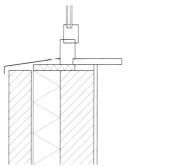

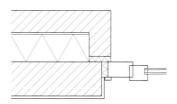

2.6.34   The function of translucent thermal insulation compared to opaque thermal insulation

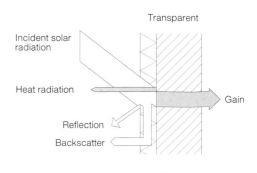

Transparent

Incident solar radiation

Heat radiation

Gain

Reflection

Backscatter

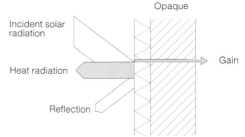

Opaque

Incident solar radiation

Gain

Heat radiation

Reflection

or common external walls ge climatic conditions [213] mon external wall		
	t colour	Dark colour
South	4	0.12
East/west	.03	0.07
North	0.02	0.06

2.6.36 Heat penetration coefficients for some building materials

Building material	Heat penetration coefficient $J/s^{0.5}m^2K$
Normal-weight concrete depending on gross density	1600 to 2400
Lightweight concrete depending on gross density	250 to 1600
Clay bricks	1000 to 1300
Timber	500 to 650
Foamed plastics	30 to 45

2.6.37 Chronological progression of interior surface temperature ϑ_{oi} for various external walls with approximately equal thermal resistances after increasing or decreasing the internal air temperature ϑ_{Li} by 15 K (°C) [62]

R = 1.50 m² K/W

Wall 1 — 240 mm aerated concrete 500 kg/m³

λ = 0.16 W/(mK)

ϑ_{oi}

ϑ_{La} = 5°C γ_{Li}

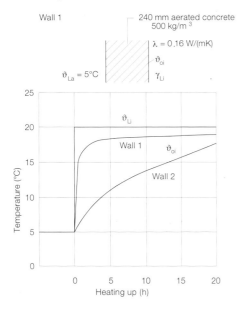

R = 1.55 m² K/W — 60 mm polystyrene, 30 kg/m³ λ = 0.040 W/(mK)

Wall 2 — 100 mm normal-weight concrete 2500 kg/m³ λ = 2.1 W/(mK)

ϑ_{oi}

ϑ_{La} = 5°C ϑ_{Li}

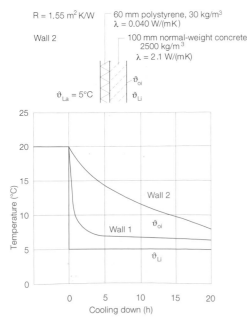

requirement for heating or cooling,
• the effects of intermittent heating or cooling.

Thermal bridges

These are weak points in the thermal insulation of the building envelope at which – compared to undisturbed, neighbouring sections of the component – additional heat losses and lower internal surface temperatures occur. Various types of thermal bridges are possible depending on the way in which they are formed:
• Geometric thermal bridges ensue when the heat-absorbing and heat-radiating surfaces of the component are of different sizes. The classic example of a geometric thermal bridge is the corner of an external wall.
• Material-related thermal bridges depend on the construction of the building and the arrangement and combination of components with materials of different thermal conductivity. Typical thermal bridges of this kind are roof bearings, parapets, balcony floor slabs and columns in external walls.
• Detail-related thermal bridges can ensue in components due to mechanical connections which penetrate or bypass the thermal insulation. These include anchors in concrete sandwich walls and multi-leaf walls, and all constructions in metal and timber.

Measures for avoiding or reducing thermal bridges are certainly necessary to avoid condensation on internal surfaces, and such measures are generally taken. However, the remaining – in energy terms – weak points with higher heat losses are usually not taken into account when assessing thermal performance and the heating requirement of a building. To some extent the additional heat losses via thermal bridges are balanced by the fact that the transmission heat losses of a building are calculated with reference to the outer surface, which is too large, particularly in the case of thick, monolithic masonry constructions. As the standard of thermal insulation of the building envelope rises and the thermal transmittance values drop, so the thermal bridges play an increasingly significant role. Therefore, the increased heat losses must be investigated at the planning stage when calculating the heating energy requirement for the building. This can be done in different ways. Thermal bridges due to the structure itself, e.g. edges, corners, roof bearings, balcony floor slabs etc., can only be calculated accurately with the help of computer techniques. However, for the preliminary design of a building and assessment of the energy effects of the building envelope, it must be possible to estimate the effects of thermal bridges without major mathematical analyses. With the help of correction values to take into account continuous and discrete thermal bridges, DIN EN ISO 14683 gives the thermal conduction of the building envelope as

$$L = \Sigma U_i \times A_i + \Sigma \Psi_K \times l_K + \Sigma \chi_j$$

where:
L   thermal conduction in W/K
U_i thermal transmittance of building envelope component i in W/m²K
A_i surface area applicable for U_i
Ψ_K thermal transmittance of continuous thermal bridge k in W/mK
l_K length applicable for Ψ_K
χ_j thermal transmittance of discrete thermal bridge j in W/K.

The thermal transmittance Ψ is normally taken from thermal bridge catalogues. The examples of building details contained in these catalogues are essentially based on fixed parameters (e.g. dimensions and materials) and are therefore less flexible than calculations. The catalogue examples often do not correspond exactly with the component being investigated. Consequently, the use of Ψ-values from catalogues leads to uncertainties about those details. Nevertheless, the Ψ-value from a catalogue can be used, provided the dimensions and the thermal properties of the catalogue example are similar to those of the building detail, or the catalogue example is less favourable in thermal terms than the building detail. The Ψ-values in a thermal bridge catalogue must have been derived from numerical calculations according to DIN EN 10211 part 2. Thermal bridge catalogues offer solutions to details from basement to roof – for wall, window, floor and balcony junctions (see fig. 2.6.38). DIN 4108 supplement 2 contains design and construction examples for thermal bridge details; the masonry details include junctions for monolithic external walls with external and cavity insulation. Figure 2.6.39 shows the junction details for ground slab, basement roof (ground floor), upper floor slabs and flat roof with parapet for a monolithic external masonry wall 365 mm thick. A balcony floor slab projecting from the structure acts like a cooling fin owing to the increase in the external surface area; figure 2.6.40 shows how the balcony junction can be thermally isolated from the floor slab. The layer of thermal insulation is only penetrated at individual points by the reinforcing bars. This cuts the thermal transmittance Ψ by 50% compared to a continuous concrete slab. A steel curtain wall construction connected to the floor slab by a tension rod exhibits a similar reduction in thermal bridge losses. Applying thermal insulation to the top and bottom of the cantilevering balcony slab brought practically no worthwhile success. In terms of the thermal bridge effect of a whole variety of construction details for balcony junctions, there is no difference between single-leaf walls, walls with thermal insulation composite system and multi-layer external walls.

The thermal influence range of thermal bridges can lead to noticeably lower surface temperatures on the inside and to condensation, which may lead to the growth of mould. Specifying the interior surface temperatures in °C determines – to a limited extent – the additional stipulation of external and internal air temperature. As very different boundary conditions may be chosen depending on use and meteorological circumstances, the surface temperature is used in a dimensionless form by DIN EN ISO 10211 part 2 according to the following definition:

$$f_{Rsi} = (\vartheta_{si} - \vartheta_e) / (\vartheta_i - \vartheta_e)$$

where:
f_{Rsi} temperature factor at location of thermal bridge
ϑ_{si} internal surface temperature
ϑ_i internal air temperature
ϑ_e external air temperature.

To avoid the growth of mould, according to DIN 4108 part 2, the minimum requirement fRsi ≥ 0.70 must be fulfilled assuming an internal air temperature of 20°C and 50% relative humidity for an external air temperature of -5°C – a not infrequent occurrence in Germany under average meteorological limits. In this context the minimum thermal resistance for an external wall R = 0.55 m²K/W must be increased to R = 1.2 m²K/W in order to also maintain the temperature factor 0.70 at the corners of external walls according to 2.6.41 assuming an internal surface resistance R_{si} = 0.25. This means maintaining an internal surface temperature of ϑ_{si} ≥ 12.6°C for the said limits. As a rule, the stipulation in DIN 4108 part 2 that all constructional, form-related and material-related thermal bridges given as examples in DIN 4108 supplement 2 can be regarded as providing adequate thermal insulation forms a simple criterion for the avoidance of mould for the designer and operator of a building. In the case of thermal bridges in components adjoining the soil or unheated basement rooms and buffer zones, we must assume the conditions given in fig. 2.6.42.

The *establishment of thermal bridges* can be carried out by experiment or by analytical means. The simplest method is the determination of the internal surface temperatures in the region of a thermal bridge by way of discrete measurements and reference to the temperature limits on both sides of the external component. Thermographic techniques involve the use of an infrared camera to provide a thermal image of the exterior of a building elevation or the internal surfaces of individual rooms. This method supplies important information about the condition and quality of thermal insulation. Defective workmanship or the success of upgrading the insulation to a building can be made visible. However, an infrared photograph cannot help us to make quantitative statements

about the extent of thermal losses. Temperature distribution and heat transfer can be determined for faithful replicas of components in laboratory tests according to DIN EN ISO 8990, in which the component is incorporated as a partition between two spaces at different temperatures. The mathematical determination of the effects of multidimensional thermal bridges is carried out by calculating the temperature zone and heat flow using the numerical solution of the three-dimensional thermal conduction equation. If adequate for the particular case, the calculation for two-dimensional plane relationships is carried out and, in the case of clear three-dimensional temperature and heat flow zones, extended to three-dimensional structures.

2.6.38   Some details used in a thermal bridge catalogue (Hauser) for specifying Ψ- and f-values

Wall junction

Floor junction

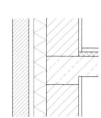

Window junction

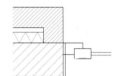

Balcony junction

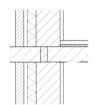

2.6.39   Junction details for a single-leaf external wall according to DIN 4108 supplement 2

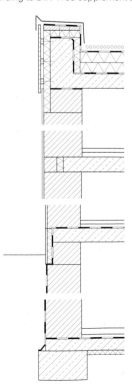

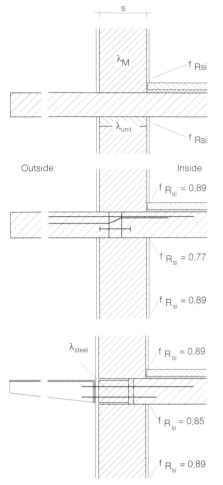

2.6.40 Improving the thermal performance of balcony floor slab junctions

λ_M
f_{Rsi}
λ_{unit}
f_{Rsi}

Outside   Inside

$f_{Rsi} = 0.89$

$f_{Rsi} = 0.77$

$f_{Rsi} = 0.89$

λ_{steel} $f_{Rsi} = 0.89$

$f_{Rsi} = 0.85$

$f_{Rsi} = 0.89$

2.6.41 The temperature factor at an external wall corner as a function of the thermal resistance of the external wall for two different thermal transmittance values

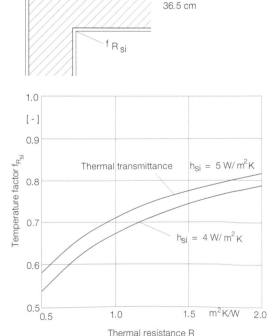

36.5 cm

f_{Rsi}

Airtightness[1]

As the requirements for thermal insulation increase, so the airtightness of the building envelope becomes more and more important. A high degree of imperviousness is necessary in order to really achieve the desired reduction in heating energy requirement and avoid damage to the building as well as a drop in the standard of comfort. Uncontrolled leakage from the building wrecks all other measures for increasing the thermal insulation. Therefore, partial optimization, like minimizing U-values without taking into account such leaks, are totally ineffective in practical terms. The airtightness of a structure must be considered independently of the exchange of internal and external air. This exchange of air is necessary to maintain a hygienic internal climate and is taken into account when calculating the heating energy requirement by way of the ventilation heat losses with a defined air change rate. The air change rate is accomplished naturally by opening the windows or by way of mechanical ventilation systems. So, leaks in external components represent additional uncontrolled ventilation heat losses which can be avoided or at least minimized according to the state of the art.
A non-airtight building envelope usually results in several unwanted effects:

• Draughts impairing the comfort of occupants
• Condensation damage resulting from water vapour convection of the moist internal air to cold external zones of enclosing components
• Lowered sound insulation against external noise
• Energy losses that form a considerable part of the total energy losses of a building.

The airtightness of buildings as well as individual residential units or rooms within a finished building is determined according to DIN EN ISO 9972 (blower door). This international standard specifies the use of mechanical overpressure or underpressure applied to buildings. The airtightness is generally defined by the remaining air change rate of the building or part of the building at a pressure difference of 50 Pa (n_{50}-value). The airtightness can be assessed on the basis of the n_{50} air change rates given in table 2.6.44. Thresholds for the air change rate were first laid down in DIN 4108 part 7. The n_{50}-value for buildings with natural ventilation is limited to 3.0 per hour, for buildings with mechanical ventilation 1.0 per hour. In addition to the requirements of the standard, it is considered adequate, taking into account practical building tolerances, when the measured air flow rate, related to the volume of air in the room, exceeds the threshold given in the standard by up to 0.5 per hour at a pressure difference of 50 Pa.
As might be may expected, masonry buildings generally have a better airtightness than lightweight types of construction. However, even in the case of masonry, penetration of the internal plaster, window junctions, false wall installations and roof junctions must be carefully detailed. DIN 4108 part 7 contains important and useful design and construction recommendations, and shows – see fig. 2.6.43 details of overlaps, junctions, penetrations and joints in the plane of imperviousness.

Requirements for thermal insulation
The design, calculation and measuring standards provided in CEN/TC 89 "Thermal performance of buildings and building components" form the basis for the National Application Documents of the series of standards belonging to DIN 4108 "Thermal insulation and energy economy in buildings". The type and extent of requirements is still a matter for the individual countries. In order to maintain minimum requirements and plan energy-saving measures, the following parts of DIN 4108 must be adhered to:

part 2: Minimum requirements for thermal insulation
part 4: Characteristic values relating to thermal insulation and protection against moisture
part 6: Calculation of annual heat and annual energy use
part 7: Airtightness of building components and connections; recommendations and examples for planning and performance
supp. 2: Thermal bridges – examples for planning and performance

DIN 4108 part 2 specifies the minimum requirements for the thermal insulation of components and thermal bridges in the building envelope. It also contains advice pertinent to thermal insulation for the design and construction of occupied rooms in buildings, the use of which requires they be heated to common internal temperatures ($\geq 19°C$). Minimum thermal insulation is understood to be a measure that guarantees a hygienic interior climate, with adequate heating and ventilation assuming a conventional usage, at every point on the internal surfaces of the building envelope so that no condensation forms over the whole area, nor in corners. Apart from that, the risk of mould growth is diminished. Major changes in the 2000 edition compared to the 1981 edition involve practically the doubling of the minimum value for the thermal resistance of external walls from $R \geq 0.55$ to $R \geq 1.2$ m²K/W, the more detailed treatment of thermal bridges, measures for avoiding the growth of mould and the simplified assessment of minimum thermal insulation for heavy and lightweight components. We now only distinguish between components with a surface-related total mass of at least 100 kg/m³ and components with a lower total mass without taking into account the position of layers of insulation and their effect on heating and cooling processes. The fact that lower storage mass is compensated for by better thermal insulation is solved simply by applying enhanced requirements with $R \geq 1.75$ m²K/W for components < 100 kg/m³, which corresponds to the former maximum value for lightweight components. In the case of structural frames, the value applies only to the infill panels. In these cases an average of $R \geq 1.0$ m²K/W is to be maintained in addition for the entire component. Further details have already been described in the sections on thermal bridges and airtightness.

Energy-savings Act
Putting figures to the requirements for energy-saving thermal performance is the object of public-law statutes aimed at energy-saving construction. The stipulation of an annual energy requirement in the Energy-savings Act corresponds to a performance class for different methods of energy-saving defined in principal document No. 6 "Energy economy and heat retention". The European standard DIN EN 832 serves for its technical implementation. This standard refers to a series of further design standards, such as the calculation of the specific heat loss coefficient, heat transfer to the soil, dynamic thermal parameters and the treatment of thermal bridges. The raw data for the design standards includes product features, e.g. the thermal conductivity of insulation materials and masonry constructions. The logical connection between the various design, product and measuring standards is illustrated in fig. 2.6.45. Furthermore, national boundary conditions, e.g. climate data, solar gains, internal heat sources and air change rate in DIN 4108 part 6, as well as provisions for dealing with total heat losses from a heating system and the heating requirement for hot water supplies to DIN 4701 part 10, still have to be specified in order to finalize the European method of analysis.
Experience has shown that ambiguous designations and confusion often arise when describing thermal insulation and energy properties. Therefore, the following definitions are intended to provide clarity:
• Heating requirement: heat to be delivered to the heated space to maintain the temperature over a period of time.
• Heating energy requirement: the calculated amount of energy that must be fed into the heating system of a building to be able to cover the heating requirement.
• Heating energy consumption: the amount of heating energy (energy carrier) measured over a certain period which is required to maintain a certain temperature in a zone.
• Final energy requirement: the amount of energy which is required to cover the annual heating energy requirement and the heating requirement for the provision of hot water, determined at the system boundary of the building under consideration.

• Primary energy requirement: the amount of energy required to cover the final energy requirement, taking into account the additional amounts of energy consumed by upstream process chains beyond the system boundary of the building during the production, conversion and distribution of the fuel used.

Up to now, the heating requirement has been subject to certain stipulations, but the new standard is coupled to the heating energy requirement, i.e. the primary energy evaluation, in order to incorporate the efficiency of the plant and the energy carrier used. This means that the balance framework, which previously ended at the radiator, now extends back to the power station or to the supply of gas or oil. One key element in the Energy-savings Act is the stricter framework of requirements for energy-saving construction, the aim of which is to cut consumption by an average of 30% for new building work and to bring the previous thermal insulation and technical plant requirements and upgrading rules, as applied to the existing building stock, up to the current technological level. As in the Thermal Insulation Act, this act covers buildings with normal internal temperatures (min. 19°C); the definition for buildings with lower internal temperatures remains unchanged.
Buildings with normal internal temperatures must comply with maximum figures for the annual primary energy requirement (see fig. 2.6.46), depending on the type of building A/Ve. The specification of the primary energy is intended to create a clear link to the political objective of reducing carbon dioxide emissions and avoid a distortion of the market for competing energy systems. On the other hand, the calculated final energy provides valuable information for the user as a standardized prediction of the consumption to be expected and at the same time forms a parameter in an "energy requirement pass" specific to the building. The additional ancillary requirement covering the maximum annual heating requirement is intended to ensure that the previous standard of thermal insulation to the building envelope is maintained.
Requirements for the imperviousness of external windows and glazed doors remain unchanged. The imperviousness of the building envelope is dealt with more precisely by providing information on a suitable method of measurement and permissible leakage rates. To guarantee energy-saving summer thermal insulation, the previous provisions have been improved and tightened up in line with technical progress.
A limit to the cooling requirement has been imposed on buildings which, because of their function, demand a particular type of facade and cooling in the summer. The minimum energy requirements for starting up heating boilers,

2.6.42 Temperature limits to DIN 4108 part 2 for thermal bridge calculations

Part of building or surroundings	Temperature θ °C
Basement	10
Soil	5
Unheated buffer zone	10
Unheated roof space	−5

2.6.43 Examples of sealing to DIN 4108 part 7

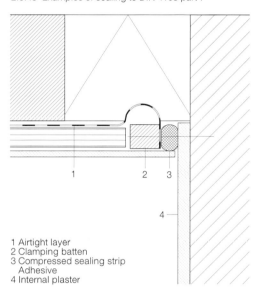

1 Airtight layer
2 Clamping batten
3 Compressed sealing strip
  Adhesive
4 Internal plaster

Junction between roof and plastered masonry wall

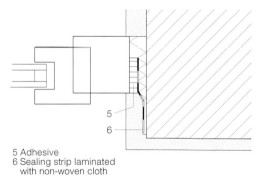

5 Adhesive
6 Sealing strip laminated
  with non-woven cloth

Junction between window frame and masonry wall

2.6.44 Air change rates for airtightness test

Recommended values

Airtightness of building	Air change rate at 50 pa/h	
	Apartment block	Detached house
very airtight	0.5–2.0	1.0–3.0
moderately airtight	2.0–4.0	3.0–8.0
less airtight	4.0–10.0	8.0–20.0

Threshold values

Building with	Air changes per h
natural ventilation	$n_{50} \leq 3$
mechanical extraction	$n_{50} \leq 1.5$

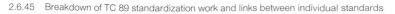

2.6.45   Breakdown of TC 89 standardization work and links between individual standards

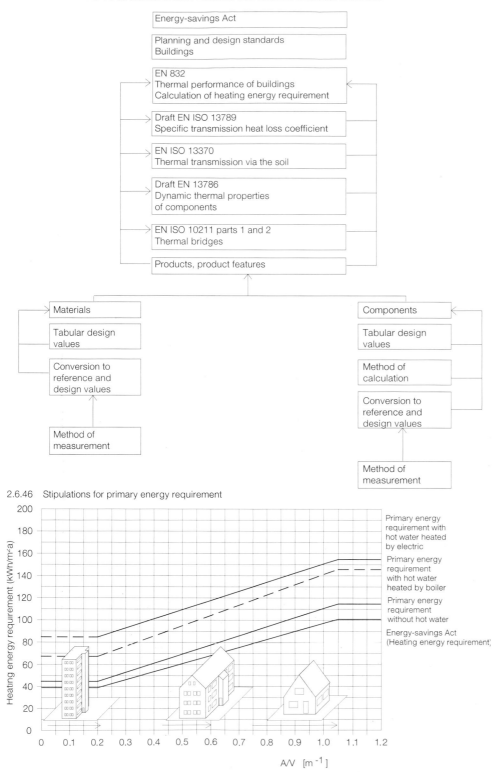

distribution apparatus and hot water systems stipulated in the Heating Plants Act have been incorporated essentially en bloc.

As before, buildings with low internal temperatures only have to comply with a maximum annual transmission heating requirement because for these buildings the air change rate and internal heat sources can fluctuate quite considerably depending on use.

Changes to existing buildings necessitated the previous provisions to be adjusted to the requirements for the thermal transmittance of individual components according to fig. 2.6.47. Tighter stipulations for thermal insulation measures to be carried out during refurbishment work were created so that corresponding improvements affecting energy requirements would find a wide range of applications among the existing building stock. Within a specified period, the heating distribution pipes of a heating system in an existing building must be insulated and the boiler itself brought up to the standard of new building work.

Method of calculation

The calculation of the heating and heating energy requirements is carried out by using the European standard DIN EN 832 in conjunction with the National Application Document DIN 4108 part 6 and DIN 4701 part 10. The method of calculation according to DIN EN 832 is based on a stationary energy balance but does, however, take into account internal and external temperature changes as well as the dynamic effect of internal and solar heat gains. The annual heating energy requirement is calculated according to fig. 2.6.48 by drawing up a balance sheet of the loss and gain variables involved. Apart from the heating requirement depending on the building, the heating energy requirement also includes the technical losses of the heating system, the energy requirements for hot water and possible gains from regenerative systems. The losses of the system can be calculated accurately according to DIN 4701 part 10 by way of quantity figures for heat transfer, distribution, storage, generation and primary energy conversion for each individual case according to the plans available for the technical services or by using a quantity figure e_p for the entire system related to the primary energy. Two methods are available for determining the heating requirement. The simpler period balance method, also possible without the use of a computer and restricted to residential buildings, uses the equation

$$Q_h = Q_{l,HP} - \eta_{HP} \times Q_{g,HP}$$

where:

Q_h the heating requirement for the heating season

$Q_{l,HP}$ the heating losses during the heating season

2.6.46   Stipulations for primary energy requirement

2.6.47   Energy-savings Act (EnEV): measures for existing building stock

Component	U-value W/m²k EnEV
External walls (internal insulation, renewing of infill walls)	0.45
External walls	0.35
Windows	1.70
Floors, roofs, pitched roofs (steep)	0.30
Floors, roofs, pitched roofs (shallow)	0.25
Roofs and walls to unheated interiors or soil (insulation on cold side)	0.40
Roofs and walls to unheated interiors or soil (insulation on warm side)	0.50

$Q_{g,HP}$ the heating gains (internal, solar) during the heating season

η_{HP} the degree of utilization.

The more accurate monthly balance method takes into account further variables influencing the heating energy requirement and broadens the planning options. The annual heating requirement Q_h is obtained by adding together the individual monthly balances, provided there have been positive values for each month, using the equation

$$Q_h = \Sigma Q_{H,M_{pos}}$$

and

$$Q_{h,M} = Q_{I,M} - \eta_M \times Q_{g,M}$$

DIN 4108 part 6 contains the limits for the heating degree days, the average available solar radiation and the average monthly external temperatures and intensity of solar radiation necessary for both methods of calculation. An analysis of thermal insulation according to public-law requirements must also apply the conditions described in DIN 4108 part 6.

The advantages of the monthly balance method are that the influences of lighter or heavier types of construction on the degree of utilization of the heat gains and the effect of the night-time drop in temperature, as well as solar gains via glazed sections, opaque components and translucent thermal insulation can all be taken into account. The air change rate of $n = 0.7$ per hour for natural ventilation, and its reduction to $n = 0.6$ per hour if an airtightness test is carried out and the condition $n_{50} < 3$ per hour is thereby fulfilled, has a decisive influence on the heat losses. A further reduction in ventilation losses can be achieved by using mechanical ventilation with heat recovery.

In the period balance method the influence of thermal bridges is determined by a global surcharge on the specific transmission heat loss H_T:

$$H_{WB} = \Delta U_{WB} \times A$$

$\Delta U_{WB} = 0.05$ W/m²K can be used for constructions comparable in thermal terms with DIN 4108 supplement 2. The monthly balance method also permits thermal bridge losses to be calculated using thermal transmittance values (ψ-values).

In addition, quick implementation of DIN EN 832 is made possible by means of global reduction methods or correction values derived from comprehensive European standards requiring intensive mathematical analysis. This simplification has an effect on temperature correction factors for areas in a heated basement in particular.

Calculations carried out for individual types of buildings confirm that single-leaf masonry walls are still possible with a higher standard of heat-

ing system (low-temperature boiler, condensing technology), with verified imperviousness, night-time drop in temperature, optimized double glazing and a high standard of insulation to roof and basement areas.

In such cases the thermal transmittance of the external wall should not exceed U = 0.40 W/m²K. Twin-leaf masonry with additional thermal insulation, single-leaf walls with thermal insulation composite systems or thermally insulated constructions with ventilated outer leaves are all possible without any problems.

All the main energy requirement segments of a building are covered by an "energy requirement pass" for the following purposes:

- To provide the user with information about the energy consumption to be expected.
- To improve clarity in the housing and property market with respect to the quality of buildings in terms of energy aspects.
- To support the implementation of the Act by putting the user in the position to check the features of his building relevant to energy, and to investigate unusual aspects.

A simple summary shows that the heating energy requirement of a building is determined by four factors:

- Climate: location of building, external temperature, incident solar radiation
- Building: shape, volume, plan layout, orientation, construction of external components, type of construction
- Heating system: heat generation, regulation, distribution, hot water supply
- Use: internal temperature, air change rate, usable waste heat.

Thermal comfort

The thermal comfort in a heated room essentially depends on the surface temperatures of the surfaces enclosing the room and on the air temperature within the room. The velocity and humidity of the air, the activities of people in the room and clothing also play a role. The comfort ranges of the individual factors are linked. The air and surface temperatures influence the temperature perceived by an occupant such that – within certain limits – a lower air temperature can be compensated for by a higher surface temperature (see fig. 2.6.49). There is a connection between the desired humidity of the air and its temperature, which can also be presented as a comfort range (see fig. 2.6.50). The degree of comfort perceived by an occupant must be assessed differently for each individual. Based on essentially physical processes such as radiation exchange, conduction and evaporation, as well as generally applicable experiences, a favourable internal climate prevails when the following factors are present:

- The external components – with good thermal insulation – have an internal surface temperature of about 18°C.

- The difference between the air temperature and the surface temperature of enclosing components does not exceed 2 K.
- The relationship between air temperature and relative humidity lies, and is appropriately balanced, in the range of $\vartheta = 18\text{-}24°C$ and $\varphi = 40\text{-}60\%$.
- The air circulating in the interior does not exceed a velocity of 0.10-0.20 m/s.

Thermal insulation in summer

With suitable construction, mechanical cooling systems are generally unnecessary in buildings containing apartments or individual offices and other buildings with similar uses.

Thermal insulation in summer essentially depends on the total energy transmittance of transparent external components, their compass orientation and, in the case of roof windows, their inclination. Other factors are the ventilation options in the rooms, the heat storage capacity (particularly internal components), and the heat conduction properties of opaque external components subject to nonconstant boundary conditions. Effective sunshades for transparent external components can be integrated into the construction by way of overhanging roofs or balconies, by external or internal blinds or by using solar-control glass. The purpose of limiting the ingress of solar radiation in the summer is to guarantee comfortable interior temperatures, i.e. to avoid exceeding certain threshold temperatures for more than 10% of the occupancy time. In order to keep within temperature limits in warmer climatic regions (with sunshades provided), the following requirements have been laid down:

- summer climate region A; cool summer regions 25°C
- summer climate region B; moderate regions 26°C
- summer climate region C; hot summer regions 27°C

The fixed threshold of the dimensionless solar heat penetration S_{max} must not be exceeded in an analysis. This value is calculated from the total energy transmittance of the glass g, the proportion of window area f in an elevation, and the reduction factor F_c for sunshades as well as the window frame component F_F:

$$S_{max} \geq S = f \times g \times F_c (1 - F_F)/0.7$$

The threshold is calculated from a basic value S_0 for the applicable summer climate region as well as correction factors depending on construction and use according to table 2.6.51:

$$S_{max} \geq S_0 + \Sigma_i \Delta S_i$$

The following values apply for the design value S_0:

2.6.48 EN 832 (thermal performance of buildings): calculation of heating energy requirement Q (final energy) and primary energy requirement Q_p for residential building.

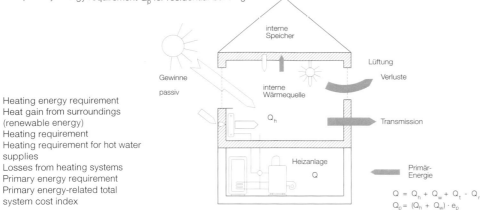

Q Heating energy requirement
Q_r Heat gain from surroundings (renewable energy)
Q_h Heating requirement
Q_w Heating requirement for hot water supplies
Q_t Losses from heating systems
Q_p Primary energy requirement
e_p Primary energy-related total system cost index

$$Q = Q_h + Q_w + Q_t - Q_r$$
$$Q_p = (Q_h + Q_w) \cdot e_p$$

summer climate region A $S_0 = 0.18$
summer climate region B $S_0 = 0.14$
summer climate region C $S_0 = 0.10$

According to DIN 4108 part 2, only the basic value $S_0 = 0.18$ for cool summer regions is used as the minimum requirement for thermal insulation in summer. If the proportion of windows in a west to south to east orientation is less than 20%, or less than 30% for a northeast to north to north-west orientation, or less than 15% for sloping windows, an analysis is not necessary.

In the *differentiated method* according to DIN 4108 part 6, the specified threshold for the so-called standardized, non-usable heat gains (which can also be interpreted as overtemperature degree hours) must not be exceeded. The method of calculation makes it possible to take into account various factors, e.g. internal heat loads, orientation of facade, air change rate etc., accurately. The differentiated method is particularly suitable for buildings with high internal loads or enhanced passive solar energy use. Buildings with interior cooling should be initially designed and constructed in such a way that the stipulations for thermal insulation in summer are complied with and the residual heat is removed by using mechanical systems (see fig. 2.6.36).

2.6.49 Relationship between interior air temperature and surface temperature with respect to the comfort of occupants [15]

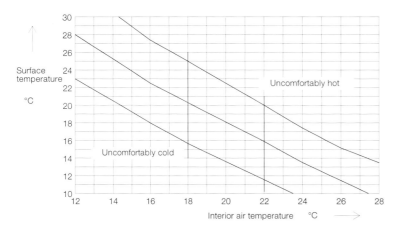

2.6.50 Relationship between interior air temperature and relative humidity with respect to the comfort of occupants [16]

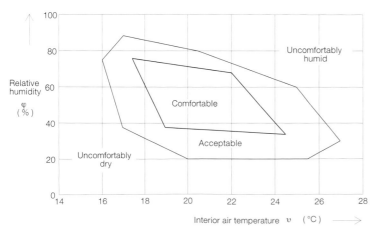

2.6.51 Correction values ΔS for basic characteristic value S_0 for solar heat penetration

Influencing variables i to be considered	ΔS_i
Lightweight construction: timber studding, lightweight partitions, suspended ceilings	– 0.03
Extremely lightweight construction: primarily internal insulation, large hall, few internal components	– 0.10
Solar-control glass[1] with g < 0.4	+ 0.04
Increased night-time ventilation (night n ≥ 1.5 /h during 2nd half of night)	+ 0.03
Proportion of window area in facade > 65%	– 0.04
Rooms facing north (NW-N-NE)	+ 0.10
Inclined windows (0°-60° to the horizontal)	– 0.06

Climate-related moisture control

The effects of moisture caused by building work, normal living conditions, rain and condensation remain a problem in the construction industry. Therefore, measures have to be taken to keep moisture of any kind away from the building or reduce it to a safe minimum. Inadequate moisture control decreases the level of thermal insulation and can lead to later damage to the masonry through corrosion, frost, mould growth and efflorescence. Figure 2.6.52 is a diagramn of the moisture loads on a building.

From outside we have the effects of:
- rain, snow, moist external air
- moist soil, seepage water, a build-up of water, groundwater

From inside we have the effects of:
- moisture from new building work
- water in kitchens and bathrooms
- dampness caused by the household, plants and washing, and moisture evaporating from the occupants
- moisture condensing on the internal surfaces of components or within the components.

The physical variables, symbols and units relevant to the assessment of moisture protection are given in table 2.6.53.

Humidity

The air in the atmosphere always contains water vapour from the evaporation of water. Depending on the temperature, air can hold only a certain amount of water vapour, and this increases as the temperature rises (see fig. 2.6.54). As moist air cools, the dew point (or saturation value) is reached. The saturation content of water vapour in the air corresponds to a saturation vapour pressure depending on temperature. This also increases as the temperature rises to the same degree as the capacity to hold water vapour.

In the majority of cases the air contains slightly more water vapour than the respective saturation content allows. The relative humidity ϕ serves to designate the water content of the air. This is the ratio between the actual amount of water vapour present W and the saturation quantity W_s or the ratio between the prevailing water vapour partial pressure p and the saturation pressure p_s, given by

$$\phi = W/W_s = p/p_s$$

For saturated air $\phi = 1.0$ or 100%. As moist air heats up in a room without the addition or extraction of air, so the relative humidity drops because the possible saturation quantity rises for a constant quantity of water vapour. In the reverse situation – moist air cooling – the relative humidity increases until the value of 100%,

i.e. saturation, is reached. If the air cools further, the water must be separated out from the air, because the air at that temperature can no longer hold that amount of water in vapour form. Mist forms in a gaseous atmosphere or condensation on solid surfaces. The temperature at which this process begins is known as the dew point temperature, or simply dew point. Constructional measures to avoid the temperature falling below the dew point on internal surfaces have been dealt with in the section "Thermal insulation" in conjunction with thermal bridges.

Hygroscopic moisture

Porous bodies absorb moisture in the form of water vapour from the surrounding air according to their physical and chemical properties. Adsorption may cause water molecules to collect on the surface of a material in one or more layers, according to the relative humidity. And in porous materials with a capillary-like structure, water can also accumulate on internal surfaces. If the water vapour in these capillaries condenses, the water moves according to the laws of capillarity. This process is known as capillary condensation. These two mechanisms come under the general heading of "sorption". The hygroscopic properties of building materials are described by sorption isotherms, which provide information on the moisture content in each case depending on the relative humidity (see fig. 2.6.55). The temperature of the ambient air has only a small influence. The hygroscopic water content that becomes established under normal ambient conditions is important for assessing moisture ratios in a material in practice. The hygroscopic equilibrium moisture contents of various building materials are given in table 2.6.23 (for reference climatic conditions of 23°C and 80% relative humidity). Besides the final values for sorption moisture which become established in the constant state, the non-constant behaviour of surface layers is also interesting since they act as buffer zones for fluctuating internal humidities. Künzel [62] has shown that it is the properties of the outermost surface layers that are particularly relevant for short-term moisture changes, and that the substance of the wall beneath plaster or wallpaper no longer has any influence. On the other hand, furnishings with a high textile content, e.g. upholstery, carpets, curtains etc., have a high sorption capacity, which means that no significant moisture fluctuations should be expected in living rooms and bedrooms, and the sorption behaviour of building materials is unimportant.

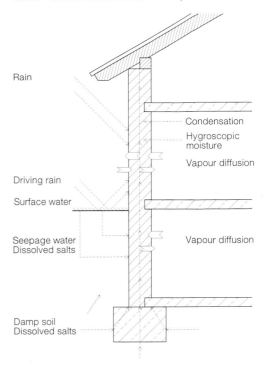

2.6.52   Moisture loads on external components

Rain

Condensation
Hygroscopic moisture
Vapour diffusion

Driving rain

Surface water

Vapour diffusion

Seepage water
Dissolved salts

Damp soil
Dissolved salts

2.6.53   Variables, symbols and units used in moisture control

Physical variable	Symbol	Unit
Water vapour partial pressure	p	Pa
Relative humidity	$\emptyset$	1
Mass-related moisture content	u	kg/kg
Water vapour diffusion coefficient	D	m²/h
Water vapour diffusion flow rate	g	kg/m²h
Water vapour diffusion resistance	Z	m² hPa/kg
Water vapour diffusion conduction coefficient	δ	kg/mh Pa
Water vapour diffusion resistance index	μ	1
Water absorption coefficient	w	kg/m²h⁰·⁵
Water vapour diffusion-equivalent air layer thickness	s_d	m
Area-related condensation mass	$m_{W,T}$	kg/m²
Area-related evaporation mass	$m_{W,V}$	kg/m²

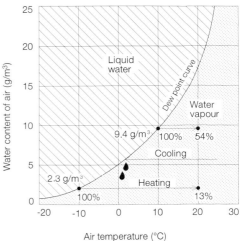

2.6.54   Water saturation or dew point graph

Liquid water

Water vapour

9.4 g/m³   100%   54%

Cooling

2.3 g/m³   Heating

100%   13%

Water content of air (g/m³)

Dew point curve

Air temperature (°C)

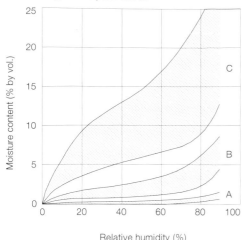

2.6.55 Ranges of sorption curves

A Clay bricks, gypsum
B Normal-weight concrete, lightweight concrete, auto-
   claved aerated concrete, calcium silicate
C Timber, organic fibrous materials

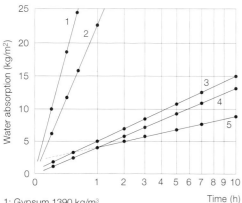

2.6.56 Capillary water absorption of various building
       materials in relation to the square root of the
       time (after Künzel)

1: Gypsum 1390 kg/m³
2: Solid clay bricks 1730 kg/m³
3: Autoclaved aerated concrete 640 kg/m³
4: Calcium silicate 1780 kg/m³
5: Pumice concrete 880 kg/m³

2.6.57 Water vapour transport through an external com-
        ponent
        ∂ temperature gradient
        p Water vapour partial pressure gradient

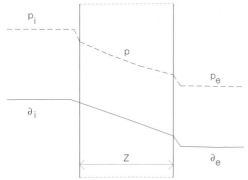

Capillarity

In water-filled pores and tube-like material structures in building materials, capillary tensile forces occur due to the surface tension of water, depending on the concave radius of the meniscus and the wettability of the solid material. The capillary suction can have either a positive or negative effect on the building, depending on the moisture load and the associated moisture movement. The absorption of water and conveyance by capillary action due to driving rain or moist soil must be avoided. On the other hand, the capillarity of a building material promotes the transport of water from within a building component to the surface, where it then has the chance to evaporate. This accelerates the removal of moisture from the building process from masonry. In the case of condensation forming within the masonry due to water vapour diffusion, the amount of condensation can be reduced by capillary action and the chance to dry out improved. A standardized test in DIN EN ISO 15148 is suitable for establishing the water absorption of a capillary-type porous material. In this test a sample surface is immersed in water and the increase in mass determined as a function of the absorption time. The water absorption increases linearly in proportion to the square root of the immersion time (see fig. 2.6.56). The curve corresponds to the water absorption coefficient specific to the material:

$$W = w \times \sqrt{t}$$

where:
W = the quantity of water absorbed for a unit
      surface area in kg/m²
t = the absorption time in h
w = the water absorption coefficient in
      kg/m²h⁻⁰·⁵

Table 2.6.58 gives w-values for materials typically used for building walls.

Water vapour diffusion

In physical terms, air is a mixture of gases in which the nitrogen, oxygen and water vapour molecules circulate independently. Each individual gas exerts the same partial pressure it would exert at the same temperature if the other gases were not present. Existing moisture differences in two blocks of air are balanced by water vapour diffusion in the direction of the potential gradient. This diffusion should not be confused with a flow which occurs as a result of a total pressure difference. In diffusion processes, the same total pressure is generally present on both sides of a separating layer. The external components of heated interiors are subjected to water vapour diffusion processes because they separate blocks of air with different temperatures and moisture contents. The diffusion process with-

out occurrence of condensation is easily illustrated for a single-layer component (see fig. 2.6.57). The water vapour diffusion flow rate g in kg/m²h through a component in the constant state is calculated using the equation below. To do this, we must know the water vapour partial pressures p_i and p_e in Pa on both sides of the component as well as the water vapour diffusion resistance Z of the component. At a reference temperature of 10°C, Z can be calculated from

$$Z = 1.5 \times 10^6 \times \mu \times d$$

Consequently, the diffusion flow rate is indirectly proportional to the diffusion resistance generally applicable and the thickness of the building material. The dimensionless material property μ specifies by how much the diffusion resistance of a material is greater than the stationary air. The μ-value of air is therefore 1. As the thickness is of course important for calculating the diffusion resistance of a component or layer of a component, in practice we use the diffusion-equivalent air layer thickness

$$s_d = \mu \times d$$

This unit is specified in m. In some cases this characterizes the diffusion properties of a building material layer better than the μ-value on its own. This is particularly true for thin layers and vapour barriers (see table 2.6.59). The diffusion-equivalent air layer thicknesses of thin layers have recently been defined in DIN 4108 part 3 as follows:

– open diffusion layer with $s_d \leq 0.5$ m
– diffusion-resistant layer with
  0.5 m $< s_d \leq 1500$ m
– closed diffusion layer with $s_d > 1500$ m.

Water vapour diffusion resistances for building materials and masonry are specified in DIN 4108 part 4 and DIN EN 12524. Two values are given in DIN 4108 part 4 in order to take account of the scatter for type of material or type of masonry. In calculating the diffusion, the less favourable water vapour diffusion resistance should always be used for the condensing period. This means that when condensation occurs within a type of structure, the lower μ-values should be used for calculating the quantity of condensation on the inner (warm) side of the condensation plane or condensation zone, and the higher μ-values for the outer (cold) side. However, the values used for calculating the mass of condensation should be retained for calculating the evaporation options. Table 2.6.60 provides an overview of the water vapour diffusion resistances for masonry and plaster given in DIN 4108 part 4. In contrast, the European standard DIN EN 12524 distinguishes between water vapour diffusion resistances determined according to the dry and moist zone method of DIN EN ISO 12572. In the first case the material is essentially dry during the test because the humidities on both sides of the sample are approx. 0% and 50%, but in the second case about 50% and 95%, so that for hygroscopic materials an appropriate moisture content becomes established and influences the μ-value through the transport of the sorbed water (see fig. 2.6.61). Corresponding figures for building materials can be found in table 2.6.62. It can be seen that the μ-values for the moist zone with the greater flow of sorbed water are lower than those for the dry zone.

Calculating the quantity of condensation within components

The quantity of condensation accumulating within a component and the chance of drying out can only be estimated and not accurately calculated owing to the assumptions concerning the climatic boundary conditions and the wide scatter of material parameters. Even subsequent calculations, carried out within the scope of assessing damage, are fraught with uncertainties. The water vapour diffusion resistance is the most important material property but can vary considerably in practice due to utilization effects. In the case of hygroscopic materials the water vapour diffusion is concealed by sorption processes and flows of adsorbate films.

Several methods – with different claims to accuracy – are known for investigating the possible saturation of components by the formation of condensation, which results from the difference between the amount of water accumulating and the amount able to dry out. The *Glaser method* is covered by a standard. This is a simple graphic method for estimating possible moisture bleeding within the cross-section of a wall and the possible drying-out based on a constant state for the temperature zone and the vapour partial pressure gradient. With constant climatic conditions for the condensing period over two winter months and the evaporating period over three summer months, we also speak of the block method. Figure 2.6.63 is a schematic presentation of a simple diffusion diagram with a condensation plane between layers 2 and 3, as would be the case, for example, in a twin-leaf masonry wall with cavity insulation. However, owing to the misunderstandings which often occur in practice, it must be emphasized that the DIN method is an estimate of the accumulation of condensation and its possible drying-out as well as a check – proved over decades – of the absolute safety of a component subjected to standard conditions. The climatic boundary conditions and the method of analysis are described in detail in DIN 4108 part 3. The basic requirement is that the formation of condensation within components, which leads to damage or impairment of

---

2.6.58 Water absorption coefficient of building materials (after Künzel)

Material		Gross density kg/m³	Water absorption coefficient kg/m²h$^{0.5}$
Clay bricks	solid	1750	25
	solid	2175	2.9
	vertically perforated	1155	8.3
	vertically perforated	1140	8.9
Calcium silicate normal-weight lightweight concrete	solid calcium silicate	1635	7.7
	solid calcium silicate	1760	5.5
	solid calcium silicate	1920	3.2
	pumice concrete	845	2.9
	pumice concrete	1085	1.9
	autoclaved aerated concrete	535	4.0
	autoclaved aerated concrete	600	4.2
	autoclaved aerated concrete	630	4.6
	normal-weight concrete	2290	1.8
	normal-weight concrete	2410	1.1

2.6.59 Water vapour diffusion-equivalent air layer thickness to DIN EN 12524 of thin layers

Product/material	Water vapour diffusion-equivalent air layer thickness S_d m
Polyethylene 0.15 mm	50
Polyethylene 0.25 mm	100
Polyester sheet 0.2 mm	50
PVC sheet	30
Aluminium foil 0.05 mm	1500
Polyethylene sheet (stacked) 0.15 mm	8
Bitumenized paper 0.1 mm	2
Aluminium composite foil 0.4 mm	10
Roofing felt for walls	0.2
Coating material	0.1
High-gloss lacquer	3
Vinyl wallpaper	2

Note: The water vapour diffusion-equivalent air layer thickness of a product is specified as the thickness of a stationary layer of air with the same water vapour diffusion resistance as the product. The thickness of the product in the table is not normally measured and can be related to thin products with a water vapour diffusion resistance. The table specifies nominal thickness values as an aid to identifying the product.

2.6.60 Recommended values for diffusion resistance indexes to DIN 4108 part 4; upper and lower limits of material scatter

Material	Recommended value for water vapour diffusion resistance index (m)
Plasters	
Plastering mixes of lime, lime-cement and hydraulic lime	15/35
Plastering mixes of lime-gypsum, gypsum, anhydrite and lime hydrite	10
Lightweight plasters	15/20
Gypsum plasters	10
Thermal insulation plaster	5/20
Synthetic resin plaster	50/200
Masonry of	
solid engineering bricks, vertically perforated engineering bricks high-strength engineering bricks	50/100
solid clay bricks, vertically perforated clay bricks lightweight vertically perforated clay bricks	5/10
calcium silicate, gross density 1.0-1.4	5/10
calcium silicate, gross density 1.6-2.2	15/25
granulated slag aggregate units	70/100
autoclaved aerated concrete	5/10
lightweight concrete	5/10

2.6.61 Diagram of direction of diffusion upon measuring the water vapour permeability in the dry and moist zones, and specification of the water content in the samples and sorbate water transport for a hygroscopic material with the given sorption curve (after Kunzel)

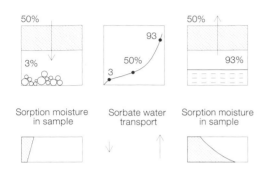

Sorption moisture in sample | Sorbate water transport | Sorption moisture in sample

2.6.62 Water vapour diffusion resistance indices for the dry and moist zones to DIN EN 12524

Material	Water vapour diffusion resistance index μ	
	dry	moist
Plastering mix	20	10
Clay brick	16	10
Calcium silicate	20	15
Concrete with expanded clay aggregates	6	4
Concrete with lightweight aggregates	15	10
Autoclaved aerated concrete	10	6

2.6.63 Water vapour diffusion with condensation occurring in one plane of the building component

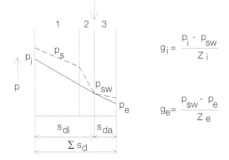

Diffusion diagram for condensation case

$$g_i = \frac{p_i - p_{sw}}{Z_i}$$

$$g_e = \frac{p_{sw} - p_e}{Z_e}$$

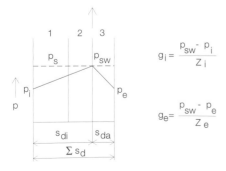

Diffusion diagram for evaporation case

$$g_i = \frac{p_{sw} - p_i}{Z_i}$$

$$g_e = \frac{p_{sw} - p_e}{Z_e}$$

the function due to the increase in moisture contained in building and insulating materials, should be avoided. This is generally the case when the following conditions are satisfied:
· Building materials that come into contact with condensation should not suffer any damage (e.g. through corrosion, mould growth).
· Water accumulating within the component during the condensing period must be able to escape to the surroundings again during the evaporating period.
· The area-related quantity of condensation should not exceed 1.0 kg/m² for roof and wall constructions.
· If condensation occurs at the contact faces of capillary, non-absorbent layers, the permissible condensation mass may be reduced to 0.5 kg/m²; provisions covering timber components are given in DIN 68800 part 2.
· An increase in the mass-related moisture content u exceeding 5% is not permitted for timber (3% for timber derivatives); wood-wool and multi-ply lightweight building boards to DIN 1101 are excluded from this.

In contrast to the DIN method, the *Jenisch method* takes into account the temperature relationships at the location of the building [90]. This makes use of the mean annual figure and the frequency of the daily average for the external air temperature in certain climatic zones in order to establish whether the mass of condensation occurring in a component can dry out again during one year. This method is slightly more involved than the DIN method but supplies a more accurate annual balance for the occurrence of condensation and the chance of it drying out.
The *COND method* [72] enables a moisture profile in multi-layer enclosing constructions to be calculated on the basis of the coupled heat, water vapour and capillary water transport, and hence forms a solid foundation for – in terms of moisture – a correct and differentiated approach to the physics of the building structure. Starting with a simple block climate for winter and summer, similar to DIN 4108 part 3, the capillarity and hygroscopicity of the building material are taken into account in addition to the water vapour diffusion. As the cold season begins, the difference between water vapour quantities diffusing into and out of the material, initially without formation of condensation, is used to create a hygroscopic load within the component. Once the water vapour saturation pressure is finally reached, condensation does form but, at the same time, capillary relief begins. The balance of vapour and capillary water flows leads to a reduced moisture load compared to the pure diffusion method. During the warm part of the year the material is relieved by water vapour and capillary water transport – until the condensation has dried out. Finally, further drying takes place until hygroscopic moisture content equilibrium with

the surrounding air is achieved.
Moisture transport in components taking into account sorption, diffusion and capillarity effects subjected to non-constant climatic conditions is reflected in the *Kießl method* [94]. The associated computer program "WUFI" [219] takes into account the conditions of the temperature and relative humidity of the internal and external air as well as the rain load and the radiation loss according to the inclination and orientation of the component. This information can be obtained from measured weather data or from test reference years. Material data such as porosity, specific heat capacity, thermal conductivity, diffusion resistance, moisture storage function and fluid transport coefficient are all put into the calculation. The computer program then determines the chronological progression of the temperature and moisture zone within the component.

Moisture behaviour of masonry

DIN 4108 part 3 describes components that, in the light of experience, can be regarded as absolutely safe with respect to saturation, and for which a mathematical analysis of condensation is not required. The condition for this is adequate minimum thermal insulation according to DIN 4108 part 2 and normal interior climates. Figure 2.6.64 provides an overview of external wall constructions which are absolutely safe in terms of the formation of condensation internally.

The masonry walls are made up as follows:

· Single-leaf masonry to DIN 1053 part 1 and walls of autoclaved aerated concrete to DIN 4223 with internal plaster and the following external layers:
  – rendering to DIN 18550 part 1
  – claddings to DIN 18515 parts 1 and 2 attached by mortar or bonding with a joint proportion of at least 5%
  – ventilated external wall claddings to DIN 18516 part 1 with and without thermal insulation
  – external insulation to DIN 1102 or DIN 18550 part 3 or an approved thermal insulation composite system
· Twin-leaf masonry to DIN 1053 part 1, also with cavity insulation
· Walls of masonry with internal insulation subject to the following limitations:
  – internal insulation with a thermal resistance of the thermal insulation layer R ≤ 1.0 m²K/W as well as a value for the water vapour diffusion-equivalent air layer thickness of the thermal insulation layer with internal plaster or internal cladding $s_{di} > 0.5$ m
  – internal insulation of plaster or clad wood-wool lightweight building boards to DIN 1101 with R ≤ 0.5 m²K/W without any further requirement for the s_{di}-value

• External basement walls of single-leaf masonry to DIN 1053 part 1 or concrete to DIN 1045 with external thermal insulation.

These provisions in the standards are based on many years of experience and, as a rule, lie on the safe side. If a construction deviates from the details given in the catalogues, this does not necessarily mean that the construction will fail. A number of selected investigations of external walls show the serviceability of facade claddings with limited ventilation, the use of various combinations of materials for twin-leaf masonry with cavity insulation and the absence of problems – in terms of moisture protection – with internal insulation. The wall protected by an *external cladding*, with or without additional thermal insulation, is a proven form of wall construction. The transport of moisture from the wall to the outside is achieved as shown in fig. 2.6.65 by ventilation to the rear of the cladding in conjunction with the formation of condensation on the inner face of the cladding, which then drains away. The mechanism which applies depends on the degree of ventilation. Tile-like, small-format elements also benefit from a considerable moisture exchange by way of the perviousness of the cladding [131]. Therefore, if a cladding is not ventilated according to DIN 18516, this does not represent a defect, provided the condensation on the rear face of the cladding can drain away and does not lead to damage to the load-bearing construction [130].

In a *full-fill cavity wall*, thermal insulation materials with any water vapour permeability can be combined with all relevant building materials for the inner leaf and an outer leaf of clay or calcium silicate facing bricks [5].

When calculating the diffusion according to DIN 4108 part 3, the amount of condensation according to figure 2.6.66 lies below the maximum permissible condensation mass of 1000 g/m^2, even for the most unfavourable case of thermal insulation open to diffusion (e.g. mineral wool, loose insulation) and a thin inner leaf. Only for an outer leaf of engineering bricks must water occurring within the component during the condensing period be able to escape again to the surroundings during the evaporating period (m_{WT}:$m_{WV} \leq 1$) not fulfilled – on paper – for insulating materials open to diffusion (see fig. 2.6.67). Taking into account laboratory tests on samples of wall in a Munich-based thermal insulation research centre, further practical investigations [53] and the fact that the condensation that occurs is only a fraction of the amount of driving rain that penetrates an outer leaf, a full-fill cavity wall can be regarded as absolutely safe, even when using engineering bricks, with respect to the formation of condensation within the wall.

Practical studies of the formation of condensation within components with internal insulation have been carried out on common forms of

2.6.64 External masonry walls for which a mathematical analysis of condensation is not necessary

masonry with different types of internal insulation in laboratory tests under the climatic conditions according to DIN 4108 part 3 [4]. Masonry walls made from no-fines lightweight concrete, calcium silicate and clay bricks with diffusion-permeable insulating materials such as mineral fibres, even those without vapour barrier, are absolutely safe with respect to saturation in winter. The thermal insulation remains dry during the condensing period. However, the increase in the water content of the masonry exceeds the limit of 1.0 kg/m^2 according to DIN 4108 part 3. The necessary drying-out during the evaporating period is achieved. Theoretical studies with a constant internal climate and practical external climate [95] confirm this assumption for certain types of masonry. As in the laboratory tests, they produce higher moisture fluctuations in the masonry compared with the use of denser insulation materials or vapour barriers. Butt joints near the covering on the inner face in conjunction with rigid expanded foams or mineral fibre boards, with vapour barriers interrupted at the butt joints, have no measurable effect on the water content of the masonry. Investigations carried out on existing structures confirm the laboratory measurements. Insulating materials with active capillaries, e.g. calcium silicate, have recently been favoured for the internal insulation of buildings with facades worth preserving [73]. A thickness of just 40 mm can

halve the thermal transmittance values often encountered in old buildings. A diffusion resistance μ = 5 allows the construction to remain open to diffusion. Possible condensation behind the insulation is dispersed and relieved by the high capillary action so that diffusion-resistant layers are unnecessary. Apart from that, the pH value of calcium silicate makes it resistant to mould growth and its hygroscopicity is a help in regulating the internal climate, i.e. moisture load peaks in the interior are buffered.

2.6.65 Schematic presentation of moisture loss in external walls with claddings. With ideal ventilation ($\vartheta_a = \vartheta_z$), the wall moisture is carried away with the air (right). With less than ideal or no ventilation ($\vartheta_a < \vartheta_z$), some moisture diffusing out of the wall can condense and drain away (left) [7]

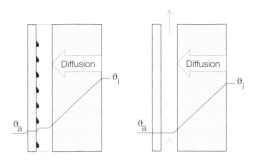

2.6.66 Condensation mass m_{WT} in relation to diffusion-equivalent air layer thickness of inner leaf
Thermal insulation layer: mineral fibre boards
Outer leaf: clay facing bricks

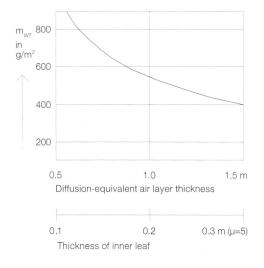

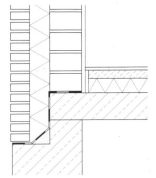

Water vapour convection

Walls and roofs must be airtight to prevent the through-flow and convection of internal humidity, which can lead to the formation of condensation. Special attention should be paid to the airtightness of junctions with other components and service penetrations. Transverse flows in ventilation layers within a construction between rooms heated to different temperatures should also be avoided. Facing masonry and timber frames, as well as masonry to DIN 1053 part 1, are not airtight without further treatment. These types of walls must be given a coat of plaster to DIN 18550 part 2 on one side or made airtight by other suitable measures. Plasters to DIN 18550 part 2 or 18558 are classed as airtight layers.

Protection against driving rain

Driving rain loads on walls are caused by the simultaneous effect of rain and wind blowing against the facade. The rainwater can be absorbed by the wall by way of the capillary action of the surface or enter via cracks, gaps or defective seals as a result of the pressure build-up. It must be ensured that the water entering the construction can escape again to the outside air. Providing a wall with protection against driving rain in order to limit the absorption of water by capillary action and to guarantee evaporation opportunities can be achieved through constructional measures (e.g. external cladding, twin-leaf masonry) or through rendering or coatings. The measures to be taken depend on the intensity of the driving rain load, which is determined by the direction of the wind and the level of precipitation as well as the local situation and type of building. Accordingly, three loading groups are defined in DIN 4108 part 3 in order to assess the behaviour of external walls subjected to driving rain. A rainfall map of Germany provides general information about precipitation levels. However, this is only the starting point for assessing driving rain because the local circumstances, altitude and form of the building (roof overhang, height of building) must also be taken into account (see fig. 2.6.68). Therefore, the loading groups for Germany are defined with associated explanations:

Loading group I – low driving rain load
As a rule, this loading group applies to regions with annual precipitation levels < 600 mm but also to locations well protected from the wind in regions with higher levels of precipitation.

Loading group II – moderate driving rain load
As a rule, this loading group applies to regions with annual precipitation levels of 600-800 mm as well as to locations well protected from the wind in regions with higher levels of precipitation and to tall buildings or buildings in exposed positions in regions where the local rain and wind conditions would otherwise cause them to be allocated to the low driving rain loading group.

Loading group III – high driving rain load
As a rule, this loading group applies to regions with annual precipitation levels > 800 mm or to windy regions, even those with lower levels of precipitation (e.g. coastal areas, hilly and mountainous regions, the foothills of the Alps), as well as to tall buildings or buildings in exposed positions in regions where the local rain and wind conditions would otherwise cause them to be allocated to the moderate driving rain loading group.

External walls with rain protection provided by rendering or coatings are assessed using the water absorption coefficient w for water absorption during rainfall and the diffusion-equivalent air layer thickness sd of the layer providing rain protection for the loss of water during dry periods [106]. In order to limit the short-term increase in moisture during rainfall, the water absorption coefficient should not exceed a certain value, even when drying-out is guaranteed in the long term. The lower the diffusion-equivalent air layer thickness s_d of the surface layer, the more quickly the component loses water – which entered during driving rain – in the dry period. So such a surface layer should be water-resistant or water-repellent with respect to rain protection, but at the same time remain as permeable as possible for water vapour to allow the moisture which has penetrated to escape quickly. The requirements for rain protection provided by rendering and coatings are defined in DIN 4108 part 3 (see table 2.6.69).
The rain protection is confined to the outer leaf in the case of twin-leaf walls with an air space or masonry with a ventilated cladding. Airtightness and thermal insulation are the tasks of the inner leaf. In a full-fill cavity wall, the cavity insulation should not impair the resistance to driving rain, and moisture should not be able to reach the inner leaf via the insulation. The cavity insulation must be covered by a standard, otherwise its serviceability will have to be verified in accordance with building authority regulations. Loose materials and mineral fibre boards must possess hydrophobic properties to repel the water. An overlapping stepped joint is adequate for plastic foams in order to guarantee that the water drains to the base of the wall. If loose cavity insulation materials are employed, suitable measures must be taken at the openings at the base of the external leaf in order to prevent material from escaping. As with a cavity wall, a damp proof course must be provided at the base and above all openings together with weep holes to allow driving rain which has penetrated the outer leaf to drain away.
When using thermal insulation composite systems, cracks in the rendering could endanger

the driving rain protection and impair the thermal insulation mainly provided by the external thermal insulation layer. The effects of cracks in rendering have been investigated on external walls subjected to natural weather conditions at the open-air test centre of the Fraunhofer Institute for Building Physics [14]. After three years of exposure to the weather, it can generally be said that for rendering on rigid expanded polystyrene and polyurethane foam sheets as well as hydrophobic mineral fibre boards, cracks with a width of approx. 0.2 mm do not impair the function of the rendering as rain protection to any significant extent, provided the substrate does not conduct through capillary action or is water-resistant. As a simple planning aid, DIN 4108 part 3 gives examples of the classification of standard types of wall according to the three loading groups (see 2.6.70). However, this does not rule out the use of other types of construction proved by years of practical experience.

2.6.67 Drying-out opportunities in relation to the diffusion-equivalent air layer thickness of insulation material when using outer leaves of clay facing bricks and engineering bricks

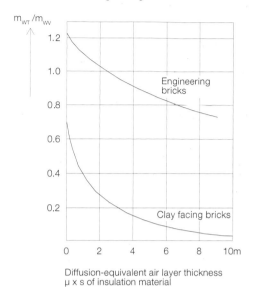

Diffusion-equivalent air layer thickness μ x s of insulation material

2.6.68 Allocation of driving rain groups according to position and form of building

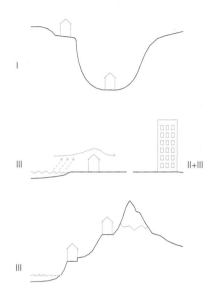

2.6.69 Requirements for rain protection to rendering and coatings according to DIN 4108 part 3

Rain protection requirement	Water absorption coefficient w kg/m²h$^{0.5}$	Diffusion-equivalent air layer thickness s_d m	Product w x s_d kg/mh$^{0.5}$
Water-resistant	0.5 < w < 2.0		–
Water-repellent	w ≤ 0.5	≤ 2.0	≤ 2.0

2.6.70 Examples of the allocation of standard wall types and loading groups according to DIN 4108 part 3

Loading group I low driving rain load	Loading group II moderate driving rain load	Loading group III high driving rain load
Rendering to DIN 18550 pt 1 without special requirements for driving rain protection • External walls of masonry, wall panels, concrete or similar • Wood-wool lightweight boards (with reinforced joints) • Multi-ply lightweight boards (reinforced over entire surface) to DIN 1101, installed according to DIN 1102	Water resistant rendering to DIN 18550 pt 1 on • External walls of masonry, wall panels, concrete or similar • Wood-wool and multi-ply lightweight boards to DIN 1101, installed according to DIN 1102	Water-repellent rendering to DIN 18550 pts 1-4 or synthetic resin plaster to DIN 18550 on
Single-leaf masonry to DIN 1053 pt 1, 310 mm thick (with internal plaster)	Single-leaf masonry to DIN 1053 pt 1, 375 mm thick (with internal plaster)	Twin-leaf facing masonry to DIN 1053 pt 1 with partial- or full-fill cavity (with internal plaster)
External walls with tiles or panels to DIN 18515 pt 1 applied in thick- or thin-bed mortar		External walls with tiles or panels to DIN 18515 pt 1 applied in water-repellent mortar
External walls with dense microstructure outer layer of concrete to DIN 1045 and DIN 1045 pt 1 (draft) as well as DIN 4219 pts 1 & 2		
Walls with ventilated external claddings to DIN 18516 pts 1, 3 & 4		
Walls with external insulation by means of a thermal insulation plaster system to DIN 18550 pt 3 or an approved thermal insulation composite system		
External walls in timber with weather protection according to section 8.2 of DIN 68800 pt 2 (May 95)		
Note: Drained joints between cladding panels do not impair rain protection.		

2.6.71 Sound levels of various sources

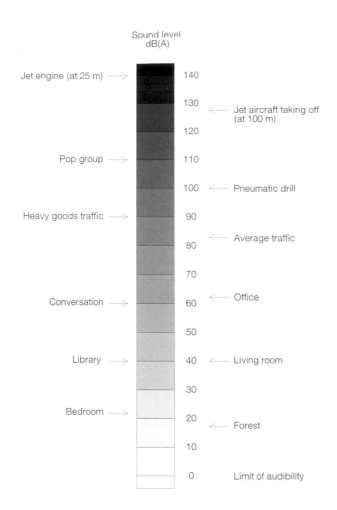

Sound level
dB(A)

Jet engine (at 25 m) ⟶   140

130 ⟵ Jet aircraft taking off (at 100 m)

120

Pop group ⟶   110

100 ⟵ Pneumatic drill

Heavy goods traffic ⟶   90

80 ⟵ Average traffic

70

Conversation ⟶   60 ⟵ Office

50

Library ⟶   40 ⟵ Living room

30

Bedroom ⟶   20 ⟵ Forest

10

0   Limit of audibility

2.6.72 Airborne and structure-borne sound

Excitation of airborne sound

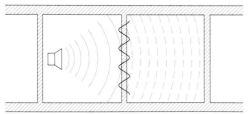

Excitation of structure-borne sound

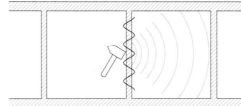

2.6.73 Frequency ranges

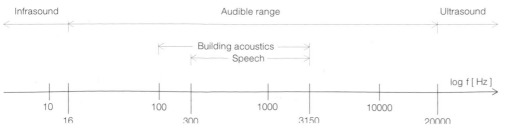

Infrasound   Audible range   Ultrasound

Building acoustics
Speech

log f [Hz]

10   100   1000   10000
16   300   3150   20000

Sound insulation

Sound insulation is becoming more and more important throughout the building industry. This primarily concerns questions relating to the health and well-being of people. Sound insulation is particularly important in housing because this is where people relax and rest and need to be shielded from the everyday noises of their neighbours. And sound insulation is an indispensable part of the building system if schools, hospitals and offices are to be used properly. Sound insulation in buildings begins at the design stage. For instance, noise-sensitive rooms like bedrooms and living rooms should be placed within the plan layout so that they are unlikely to be affected by unacceptable external noise; a useful expedient is to group those rooms with similar functions together. Besides careful planning, sound insulation measures can only be successful when great care is exercised during construction. Even minor flaws in workmanship can lead to, for example, acoustic bridges for structure-borne noise, which then practically nullify the entire sound insulation measures. Putting right such problems subsequently is in many cases impossible or at best extremely expensive.

Terms and definitions

Sound insulation is the protection against sound which is conveyed in various ways (see fig. 2.6.72):

- Airborne sound is sound which propagates in air (a gaseous medium). Upon striking a solid body (building component), part of the airborne sound is reflected and part is absorbed or attenuated.
- Structure-borne sound is sound which propagates in solid materials. In buildings these are frequently noises caused by building services and machinery which are then conveyed via the construction.
- Impact sound is a special form of structure-borne sound caused by people walking across the floor.

Sound is the mechanical vibration of an elastic medium whose frequency lies within the audible range of the human ear (between 16 and 20 000 Hz). Frequency f is defined as the number of vibrations per second. As the frequency increases the pitch rises. A doubling of the frequency corresponds to one octave. In building acoustics we are generally concerned with a range of five octaves – from 100 to 3150 Hz (see fig. 2.6.73). The periodic sound vibration generates an alternating pressure in air or fluids known as *sound pressure* p. The sound pressure is superimposed on the static pressure present in the respective medium and can be measured by using a microphone. The *sound pressure level* L describes sound events in building acoustics. As the human ear is in a position to perceive a range equal to 1 x 10^6, the sound pressure level (often abbreviated to SPL) is described using a logarithmic scale. This is the base 10 logarithm of the ratio of the square of the respective sound pressure p to the square of the reference sound pressure p_0:

$$L = 10 \log_{10} (p^2/p_0^2)$$

The unit of sound pressure or sound level difference is the decibel (dB). The sound level is specified using the A-scale dB(A); this is based on the A-weighting network, which approximates to a scale of volume comparable to that of the sensitivity of the human ear. A sound that increases by 10 dB is perceived to be twice as loud. The sound level extends from the limit of audibility 0 dB(A) to the pain threshold . A number of typical sound levels are given in fig. 2.6.71. So sound insulation means reducing the sound levels of sound sources to an acceptable level when they cannot be diminished. The sound reduction index R describes the insulating effect of components against airborne sound. This is calculated from the sound level difference between two rooms (source and receiving rooms) taking into account the absorption surface A of the receiving room and the test surface of the component S:

$$R = L_1 - L_2 + 10 \log_{10} (S/A)$$

The *airborne sound insulation index* R_w is a single value for the simple identification of building components. As shown in fig. 2.6.74, a curve B, the shape of which takes into account the sensitivity of the human ear, above the line of measured frequencies M, is displaced downwards in steps of 1 dB until the average undershoot U of the displaced grade curve below the measured curve is max. 2 dB. The sound reduction index of the displaced grade curve at 500 Hz is taken as the single identifying value.

In practice the airborne sound insulation index is specified taking into account the sound transmission via flanking components (see fig. 2.6.75). Flanking transmission is that part of the airborne sound transmission between two adjacent rooms which does not take place directly via the separating component but instead via auxiliary paths through adjoining components. *Impact sound* is structure-borne sound generated by walking or similar excitation of floors or stairs, and is transmitted to the rooms below partly directly as airborne sound or via flanking components as structure-borne sound waves. Impact sound insulation is usually improved by a two-layer arrangement in the form of the floor finish being supported by a "floating" construction on the structural floor.

A floating screed is a supporting layer which is separated from the structural floor, and from

the walls on all sides as well as door frames and service penetrations, by a resilient insulating layer.

Requirements

Minimum requirements for sound insulation have been laid down in a number of construction law documents. DIN 4109 specifies requirements for airborne and impact sound insulation between individual functional units in buildings and requirements for protection against external noise. It should be noted here that the requirements apply only to the sound performance of separating components between different residential or office premises; there are no minimum requirements for sound insulation within residential or office premises. Supplement 1 to DIN 4109 (examples of details and methods of calculation) has been implemented by the building authorities. Supplement 2 to DIN 4109 (recommendations for enhanced sound insulation and suggestions for sound insulation within premises) has not been implemented by the building authorities, and necessitates a special agreement between developer and architect. Bearing in mind the increasing quality awareness of users, the designer should check whether the enhanced sound insulation measures of supplement 2 can be implemented taking into account technical and economic aspects. A guide to the contents of DIN 4109 and the supplements is given in fig. 2.6.76. Work on European standardization is being carried out by the technical committee CEN/TC 126 "Acoustic properties of building products and of buildings".

The European standard is essentially concerned with the harmonization of testing methods (laboratory and in situ), the evaluation of test results and the drawing-up of methods of calculation for determining the acoustic performance of buildings based on the properties of their components. The standards being produced for this by CEN will have a direct influence on the provisions of DIN 4109. The German building acoustics standardization concept will have to undergo a fundamental overhaul. The DIN study groups responsible are currently working on a standardization concept that takes the harmonized codes into account. Both DIN 4109 and supplement 1 will need to be revised.

The work to be carried out essentially involves the following areas:

- A revision of DIN 4109 while retaining the current level of requirements.
- The production of a building component catalogue.
- The integration of the harmonized method of calculation in the German building acoustics concept, including the drawing-up of instructions.

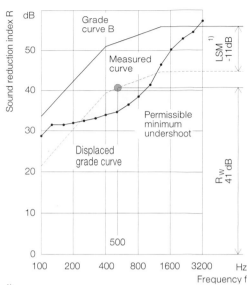

2.6.74 Example of formation of average value with the aid of the evaluation curve

[1] LSM = airborne sound insulation margin

2.6.75 Transmission paths for airborne sound

Besides transmission through the separating wall (path 1), the airborne sound is also transmitted via paths 2, 3 and 4.

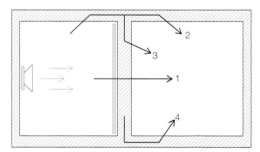

Flanking transmission

2.6.76 Requirements and recommendations for sound insulation

Designation	Implemented by building authorities	Content
DIN 4109	Yes	Protection of occupied rooms against • noises from rooms not belonging to the same premises • noises from building services and operations on the same premises • external noise and the noise of commercial or industrial operations
Supplement 1 to DIN 4109	Yes	Examples of construction details and methods of calculation
Supplement 2 to DIN 4109	No	Advice on design and construction and recommendations for enhanced sound insulation

2.6.77 Airborne sound insulation for walls and doors to prevent sound transmission from other residential or working areas

Component	Requirements to DIN 4109[1] reqd R'_w dB	Recommendations for enhanced sound insulation according to supplement 2[2] reqd R'_w dB
1. Multistorey buildings with apartments and work rooms		
Party walls between apartments and walls between separate work premises	53	≥ 55
Staircase walls and walls adjacent to communal corridors	52[3]	≥ 55
Walls adjacent to driveways, entrances to common garages etc.	55	–
Walls to games or similar community rooms	55	–
Doors		
• which lead from communal corridors or stairs to corridors and hallways in apartments and residential homes or from work rooms;	27	≥ 37
• which lead from communal corridors or stairs directly to occupied rooms – except corridors and hallways – in apartments	37	–
2. Semidetached or terraced houses		
Party walls	57	≥ 67
3. Hotels etc.		
Walls between		
• bedrooms	47	≥ 52
• corridors and bedrooms	47	≥ 52
Doors		
• between corridors and bedrooms	32	≥ 37
4. Hospitals, clinics		
Walls between	47	≥ 52
• patients' rooms		
• corridors and patients' rooms		
• examination or consultation rooms		
• corridors and examination or consultation rooms		–
• patients' rooms and work or nursing rooms		
Walls between		
• operating theatres or treatment rooms	42	–
• corridors and operating theatres or treatment rooms		
Walls between	37	–
• intensive care rooms		
• corridors and intensive care rooms		
Doors between		
• examination or consultation rooms	37	–
• corridors and examination or consultation rooms		
• corridors and patients' rooms	32	≥ 37
• operating theatres or treatment rooms		–
• corridors and operating theatres or treatment rooms		
5. Schools and similar places of education		
Walls between	47	–
• classrooms or similar rooms		
• corridors and classrooms or similar rooms		
Walls between	52	–
• stairs and classrooms or similar rooms		
Walls between	55	–
• "particularly noisy" rooms (e.g. sports halls, music rooms, work rooms) and classrooms or similar rooms		
Doors between	32	–
• corridors and classrooms or similar rooms		

1) Extract from table 3 of DIN 4109
2) Extract from table 2 of supplement 2 to DIN 4109
3) The following applies to walls with doors: R'_w(wall) = R_w(door) + 15 dB; wall widths ≤ 300 mm are not considered here.

The necessary work will involve masonry and reinforced concrete, steel and other frames, timber construction, elements (windows, doors etc.) and building services.

In Germany, supplement 3 to DIN 4109 has been prepared for the transition period. This contains a method for converting the airborne sound insulation index R_w determined in the laboratory without flanking transmission into a value R'_w, which is still required at present for the German system. The reverse procedure, i.e. converting R'_w to R_w, is also included in the supplement.

The level of requirements for sound insulation in buildings is not affected by the European standard. The establishment of requirements remains exclusively the province of national bodies and can therefore be adjusted to the respective national traditions and developments in the construction industry. Accordingly, DIN 4109 is not threatened in this respect by developments at European level.

Sound insulation against internal noise

Table 2.6.77 lists the requirements of DIN 4109 and the recommendations of supplement 2 to DIN 4109 for a number of selected walls for protecting occupied rooms against sound transmission from other residential or working premises. Sound insulation for occupants is also important within the same residential and working premises when rooms serve different purposes, or different working and resting periods apply, or enhanced insulation requirements are desirable. Supplement 2 to DIN 4109 contains recommendations for standard and enhanced sound insulation. Table 2.6.79 provides an overview of the corresponding suggestions for residential and office buildings. DIN 4109 stipulates values for the permissible sound level in noise-sensitive rooms in order to provide *protection against noise from building services and operations*. In order to maintain these values, requirements are laid down for the airborne and impact sound insulation of components between "particularly noisy" rooms and those sensitive to noise (see table 2.6.80). The latter are understood to be living rooms, bedrooms, hospital wards, classrooms and offices. "Particularly noisy" rooms are:

• Rooms with "particularly noisy" building plant or services if the maximum sound pressure level of the airborne sound in these rooms frequently exceeds 75 dB(A).
• Rooms housing containers for rubbish chutes and access corridors to such rooms from the outside.
• Rooms for craft or commercial activities, including sales activities, if the maximum sound pressure level of the airborne sound in these rooms frequently exceeds 75 dB(A).
• Restaurants, cafés, snack bars and the like.

- Bowling alleys
- Kitchens for hotels etc., hospitals, clinics, restaurants; not included here are small kitchens, preparation rooms and communal kitchens.
- Theatres
- Sports halls
- Music and work rooms.

In many cases it is necessary to provide additional structure-borne insulation to machines, apparatus and pipes opposite soffits and walls of the building. No figures can be specified here because it depends on the magnitude of the structure-borne sound generated by the machine or apparatus, which is very different in each case. Supplement 2 to DIN 4109 provides general design advice. There is no requirement with respect to the airborne sound insulation index for the sound insulation of walls built to conceal building services and plant if the area-related mass of the wall is at least 220 kg/m² – such walls comply with the permissible sound level for noises generated by water pipes (including waste water pipes). Walls with an area-related mass < 220 kg/m² must be verified by a suitability test to prove that they are adequate. Excessive noise transmission in such situations can be effectively reduced by attaching a non-rigid facing of mineral fibre board and plasterboard on the side of the noise-sensitive room. Modern systems for such walls, with a facing or cladding the full height of the room, provide very good sound insulation.

Sound insulation against external noise
Various noise level ranges, classified according to the actual or expected "representative external noise level", form the basis of the provisions for the required airborne sound insulation of external components to protect against external noise. Different requirements have been laid down for the bedrooms in hospitals and clinics, occupied rooms in residential accommodation, hotel bedrooms and classrooms as well as offices (see table 2.6.81). As the enclosing external components usually consist of several different surfaces with different sound insulation properties, the requirements apply to the resulting sound reduction index $R'_{w,res}$ calculated from the individual sound reduction indexes of the different surfaces. The required sound reduction indices have to be increased or decreased depending on the ratio of the total external surface of a room to the plan area of the room. For instance, for a standard ceiling height of 2.5 m, the requirements given in table 2.6.81 are already acceptable for a room depth of 3 m and reductions of up to -3 dB may be exploited for greater room depths.
The requirements for the resulting sound reduction index for rooms in residential buildings

2.6.78   The airborne sound insulation index R'_w according to the mass law

2.6.79   Suggestions for sound insulation within residential or working premises according to DIN 4109 supplement 2

Component	Suggestions for standard sound insulation reqd R'_w dB	enhanced sound insulation reqd R'_w dB
Residential building		
Walls without doors between "noisy" and "quiet" rooms with different uses, e.g. between living room and child's bedroom.	40	≥ 47
Office buildings		
Walls between rooms for normal office activities	37	≥ 42
Walls between corridors and rooms for normal office activities	37	≥ 42
Walls to rooms for intensive mental activities or for handling confidential matters, e.g. between director's office and anteroom	45	≥ 52
Walls between corridors and rooms for intensive mental activities or for handling confidential matters	45	≥ 52
Doors in walls between rooms for normal office activities or in walls between corridors and such rooms	27	≥ 32
Doors in walls to rooms for intensive mental activities or for handling confidential matters or in walls between corridors and such rooms	37	–

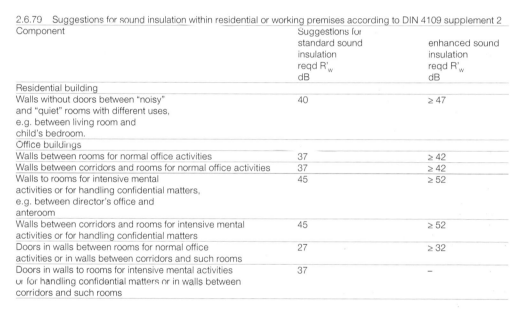

2.6.80   Requirements for airborne sound insulation of walls and floors between "particularly noisy" rooms and those needing to be insulated

Type of room	Airborne sound insulation index R'_w reqd dB	
	Sound level L_{AF} = 75- 80 dB(A)	Sound level L_{AF} = 81- 85 dB(A)
Rooms with "particularly noisy" building plant or services	57	62
Rooms for craft or commercial activities, including sales activities	57	62
Kitchens for hotels etc., hospitals, clinics, restaurants, snack bars etc.	55	
Kitchens as above but also in operation after 10 p.m.	57	
Restaurants etc. not occupied after 10 p.m.	55	
Restaurants etc. – max. sound level L_{AF} < 85 dB(A) – also occupied after 10 p.m.	62	
Bowling alleys	67	
Restaurants etc. – max. sound level 85 dB(A) ≤ L_{AF} ≤ 95 dB(A) e.g. with electroacoustic system	72	

Note: L_{AF} = time-related sound level, which is measured with the frequency evaluation A and the time evaluation F (= fast) as a function of the time.

2.6.81 Noise level ranges and sound reduction index
        $R'_{w,res}$ to be maintained

Noise level range	Critical external noise level dB(A)	$R'_{w,res}$ reqd for external component (in dB)		
		Bed-rooms	Occupied rooms	Offices[1]
I	≤ 55	35	30	–
II	56 – 60	35	30	30
III	61 – 65	40	35	30
IV	66 – 70	45	40	35
V	71 – 75	50	45	40
VI	76 – 80	[2]	50	45
VII	> 80	[2]	[2]	50

[1] There are no stipulations for the external components of rooms in which, owing to the nature of the activities carried out in those rooms, external noise which enters such rooms makes only a minor contribution to the internal noise level.
[2] The requirements in these cases are to be established according to the local circumstances.

2.6.82 Airborne sound insulation index of party walls
        without plaster, after Gösele

	R'_w [dB]	
	without	with plaster
240 mm vertically perforated clay bricks	50	53
250 mm in-situ concrete	11	53
240 mm hollow blocks of pumice concrete	16	49
200 mm storey-height aerated concrete panels	45	47

2.6.83 Different sound insulation of vertically perforated
        clay brick walls with approximately equal area-
        related mass but different perforations, after
        J. Lang

Unit cross-section

Web cross-section (schematic)

A: $m' = 435$ kg/m^2, $R_w = 59$ dB
   (continuous webs from outside to inside)
B: $m' = 420$ kg/m^2, $R_w = 49$ dB
   (webs offset with respect to each other)

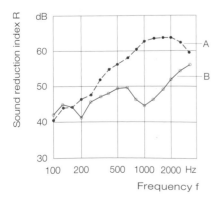

Frequency f

with a standard ceiling height of 2.5 m, room depths of at least 4.5 m, and 10-60% window area, are deemed to be fulfilled when the individual sound reduction indices given in tables in DIN 4109 – according to the proportion of window area – are maintained for the wall and window.

The sound reduction indices of ventilation ducts and roller blind boxes and the associated reference area should be taken into account when calculating the resulting sound reduction index. Facilities for temporary ventilation (e.g. opening lights and flaps) are evaluated in the closed condition, those for permanent ventilation (e.g. sound-attenuated ventilation openings) in the operating condition.

The representative external noise level is determined for the various noise sources using appropriate methods of measurement and evaluation. DIN 4109 contains a traffic noise nomogram in which the average level can be read off depending on the volume of traffic and the distance of the building from the centre of the road. Special analyses for traffic situations in which the nomogram cannot be used as well as for rail and waterborne traffic are covered by DIN 18005 part 2.

For air traffic, i.e. airports, the "Law governing protection against aircraft noise" lays down noise protection zones. The provisions of this law, or more rigorous national regulations, apply within these protected zones.

The representative external noise level for commercial and industrial operations makes use of the daily immissions value given in the development plan for the respective area category according to Germany's Noise Abatement Act.

Single-leaf walls
The sound insulation of thick, single-leaf, homogeneous walls depends in the first instance on their area-related mass. The relationship between the airborne sound insulation index R'_w and the area-related mass is shown in fig. 2.6.78. The prerequisite for the correlation between the airborne sound insulation and the area-related mass of a single-leaf wall is a closed microstructure and sealed construction. If this requirement is not fulfilled, then the wall must be sealed on at least one side by a complete covering of firmly adhering plaster or corresponding coating to insulate against direct sound transmission [62]. Table 2.6.82 shows the difference in the airborne sound insulation indices for walls with and without plaster. The curve in fig. 2.6.78 does not apply to lightweight components < 85 kg/m^2 and, according to DIN 4109, with an area-related mass > 630 kg/m^3 can only be used to describe the behaviour of twin-leaf walls with continuous separating joint because in this range the achievable sound insulation is limited by the flanking components. The given sound reduction indices are achieved only if the average area-related mass

of the flanking components can be assumed to be approx. 300 kg/m^3.

Besides the fact that sound insulation generally depends on mass, the internal attenuation (material attenuation) of the material used is also important to a certain extent. This attenuation is understood to be the ability of the material to convert part of the vibration energy into heat and hence remove some of the energy from the vibration. Investigations carried out by the Fraunhofer Institute for Building Physics have shown that the airborne sound insulation index can be set 2 dB higher thanks to this material attenuation effect for plastered walls of autoclaved aerated concrete and lightweight concrete containing aggregates of pumice or expanded clay with gross densities ≤ 800 kg/m^3 and an area-related mass ≤ 250 kg/m^2.

Acoustic studies at Braunschweig University have established this 2 dB bonus for plastered walls of calcium silicate with gross densities ≤ 800 kg/m^3 as well.

J. Lang [107] showed long ago that clay brick walls with comparable masses but different perforations exhibited differences in their airborne sound insulation index of up to 10 dB (see fig. 2.6.83). Gösele discovered one explanation for this in the effect of thickness resonances [62]. The measured deviations were attributed to the arrangement of the webs within the masonry units. In one case the webs pass through the unit in a straight line and serve to stiffen the unit; in another they are offset with respect to each other and work like a set of springs in series. More recent studies have revealed that the sound insulation of walls made from perforated units depends not only on the arrangement of perforations in the units but also on numerous other factors, such as the type of mortar bed, thickness of plaster and format of the unit [176]. Figure 2.6.84 shows the difference between the measured and calculated sound reduction indices for walls of perforated units with different area-related masses and different proportions of perforations. The effects of the various influencing variables on the sound insulation are summarised in table 2.6.85.

Positive effects are brought about by:
• harder mortar
• thicker coats of plaster
• shorter masonry units
• coarsely structured perforations with thick webs.

The problems associated with perforated masonry units appeared in clay, calcium silicate and concrete units, and – according to current findings – are not restricted to a certain building material.

Table 2.6.87 provides an overview of the characteristic airborne sound insulation indices for masonry with normal-weight and lightweight mortar and plastered both sides. These values must be reduced by 100 kg/m^3 for a gross density > 1000 kg/m³ and 50 kg/m³ for a gross density < 1000 kg/m³ for walls of lightweight or autoclaved aerated concrete panels, as well as for gauged brickwork using thin-bed mortar. Another possibility of improving the sound insulation of internal walls – also subsequently – is to combine the solid wall skin with a non-rigid cladding on the "noisy" side of the separating wall. We distinguish between two groups depending on the connection to the rigid wall (see fig. 2.6.88). Claddings of group A are fixed to the heavy wall via a supporting framework, while those of group B are free-standing or bonded to the substrate via a resilient connection using mineral fibre boards. Table 2.6.86 specifies airborne sound insulation indices for solid walls with a cladding on one side. If, for example, for thermal insulation reasons, insulating batts with a high dynamic stiffness are attached to a single-leaf rigid wall either fully bonded over the whole surface or just at discrete points, this can degrade the sound insulation if the insulating batts are covered by plaster.

Twin-leaf party walls

Party walls of two heavy, rigid leaves with a continuous separating joint bring about a considerable reduction in the sound transmission between, for example, adjoining apartments. The sound reduction index of a twin-leaf party wall with continuous joint is determined from the area-related mass of both leaves, including coats of plaster, similarly to single-leaf components. The direct sound transmission (without flanking transmission) of a twin-leaf wall of solid leaves is 12 dB higher than could be expected for a single-leaf solid wall with the same mass. The joint extends without interruption from top of foundation to roof covering (see fig. 2.6.90). A joint passing through the foundation leads to better sound insulation in the basement but as this is a problem in terms of sealing the building, this arrangement remains an exception. The 12 dB bonus may only be taken into account when the following conditions are complied with:

- The area-related mass of each leaf must be at least 150 kg/m² and the distance between the leaves at least 30 mm.
- With a separating joint ≥ 50 mm, the area-related mass of each leaf may be reduced to 100 kg/m².
- The joint must be filled completely with tightly jointed resilient boards, e.g. mineral fibre impact sound insulation boards.
- Such fibre boards are not required when the area-related mass of each leaf is ≥ 200 kg/m².

The joint between the leaves should not be made too thin as this can very quickly lead to acoustic bridges. On the other hand, the optimum leaf spacings in terms of sound insulation are higher than the minimum values given in

2.6.84 Difference between measured and calculated (to DIN 4109 supplement 1) airborne sound insulation indices in relation to proportion of perforations for various walls of perforated masonry units, after Scholl

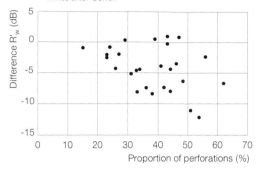

2.6.85 Influence of masonry unit geometry and type of construction on the sound insulation of walls of perforated units, after Scholl

Influencing variable	ΔR_{max}
Arrangement of perforations	10–15 dB
Type of mortar	approx. 5 dB
Thickness of bed joints	approx. 5 dB
Thickness of plaster	5–10 dB
Unit format	approx. 5 dB

The figures given here represent the maximum change in sound insulation ΔR_{max} that occurred upon changing the respective influences for a constant wall mass in the measurement data available.

2.6.86 Airborne sound insulation index R'_w of single-leaf rigid walls with a non-rigid cladding; characteristic values according to DIN 4109 supplement 1

Area-related mass of solid wall kg/m²	Airborne sound insulation index R'_w[1] without cladding dB	with cladding group A dB	with cladding group B dB
100	37	48	49
200	45	49	50
300	47	53	54
400	52	55	56
500	55	57	58

[1] Applies to flanking components with an average area-related mass $m'_{L,mean}$ of 300 kg/m². The values are reduced by 1 dB for a "rigid" connection between cladding and wall.

2.6.87 Airborne sound insulation index R'_w of walls plastered both sides in relation to the bulk density class and wall thickness

Gross density class	Wall thickness mm	Airborne sound insulation index [1][2] R'_w (dB) Normal mortar	Lightweight mortar	Gross density class	Wall thickness mm	Airborne sound insulation index [1][2] R'_w (dB) Normal mortar	Lightweight mortar
0.5	175	40	39	1.0	175	45	[3]
	240	43	42		240	48	
	300	45	44		300	51	
	365	47	45		365	53	
0.6	175	41	40	1.2	175	47	[3]
	240	44	43		240	50	
	300	46	45		300	52	
	365	48	47		365	54	
0.7	175	43	42	1.4	175	48	[3]
	240	45	45		240	52	
	300	47	47		300	54	
	365	50	49		365	56	
0.8	175	44	43	1.6	175	50	[3]
	240	46	46		240	53	
	300	49	48		300	55	
	365	51	50		365	57	
0.9	175	45	44	1.8	175	51	[3]
	240	48	47		240	54	
	300	50	49		300	57	
	365	52	51		365	59	

[1] Applies to flanking components with an average weight of 300 kg/m².
[2] A total of 40 kg/m² has been taken into account for the coats of plaster.
[3] These gross densities are not generally combined with lightweight mortar.

2.6.88 Sound performance of favourable claddings to DIN 4109 supplement 1

Group[1]	Wall construction	Description
B (no connection or resilient connection to wall)	≥ 20, ≥ 60, ≥ 500	Cladding of wood-wool lightweight boards to DIN 1101, thickness ≥ 25 mm, plastered, gap between wall and timber studding ≥ 20 mm, free-standing in front of heavy wall, construction to DIN 1102.
	≥ 20, ≥ 60, ≥ 500	Cladding of plasterboard to DIN 18180, thickness 12.5 or 15 mm, construction to DIN 18181 (currently in draft form), or of chipboard to DIN 68763, thickness 10-16 mm, gap between wall and timber studding ≥ 20 mm, free-standing[2] in front of heavy wall, with cavity filled[3] between timber studding.
	≥ 30 to 50, ≥ 50	Cladding of wood-wool lightweight boards to DIN 1101, thickness ≥ 50 mm, plastered free-standing with 30-50 mm gap in front of heavy wall, construction to DIN 1102, a 20 mm gap is sufficient when filling the cavity according to footnote 3.
	≥ 40	Cladding of plasterboard to DIN 18180, thickness 12.5 or 15 mm, and fibre insulation boards[4], construction to DIN 18181 (currently in draft form), discrete or linear fixing to heavy wall.
A (with connection to wall)	≥ 60, ≥ 500	Cladding of wood-wool lightweight boards to DIN 1101, thickness ≥ 25 mm, plastered, timber studding fixed to heavy wall, construction to DIN 1102.
	≥ 60, ≥ 500	Cladding of plasterboard to DIN 18180, thickness 12.5 or 15 mm, construction to DIN 18181 (currently in draft form), or of chipboard to DIN 68763, thickness 10-16 mm, with cavity filling[3], timber studding fixed to heavy wall[2]).

[1] In a wall test rig without flanking transmission (test rig DIN 52210-P-W), the airborne sound insulation index $R_{w,P}$ of a single-leaf, rigid wall is improved by at least 15 dB when adding claddings of group B, and by at least 10 dB for claddings of group A.

[2] In these examples the timber studding may be replaced by sheet steel C wall sections to DIN 18182 pt 1.

[3] Fibre insulation materials to DIN 18165 pt 1, nominal thickness between 20 and 60 mm, linear flow resistance $\Xi \geq 5$ kNs/m^4.

[4] Fibre insulation materials to DIN 18165 pt 1, application type WV-s, nominal thickness ≥ 40 mm, s' ≥5 MN/m^3.

2.6.89 Examples of twin-leaf walls – two leaves employing normal-weight mortar with continuous separating joint between buildings – in relation to gross density classes to DIN 4109 supplement 1

Airborne sound insulation index $R'_{W,R}$ (dB)	Gross density class of unit and min. wall thickness of leaves for twin-leaf masonry					
	Facing brickwork both sides		10 mm plaster P IV both sides (lime-gypsum or gypsum plaster) 2 x 10 kg/m²		15 mm plaster P I, P II or P III both sides oder P III (lime, lime-cement or cement plaster) (2 x 25 kg/m²)	
	Unit gross density class	Min. thickness of leaves without plaster mm	Unit gross density class	Min. thickness of leaves without plaster mm	Unit gross density class	Min. thickness of leaves without plaster mm
57	0.6	2 x 240	0.6[1]	2 x 240	0.7[2]	2 x 175
	0.9	2 x 175	0.8[2]	2 x 175	0.9[4]	2 x 150
	1	2 x 150	1.0[3]	2 x 150	1.2[4]	2 x 115
	1.4	2 x 115	1.4[5]	2 x 115	–	–
62	0.6	2 x 240	0.6[6]	2 x 240	0.5[6]	2 x 240
	0.9	175 + 240	0.8[7]	2 x 175	0.8[7]	2 x 175
	0.9	2 x 175	1.0[7]	2 x 150	0.9[7]	2 x 150
	1.4	2 x 115	1.4	2 x 115	1.2	2 x 115
67	1	2 x 240	1.0[8]	2 x 240	0.9[8]	2 x 240
	1.2	175 + 240	1.2	175 + 240	1.2	175 + 240
	1.4	2 x 175	1.4	2 x 175	1.4	2 + 175
	1.8	115 + 175	1.8	115 + 175	1.6	115 + 175
	2.2	2 x 115	2.2	2 x 115	2	2 x 115

[1] The gross density class may be 0.2 less when spacing between leaves is ≥ 50 mm and weight of each individual leaf is ≥ 100 kg/m².

[2] The gross density class may be 0.3 less when spacing between leaves is ≥ 50 mm and weight of each individual leaf is ≥ 100 kg/m².

[3] The gross density class may be 0.4 less when spacing between leaves is ≥ 50 mm and weight of each individual leaf is ≥ 100 kg/m².

[4] The gross density class may be 0.5 less when spacing between leaves is ≥ 50 mm and weight of each individual leaf is ≥ 100 kg/m².

[5] The gross density class may be 0.6 less when spacing between leaves is ≥ 50 mm and weight of each individual leaf is ≥ 100 kg/m².

[6] For leaves of gas concrete units or panels to DIN 4165 or 4166, as well as lightweight concrete units with expanded clay aggregate to DIN 18151 or 18152, the gross density class may be 0.1 less when spacing between leaves is ≥ 50 mm and weight of each individual leaf is ≥ 100 kg/m².

[7] For leaves of gas concrete units or panels to DIN 4165 or 4166, as well as lightweight concrete units with expanded clay aggregate to DIN 18151 or 18152, the gross density class may be 0.2 less when spacing between leaves is ≥ 50 mm and weight of each individual leaf is ≥ 100 kg/m².

[8] The gross density class may be 0.2 less for leaves of gas concrete units or panels to DIN 4165 or 4166, as well as lightweight concrete units with expanded clay aggregate to DIN 18151 or 18152.

meet requirements when it is used as the surface of a component (e.g. wall and soffit cladding); second, when used as part of the construction of a component. The essential parts of fire-resistant components must consist of incombustible materials.

The European classes for the fire behaviour of building products have now been accepted by the Standing Committee for the Construction Industry. They will be published after work on the standard and the associated test methods has been completed. A comparison between the European and German building materials classes could well look something like table 2.6.98.

Fire resistance classes

The safety of a structure during a fire depends not only on the combustibility of the materials but also – in particular – on the duration of fire resistance of the components. The fire resistance class of a component is defined as the minimum duration in minutes for which the component withstands a specified fire test. In a fire test the sample is subjected to a precisely defined temperature gradient, the internationally standardized standard temperature curve (see fig. 2.6.100), and is assessed according to the following chief test criteria:

· Maintaining the load-carrying capacity (stability) – under load for loadbearing components or self-weight for non-loadbearing components.
· Maintaining a maximum permissible rate of deflection in the case of components on statically determinate supports.
· Maintaining the room enclosure (integrity and insulation) in the case of walls so that no ignitable gases can escape and no cracks can form which might lead to ignition. The increase in temperature on the side remote from the fire should not exceed 140°C on average and 180°C at individual measuring points.

As can be seen in fig. 2.6.99, the duration of fire resistance is essentially determined by the behaviour of the material and influences specific to the component. In the case of masonry, failure takes place due to the reduction in cross-section resulting from temperature-related fatigue of the masonry units and dehydration of the mortar. The duration of fire resistance enables a component to be assigned to a fire resistance class (see table 2.6.97). Component classifications can be coupled to material requirements with respect to building materials classes according to fig. 2.6.101 in individual cases.

The fire resistance classes are designated with different letters depending on the type of component (see table 2.6.102).

2.6.100   Standard temperature curve

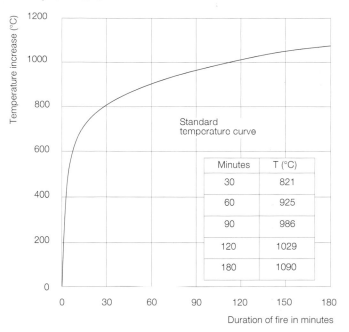

Minutes	T (°C)
30	821
60	925
90	986
120	1029
180	1090

Duration of fire in minutes

2.6.101   Designation of fire resistance classes in conjunction with materials used according to DIN 4102 part 2

Fire resistance class to table 2.2.3-2	Building materials class to DIN 4102 pt 1 of the materials used for		Designation[2]	Code
	essential parts[1] of components	other parts not classed as essential parts[1] of components	Components of	
F 30	B	B	Fire resistance class F 30	F 30-B
	A	B	Fire resistance class F 30 and with essential parts made from incombustible materials[1]	F 30-AB
	A	A	Fire resistance class F 30 and made from incombustible materials	F 30-A
F 60	B	B	Fire resistance class F 60	F 60-B
	A	B	Fire resistance class F 60 and with essential parts made from incombustible materials[1]	F 60-AB
	A	A	Fire resistance class F 60 and made from incombustible materials	F 60-A
F 90	B	B	Fire resistance class F 90	F 90-B
	A	B	Fire resistance class F 90 and with essential parts made from incombustible materials[1]	F 90-AB
	A	A	Fire resistance class F 90 and made from incombustible materials	F 90-A
F 120	B	B	Fire resistance class F 120	F 120-B
	A	B	Fire resistance class F 120 and with essential parts made from incombustible materials[1]	F 120-AB
	A	A	Fire resistance class F 120 and made from incombustible materials	F 120-A
F 180	B	B	Fire resistance class F 180	F 180-B
	A	B	Fire resistance class F 180 and with essential parts made from incombustible materials[1]	F 180-AB
	A	A	Fire resistance class F 180 and made from incombustible materials	F 180-A

[1] Essential parts include:
a) All loadbearing parts and those contributing to stability; for non-loadbearing parts also the parts that contribute to their stability (e.g. frames for non-loadbearing walls).
b) In enclosing components a continuous layer in the component plane that may not be destroyed in the test according to this standard.
In floors this layer must be at least 50 mm thick in total; voids within this layer are permissible.
When assessing the fire behaviour of materials, surface coatings or other surface treatments need not be considered.

[2] This designation concerns only the fire resistance of the component; the building authority requirements for materials used in fitting out the interior, and which are connected to the component, are not affected by this.

2.6.102   Codes for designating components when specifying the fire resistance class

Component	Code for designating fire resistance class
Walls, floors, columns, beams	F
External walls	W
Fire protection closures, e.g. fire doors	T
Ventilation ducts, fire stops (fire protection closures)	L/K
Glazing	G

2.6.103   Types of walls: examples of plan layouts for residential and industrial buildings, after Hahn

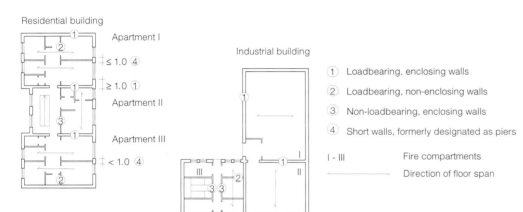

2.6.104   Overview of building authority fire protection regulations

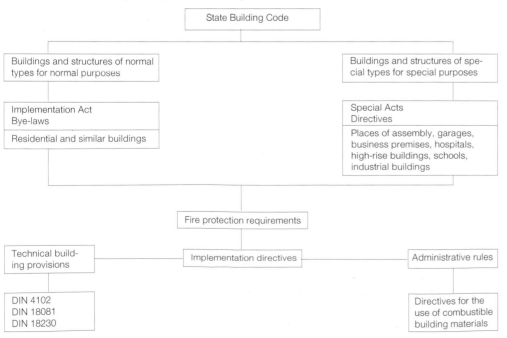

Types and functions of walls

In terms of the function of a wall, for fire protection purposes we distinguish between loadbearing and non-loadbearing, and between enclosing and non-enclosing walls. Figure 2.6.103 illustrates these terms using practical examples [68].

A *non-loadbearing wall* is a plate-type component that – also in the case of fire – is essentially loaded by its own weight and does not provide buckling restraint to loadbearing walls. However, it must transfer wind loads acting on its surface to loadbearing components.

A *loadbearing wall* is a plate-type component mainly loaded in compression for carrying both vertical and horizontal loads. Walls contributing to the stability of the building or other loadbearing components are to be considered as loadbearing walls from the point of view of fire protection.

An *enclosing wall* is a wall, for example, along an escape route, adjacent to a staircase, or a party wall or fire wall. Such walls serve to prevent fire spreading from one room to the next and are therefore subjected to fire on only one side. Enclosing walls may be loadbearing or non-loadbearing.

A *non-enclosing wall* is a wall subjected to fire on two, three or four sides during a fire.

Requirements

The fundamentals of building authority fire protection requirements are contained in the respective State Building Codes and the associated statutes, as well as in technical building provisions and administrative rules. Figure 2.6.104 explains the relationships and mutual influences. All State Building Codes, the corresponding implementation acts and administrative rules make a distinction between normal buildings for normal purposes, e.g. housing, and those of special construction for special purposes, e.g. places of assembly, hospitals, industrial buildings.

Normal buildings for normal purposes make a distinction between the different types of buildings. The classification in building classes according to fig. 2.6.105 depends on ladder access for the fire brigade and so is directly related to the height of the building.

Buildings of special construction or for special purposes are dealt with only in principle in the building codes. The State Building Codes are complemented by special acts and directives that take into account the special circumstances of high-rise buildings, places of assembly, restaurants, hospitals, business premises, schools and industrial buildings. The relationship between the requirements partly described in the State Building Codes and the abstract classification according to part 2 and other parts of DIN 4102 is carried out on the basis of the definitions contained in some State Building Codes, or according to the list of standard building material. The relationship between construction law and DIN 4102 is given in table 2.6.106. The primary component of the fire safety concept in the building code is the compartmentation principle: fire should be restricted to as small an area as possible. The first "fire compartment" is the functional unit, e.g. a whole apartment in an apartment block, bounded by the floors, party walls and staircase walls. At the very least, the fire should not spread to neighbouring buildings, which can be achieved by relatively high requirements being placed on the fire walls. In addition, the State Building Codes demand that large buildings themselves be subdivided into fire compartments. However, the compartmentation principle can be fully effective only when the openings necessary for the use of building are appropriately closed. This applies to building service penetrations, e.g. electric cables, pipes, as well as to openings such as flaps, doors and gates.

A number of primary fire protection requirements for components in residential buildings are given in table 2.6.107. The example given here is taken from the State Building Code for North Rhine-Westphalia (there are sometimes slight differences between the codes of the individual federal states in Germany); this building code was adopted in its entirety for all the federal states of former East Germany. Free-standing residential buildings with one housing unit (building class 1) are not included in the table because there are no requirements for the fire resistance classes of components in such buildings. However, the basic requirement, that no highly flammable building materials may be employed, still applies. Consequently, the thermal insulation materials used in walls with external or internal thermal insulation layer and twin-leaf masonry with additional thermal insulation between the masonry leaves must comply with building materials class B 2 or higher.

Fire walls

Fire walls according to DIN 4102 part 3 must comply with the following enhanced requirements:

- They must be built from materials of building materials class A to DIN 4102 part 1.
- They must comply with the requirements of fire resistance class F 90 or higher to DIN 4102 part 2; loadbearing walls must satisfy this requirement under concentric and eccentric loading.
- Fire walls must remain stable and fulfil their enclosing function after being subjected to an impact load (3 x 200 kg of lead shot in sack).

However, it is not only adequate to ensure that fire walls comply with test requirements – they must be properly located in practice and properly constructed.

2.6.105 Classification of buildings in five building classes according to the building codes

Building class				
1	2	3	4	5
Free-standing residential building 1 housing unit	Low-rise buildings Ladder access H ≤ 8 m ≤ 2 housing units	≥ 3 housing units	Other buildings H > 8 m	High-rise buildings
Fire brigade access possible with scaling ladder for FFL ≤ 7 m			For FFL > 7m ≤ 22 m	At least 1 occupied room > 22 m above FFL

2.6.106 Designations according to DIN 4102 and construction law

DIN 4102 designation	Code	Building authority designation
Fire resistance class F 30	F 30-B	Fire-retardant
Fire resistance class F 30 with essential parts made from incombustible materials	F 30-AB	Fire-retardant with loadbearing parts made from incombustible materials
Fire resistance class F 30 and made from incombustible materials	F 30-A	Fire-retardant and made from incombustible materials
Fire resistance class F 90 with essential parts made from incombustible materials	F 90-AB	Fire-resistant
Fire resistance class F 90 and made from incombustible materials	F 90-A	Fire-resistant and made from incombustible materials

2.6.107 Summary of the most important requirements for structural fire protection for components customary in buildings using the North Rhine-Westphalia Building Code as an example

Class of building		2	3	4
Type of building		Residential of low height (FFL ≤ 7 m) ≤ 2 housing units	Any building ≥ 3 housing units	Other buildings apart from from high-rise buildings
Loadbearing walls	Roof	0[1]	0[1]	0[1]
	Other	F 30-B	F 30-AB[2]	F 90-AB
	Basement	F 30-AB	F 90-AB	F 90-AB
Non-loadbearing external walls		0	0	A or F 30-B
External wall		0	0	B1
Cladding		B 2 —>suitable measures		
Building end walls		F 90-AB (F 30-B) + (F90-B)	BW F 90-AB	BW
Floors	Roof	0[1]	0[1]	0[1]
	Other	F 30-B	F 30-AB[3]	F 90-AB
	Basement	F 30-B	F 90-AB	F 90-AB
Party walls – 40 m building compartments		F 90-AB	BW F 90-AB	BW
Party walls between apartments	Roof	F 30-B	F 30-B	F 30-B
	Other	F 30-B	F 60-AB	F 90-AB
Staircase	Roof	0	0	0
	Floor	0	F 30-AB	F 90-AB
	Walls	0	F 90-AB	BW
	Cladding	0	A	A
Stairs	Loadbearing parts	0	0	F 90-A
Generally accessible corridors as escape routes	Walls	-	F 30-B	F 30-AB F 30-AB
	Cladding	-	0	A
Open walkways adjacent external walls	Walls, floors	-	0	F 90-AB
	Cladding	-	0	A

[1] Inside of roof F 30-B for buildings with gable facing the street
[2] F 30-B for buildings with ≤ 2 storeys above ground level
[3] F 30-B for buildings with ≤ 2 storeys above ground level
  F 30-B/A for buildings with ≥ 3 storeys above ground level

2.6.108   Fire protection requirements in the vicinity of fire walls

Component	Requirements
Fire walls	F 90-A
	+ impact load 3 x 3000 Nm
Loadbearing and bracing components	F 90
No. of openings	No restriction
Closures to openings	T 90 doors (self-closing mechanism)
	F 90 fire protection glazing
	S 90 fire stop to cable penetrations
	R 90 fire stop to pipe penetrations
Arrangement of fire walls	At the boundary with a neighbour
The respective Federal State Building Code	Between buildings forming a terrace
must be adhered to	Within large buildings
	Depending on height of building and roof covering:
	≤ 3 full storeys extending to underside of roof covering
	> 3 full storeys at least 300 mm above roof
	soft roof covering at least 500 mm above roof
	Components may intrude, provided the remaining cross-section
	of the wall remains sealed and stable to F 90 standard.

2.6.109   Fire protection requirements for ventilated curtain wall facades

Component	Required building materials class to DIN 4102		
	n ≤ 2 full storeys	n > 2 full storeys, < high-rise buildings	high-rise buildings
Cladding	B 2	B 1	A
Supporting construction	B 2	B 2 [1)2)]	A
Thermal insulation	B 2	B 1	A [3)]
Means of fixing	A [4)]	A [4)]	A [4)]

[1)] There are no restrictions on using B 2 building materials for frame-like supporting constructions, provided the gap between cladding and insulation does not exceed 40 mm and window/door reveals are protected by class A building materials.
[2)] The Bavarian Building Code permits timber supporting constructions for buildings up to 30 m high.
[3)] Does not apply to elements for retaining layers of insulation.
[4)] Does not apply to anchor systems covered by a building authority certificate.

2.6.110   Single- and twin-leaf fire walls to DIN 4102 part 4 table 45. Permissible slenderness, min. wall thickness and min. spacing of leaves (fire load on one side). Values in brackets apply to walls with plaster. Design to DIN 1053 parts 1 and 2 with permissible slenderness ratio h_s/d. The eccentricity e may not exceed d/3.

Type of wall		Masonry without plaster Min. thickness d (mm) for single-leaf construction	with plaster twin-leaf[6)] construction
Walls of masonry[3)] to DIN 1053 parts 1 and 2 using normal-weight mortar of mortar group II, IIa or III, IIIa.			
Masonry units to DIN 105 part 1 of gross density class	≥ 1.4	240	2 x 175
	≥ 1.0	300	2 x 200
		(240)	(2 x 175)
DIN 105 part 2 of gross density class	≥ 0.8	365[3)]	2 x 240
		(300)[3)]	(2 x 175)
Masonry units to DIN 106 part 1[1)] and DIN 106 part 1 A1[1)] as well as part 2 of gross density class	≥ 1.8	240[2)]	2 x 175[5)]
	≥ 1.4	240	2 x 175
	≥ 0.9	300	2 x 200
		(300)	(2 x 175)
	= 0.8	300	2 x 240
			(2 x 175)
Masonry units to DIN 4165 of gross density class	≥ 0.6	300	2 x 240
	≥ 0.6[4)]	240	(2 x 175)
	≥ 0.5[6)]	300	2 x 240
Masonry units to DIN 18151, 18152 and 18153 of gross density class	≥ 0.8	240	2 x 175
		(175)	(2 x 175)
	≥ 0.6	300	2 x 240
		(240)	(2 x 175)

[1)] Also with thin-bed mortar.
[2)] d = 175 mm when using thin-bed mortar and gauged brickwork.
[3)] Utilization factor α_2 ≤ 0.6 when using lightweight mortar.
[4)] Applies to thin-bed mortar and gauged brickwork with mortar to perpends and bed joints.
[5)] d = 150 mm when using thin-bed mortar and gauged brickwork.
[6)] Applies to thin-bed mortar and gauged brickwork with tongue and groove only in the case of mortar to perpends and bed joints.

The fire protection requirements for fire walls are summarized in 2.6.108. DIN 4102 part 4 contains details of permissible slenderness ratios and minimum thicknesses of fire walls and their junctions with other components.

Complex party walls
Complex party walls are merely referred to in a footnote in DIN 4102 part 3 because this is an insurance industry term. The main point to be noted is that the provisions of the insurers, with limitations on openings, call for fire resistance class F 180. Complex walls must pass through all storeys without any offsets. Components may not intrude into nor bypass these walls.

Classification of proven components
DIN 4102 part 4 contains details of building materials, components and special components whose fire behaviour has been classified on the basis of tests. The products included in the standard have already been verified in terms of their behaviour in fire. The fire protection classification of the walls is carried out according to:

· wall material
· wall thickness
· type of fire (from just one side or from more than one side)
· utilization of the load-carrying capacity of the wall

If a component is not fully utilized, its load-carrying capacity during a fire is greater than when it is utilized 100%. Therefore, in the standard we distinguish between the utilization factors α_2 = 1.0 (100% utilization), α_2 = 0.6 (60% utilization) and α_2 = 0.2 (20% utilization). The classification of walls, shallow lintels and channel blocks filled with concrete can be found in tables 38-42 of DIN 4102 part 4. The information in the tables applies to masonry according to DIN 1053. Plaster on the side facing the fire prolongs the duration of fire resistance. The values in brackets in the tables relating to wall thicknesses refer to plastered walls because certain plasters have a positive influence on the fire behaviour of masonry walls. Twin-leaf walls only require plaster on the outer faces. The tables are valid for all types of perpends according to DIN 1053 part 1, i.e. for perpends fully filled with mortar, for "tipped and tailed" perpends, and perpends without mortar (interlock or tongue and groove). Perforations in masonry units or wall panels may not run perpendicular to the plane of the wall. Masonry readily satisfies the requirements of fire protection, generally through the wall thickness required for structural or building science reasons. Therefore, the extensive tables in DIN 4102 part 4 can be considerably reduced by specifying fire resistance class F 90 and 100%

degree of utilization. Tables 2.6.111-113 specify the minimum thicknesses required to achieve fire resistance class F 90 employing masonry of standard units. Besides the fire resistance class, fire walls must also comply with the conditions given in table 2.6.110 with regard to slenderness ratio and wall thickness. Claddings may not be used in order to reduce the specified wall thicknesses. Thinner walls than those given in DIN 4102 part 4 have been proved for fire walls of clay, calcium silicate, autoclaved aerated concrete and lightweight concrete units in tests to DIN 4102 part 3 [7, 76, 134, 209]. Reference [67] contains comprehensive information on fire protection in masonry structures with practical examples.

External walls with thermal insulation
Single-leaf external walls with an external, rendered thermal insulation layer (thermal insulation composite system) are assessed in fire protection terms according to the type of insulation material used.

Thermal insulation composite systems with insulation materials of not readily flammable polystyrene particle foam (building materials class B 1) and a maximum thickness of 100 mm complying with a general building authority certificate may be used on masonry up to the high-rise building limit. Thermal insulation composite systems using mineral materials, e.g. mineral wool products of building materials class A 1 or A 2, are considered as a coat of plaster when classifying the wall. In terms of fire protection, the external wall is equivalent to a plastered wall without thermal insulation. Thermal insulation composite systems with insulation materials of building materials class B 2 may be employed only on buildings with a maximum of two full storeys. The fire protection requirements for curtain wall ventilated facades depend on the height of the building; the requirements with respect to building materials classes for facade components are summarized in table 2.6.109. The fire protection requirements still apply for ventilated external

wall claddings upon which doubt has been cast by certain tests [22].
Thermal insulation materials of building materials class B 2 may be used up to the high-rise building limit for partial- or full-fill cavity walls. In contrast to this, buildings of medium height (7-22 m) require that continuous layers of F 30-AB and F 90-AB components must consist of class A building materials.
Flammable insulation materials of building materials class B 2 are permitted in the case of internal insulation for buildings up to 22 m height. Special regulations apply to escape routes.

2.6.111 Loadbearing, enclosing walls of masonry to DIN 4102 part 4 table 39. Values in brackets apply to walls plastered both sides. Utilization factor $\alpha_2 = 1.0$

Construction features	Min. thickness (mm) for fire resistance class F 90
d_1 / d / d_1	
Walls	
Autoclaved aerated concrete Blocks & gauged brickwork to DIN 4165	175
Gross density class ≥ 0.5 using [1][2]	(150)
Lightweight concrete Hollow blocks to DIN 18151 Solid bricks & blocks to DIN 18152	175
Concrete masonry units to DIN 18153 Gross density class ≥ 0.6 using [1][3]	(140)
Clay bricks Solid & vertically perforated to DIN 105 pt 1 using [1]	175
	(115)
Clay bricks Lightweight & vertically perforated to DIN 105 pt 2 Gross density class ≥ 0.8 using [1][3]	
Perforation types A & B	(115)
Lightweight vertically perforated bricks type W	(240)
Calcium silicate Solid, perforated, blocks, hollow blocks & gauged brickwork to DIN 106 pt 1 & 1 A1	115
	(115)
Facing bricks to DIN 106 pt 2 using [1][2][4]	

[1] Normal-weight mortar
[2] Thin-bed mortar
[3] Lightweight mortar
[4] The values apply only to masonry of solid bricks, blocks and gauged brickwork when 3.0 < exist σ ≤ 4.5 N/mm².

2.6.112 Min. thickness d of loadbearing, non-enclosing walls of masonry to DIN 4102 part 4 table 40 (fire load on more than one side). Values in brackets apply to walls plastered both sides. Utilization factor $\alpha_2 = 1.0$

Construction features	Min. thickness (mm) for fire resistance class F 90
d_1 / d / d_1	
Autoclaved aerated concrete Blocks & gauged brickwork to DIN 4165	240
Gross density class ≥ 0.5 ucing [1][2]	(175)
Lightweight concrete Hollow blocks to DIN 18151 Solid bricks & blocks to DIN 18152	240
Concrete masonry units to DIN 18153 Gross density class ≥ 0.6 using [1][3]	(175)
Clay bricks Solid & vertically perforated to DIN 105 pt 1 1 using [1]	240
	(115)
Clay bricks Lightweight vertically perforated to DIN 105 pt 2 Gross density class ≥ 0.8 using 1)3)	
Perforation types A & B	(115)
Lightweight vertically perforated bricks type W Utilization factor $\alpha_2 = 1.0$	(240)
Calcium silicate Solid, perforated, blocks, hollow blocks & gauged brickwork to DIN 106 pt 1 & 1 A1 DIN 106 pt 1 A1	140
	(115)
Facing bricks to DIN 106 pt 2 using [1][2]	

[1] Normal-weight mortar
[2] Thin-bed mortar
[3] Lightweight mortar
[4] The values apply only to masonry of solid bricks, blocks and gauged brickwork when 3.0 < exist σ ≤ 4.5 N/mm².

2.6.113 Non-loadbearing, enclosing walls of masonry or wall panels to DIN 4102 part 4 table 38. Values in brackets apply to walls plastered both sides

Construction features	Min. thickness (mm) for fire resistance class F 90
Walls	mm
Autoclaved aerated concrete	100[1]
Blocks & gauged brickwork to DIN 4165	(75)
Panels & gauged brickwork elements to DIN 4166	
Lightweight concrete	95
Hollow wall elements to DIN 18148	(70)
Hollow blocks to DIN 18151 Solid bricks & blocks to DIN 18152 Wall elements to DIN 18162 Concrete masonry units to DIN 18153	
Clay bricks	115
Solid & vertically perforated to DIN 105 pt 1	(100)
Lightweight vertically perforated to DIN 105 pt 2 High-strength bricks & engineering bricks to DIN 105 pt 3 High-strength engineering bricks to DIN 105 pt 4	
Calcium silicate	115
Solid, perforated, blocks, hollow blocks & gauged brickwork to DIN 106 pt 1 & 1 A1	(100)
Gauged brickwork to DIN 106 pt 1 & DIN 106 pt 1 A1 Facing bricks to DIN 106 pt 2	

[1] d ≥ 50 mm when using thin-bed mortars.

Units and symbols for building science

Symbol	Designation	Unit
A	Area	m^2
F_m	Moisture correction factor	–
F_C	Reduction factor for sunshading	–
H_T	Specific transmission heat loss	W/K
L	Heat conduction	W/K
Q	Heat, heat energy	J or Ws
Q	Annual heating energy requirement	kWh/a
Q_h	Annual heating requirement	kWh/a
Q_g	Heat gain	kWh/a
Q_l	Heat loss	kWh/a
Q_p	Primary energy requirement	kWh/a
Q_r	Energy requirement from renewable sources	kWh/a
Q_t	Total heat losses due to heating system	kWh/a
Q_w	Energy requirement for hot water provision	kWh/a
R	Thermal resistance	m^2K/W
R_{si}, R_{se}	Internal/External surface resistance	m^2K/W
R_T	Total thermal resistance (air-to-air resistance)	m^2K/W
S	Solar heat penetration	–
U (formerly k in Germany)	Thermal transmittance	W/m^2K
U_f	Thermal transmittance, window frame	W/m^2K
U_g	Thermal transmittance, glazing	W/m^2K
U_w	Thermal transmittance, window	W/m^2K
V	Volume	m^3
Z	Water vapour diffusion resistance	m^2hPa/kg
a	Temperature diffusivity	m^2/s
b	Heat penetration coefficient	$J/m^2Ks^{0.5}$
c	Specific heat capacity	J/kgK
d	Thickness	m
e, e_p	Cost index related to primary energy requirement	–
f_{Rsi}	Temperature factor	–
g	Solar total energy transmittance	–
g	Water vapour diffusion flow rate	kg/m^2h
h	Thermal surface resistance coefficient	W/m^2K
m	Mass	kg
$m_{W,T}$	Area-related condensation mass	kg/m^2
$m_{W,V}$	Area-related evaporation mass	kg/m^2
n	Air change rate	No./h
p, p_s	Water vapour partial pressure, water vapour saturation pressure	Pa
p_i, p_e	Water vapour partial pressure, internal/external	Pa
q	Heat flow rate	W/m^2
s_d	Water vapour diffusion-equivalent air layer thickness	m
t	Time	d
u	Mass-related moisture content	kg/kg
w	Water absorption coefficient	$kg/m^2h^{0.5}$
η (eta)	Degree of utilization	–
ϑ (theta)	Temperature	°C
ϑ_i, ϑ_e	Air temperature, internal/external	°C
ϑ_{si}	Internal surface temperature	°C
λ (lambda)	Thermal conductivity	W/mK
μ (my)	Water vapour diffusion resistance index	–
ρ (rho)	Gross/bulk density	kg/m^3
ϕ (phi)	Heat flow	W
ϕ	Relative humidity	–
χ (chi)	Discrete thermal transmittance	W/K
ψ (psi)	Linear thermal transmittance	W/mK
ψ	Volume-related moisture content	m^3/m^3
J	Sound intensity	W/m^2
L	Sound pressure level, sound level	dB
R	Sound reduction index	dB
R_W	Airborne sound insulation index	dB
f	Frequency	Hz
p	Sound pressure	Pa

m	metre
W	Watt
K	Kelvin
J	Joule
a	year
s	second
h	hour
P	Pascal
kg	kilogram
d	day
°C	degree Celsius
dB	decibel
Hz	Hertz

Part 3 · Construction details

Contents

Preliminary remarks

Masonry continues to be the most popular form of construction in Central Europe, especially for housing. With its diverse architectural options and rich variety of different types of construction, masonry is just as fashionable as ever. Indeed, its good building science properties have increased the vocabulary of its architectural manifestations. The following chapter, "Construction Details", illustrates the diverse applications of masonry. Three different types of wall were chosen for the details:

• A single-leaf rendered wall

• A partial-fill cavity wall (outer leaf of facing masonry, air space, insulation, inner load-bearing leaf)

• A full-fill cavity wall (outer leaf of facing masonry)

A schematic overview of the details presents the most important building details for the three different types of wall. The details shaded grey are shown enlarged at a scale of 1:10 in the subsequent catalogue.
In designing these details, the prime objectives were dependable engineering qualities and architectural clarity.
Energy-efficient building demands alternative types of wall construction with ever better, ever thicker thermal insulation. Therefore, cavity insulation in conjunction with an independent outer leaf 240 mm thick was included in the catalogue of details as this form of wall construction is becoming increasingly widespread. It provides – in masonry – a reliable form of construction in terms of building science but still permits all the options of facing masonry in the design of the actual masonry skin.

Roof constructions include diffusion-tight layers where necessary. In the other cases the details employ diffusion-resistant membranes. The use of roofing felts sufficiently open to diffusion means that a membrane on the inside is no longer necessary, provided the layers of the construction below the thermal insulation, e.g. chipboard, plasterboard, form an adequate barrier to diffusion. However, it should not be forgotten that the necessary degree of airtightness must still be guaranteed.

The details shown do not relate to specific construction projects but instead, in conjunction with the explanatory texts, are intended to draw attention to possible problem zones and illustrate feasible solutions. Their suitability for the respective climatic conditions must be checked in each individual case. Details which only vary as a result of the different types of wall construction are shown schematically in the overview of the details.

3.1. **Flat roof**

Parapet to warm deck
with sheet metal capping

3.2. **Flat roof**

Parapet to warm deck
with precast concrete
coping

3.3 **Flat roof**

Parapet to warm deck
with steel section

**Single-leaf rendered
masonry**

365 mm masonry

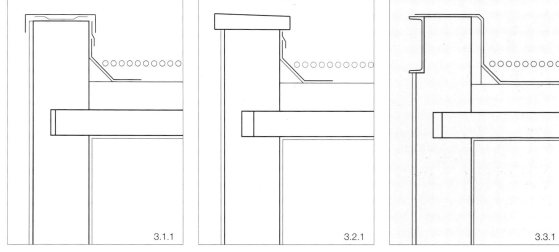

3.1.1

3.2.1

3.3.1

Partial-fill cavity wall

115 mm outer leaf of facing
brickwork
55 mm air space
80 mm insulation
240 mm inner leaf

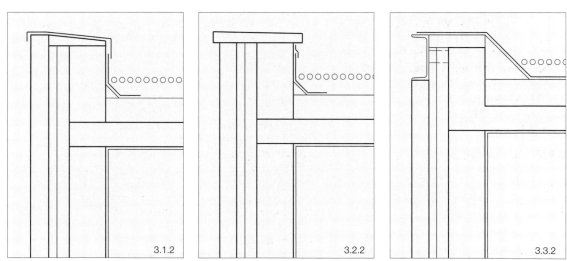

3.1.2

3.2.2

3.3.2

Full-fill cavity wall

240 mm outer leaf of facing
brickwork
135 mm insulation
175 mm inner leaf

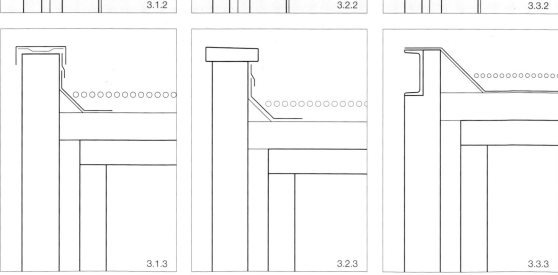

3.1.3

3.2.3

3.3.3

	3.4 Shallow pitched roof Parapet to cold deck with sheet metal capping	**3.5 Pitched roof** Eaves	**3.6 Pitched roof** Verge without roof overhang
Single-leaf rendered masonry 365 mm masonry	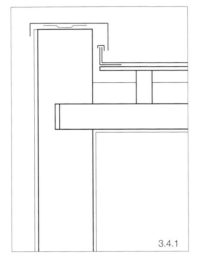 3.4.1	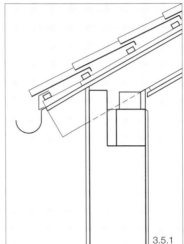 3.5.1	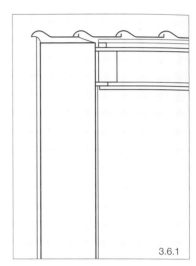 3.6.1
Partial-fill cavity wall 115 mm outer leaf of facing brickwork 55 mm air space 80 mm insulation 240 mm inner leaf	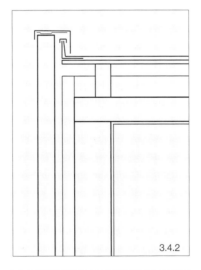 3.4.2	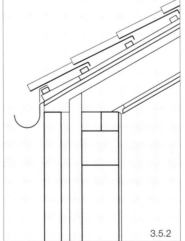 3.5.2	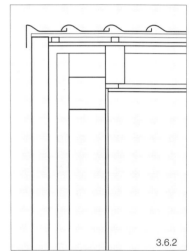 3.6.2
Full-fill cavity wall 240 mm outer leaf of facing brickwork 135 mm insulation 175 mm inner leaf	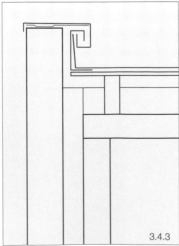 3.4.3	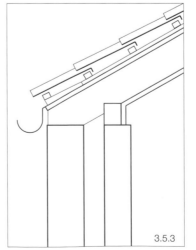 3.5.3	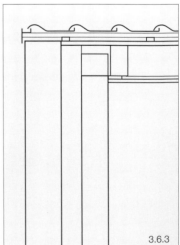 3.6.3

| 3.7 | **Pitched roof** | 3.8 | **Pitched roof** | 3.9 | **Pitched roof** | 3.10 | **Pitched roof** |

Verge
with roof overhang

Verge
with masonry parapet

Junction with wall

Chimney

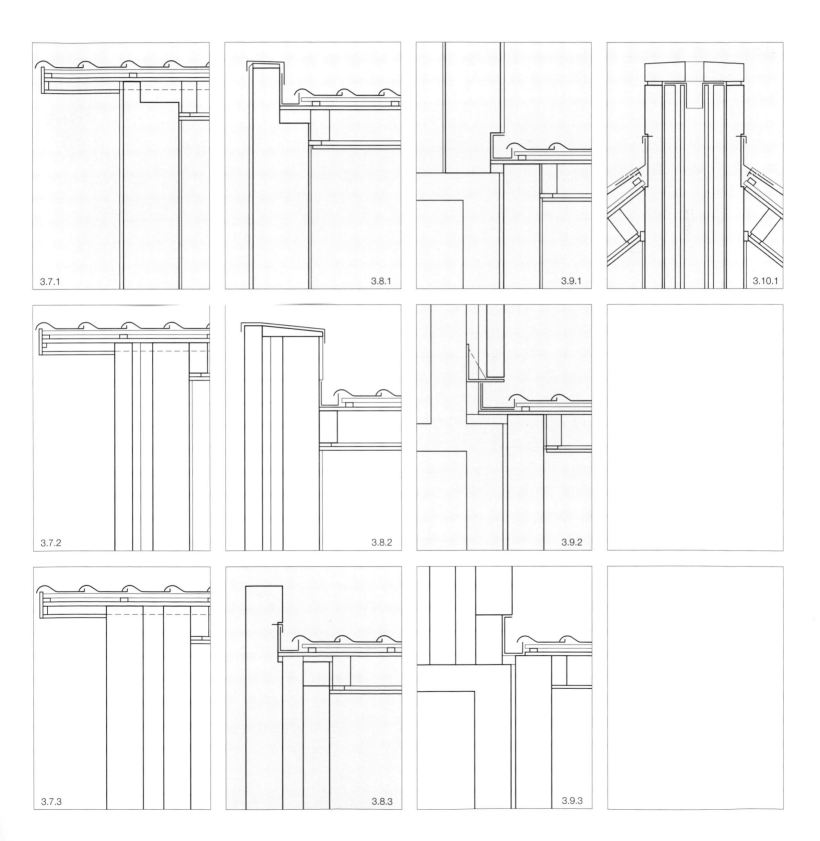

3.7.1

3.8.1

3.9.1

3.10.1

3.7.2

3.8.2

3.9.2

3.7.3

3.8.3

3.9.3

	3.11 Floor junction	**3.12 Openings** Window head and reveals without shoulder	**3.13 Openings** Window head and reveals without shoulder with roller blind

Single-leaf rendered masonry

365 mm masonry

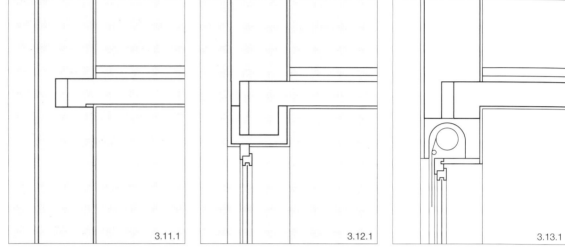

3.11.1 · 3.12.1 · 3.13.1

Partial-fill cavity wall

115 mm outer leaf of facing brickwork
55 mm air space
80 mm insulation
240 mm inner leaf

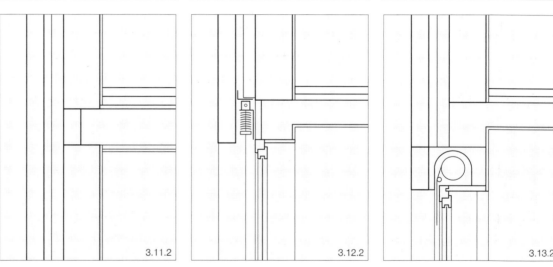

3.11.2 · 3.12.2 · 3.13.2

Full-fill cavity wall

240 mm outer leaf of facing brickwork
135 mm insulation
175 mm inner leaf

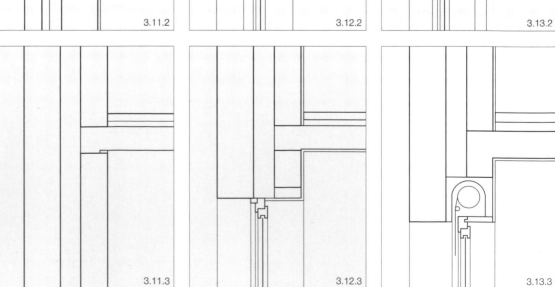

3.11.3 · 3.12.3 · 3.13.3

3.14 Openings

Window fitted behind
shoulder

3.15 Openings

Window
with peripheral sheet
metal lining

3.16 Openings

Door head and jambs
without shoulder

3.17 Openings

Door head and jambs
with shoulder

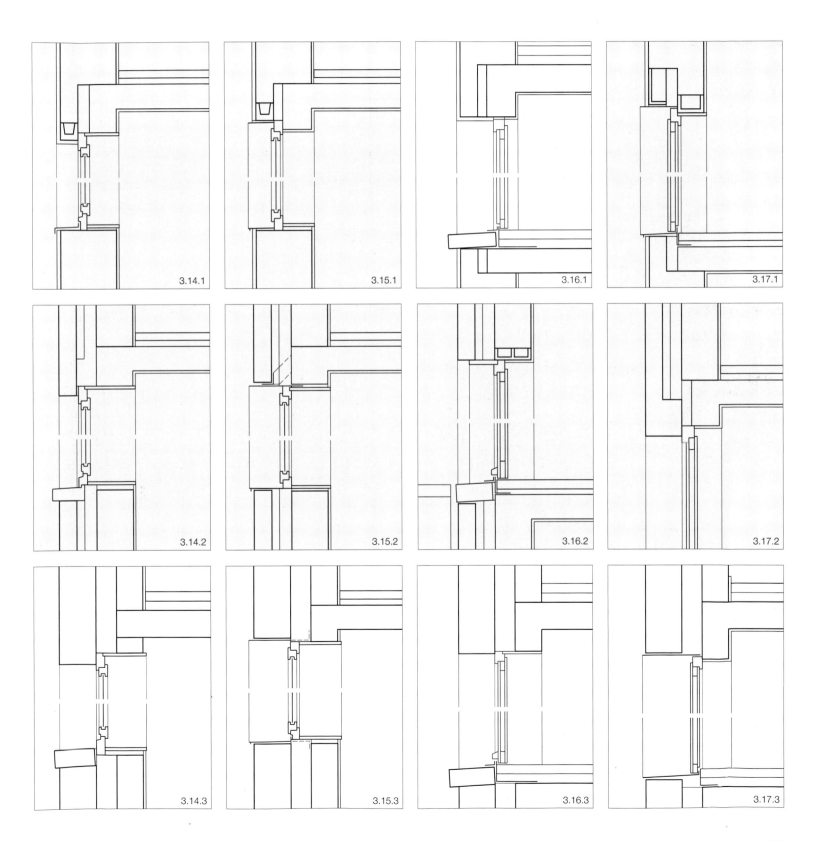

3.14.1

3.15.1

3.16.1

3.17.1

3.14.2

3.15.2

3.16.2

3.17.2

3.14.3

3.15.3

3.16.3

3.17.3

3.18 Openings

Door to terrace

3.19 Balconies

3.20 Junction with terrace

Outer edge

Single-leaf rendered masonry

365 mm masonry

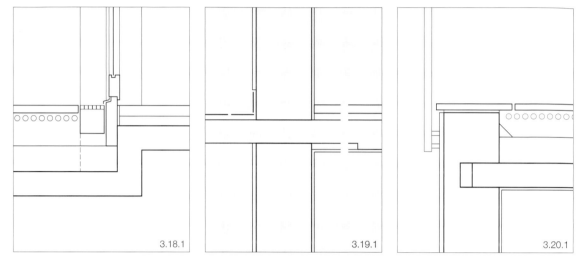

3.18.1

3.19.1

3.20.1

Partial-fill cavity wall

115 mm outer leaf of facing brickwork
55 mm air space
80 mm insulation
240 mm inner leaf

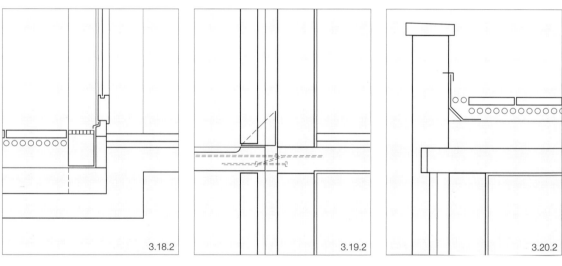

3.18.2

3.19.2

3.20.2

Full-fill cavity wall

240 mm outer leaf of facing brickwork
135 mm insulation
175 mm inner leaf

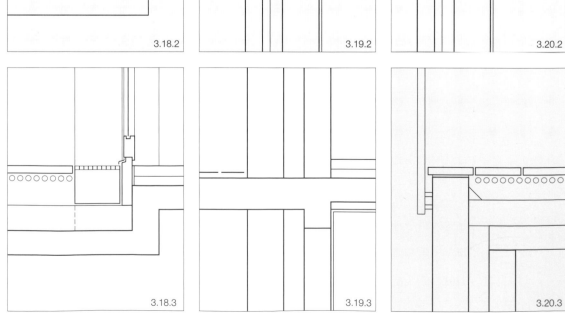

3.18.3

3.19.3

3.20.3

3.21 Plinth

Masonry basement
Junction with plinth

3.22 Stairs

Internal stairs
Entrance to building
Stairs to basement

3.23 Special details

Re-entrant corner
Corner
Free-standing walls

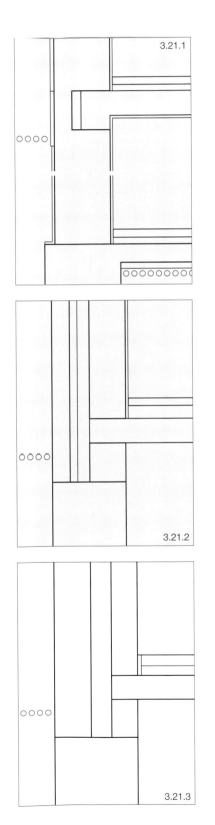

3.21.1

3.21.2

3.21.3

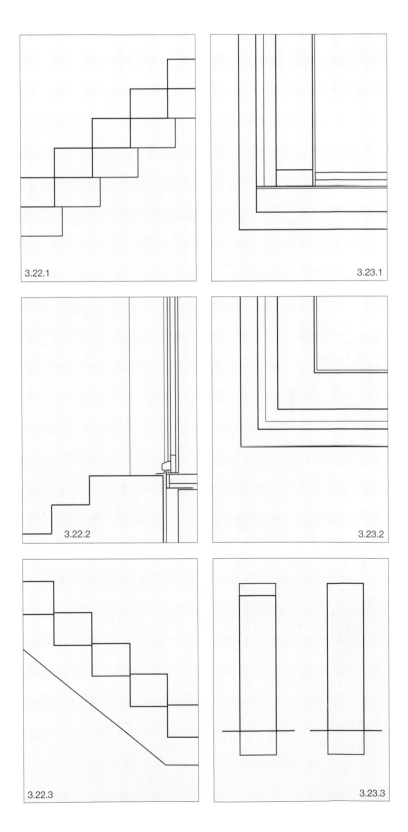

3.22.1

3.23.1

3.22.2

3.23.2

3.22.3

3.23.3

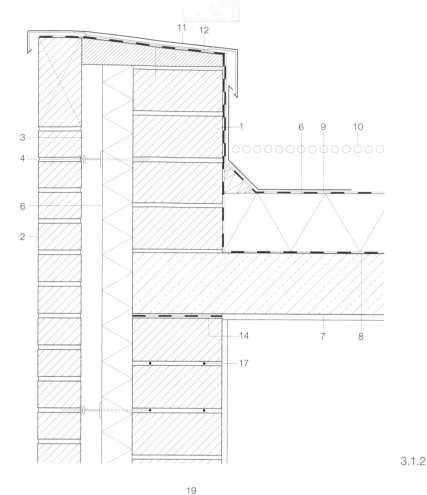

3.1.2

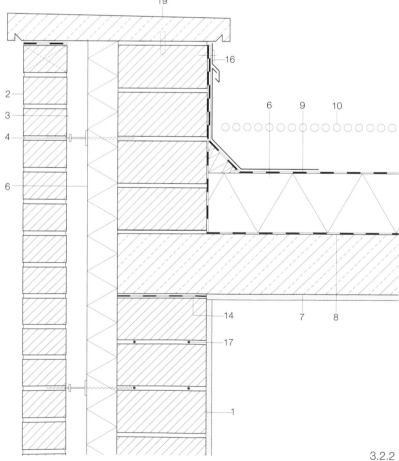

3.2.2

Flat roof
Parapet to warm deck

3.1.2 Parapet with sheet metal capping on twin-leaf masonry
3.2.2 Parapet with stone coping on twin-leaf masonry
3.3.1 Parapet with steel section on single-leaf masonry
3.3.2 Parapet with steel section on twin-leaf masonry

The most common finish to the top of a masonry wall is the capping of sheet metal – copper, titanium-zinc or galvanized steel. This is usually fitted over a suitably sized and shaped timber section, which should be fixed only to the loadbearing inner leaf and may not transfer any load to the outer leaf of facing brickwork. The capping should be designed with a fall towards the roof surface. In architectural terms it is primarily the height of the visible front lip of the capping which is relevant, as this forms the upper boundary of the facade. It is also possible to provide a welted edge at this point, although this does deviate from the stipulations of the DIN standard.

Finishing the top of a wall with a prefabricated coping creates a distinct boundary, often of a different colour. Prefabricated elements offer diverse architectural options in terms of shape and material – from a simple precast concrete coping to dressed natural stone.
When providing a prefabricated coping to a twin-leaf wall, it must be ensured that it is fixed only to the loadbearing 240 mm wall; it must be able to slide where it bears on the outer leaf. It is advisable for the coping to have a fall to the inside. The expansion joints between the individual coping elements must be designed and carefully built so that no water can penetrate through to the masonry. A stepped joint or a damp proof course beneath the coping is advisable.
To reduce the thermal bridge effect, it is recommended to use masonry units with a low gross density (thermal conductivity) for building the parapet.

Please refer to "Part 2 · Fundamentals" for details of the ring beam.

The inclusion of a steel section adds a special emphasis to the edge of a flat roof on a masonry building. The top of the wall is highlighted and, with an appropriate choice of colour, can contrast with the wall below. However, this detail is not without its problems.

A steel section can be fixed directly to the top of a single-leaf, rendered masonry wall. However, it must be ensured that the steel section includes expansion joints and that the fixings can accommodate the movement. The movement joint between a steel section and a rendering stop bead must be sealed with a permanently elastic compound to prevent moisture from penetrating through to the masonry. It is essential to provide a covering to the steel section to stop water entering the expansion joint. The detail proposed here with UV-resistant sheeting and a clamping bar fitted to the steel section places particular demands on the sealing. Great care must be taken to ensure that the connection to the clamping bar is properly executed.

If the parapet on a building employing twin-leaf wall construction (with facing brickwork) is to be terminated with a steel section, then the detail must be carefully adapted to suit (3.3.2). First, care must be taken to ensure that the fixing of the steel section to the loadbearing leaf permits adjustment (elongated hole) and that the section can accommodate expansion. There must be no direct connection with the outer leaf. This joint must be watertight, i.e. a damp proof course must be carefully bonded to the top of the outer leaf and the steel section must be able to slide on this. The steel section must be covered as described for detail 3.3.1. Instead of UV-resistant sheeting, an additional sheet metal capping can be used, but this is a considerably more elaborate and costly detail (see "Built examples in detail", example 12).

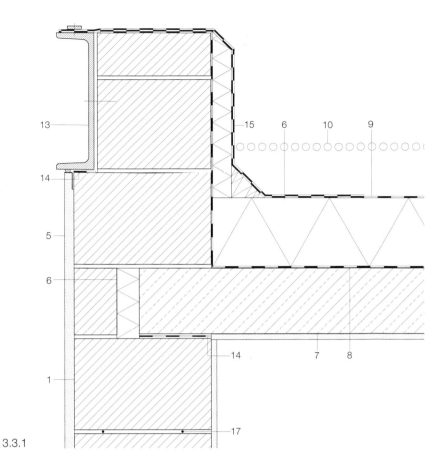

3.3.1

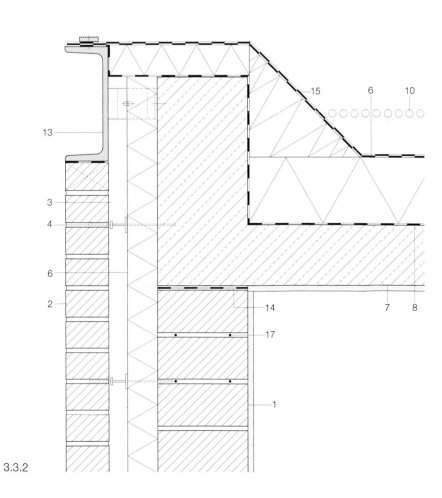

3.3.2

1   Loadbearing masonry
2   Facing brickwork
3   Air space
4   Wall tie
5   Rendering
6   Thermal insulation
7   Reinforced concrete slab
8   Diffusion-tight membrane
9   Roofing felt
10 Stone chippings
11 Sheet metal capping
12 Profiled timber section
13 Steel section
14 Foil slip joint
15 UV-resistant roofing felt
16 Clamping bar
17 Ring beam, or ring beam reinforcement

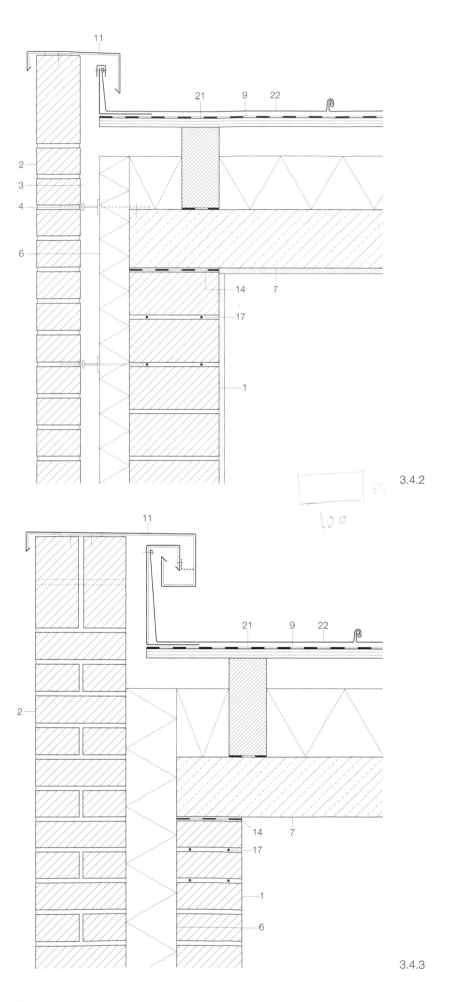

3.4.2

3.4.3

Shallow pitched roof
Parapet to cold deck

3.4.2 Parapet to cold deck on partial-fill
cavity wall
3.4.3 Parapet to cold deck on full-fill
cavity wall

Terminating a non-loadbearing outer leaf in the
form of a parapet to a cold deck requires provision to be made for adequate ventilation of
both the outer leaf and the roof construction.
However, it should be ensured that the last wall
tie for the outer leaf is fixed to the loadbearing
structure as near as possible to the top edge
of the outer leaf. The detail shown here applies
to sections of roof which fall only a short distance. If the parapet needs to be higher, then it
should be built as a twin-leaf construction to
anchor the outer leaf properly.

The parapet to a full-fill cavity wall is shown in
detail 3.4.2. In this case it is not necessary to
stabilize the outer leaf. The required cross-
section for ventilation of the cold deck
depends on the pitch of the roof. The roof covering of sheet metal with double-welted seams
is possible for a pitch $\geq 7°$. The metal roof covering is given more elaborate treatment here to
provide better protection against driving snow.

1   Loadbearing masonry
2   Facing brickwork
3   Air space
4   Wall tie
5   Rendering
6   Thermal insulation
7   Reinforced concrete slab
8   Diffusion-tight membrane
9   Roofing felt
11 Sheet metal capping
14 Foil slip joint
17 Ring beam, or ring beam reinforcement
21 Timber boarding of cold deck
22 Roof covering of metal sheeting with standing seams
23 Rafter
24 Gutter
25 Roof tiles
26 Roofing felt, open to diffusion
27 Wall plate (eaves purlin)
28 Timber boarding
29 Roofing felt, diffusion-resistant
30 Tiling battens
31 Clamping bar
37 Insect screen

Pitched roof

Pitched roof – eaves

3.5.1 Eaves detail for single-leaf masonry
3.5.2 Eaves detail for twin-leaf masonry

The eaves detail for a single-leaf, rendered masonry wall makes use of facing brickwork to conceal the ring beam and wall plate. An overhanging roof requires the rendering to continue up to the top edge of the rafters. With a parapet to the gable wall (see details 3.8.1 and 3.8.3), the verge gutter should discharge into the eaves gutter.
On the inside it must be ensured that there is an airtight connection between the diffusion-resistant roofing felt and the masonry. The example shown here employs a clamping bar.

The wall plate of the roof construction in detail 3.5.2 is placed on the outside edge of the loadbearing leaf. Masonry units are laid on top of the ring beam to conceal the wall plate and provide a consistent substrate for the plaster. The reader's attention is drawn to the airtight connection between the diffusion-resistant roofing felt and the masonry (tucked into the plaster). The remaining cross-section of the rafter above the outer leaf must be sufficient for fixing the timber boarding. The outer leaf is ventilated at the eaves. The ventilation opening must include a screen to protect against insects. With a parapet to the gable wall (see details 3.8.1 and 3.8.3), the verge gutter should discharge into the eaves gutter.
As the outer leaf forms the actual weather protection, the roof does not need to overhang the wall.

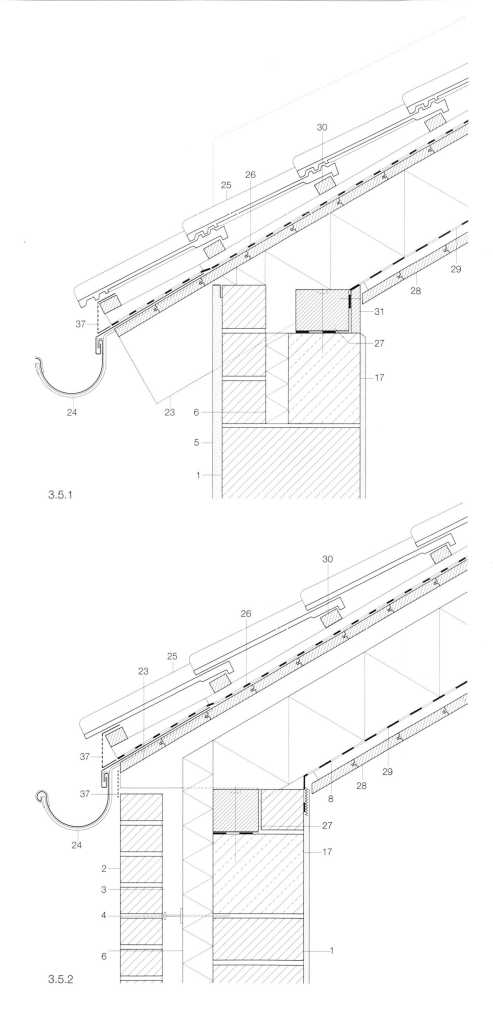

3.5.1

3.5.2

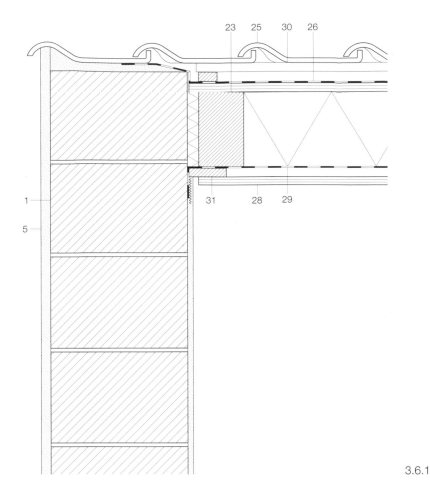

23 25 30 26

1
5

31 28 29

3.6.1

Pitched roof – verge

3.6.1 Single-leaf masonry with roof tile
 bedded in mortar
3.6.2 Partial-fill cavity wall with verge tile
3.6.3 Full-fill cavity wall with metal trim
3.7.1 Single-leaf masonry with bargeboard
 and roof overhang

The detail in which the rendering is taken right
up to the underside of a roof tile bedded in
mortar has become less common. However, it
still remains a typical masonry detail and merely requires a good standard of workmanship in
order to be successful. It is important that the
roof tile at the edge is solidly bedded in mortar
(mortar group II) and that the roofing felt is
fixed to this. On the outside, the individual
masonry units must be properly jointed with
mortar in order to provide a solid substrate for
the rendering.
Detail 3.6.1 is suitable for low-rise buildings
that do not require a ring beam.

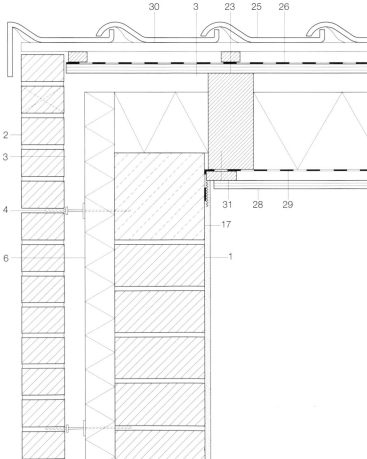

30 3 23 25 26

2
3
4
6

31 28 29
17
1

3.6.2

The use of a verge tile permits the creation of
an almost flush junction with this twin-leaf
masonry wall.
A number of variations may be employed for
the top course of the outer leaf (compare detail
3.8.3). If the topmost course of masonry units
is to be cut off at an angle to match the pitch of
the roof, this can be partly concealed by the
verge tile. However, ventilation for the outer
leaf must still be guaranteed. The last tiling
batten can be fixed to the boarding cantilevering beyond the last rafter. This detail can also
be used in a similar way for single-leaf, rendered masonry walls.

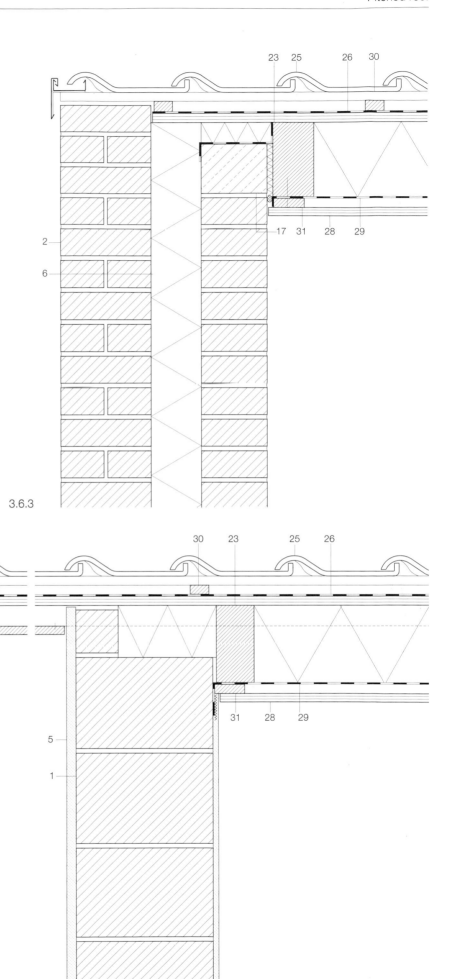

A folded metal profile creates a neat termination to the edge of a tiled roof as it conceals the edges of the roof tiles. The metal profile acts as a sort of "mini-gutter" and slips under the last row of tiles. It also conceals the top edge of the uppermost course of facing brickwork, which is cut to match the pitch of the roof.
The metal profile must include a drip positioned clear of the face of the masonry.
As it acts as a gutter, the metal profile must be able to discharge into the eaves gutter.

3.6.3

The most common verge detail with a timber bargeboard can be used with different lengths of roof overhang. If the overhang is large, then a robust supporting construction with tail beams is called for.
The soffit board(s) can be fixed to battens attached to the purlins and/or tail beams. But these are not installed until after the rendering is complete. Detail 3.7.1 is suitable for low-rise buildings that do not require a ring beam.

1   Loadbearing masonry
2   Facing brickwork
3   Air space
4   Wall tie
5   Rendering
6   Thermal insulation
8   Diffusion-tight membrane
11 Sheet metal capping
17 Ring beam, or ring beam reinforcement
23 Rafter
25 Roof tiles
26 Roofing felt, open to diffusion
28 Timber boarding
29 Roofing felt, diffusion-resistant
30 Tiling battens
31 Clamping bar
81 Bargeboard

3.7.1

217

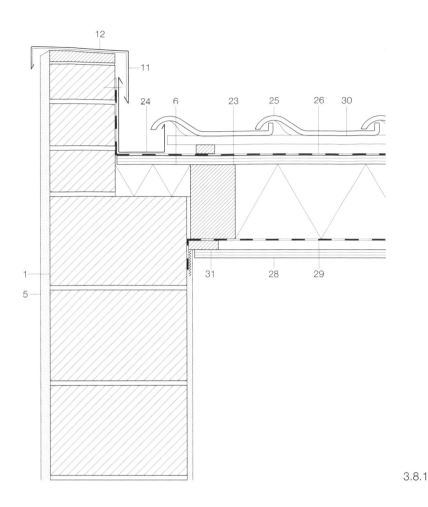

3.8.1

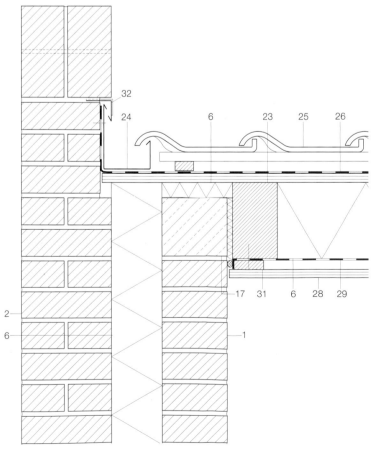

3.8.3

Pitched roof – verge

3.8.1 Single-leaf masonry with masonry parapet and sheet metal capping

3.8.3 Twin-leaf masonry with masonry parapet

The masonry parapet with internal sheet metal gutter is a well-established architectural means for achieving a plain edge to the roof. The top of the rendered parapet can be finished with a sheet metal capping or with precast concrete or natural stone copings.

The masonry parapet should be at least 175 mm thick.

The metal gutter behind the masonry parapet must be able to discharge into the eaves gutter (see detail 3.5.1).

Finishing the top of the wall with a brick-on-edge or soldier course can be accomplished only with an outer leaf of facing masonry 240 mm thick. In this case the courses of brickwork below the soldier course should be cut back so that the metal drip below the soldier course overhangs the internal sheet metal gutter. No further flashings are necessary, provided the work is carried out to a good standard of workmanship and all joints are fully filled with mortar (if necessary with water-repellent mortar). It is always the bricks below the brick-on-edge or soldier course which are cut to match the pitch of the roof.

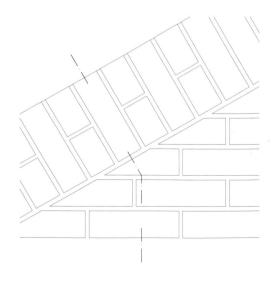

Pitched roof – junction with wall

3.9.1   Junction with single-leaf masonry wall
3.9.2   Junction with twin-leaf masonry wall

Details 3.9.1 and 3.9.2 illustrate junction details for buildings with different numbers of storeys, or which are offset with respect to each other. Great care must always be exercised at any wall-roof junction. The position of the edge tiles must be coordinated with that of the tiles at the eaves. The start of the gutter and its flashing should the aligned with the end of the wall for a facade of varying height. On a rendered wall, the gutter must terminate at the base of the rendering. The rendering should be isolated from the gutter by means of a stop bead and near the junction with the roof should be of a type suitable for use on ground level plinths (mortar group II).
The wall construction should be chosen such that the continuous slot for the gutter does not impair the structural stability of the wall.

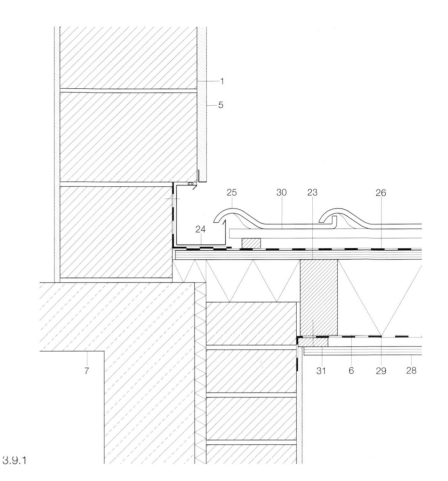

3.9.1

In detail 3.9.2 the outer leaf of facing brickwork is supported on a continuous bracket. In this case the facing brickwork can follow the pitch of the roof exactly. It is recommended to construct the base course as a brick-on-edge or one-brick course and to cut the bricks of the next course to match the pitch of the roof. This recommendation also applies to detail 3.9.3 (see p. 207). In that case the lower junction behind the gutter could also be cast in concrete.

 1   Loadbearing masonry
 2   Facing brickwork
 4   Wall tie
 5   Rendering
 6   Thermal insulation
 7   Reinforced concrete slab
 8   Diffusion-tight membrane
11   Sheet metal capping
12   Profiled timber section
16   Clamping bar
17   Ring beam, or ring beam reinforcement
23   Rafter
24   Gutter
25   Roof tiles
26   Roofing felt, open to diffusion
28   Timber boarding
29   Roofing felt, diffusion-resistant
30   Tiling battens
31   Clamping bar
32   Metal drip
33   Steel angle bracket

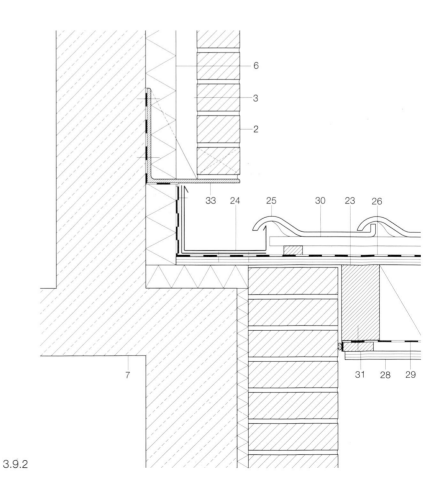

3.9.2

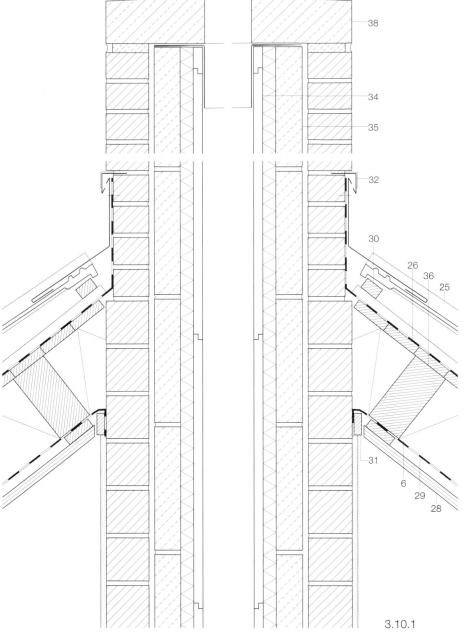

Pitched roof – chimney

3.10.1 Top of chimney with metal flashings
3.10.2 Roof tiles bedded in mortar

Chimneys passing through pitched roofs must be flashed to prevent ingress of water into the roof space. Ideally, chimneys should be positioned to pass through the ridge in order to avoid forming an acute angle on one side. This preferred detail is shown in 3.10.1. The chimney with refractory clay flue lining, insulation and flue blocks passes between trimmers incorporated in the timber roof construction. The flue blocks are also available with corbal bricks for the facing brickwork, which means that the facing brickwork only needs to continue down to just below the trimmers. The metal flashings and roofing felt are easier to attach to the facing brickwork when the corresponding courses are cut back approx. 30-40 mm. The roofing felt and metal flashings with drip above can be neatly fixed and sealed in the resulting recess in the masonry. A precast concrete cap protects the top of the chimney.

If the top of the chimney is to have facing brickwork 240 mm thick, the roof tiles can be bedded in mortar in a recess on all sides, provided the climatic conditions allow. A fibre-reinforced mortar is recommended. The 240 mm facing brickwork can then be easily laid on the 115 mm masonry below owing to the bond laid in a ring around the chimney.

3.10.1

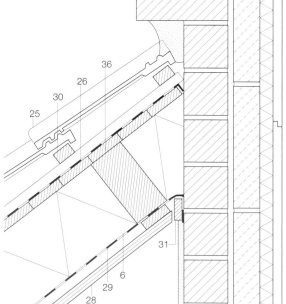

3.10.2

Floor junction

3.11.1 Junction between reinforced concrete floor and single-leaf masonry
3.11.2 Junction between timber joist floor and partial-fill cavity wall
3.11.3 Junction between reinforced concrete floor and full-fill cavity wall

All floor junctions should be constructed in such a way that an adequate thermal break is assured. In the case of single-leaf, rendered masonry (3.11.1), the closing brick sealing the edge of the floor slab should always be made from the same material as the rest of the wall. This creates a consistent substrate for the rendering. A strip of compressible material at the inside edge of the floor support protects the corner of the topmost course of masonry units below the floor against excessive bearing pressure.

The insulation in the partial-fill cavity wall (3.11.2) automatically creates the necessary thermal break. This detail also applies when using facing masonry for the inner, loadbearing leaf as well.

A timber floor requires the timber joists to bear on the masonry via a separating membrane. In addition, air bricks must be built into the wall adjacent the ends of the timber joists.

1   Loadbearing masonry
2   Facing brickwork
3   Air space
4   Wall tie
5   Rendering
6   Thermal insulation
7   Reinforced concrete slab
8   Diffusion-tight membrane
17 Ring beam, or ring beam reinforcement
25 Roof tiles
26 Roofing felt, open to diffusion
28 Timber boarding
29 Roofing felt, diffusion-resistant
30 Tiling battens
31 Clamping bar
32 Metal drip
34 Refractory clay flue lining
35 Flue block
36 Trimmer
38 Precast concrete chimney cap
39 Impact sound insulation
40 Floating screed
41 Compressible plastic strip
42 Timber floor joist
43 Air brick

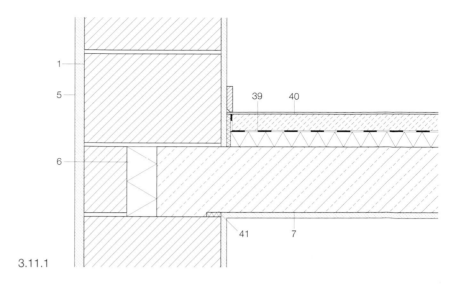

3.11.1

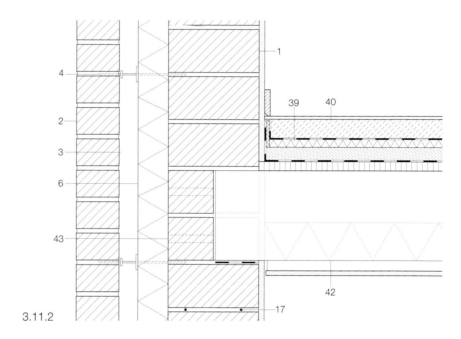

3.11.2

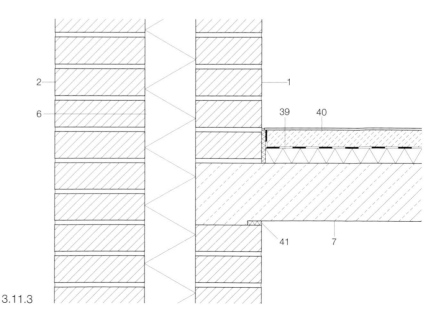

3.11.3

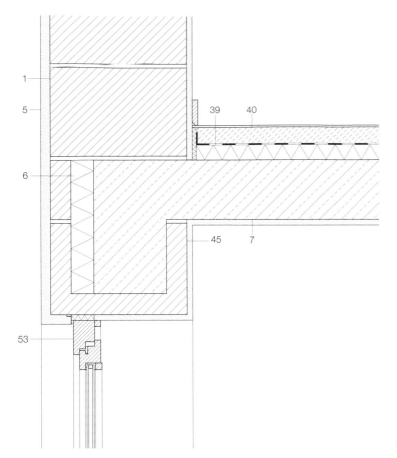

3.12.1

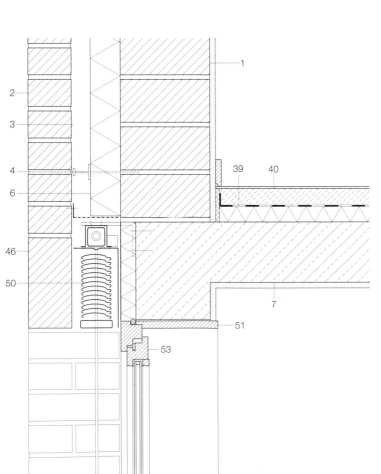

3.12.2

Openings
Window head and reveals without shoulder

3.12.1 Lintel over window in single-leaf masonry
3.12.2 Lintel over window in partial-fill cavity wall, with louvre blind
3.12.3 Lintel over window in full-fill cavity wall
3.13.2 Lintel over window in partial-fill cavity wall, with roller blind box

It is possible to install windows without a step or shoulder in the opening, but special attention should be paid to achieving a good seal to the peripheral joint between window frame and structure. Various prefabricated lintels are available from building materials suppliers. All the details require the inclusion of adequate thermal insulation. Detail 3.12.1 shows channel blocks filled with (reinforced) concrete and a layer of insulation. The channel blocks must be made from aerated clay. Window details without step or shoulder will become increasingly problematic as the thermal insulation regulations are tightened further.

Twin-leaf masonry (3.12.2) enables a sunshade (in this case a louvre blind) to be incorporated in the cavity between loadbearing leaf and facing brickwork. Care must be taken to ensure that the reinforced concrete lintel is adequately insulated; the insulation should be protected by a sheet metal cover. The operating mechanism for the blind should certainly be motorized with this type of detail. The facing brickwork outer leaf can be supported by means of a cambered arch for spans up to 2 m; larger spans require the use of steel sections.

1 Loadbearing masonry
2 Facing brickwork
3 Air space
4 Wall tie
5 Rendering
6 Thermal insulation
7 Reinforced concrete slab
39 Impact sound insulation
40 Floating screed
41 Compressible plastic strip
42 Timber floor joist
43 Air brick
44 Open perpend
45 Lightweight clay channel block lintel
46 Masonry lintel
47 Shallow lintel
48 Precast concrete lintel
49 Prefabricated lintel
50 Blind
51 Wooden lining
52 Roller blind with box
53 Window with wooden frame

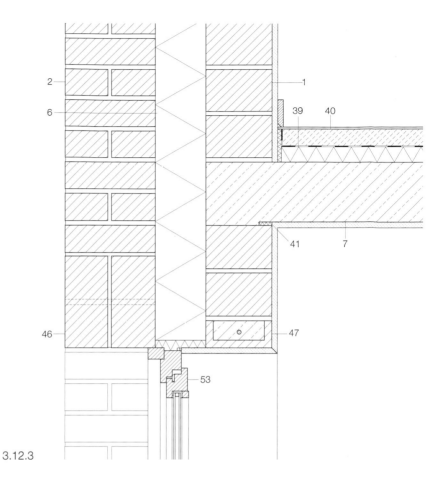

A window detail without step or shoulder in a full-fill cavity wall (3.12.3) is best achieved by positioning the window in the plane of the insulation. A prefabricated shallow lintel can be used as the lintel supporting the inner leaf. Special attention must be given to achieving a good junction with the insulation at the frame. The solution illustrated here presupposes that after installing the subframe, the gap between the cavity insulation and the window frame is filled with insulation (polyurethane foam) and the opening closed with a continuous profiled strip. The window reveal is clad with plasterboard.

3.12.3

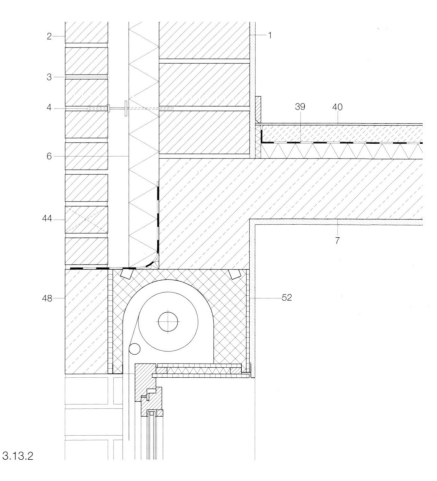

The roller blind industry provides box elements which comply with all the thermal insulation requirements.
For single-leaf masonry there is a roller blind box with a rendering support along its outer edge. Roller blind boxes are available for all the common wall thicknesses.
In twin-leaf masonry the roller blind box should be positioned behind the outer leaf of facing brickwork.
The detail shown here assumes a concrete lintel left exposed, which bears on the masonry on both sides of the opening.
The outer leaf has to be ventilated above the roller blind box. A damp proof course must be provided at the base of the cavity.

3.13.2

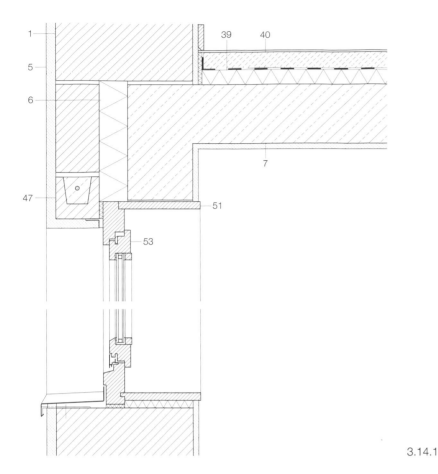

3.14.1

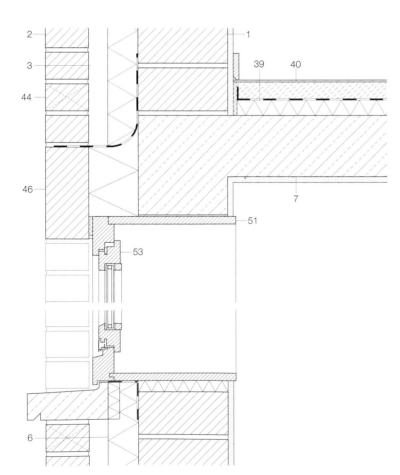

3.14.2

Openings
Window fitted behind shoulder

3.14.1 Single-leaf masonry
3.14.2 Twin-leaf masonry

Windows fitted behind a step or shoulder can be sealed easier and more reliably. The joints to be sealed can be hidden and are not visible from the outside. The subframe may need to be suitably enlarged if an identical width of frame on all sides is desired on the outside face. The lintel arrangement shown in detail 3.14.1 may employ a shallow lintel, provided the span is not too large. It is necessary to ensure adequate insulation between the lintel/masonry and the concrete lintel on the inside face. The wood finish to the window reveal shown in this detail covers the thermal insulation on the inside of the window. The external window sill, in this case of sheet metal, could also be made of precast concrete or natural stone.

Detail at end of sheet
metal window sill

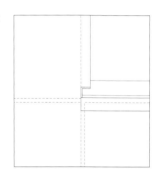

For a twin-leaf masonry wall (3.14.2), the window is installed similarly to detail 3.14.1. If the opening is not too wide, then a cambered arch may be used to support the outer leaf; spans > 2 m require additional support in the form of steel sections. Ventilation (open perpends) to the outer leaf must be provided above the bricks of the arch.
The window sill in detail 3.14.2 is shown as a precast concrete element. However, a brick-on-edge course could be used instead.

Detail at end of
precast concrete
window sill

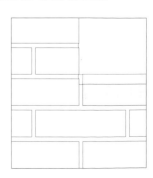

Openings

Window with peripheral sheet metal lining

3.15.1 Sheet metal lining in single-leaf masonry for window fitted in front of shoulder

3.15.2 Sheet metal lining in twin-leaf masonry for window openings without shoulder

Windows opening outwards or at least fitted on the outside are common and indeed advisable in northern Europe. However, adequate protection against driving rain must be guaranteed, especially for the detail at the head of the frame. Detail 3.15.1 shows a peripheral sheet metal lining, which at the same time functions as the window sill. In single-leaf masonry care must be taken to ensure that the window is positioned in the plane of the insulation behind the outer lintel. It is important to provide a carefully detailed permanently elastic joint, incorporating a stop bead, at the junction between rendering and sheet metal lining.

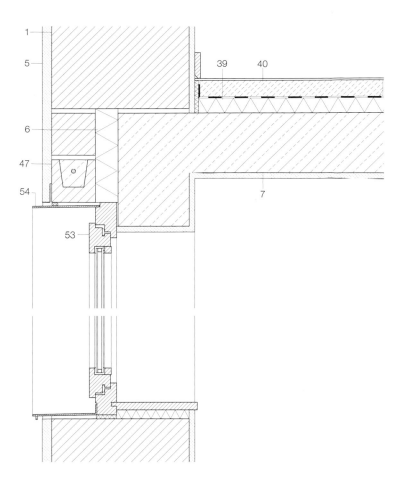

3.15.1

The sheet metal lining in a twin-leaf masonry wall (3.15.2) fulfils the same requirements as in detail 3.15.1. Detail 3.15.2 shows an arrangement without a step or shoulder in the window opening. Once again, the sheet metal lining also acts as the window sill, projecting a sufficient distance beyond the face of the outer leaf.

1 Loadbearing masonry
2 Facing brickwork
3 Air space
4 Wall tie
5 Rendering
6 Thermal insulation
7 Reinforced concrete slab
39 Impact sound insulation
40 Floating screed
41 Compressible plastic strip
42 Timber floor joist
43 Air brick
44 Open perpend
46 Masonry lintel
47 Shallow lintel
51 Wooden lining
53 Window with wooden frame
54 Sheet metal lining

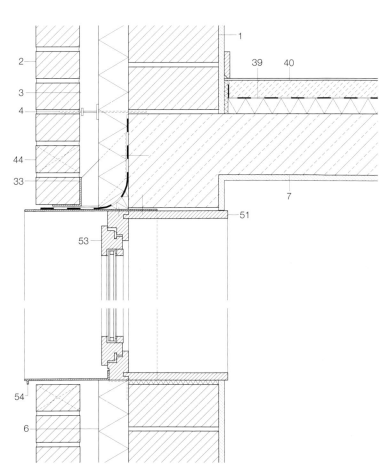

3.15.2

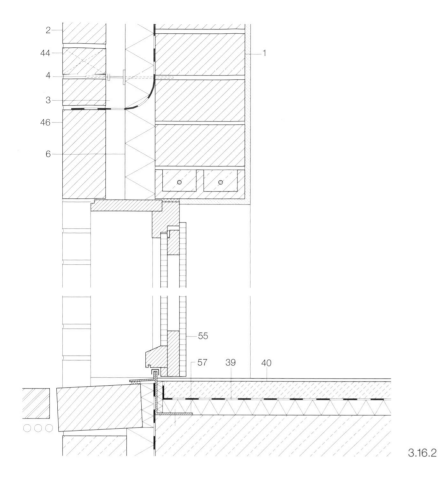

3.16.2

Door openings without a shoulder are subject to similar conditions to window openings without a shoulder. The door is best positioned flush with the outside face of the loadbearing leaf in order to provide a neat junction with the floor. The edge of the floor construction is finished with a steel section, which also functions as the weather bar at the bottom of the door. The brick-on-edge course forming the threshold requires its own support. The insulation is covered by a wooden lining fixed on the outside to the sides and top of the opening. A cambered masonry arch may be used as the lintel for normal door widths. Ventilation (open perpends) for the outer leaf is required above the arch. The damp proof course above the wooden lining must be built into the outer leaf below the open perpends.

A door fitted in front of a shoulder (3.17.1) requires careful detailing to provide protection against rain, especially at the head of the door (as for details 3.15.1 and 3.15.2). The peripheral sheet metal lining provides the necessary protection, while acting as threshold and weather bar. Therefore, this sheet metal should be thick enough to withstand being walked upon.
In twin-leaf masonry the sheet metal lining should be separated from the outer leaf. This means that a gap can be formed to permit ventilation of the outer leaf.

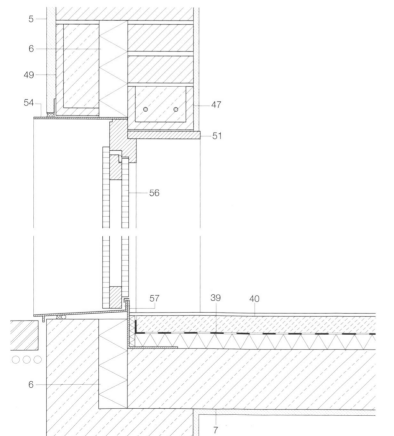

3.17.1

1 Loadbearing masonry
2 Facing brickwork
3 Air space
4 Wall tie
5 Rendering
6 Thermal insulation
7 Reinforced concrete slab
14 Foil slip joint
17 Ring beam, or ring beam reinforcement
19 Precast concrete capping
39 Impact sound insulation
40 Floating screed
41 Compressible plastic strip
42 Timber floor joist
43 Air brick
44 Open perpend
46 Masonry lintel
47 Shallow lintel
49 Prefabricated lintel
51 Wooden lining
54 Sheet metal lining
55 Wooden door with weather bar
56 Wooden door opening outwards
57 Steel section as weather bar
58 Paving to terrace
60 Glazed door with wooden frame
64 Drainage channel with grating

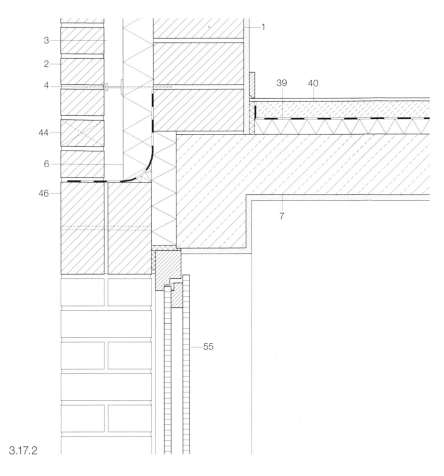

3.17.2

Detail 3.17.2 shows a masonry arch lintel 240 mm thick. The masonry at the sides of the opening remains exposed. The door frame is positioned behind the jambs and the lintel. In this detail care must be taken to ensure that the lintel is adequately insulated and that a damp proof course is incorporated.

Doors leading to outside terraces often incorporate steps. However, detail 3.18.2 shows an arrangement where the outside terrace is at the same level as the floor inside the building. The structural floor is stepped at this point. This detail shows only the form of the transition at the opening.
The outer leaf of the twin-leaf wall is carried on a continuous bracket above the insulation on top of the concrete slab supporting the terrace. The transition from the door opening to the terrace includes a drainage channel covered by a grating; this is connected to the drainage system.

Single-leaf, rendered masonry, as shown schematically in detail 3.18.1, p. 210, may be built directly on the concrete slab.
The 240 mm outer leaf of a full-fill cavity wall is also supported on a continuous bracket (see detail 3.18.3, p. 210).

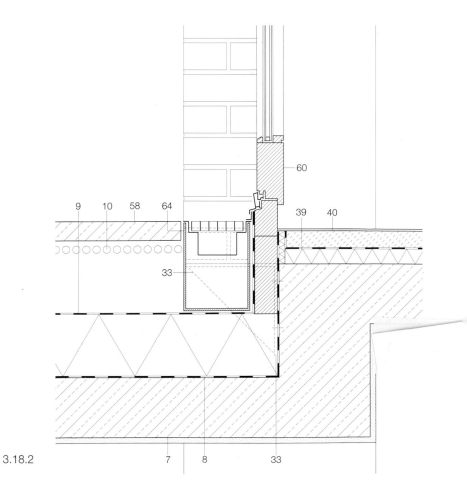

3.18.2

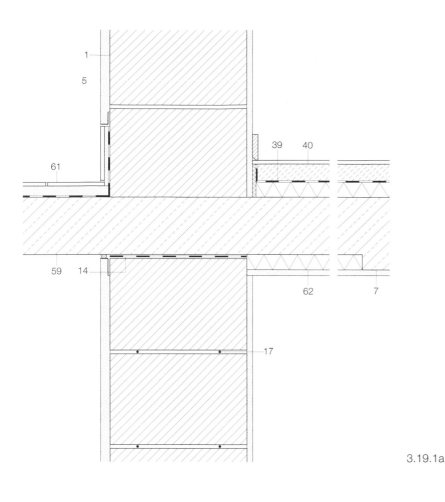

3.19.1a

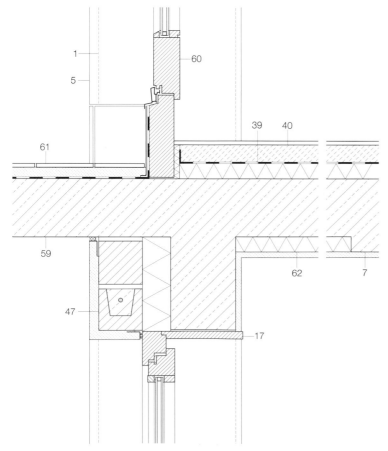

3.19.1b

Balconies

3.19.1 Continuous balcony floor slab
3.19.2 Balcony floor slab with thermal break

Balconies whose loadbearing construction is integral with the floor slab inside the building are always a problem. In building science terms it is better to provide the balcony construction as an independent item in front of the external wall.

However, in the case of single-leaf masonry, the floor construction often continues through the wall to the outside. If this is done, then the floor slab inside must be adequately insulated (3.19.1a). A sufficient width (min. 500 mm) of insulation must be provided across the full width of the slab where it passes through the wall in order to reduce thermal bridge losses. It should be noted, however, that this causes the surface temperatures at the junction between floor and wall to drop by about 2 K (2°C). The detail can be substantially improved by extending the thermal insulation 20 mm into the external masonry. Similar positive effects can be obtained by placing a strip of insulation approx. 100 mm wide vertically in the masonry beneath the floor slab.

A slip joint should be provided between floor slab and masonry to allow for the differential deformation.

Openings (3.19.1b) should be treated similarly. In doing so, the outer lintel should also be of masonry in order to achieve a consistent substrate for the rendering. This lintel must be properly insulated. A small step from inside to outside is unavoidable in this detail; elaborate measures are required to avoid such a step (by way of different floor slab thicknesses). At the sides of the opening, the damp proof membrane below the balcony floor finish must extend up the wall as far as the bottom edge of the rendering. The damp proof membrane is then covered with a plinth of the same material as the balcony floor finish.

A better detail for the balcony floor junction is one with an intended thermal break (3.19.2a). One of the advantages of this type of construction is that the balcony can be formed as a prefabricated unit with an integral surface finish. It is useful to match the thickness of the balcony floor slab to the size of the masonry units in the case of twin-leaf masonry.

The outer leaf should be supported on a continuous bracket and should not bear directly on the balcony. Likewise, there should be a compressible joint between the top course of bricks below the balcony and the underside of the balcony floor slab. At an opening (3.19.2b) the masonry lintel should also be separated from the balcony. Here, the bricks are carried on a steel section, which is supported at the sides of the opening.

It is advisable to position the window in the plane of the insulation in order to avoid cold bridges. The sheet metal threshold shown in detail 3.19.2b should be made from hot-dip galvanised steel of adequate thickness (4mm). There must be a good seal below this threshold, connecting balcony floor slab to bottom rail of door frame.

The detail shown here has a considerable difference in level between inside and outside and is therefore not suitable for disabled persons.

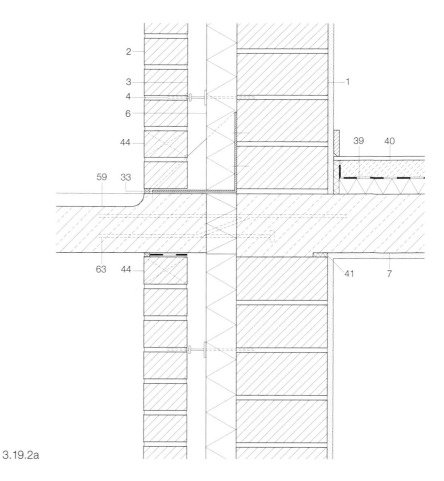

3.19.2a

1   Loadbearing masonry
2   Facing brickwork
3   Air space
4   Wall tie
5   Rendering
6   Thermal insulation
7   Reinforced concrete slab
14 Foil slip joint
17 Ring beam, or ring beam reinforcement
33 Steel angle bracket
39 Impact sound insulation
40 Floating screed
41 Compressible plastic strip
44 Open perpend
59 Reinforced concrete balcony floor slab
60 Glazed door with wooden frame
61 Balcony floor finish
62 Thermal insulation incorporated in formwork
63 Reinforcement, with thermal break

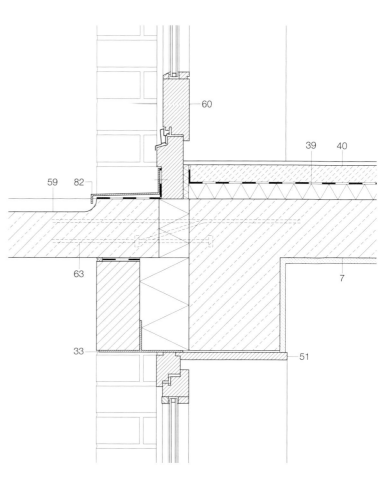

3.19.2b

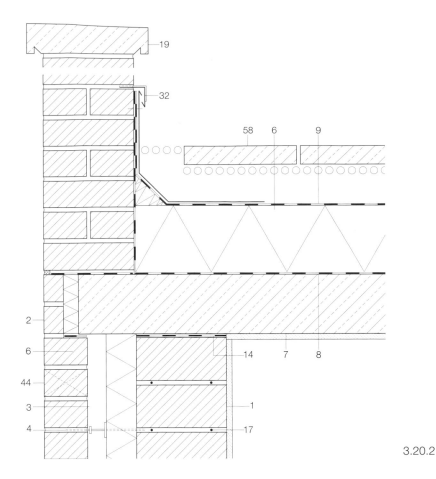

3.20.2

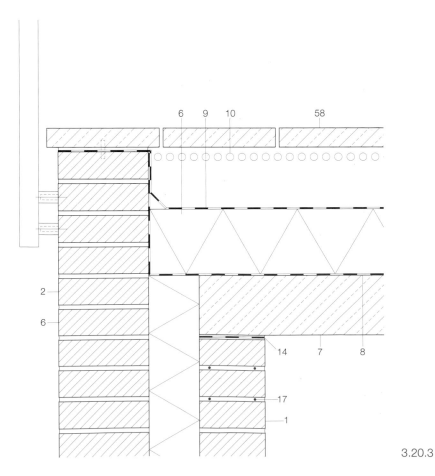

3.20.3

Junction with terrace
Outer edge of terrace

3.20.2 Masonry parapet above partial-fill cavity wall
3.20.3 Balustrade fixed to full-fill cavity wall

The detail at the outer edge of a terrace supported on twin-leaf masonry can be the same as that for a flat roof parapet. Detail 3.20.2 shows a masonry wall (i.e. parapet) forming the boundary to the terrace because it not possible to fix a balustrade to the facing brickwork – which is shown in detail 3.20.3. The masonry parapet should be at least
175 mm thick – 240 mm is better. The top can be finished with a precast concrete or natural stone coping, or a soldier course (see detail 3.8.3, p. 218). A compressible joint should be incorporated between the masonry parapet and the facing brickwork. This joint – a "predetermined breaking point" – should be sealed with a permanently elastic compound. If, for architectural reasons, such a special joint is not desirable, there is no alternative to building the entire parapet in twin-leaf masonry (similar to detail 3.2.2, p. 212).
Adequate insulation must be incorporated between the edge of the floor slab and the outer leaf. Open perpends are included below this insulation to ensure ventilation.
The waterproof sheeting must be extended up the side of the parapet to a level at least
150 mm above the water run-off layer (in this case gravel). The peripheral metal sheet with its fixing and the metal drip could be incorporated somewhat more attractively – but at higher cost – by cutting out a recess in the masonry similar to detail 3.8.3.

The terrace edge detail shown in 3.20.3 calls for a firm bond between the edge of the waterproof sheeting where it joins the masonry and the top of the outer leaf above the level of the concrete slab supporting the terrace. Care must be taken to guarantee that the paving slabs forming the floor of the terrace and the slabs on top of the outer leaf – which must be securely fixed – finish at the same level.

Plinth

3.21.1 Masonry basement
3.21.2 Plinth detail for twin-leaf masonry

In principle, masonry basements must comply
with the protective measures for non-pressurized water – a situation which occurs in most
construction projects – as laid down in DIN
18195 part 5. This is accomplished by using
bonded waterproof layers of bitumen or plastic
sheeting or thick bitumen coats (see "Part 2 ·
Fundamentals"). The horizontal layer of waterproofing must be properly joined to the vertical
layer. In order to provide extra protection, a
second waterproof layer can be incorporated
horizontally above the second course of
masonry. Only rendering made from pure
cement mortar of mortar group II may be used
in contact with the ground and on the waterproof layers. This rendering should extend at
least 150 mm above ground level. The lime-
cement mortar rendering above this should be
separated by a slit cut with a trowel. In twin-
leaf wall construction the waterproof layer
should extend over the foundation and as far
as the top of the second course of masonry.
The outer leaf can then be built on the foundation. The base course of the outer leaf must
include open perpends to allow moisture to
drain away. Ventilation of the outer leaf is guaranteed by way of open perpends in the third
course above ground level; a horizontal damp
proof course should be included below the
open perpends.

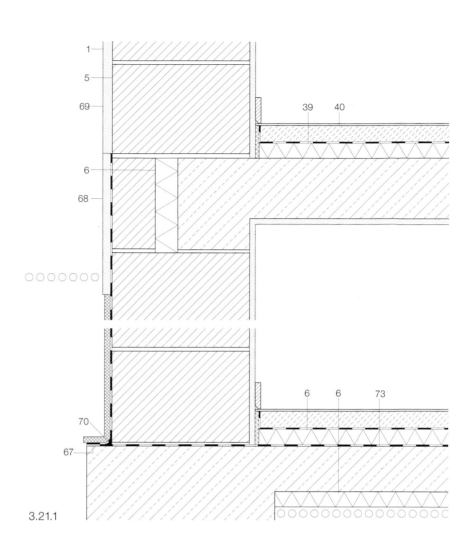

3.21.1

1   Loadbearing masonry
2   Facing brickwork
3   Air space
4   Wall tie
5   Rendering
6   Thermal insulation
7   Reinforced concrete slab
8   Diffusion-tight membrane
9   Roofing felt
10 Stone chippings
13 Steel section
14 Foil slip joint
17 Ring beam, or ring beam reinforcement
58 Paving to terrace
65 Waterproofing
66 Protective mat
67 Horizontal damp proof course/membrane
68 Cement mortar rendering
69 Lime-cement mortar rendering
70 Concave fillet
71 Concrete foundation
73 Reinforced concrete ground slab

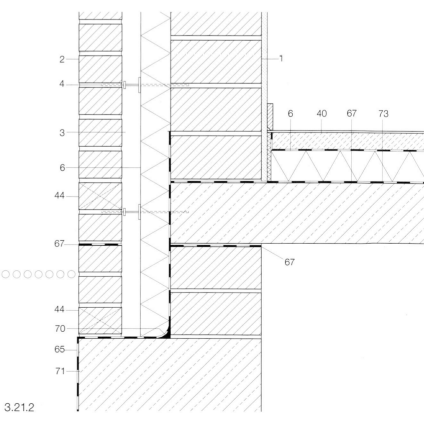

3.21.2

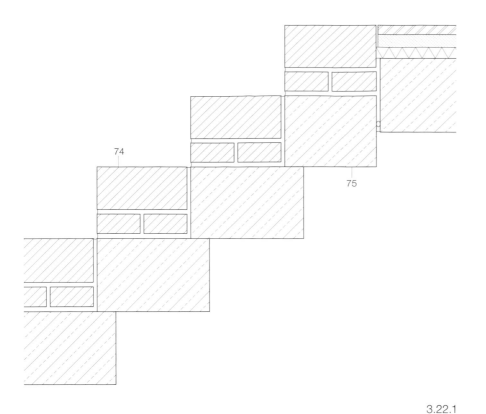

Stairs

Stairs

3.22.1 Internal stairs
3.22.2 Stairs at entrance to building
3.22.3 Stairs to basement

3.22.1

Masonry stairs inside buildings may be constructed using various combinations of masonry unit formats depending on the pitch.
In principle, the supporting construction can make use of loadbearing masonry walls with segmental arches, precast concrete elements or reinforced concrete stairs. The stair treads are then placed on this. Detail 3.22.1 shows treads formed from DF units laid horizontally and also on edge.
This example shows precast concrete steps which are incorporated without sound insulation at the ends. To satisfy sound insulation requirements, it is recommended to use a continuous reinforced concrete stair flight with sound insulation at the supports.

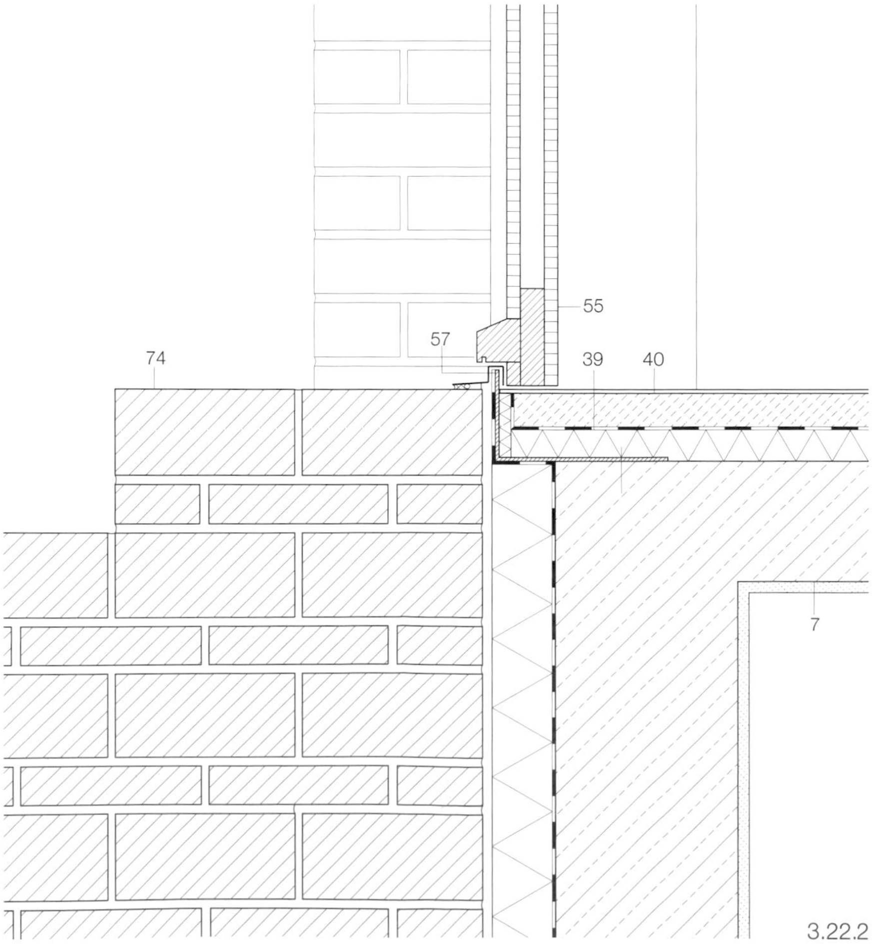

Masonry entrance stairs can be constructed as a solid block located completely within the width between the reveals of the door opening. The size of the landing depends on the nature of the entrance door and the design of the entrance.
The example shown here includes a modest landing just 490 mm deep in front of an entrance door opening inwards. It is essential to provide an adequately sized foundation to the stair block, if necessary separate to the loadbearing construction of the basement. The internal floor finish terminates at a steel section, which also functions as the weather bar for the door.

3.22.2

1 Loadbearing masonry
2 Facing brickwork
3 Air space
4 Wall tie
6 Thermal insulation
7 Reinforced concrete slab
39 Impact sound insulation
40 Floating screed
44 Open perpend
55 Wooden door with weather bar
57 Steel section as weather bar
74 Brick-on-edge course
75 Reinforced concrete treads
76 Reinforced concrete stair flight
77 Insulating masonry unit
78 Masonry units laid in bond in formwork

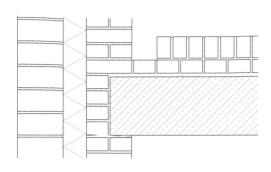

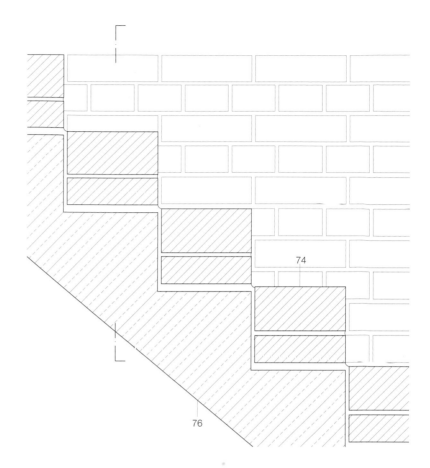

The masonry external basement stairs shown in detail 3.22.3 are supported on a reinforced concrete stair flight. This is cast against the soil as a self-supporting flight spanning from top to bottom. Normally, the basement walls and the wall on the other side of the stairs separating them from the soil are constructed independently from the stairs.

The external wall to the basement in this example makes use of English bond and is at least 240 mm thick. The facing brickwork to the concrete wall on the opposite side facing the soil can be constructed similarly. The stairs are then constructed independently between the two walls. The joints at the sides can be left open.

3.22.3

Re-entrant corner

3.23.1 Re-entrant corner with masonry soffit

The masonry re-entrant corner is not unknown in masonry construction. Höger and Schumacher have used this particular feature on many occasions. This detail increasingly appears in re-entrant facades, offset storeys, arcades and covered passages or driveways in the examples of modern masonry construction. A one-brick-thick skin is built in a proper bond in the bottom of the formwork for the reinforced concrete slab and anchored to the reinforced concrete with mechanical fixings. The reinforcement is then positioned and the concrete slab cast on top of the brickwork. To avoid a cold bridge, it is necessary to construct the base course of the loadbearing leaf above the floor slab using insulating masonry units. The damp proof course in the cavity is built into the outer leaf above the concrete slab.

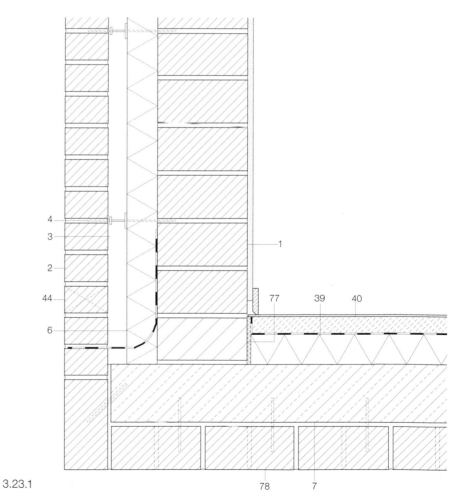

3.23.1

233

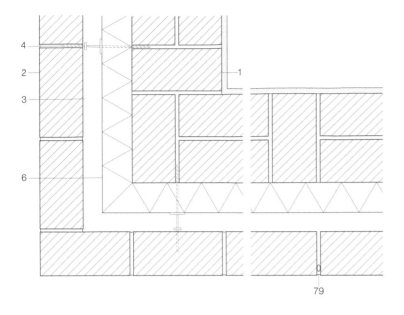

79

Corner

3.23.2 Horizontal section through external corner of twin-leaf masonry

The provision of movement joints at building corners is relevant only for the 115 mm outer leaf. The separation of the outer leaf at the corner which is normally carried out reveals the thinness of the outer leaf and hence demonstrates the – often – wallpaper-like quality of the cladding.

However, the corner can also be built in a proper bond. A movement joint must then be incorporated into the main body of the wall. When doing so, it should be ensured that the distance between the corner and the joint does not exceed half the maximum recommended joint spacing. If this rule is observed, then the joint can be located satisfactorily within the wall.
The joint may be vertical or may zigzag (vertically) following the joints in the masonry.

In contrast to this, an example of a negative corner incorporating a steel section is also shown. This emphasizes the corner. The steel section must be carefully fixed to the corner of the loadbearing leaf.

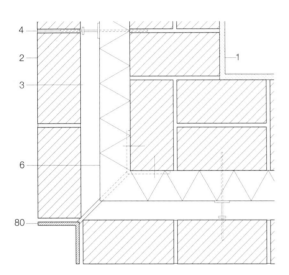

3.23.2

Free-standing walls

3.23.3 Finishing the tops of free-standing masonry walls

Free-standing masonry walls of facing brickwork are usually topped by a precast concrete coping, or a brick-on-edge or soldier course. Good-quality workmanship with joints fully filled with mortar (if necessary water-repellent mortar) makes any further protection unnecessary. Sheet metal cappings similar to those used on masonry parapets (see detail 3.1.1) are, in the opinion of the authors, not suitable in this situation.

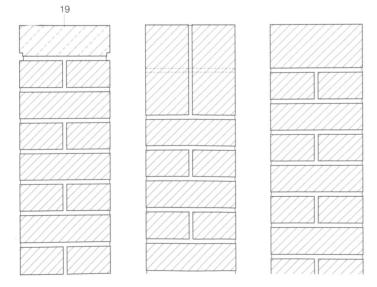

3.23.3

1	Loadbearing masonry
2	Facing brickwork
3	Air space
4	Wall tie
6	Thermal insulation
19	Precast concrete capping
79	Movement joint
80	Steel angle as corner profile

Part 4 · Built examples in detail

Günter Pfeifer

The buildings documented on the following pages illustrate the multitude of applications for masonry.

Modern masonry construction has many faces. This is reflected not only in the design of facing brickwork and a changing architectural expression, but also in the structural treatment of slender loadbearing constructions right up to thick solid walls used for reasons of energy efficiency. In the choice of examples, attention was given to the various materials used for facades: rendering, clay, calcium silicate and concrete bricks, and natural stone. But an equal amount of attention was also devoted to the resulting, different types of wall construction. However, the chief criteria for selecting a project were its engineering and architectural qualities.

The examples shown here come from different locations with different conditions in terms of climate, construction law and building regulations. Likewise, there are also examples from times when other thermal insulation requirements applied. For this reason, the details recorded here cannot necessarily be used elsewhere without being modified to suit the respective situation.

The typical engineering and architectural details were selected from the planning documents of the examples shown here and redrawn in a standard format. To help in identifying the relationships, basic information such as location plan, floor layouts, sections and general explanations were added.

No.	Page	Architect(s)	Project	External wall	Material(s)
1	238	Walter Stolz, Rosenheim	House in Hallertau, D	Single-leaf, rendered	Lightweight clay
2	242	Hartwig N. Schneider, Stuttgart	Housing complex in Ludwigsburg, D	Single-leaf, rendered	Lightweight clay
3	246	Rolf Ramcke, Hannover	Sewage works building in Hannover, D	Single-leaf	Clay
4	250	Burkard, Meyer + Partner, Baden	Extension to school in Gebenstorf, CH	Single-leaf	Clay + lightweight clay in common bond
5	256	Günter Pfeifer, Lörrach	House in Bad Säckingen, D	Partial-fill cavity wall	Calcium silicate / calcium silicate
6	258	Frederiksen + Knudsen, Copenhagen	House in Hellerup, DK	Full-fill cavity wall	Clay / clay
7	262	Heinz Bienefeld, Swisttal-Ollheim	House in Brühl, D	Single-leaf	Clay + lightweight clay in common bond
8	267	Günter Pfeifer, Lörrach	Housing complex in Lörrach, D	Partial-fill cavity wall	Concrete (bricks) / calcium silicate
9	272	Claus + Kaan, Amsterdam	Housing complex in Groningen, NL	Partial-fill cavity wall	Clay / calcium silicate
10	276	Heide + Beckerath, Berlin	Two apartment blocks in Berlin, D	Partial-fill cavity wall	Clay / calcium silicate
11	278	Hans Kollhoff, Berlin	Housing complex in Amsterdam, NL	Partial-fill cavity wall	Clay / calcium silicate
12	284	Schattner, Schmitz, Eichstätt	Extension to palace near Beilngries, D	Partial-fill cavity wall	Concrete (bricks) / reinforced concrete
13	288	Rudolf Hierl, Munich	Youth hostel in Dachau, D	Partial-fill cavity wall	Concrete (bricks) / reinforced concrete
14	293	Schunck–Ullrich–Krausen, Munich	School in Munich, D	Partial-fill cavity wall	Concrete (bricks) / reinforced concrete
15	298	Lederer, Ragnarsdóttir, Oei, Stuttgart/Karlsruhe	School in Ostfildern, D	Partial-fill cavity wall	Clay / reinforced concrete
16	304	Ernst Gisel, Zürich	Town hall in Fellbach, D	Partial-fill cavity wall	Clay / reinforced concrete
17	308	Hillebrandt + Schulz, Cologne	Office building in Lünen, D	Partial-fill cavity wall	Clay / autoclaved aerated concrete
18	311	Heinz Mohl, Karlsruhe	Computer centre in Karlsruhe, D	Partial-fill cavity wall	Concrete (bricks) / concrete (bricks)
19	314	Haessig + Partner, Zürich	Mixed-use building in Zürich, CH	Full-fill cavity wall	Calcium silicate / reinforced concrete
20	318	Petra und Paul Kahlfeldt, Berlin	Mixed-use development in Berlin, D	Full-fill cavity wall	Clay / reinforced concrete
21	322	Lederer, Ragnarsdóttir, Oei, Stuttgart/Karlsruhe	Extension to office building in Stuttgart, D	Partial-fill cavity wall	Clay / reinforced concrete
22	328	Maccreanor, Lavington, London	Business premises in London, GB	Framework	Precast concrete elements, clay facing brickwork
23	331	Hegger, Hegger, Schleiff, Kassel	Business start-up centre in Hamm, D	Partial-fill cavity wall	Recycled clay / calcium silicate
24	334	Atelier Zeinstra, van der Pol, Amsterdam	Housing complex in Amsterdam, NL	Partial-fill cavity wall	Clay infill panels / lightweight timber construction
25	338	Lundgaard + Tranberg, Copenhagen	Housing development in Rungsted, DK	Full-fill cavity wall	Clay / precast concrete elements
26	342	Jesús María Aparicio Guisado, Madrid	Apartment block in Salamanca, E	Full-fill cavity wall	Clay / horizontally perforated clay
27	346	Baumschlager + Eberle, Lochau	Community centre in Lochau, A	Partial-fill cavity wall	Clay / reinforced concrete frame
28	352	Hahn, Helten, Aachen	Church, community centre in Neu-Anspach, D	Partial-fill cavity wall	Concrete (bricks) / reinforced concrete
29	357	Raffaele Cavadini, Locarno	Community buildings in Iragna, CH	Full-fill cavity wall	Natural stone / clay
30	360	Kaag und Schwarz, Stuttgart	Bank extension in Schönaich, D	Partial-fill cavity wall	Natural stone / reinforced concrete
31	364	de Blacam + Meagher, Dublin	Library in Cork, IRL	Diaphragm wall	Clay / concrete (bricks)
32	369	Adalberto Dias, Porto	Faculty building in Aveiro, P	Partial-fill cavity wall	Clay / reinforced concrete
33	374	Eckert Negwer Sommer Suselbeek, Berlin	Office building in Essen, D	Full-fill cavity wall	Clay / calcium silicate
34	378	Fink + Jocher, Munich	Housing complex in Hannover, D	Partial-fill cavity wall	Clay / reinforced concrete

Example 1

House in Hallertau, Germany

1999

Architect:
Walter Stolz, Rosenheim
Assistants:
Georg Trengler,
Elisabeth Mehrl (colour scheme), Hofberg
Structural engineers:
Bauer Ingenieure, Landshut

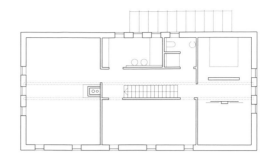

The plot is located in a new development with heterogeneous, detached family houses on the edge of this little town in Bavaria. The house and garage are positioned at the top end of this gently sloping site. Together with the wall in between, they form a boundary on the road side and enclose the west-facing garden with its view towards the town in the valley. The north elevation of the main building has very few openings but includes a glazed porch, which acts as a climate buffer and lobby for the entrance to the house. The living room is a few steps below the level of the rest of the open-plan ground floor layout in order to follow the slope of the garden outside. The careful choice of materials and the simple, precise detailing have created a building that relates to both contemporary architecture and regional building traditions. The walls are of 365 mm lightweight clay brickwork with three-coat lime rendering painted sienna red. The shallow reveals of the windows leave them almost flush with the outside face and the amount of in-coming sunlight can be regulated by means of louvre blinds fitted internally. The natural-colour concrete roof tiles terminate at the eaves and verges without an overhang, simply with sheet metal flashings.

The pitched roof is supported on two glulam purlins. There is glazing to part of the ridge between these two purlins. The roof structure appears once again above the ground floor in the form of two steel beams spanning length-wise to shorten the span of the timber joist floor.

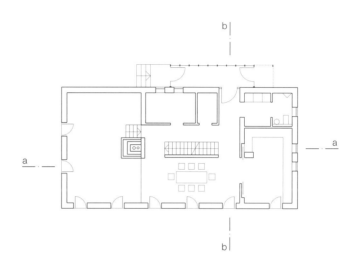

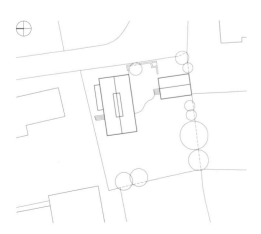

Site layout
scale 1:1000
1st floor
Ground floor
Sections
scale 1:250

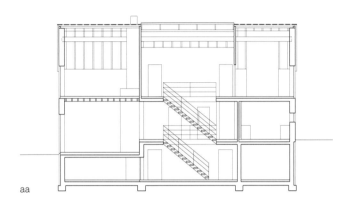

aa

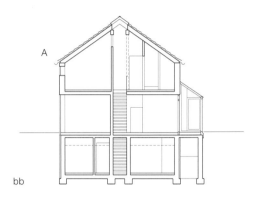

A

bb

Example 1

Sections
Verge
scale 1:20

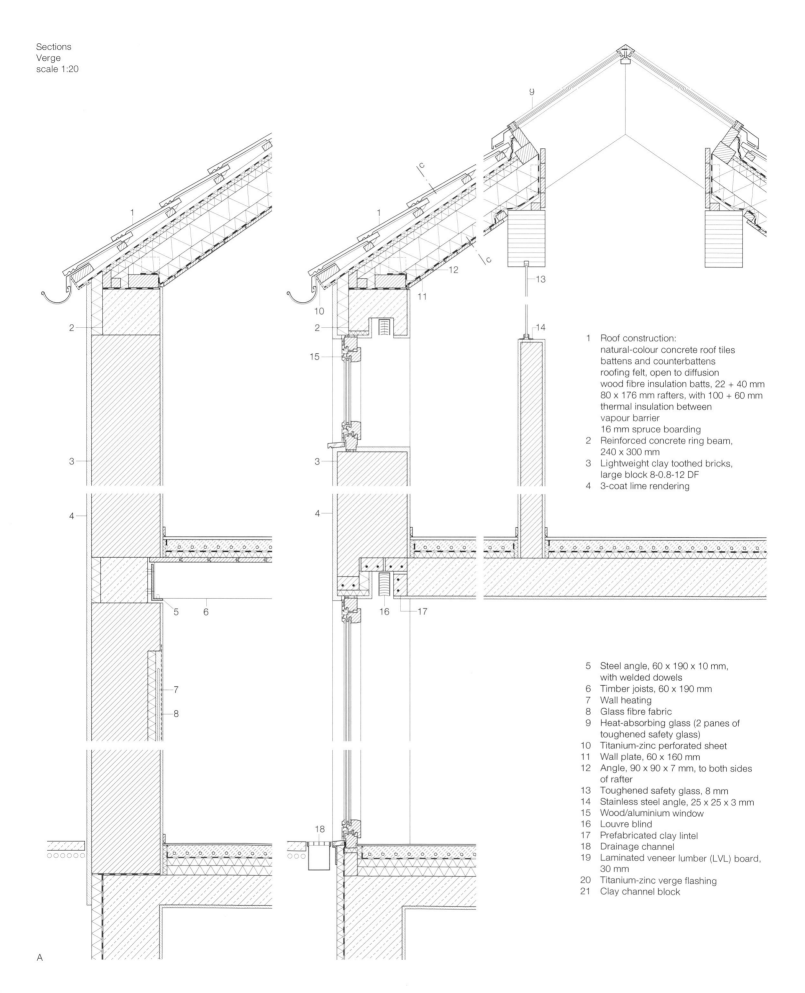

1   Roof construction:
    natural-colour concrete roof tiles
    battens and counterbattens
    roofing felt, open to diffusion
    wood fibre insulation batts, 22 + 40 mm
    80 x 176 mm rafters, with 100 + 60 mm
    thermal insulation between
    vapour barrier
    16 mm spruce boarding
2   Reinforced concrete ring beam,
    240 x 300 mm
3   Lightweight clay toothed bricks,
    large block 8-0.8-12 DF
4   3-coat lime rendering

5   Steel angle, 60 x 190 x 10 mm,
    with welded dowels
6   Timber joists, 60 x 190 mm
7   Wall heating
8   Glass fibre fabric
9   Heat-absorbing glass (2 panes of
    toughened safety glass)
10 Titanium-zinc perforated sheet
11 Wall plate, 60 x 160 mm
12 Angle, 90 x 90 x 7 mm, to both sides
    of rafter
13 Toughened safety glass, 8 mm
14 Stainless steel angle, 25 x 25 x 3 mm
15 Wood/aluminium window
16 Louvre blind
17 Prefabricated clay lintel
18 Drainage channel
19 Laminated veneer lumber (LVL) board,
    30 mm
20 Titanium-zinc verge flashing
21 Clay channel block

A

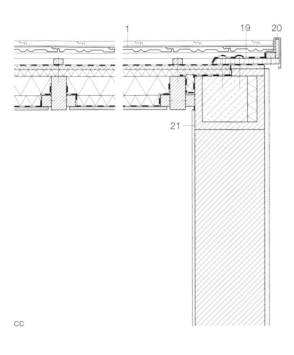

cc

Horizontal sections through chimney
1st floor · Ground floor
scale 1:50

22 Seat
23 Refractory clay brickwork, sharp-edge moulding, 70 mm
24 Wood-burning oven
25 2 No. 60 x 190 x 10 mm angles as support for floor joists

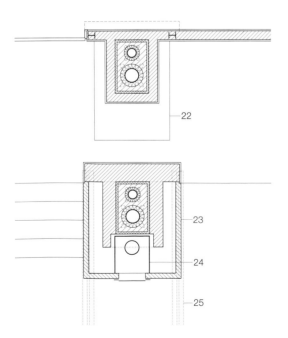

Example 2

Housing complex in Ludwigsburg, Germany

1998

Architects:
Hartwig N. Schneider, with Gabriele Mayer,
Stuttgart
Project architects:
Andreas Gabriel, Ingo Pelchen
Assistant:
Franz Lutz

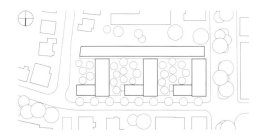

This housing complex, comprising a total of
60 rented apartments distributed according to
type among the group of three-storey blocks, is
located on the eastern edge of Ludwigsburg's
city centre. There is one main block over 80 m
long which faces south. Attached to this are
three L-shaped wings on the road side, whose
end facades break up the streetscape. The
open spaces between these wings contain the
entrances to the basement garages and the
outside stairs to the landscaped courtyards
over the garages.
The building follows the topography with very
small changes in height between the different
parts of the complex. Access to the apartments
is by way of various staircase arrangements or
an open walkway. All the housing units receive
daylight from at least two sides and face either
onto the semi-public courtyards or the garden
to the south. Further differentiation is provided
by the different facade elements: ribbon windows with sliding wooden shutters alternate
with regular fenestration, cedar-clad access
blocks contrast with the areas of dark rendering.
The walls of the blocks comprise, in the main,
300 mm aerated clay brickwork covered with a
coloured mineral rendering. The junctions
between the areas of rendering and adjoining
elements, such as windows and plinths, are
carefully detailed. The masonry on the long
south elevation facing the garden is clad with
cedar wood elements. Similar elements serve
as sliding shutters to the room-height glazing.
The balconies are precast concrete units suspended in front of the facade and
provided with a thermal break.

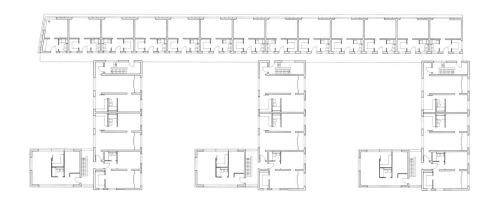

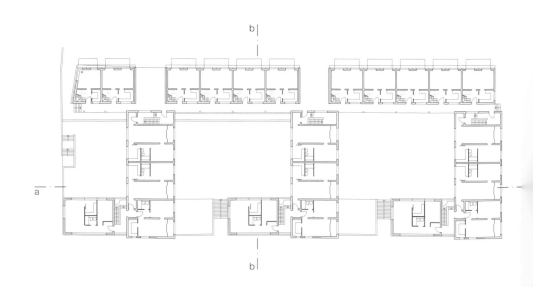

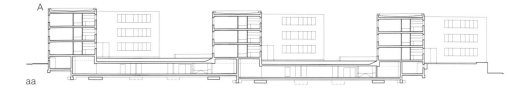

Location plan   scale 1:2500

2nd floor · Ground floor
North elevation · Section
scale 1:750

Example 2

A

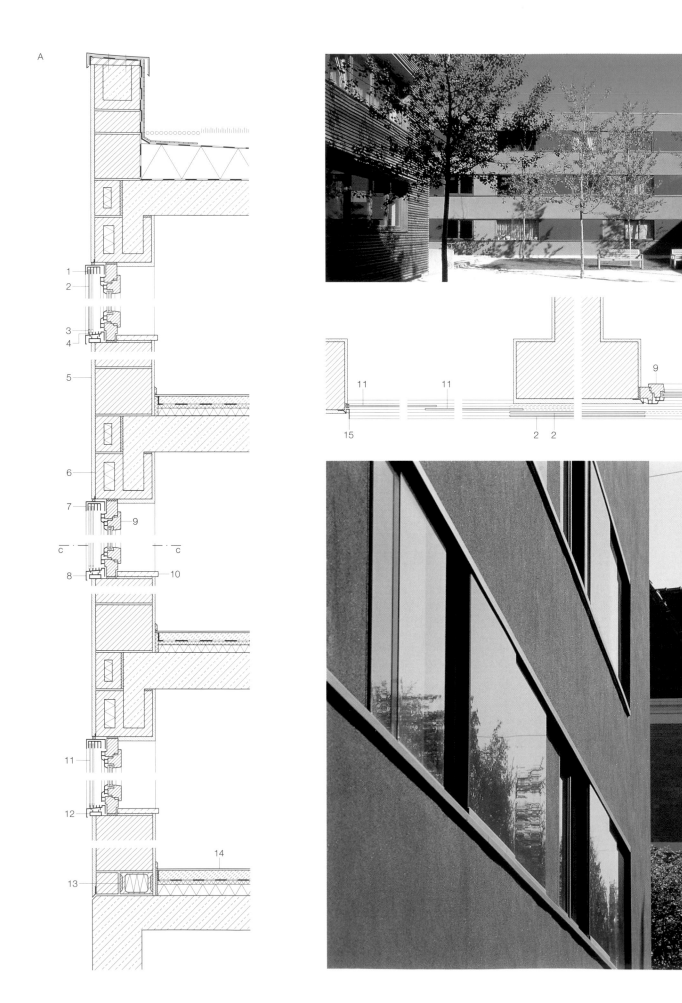

1
2
3
4
5
6
7
9
8   10
c   c
11
12
14
13

11   11
15   2 2   9   cc

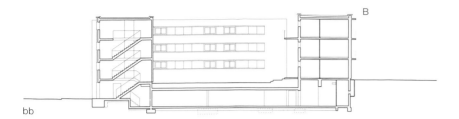

bb

Section through west facade
Horizontal section through sliding glazing in
rendered facade   scale 1:20
Section   scale 1:500
Section through south facade   scale 1:20

1 Aluminium track, with brushes
2 Toughened safety glass, 8 mm,
   rear face enamelled
3 Aluminium guide shoe, with guide wheel
4 Aluminium track
5 Wall construction:
   20 mm mineral rendering
   300 mm Hlz lightweight clay bricks
   15 mm internal plaster
6 Lightweight clay channel block, 300 mm
7 Aluminium channel, 100 x 50 x 5 mm
8 Aluminium external window sill
9 Wood/aluminium window with insulating glazing
10 Reconstituted stone internal window sill
11 Toughened safety glass, 8 mm
12 Steel hollow section, 60 x 20 x 3 mm, galvanized
13 Thermal insulation element, loadbearing

14 Floor construction:
   5 mm floor covering
   50 mm cement screed
   0.2 mm polyethylene separating membrane
   20 mm impact sound insulation
   60 mm thermal insulation
   180 mm reinforced concrete slab
15 Aluminium angle, 60 x 30 x 5 mm
16 Parapet cladding: 14 mm cement-bound
   wood fibre board
17 Upper track for sliding shutters
18 Lower track
19 Cedar wood shutters, 58 mm
20 Wall construction:
   15 mm internal plaster
   240 mm Hlz lightweight clay bricks
   80 mm mineral wool thermal insulation
   protective covering (non-woven fabric)
   prefabricated cedar wood cladding, 58 mm
21 Timber closing piece, 220 x 48 mm
22 Precast concrete element, coloured
23 Balustrade of steel sections, galvanized,
   colour-coated

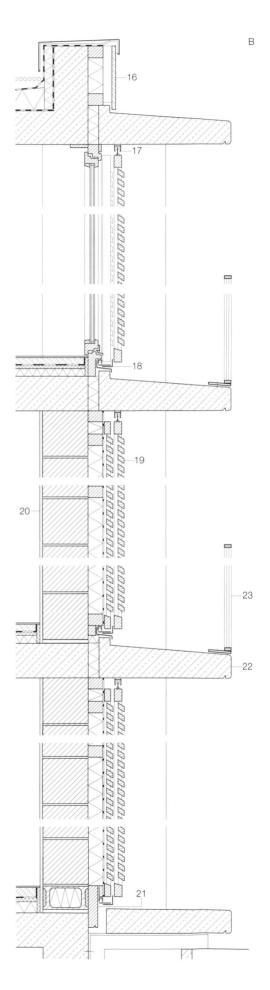

Example 3

Screens and sand catcher facility to sewage works in Hannover, Germany

1994

Architect:
Rolf Ramcke,
Hannover Municipal Building Authority
Structural engineers:
Schülke & Gerke, Erich Schülke, Hannover

Situated on the raised bank of the River Leine, this utility building appears as a concise statement dominating the recreational zone of the Leine flood plain.

This plant and processing building houses the mechanical preliminary sedimentation of the city's waste water. The building is divided into two sections to match the processing of the waste water: separating out solids by means of coarse and fine screens and the subsequent separation of the deposits via sand catcher lines, as well as the collection of mineral settling material for further processing in the waste water treatment plant. The waste water passes through the two sections in open channels.

The unheated processing areas have a constant internal temperature of 12 °C and a relative humidity of approx. 90%. Added to the extreme building science conditions are the loads generated by the aggressive gases from the waste water. Temperatures below the dew point are unavoidable in this situation, which is why all the walls were built in single-leaf facing masonry of solid engineering bricks.

The clearly arranged complex with the external walls and stairs matched to the main building lives from the use of the changing colours of the Bockhorn engineering bricks built in an irregular bond. The small number of formal interventions are restricted to the arrangement of the vertical windows, which are formed with approx. 10 mm thick profiled piers. All window openings employ glass bricks. The south-east corner is particularly emphasized by dog-toothing at an angle of 45°. This sedate structure with its long masonry walls and handful of interruptions to edges and enclosures represents simple but powerful industrial architecture.

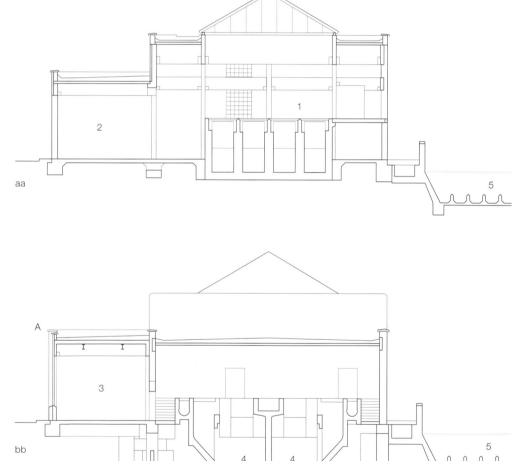

Section through screens building
Section through sand catcher
scale 1:250

South elevation
Plan
scale 1:750

1 Screens building
2 Screens containers
3 Sand screening
4 Sand catcher lines I and II
5 Rainwater retention basin
6 Inlet pumping plant I

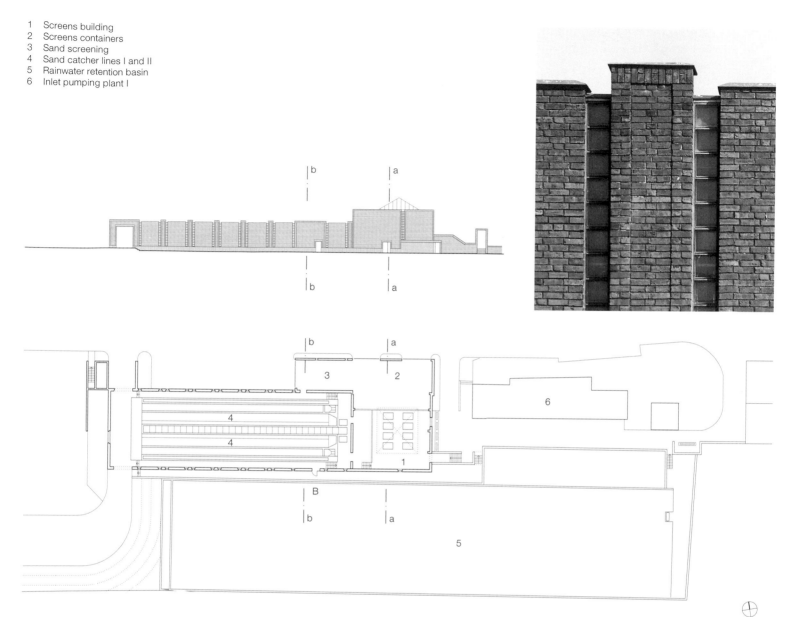

Example 3

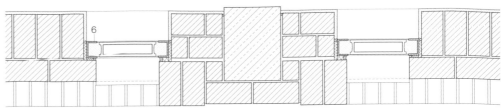

Section through north facade
Horizontal section through windows
Elevation on and section through door
scale 1:20

1 Sheet metal capping
2 NF engineering bricks
3 Thermal insulation, 40 mm
4 Roof construction:
   50 mm gravel
   waterproofing, 3 layers
   thermal insulation with 1.5% fall,
   150-270 mm
   vapour barrier

vapour pressure compensation
membrane
200 mm lightweight concrete
planks
5 Floor construction:
   50 mm reconstituted stone tiles
   30 mm mortar bed
   polyethylene separating membrane
6 Stainless steel channel, 80 mm

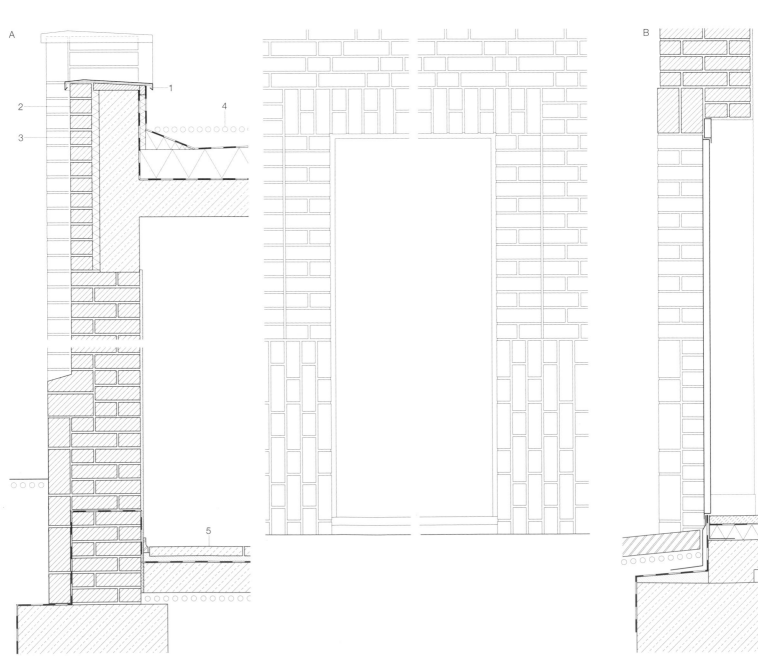

Example 4

Extension to school in Gebenstorf, Switzerland

1997

Architects:
Urs Burkard, Adrian Meyer & Partner, Berlin
Assistants:
Daniel Krieg, Adrian Streich
Structural engineers:
Gerber + Partner, Munich

This extension to the existing school complex consists of two sections: a three-storey classroom wing facing south, and to the east a two-storey block with staff-room and library plus the school kitchen on the upper floor. The north facade of the three-storey block forms the boundary to the school yard and features storey-height glazing, which permits a view of the stairs and the internal walls with their windows to the classrooms.

The buildings, the proportions of which remind us of bricks, are built entirely of masonry: single-leaf 610 mm external walls clad internally, and 250 mm internal walls with facing brickwork on both sides. The tension which results from the heaviness of the brick volumes and the lightness of the glazing helps to create this impressive architectural statement.

The 320 mm reinforced concrete floor slabs are prestressed to support the cantilever. Their good heat storage capacity reinforces the simple energy concept of the building. The single-leaf wall construction employs a precisely specified two-layer composite. Hard clay bricks on the outside with a bulk density of 1800 kg/m³ have been combined with aerated masonry units with a bulk density of 1400 kg/m³. Within the masonry bond, every fourth course of engineering bricks penetrates deeper into the external wall. This construction achieves a U-value of 0.34 W/m²K, which lies within the statutory requirements for this type of building. The advantages of this system found expression in the architecture – the south elevation, with tall, simple window slits and deep reveals, does not require any sunshading. The classroom walls adjacent to the corridors also include window openings to enable those passing to observe the activities within. This school has pointed a new way forward for masonry construction in terms of the precise implementation of the building concept and the credibility of the design and the details.

Location plan scale 1:1000
2nd floor
1st floor
Ground floor
scale 1:400

1 Library
2 Staffroom
3 Hall
4 Cloakroom
5 Workshop

6 Textiles workshop
7 School kitchen
8 Dining room
9 Classroom
10 Group room

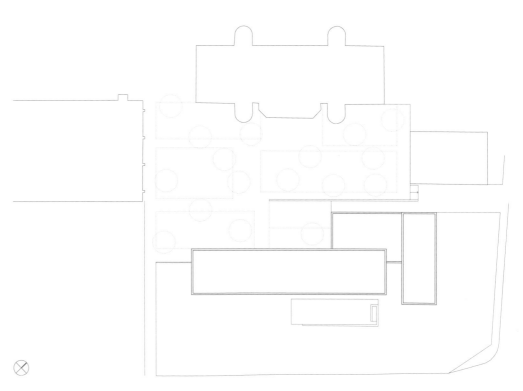

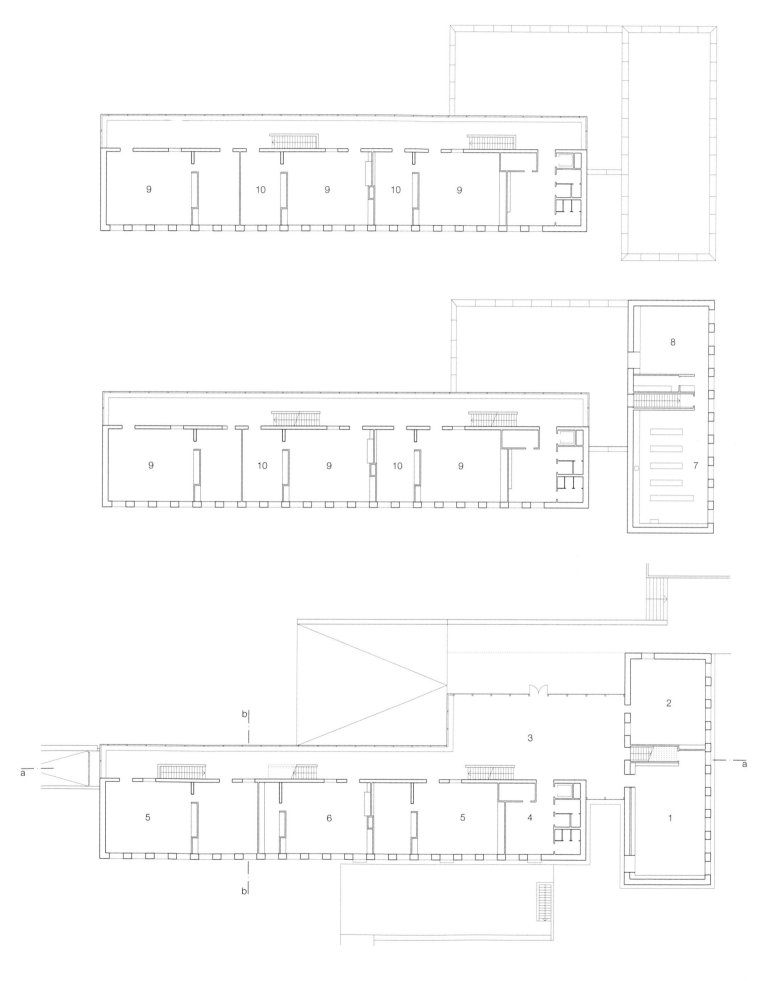

Example 4

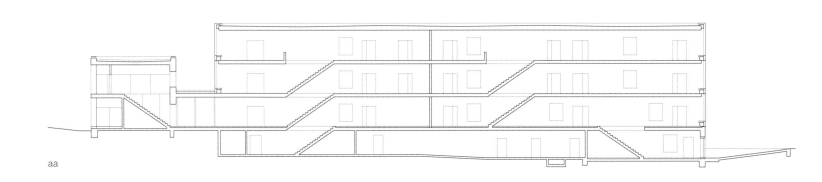

aa

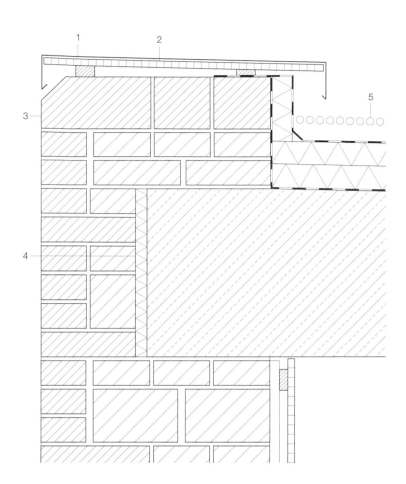

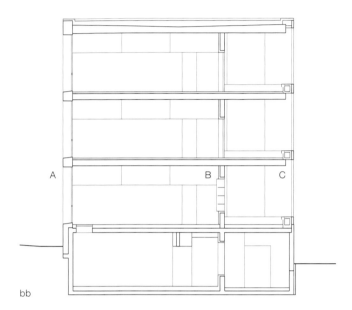

bb

Section
South-east elevation
scale 1:400
Section
scale 1:200
Section through parapet
scale 1:10

1 Aluminium capping, 2 mm
2 Waterproof chipboard laid to fall, 18 mm
3 Brick-on-edge course of facing cant bricks
4 Thermal insulation, rigid expanded foam, 30 mm
5 Roof construction:
60 mm gravel
waterproofing, 2 layers of bitumen sheeting
thermal insulation, 100 mm rigid expanded foam
vapour barrier
320-440 mm reinforced concrete slab

Example 4

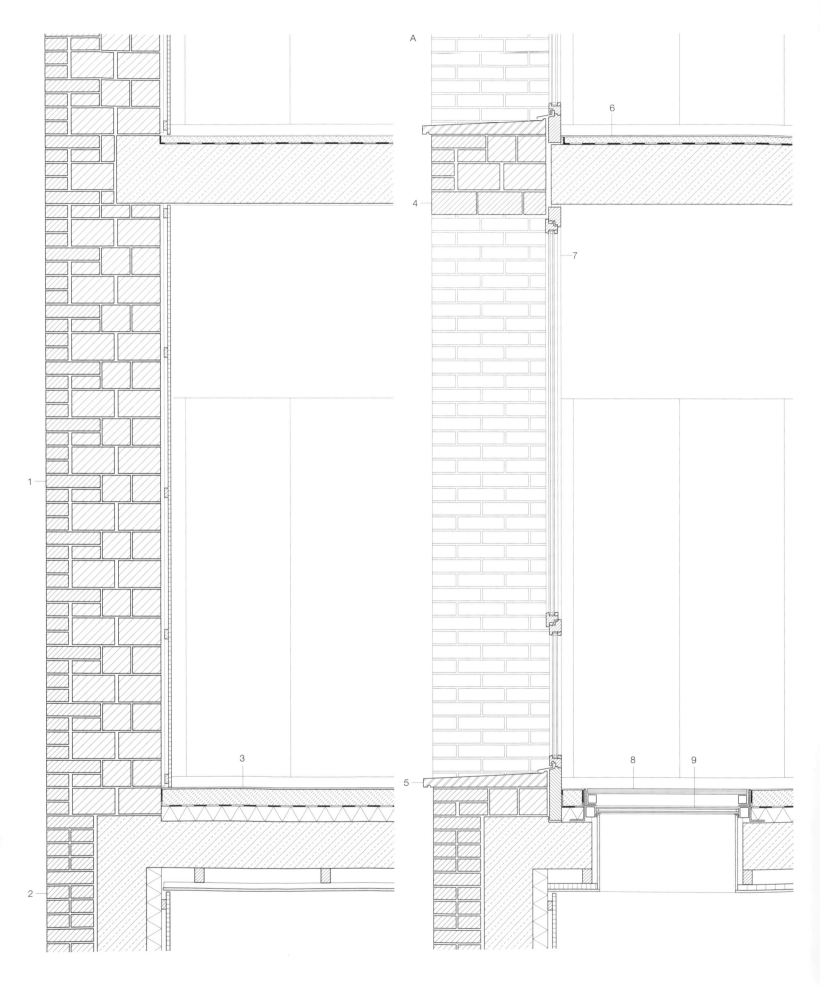

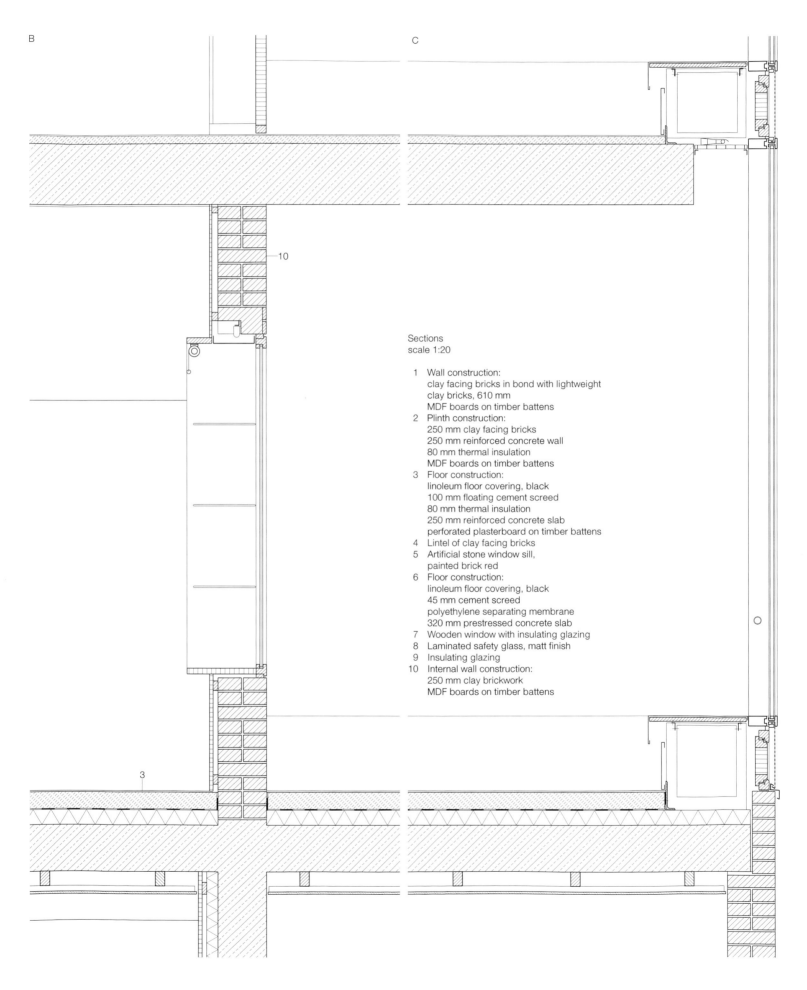

B

C

10

3

Sections
scale 1:20

1 Wall construction:
   clay facing bricks in bond with lightweight
   clay bricks, 610 mm
   MDF boards on timber battens
2 Plinth construction:
   250 mm clay facing bricks
   250 mm reinforced concrete wall
   80 mm thermal insulation
   MDF boards on timber battens
3 Floor construction:
   linoleum floor covering, black
   100 mm floating cement screed
   80 mm thermal insulation
   250 mm reinforced concrete slab
   perforated plasterboard on timber battens
4 Lintel of clay facing bricks
5 Artificial stone window sill,
   painted brick red
6 Floor construction:
   linoleum floor covering, black
   45 mm cement screed
   polyethylene separating membrane
   320 mm prestressed concrete slab
7 Wooden window with insulating glazing
8 Laminated safety glass, matt finish
9 Insulating glazing
10 Internal wall construction:
   250 mm clay brickwork
   MDF boards on timber battens

Example 5

House in Bad Säckingen, Germany

1978

Architect:
Günter Pfeifer, Lörrach
Assistant:
Rolf Bühler
Structural engineer:
Jürgen Bähr, Schopfheim

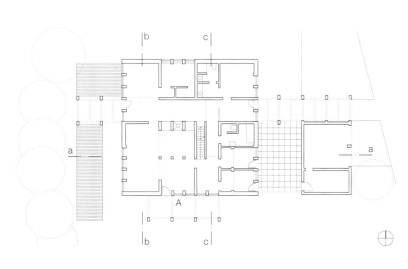

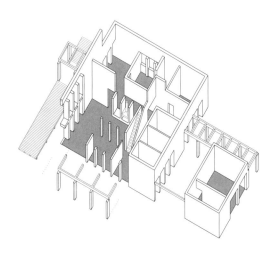

This house stands on the north-west boundary of a plot where in the past it formed a counter-weight to a villa dating from the Bauhaus era, which has since been demolished. The owners possess an extensive collection of contemporary art.

In order to provide an appropriate setting for the paintings, with differentiated lighting, the internal rooms are of different heights.

The shape of the house is based on a square plan which includes large rooftop terraces on two sides.

The garage and a pergola, which denote the entrance, enclose a small play area in front of the children's bedrooms. The building is set out on a 1.25 m grid. The calcium silicate masonry left exposed internally and externally was whitewashed after the joints were finished in the same operation as the bricklaying.

Just two different window sizes with blinds behind the soldier course lintels determine the simplistic appearance of the house.

The details which would today no longer be acceptable from the building science viewpoint have not led to any damage to the building thanks to the extensive low-temperature heating at ground floor level.

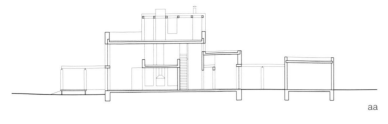

aa

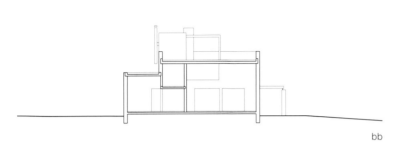

bb

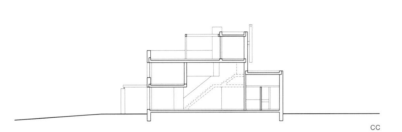

cc

Axonometric view
not to scale

Plans
Sections
scale 1:400

Section through facade
Scale 1:10

1   Titanium-zinc sheet
    capping
2   Soldier course, calcium
    silicate 2 DF bricks
3   Titanium-zinc flashing
4   Roof construction:
    gravel
    waterproofing
    80 mm thermal insulation
    vapour barrier
    180 mm reinforced
    concrete slab
5   Steel angle, galvanized,
    90 x 75 x 7 mm
6   Wooden window, red
    cedar with insulating
    glazing
7   Louvre blind
8   Wall construction:
    115 mm calcium silicate
    2 DF bricks, without
    rendering, with white-
    wash finish
    15 mm air space
    50 mm mineral fibre
    thermal insulation
    240 mm calcium silicate
    2 DF bricks, with white-
    wash finish
9   Floor construction:
    18 mm quarry tiles in
    thin-bed mortar
    70 mm screed with
    underfloor heating pipes
    40 mm thermal insulation
    damp proof membrane
    100 mm reinforced
    concrete slab

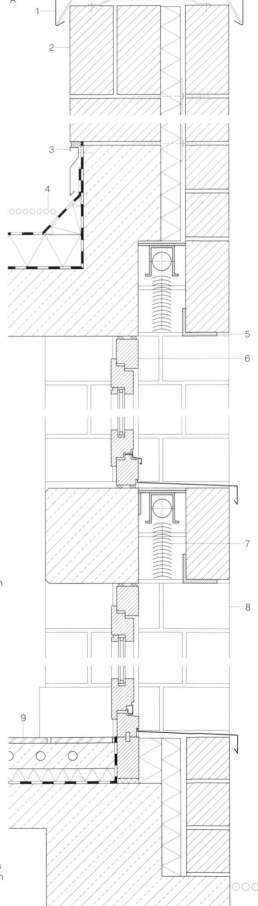

257

Example 6

House in Hellerup, Denmark

1995

Architects:
Frederiksen & Knudsen, Copenhagen
Assistants:
Ulrik Schwanenflügel,
Carsten Nøhr Larsen
Structural engineer:
Kurt Thybo, Hellerup

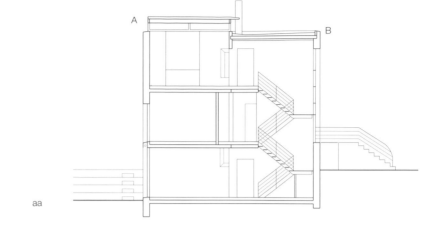

aa

The captivating design of this three-storey detached house is due to its distinctive position within the streetscape, its forecourt enclosed by masonry walls, the capacious setting of the entrance and the clear lines of the building itself. The house was sited towards the rear of the plot in order to retain an existing bay which determined the atmosphere of the location. The simple plan layout results from a distinct north-south zoning of the functional areas of the house. Arranging the levels of the house offset by half a storey with respect to the surrounding ground level places the entrance on the level of the children's bedrooms. Dining area and kitchen look out onto a sunken terrace in the garden on the southern side. The spacious living room with fireplace is located on the second floor; it faces south and commands a good view across the waters of The Sound. The second floor also contains a study and the master bedroom.

The skill of the design is not apparent at first sight. The external walls of the house are constructed from two 110 mm leaves with 130 mm cavity insulation, while the single-leaf load-bearing transverse wall is 170 mm thick. Precast concrete planks were used for the floors, the roof structure is of timber. Large spans, like over the window openings of the south elevation, make use of additional steel members. The other openings have been kept small and correspond to the structural requirements of the 110 mm masonry. The unorthodox facade arrangement is explained by the fact that the fenestration was chosen to suit the atmosphere of the interior and provide certain picturesque views.

The whitewashed masonry is left exposed internally as well, with the exception of the blue walls to the staircase.

This project shows that careful planning, particularly with respect to the building services normally encountered in the walls, and accurate structural analysis can provide a future for masonry in a "slimline" construction as well.

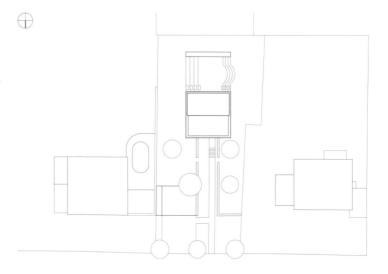

Location plan
scale 1:750
Sections
Upper floor
Ground floor
Basement
scale 1:200

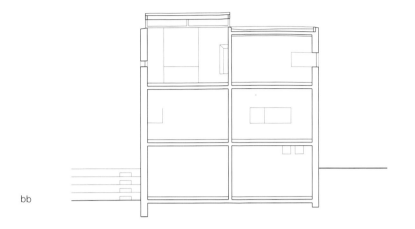

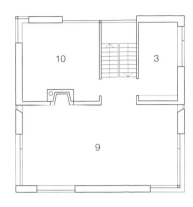

1 Lobby
2 Hall
3 Room
4 Bathroom
5 Kitchen
6 Dining area
7 Guest's bedroom
8 Wine cellar
9 Living room
10 Bedroom

bb

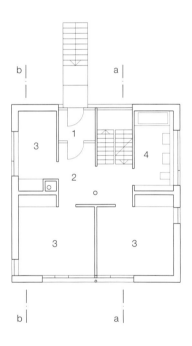

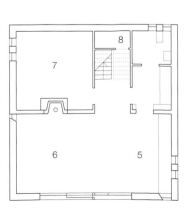

Example 6

A

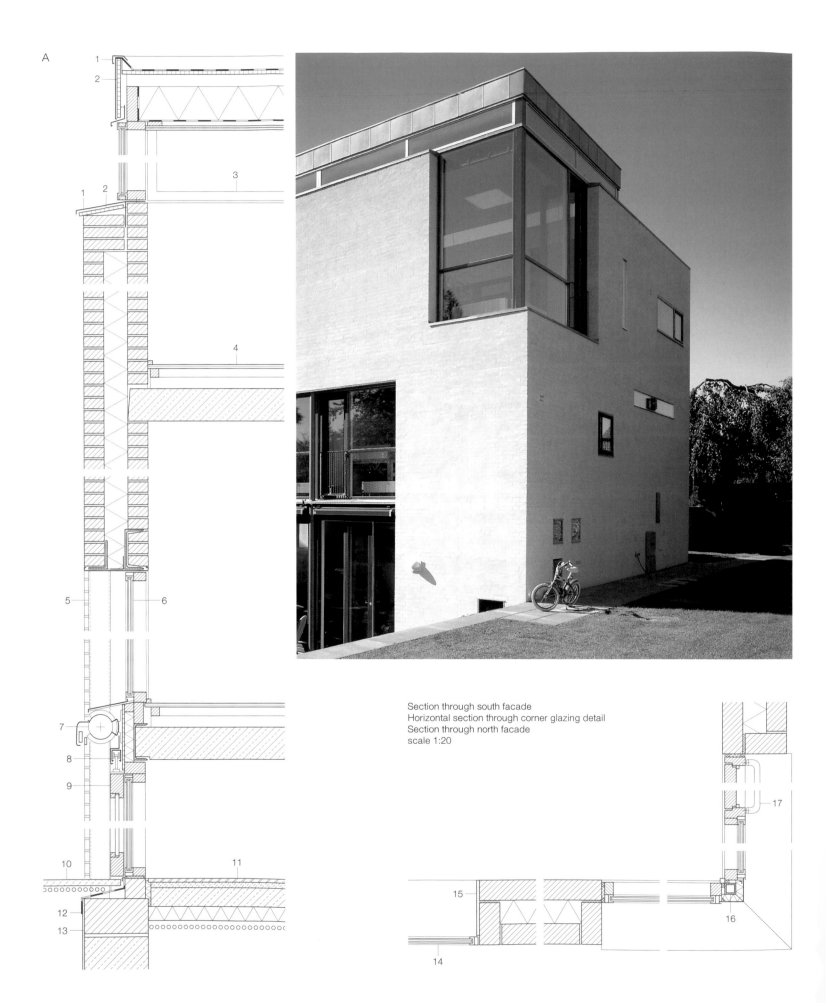

Section through south facade
Horizontal section through corner glazing detail
Section through north facade
scale 1:20

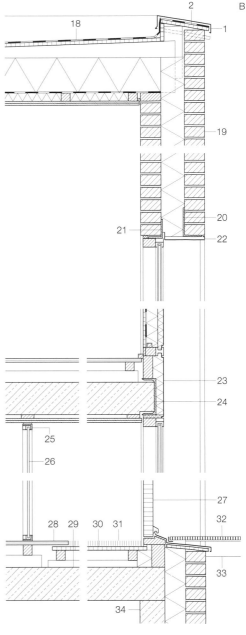

1	Sheet zinc capping
2	Laminated veneer lumber (LVL), 16 mm
3	Window frame,
	50 x 100 x 3.2 mm steel hollow section
4	Floor construction:
	20 mm wooden planks
	50 x 50 mm timber supporting construction
	timber levelling layer
	180 mm lightweight concrete slab
5	Column, 115 mm dia. steel circular hollow section
6	Wood/aluminium window, with insulating glazing
7	Extending marquise
8	Sliding door fittings
9	Sliding door
10	Concrete paving slabs
11	Floor construction:
	20 mm natural stone tiles in varying lengths
	30 mm mortar bed
	100 mm reinforced concrete
	75 mm rigid mineral wool
	200 mm gravel
12	Bitumen sheeting, welded on
13	Lightweight concrete brickwork
14	Insulating glazing, flush with outside face

15	Reinforced plaster
16	Corner column, 60 x 60 x 4 mm steel hollow section
17	Guard rail mounted on window frame
18	Roof construction:
	waterproofing
	21 mm waterproof LVL
	Firring pieces
	75 x 200 mm rafters
	thermal insulation, 180 mm mineral wool
	vapour barrier
	50 x 50 mm battens
	13 mm plasterboard, 2 layers
19	Wall construction:
	115 mm clay brickwork with whitewash finish
	110 mm thermal insulation
	115 mm clay brickwork with whitewash finish
20	Steel angle, 100 x 150 x 10 mm
21	Steel angle, 75 x 100 x 9 mm
22	Cavity closer, 2 mm aluminium sheet
23	Cladding, aluminium sheet
24	Steel channel, 220 mm
25	Steel angle, 50 x 30 x 4 mm, with white coating
26	Glass door to lobby
27	Entrance doors

28	Wooden planks, courbaril
29	Lightweight concrete slab, 180 mm
30	Chipboard, 20 mm
31	Doormat
32	Steel open-grid flooring
33	Steel angle, 80 x 80 mm
34	Reinforced concrete wall, 135 mm

Example 7

House in Brühl, Germany

1997

Architect:
Heinz Bienefeld, Swisttal-Ollheim
Structural engineer:
R. Mertens, Cologne

The fully glazed east side, together with the roof, seems to enclose and shelter the large, stepped masonry block. Heinz Bienefeld's house, completed in 1997, has also become his legacy – the archetypal form of the house in which the experiences and thoughts of the architect are portrayed. The stepped form of the masonry block, adjacent to the large open hall rising to the roof, guarantees internal perspectives which vary from floor to floor. Our attention is drawn again and again to the solid masonry block. The size of this hall is made all the more obvious by the dramatic change between this commodious volume and the relatively small, separate rooms. This experience is reflected in the appearance of the structure, in the immediate legibility from inside and outside.

The setting directs our view to the essential components, to the depth of the three-dimensional encounter and the spatial perception. The two longitudinal elevations of the house exhibit very different characters. To the southwest there is the regimental fenestration of the clay brick facade with only minor differences in the sizes of the openings. At almost 500 mm thick, the mass of wall with its seemingly detached roof and multilevel lintels has an almost physical presence.

Contrasting with this is the glazed lightness of the north-east facade, which, paradoxically, supports the large roof of clay tiles, which conveys a more heavyweight impression. However, the glass facade is merely a "second skin", a concession to the climatic conditions. Inside, behind the glass, there is the external wall of the masonry structure with the "open-air stairs" leading to the upper floors, and the cascade-like profile of the brickwork.

Bienefeld's belief that "the effects of the surfaces are part of the architecture" has been proved to still hold true in this building with its precise detailing.

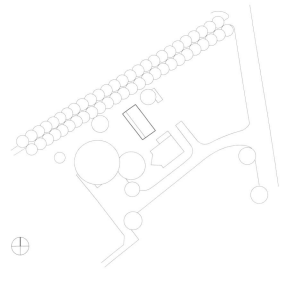

Location plan
scale 1:2000

South-west elevation
Attic floor
1st floor
Ground floor
Basement
scale 1:250

1 Master bedroom
2 Bathroom
3 Child's bedroom
4 Kitchen
5 Living room
6 Study
7 Hall
8 WC
9 Hobby room
10 Workshop
11 Sauna

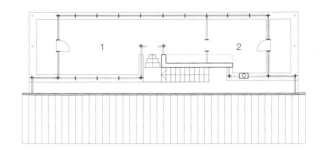

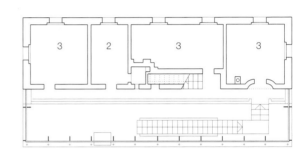

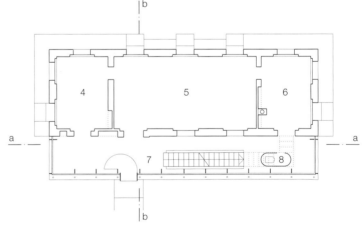

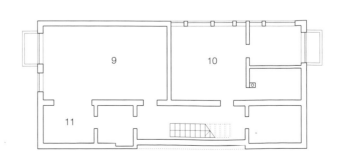

Example 7

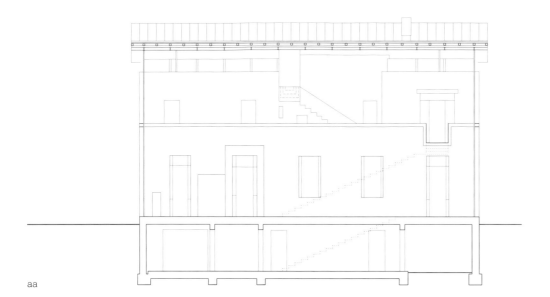

Longitudinal section
through hall
North-west elevation
Section
scale 1:200

aa

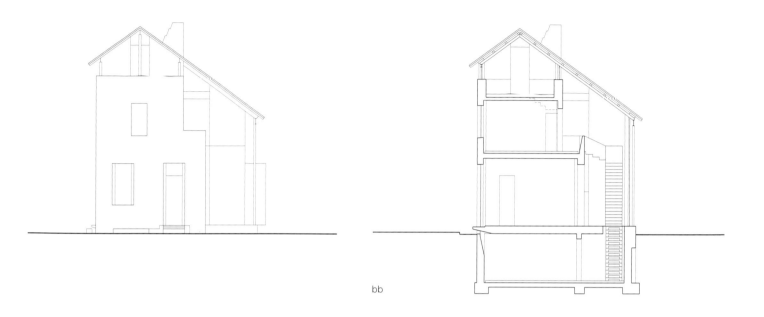

bb

Example 7

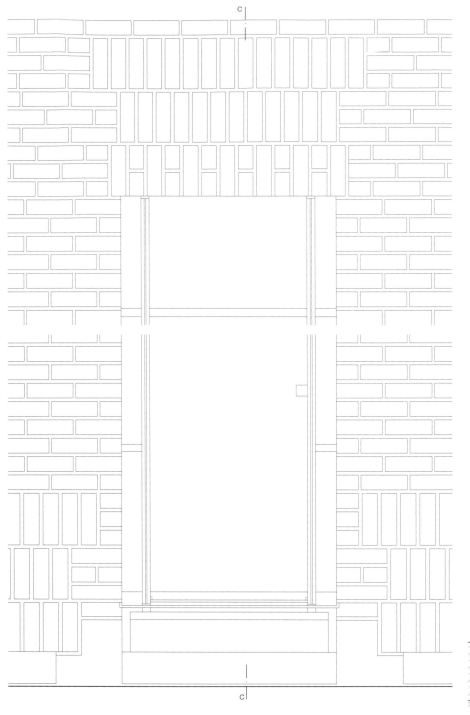

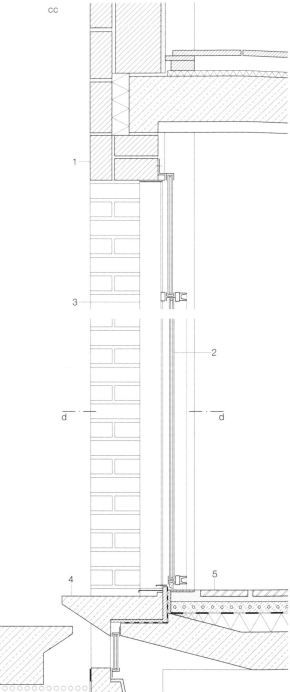

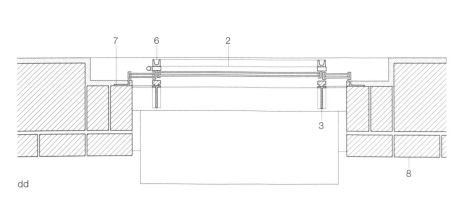

Glazed door
Elevation · Section
Horizontal section
scale 1:20

1 Cambered arch lintel,
   15 mm rise
2 Galvanized steel glazed
   door, micaceous iron oxide
   finish, with insulatingglazing
3 Column, 120 x 40 x 8 mm
   galvanized steel channel,
   micaceous iron oxide
   finish
4 Precast concrete step
5 Floor construction:
   clay tiles
   60 mm mortar bed
   60 mm screed with under

floor heating pipes
80 mm thermal insulation
separating membrane
200 m reinforced concrete slab
6 Steel channel, 40 x 35 mm,
   integrated in steel hollow
   section, 50 x 25 mm
7 Fixing lug, bent steel flat,
   200 mm long
8 Wall construction:
   facing bricks
   Taunus stone, NF, 115 mm,
   with 20 mm bed joints
   20 mm mortar wall joint
   lightweight clay brickwork
   25 mm lime plaster
   neat lime finish with
   marble dust

Housing complex in Lörrach, Germany

1993

Architect:
Günter Pfeifer
in partnership with Roland Mayer, Lörrach
Assistants:
Peter Bährle, Hermann Vester,
Elke Hudetz
Structural engineers:
Greschik & Falk, Lörrach

The building is situated on a main road leading into the border town of Lörrach. The urban approach and the triangular shape of the plot – brought about by its position between a fork in the road – led to the building's striking form of a semicircle plus a straight wing placed tangentially on one side.

In keeping with the geometrical appearance, the building is divided into two parts. First, the semicircular section contains seven housing units. These are arranged radially so that living rooms and balconies face more or less west, while access is via the semicircular courtyard to the east. Second, there are another five housing units in the straight wing. These have basically the same internal layout but here the units are aligned in a north-south direction, with access via an open walkway on the northern side and the living rooms and balconies facing south. The positions of the small, walled gardens change likewise. An open passageway at the junction between the two blocks links the basement garages with the courtyard. This feature is both entrance and link, and illustrates the reversal of the layouts in an attractive, tangible manner. The different finishes to the external walls clarify the changing alignment and hence help the observer to comprehend the internal zoning of the building. The three-storey south elevation makes use of rendered 300 mm lightweight clay brickwork, while concrete brickwork with air space, insulation and a 175 mm calcium silicate loadbearing leaf was preferred for the two-storey entrance elevation facing north. The 240 mm thick dividing walls to the walled gardens repeat the exposed masonry of the access zone.

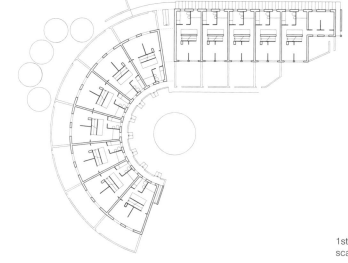

1st floor · Ground floor
scale 1:600

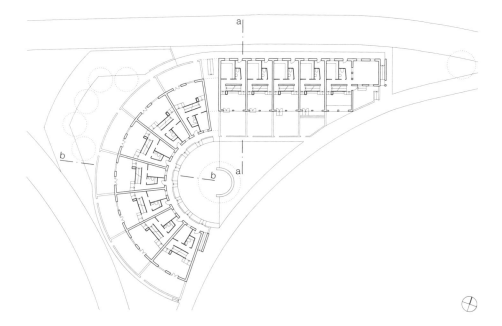

Example 8

Sections
scale 1:200
Elevation · Section
Concrete brickwork facade
scale 1:50

1   Concrete lintel
2   Wooden window with insulating glazing
3   Wall construction:
    90 mm concrete bricks in stretcher bond
    40 mm air space
    60 mm thermal insulation
    175 mm calcium silicate bricks
    15 mm lime-cement plaster

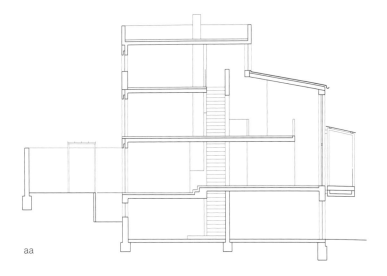

aa

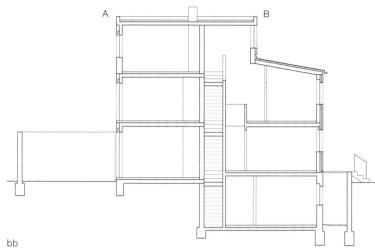

bb

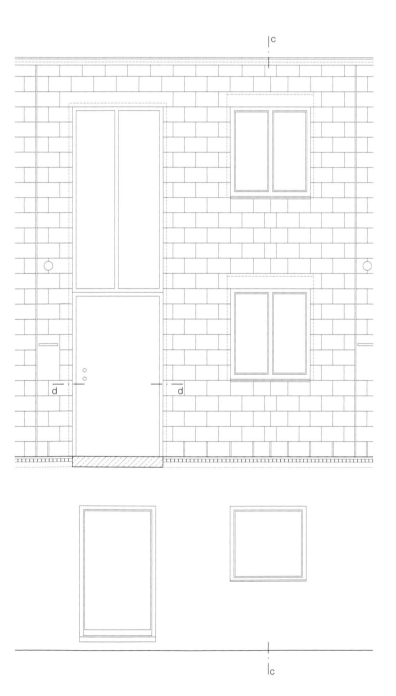

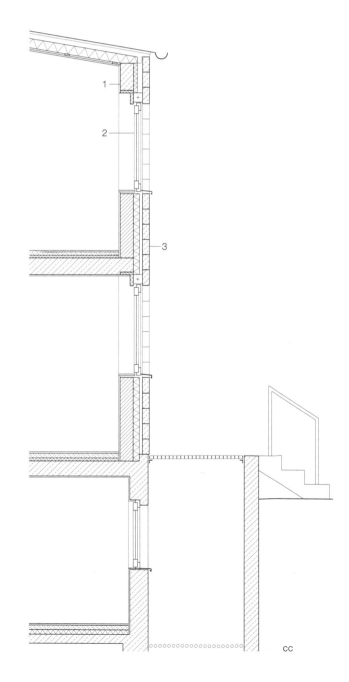

cc

Example 8

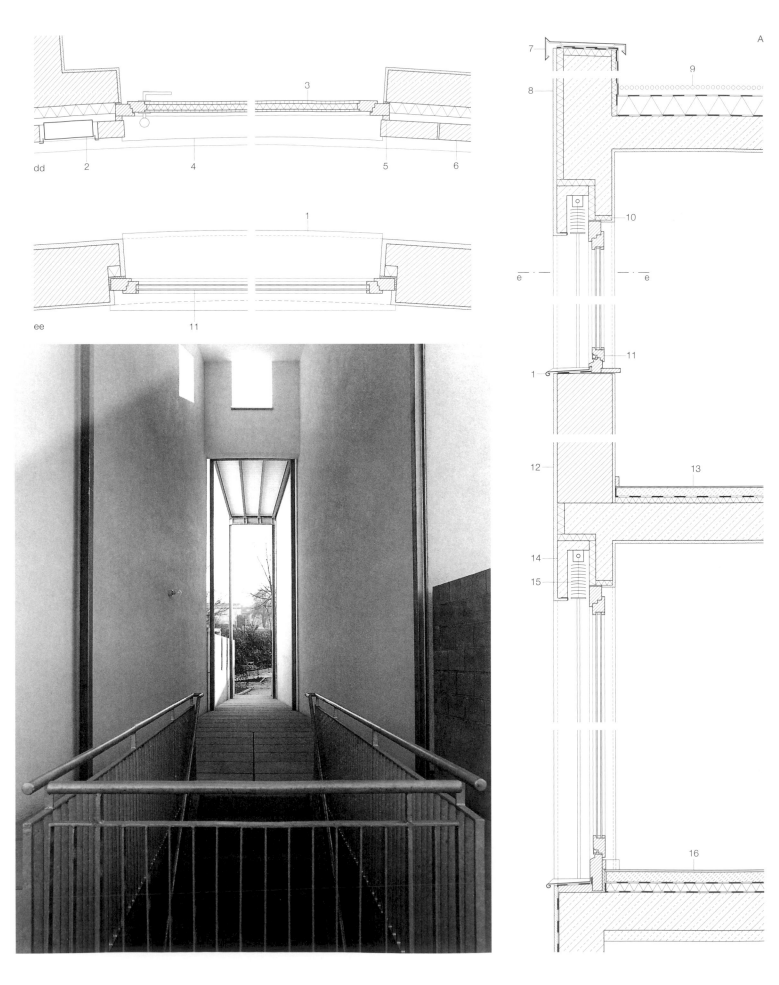

1 Window sill, titanium-zinc sheet
2 Letter box
3 Entrance door
4 Door threshold, 5 mm galvanized steel sheet
5 Cavity closer
6 Wall construction:
 90 mm concrete bricks
 40 mm air space
 60 mm thermal insulation
 175 mm calcium silicate bricks
 15 mm lime-cement plaster
7 Parapet capping, titanium-zinc sheet
8 Parapet construction:
 20 mm rendering
 thermal insulation, 35 mm rigid expanded foam
 reinforced concrete wall
 thermal insulation, 25 mm rigid expanded foam
 waterproofing

9 Roof construction:
 50 mm gravel
 waterproofing
 thermal insulation,
 100 mm rigid expanded foam
 vapour barrier
 180 mm RC slab
 15 mm lime-cement plaster
10 Thermal insulation, 25 mm
11 Wooden window with insulating glazing
12 Wall construction:
 20 mm rendering
 300 mm ltwt clay bricks
 15 mm lime-cement plaster
13 Floor construction:
 linoleum
 45 mm screed
 separating membrane
 30 mm thermal insulation
 200 mm RC slab
 15 mm lime-cement plaster
14 Precast concrete lintel
15 Blind
16 Floor construction:
 linoleum

 55 mm screed
 separating membrane
 60 mm thermal insulation
 waterproofing, bitumen sheeting
 200 mm RC slab
 blinding
17 Wall construction:
 20 mm rendering
 thermal insulation, 50 mm rigid expanded foam
 240 mm RC wall
 15 mm lime-cement plaster
18 Flashing, titanium-zinc sheet
19 Titanium-zinc sheet, plastic-laminated
20 Monopitch roof construction:
 waterproofing
 24 mm timber boarding
 120 x 180 mm rafters
 120 mm thermal insulation
 25 mm timber battens
 15 mm plasterboard
21 Roller blind box, 100 x 100 mm
22 Steel angle, 120 x 80 x 8 mm

B

Horizontal sections
Concrete brick facade ·
Rendered facade
Vertical sections
scale 1:20

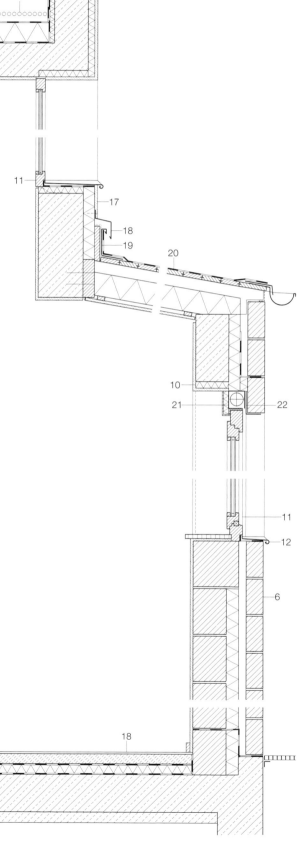

Example 9

**Housing complex in Groningen,
The Netherlands**

1993

Architects:
Felix Claus, Kees Kaan, Amsterdam
Assistant:
Andrew Dawes
Structural engineers:
Ingenieurbüro Wassenaar, Haren

The surrounding streets and paths determine
the urban arrangement of the whole complex,
which forms an intermittent boundary on two
sides of a triangular park open at the west end.
On the south-west side there are terraced
houses with walled gardens, while on the north-
east side there are three blocks containing
apartments. These form the backbone of the
complex, split up by the intervening access
paths and play areas. On the southern side
facing the park, the apartments are fully glazed
with slim balconies. On the other side, facing
the road, the open walkways on the upper
floors are well lit via the generous expanse of
glazing. The slim apartments contain two deep
rooms facing south-west, which can be used
as living room, bedroom or study as required.
The kitchen and a further room lie on the walkway side.
The terraced houses on the southern boundary
of the site are arranged in groups of six, separated from each other by narrow access
passageways.
The loadbearing construction consists of twin-
leaf masonry walls with precast concrete floors.
The external surfaces – red facing brickwork
adjacent the alleyways, vertical timber boarding facing the gardens and on the gables – are
skilfully related to each other. On the ground
floor the almost square houses are divided into
an entrance lobby, kitchen and living/dining
area. A winding stair leads from the lobby up to
the first floor, which contains three rooms and a
small, separate toilet, plus bathroom. The plan
layouts are such that the houses could be
divided into separate apartments on ground
floor and first floor at a later date. The apartment blocks are differentiated in a similar fash-
ion: storey-height sliding windows in front of
glass facades on the park side, clay brickwork
to the gables. The ground floor "plinth"
facing the road is likewise built in red brickwork. A partial-fill cavity wall is used throughout, with the stretcher bond also continuing
across the lintels. The windows, with wooden
subframes and inset casements, are positioned
in the plane of the thermal insulation and air
space. They employ a contrasting colour near
the entrances and are divided up with a few
reinforced concrete elements.

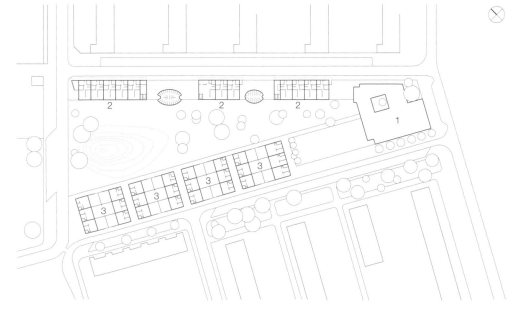

Location plan scale 1:2000
Sheltered housing
West elevation · Ground floor
scale 1:250

1 Existing church
2 48 sheltered housing units
3 24 houses with walled gardens

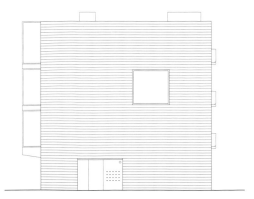

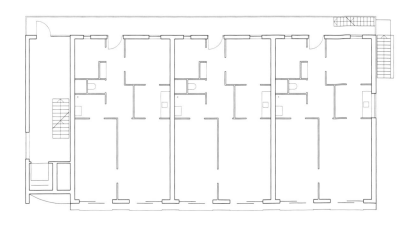

Example 9

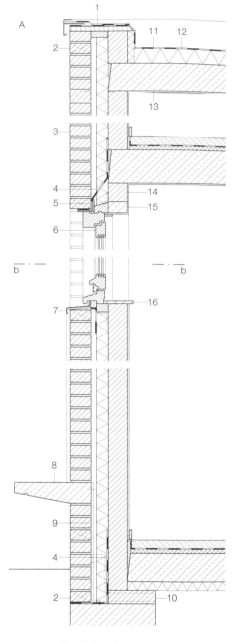

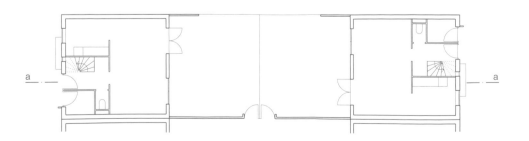

Houses will walled gardens
Section · Ground floor
scale 1:250
Sections
scale 1:20

1 Laminated veneer lumber (LVL)
   board, with bitumen sheet waterproofing
2 Open perpend
3 Wall construction:
   102 mm facing clay brickwork
   28 mm air space
   60 mm thermal insulation
   100 mm calcium silicate brickwork
   15 mm plaster
4 Damp proof course
5 Steel angle, 80 x 80 x 8 mm
6 Wooden window, with insulating
   glazing
7 Window sill, aluminium sheet
8 Built-in bench, precast concrete
9 Bracket, bent steel sheet,
   500 x 80 mm
10 Ventilation pipe, grille in facade
11 Waterproofing, bitumen sheeting, 1 layer

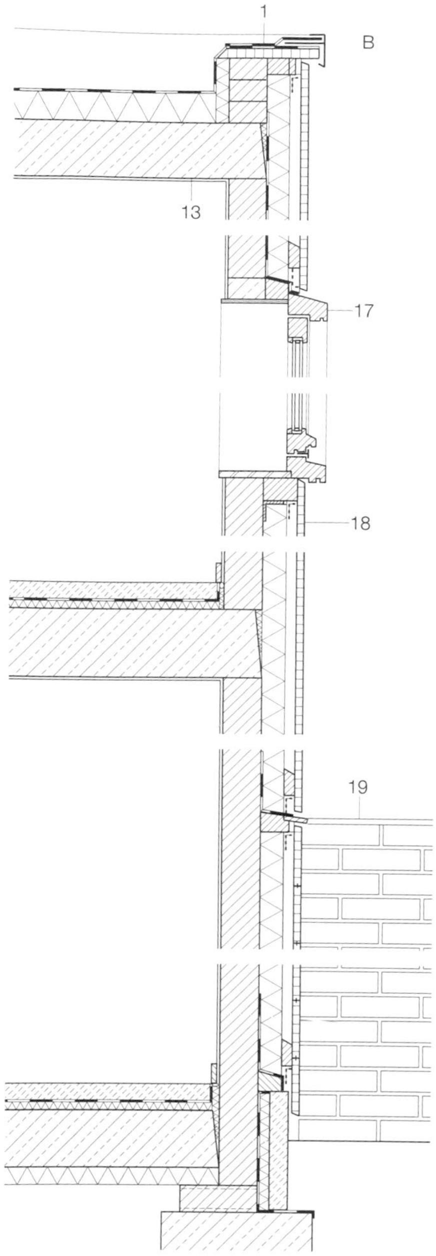

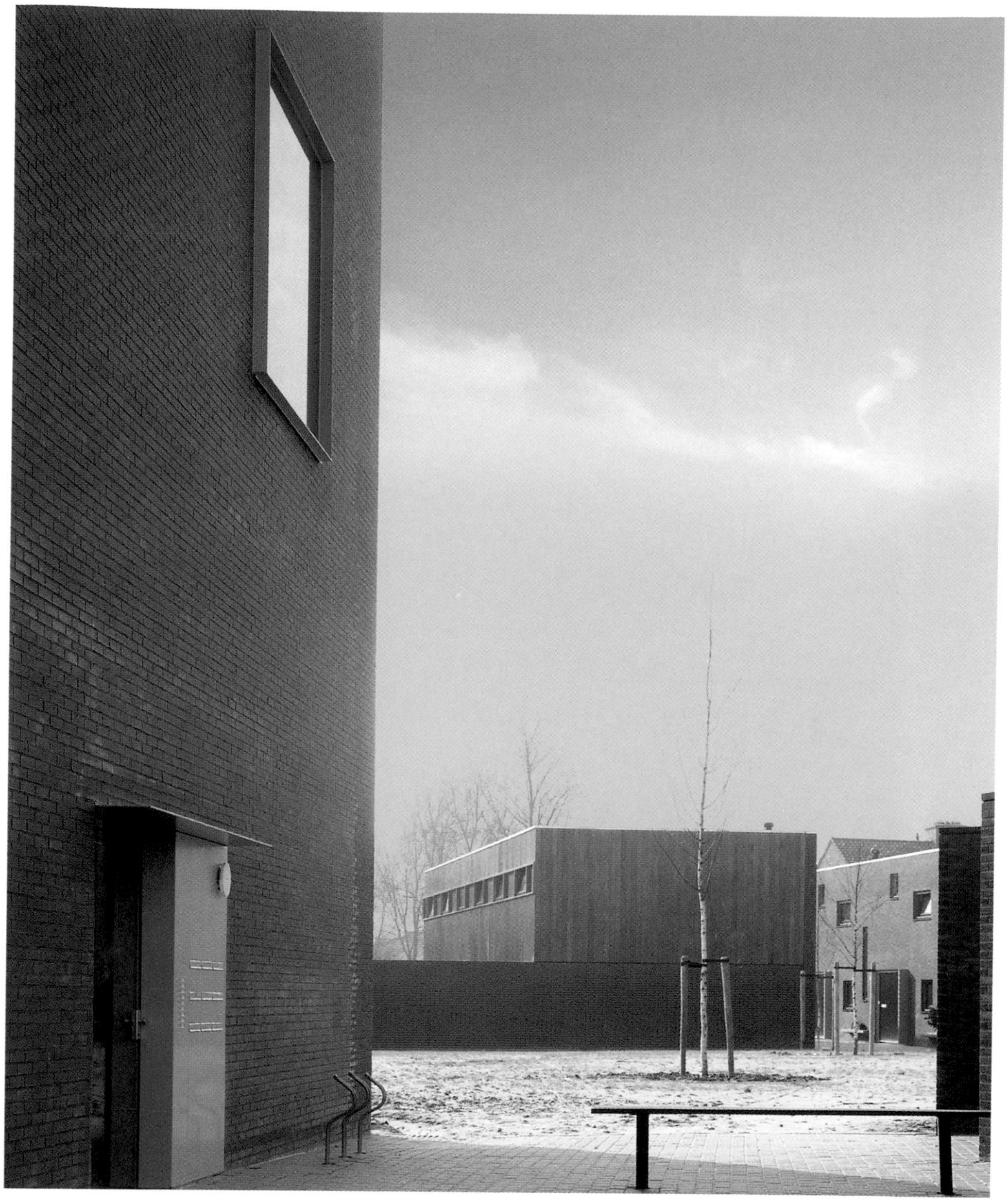

12 Thermal insulation, 60-80 mm
13 Reinforced concrete slab, 150 mm
14 Reinforced clay brickwork
15 Precast concrete element
16 Reconstituted stone window sill
17 Wooden window, with external lining and insulating glazing

18 Wall construction:
profiled boarding, 19 mm western red cedar
28 x 46 mm timber battens with cut-outs for ventilation
44 x 63 mm timber studs
60 mm thermal insulation
100 mm calcium silicate masonry, 15 mm plaster

19 Reconstituted stone coping
20 Movement joint, 2-3 mm
21 Door element
22 Precast concrete element with built-in lights
23 Thermal insulation, 60 mm

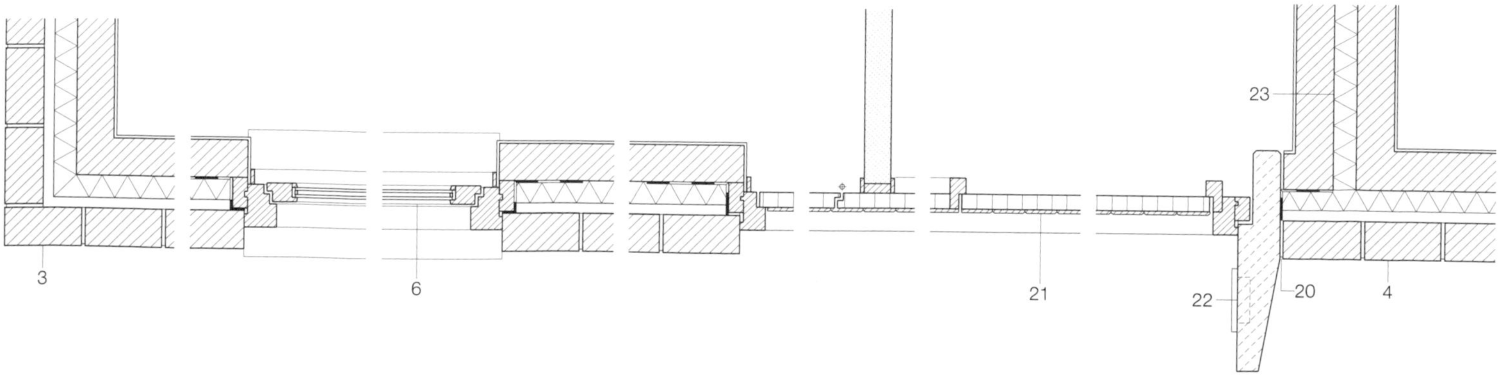

Example 10

Two apartment blocks in Berlin, Germany

1997

Architects:
Tim Helde and Verena von Beckerath, Berlin
Assistants:
Rainer Schmitz (project manager),
Heike Lauterbach, Wolfgang Rehn
Site manager:
Wolfgang Gärsch, Berlin
Structural engineer:
Jörg Wiese, Berlin

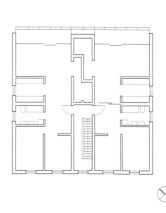

Following on from the inter-city housing developments of the 1980s, housing estates continued to be built and added to on the north-east boundary of Berlin after German unification. New urban development strategies were intended to do justice to the great demand for housing. These two isolated blocks are part of a general plan. The four-storey buildings without basements both contain three apartments on each upper floor (each with three rooms plus kitchen, bathroom) and two smaller apartments on the ground floor, which leaves space for ancillary rooms.

The simple two-apartment format was developed within the scope of the guidelines for publicly assisted housebuilding. The staircase and the ground floor storage rooms, which replace cellars, form the central core. This arrangement enables a slim plan layout and enables occupants to utilize the space to the full. The spacious hallways can be used for different purposes as required and may also be subdivided by way of a sliding door. Bathrooms and kitchens are placed on external walls to permit natural lighting and ventilation. Walls of calcium silicate masonry with reinforced concrete floors and beams form the loadbearing structure. The outer leaf, with air space behind, of blue-brown, facing bricks, hard-burned almost to vitrification, forms the finish on three sides of each block; on the garden elevation all floors have full-width balconies. The masonry facades are regular and identical. The room-height glazing is positioned in the plane of the thermal insulation and is combined with a sliding shutter of perforated stainless steel and a galvanized steel balustrade. The shutter finishes flush with the facade and can be slid into a shallow recess in the masonry, which results from the outer leaf of masonry being set back into the cavity.

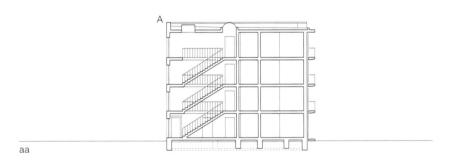

aa

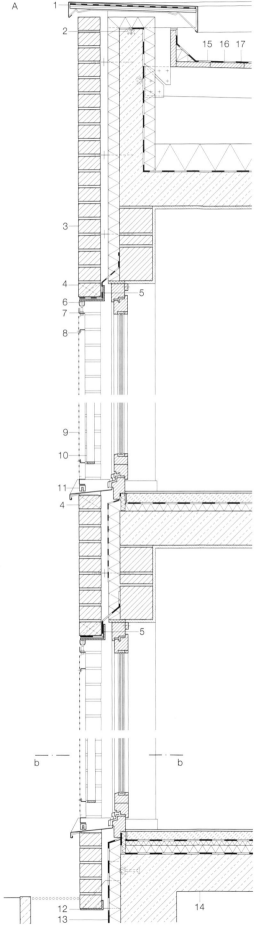

Ground floor · Upper floor
Section
scale 1:400

Facade details
Horizontal section · Vertical section
scale 1.20

1 Titanium-zinc sheet capping
2 Cast-in slot
3 Wall construction:
115 mm facing brickwork
40 mm air space
thermal insulation, 60 mm mineral wool
or 60 mm external insulation behind sliding
elements
175 mm calcium silicate brickwork
15 mm plaster
4 Open perpend
5 Galvanized steel angle, 80 x 130 x 10 mm
6 Rustproof track for twin-wheel roller
7 Galvanized steel angle, 30 x 30 x 3 mm

8 Galvanized steel angle, 20 x 30 x 3 mm
9 Stainless steel sheet with elongated perforations, 1 mm, edges not perforated
10 Spandrel element of 10 x 40 mm
galvanized steel sections
11 Plastic track
12 Support bracket fixed to cast-in slot
13 External insulation, 60 mm rigid expanded
foam
14 Reinforced concrete ground slab
15 Waterproofing, bitumen sheeting
16 Timber boarding, 28 mm
17 Rafters, 100 x 160 mm

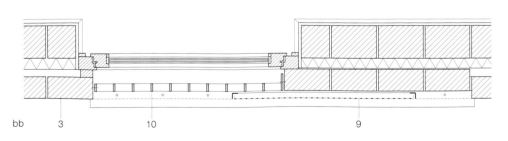

bb   3   10   9

Example 11

**Housing complex in Amsterdam,
The Netherlands**

1994

Architect:
Hans Kollhoff, Berlin
with Christian Rapp, Berlin/Amsterdam
Structural engineers:
Heijckmann Consulting Engineers, Amsterdam

This extensive building complex, on a former
docks and industry island not far from the centre of Amsterdam, is part of an urban redevelopment programme. This programme allows
for individual large buildings to respond differently to the local conditions, existing buildings
and their position in relation to the water. The
basic outline of this four- to nine-storey structure is determined by an existing building on
the southern side of the plot.
There are more than 300 apartments accessible via a network of staircases, various open
walkways and individual stairs. The very deep
apartments in most cases receive daylight from
both sides when they are not located on one of
the – sometimes – very long access corridors.
The entire building complex was built using
twin-leaf facing masonry with 100 mm hard-
burned bricks. Standard stretcher bond was
used throughout, even for the single-leaf
240 mm facing masonry of the balcony walls
and the walls adjacent the open walkways. In
these instances two 115 mm walls were built,
one directly behind the other, and the under-
sides of balconies and loggias adapted to suit
the window lintels. Therefore, the entire building has been given a consistent masonry texture which reinforces the placid immensity of
the complex. The edges of the roofs are finished with folded aluminium sheet with the
gutters placed internally. The wooden windows
are set back in the plane of the insulation, while
the steel windows to the loggias are fitted flush
with the masonry facade in a steel lining with
peripheral ventilation joint. The folding mechanism of these windows allows them to be
opened outwards and thus create an ever-
changing pattern, which animates this huge
sculpture.

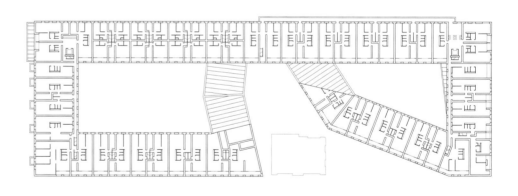

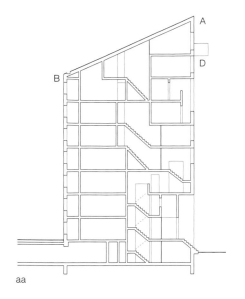

aa

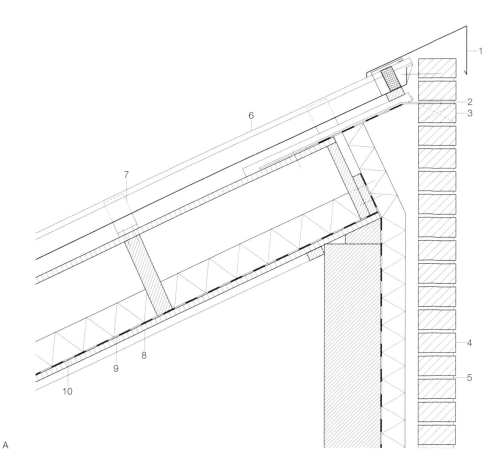

A

North elevation
4th floor · Ground floor
scale 1:1250
Section
scale 1:400
Sections through verge and eaves
scale 1:10

1   Aluminium sheet capping
2   Galvanized steel flat, 20 x 2 mm
3   Open perpend
4   Wall construction:
    100 mm variegated blue facing bricks, hard-burned
    35 mm air space
    thermal insulation, 65 mm rockwool
    150 mm calcium silicate brickwork
5   Joints recessed 5 mm
6   Sheet aluminium roof covering,
    with double-lock welted joints
7   Cleat
8   Laminated veneer lumber (LVL), 10 mm
9   Vapour barrier, 0.15 mm
10 Thermal insulation, 80 mm mineral wool
11 Aluminium sheet capping
12 Aluminium sheet gutter
13 LVL, 18 mm
14 Timber section, 146 x 71 mm
15 Galvanized steel flat, 40 x 6 mm
16 Calcium silicate brickwork, 150 mm
17 Thermal insulation, 40 mm rockwool
18 Floor construction:
    50 mm cement screed
    180 mm reinforced concrete slab
19 Thermal insulation,
    multilayer lightweight board,
    with plaster, 60 mm
20 Rainwater downpipe, 125 mm NB

B

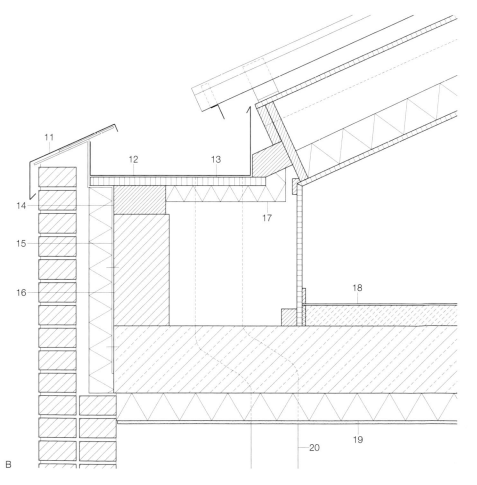

Example 11

C

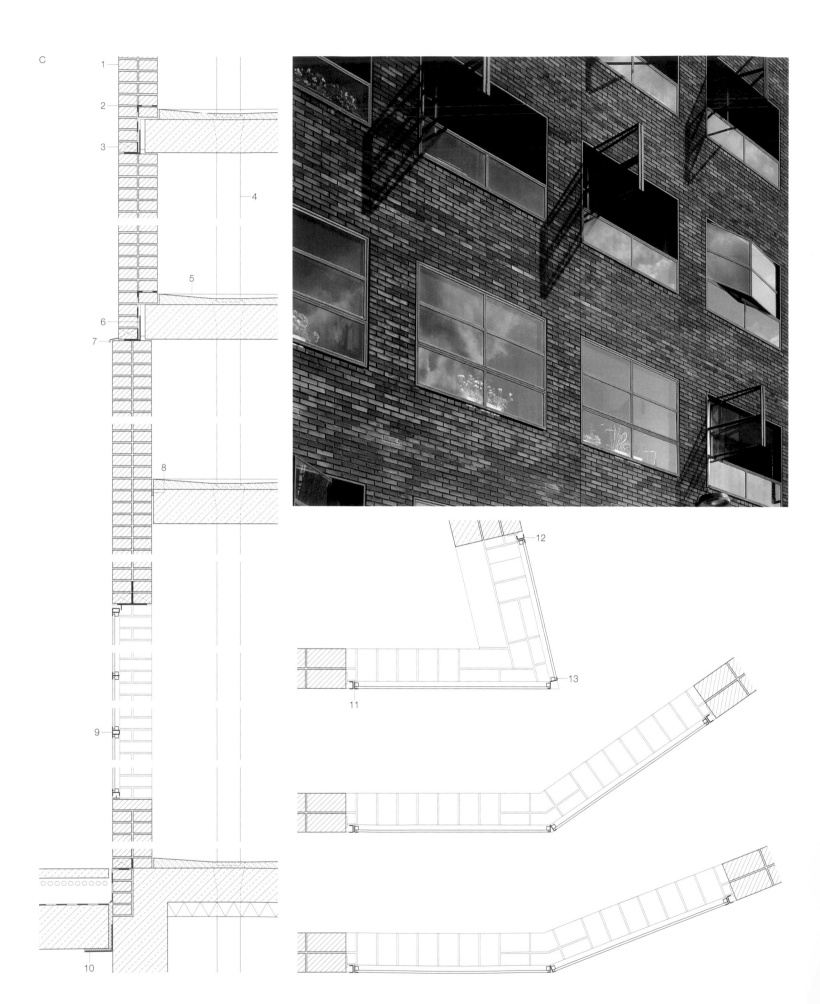

1

2

3

4

5

6

7

8

9

10

11

12

13

Section through external wall
Horizontal sections through corners of building with steel
windows: 76.58° – 144.92° – 158.38°
Elevation on steel window
Horizontal section through steel window
scale 1:20

1 Wall construction:
 208 mm variegated blue facing bricks,
 hard-burned
2 Joints recessed 5 mm
3 Open perpend
4 Rainwater downpipe, 125 mm NB
5 Floor construction:
 cement screed laid to falls, coated
 180 mm reinforced concrete slab
 cut-out for drainage
6 Steel angle
7 Titanium-zinc sheet flashing
8 Compressible sealing strip
9 Steel window, powder coated,
 4 mm toughened safety glass
10 Steel angle, 150 x 150 x 15 mm, with slip joint
11 Steel angle, 40 x 20 x 4 mm
12 Steel channel, 40 x 20 x 4 mm
13 2 No. steel angles, 40 x 20 x 4 mm

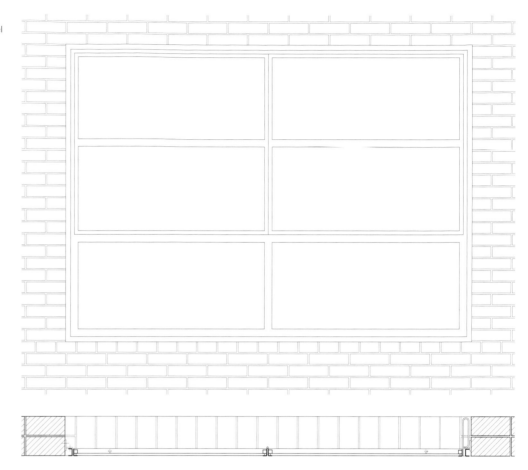

Example 11

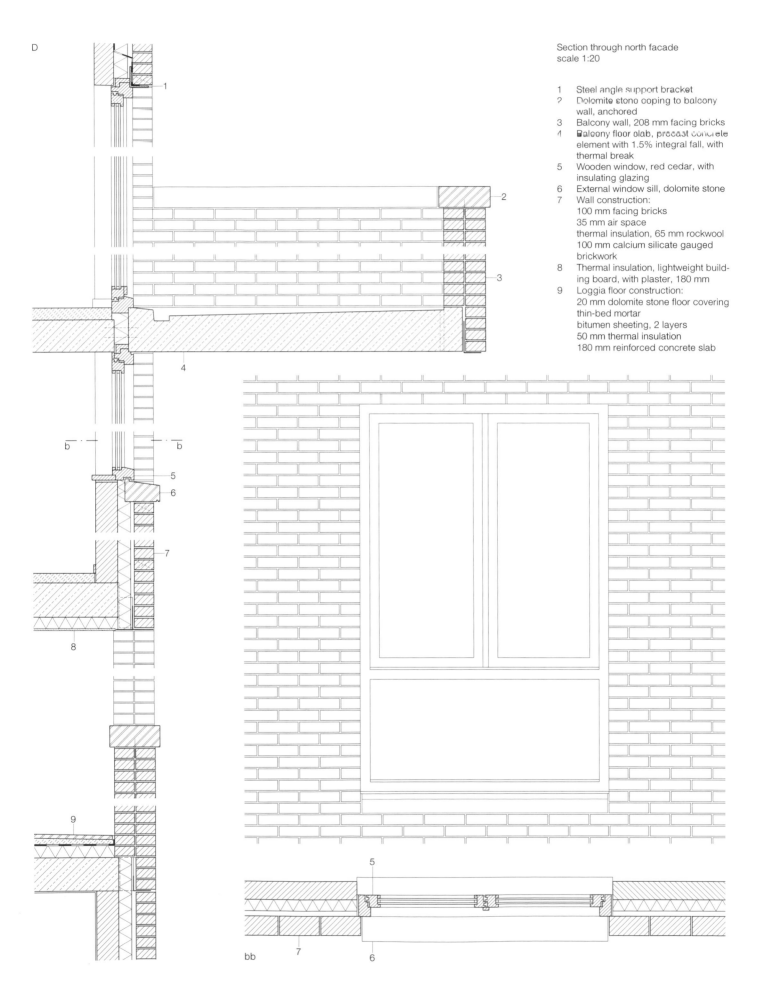

D

Section through north facade
scale 1:20

1   Steel angle support bracket
2   Dolomite stone coping to balcony
    wall, anchored
3   Balcony wall, 208 mm facing bricks
4   Balcony floor slab, precast concrete
    element with 1.5% integral fall, with
    thermal break
5   Wooden window, red cedar, with
    insulating glazing
6   External window sill, dolomite stone
7   Wall construction:
    100 mm facing bricks
    35 mm air space
    thermal insulation, 65 mm rockwool
    100 mm calcium silicate gauged
    brickwork
8   Thermal insulation, lightweight build-
    ing board, with plaster, 180 mm
9   Loggia floor construction:
    20 mm dolomite stone floor covering
    thin-bed mortar
    bitumen sheeting, 2 layers
    50 mm thermal insulation
    180 mm reinforced concrete slab

bb

Example 12

**Extension to Hirschberg Palace near
Beilngries, Germany**

1992

Architects:
Karljosef Schattner
and Karl-Heinz Schmitz, Eichstätt
Structural engineers:
Sailer, Stepan, Bloos, Munich

The symmetrical palace structure dating from the 18th century stands on a narrow hilltop and therefore offered little scope for any extension. This completely refurbished building is used by the church for spiritual exercises and education. Besides extensive conversion work, a new annex was built to accommodate kitchen, dining hall and storage facilities.

The new section is positioned in front of the south wing of the palace and is partly built into the side of the hill. A row of tall concrete columns supports the long, slim structure clear of the slope and hence emphasizes the contrast with the strictly uniform, rendered finish to the palace. Fair-face concrete and concrete bricks for the outer leaf of the partial-fill cavity wall underline the independence of the new structure. A long, narrow, steel-and-glass hall provides a clear demarcation between old and new.

The outer leaf is clearly distinguished from the rest of the construction; there is an air space behind and therefore the leaf is positioned 40 mm proud of the reinforced concrete wall and the row of columns. Grey steel angles mark the corners of the facing brickwork, and a steel channel forms an elegant finish to the top of the walls. The deeply recessed, narrow, vertical window slits are also framed in grey steel which projects beyond the facade and so conveys the impression of very precisely located cut-outs. The steel external stair employs a particularly delicate construction in order not to disturb the careful balance between harmonization and independence.

All these clear, simple details lend the annex a lightness and obvious language which is quite distinct from that of the old palace.

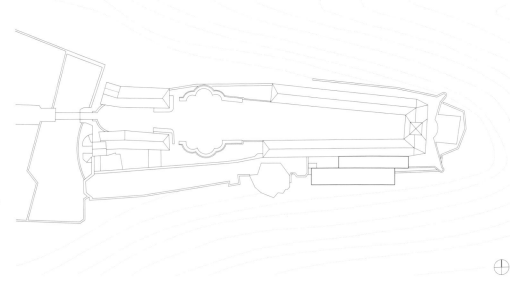

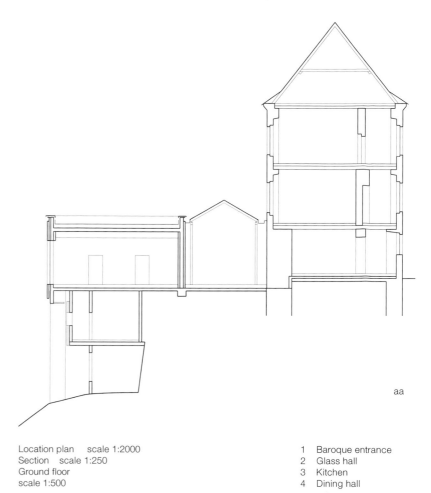

aa

Location plan   scale 1:2000
Section   scale 1:250
Ground floor
scale 1:500

1   Baroque entrance
2   Glass hall
3   Kitchen
4   Dining hall

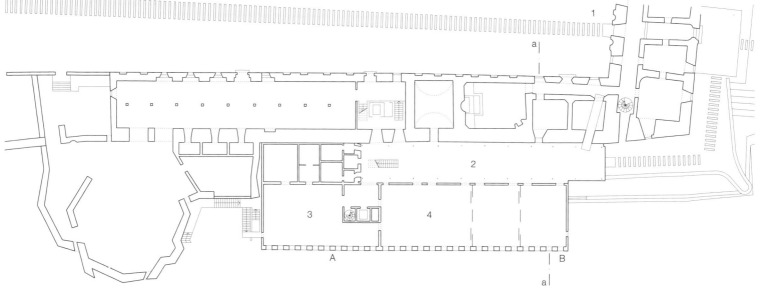

Example 12

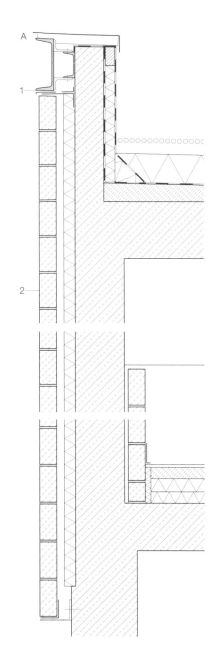

A

1

2

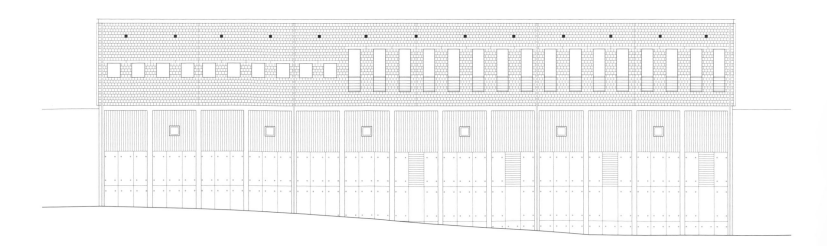

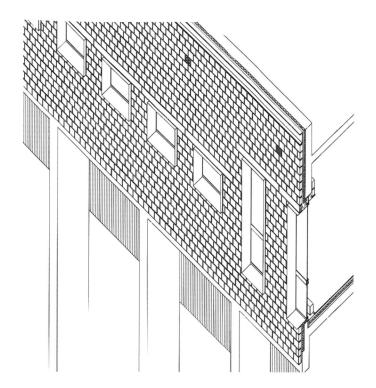

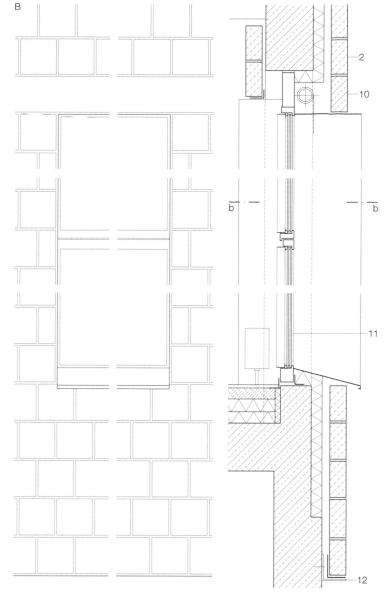

Vertical section through external wall
scale 1:20
South elevation
scale 1:250
Axonometric view
not to scale
Detail of parapet
scale 1:5
Window
Elevation · Vertical section ·
Horizontal section
scale 1:20

1   Steel channel, 280 mm
2   External wall construction:
    concrete bricks, 200 x 200 x 90 mm
    40 mm air space
    60 mm thermal insulation
    160 mm reinforced concrete
3   Steel angle, 100 x 65 x 9 mm
4   Screw fixing, M12
5   Steel channel, 140 mm
6   Steel T-section, 50 mm
7   Sheet steel capping, galvanized, 2 mm
8   Timber section, 100 x 60 mm
9   Thermal insulation, 60 mm
10 Reinforced concrete lintel
11 Window: steel frame with insulating
    glazing in sheet steel lining
12 Steel angle support bracket

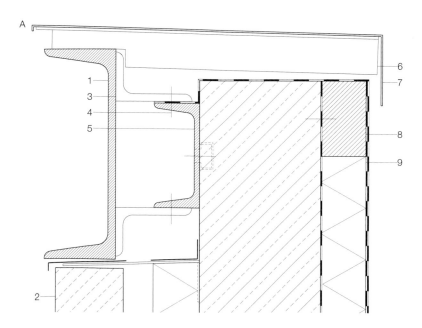

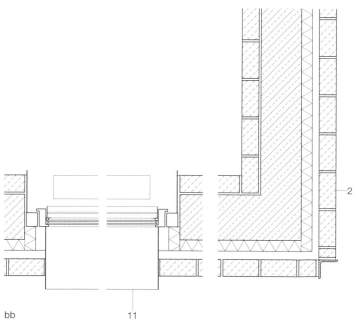

Example 13

Youth hostel in Dachau, Germany

1998

Architect:
Rudolf Hierl, Munich
Assistants:
Peter Hofman (project manager),
Dominik Fischer, Maleen Fromm,
Nadja Herrmann, Michaela Oswald,
Jeannette Quecke, Ulrike Rechler,
Bernhard Schambeck, Oliver Schubert,
Tanja Wienecke
Structural engineer:
Hans Tischner, Dachau

This facility, run by the German Youth Hostels Association, is more than just a youth hostel. Situated near the former Nazi concentration and extermination camp, it acts as a centre for getting to grips with the dark side of Germany's history. The architectural form is intended to reflect both the functions of the building but also this special task. Apart from the main building, there is also a building for the staff and the separate "Raum der Stille" (Room of Silence). These three structures frame a tranquil inner courtyard – a garden and structured space, which is ideal for understanding and experiencing the serious issues that dominate this place. The restrained architecture responds to its surroundings by limiting the materials used to timber and facing brickwork of light-coloured concrete bricks. The texture of the building emphasizes the low-rise, elongated form; both in terms of the size and the style of the facade. The main building covers a large area and so two storeys are adequate. It measures 24.5 x 60 m and is arranged as two parallel blocks either side of a central circulation zone. The architectural setting distinguishes between the different materials. For instance, on the west side of the building, the wooden recesses for windows and sunshades on the ground floor are juxtaposed with the concrete masonry lintels and spandrel panels of the upper floor. Placing the masonry above the timber is a reversal of our customary ideas and introduces a different reality to challenge the perception of the observer. This is an artistic contrivance for reminding us of the special importance of this place. The wall construction is conventional – partial-fill cavity wall with outer leaf supported on individual brackets – but incorporates special details that emphasize and preserve the restful uniformity of the stretcher bond. Such details include the mortar joints raked out to a depth of 15 mm and the movement joints which zigzag to follow the bond.

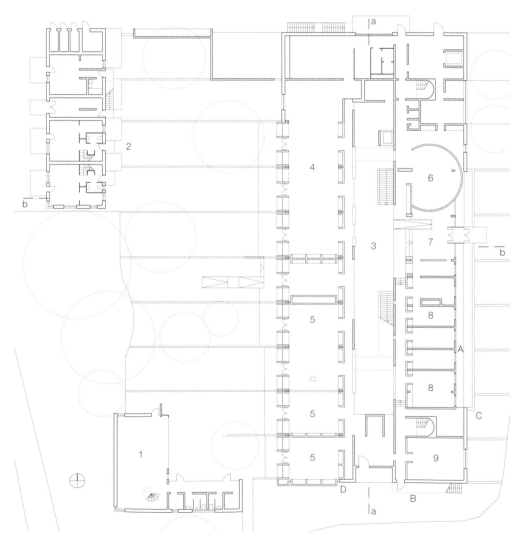

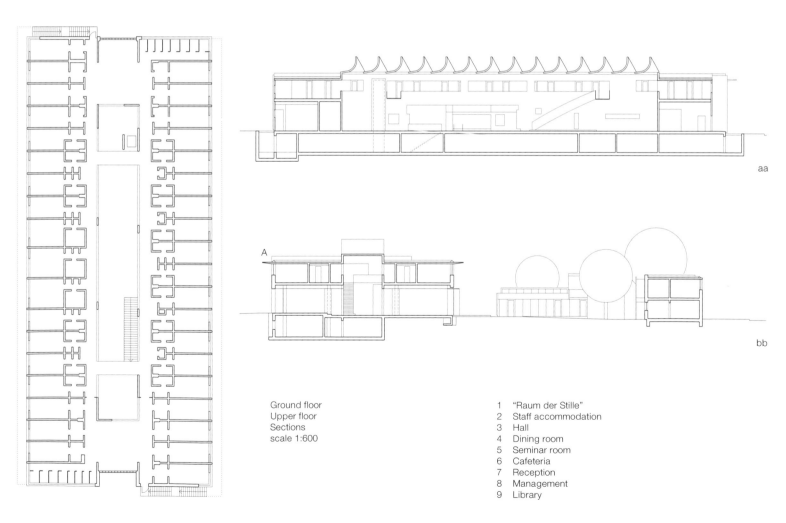

Ground floor
Upper floor
Sections
scale 1:600

1   "Raum der Stille"
2   Staff accommodation
3   Hall
4   Dining room
5   Seminar room
6   Cafeteria
7   Reception
8   Management
9   Library

aa

bb

A

Example 13

Section through east facade   A
scale 1:20

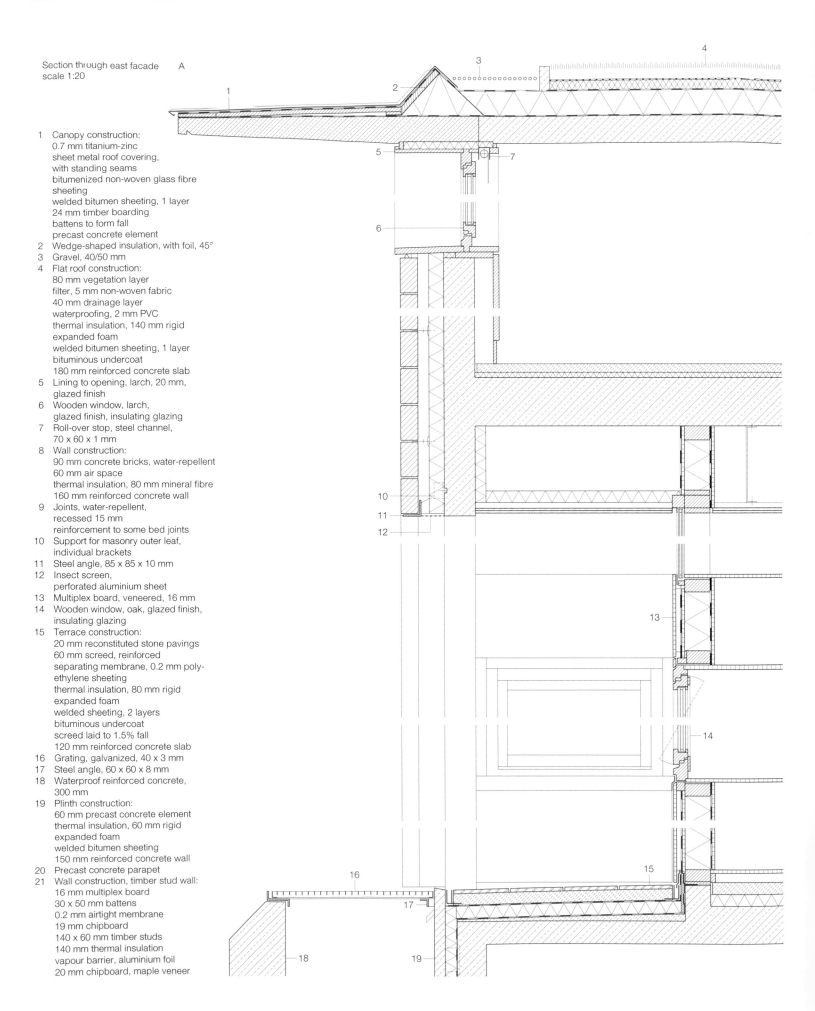

1 Canopy construction:
   0.7 mm titanium-zinc
   sheet metal roof covering,
   with standing seams
   bitumenized non-woven glass fibre
   sheeting
   welded bitumen sheeting, 1 layer
   24 mm timber boarding
   battens to form fall
   precast concrete element
2 Wedge-shaped insulation, with foil, 45°
3 Gravel, 40/50 mm
4 Flat roof construction:
   80 mm vegetation layer
   filter, 5 mm non-woven fabric
   40 mm drainage layer
   waterproofing, 2 mm PVC
   thermal insulation, 140 mm rigid
   expanded foam
   welded bitumen sheeting, 1 layer
   bituminous undercoat
   180 mm reinforced concrete slab
5 Lining to opening, larch, 20 mm,
   glazed finish
6 Wooden window, larch,
   glazed finish, insulating glazing
7 Roll-over stop, steel channel,
   70 x 60 x 1 mm
8 Wall construction:
   90 mm concrete bricks, water-repellent
   60 mm air space
   thermal insulation, 80 mm mineral fibre
   160 mm reinforced concrete wall
9 Joints, water-repellent,
   recessed 15 mm
   reinforcement to some bed joints
10 Support for masonry outer leaf,
   individual brackets
11 Steel angle, 85 x 85 x 10 mm
12 Insect screen,
   perforated aluminium sheet
13 Multiplex board, veneered, 16 mm
14 Wooden window, oak, glazed finish,
   insulating glazing
15 Terrace construction:
   20 mm reconstituted stone pavings
   60 mm screed, reinforced
   separating membrane, 0.2 mm polyethylene sheeting
   thermal insulation, 80 mm rigid
   expanded foam
   welded sheeting, 2 layers
   bituminous undercoat
   screed laid to 1.5% fall
   120 mm reinforced concrete slab
16 Grating, galvanized, 40 x 3 mm
17 Steel angle, 60 x 60 x 8 mm
18 Waterproof reinforced concrete,
   300 mm
19 Plinth construction:
   60 mm precast concrete element
   thermal insulation, 60 mm rigid
   expanded foam
   welded bitumen sheeting
   150 mm reinforced concrete wall
20 Precast concrete parapet
21 Wall construction, timber stud wall:
   16 mm multiplex board
   30 x 50 mm battens
   0.2 mm airtight membrane
   19 mm chipboard
   140 x 60 mm timber studs
   140 mm thermal insulation
   vapour barrier, aluminium foil
   20 mm chipboard, maple veneer

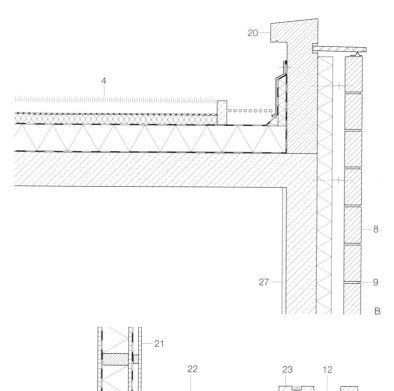

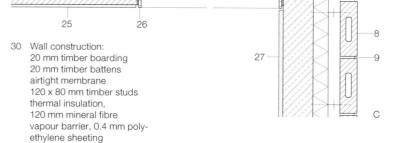

Section through parapet
Horizontal sections
scale 1:20

22 6 mm laminated safety glass +
8 mm toughened safety glass
outside
23 Precast concrete element,
150 x 180 mm
24 Thermal insulation, 60 mm rigid
expanded foam
25 Clay brickwork internal wall,
plastered both sides, 115 mm

26 Removable lining to window
opening, laminated veneer lumber
(LVL), 136 x 15 mm
27 Internal plaster, 20 mm
28 Built-in cupboard
29 Wall construction, return wall:
20 mm multiplex board
0.2 mm airtight membrane
120 x 100 mm timber studs
therm. insulation, 100 mm min. fibre
vapour barrier, 0.4 mm polyethylene sheeting
20 mm multiplex board, screwed
and glued to timber frame

30 Wall construction:
20 mm timber boarding
20 mm timber battens
airtight membrane
120 x 80 mm timber studs
thermal insulation,
120 mm mineral fibre
vapour barrier, 0.4 mm polyethylene sheeting
30 mm multiplex board

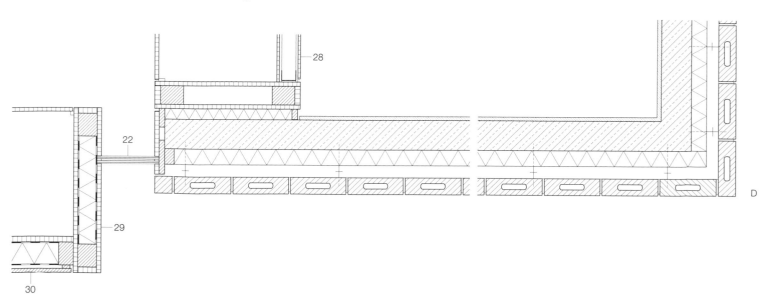

Example 13

School in Munich, Germany

1999

Architects:
Schunck-Ullrich-Krausen, Munich
Project partner:
Norbert Krausen
Project manager:
Martin Kerling
Assistants:
Robert Kellner, Martina Wulf
Structural engineers
Sailer, Stepan & Partner, Munich

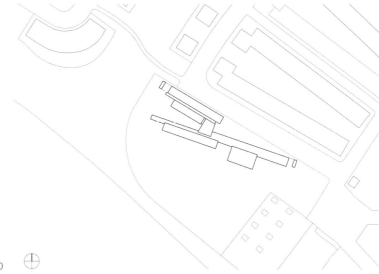

Location plan   scale 1:4000

The ensemble of buildings forming this primary school is well spaced out on this site on the outskirts of Munich. To the south there is a landscaped noise barrier screening the school from the adjacent railway line, and to the east and north-west the school is bounded by housing. The random arrangement of the long, low-rise buildings defines courtyards and semi-enclosed spaces, thereby allowing the school to mesh with its surroundings.

The quality of the architecture is evident on the inside as well, with brightly lit passages and corridors, which structure the layout and incorporate the landscape, as well as in the careful design and construction of the details.

The different facades are part of an energy concept: while the classrooms facing south employ full-height glazing (which leads to corresponding solar gains), the other facades are mainly built using a highly insulated solid construction. Their appearance is governed by the partial-fill cavity wall with concrete brick (290 x 190 x 90 mm) outer leaf built in a variation of raking stretcher bond.

The building materials used have essentially been left untreated. Inside, the rough concrete bricks contrast with the few wooden surfaces and a number of coloured elements which have been very carefully and discreetly incorporated. Outside, the concrete surfaces, the concrete bricks, the galvanized steel and the light-coloured anodized aluminium window frames enter into a dialogue with the green surroundings.

Using minimal architectural means, the school succeeds in conveying an impression of playful and charming attractiveness. The masonry units of this building, left untreated, give the school a "tangible" texture.

Example 14

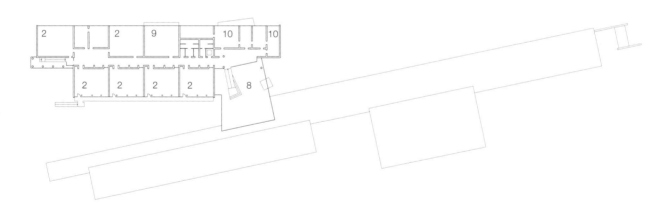

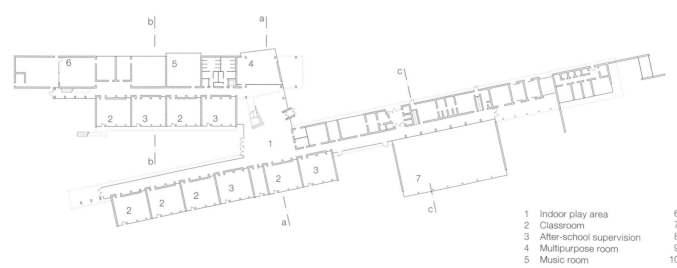

1	Indoor play area	6	Workshop
2	Classroom	7	Sports hall
3	After-school supervision	8	Void
4	Multipurpose room	9	Staffroom
5	Music room	10	Management

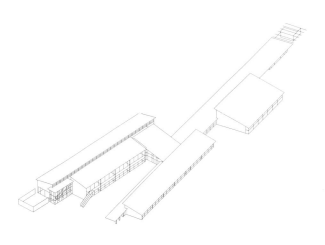

Upper floor ·
Ground floor
scale 1:1000

Isometric view of buildings
Isometric view of facade
not to scale

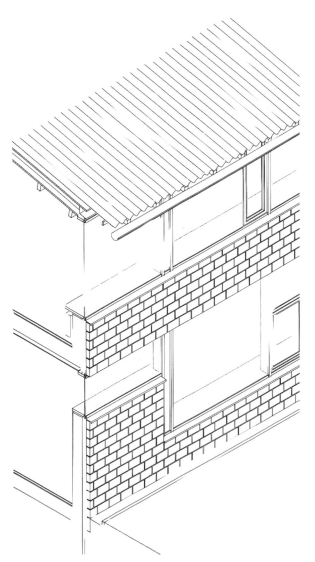

Example 14

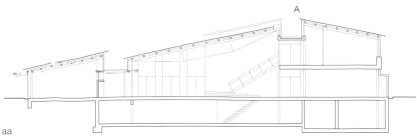

aa

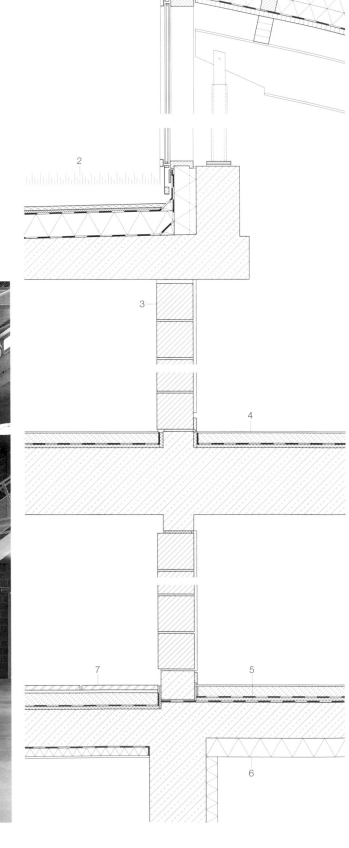

1   Monopitch roof construction:
    corrugated aluminium sheeting,
    177 x 55 mm
    50 mm battens and counterbattens
    waterproofing, 3 mm bitumen
    sheeting
    24 mm timber boarding
    80 mm air space
    thermal insulation, 160 mm mineral
    fibre
    vapour barrier, polyethylene sheeting
    28 mm timber boarding
    glulam purlin, 14 x 8 mm
    steel beam, IPE 270

2   Flat roof construction:
    100 mm vegetation layer
    20 mm drainage mat, with non-woven
    fabric
    15 mm structure protection mat
    waterproofing, 5 mm plastic sheeting,
    resistant to root penetration
    120 mm rigid expanded polyurethane
    insulation
    vapour barrier
    200 mm reinforced concrete slab, top
    surface cast to 2% fall
3   Internal wall, concrete bricks, white,
    290 x 190 x 190 mm

Section through hall
scale 1:400
Section through clerestory over internal wall
section through external wall
scale 1:20
Section through classroom wing
Section through sports hall
scale 1:400

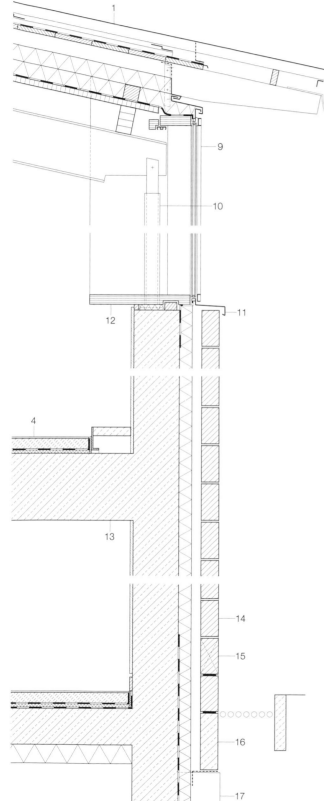

4 Floor construction:
   5 mm linoleum
   55 mm cement screed, reinforced
   separating membrane, polyethylene
   sheeting
   10 mm impact sound insulation
5 Damp proof membrane on ground floor
   slab, 200 mm reinforced concrete slab
6 Thermal insulation, 100 mm rigid
   expanded foam
7 Floor construction:
   25 mm natural stone tiles laid in thin
   bed
   65 mm screed
   separating membrane, polyethylene
   sheeting
   10 mm impact sound insulation
   200 mm reinforced concrete slab
   50 mm multiplex lightweight mineral
   building board
8 Aluminium gutter
9 Post-and-rail facade:
   50 mm laminated veneer lumber (LVL),
   birch, clear lacquer to exposed face
   insulating glazing, aluminium cover
   profile, natural-colour anodized
10 Column, steel circular hollow section,
   82.5 dia. x 3.6 mm
11 Aluminium sheet, natural-colour
   anodized
12 LVL rail, birch, 530 x 50 mm
13 Reinforced concrete slab, 350 mm
14 Wall construction:
   outer leaf of concrete bricks, white,
   raking stretcher bond 290 x 190 x 90 mm
   50 mm air space
   thermal insulation, 60 mm mineral wool
   240 mm reinforced concrete wall
   15 mm internal plaster
15 Open perpend
16 Precast concrete beam,
   300 x 90 x 2585 mm
17 Reinforced concrete corbel,
   210 x 250 x 250 mm

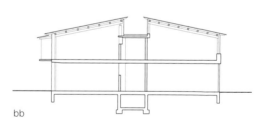

bb

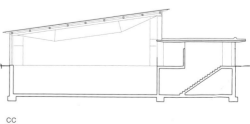

cc

Example 15

School in Ostfildern, Germany

1999

Architects:
Arno Lederer, Jórunn Ragnarsdóttir, Marc Oei,
Stuttgart/Karlsruhe
Assistants:
Judith Haas (project manager),
Alexander Mayer-Steudte (project manager),
Ulrike Hautau, Cornelia Hund
Structural engineers:
Müller + Müller, Ostfildern

Scharnhauser Park is a redevelopment scheme on the site of a former military barracks. The north-east boundary of the site is a sweeping curve – determined by the new rapid transit light railway line. The design for this new school originated from a competition. The curving boundary is integrated in the outside facilities of the school and the structures clearly follow the grid of the development plan. The school building itself, with three storeys in the south and two in the north, is a simple twin parallel block system with a central, longitudinal circulation zone, which is broken up by the single flights of stairs of fair-face concrete and the circular rooflights. The bright upper floor benefits from the rooflights in the V-shaped roof, which like the stairs follows the longitudinal axis. The windows to the classrooms are no larger than is necessary to admit sufficient daylight. This is both a contribution to thrifty and energy-efficient construction, and this simple, strict design rule leads to a clearly defined interface between interior and exterior. For reasons of cost, an inexpensive brick fired in a circular kiln was chosen whose edges are not so sharp and whose colour can vary from light brown to light red. During bricklaying, attention was given to producing wide joints finished in one operation with the bricklaying. The sand-coloured mortar was deliberately "smeared" almost amateurishly, which resulted in a rough, coarse surface finish. This texture was continued internally along the corridors; merely at the entrances to the classrooms was this surface somewhat "improved". There is a large school-yard between the main building and the sports hall, terraced to follow the slope of the land. This resulted in a close harmony, partly brought about by the homogeneity of the material.

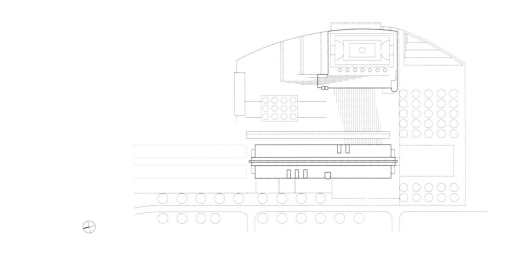

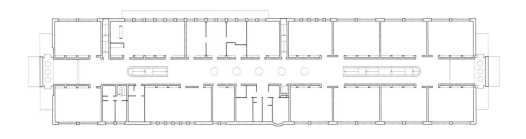

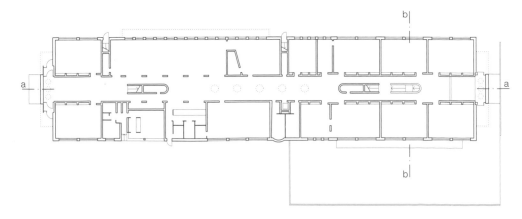

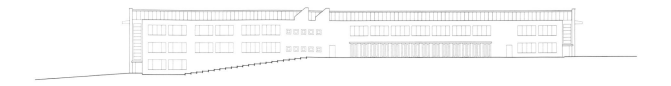

Location plan
scale 1:2500
Upper floor · Ground floor
East elevation
Section through school building
scale 1:800

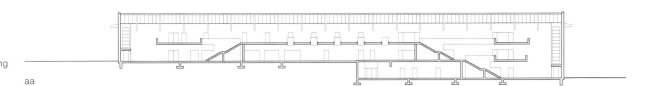

aa

Example 15

A

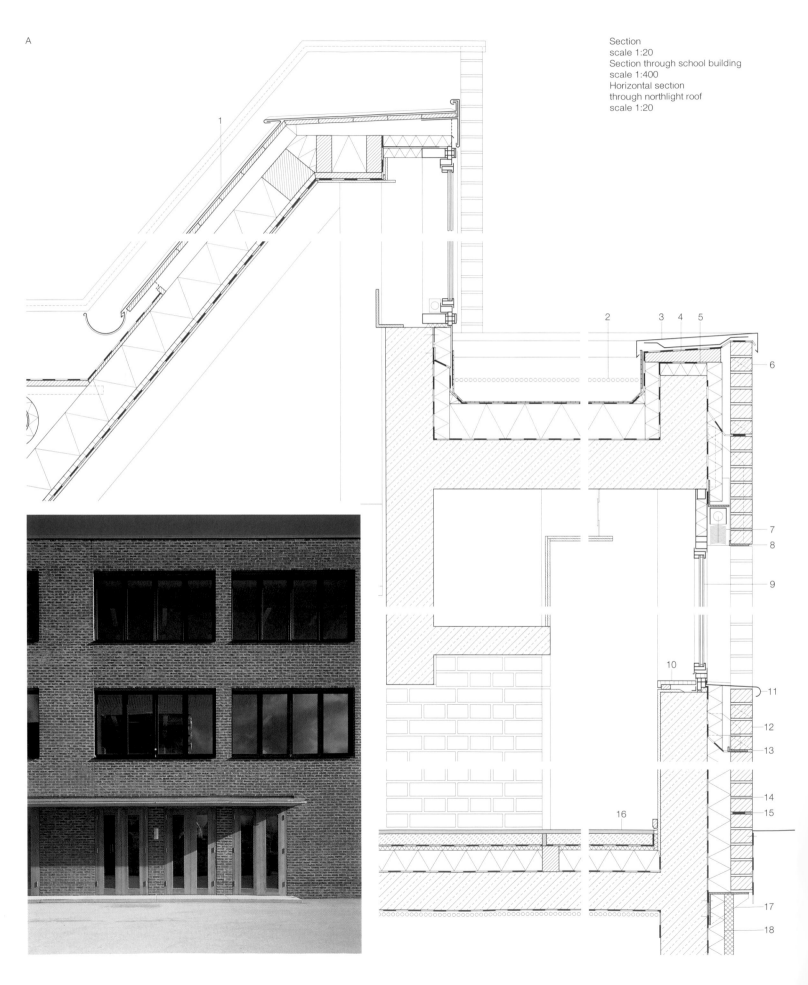

Section
scale 1:20
Section through school building
scale 1:400
Horizontal section
through northlight roof
scale 1:20

1

2   3   4   5

6

7

8

9

10

11

12

13

14

15

16

17

18

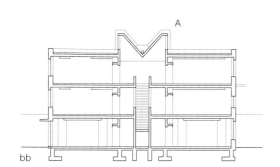

bb

1 Roof construction:
   0.7 mm titanium-zinc sheet, with standing seams
   24 mm timber boarding
   80 x 80 mm counterbattens (80 mm air space
   between)
   200 x 120 mm rafters (200 mm mineral fibre
   insulation between)
   200 x 120 mm purlin
   24-32 mm oriented strand board (OSB)
   vapour barrier, 0.4 mm polyethylene sheeting
   12.5 mm plasterboard
2 Roof construction:
   extensive planting,
   min. 120 mm vegetation layer
   protection and storage mat
   waterproofing, bitumen sheeting, 2 layers, top layer
   resistant to root penetration
   190 mm thermal insulation
   vapour barrier
   260 mm reinforced concrete slab
3 Parapet capping, 0.7 mm titanium-zinc sheet
4 Timber section
5 Thermal insulation, 60 mm mineral fibre
6 Open perpend
7 Blind, natural-colour aluminium, 50 mm
8 Bracket, stainless steel angle
9 Aluminium window with insulating glazing
10 Window sill, MDF board, lacquered
11 Window sill, bent 3 mm aluminium sheet,
   front edge rounded
12 Wall construction:
   115 mm clay facing brickwork
   45 mm air space
   thermal insulation, 80 mm mineral fibre
   250 mm reinforced concrete wall
   15 mm internal plaster
13 Movement joint
14 External insulation, 120 mm
15 Damp proof course
16 Parquet flooring, oak, 20 mm
17 Support bracket, stainless steel sheet
18 External insulation, 80 mm

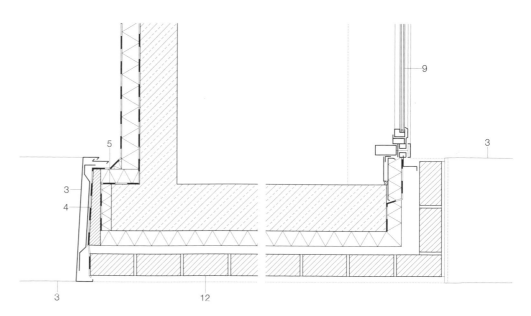

Example 15

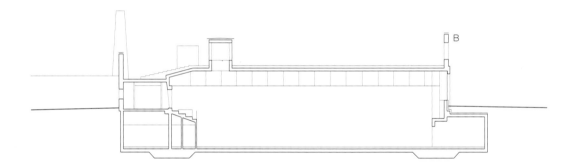

Section through sports hall
scale 1:400
Section through east facade of sports hall
scale 1:20

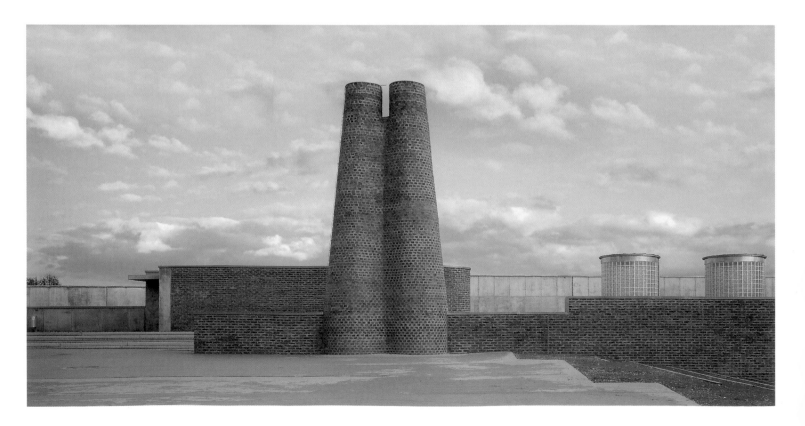

B

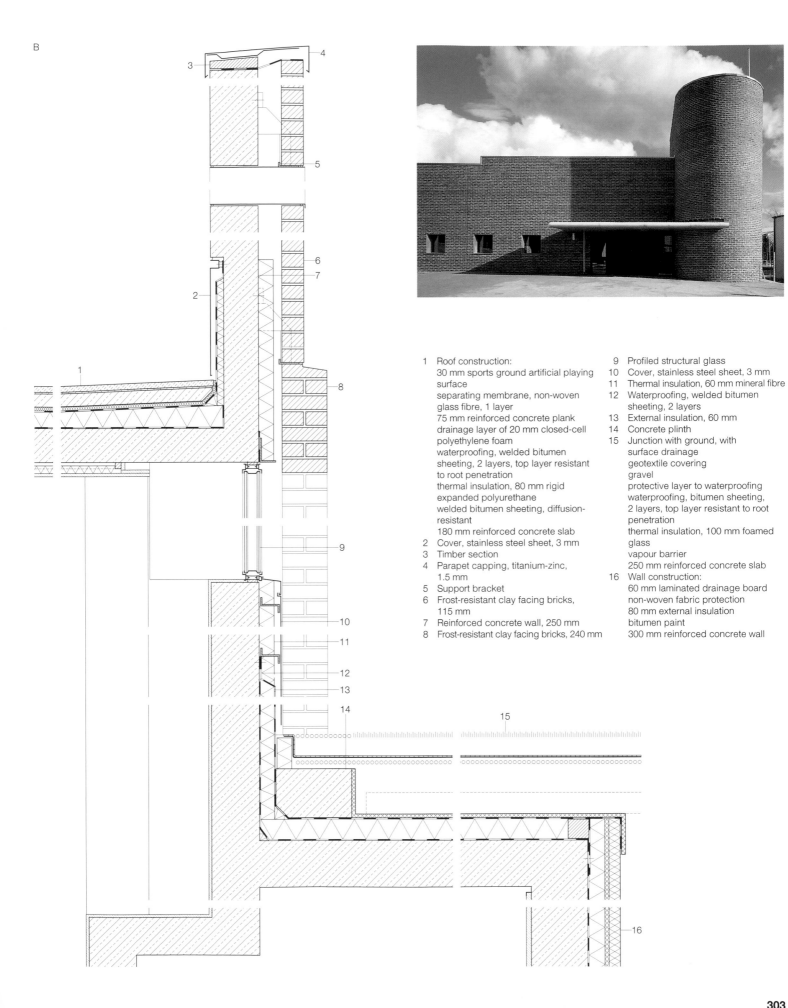

1   Roof construction:
    30 mm sports ground artificial playing
    surface
    separating membrane, non-woven
    glass fibre, 1 layer
    75 mm reinforced concrete plank
    drainage layer of 20 mm closed-cell
    polyethylene foam
    waterproofing, welded bitumen
    sheeting, 2 layers, top layer resistant
    to root penetration
    thermal insulation, 80 mm rigid
    expanded polyurethane
    welded bitumen sheeting, diffusion-
    resistant
    180 mm reinforced concrete slab
2   Cover, stainless steel sheet, 3 mm
3   Timber section
4   Parapet capping, titanium-zinc,
    1.5 mm
5   Support bracket
6   Frost-resistant clay facing bricks,
    115 mm
7   Reinforced concrete wall, 250 mm
8   Frost-resistant clay facing bricks, 240 mm

9   Profiled structural glass
10 Cover, stainless steel sheet, 3 mm
11 Thermal insulation, 60 mm mineral fibre
12 Waterproofing, welded bitumen
    sheeting, 2 layers
13 External insulation, 60 mm
14 Concrete plinth
15 Junction with ground, with
    surface drainage
    geotextile covering
    gravel
    protective layer to waterproofing
    waterproofing, bitumen sheeting,
    2 layers, top layer resistant to root
    penetration
    thermal insulation, 100 mm foamed
    glass
    vapour barrier
    250 mm reinforced concrete slab
16 Wall construction:
    60 mm laminated drainage board
    non-woven fabric protection
    80 mm external insulation
    bitumen paint
    300 mm reinforced concrete wall

Example 16

Town hall in Fellbach, Germany

1987

Architect:
Ernst Gisel, Zürich
Assistants:
Othmar Brügger, Heinrich Gerster,
Harry Moor, Heinz Schmid, Leo Schweitzer
Site manager:
Peter Zimmermann, Filderstadt
Structural engineer:
Heinrich Bechert, Fellbach

Location plan
scale 1:1500
Section · Ground floor
scale 1:750

"Architecture that creates the town." Ernst Gisel's
work in Fellbach could be viewed in this light.
The prosperous town of Fellbach with its fast-
growing population and the usual outgrowths
of the 1950s and 1960s, also not unknown in
other towns, was looking for a nucleus. The
area around the Lutheran church, once shielded by a fortified wall, provided an adequate
setting for the 1979 competition to redesign the
centre of the town. The brief was to "create,
together with a marketplace, not only a centre
for the local authority but also a lively zone
which would be frequented by the citizens".
The jury chose Gisel's design because of its
"agreeable matter-of-factness". Well structured, clearly arranged, decisive in its language, Ernst Gisel's solution makes excellent
use of both the internal and external spaces of
this urban node, clarifying and structuring the
outer contours. The configuration of the inner
courtyards with their small alleyways and the
square in front of the town hall themselves provide a high urban quality.
It seemed a natural choice to opt for a twin-leaf
masonry construction with a 240 mm loadbearing outer leaf. However, the thickness of
the thermal insulation used would these days
no longer satisfy the statutory requirements.
The building exploits the advantages of a self-
supporting masonry wall to the full: lesenes,
corbels and columns in real masonry bond,
robust detailing at the window reveals, plus
masonry stairs and semicircular arches.
The masonry is complemented by natural
stone for the window sills and lintels as well as
for the clearly differentiated plinth.
Designed in an age of flourishing post-
modernism, the architect has created an authen-
tic setting without superfluous comments which,
owing to its internal and external spatial qualities, its correct use of the materials and attention to detail, has lost nothing of its topicality.

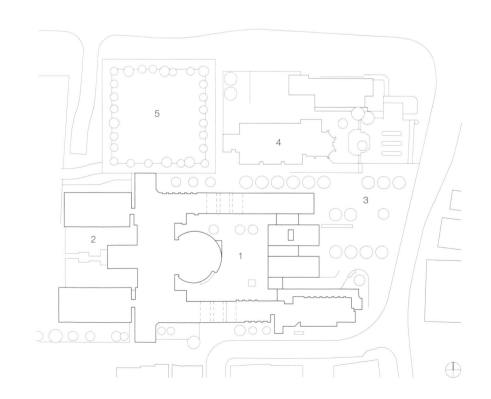

1 Town square
2 Garden
3 Marketplace
4 Lutheran church
5 Churchyard
6 Main entrance
7 Foyer

8 Room for civil marriage
  ceremonies
9 Council services
10 Offices
11 Information centre
12 Restaurant
13 Café
14 Shop

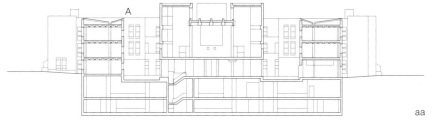

aa

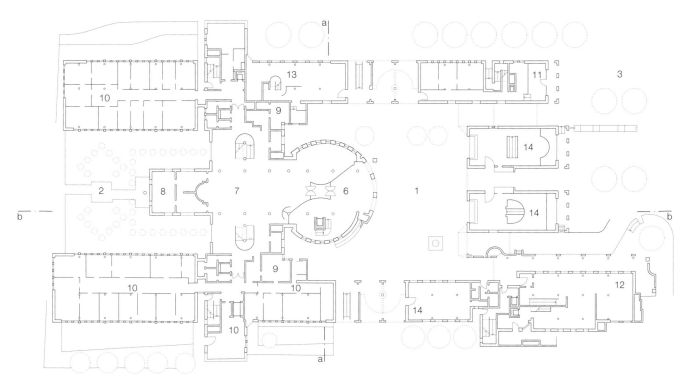

Example 16

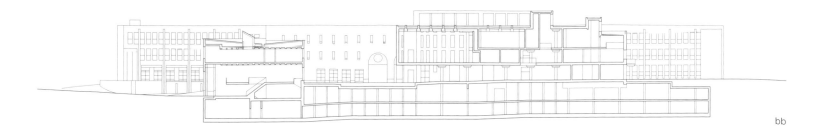

bb

Section
scale 1:750
Part-elevation · Section
scale 1:20

1 Cold deck roof construction, 5.4° pitch:
  copper sheet roof covering, 670 x 0.7 mm,
  double-lock welted joints
  roofing felt
  24 mm timber boarding
  160 x 80 mm rafters
  air space
  thermal insulation, 100 mm mineral wool
  reinforced concrete waffle slab,
  with white cement
2 Trim, 0.7 mm copper sheet
3 Closure strip, 60 x 40 mm
4 Lower trim, 0.7 mm copper sheet on
  building paper
5 Flashing, 0.7 mm copper sheet
6 Wall plate, 120 x 120 mm
7 Soldier course, NF facing bricks
8 Reinforced concrete upstand beam
9 Stone coping to lesene, Lodrino gneiss
10 Thermal insulation, 50 mm mineral fibre
11 Damp proof membrane
12 Fixing plate, galvanized steel, 140 x 5 mm
13 Stone lintel, Lodrino gneiss
14 Box for sunshade, 1.5 mm copper sheet
15 Cavity closer as inspection flap, 1.5 mm copper
   sheet, fixed with stainless steel screws in sleeves
16 Wooden window, with insulating glazing
17 Column, 300 mm dia.
18 Water channel
19 Stone window sill, Lodrino gneiss
20 Wall construction:
   240 mm yellow facing bricks in English bond
   42 mm air space
   thermal insulation, 50 mm mineral fibre
   100 mm in-situ concrete spandrel panel
   steel sheet cladding to spandrel panel
21 Waffle slab, reinforced concrete,
   with white cement
22 Guide cable for sunshade
23 Window sill, 1.5 mm copper sheet
24 Steel angle, 55 x 75 x 5 mm, galvanized
25 Cladding to plinth, Maggia granite, exposed
   surfaces knapped, 50 mm

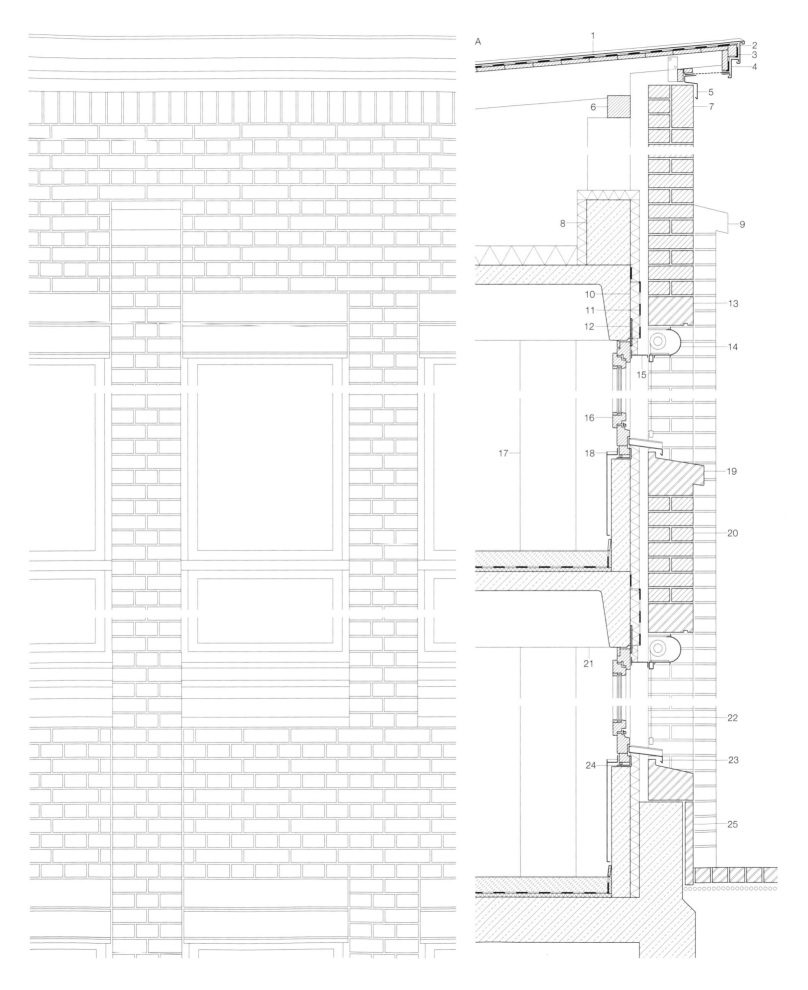

A
1
2
3
4
5
6
7
8
9
10
11
12
13
14
15
16
17
18
19
20
21
22
23
24
25

Example 17

Office building in Lünen, Germany

1995

Architects:
Hillebrandt + Schulz, Cologne
Structural engineers:
Kleinwechter, Dortmund

This office building is located on a new business estate in Lünen on the north-eastern edge of Germany's Ruhr district.

The design brief of the municipal building authority called for "a road-side facade of facing brickwork". The architects responded with a long, low-rise building on this slightly elevated plot in which the "facing brickwork" stipulation became an agenda: a subtly designed, articulate building which attains a high quality with respect to daylighting through the special arrangement of the openings. Each elevation of the structure responds differently to the environment. At the north-west corner the glass, framed in steel, protrudes quite noticeably from the building. On the south side the windows extend over two storeys and are framed by projecting brickwork. The small staircase foyer has walls which vary in thickness and an over-sized window with splayed reveals, which provides a special setting for the lighting and view of the outside. The differentiated building design is accompanied by well-thought-out window details and rooflights in the form of semi-cupolas at a regular spacing. The primary loadbearing construction consists of 300 mm lightweight concrete masonry which is given a coat of gypsum plaster and in some areas finished with several coats of lime plaster. The window lintels are of in-situ concrete insulated with polystyrene. Thin-format Wittmunder peat-fired clay bricks in a random bond are employed for the 115 mm facing brickwork of the outer leaf. There is a 50 mm air space behind the outer leaf. Located in front of the ground floor meeting room is a terraced pond feature with masonry walls; the play of light on its surface is an agreeable reflection of the atmosphere of the interior. The use of a single masonry material throughout fuses the building and the car park and entrance steps into one entity and conveys the notion of spaciousness as a subtle means of representation.

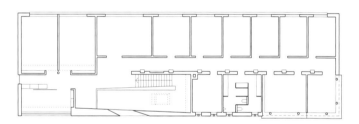

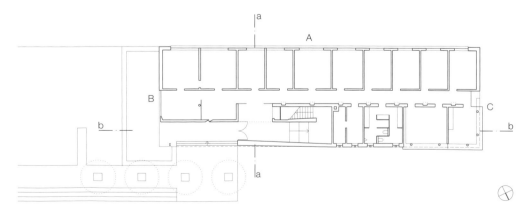

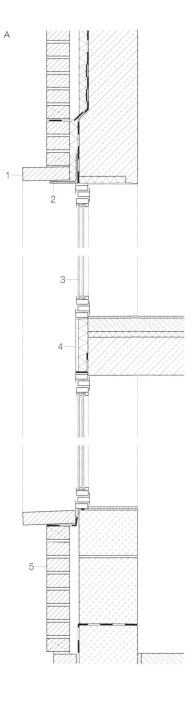

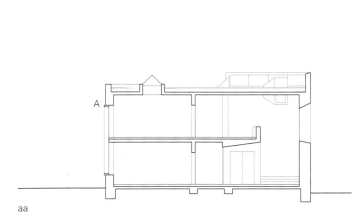

aa

1st floor · Ground floor
scale 1:500
Sections
scale 1:250
Section through south facade
scale 1:20

1 Masonry frame in trass cement
2 Steel angle, 150 x 150 x 12 mm
3 Steel window, with insulating
  glazing
4 Panel construction:
  15 mm cement rendering,
  flush with window, painted
  thermal insulation, multiplex
  lightweight board, 50 mm
5 Wall construction:
  facing bricks, Wittmunder
  peat-fired clay DF, 115 mm
  50 mm air space
  300 mm lightweight concrete
  masonry, with skim plaster coat

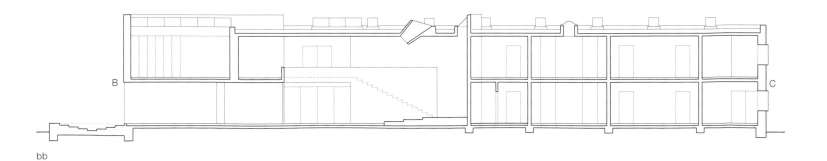

bb

Example 17

Section through east facade
Section through west facade
scale 1:20

1 Wall construction:
   cement rendering, reinforced,
   finished with several coats of
   smooth, coloured lime rendering
   thermal insulation, multiplex lightweight board, 50 mm
   250 mm reinforced concrete lintel
   15 mm internal plaster, painted
2 Steel window, with tilting opening
   light, insulating glazing
3 Bitumen waterproofing
4 Floor construction:
   carpet
   60 mm screed
   80 mm thermal insulation
   vapour barrier
   160 mm reinforced concrete slab
5 Steel window in steel flat reveal
6 Wooden reveal, laminated with
   damp proof membrane
7 Thermal insulation, 50 + 30 mm
   rigid expanded foam

B

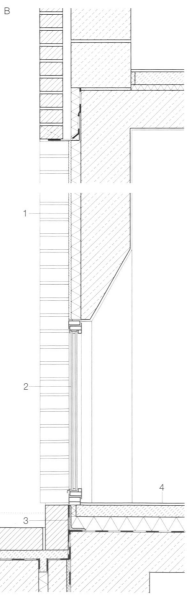

C

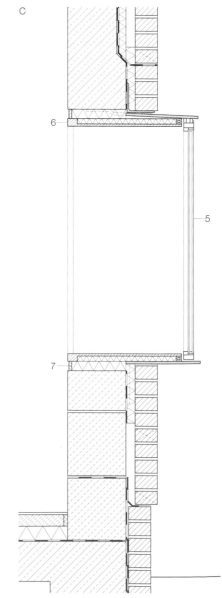

Computer centre in Karlsruhe, Germany

1992

Architect:
Heinz Mohl, Karlsruhe
Project manager:
Peter Litzlbauer
Assistants:
M. Bertram, K. Böhm, H. Döbbeling, G. Döring,
N. Fostiropolous, S. Hirschfeld, R. Preisser,
S. Özcam, J. Schneider, M. Wagner, I. Walser,
T. Weiler
Site management:
Stieff + Trunzler, Karlsruhe
Structural engineers:
Ingenieurgruppe Bauen, Karlsruhe

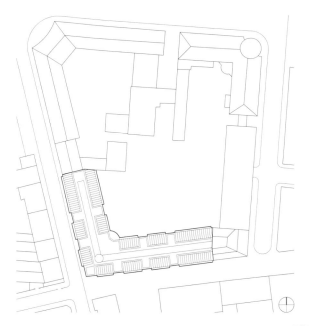

Location plan
scale 1:2000

The fan-shaped structure of the city of Karlsruhe, radiating out from the palace, is dominated by this late-Baroque or classicistic idealistic plan. Within this historical radius, the shape and proportions of every new development must comply with this overriding geometry. However, respect for the city does not exclude the use of modern forms of construction and modern materials, as the example of the computer centre makes abundantly clear. This striking building of facing masonry is situated in the direct vicinity of the well-known church designed by Friedrich Weinbrenner. The number of storeys and height of the eaves match the neighbouring buildings. But the large rooftop structures and set-back features of the surroundings are also reflected in the new building, true to scale and with a new interpretation.

The primary loadbearing construction consists of a reinforced concrete frame with infill panels of concrete bricks. The bricks are left exposed on the spandrel panels and some of the internal walls. Concrete bricks were also chosen for the 90 mm outer leaf (with air space behind). The consistent masonry bond lends the facade an even texture. Merely the lintels over windows, doors and other openings are emphasized by the brick-on-end courses. The complex details at the junctions have been worked out exactly and in harmony with the pattern of the bond. This also applies to the overhanging canopies at the top of the facade, the taller building sections rising above roof level, and the precast concrete elements, both decorative and structural.

The restrained colouring of the different shades of grey used – from the light grey concrete bricks to the anthracite window frames – binds this structure into the context of the city without denying its independent character.

Example 18

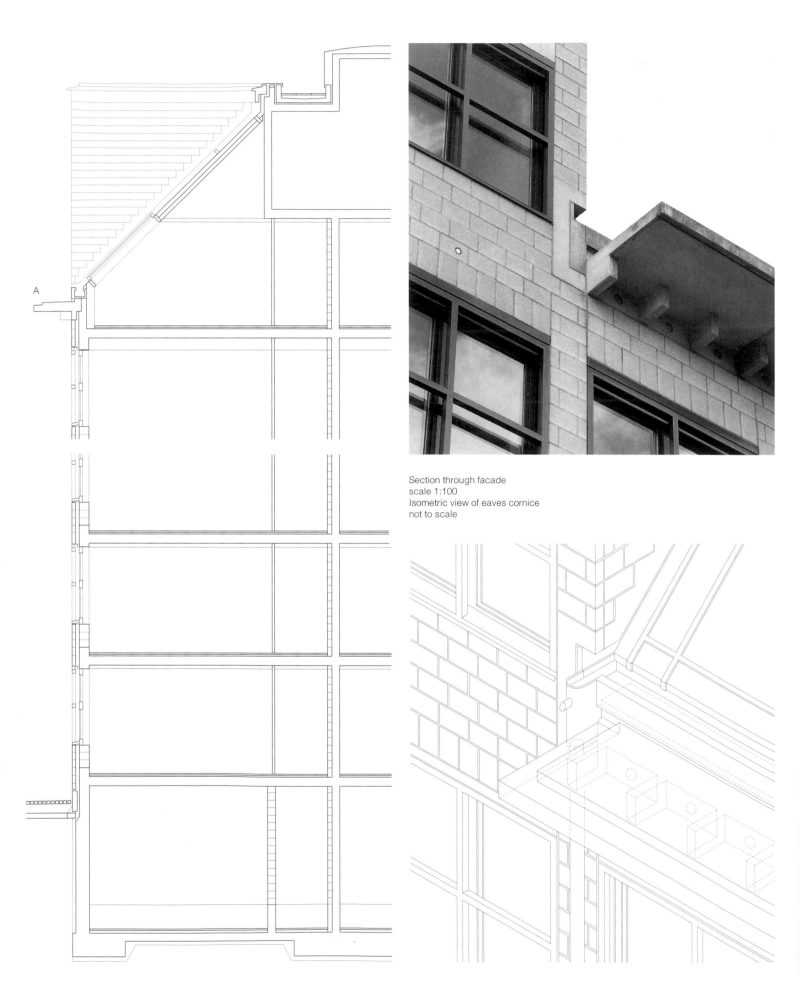

Section through facade
scale 1:100
Isometric view of eaves cornice
not to scale

A

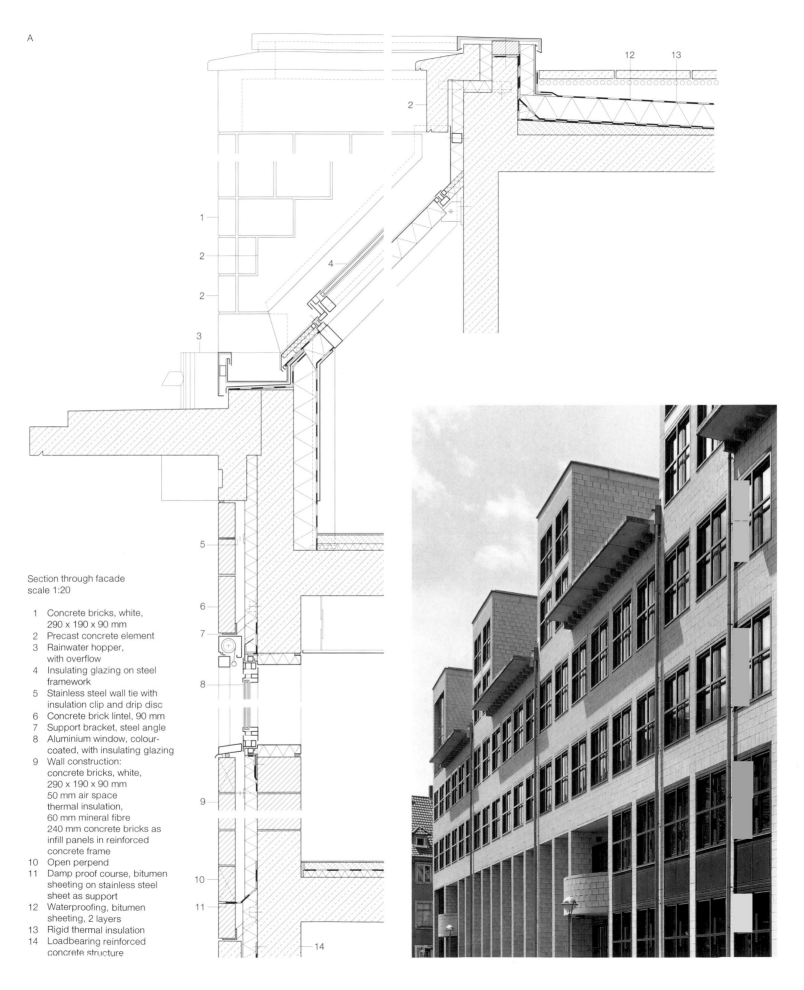

Section through facade
scale 1:20

1 Concrete bricks, white,
   290 x 190 x 90 mm
2 Precast concrete element
3 Rainwater hopper,
   with overflow
4 Insulating glazing on steel
   framework
5 Stainless steel wall tie with
   insulation clip and drip disc
6 Concrete brick lintel, 90 mm
7 Support bracket, steel angle
8 Aluminium window, colour-
   coated, with insulating glazing
9 Wall construction:
   concrete bricks, white,
   290 x 190 x 90 mm
   50 mm air space
   thermal insulation,
   60 mm mineral fibre
   240 mm concrete bricks as
   infill panels in reinforced
   concrete frame
10 Open perpend
11 Damp proof course, bitumen
   sheeting on stainless steel
   sheet as support
12 Waterproofing, bitumen
   sheeting, 2 layers
13 Rigid thermal insulation
14 Loadbearing reinforced
   concrete structure

Example 19

Mixed-use building in Zürich, Switzerland

1993

Architects:
Haessig + Partner, Zürich
Felix B. Haessig, Peter C. Haessig,
Bruno Clausen
Structural engineers:
Schubiger AG, Zürich

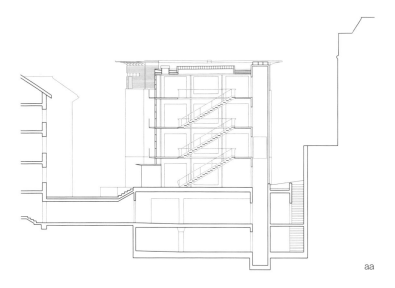

aa

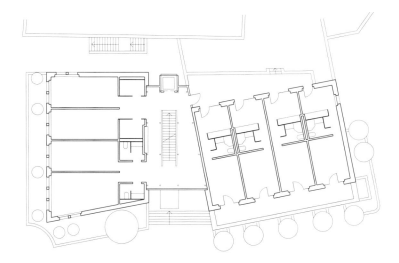

The north-west boundary of the grounds to
Zürich Hospital is denoted by a loosely spaced
row of buildings. One of the gaps was filled
with two new structures positioned at a slight
angle to each other, one with apartments, the
other with laboratories, joined by a glazed
access block. The geometry and alignment of
both buildings follow the existing lines of the
surrounding buildings. The architectural language of the two components is related but
varied slightly to reflect the different functions.
In terms of volume and scale they echo the
regular urban structure of the existing building
stock. Like the neighbouring structures, there
is a plinth which can adapt to the existing
topography. Clad in granite slabs, the plinth
forms a common foundation to the two buildings; likewise, the large overhanging eaves
create a common termination to the walls. To
establish a difference, the western uppermost
story is set back and provided with a cladding
of corrugated aluminium sheeting. The remaining facades are, in the main, of calcium silicate
bricks, 120 mm thick, built in stretcher bond.
There is an air space and 100 mm of thermal
insulation between the facing brickwork of the
outer leaf and the reinforced concrete loadbearing structure. Window lintels, mullions and
sills comprise precast concrete elements clad
in 30 mm thick calcium silicate brick slips. All
the masonry is pointed throughout with a grey
cement mortar, even at the junctions between
the prefabricated and in-situ walls, to create
the impression of a seamless masonry structure. The interior of the building also employs
prefabricated facing masonry erected with the
same precision as the exterior.

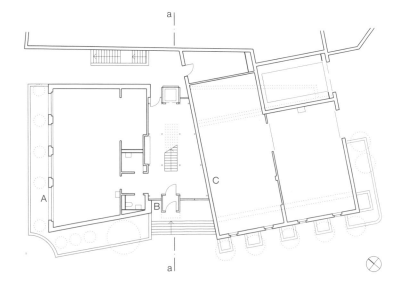

Section
1st floor · Ground floor
North-west elevation
scale 1:400

Example 19

Horizontal section through windows
Section through west facade
Horizontal section through plinth at entrance
Horizontal section through standard storey at entrance
Section through staircase wall
scale 1:20

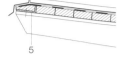

A

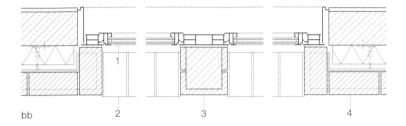

bb   2   3   4

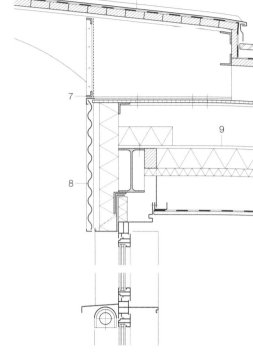

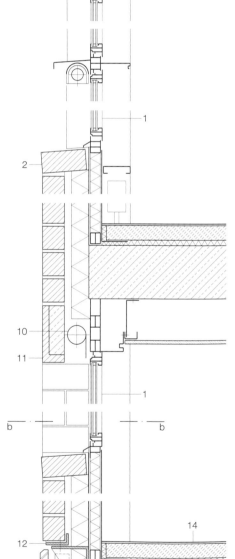

1   Aluminium window, micacious iron oxide finish, with insulating glazing
2   Window sill, calcium silicate element
3   Reinforced concrete mullion with calcium silicate cladding
4   Wall construction:
120 mm calcium silicate bricks
40 mm air space
thermal insulation, 100 mm mineral wool
5   Steel angle, 100 x 30 x 3.5 mm
6   Canopy construction: titanium-zinc sheet roof covering, 0.7 mm, with double-lock welted joints
roofing felt
100 x 40 mm timber boarding screwed to fin
7   Steel angle, 30 x 30 x 4 mm
8   Corrugated aluminium sheeting, mill-finished, 18 x 76 mm
9   Roof construction: steel beam, IPE 240
thermal insulation, 140 mm mineral wool
void
vapour barrier
18 mm plasterboard
10   Sunshade, fabric blind
11   Reinforced concrete lintel with calcium silicate cladding
12   Steel angle, 120 x 60 x 12 mm
13   Stainless steel bracket

B

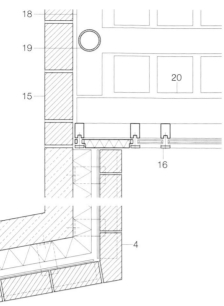

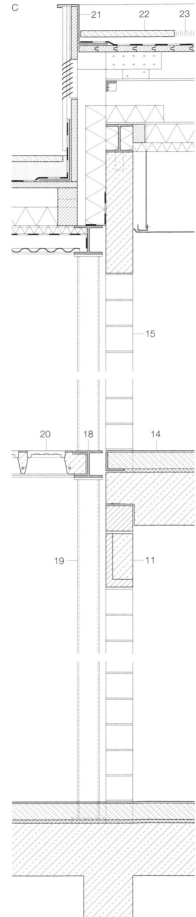

C

14 Floor construction:
    5 mm linoleum
    95 mm cement screed
    10 mm impact sound
    insulation
    280 mm reinforced
    concrete slab
15 Calcium silicate
    brickwork, 120 mm,
    without plaster
16 Aluminium section, stove
    enamelled, with insulat-
    ing glazing
17 Plinth wall construction:
    40 mm granite slabs,
    retaining
    and fixing anchors of
    stainless steel
    100 mm thermal
    insulation
    180 mm reinforced
    concrete
18 Steel beam, HEA 140
19 Steel circular hollow
    section, 101.6 dia. x 5 mm
    with 140 x 140 x 10 mm
    plates top and bottom
20 Glascrete element
21 Copper sheet
22 Concrete paving slab,
    40 mm
23 Roof construction:
    extensive planting
    waterproofing, bitumen
    sheeting, 3 layers
    40 mm spruce boarding
    tapering timber joists,
    140-180 x 100 mm
    steel beam, IPE 240
    thermal insulation,
    140 mm mineral wool
    suspended ceiling

Example 20

Mixed-use development in Berlin, Germany

1996

Architects:
Petra and Paul Kahlfeldt, Berlin
Assistants:
Anja Herold, Christoph Haag,
Yves Minssart, Michael Fuchs,
Jörn Pötting, Thomas Kälber, Conor Moran,
Frauke Hellweg, Martin Oestlund
Structural engineers:
Ingenieurbüro Fink, Berlin

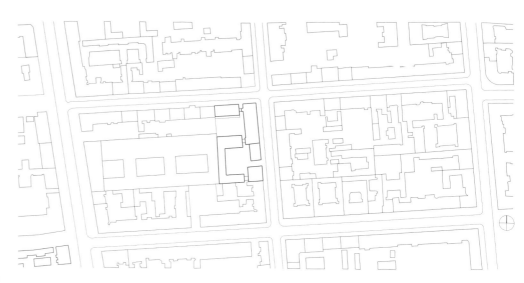

This ensemble of residential and commercial buildings – "Engelhardt Hof" – lies in a densely developed inner-city district in the immediate proximity of Charlottenburg Palace.

The surrounding buildings originate from the second half of the 19th century and survived the war more or less undamaged. The plot within this block belonged to a brewery up until the mid-1980s. After production ceased, only the original office building and warehouse remained.

The new development is divided into three parts. At the north-west corner a block with offices forms the transition from the surrounding housing to the inner courtyard, a U-shaped commercial development joins on at the fire-walls, and an apartment building echoes the historical perimeter block development – and in so doing closes off the courtyard to the south.

The common design feature linking all the buildings is the masonry of light-yellow facing bricks. The external walls are full-fill cavity walls. The different facade treatments, corresponding to each building's utilization, distinguish the appearance of the whole complex. The office building has an outer leaf in header bond with an inset steel-and-glass facade which leads from the public road to the courtyard. The external, fixed glazing protects the delicate wooden windows behind against the effects of the weather and offers sound and thermal insulation. The opening lights of the inner leaf provide a means of natural ventilation for the offices.

In contrast, the masonry construction of the commercial block in the courtyard is reduced to little more than a frame with infill panels comprising generous expanses of glazing in wooden frames. The outer leaf here on these facades has become columns and lintels in English bond. The side of the apartment block facing the landscaped inner courtyard has been given continuous balconies; the large areas of glazing are broken up vertically by narrow columns of facing brickwork. On the road side the coupled windows are set into the rendered facade.

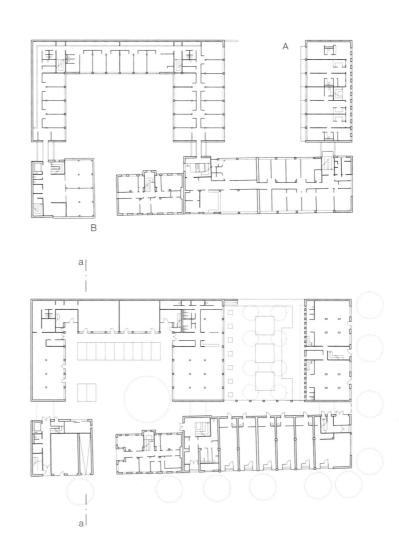

Location plan
scale 1:4000
Upper floor · Ground floor
scale 1:1000
Section
scale 1:500

Example 20

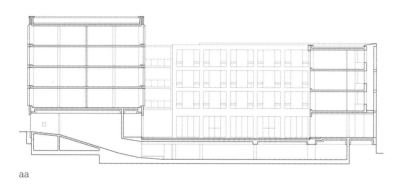

aa

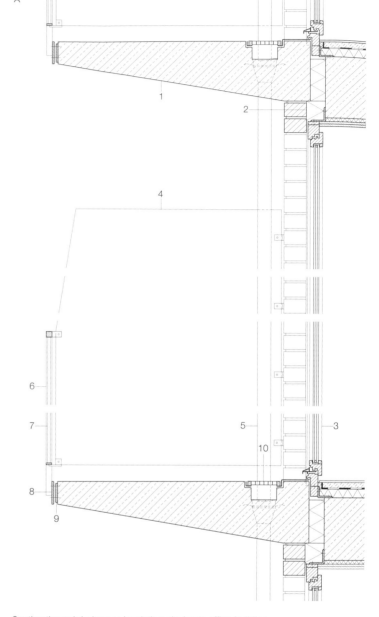

A

Section through balcony · Insulating glazing to office building
Horizontal section · Vertical section
scale 1:20

1   Precast concrete element,
    1203 mm
2   Thermal insulation, 100 mm
3   Wooden window, 3-part,
    with insulating glazing
4   Divider, acrylic
5   Rainwater downpipe, 70 mm dia.
6   Steel section, 30 x 30 mm
7   Steel section, 20 mm
8   Steel section, 120 x 10 mm
9   Anchor plate, 150 x 100 x 10 mm
10 Grating, cast iron, to cover
    drainage channel
11 Wall construction:
    115 mm facing brickwork
    100 mm thermal insulation
    vapour barrier
    240 mm reinforced concrete wall
12 Parapet capping, zinc sheet
13 Timber section, 300 x 40 mm
14 Concrete, 200 x200 mm, as
    crenellations at 900 mm centres

15 Waterproofing, bitumen
    sheeting
16 Roof waterproofing, bitumen
    sheeting, 3 layers
17 Thermal insulation, 140 mm
18 Vapour barrier
19 Reinforced concrete slab,
    200 mm
20 Gutter
21 Reinforced concrete upstand
22 Thermal insulation, 30 + 30 mm
23 Steel bracket for supporting
    outer leaf
24 Blind
25 2 No. steel sections, with single
    glazing
26 Ventilation
27 Wooden window, with
    insulating glazing
28 Reinforced concrete column,
    240 x 240 mm

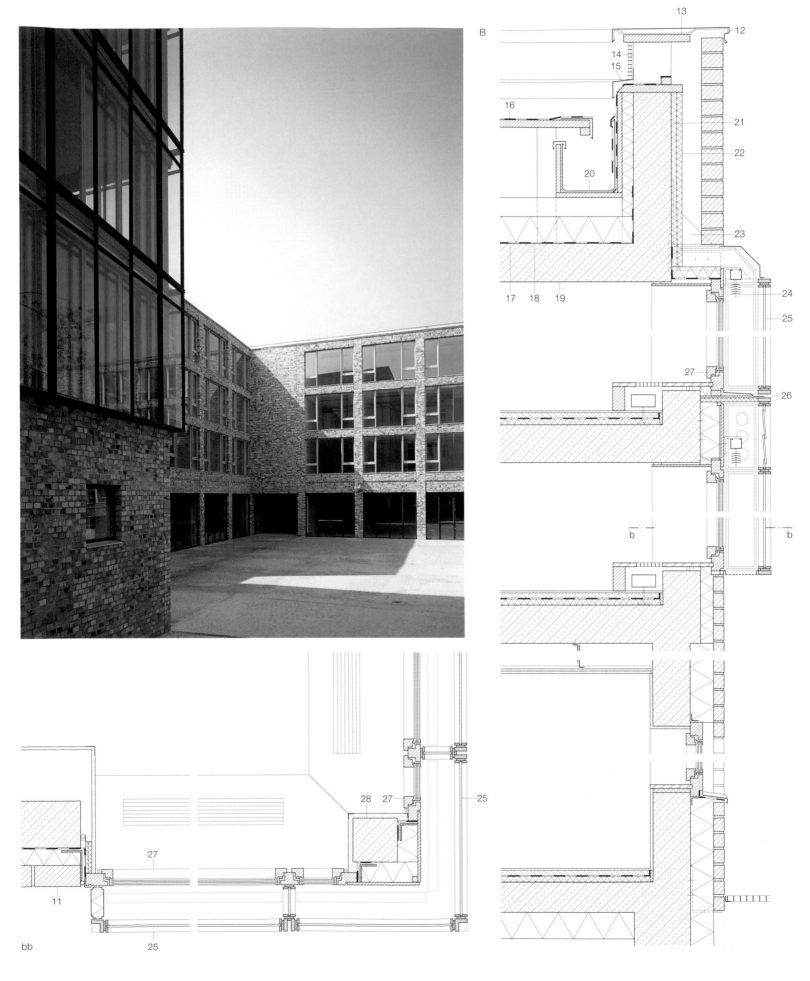

B

13

12

14

15

16

20

21

22

23

17 18 19

24

25

27

26

b b

28 27 25

27

11

bb 25

Example 21

Extension to office building in Stuttgart, Germany

1998

Architects:
Arno Lederer, Jórunn Ragnarsdóttir, Marc Oei,
Stuttgart/Karlsruhe
Assistants:
Marko García-Barth, Sabine Birk,
Andy Brauneis, Oliver Cyrus, Roland Göppel,
Alf Hoinkis, Thilo Holzer, Marc Losch,
Alexander Mayer-Steudte, Boris Miklautsch,
Dorothee Strauss
Structural engineers:
IBA – Acatürk + Kiesel, Stuttgart

The new building extends the headquarters of
the local power company, which dates from
the 1970s. That structure, by the architects
Kammerer, Belz, Kucher + Partner, was the
expression of a technically oriented architecture, which emphasized the very latest materials. The loadbearing framework is clad in glass
and dark, anodized aluminium panels. Ventilation and climate control are mechanical.
In contrast to this, the architects of the extension designed a passive, ecological energy
concept. The great mass of the building with
its multilayer external skin – with clay facing
brickwork and reinforced concrete loadbearing
structure – achieves, on the one hand, a high
thermal inertia, and on the other, forms a thermal buffer between interior and exterior by way
of the coupled windows.
The confines of this urban site made it necessary to accommodate the offices on the sides
with good lighting. Specially developed
coupled windows guarantee, besides additional protection against heat, the desired degree
of sound insulation and natural ventilation.
The building envelope is formed by a partial-fill
cavity wall with a 115 mm anthracite-colour
clay brickwork (KMz 28/1.8 NF) outer leaf. The
plinth makes use of particularly resistant bricks
and rounded specials are used adjacent the
entrance doors. Each storey of the stretcher-
bond masonry is supported on stainless steel
brackets adjustable for height. The cavity
measures 125 mm in total – 80 mm thermal
insulation plus 45 mm air space. Pointing of the
walls was carried out in a second operation
using coloured mortar – white for the bed joints
and black for the perpends. The anthracite
bricks with their light metallic sheen and the
two-colour pointing gives the extension a very
special character but also allows it to blend
harmoniously with the existing building.

Location plan
scale 1: 2000
Sections 2nd floor
scale 1: 1000

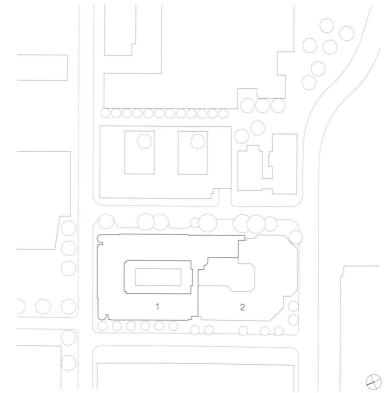

1   New extension
2   Existing building

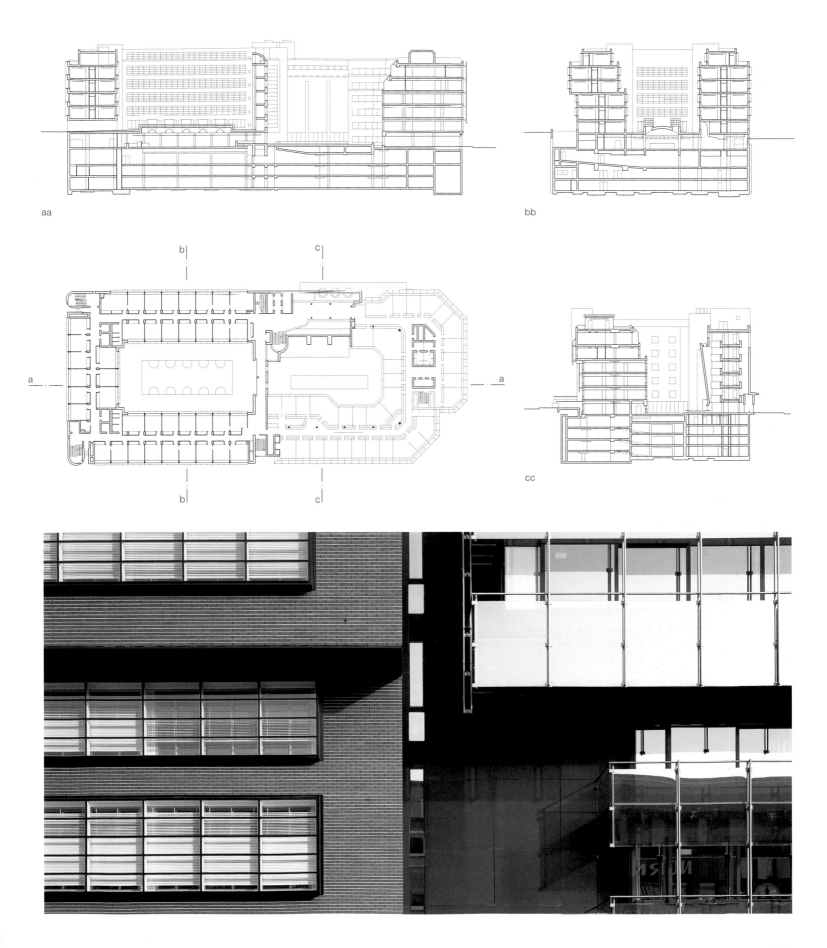

aa

bb

cc

Example 21

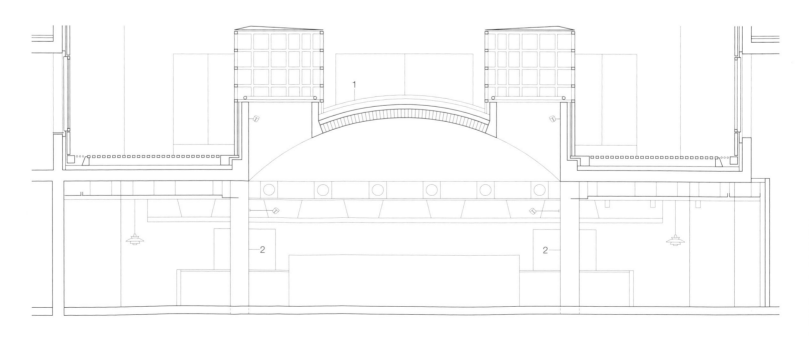

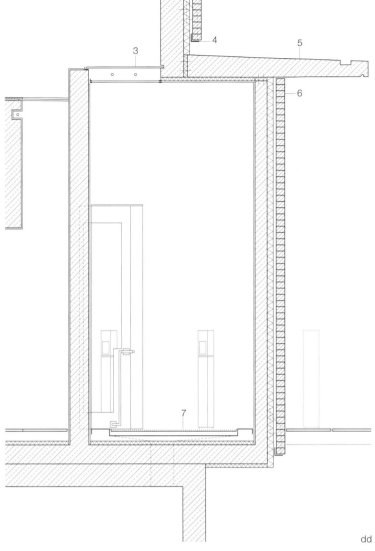

dd

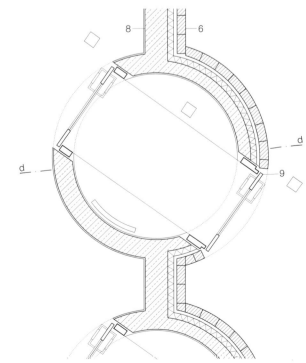

Section through restaurant
scale 1: 100
Entrance lobby
Vertical section
Horizontal section
scale 1:50

1 Barrel-vault roof construction (with
extensive planting):
200 mm vegetation and drainage layer
non-woven fabric as protection and
filter
protective mat, granulated rubber
waterproofing, 2 layers
thermal insulation, 100 mm foamed glass
waterproof sheeting as temporary roof
covering
150 mm lean-mix concrete
240 mm clay brickwork
2 Loadbearing column, 490 x 490 mm
facing brickwork

3 Lighting units forming top of lobby:
2 panes of glass, sand-blasted
fluorescent tubes
4 Steel angle as support to outer leaf
of facing brickwork
5 Canopy with drainage channel,
in-situ reinforced concrete
6 Wall construction:
115 mm facing brickwork
45 mm air space
thermal insulation, 80 mm mineral wool
250 mm reinforced concrete wall
15 mm internal plaster
7 Floor construction:
mat in matwell (non-slip steel tray
with drainage)
60 mm thermal insulation
250 mm reinforced concrete slab
8 300 mm reinforced concrete wall
9 Lobby element:
doors in steel frame
door leaves of steel with wooden
planks and glass elements

325

Example 21

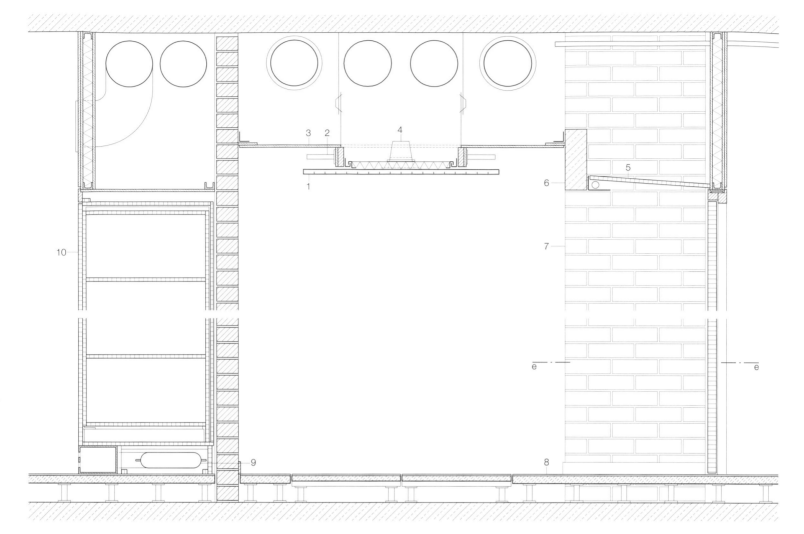

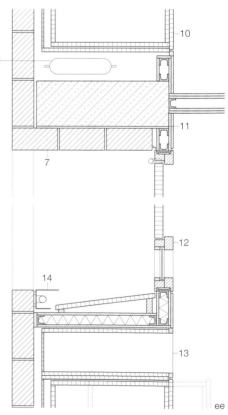

Section through corridor
adjacent offices
Horizontal section through alcove
in office
Section through facade
Horizontal section through
coupled window
scale 1:20

1 Acoustic ceiling panels:
removable slit MDF
boards laminated with
non-woven fabric, foam
absorber
2 Energy-saving fluores-
cent bulbs
3 Plasterboard, 12.5 mm
4 Loudspeaker
5 Laminated veneer
lumber (LVL) board,
beech, removable for
inspection
6 Concrete lintel
7 Facing brickwork,
yellow, 115 mm
8 Cavity floor with carpet
floor covering, removable
access panels adjacent
doors

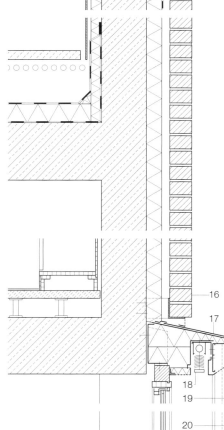

9 Fresh-air vent
10 Pull-out "pharmacist's
   cupboard", LVL board,
   beech
11 Concrete column
12 Door element, beech
   veneer, with side lights
13 Open shelving
14 Stainless steel section
   with strip lighting

15 Parapet capping, coated
   steel sheet, 4 mm
16 Wall construction:
   115 mm facing brickwork
   45 mm air space
   thermal insulation,
   80 mm mineral wool
   250 mm reinforced concrete wall
17 Cover plate, powder-coated
   aluminium, 2 mm, black

18 Louvre blind
19 Glass louvres, 10 mm
   toughened safety glass
20 Aluminium section
21 Insulating glazing
22 Window frame, LVL,
   beech
23 Drive motor
24 Cupboard unit, LVL
   board, beech

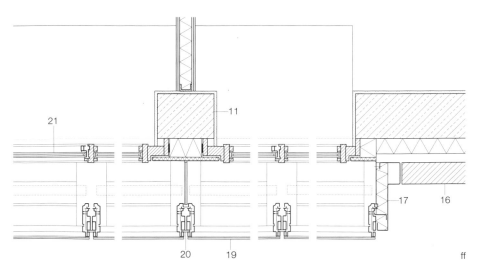

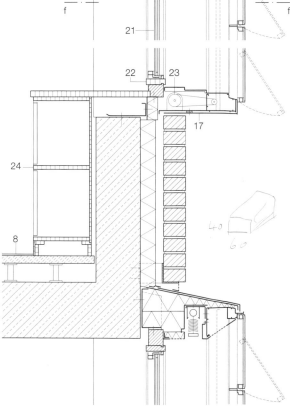

Example 22

Business premises in London, UK

1998

Architects:
MacCreanor Lavington Architects, London
Assistants:
Tim Anstey, Marie Brunborg, Alexis Burrus,
Nichola Dunlop, Jeremy King,
Richard Lavington, Gerard MacCreanor,
Aidan Williams
Structural engineers:
Andrew Greig, Graham Ling, London

This building is situated at the south-west
corner of Hoxton Square. It is integrated into
an existing block and is only visible on three
sides: to the east, facing the square, to the
north, facing the inner courtyard, and via a
narrow section facing Coronet Street to the
west.
The plan layout is skilfully organized on the
southern side of the plot between the three
opportunities for admitting daylight and the
small, additional lightwell. The retail premises
on the ground floor take the form of a semi-
basement and so accommodate the different
heights of the adjoining streets. The extra-high
first floor compensates for these topographic
differences and therefore possesses a special
facade structure. Columns and lintels 325 mm
thick clad in dark clay brickwork were suspended in front of the reinforced concrete construction as prefabricated facade elements.
The bricks were in some cases formed as half-
channels in the production process for the prefabricated elements.
Additions to the lintels above the ground floor
and to a number of wall sections were constructed using suspended half-brick-thick
cladding and at the parapet with 240 mm loadbearing clay brickwork walls. The thermal
break is always positioned between the prefabricated facade and the loadbearing structure. The lintels above the window openings
divide up the stretcher bond with horizontal
lines. Emphasizing the effect of the seemingly
continuous columns with the intervening window lintels makes the nature of the assembly of
the cladding very clear. The choice of materials and the careful but restrained detailing
round off the architectural character.

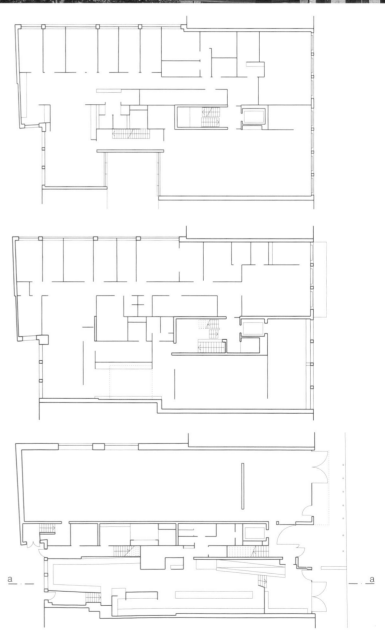

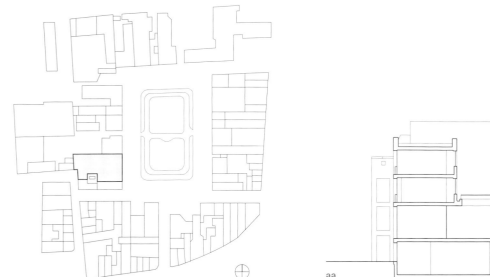

2nd floor · 1st floor
Ground floor · Section
scale 1: 400
Location plan
scale 1: 2500

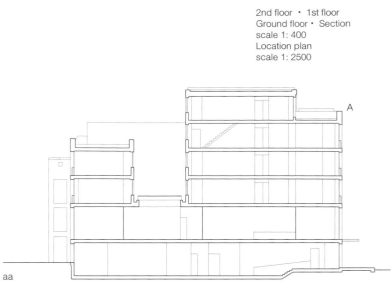

A

aa

Example 22

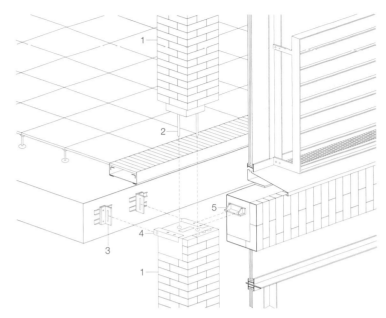

Axonometric view of facade
structure
not to scale
Section through facade
scale 1: 20

A

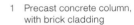

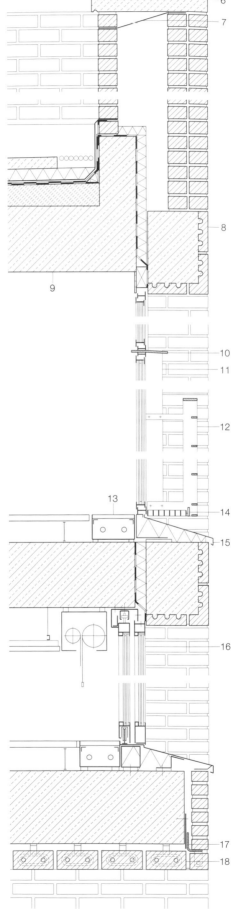

1 Precast concrete column,
 with brick cladding
2 Positioning/fixing bolts
3 Stainless steel brackets,
 with elongated holes
4 Stainless steel section,
 cast into precast element
5 Stainless steel bracket,
 cast into precast element
6 Parapet coping, precast
 concrete
7 Damp proof course
8 Beam, precast concrete,
 with brick cladding,
 325 x 450 mm
9 In-situ reinforced
 concrete slab, 350 mm
10 Steel flat, galvanized,
 200 x 8 mm, as load-
 bearing rail at steel
 window, frame galvan-
 ized and powder
 coated, with insulating
 glazing, 24 mm
11 Steel flat, galvanized,
 150 x 8 mm, as load-
 bearing post
12 Balustrade of steel flats,
 galvanized and powder
 coated
13 Heating pipes in floor
 duct
14 Steel open-grid flooring,
 galvanized
15 Aluminium plate, 4 mm
16 Sliding doors in frame of
 steel sections, galvan-
 ized and powder coated,
 with insulating glazing
17 Stainless steel support
 bracket
18 Clay bricks with stainless
 steel support system

Business start-up centre in Hamm, Germany

1998

Architects:
Hegger Hegger Schleiff, Kassel
Project manager:
Gerhard Greiner
Assistants:
Achim Dahl, Berit Schaal, Tobias Schaffrin
Structural engineer:
Reinhold Meyer, Kassel
Services engineers:
Hausladen, Kirchheim bei München

Sections
Ground floor
scale 1:1000

This business start-up centre was built on one of the countless former industrial sites that today are being put to new uses. The aim of this project was to provide assistance for ecologically oriented manual trades and service companies in the building industry. The complex consists of a four-storey office block and a number of two-storey units grouped around a courtyard. These units can be divided in a variety of ways and so can accommodate up to 24 businesses.

The four-storey office block, with circulation zone along one side, consists of 240 mm calcium silicate masonry with composite floors of boards laid on edge cast in concrete. The partial-fill cavity walls were constructed using recycled bricks from demolished buildings. The lintels were formed from bricks in stretcher bond supported on a steel angle in order to highlight the rows of windows. These are placed in the plane of the thermal insulation. Junctions with partitions are characterized by a cladding of wooden panels. The sunshades are clearly visible beneath the lintels in front of the windows.

The units are based on a steel framework with infill panels, also of recycled clay bricks. Their barrel-vault roofs comprise curved glulam ribs with thermal insulation between and extensive planting as the roof finish.

This ecologically oriented project was investigated and optimized with respect to the energy balance (consumption figures as well as primary energy consumption during production of building materials). One of the outcomes of this was the use of a four-storey air collector over the windowless south-east facade. An earth channel ensures that the air is precooled in summer. Thanks to the use of recycled facing bricks with their vivid colouring and irregularities, this building helps to remind us that this location was once the home of the local colliery.

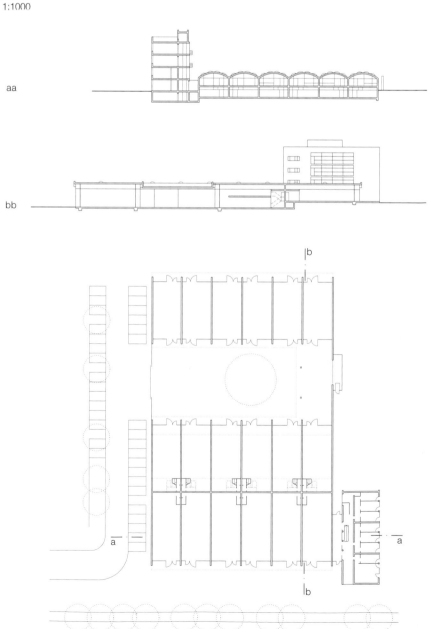

aa

bb

Example 23

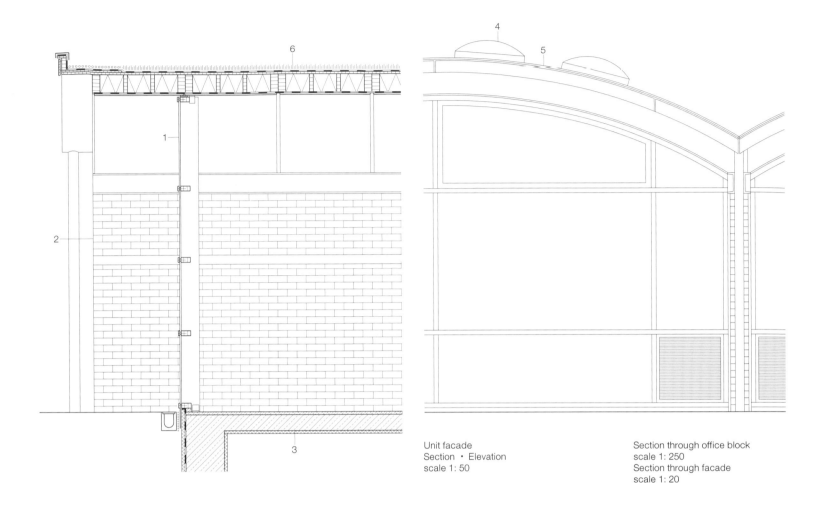

Unit facade
Section · Elevation
scale 1: 50

Section through office block
scale 1: 250
Section through facade
scale 1: 20

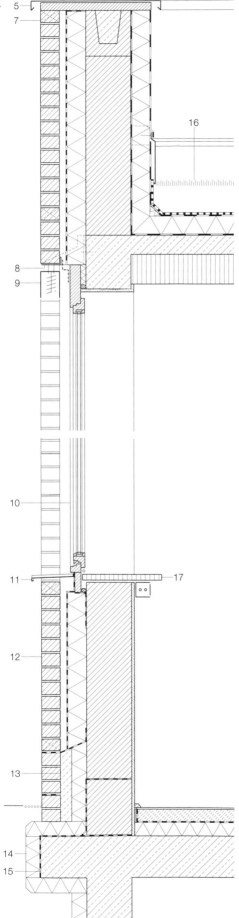

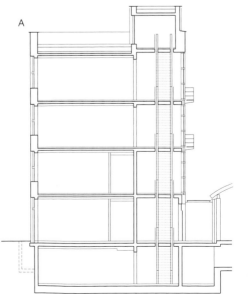

1   Post-and-rail facade, glu-
    lam, cover strips of oiled
    oak, steel beams with
    brackets
2   Recycled bricks, 240 mm
3   Reinforced concrete
    ground slab, waterproof,
    250 mm
4   Dome rooflight
5   Parapet capping, zinc
    sheet
6   Roof construction:
    50 mm vegetation layer
    sheeting, resistant to root
    penetration
    waterproofing
    22 mm plywood
    240 mm thermal insulation
    160 x 240 mm glulam rib,
    barrel-vault segment
    vapour barrier
    22 mm plywood
7   Open perpend
8   Angle bracket
9   Acrylic shell for aluminium
    sunshade
10 Wooden window, grey
    glazed finish, with insulat-
    ing glazing
11 External window sill, zinc
    sheet

12 Wall construction:
    217 x 100 x 66 mm
    recycled bricks
    50 mm air space
    airtight membrane
    90 mm thermal insulation
    240 mm calcium
    silicate brickwork
    15 mm internal plaster
13 Mortar filling, 50 mm
14 Thermal insulation,
    80 mm foamed glass
15 Concrete, waterproof,
    220 mm
16 Roof construction:
    extensive planting
    sheeting, resistant to
    root penetration
    waterproofing
    100 mm thermal
    insulation
    vapour barrier
    260 mm timber-
    reinforced concrete
    composite roof
17 Internal window sill,
    laminated veneer
    lumber (LVL) board,
    birch, 30 mm

Example 24

Housing complex in Amsterdam, The Netherlands

1998

Architects:
Atelier Zeinstra, van der Pol, Amsterdam
Project architect:
Herman Zeinstra
Assistants:
Harriet Dil, Martin Fredriks, Sjoerd Landmann,
Mechthild Stuhlmacher
Structural engineers:
Bouwstart, Amsterdam

Development of the two peninsulas of Sporenborg and Borneo for inner-city housing in the eastern part of Amsterdam's dockyards began in 1987. The docks here had not been used for many years and the buildings were occupied by squatters and artists. Refurbishment had been planned since the 1970s and was long overdue. The master plan rigorously prescribed a three-storey blanket development disected by parallel streets every 30-40 m. The development plan provided for a number of different types of housing which, however, had to comply with very strict rules. For instance, the ground floor had to be 3.5 m high in order to guarantee alternative uses, and each building had to occupy an entire plot, including parking and external facilities. And all the facades had to be uniform – finished with the same type of brick.

The "back-to-back" apartments do not have individual carports but a garage within the block instead. The constricted plan layouts measuring 4.2 m wide and 14.5 m long are lit via a patio. The second floor contains one bedroom, a small bathroom and a rooftop terrace. The short spans enable the use of 190 mm reinforced concrete slabs spanning transversely which are supported on the 230 mm concrete party walls. Consequently, the external walls on the south and north elevations can be of a lightweight timber construction. Nevertheless, the stipulation to use bricks was complied with by constructing the infill panels between the glulam beams and columns in 110 mm facing brickwork. Opening panels are incorporated in the side of a recess in the south facade. Fixed windows are positioned flush with the loadbearing timber members. The elegant interplay between brickwork, timber and glass lends these buildings their special character.

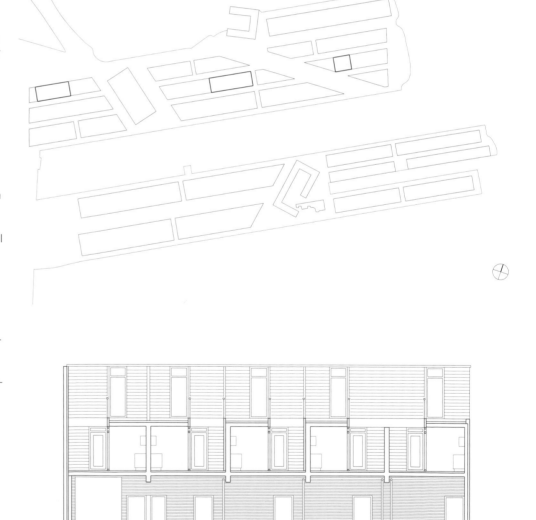

aa

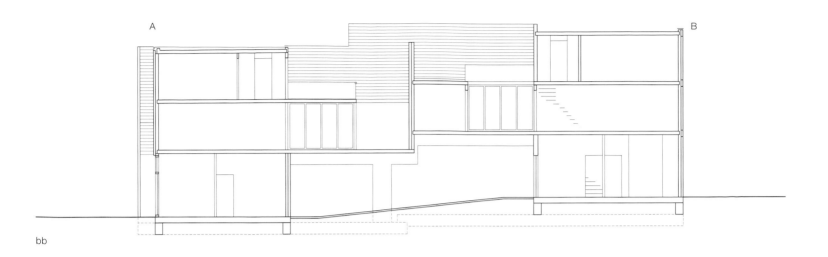

A   B

bb

Location plan
scale 1: 7500
Sections
Ground floor · 1st floor · 2nd floor
scale 1: 200

1	Hall	4	Living room	7	Bedroom
2	Storage	5	Kitchen	8	Bathroom
3	Garage	6	Patio	9	Terrace

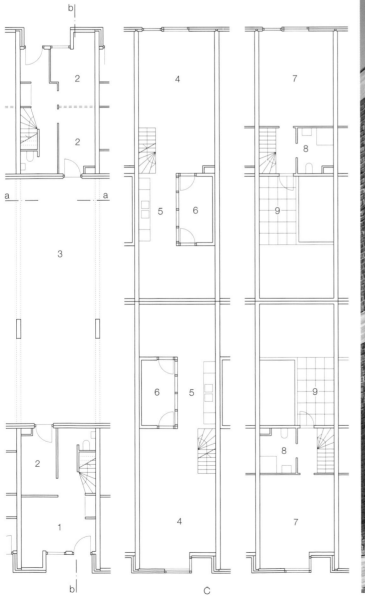

Example 24

A

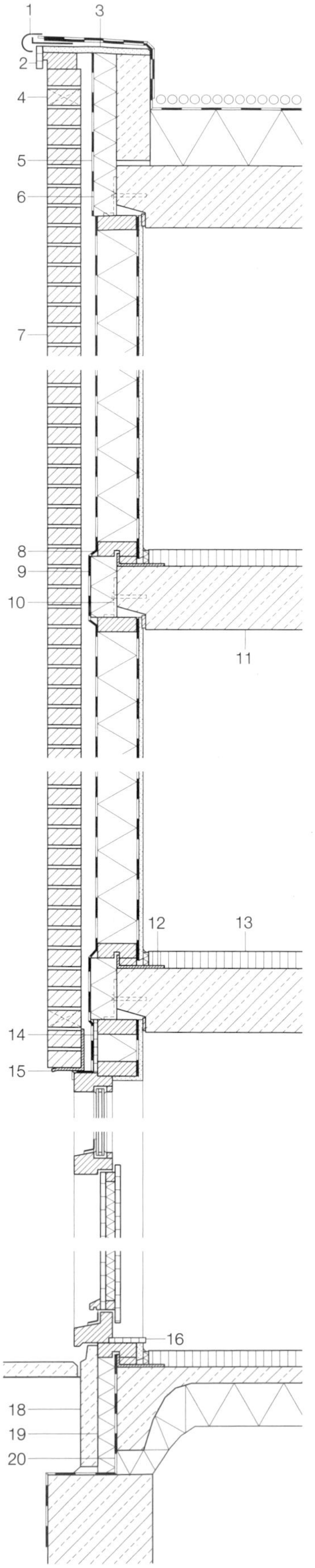

B

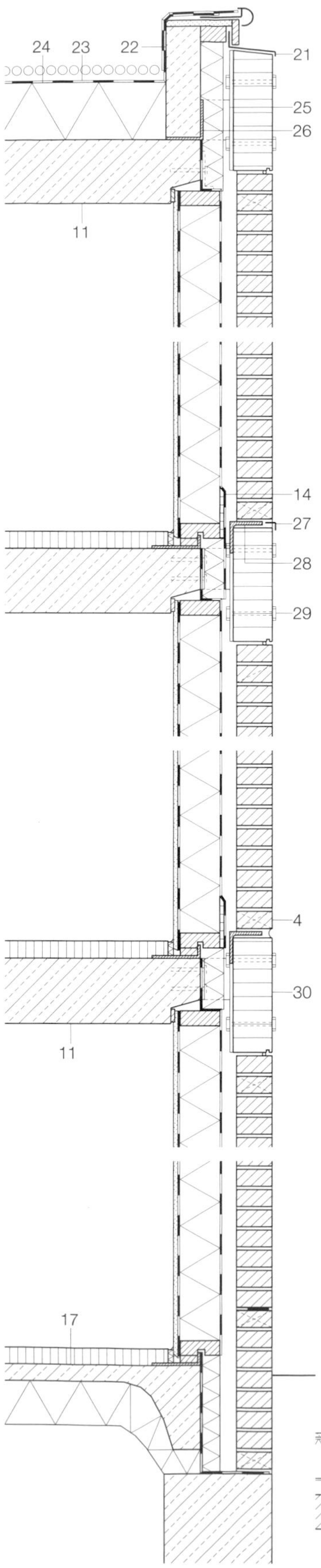

Section through facade
Horizontal section through recess in facade
scale 1: 20

1 Parapet trim, aluminium section, 40 mm dia., coated
2 Laminated veneer lumber (LVL) board, 18 mm
3 Fibre-reinforced cement board, 16 mm
4 Open perpend
5 Foil, water-repellent
6 Thermal insulation, 75 mm mineral wool
7 Wall construction:
   100 mm facing brickwork
   48 mm air space
   foil, water-repellent, open to diffusion
   timber post-and-rail construction, 119 x 38 mm
   thermal insulation, 120 mm glass wool
   vapour barrier, polyethylene sheeting
   12.5 mm plasterboard
8 Sole plate
9 Thermal insulation, 80 mm mineral wool
10 Fixing anchor, steel angle, cast in
11 Reinforced concrete slab, 190 mm
12 Steel angle, 140 x 40 x 8 mm, fixed to slab
13 Floor finish, 50 mm
14 LVL board, 12 mm
15 Steel angle support
16 LVL board, 15 mm
17 Ribbed reinforced concrete floor
18 Precast concrete element, 30 mm

19 Thermal insulation, 50 mm rigid expanded foam
20 Sheeting, water-repellent
21 Capping, bent sheet steel
22 Upstand, gas concrete, 100 mm
23 Waterproofing, 2 layers
24 Thermal insulation, rigid expanded foam with integral falls
25 Sheet steel brackets at 1000 mm centres
26 Steel angle, 100 x 120 x 10 mm
27 Flashing, lead sheet
28 Steel angle, 90 x 90 x 10 mm
29 Fixing bolts
30 Glulam beam, impregnated, 353 x 110 mm
31 Wall construction:
   100 mm facing brickwork
   45 mm air space
   thermal insulation, 75 mm mineral wool
   230 mm reinforced concrete
32 Glulam column, 316 x 110 mm
33 Construction of opening panel:
   20 mm profiled boards
   15 mm air space
   foil, water-repellent, open to diffusion
   thermal insulation, 70 mm rigid expanded foam
   vapour barrier
   LVL board, 12 mm

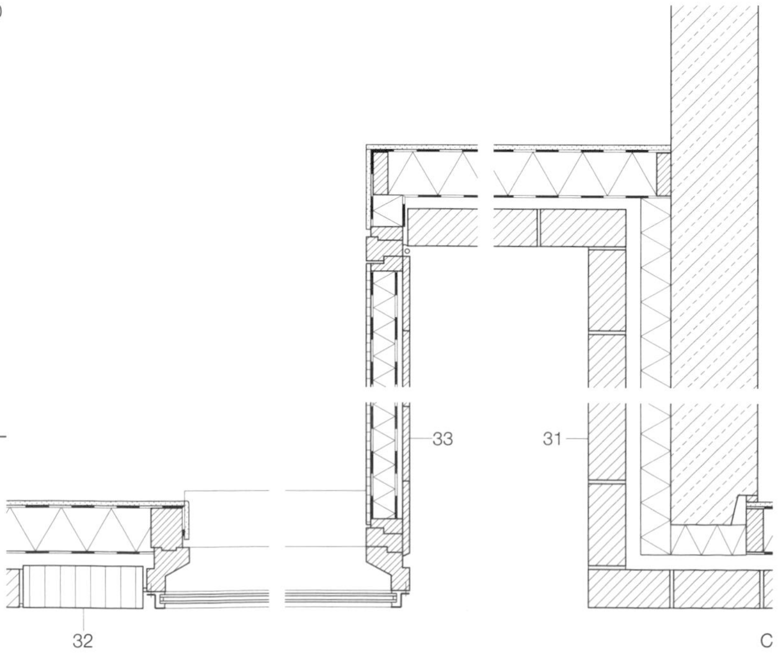

C

Example 25

Housing development in Rungsted, Denmark

1999

Architects:
Boje Lundgaard & Lene Tranberg,
Copenhagen
Assistants:
Henrik Schmidt, Niels Friis, Sören Aabling,
Merete Adler
Structural engineers:
Birch & Krogboe, Copenhagen

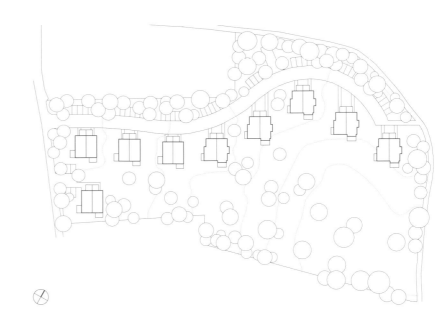

Bel Colle Park is located near the town of Hørs-holm in the vicinity of The Sound amid an undulating landscape with a good stock of large, mature trees. Locally, it is one of the most sought-after areas among house-buyers. The group of 18 two-storey semidetached properties is arranged to follow the topography of the site.

The land slopes down towards the south-east and in doing so forms a shallow depression. The houses have been carefully placed between the existing trees towards the top of the slope. Access is by means of a private driveway (cul-de-sac) on the northern side which curves to follow the topography.

Two types of house are available: semi-detached with or without bay. Further differ-ences are evident in the shape of the windows and in slight variations to the living rooms, which leads to minor differences in the usable space available. Each block of two houses is divided in the centre and the plan layouts are mirrored. Only the rooms on the first floor could be assigned alternative uses.

The loadbearing internal and external walls of the buildings comprise 120 mm precast con-crete elements, the non-loadbearing walls gas concrete panels. Hollow concrete planks form the upper floors and the roof structures are of timber. The loadbearing leaf of the external wall is enclosed by 150 mm cavity insulation, while the 115 mm outer leaf of facing brickwork employs stretcher bond with flush joints. The windows, partly fixed lights, partly opening out-wards, are positioned flush with the outside face of the masonry. The cantilevering bays are supported on steel columns and beams. These buildings with their light-coloured facing masonry, long overhanging eaves and simple timber details blend in harmoniously with their natural surroundings.

Location plan
scale 1: 20000
Type 1
Upper floor
Ground floor
Type 2
Upper floor
Ground floor
scale 1: 250

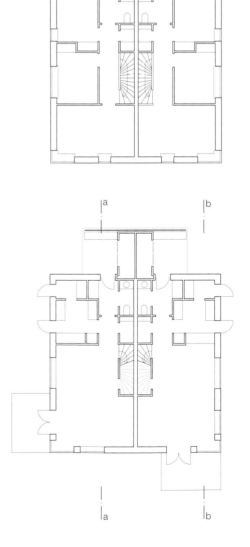

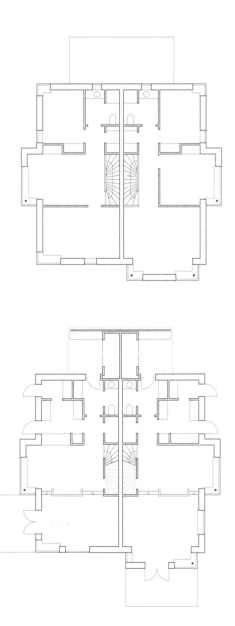

Example 25

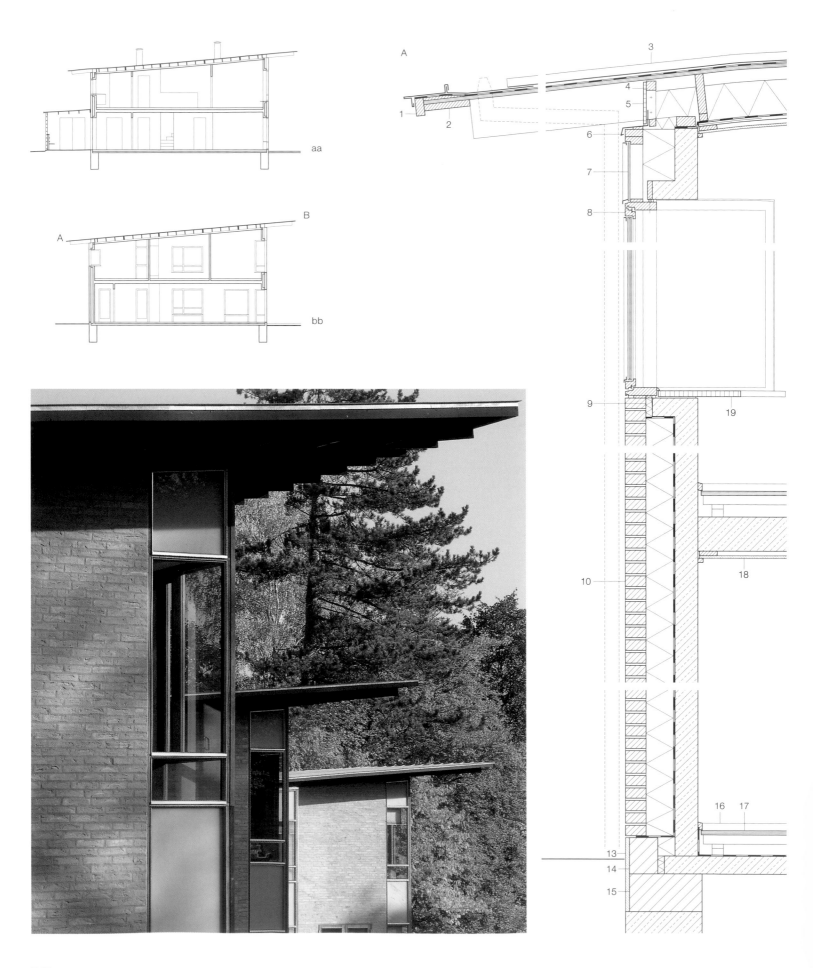

aa

bb

A

B

A

1
2
3
4
5
6
7
8
9
10
13
14
15
16
17
18
19

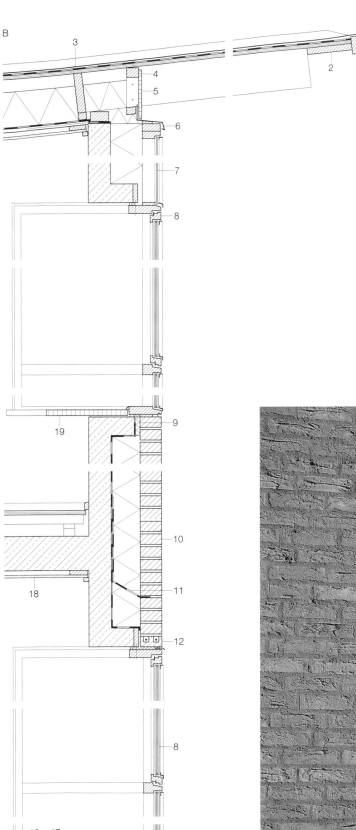

B

Sections
scale 1: 250
Section through north facade
Section through south facade
scale 1: 20

1 Timber section, 95 x 45 mm
2 Timber section, 240 x 35 mm
3 Roof construction:
 standing seam roof covering, zinc sheet
 roofing felt
 laminated veneer lumber (LVL) board, 16 mm
 220 mm rafters
 200 mm thermal insulation between rafters
 vapour barrier
 20 mm boarding
 20 mm battens
 13 mm plasterboard
4 Timber section, 50 x 50 mm
5 LVL board, 12 mm, waterproof
6 Zinc flashing
7 Single glazing, fixed
8 Hardwood frame, oiled, with insulating glazing
9 Thermal insulation, 30 mm rigid expanded foam

10 Wall construction:
 115 mm facing brickwork
 150 mm thermal insulation
 vapour barrier
 120 mm reinforced concrete
11 Damp proof course
12 Shallow lintel, clay
13 Rendering, 20 mm
14 Lightweight clay bricks, 150 x 90 mm
15 Lightweight clay bricks, 190 x 400 mmm
16 Timber section, oak
17 Floor construction:
 parquet flooring on supporting members
 damp proof membrane
 reinforced concrete slab
18 Plasterboard, 13 mm
19 Window sill, MDF board, 30 mm

Example 26

Apartment block in Salamanca, Spain

1998

Architect:
Jesús María Aparicio Guisado, Madrid
Assistants:
Luis Ignacio Aguirre López,
Daniel Huertas Nadel,
Héctor Fernández Elorza,
Carlos Pesqueira Calvo
Structural engineer:
Valeriano de Diego

This apartment block is situated in Santa Marta de Tormes, a suburb of the Spanish university town of Salamanca. Set amid the typical apartment block architecture, it stands out conspicuously from its surroundings.

This is a crisp-outlined, five-storey block, one side of which abuts a neighbouring building. Four red-brick masonry storeys are supported on a rough-finish concrete plinth. The central section is characterized by the restrained fenestration. The long ribbon windows at the ends continue around the corners of the open end of the building and terminate on the narrow side. This four units per floor layout with its elongated stair shaft contains well-structured apartments, each with three large, separate rooms of almost equal size plus a spacious living area with kitchen, bathroom, storage space and built-in cupboards.

The entrance lobbies are small but functional and well proportioned.

The top storey, with its large openings framed in concrete, guarantees a conspicuous appearance. Therefore, this storey stands out clearly from the others, signalling a usage different to that of the standard floors.

There are only two apartments on the top floor. These were given an additional external zone, with enough space for a rooftop garden and even a small pool for each apartment, by placing the external walls to the apartments back within the building. The enclosing masonry walls create a private, courtyard-type area. The large openings in the outer walls permit generous views of the surroundings. The quality of this apartment block lies in such carefully formulated, uncommon spatial situations. Their effect is reinforced by the use of just a few, coordinated materials and simple details.

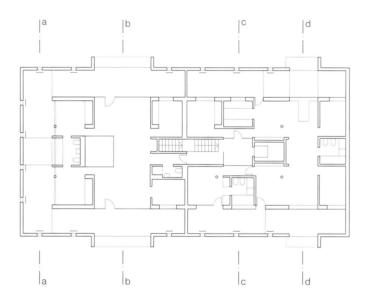

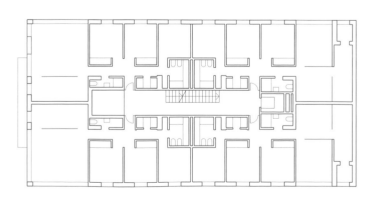

Top storey
Standard storey
Sections through top storey
scale 1:400
Location plan
scale 1:3000

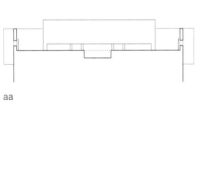

aa

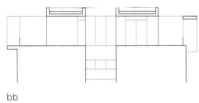

bb

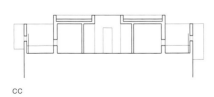

cc

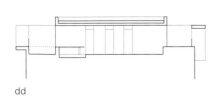

dd

Example 26

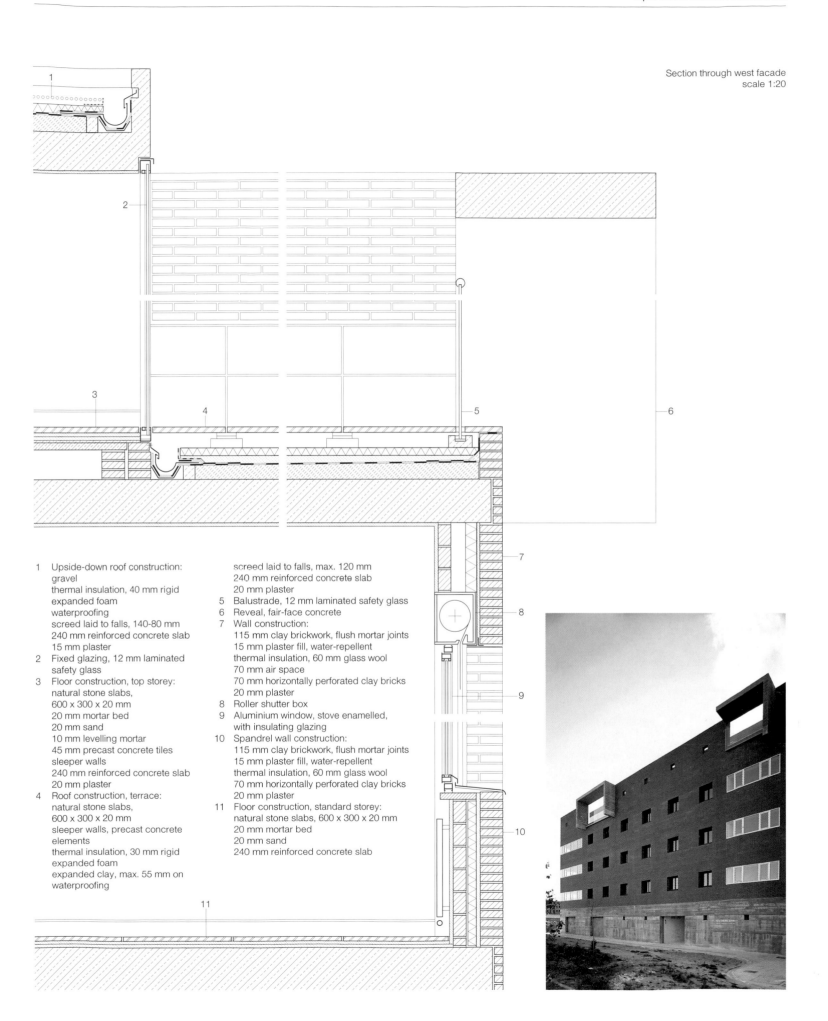

1 Upside-down roof construction:
   gravel
   thermal insulation, 40 mm rigid
   expanded foam
   waterproofing
   screed laid to falls, 140-80 mm
   240 mm reinforced concrete slab
   15 mm plaster
2 Fixed glazing, 12 mm laminated
   safety glass
3 Floor construction, top storey:
   natural stone slabs,
   600 x 300 x 20 mm
   20 mm mortar bed
   20 mm sand
   10 mm levelling mortar
   45 mm precast concrete tiles
   sleeper walls
   240 mm reinforced concrete slab
   20 mm plaster
4 Roof construction, terrace:
   natural stone slabs,
   600 x 300 x 20 mm
   sleeper walls, precast concrete
   elements
   thermal insulation, 30 mm rigid
   expanded foam
   expanded clay, max. 55 mm on
   waterproofing

   screed laid to falls, max. 120 mm
   240 mm reinforced concrete slab
   20 mm plaster
5 Balustrade, 12 mm laminated safety glass
6 Reveal, fair-face concrete
7 Wall construction:
   115 mm clay brickwork, flush mortar joints
   15 mm plaster fill, water-repellent
   thermal insulation, 60 mm glass wool
   70 mm air space
   70 mm horizontally perforated clay bricks
   20 mm plaster
8 Roller shutter box
9 Aluminium window, stove enamelled,
   with insulating glazing
10 Spandrel wall construction:
   115 mm clay brickwork, flush mortar joints
   15 mm plaster fill, water-repellent
   thermal insulation, 60 mm glass wool
   70 mm horizontally perforated clay bricks
   20 mm plaster
11 Floor construction, standard storey:
   natural stone slabs, 600 x 300 x 20 mm
   20 mm mortar bed
   20 mm sand
   240 mm reinforced concrete slab

Example 27

Community centre in Lochau, Austria

1998

Architects:
Baumschlager & Eberle
Karl Baumschlager, Dietmar Eberle,
Lochau
Project manager:
Rainer Huchler
Structural engineer:
Ernst Mader, Bregenz

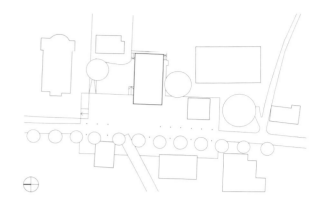

The centre of the rather rural-looking town of Lochau at the eastern extremity of Lake Constance is dominated by a busy throughroad carrying traffic to and from the nearby border. Situated on this road are the church, the council offices, a number of small hotels and the new, detached vicarage. This clarifies in a simple way the spatial relationships both to the church and to the surrounding houses, lending structure and intensity to the urban planning of the centre of the town. This no-nonsense building solves problems of function and architectural form within its simple structure.
Two arcades help to overcome the change in levels at the edge of the church square, but also create a reference point for the streetscape, the open square. At street level there is a shop behind the arcade; the floor above contains the large parish hall, which looks out onto the forecourt to the vicarage. The hall can be divided into two sections by way of a glazed sliding partition. The facades of the building are plain, without recesses or projections, the windows flush with the outside face. They convey the impression of a homogeneous envelope enclosing the building. Merely the arcades provide texture and depth. The loadbearing construction of the building consists of a reinforced concrete frame with floors of hollow concrete planks. Timber stud walls form the infill panels to the frame – with columns on a 3.0 m grid. Therefore, the 120 mm outer skin had to be built as a free-standing masonry leaf extending the full height of the building. The brickwork is connected to the concrete frame via stainless steel anchors. All lintels are carried on stainless steel angles so that the stretcher bond of the facing brickwork and hence the structure of the envelope is maintained throughout. Along the arcades the brickwork skin is reduced to a 25 mm brick slip cladding to the concrete lintels. This cladding, in a slightly different colour, is also carried around the corners of the building to match.

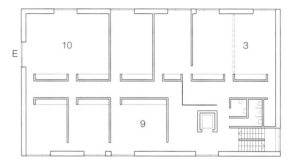

Location plan
scale 1:2000
2nd floor
1st floor
Ground floor
North elevation
South elevation
scale 1:400

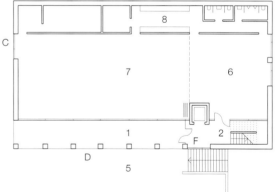

1   Arcade
2   Entrance
3   Youth activities
4   Shop
5   Forecourt to vicarage
6   Foyer
7   Parish hall
8   Kitchen
9   Parish secretariat
10 Choir room

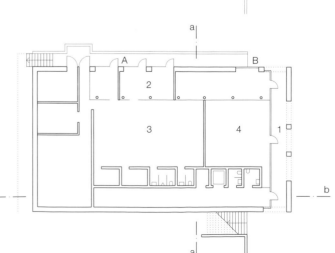

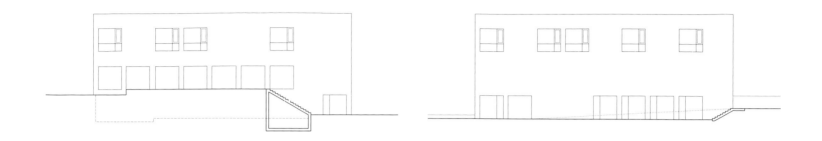

Example 27

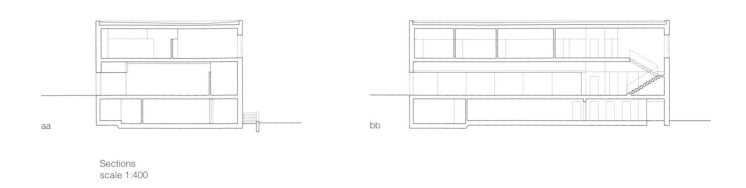

aa

bb

Sections
scale 1:400

Horiz. section through door-pier junction
Horizontal section through pier-fixed
glazing junction

Section
scale 1:20

1   Wall construction:
    127 mm facing brickwork anchored to
    concrete frame
    40 mm air space
    thermal insulation, 60 mm glass wool
    concrete frame: 200m concrete
    beams/columns
    15 mm thermal insulation
    12.5 mm plasterboard
    vapour barrier
    12.5 mm plasterboard, with skim coat
    and paint finish
2   Thermal insulation, 100 mm rigid
    expanded foam
3   Silicone joint
4   Wooden window, opening light, oak,
    with triple glazing
5   Floor construction:
    100 mm oak planking
    60 x 80 mm timber battens

    thermal insulation, 80 mm mineral wool
    360 mm hollow concrete planks, with
    skim coat and paint finish
6   Ventilation slot
7   Facing brickwork, 115 mm, with
    horizontal reinforcement every
    4th-5th course
8   Timber stud wall construction:
    5 mm hardboard
    120 x 60 mm timber studs
    thermal insulation, 120 mm mineral wool
    18 mm oriented strand board (OSB)
    services plane, with thermal insulation,
    50 mm mineral wool
    12.5 mm plasterboard
    vapour barrier
    12.5 mm plasterboard, with skim coat
    and paint finish
9   Stainless steel Z-section, with
    elongated holes

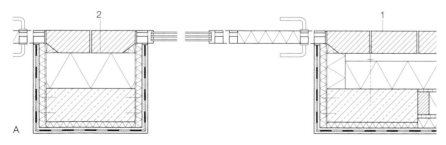

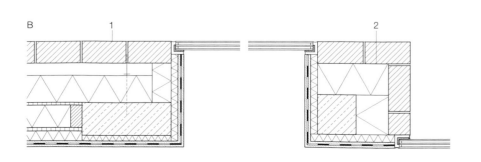

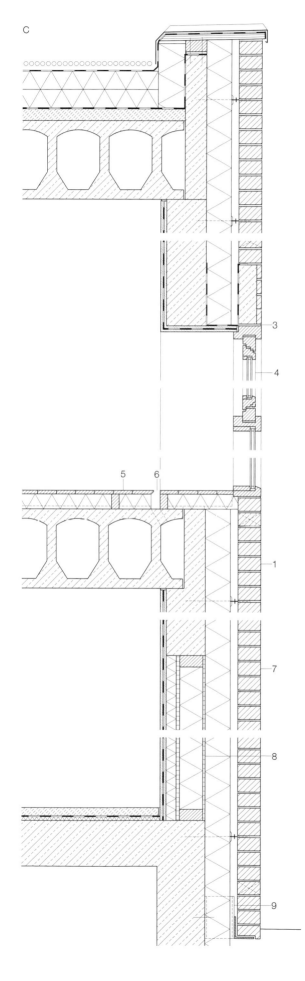

Example 27

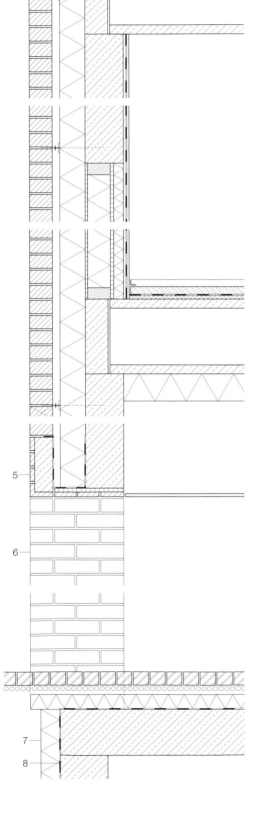

Section through arcade facade
Horizontal section through window
Horizontal section through fixed glazing
scale 1:20

1   Parapet capping, stainless steel sheet
2   Multiplex board, 25 mm
3   Roof construction:
    50 mm gravel
    waterproofing
    thermal insulation, 200 mm rigid
    expanded foam
    vapour barrier
    screed laid to falls
    360 mm hollow concrete planks, with
    skim coat and paint finish

4   Concrete upstand
5   Lintel, precast concrete, clad
    in 25 mm brick slips
6   Concrete column,
    230 x 250 mm, with facing
    brickwork cladding
7   Thermal insulation,
    120 mm rigid expanded foam
8   Reinforced concrete wall,
    waterproof, 250 mm

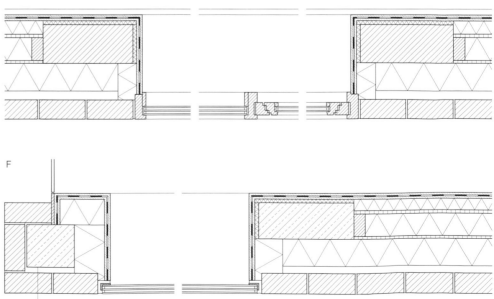

Example 28

Church and community centre in
Neu-Anspach, Germany

1998

Architects:
Hahn Helten Architekten, Aachen
Assistants:
Harald Schäfer (project manager),
Bettina Noppeney, Jutta Pieper, Dirk Lenzner,
Bettina Horn, Gregor Dewey
Structural engineers:
Stöffler-Abraham-Fäth, Darmstadt

The new community centre with church and parish hall is located in the immediate proximity of the market-place. The scale of this large, detached cube integrates well with the heterogeneous architecture of the town centre. The design and shape of the church structure provides an unobtrusive setting for introspective quietness.

The glazed foyer links the two blocks roughly equal in size: the introverted church on one side, the community centre with offices, meeting rooms and apartments on the other. The internal layout is determined by the spacious foyer. A glazed partition with large, glass sliding screens to the church, and the common roof construction create a visual bond. When the sliding screens are open, the foyer serves as an extension to the church.

Besides the graphic configuration of the overall building, the two parts are also distinguished by the choice of facade material and the openings. Reinforced concrete walls constitute the primary loadbearing structure. These enable diverse openings for windows and loggias to be positioned as required. The facades of the two parts are different: the almost completely plain surfaces of the church structure contrast with the carefully worked rendered surfaces with their precisely located windows. The rendered surfaces conceal a "thermoskin" with mineral fibre insulation. Parapet cappings and window reveals make use of narrow aluminium sheets. The church employs a partial-fill cavity wall construction; blocks of Norwegian white concrete were used for the outer leaf.

One essential charm of this fine material differentiation lies in the treatment of the white masonry. The even stretcher bond is given a pattern by the graphic arrangement of the necessary movement joints. In each case the bond restarts at the joint. The corners were built in bond in such a way that the observer is given the impression of a continuous external skin.

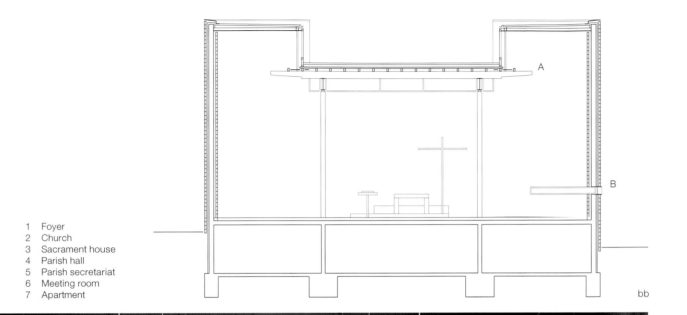

bb

Section
Upper floor
Ground floor
scale 1:500
Section
scale 1:200

1 Foyer
2 Church
3 Sacrament house
4 Parish hall
5 Parish secretariat
6 Meeting room
7 Apartment

Example 28

Section through roof
Section through facade to church
Horizontal section through window slit
scale 1:20

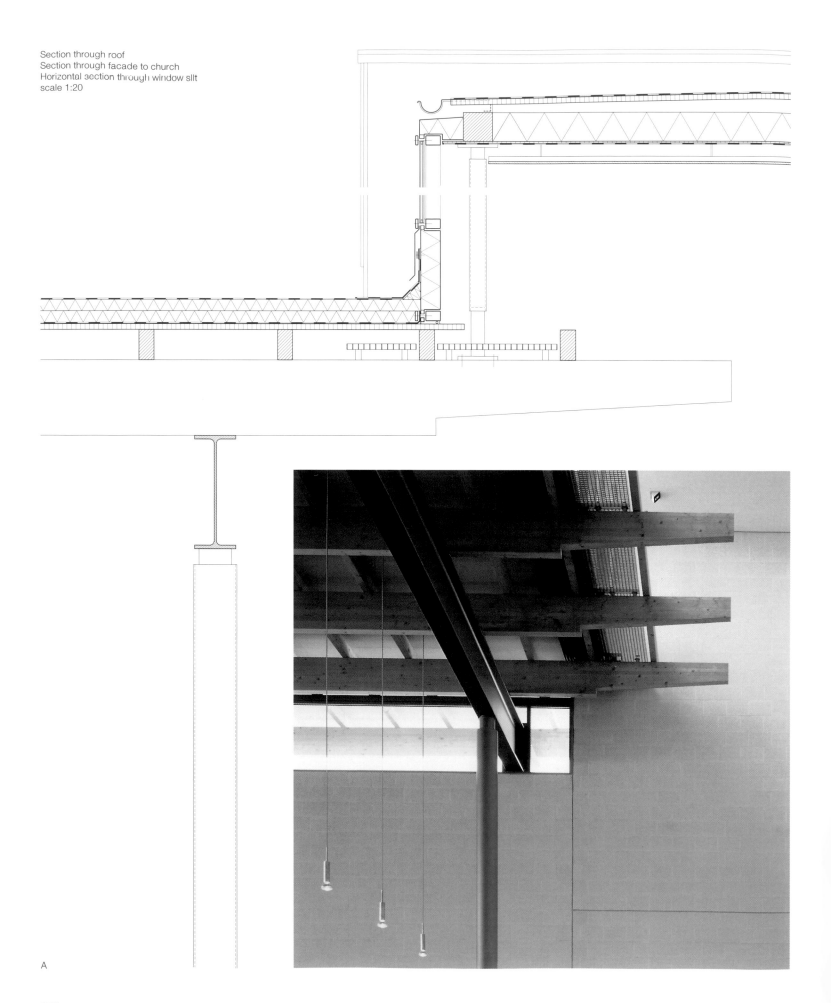

A

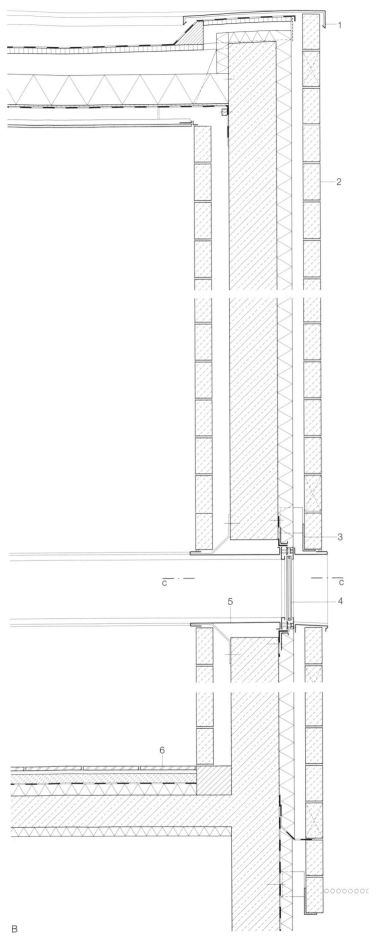

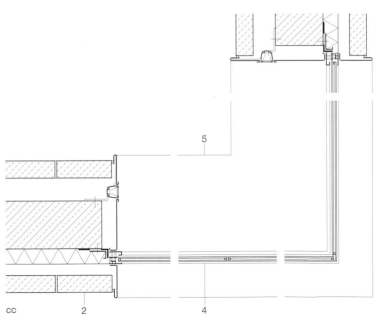

1   Parapet capping, 0.8 mm zinc sheet
2   Wall construction:
     90 mm white concrete bricks
     60 mm air space
     thermal insulation, 80 mm mineral fibre
     250 mm reinforced concrete
     95 mm air space
     115 mm white concrete bricks
3   Angle bracket, 8 mm stainless steel
4   Aluminium window, with insulating glaz-
     ing, inner pane of 8 mm laminated
     safety glass, sand-blasted

5   Aluminium sheet, 3 mm,
     bent to suit
6   Floor construction:
     20 mm natural stone slabs
     20 mm mortar bed
     50 mm cement screed
     separating membrane, 0.2 mm
     polyethylene sheeting
     impact sound insulation, 60 mm
     rigid expanded foam
     200 mm reinforced concrete slab
     50 mm thermal insualtion

Example 28

Corner window to church
Horizontal section · Vertical section
scale 1:20

1   Stainless steel angle, 8 mm
2   Aluminium sheet, 3 mm, bent to suit
3   Aluminium window, with insulating glazing,
    inner pane of 8 mm laminated safety glass,
    sand blasted
4   Ventilation grille, 50 x 15 x 2 mm aluminium
    sections

5   Fresh-air duct, 500 x 300 mm,
    sheet steel, galvanized
6   Wall construction:
    15 mm mineral rendering
    120 mm thermal insulation
    240 mm reinforced concrete wall
    15 mm internal plaster

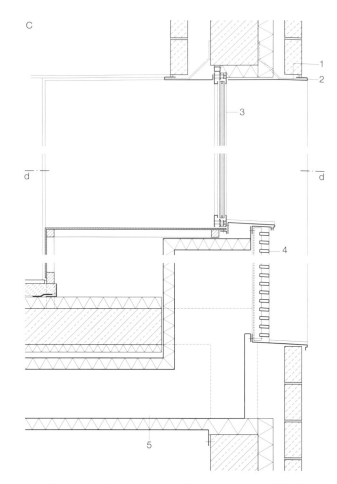

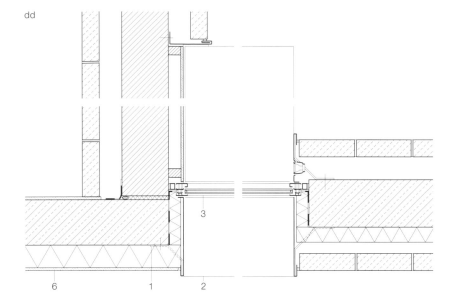

Community buildings in Iragna, Switzerland

1995

Architects:
Raffaele Cavadini, Locarno
Assistants:
Fabio Trisconi, Silvana Marzari
Structural engineers:
Giorgio Masotti, Bellinzona (town hall),
Paolo Regolati, Minusio (chapel),
Walter Perlini, Lodrino (square design)

Located between St Gotthard and Bellinzona in the Ticino Alps, a traditional granite mining district, this community was given several new buildings to meet the needs of today's infrastructure but provide a respectful complement to the old, intact, village structure. One after the other, the chapel, the town hall and the square in the southern part of Iragna were realized by the same architects. The use of the local stone with its powerful texture illustrates the bond between the new structures and the history of the village. Using simple building geometries they relate to the character of the village, although the structures themselves are a deliberate, contemporary comment on their surroundings.

The highlighting of structural elements, like the plinth in fair-face concrete or the exposed edges of the floors, serve as a stylized architectural link between tradition and modernism. This approach makes possible large ribbon windows on the town hall, likewise large panels of glass bricks. With outer leaves of natural stone, the buildings generate a reference to the authenticity of the village without intruding. The twin-leaf external walls are made from squared gneiss stones, insulation and plastered clay brickwork. The hammer-dressed natural stone masonry in Roman bond is built using cement mortar and a galvanized reinforcing lattice in front of the 80 mm thick thermal insulation. The floors which pass through the walls and act as supports are provided with strips of insulation internally (a form of construction which is hardly feasible on the north side of the Alps owing to the climate and the strict regulations). Therefore, it is possible to see the stone masonry wall not as a mere envelope but also in its structural capacity.

Location plan
scale 1:3000
1   Piazza della Posta Vecchia
2   Chapel
3   Town hall

Example 29

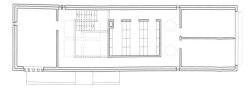

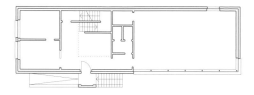

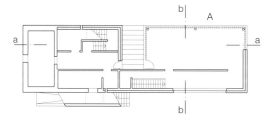

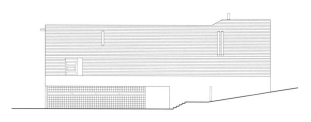

Town hall
2nd floor
1st floor
Ground floor
North elevation
Sections
scale 1:400

Section through north facade
scale 1:20
1   Roof construction:
     60 mm gravel
     protective membrane, non-woven fabric
     waterproofing and thermal insulation of 80 mm in-situ
     plastic foam
     200 mm reinforced concrete slab
     15 mm gypsum plaster
2   Capping, 0.2 mm copper sheet
3   MDF board, 15 mm
4   Wall construction:
     gneiss stone, 200-500 x 100-170 x 100-250 mm
     cement mortar with galvanized reinforcing lattice
     thermal insulation, 80 mm in-situ foam
     150 mm clay brickwork
     15 mm gypsum plaster
5   Floor construction:
     10 mm parquet flooring
     70 mm cement screed
     separating membrane
     20 mm impact sound insulation
     220 mm reinforced concrete slab
     15 mm gypsum plaster
6   Fair-face concrete surface
7   Thermal insulation, 30 mm rigid expanded foam
8   Window sill, 40 mm reconstituted stone
9   Column, steel circular hollow section, 200 dia. x 5.6 mm
10 Glass bricks, 200 x 200 x 80 mm
11 Steel channel, 120 x 80 x 5 mm
12 Precast concrete threshold
13 Granite slabs, 40 mm, on sand or cement bed

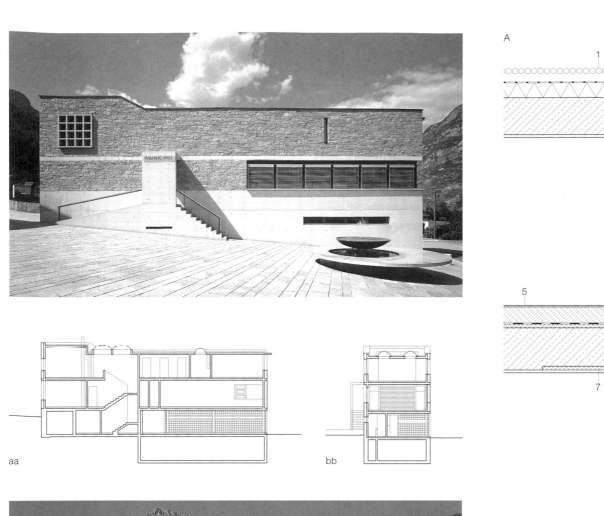

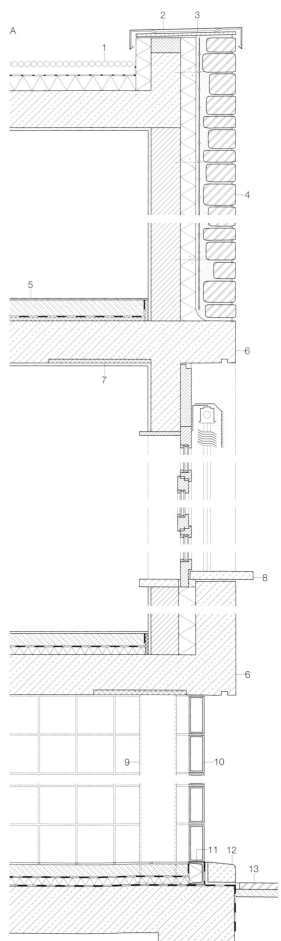

aa   bb

A

Example 30

Bank extension in Schönaich, Germany

1999

Architects:
Kaag + Schwarz, Stuttgart
Werner Kaag, Rudolf Schwarz
Assistants:
Thorsten Kock, Almut Schwabe,
Horst Fischer, Marcus Lembach
Structural engineers:
Merkt + Le, Böblingen

The special feature of this extension to an existing bank building lies in the unusual construction of the natural stone facade. It is built from 115 mm thick Gauinger travertine stone. In contrast to conventional techniques using as thin as possible a cladding of slabs , there are currently few examples of the use of this material in a proper and structurally lucid form.

The proportions of the extension are derived from the existing urban relationships and building lines. The building is made up of a stone-faced structure and a glass link which contains the vertical and horizontal access routes. The new facades embrace the forecourt adjacent the street and clearly assign this to the bank complex.

The loadbearing construction consists of reinforced concrete walls 200 mm thick and flat slabs, which can be used as heat storage media. The outermost layer of the partial-fill cavity wall construction employs large natural stone blocks with thin joints built in stretcher bond. The sizes of the stones decrease towards the tops of the walls. Near the parapet in particular, the stones are shallower and narrower. This has an economic advantage because there is less wastage, but another benefit is that this form of construction reinforces the natural and animated effect of the bush-hammered stone surfaces. Lintels to doors and windows are made from a single stone in each case. The relieving lintel above is slightly cambered, which makes it visible as a structural element and illustrates the jointing principles of a stone facade.

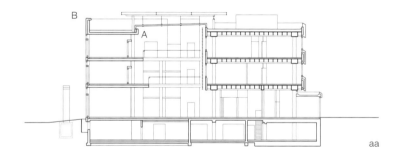

aa

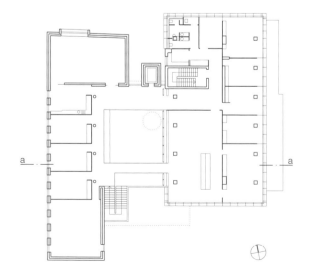

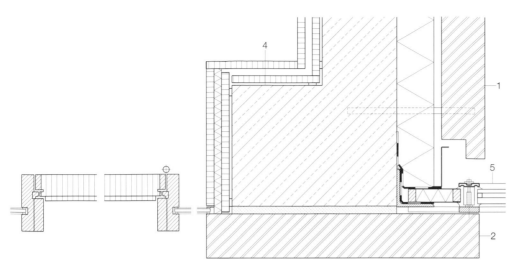

Section
2nd floor
scale 1:500
Horizontal section through door to meeting room –
internal wall on 2nd floor
Section through glass roof to central hall – parapet
scale 1:10

1   Wall construction, external:
    115 mm Gauinger travertine stone in masonry bond,
    bush-hammered surface
    20 mm air space
    thermal insulation, 100 mm mineral wool
    200 mm reinforced concrete
2   Gauinger travertine stone in masonry bond, 115 mm,
    bush-hammered surface, door lintel provided with
    camber for structural relief

3   Mortar filling, 20 mm
4   Reinforced concrete wall
5   Steel-and-glass facade of welded steel flats, with
    insulating glazing
6   Floor construction, ground floor to central hall:
    20 mm natural stone, "Tauern" green
    20 mm mortar bed
    60 mm anhydrite screed with underfloor heating
    50 mm thermal and impact sound insulation

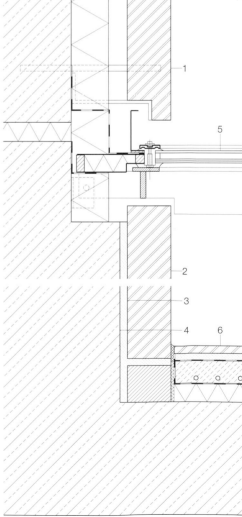

Example 30

West facade
Horizontal sections · Vertical section
scale 1:10

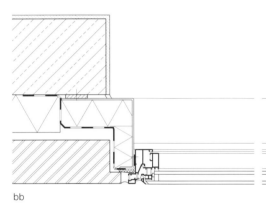
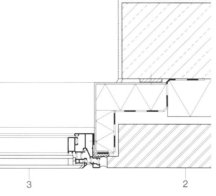
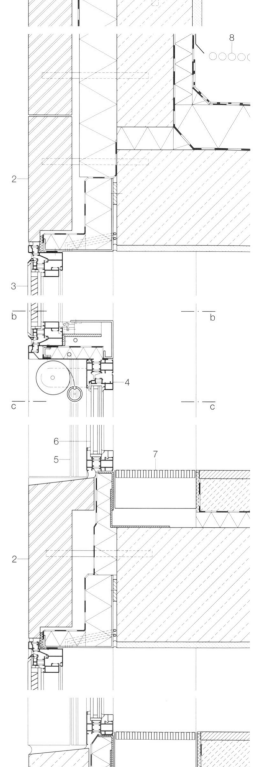

bb

3   2

cc

5   4   2

1   Parapet coping, Gauinger travertine stone,
    smooth surface
2   Lintel to uppermost row of windows, provided with
    camber, Gauinger travertine stone in masonry bond,
    115 mm, bush-hammered surface
3   Opening lights for night-time ventilation, opened
    individually as required, 10 mm toughened safety
    glass + 18 mm cavity with sunshading light-
    deflecting grid + 10 mm toughened safety glass, in
    black anodized aluminium sections, plus anti-intruder
    bars at ground floor only
4   Revolving light, black anodized aluminium,
    8 mm + 16 mm cavity + 12 mm laminated safety glass
5   Guide track for sunshade blind

6   Fixed glazing in aluminium sections, 8 mm + 16 mm
    cavity + 12 mm laminated safety glass
7   Floor duct for heating
8   Roof construction:
    extensive planting / 100 mm gravel
    sheeting, resistant to root penetration
    filter, non-woven fabric
    waterproofing, bitumen sheeting, 2 layers, top layer
    with slate granule surfacing
    thermal insulation, 140 mm rigid expanded foam
    vapour barrier
    250 mm reinforced concrete slab, with undercoat
    15 mm internal plaster

Example 31

Library of the Technological Institute in Cork, Ireland

1996

Architects:
Shane de Blacam & John Meagher
with Boyd Barrett, Murphy O'Connor, Dublin
Structural engineers:
Horgan Lynch & Partners, Cork

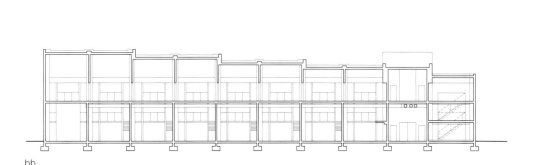

aa

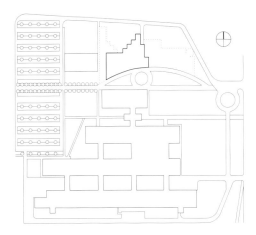

bb

Location plan
scale 1:5000
Ground floor · 1st floor
scale 1:500

1   Entrance foyer
2   Information desk
3   Reading room
4   Bookstack
5   Librarians
6   Deliveries
7   Periodicals gallery
8   Seminar rooms

The library building is part of the overall urban plan for the Technological Institute. The shape of the building with its sweeping south facade is explained by the geometry of the overall complex.

There is a very strict organization of the internal functions from south to north, which starts with the two-storey reading room and unfolds by way of lively interventions with stairs and galleries. Up to 500 students can be accommodated in the large reading room and on the galleries. The shelves have space for about 70,000 books, periodicals and video films. Likewise integrated in the linear structure are rooms for seminars and the library management. The different heights of the building and the associated changing lighting conditions give the interior an even more pronounced three-dimensional effect. Local, traditional building materials were used for the construction: clay and calcium silicate, oak for the window frames, panelling and furniture. Concrete bricks alternating with clay bricks create impressive patterns on walls and columns. Clay brickwork cladding was positioned in the formwork before casting the in-situ reinforced concrete columns and arches. The diaphragm wall construction (max. spacing between leaves 550 mm) offers numerous opportunities for projections and recesses which can be used for built-in furniture. The curving south elevation almost devoid of windows presents a stark contrast to the brightly lit and contrasting interior of the library.

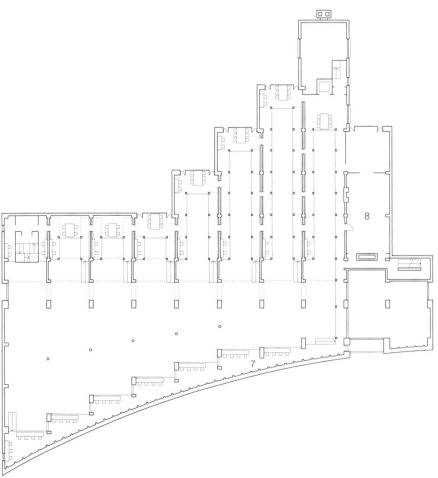

Example 31

cc

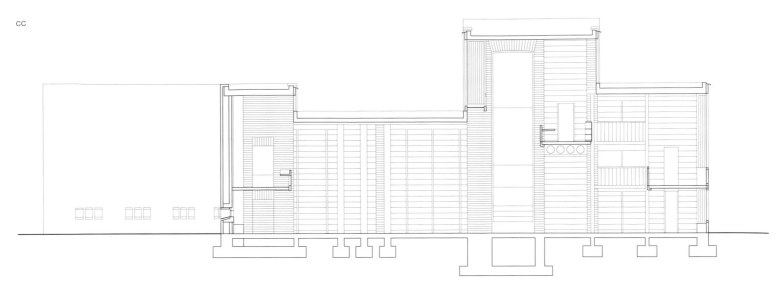

Section   scale 1:250
Facade
Elevation · Horizontal section · Vertical section
scale 1:20

1   Parapet capping, calcium silicate slab, 450 x 20 mm
2   Drip plate, stainless steel, bent to suit
3   Roof construction:
    20 mm mastic asphalt on separating membrane
    60 mm thermal insulation
    vapour barrier
    150 mm in-situ reinforced concrete
    75 mm precast concrete planks
4   Cross-ribs of concrete brickwork

5   Wall construction:
    100 mm clay brickwork
    310 mm cavity
    50 mm thermal insulation
    100 mm concrete brickwork
6   Floor construction, gallery:
    coconut fibre carpet
    150 mm in-situ concrete
    75 mm precast concrete planks
7   Built-in bookshelves, MDF board, coated
8   Precast concrete peripheral frame
9   Perforated plate element for permanent ventilation
10 Lining to reveal, oak, 150 x 25 mm
11 Wooden window, oak, with insulating glazing

12 Waterproofing, bitumen sheeting
13 Window lintel, calcium silicate block, 65 mm
14 Roofing slates, several layers
15 Roofing slates, 2 layers, laid to fall
16 Floor construction:
    coconut fibre carpet
    150 mm in-situ concrete
    separating membrane
    thermal insulation, 50 mm rigid expanded foam
    cement levelling coat
    hardcore
17 Lean mix concrete filling
18 Calcium silicate pavings externally

A

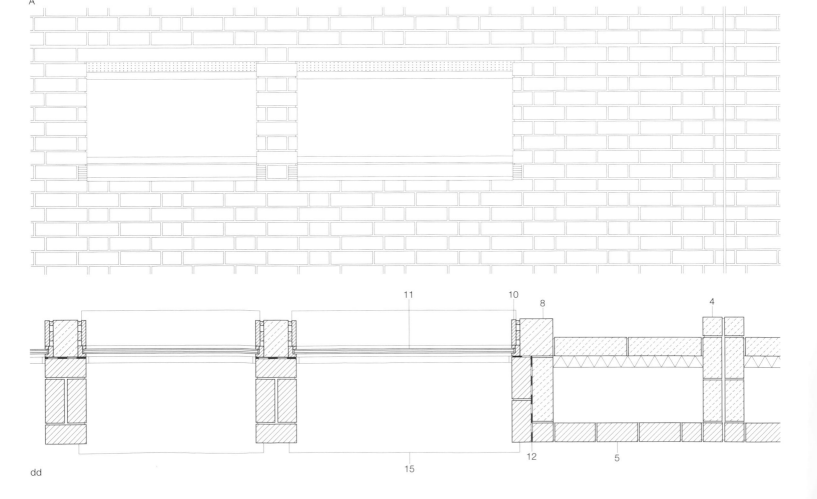

dd

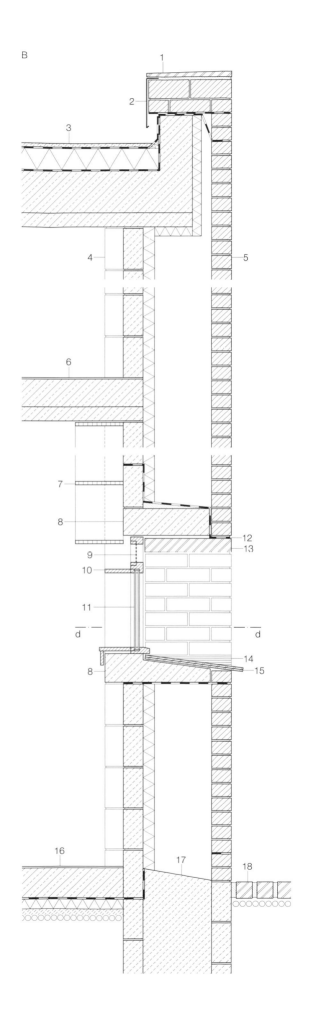

B

1
2
3
4
5
6
7
8
12
13
9
10
11
d ——————— d
14
8
15
16
17
18

Example 31

Mechanical Engineering Faculty Building of the University of Aveiro, Portugal

1996

Architect:
Adalberto Dias, Porto
Assistants:
A. Teixeira, C. Veloso, J. Eusébio, V. Gama,
J. Miguelote, N. Rocha
Structural engineer:
A. Dinis

Since 1985 a general plan has been in force for all newly erected buildings on the new campus of the University of Aveiro. One of the prime considerations was to limit the choice of architect, if feasible, to members of the "Porto School" in order to give the buildings by different architects an inner architectural coherency. The effect of this strategy is that the campus is now also a showcase for Porto's most notable architects.

The building designed by Adalberto Dias for the Mechanical Engineering Faculty is in the immediate vicinity of the buildings for geology (Eduardo Souto de Moura) and mathematics (Carlos Prata).

The predefined interior layout of the building led to an obvious solution. The south-west elevation – with virtually no openings – forms one wall to the access zone, which incorporates the stairs and is lit from above via a long, continuous rooflight. The loadbearing structure of the building consists of reinforced concrete in conjunction with steel beams and columns for walls and floors, some of which have to span quite considerable distances above the lecture theatres. The external walls are provided with a masonry outer leaf of approx. 70 mm high courses of facing brickwork built in stretcher bond. In order to emphasize the radical nature of the concept, the external masonry is given a horizontal profile. This is achieved by recessing every second course by 30 mm. To do this, the bricks were sawn to 80 mm width. Steel sections at the transition between masonry and glass facade and along the edge of the roof stress the horizontal format of the structure. The external wall alongside the rooflight also features facing brickwork on the inside; the irregularities of this masonry produce a very lively texture when illuminated by the dramatic diagonal, overhead lighting.

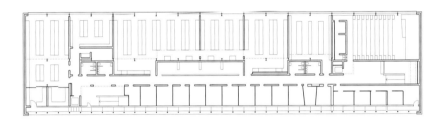

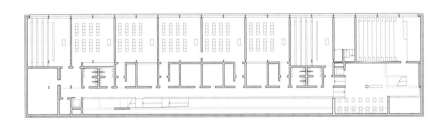

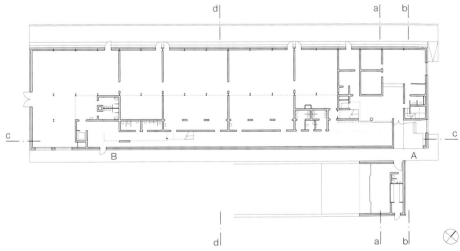

3rd floor · 2nd floor · Ground floor
scale 1:750

Example 32

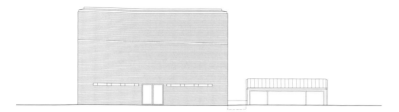

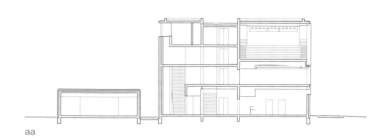

aa

South-west elevation
Sections
scale 1:500
Section through facade
scale 1:20

1 Clay bricks
2 Capping, zinc sheet on cork board
3 Steel channel, 180 mm
4 Steel round section, 75 mm dia.
5 Spandrel panel capping, zinc sheet on cork board
6 Steel channel, 160 mm
7 Spandrel panel: clay brickwork

12 mm air space
thermal insulation, 40 mm rigid expanded foam
195 mm reinforced concrete
clay bricks
30 mm synthetic resin plaster
8 Steel window, with insulating glazing
9 Window sill, natural stone

10 Floor construction:
40 mm natural stone alsbs
levelling mortar bed
thermal insulation, 30 mm rigid expanded foam
damp proof membrane
screed laid to falls
thermal insulation, 50 mm rigid expanded foam
180 mm reinforced concrete

A

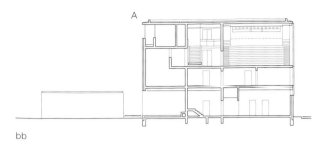

bb

11 Roof construction:
    40 mm reconstituted stone pavings
    levelling bed
    thermal insulation, 30 mm rigid
    expanded foam
    waterproofing
    screed laid to falls
    180 mm reinforced concrete slab
    40 mm synthetic resin plaster
12 Wood/steel window

13 Synthetic resin plaster, 50 mm
14 Clay bricks
15 Internal plaster, 20 mm
16 Floor construction:
    floor finish of stone slabs
    20 mm mortar bed
    40 mm screed
    180 mm reinforced concrete
    40 mm timber battens
    40 mm synthetic resin plaster

A

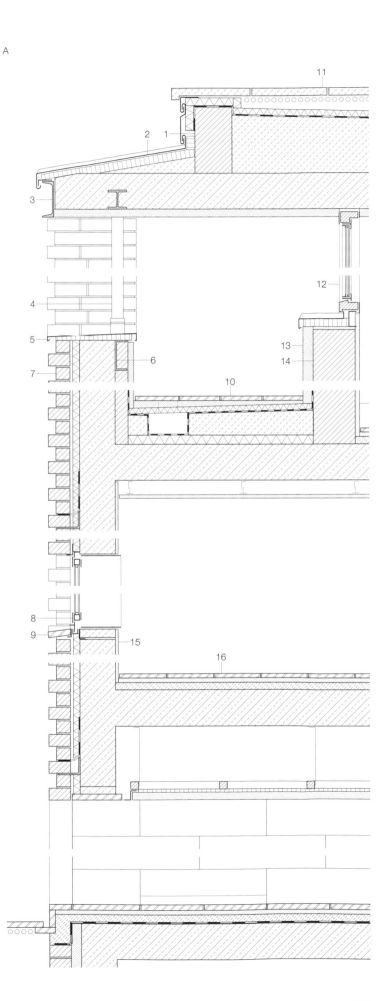

Example 32

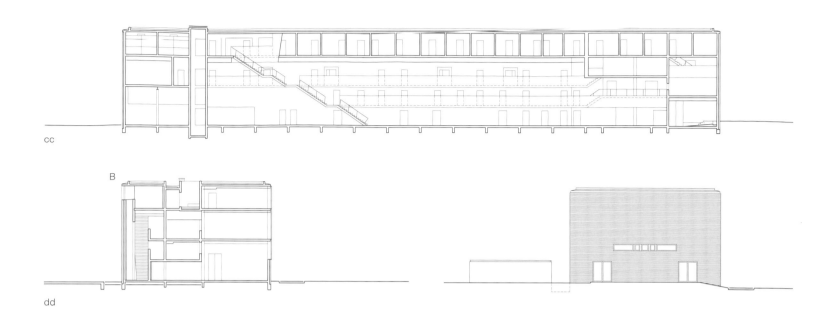

cc

B

dd

B

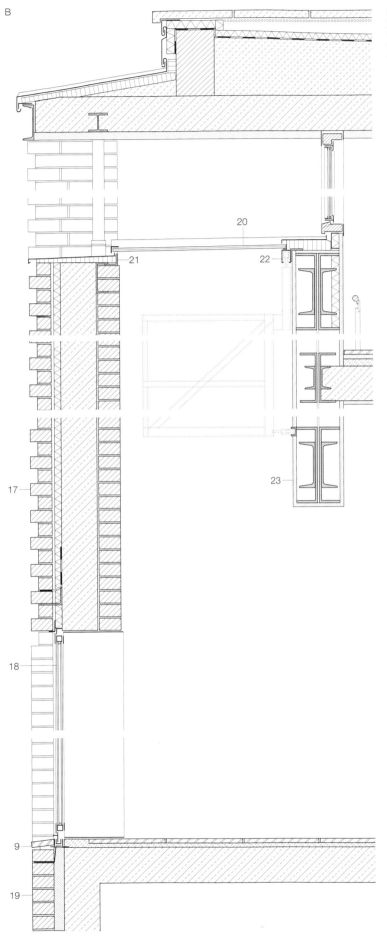

Sections
North-east elevation
scale 1:500
Section through facade
scale 1:20

17 Wall construction:
    110 x 80 mm clay bricks in stretcher
    bond
    12 mm air space
    thermal insulation, 40 mm rigid
    expanded foam
    195 mm reinforced concrete
    clay bricks in stretcher bond,
    115 mm
18 Glazed steel door

19 Plinth construction:
    clay brickwork
    50 mm mortar filling
    195 mm reinforced concrete
20 Horizontal glazing, laminated safety
    glass in steel frame
21 Steel angle, 60 x 70 x 8 mm
22 Guide rail for inspection cradle
23 Plasterboard

Example 33

Office building in Essen, Germany
1996

Architect:
Detlef Sommer of
Eckert Negwer Sommer Suselbeek, Berlin
Assistant:
Marc Jordi
Site manager:
Helmut Heimeshoff, Essen
Structural engineers:
A. Bruns, B. Szafranski, Berlin

This office building at the Christine Colliery provides a link between the once separate offices and the existing production building. The small plot made it necessary to erect a four-storey building. This contains simple plan layouts with six offices per floor as well as the associated vertical and horizontal access zones and service core. The rooms are arranged alongside a central corridor. The offset between the two halves of the building gives rise to an interesting spatial effect.

Storey-height, narrow windows break up the simple cube, while the piers provide a rhythmic structure to the facade. The layout of the masonry is such that the observer gets the impression of a framework. However, the quality of the design concept manifests itself in the skilful balance between piers and openings. Consequently, special attention was paid to careful detailing of the openings.

The facing brickwork of the outer leaf consists of Wittmunder peat-fired bricks with the Oldenburg format. Cavity insulation and loadbearing calcium silicate masonry complete the external wall construction. The window reveals are carried around the corners with a one-brick-deep bond.

The window sills consist of brick-on-edge courses, the lintels of reinforced concrete clad in facing brickwork. The windows with their fixed glazing, wooden reveals and wooden openings lights fitted behind the outer leaf form a distinct contrast to the piers in order to reinforce their effect.

Ironically, the closed openings lights, offset from the plane of the window, form their own pier within the opening and hence consummate the architectural setting.

The loadbearing walls adjacent the internal corridors are made from the same material as the outer leaves of the external walls. They illustrate the simple structural system: the exposed in-situ concrete floors spanning between external wall and corridor wall. Masonry architecture becomes contemporary when used in such an exciting, simple yet subtle way.

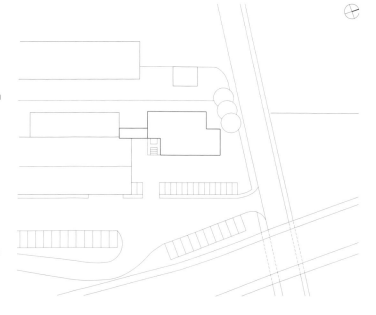

Location plan
scale 1:1250
East elevation
3rd floor
Ground floor
scale 1:250

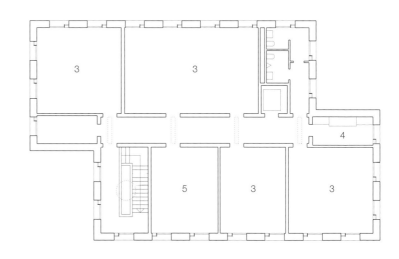

1 Lobby
2 Reception
3 Office
4 Tea kitchen
5 Meeting room
6 Existing building

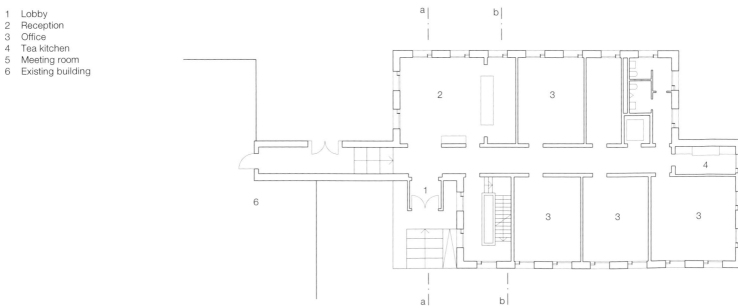

Example 33

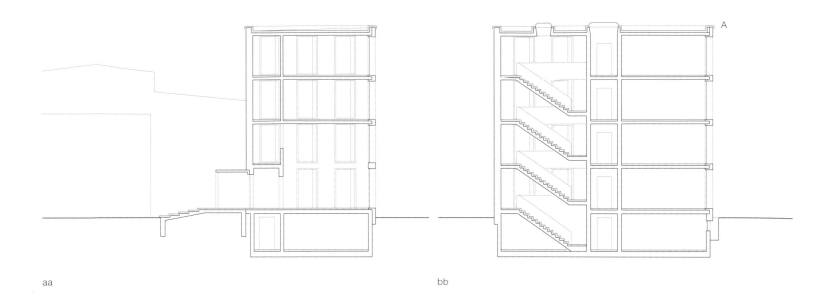

aa

bb

Sections
scale 1:250
Window
Elevation · Horizontal section
Section through facade
scale 1:20

1 Roof construction:
   50 mm gravel
   waterproofing, bitumen sheeting, 3 layers
   thermal insulation, rigid expanded foam, with
   integral falls, 300-120 mm
   220 reinforced concrete slab, soffit exposed, rough
   formwork finish
2 Laminated veneer lumber (LVL) board, 450 x 25 mm
3 Timber section, 220 x 70 mm
4 Flashing, 1 mm zinc sheet, pre-weathered
5 Parapet capping, 1 mm zinc sheet, pre-weathered,
   on separating membrane V 13
6 Concrete upstand, 160 x 400 mm
7 Wooden window, meranti with glazed finish, fixed
   glazing, insulating glazing with laminated safety
   glass

8 Floor construction:
   13 mm carpet
   60 mm screed
   separating membrane
   17 mm impact sound insulation
   220 reinforced concrete slab, soffit exposed,
   rough formwork finish
9 Brick-on-edge window sill, Wittmunder peat-fired
   bricks, Oldenburg format, 52 x 105 x 220 mm
10 Thermal insulation, 110 mm mineral fibre
11 Reinforced concrete lintel, brick slip cladding
12 Peripheral timber cover strip, 125 x 15 mm
13 Convector heating under grating
14 Opening panel with timber infill, meranti with
   glazed finish
15 Wall construction:
   facing brickwork, Wittmunder peat-fired bricks,
   Oldenburg format, 52 x 105 x 220 mm
   thermal insulation, 110 mm mineral fibre
   240 mm calcium silicate brickwork
   15 mm gypsum plaster

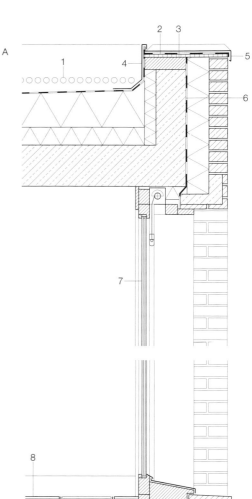

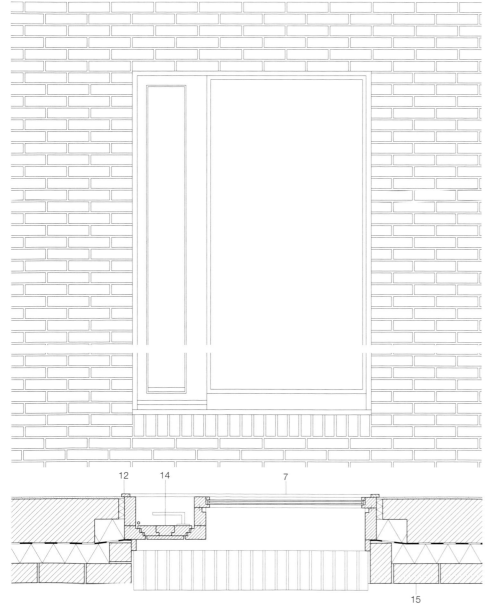

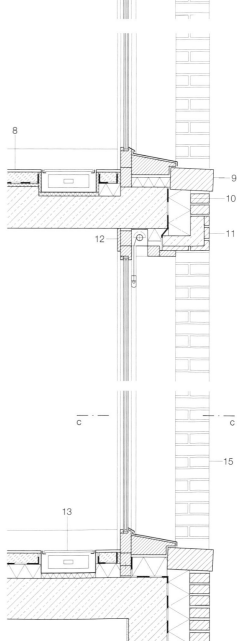

Example 34

Housing complex in Hannover, Germany

1999

Architects:
Fink + Jocher, Munich
Assistants:
Ivan Grafl, Ulrike Wietzorrek, Rüdiger Krisch
Structural engineers:
Bergmann + Partner, Hannover

Situated on the north-western edge of the development built to coincide with EXPO 2000, this urban component with 87 apartments, public amenities and shops forms the gateway to Kronsberg, an entirely new city suburb. The two main facades of the building have been given different treatments: a brickwork facade with peat-fired facing bricks and room-height French windows with folding shutters facing the city, and a timber facade behind continuous, deep loggias facing the inner courtyard. The sculptured form of the block with equal-sized window elements distributed evenly over the facade in an intriguing staggered arrangement lends the building both stability and vitality. A large number of different apartments, from simple layout with hall to open plan, offers diverse possibilities with a constant basic structure.

The entire loadbearing structure of the building was built in precast concrete. This resulted in fast erection and low building costs. There is an outer leaf of 115 mm facing bricks with a 10 mm air space and 120 mm thermal insulation. A contrasting precast concrete coping completes the parapet. The window lintels, also precast, are clad with clay bricks in stretcher bond in order to match the depth and appearance of the 240 mm reveals. Fitted into the reveals are wooden folding shutters which help to assert the character of the building. The precast concrete window sills round off the homogeneous appearance of the complex. The facades to the inner courtyard, with their deep loggias, are clad in birch plywood. These loggias raise the living standards of the complex and form the transition to the landscaped inner courtyard, generating a contrast to the urban environment.

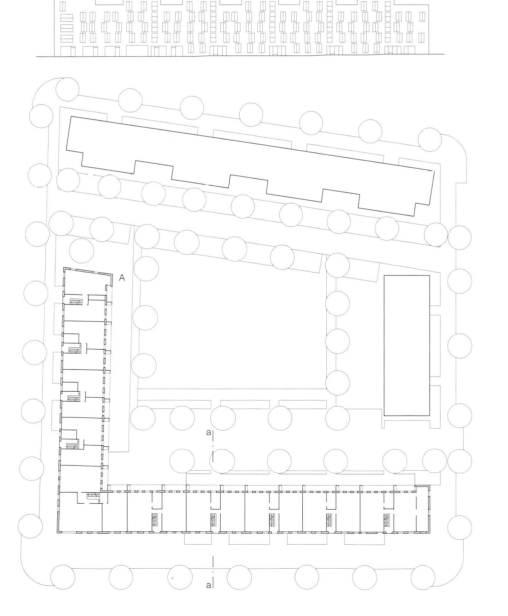

Location plan
scale 1:3000
North-west elevation
Standard floor
scale 1:1000
Apartment layouts
scale 1:500

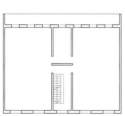

Standard layout

Hall

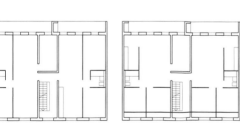

Variable

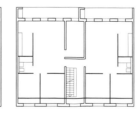

Semi-open plan

Island

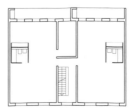

Open plan

Example 34

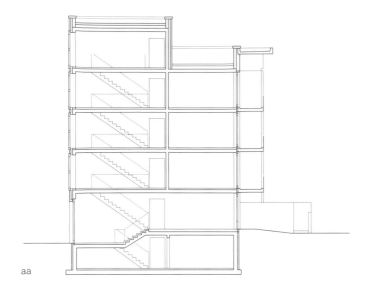

aa

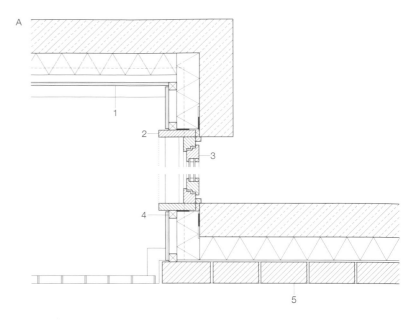

A

Section
scale 1:250
Horizontal section through junction between facing brick-
work and timber panel facade
Horizontal section through apartment window
Horizontal section through staircase window
Section through street facade
scale 1:20

1   Plywood panel, 18 mm birch, both sides coated
    with phenolic resin
2   Wooden lining, 200 x 40 mm
3   Wooden glazed door, with insulating glazing
4   Supporting construction, 40 x 40 mm timber sections
5   Wall construction:
    peat-fired facing bricks, NF 115 mm
    10 mm air space
    thermal insulation, 120 mm mineral fibre
    180 mm reinforced concrete
6   4-part folding shutters of 3-ply timber boarding, with
    edge beading in weatherproof glue, guide tracks top
    and bottom, 2 No. 15 mm
7   Balustrade of steel flats, galvanized, micacious
    iron oxide coating, 35 x 8 mm
8   Window sill, precast concrete, overhang with drip,
    50 mm
9   Wooden window, 2 lights, with insulating glazing
10 Horizontal-pivot window, with insulating glazing,
    spandrel pane fixed, inner pane of laminated
    safety glass
11 Plasterboard, 12.5 mm
12 Thermal insulation, 80 mm
13 Ring beam, autoclaved aerated concrete
    channel block
14 Rendering, 25 mm
15 Terrace construction:
    pavings in gravel bed
    15 mm impact sound insulation
    waterproofing
    200 mm thermal insulation
    vapour barrier
    220 mm reinforced concrete slab
16 Sheet metal flashing
17 Parapet/spandrel panel:
    peat-burned facing bricks in stretcher bond,
    NF 115 mm
    10 mm air space
    thermal insulation, 120 mm mineral fibre
    175 mm aerated concrete
18 Open perpend
19 Thermal insulation, 60 mm rigid expanded foam
20 Horizontal groove, with fall to outside
21 Ventilation element
22 Steel angle as support for window sill

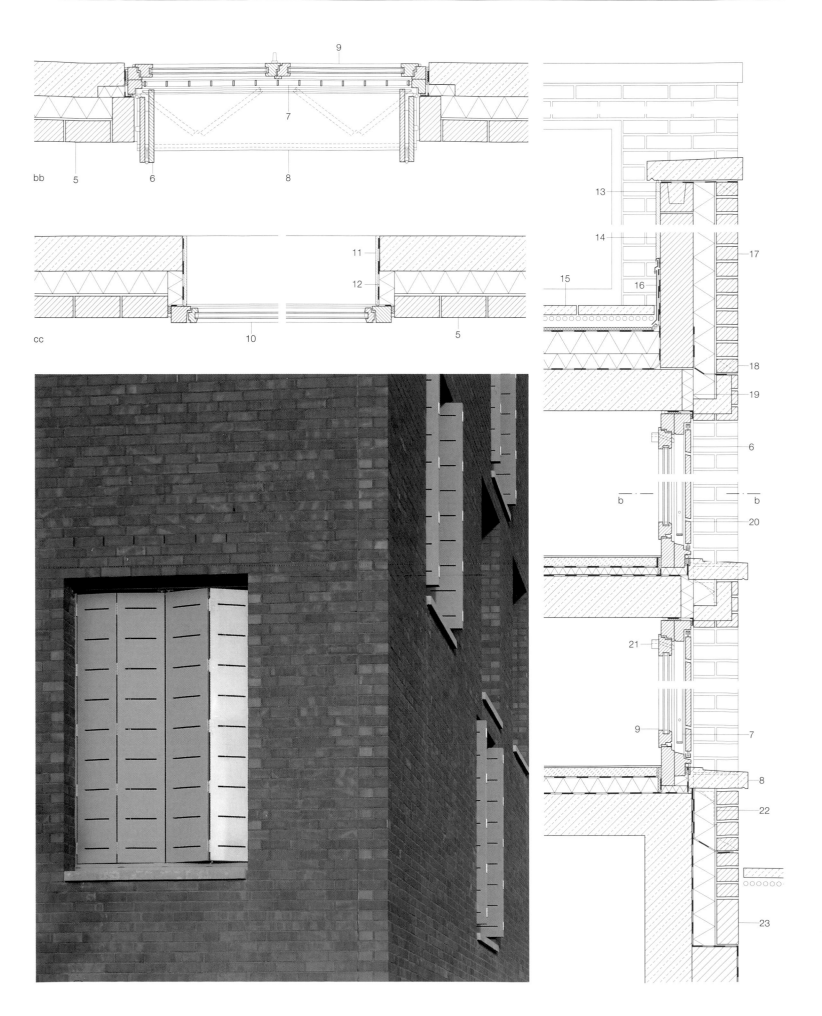

bb

5　　6　　7　　8　　9

cc

11　12　10　5

13　14　15　16　17　18　19　6

b　　b

20　21　9　7　8　22　23

Example 34

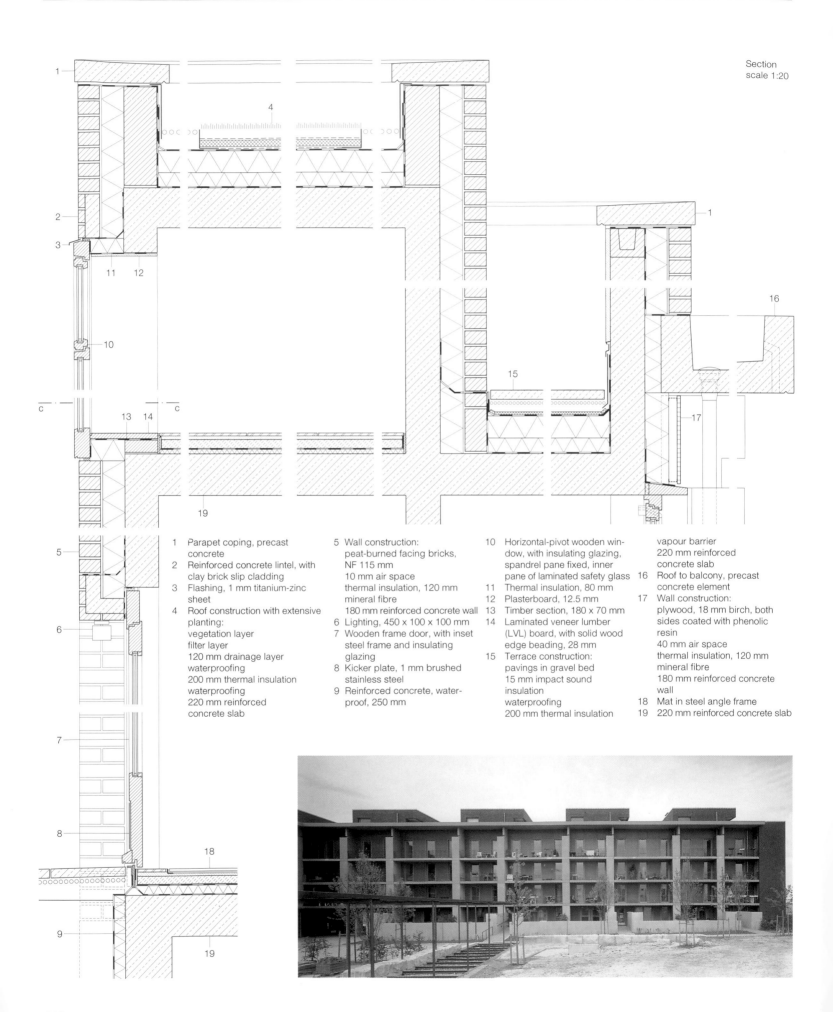

Section
scale 1:20

1 Parapet coping, precast concrete
2 Reinforced concrete lintel, with clay brick slip cladding
3 Flashing, 1 mm titanium-zinc sheet
4 Roof construction with extensive planting:
   vegetation layer
   filter layer
   120 mm drainage layer
   waterproofing
   200 mm thermal insulation
   waterproofing
   220 mm reinforced concrete slab

5 Wall construction:
   peat-burned facing bricks, NF 115 mm
   10 mm air space
   thermal insulation, 120 mm mineral fibre
   180 mm reinforced concrete wall
6 Lighting, 450 x 100 x 100 mm
7 Wooden frame door, with inset steel frame and insulating glazing
8 Kicker plate, 1 mm brushed stainless steel
9 Reinforced concrete, waterproof, 250 mm

10 Horizontal-pivot wooden window, with insulating glazing, spandrel pane fixed, inner pane of laminated safety glass
11 Thermal insulation, 80 mm
12 Plasterboard, 12.5 mm
13 Timber section, 180 x 70 mm
14 Laminated veneer lumber (LVL) board, with solid wood edge beading, 28 mm
15 Terrace construction:
   pavings in gravel bed
   15 mm impact sound insulation
   waterproofing
   200 mm thermal insulation

   vapour barrier
   220 mm reinforced concrete slab
16 Roof to balcony, precast concrete element
17 Wall construction:
   plywood, 18 mm birch, both sides coated with phenolic resin
   40 mm air space
   thermal insulation, 120 mm mineral fibre
   180 mm reinforced concrete wall
18 Mat in steel angle frame
19 220 mm reinforced concrete slab

Statutory instruments, directives and standards

Standards for masonry materials

DIN 105 pt 1 — Clay bricks; solid bricks and vertically perforated bricks. Aug 1989

DIN 105 pt 2 — Clay bricks; lightweight vertically perforated bricks. Aug 1989

DIN 105 pt 3 — Clay bricks; high-strength bricks and high-strength engineering bricks. May 1984

DIN 105 pt 4 — Clay bricks; ceramic engineering bricks. May 1984

DIN 105 pt 5 — Clay bricks; lightweight horizontally perforated bricks and lightweight horizontally perforated brick panels. May 1984

DIN 105 pt 6 (draft) — Clay masonry units – high precision units. Aug 1999

DIN 106 pt 1 — Sand-lime bricks and blocks; solid bricks, perforated bricks, solid blocks, hollow blocks. Sept 1980

DIN 106 pt 2 — Sand-lime bricks and blocks; facing bricks and hard-burned facing bricks

DIN 278 — Hollow Clay tiles (Hourdis) and hollow bricks, statically loaded. Sept 1978

DIN 398 — Granulated slag aggregate concrete blocks; solid, perforated, hollow blocks. Jun 1976

DIN 4159 — Floor bricks and plasterboards, statically active. Apr 1999

DIN 4165 — Autoclaved aerated concrete blocks and flat elements. Nov 1996

DIN 4166 — Autoclaved aerated concrete slabs and panels. Oct 1997

DIN 18148 — Lightweight concrete hollow boards. Dec 1998

DIN 18151 — Lightweight concrete hollow blocks. Sept 1987

DIN 18152 — Lightweight concrete solid bricks and blocks. Apr 1987

DIN 18153 — Normal-weight concrete masonry units. Sept 1989

DIN 18162 — Lightweight concrete wall-boards, unreinforced. Dec 1998

DIN 18554 pt 1 — Testing of masonry; determination of compressive strength and elastic modulus. Dec 1985

DIN 52252 pt 1 — Testing the frost resistance of facing bricks and clinker blocks; freezing of single bricks on all sides. Dec 1986

DIN EN 1926 — Natural stone test methods – determination of compressive strength. May 1999

DIN EN 12372 — Natural stone test methods – determination of flexural strength under concentrated load. Jun 1999

Standards for masonry mortar, plasters, binders

DIN 1060 pt 1 — Building lime – pt 1: definitions, specifications, control. Mar 1995

DIN 1164 pt 1 — Cement – pt 1: composition, specifications. Oct 1994

DIN 4211 — Masonry cement – specifications, control. Mar 1995

DIN 18550 pt 1 — Plaster; terminology and requirements. Jan 1985

DIN 18550 pt 2 — Plaster; plasters made of mortars containing mineral binders; application. Jan 1985

DIN 18550 pt 3 — Rendering; rendering systems for thermal insulation purposes made of mortars consisting of mineral binders and expanded polystyrene (EPS) as aggregate. Mar 1991

DIN 18550 pt 4 — Plasters and rendering; lightweight plasters and rendering; execution. Aug 1993

DIN 18555 pt 1 — Testing of mortars containing mineral binders; general, sampling, test mortar. Sept 1982

DIN 18555 pt 3 — Testing of mortars containing mineral binders; hardened mortars; determination of flexural strength, compressive strength and bulk density. Sept 1982

DIN 18555 pt 4 — Testing of mortars containing mineral binders; hardened mortars; determination of linear and transverse strain and deformation characteristics of masonry mortars by the static pressure test. Mar 1986

DIN 18555 pt 5 — Testing of mortars containing mineral binders; hardened mortars; determination of bond shear strength of masonry mortars. Mar 1986

DIN 18555 pt 8 — Testing of mortars containing mineral binders; freshly mixed mortar; determination of workability time and correction time of thin-bed mortar for use with masonry. Nov 1987

DIN 18555 pt 9 — Testing of mortars containing mineral binders – pt 9: hardened mortars; determination of compressive strength in the bed joint. Sept 1999

DIN 18557 — Factory mortar – production, control and delivery. Nov 1997

DIN 18558 — Synthetic resin plasters; terminology, requirements, application. Jan 1985

Application standards

DIN 1045 — Structural use of concrete; design and construction. Jul 1988

DIN 1053 pt 1 — Masonry – pt 1: design and construction. Nov 1996

DIN 1053 pt 2 — Masonry – pt 2: masonry strength classes on the basis of suitability tests. Nov 1996

DIN 1053 pt 3 — Reinforced masonry; design and construction. Feb 1990

DIN 1053 pt 4 — Masonry; buildings of prefabricated brickwork components. Aug 1999

DIN 1055 pt 3 — Design loads for buildings; live loads. Jun 1971

DIN 1055 pt 3 (draft) — Action on structures – pt 3: self-weight and imposed load in building. Mar 2000

DIN 4103 pt 1 — Internal non-loadbearing partitions; requirements, testing. Jul 1984

DIN 4149 pt 1 — Buildings in German earthquake zones; design loads, dimensioning, design and construction of conventional buildings. Apr 1981

ENV 1996-1-1 — Eurocode 6: design of masonry structures, pt 1-1: general rules for buildings – rules for reinforced and unreinforced masonry. June 1995

Masonry bonds

DIN 1057 pt 1 — Building materials for free-standing chimneys; compass bricks; requirements, testing, inspection. Jul 1985

DIN 4172 — Modular coordination in building construction. Jul 1955

DIN 18000 — Modular coordination in building. May 1984

DIN 18100 — Doors; wall openings for doors with dimensions in accordance with DIN 4172. Oct 1983

DIN 18201 — Tolerances in building – terminology, principles, application, testing. Dec 1984

DIN 18202 — Dimensional tolerances in building construction – buildings. May 1986

Thermal insulation

DIN 18165 pt 1 — Fibre insulation materials; thermal insulation materials. Jul 1991

DIN EN 1745 — Masonry and masonry products – methods for determining declared and design thermal values

DIN EN 12664 — Thermal performance of building materials and products – determination of thermal resistance by means of guarded hot plate and heat flow meter methods – dry and moist products with medium and low thermal resistance

DIN EN ISO 10456 — Building materials and products – procedures for determining declared and design thermal values (ISO 10456: 1999)

Moisture control

DIN 1101 — Wood-wool slabs and multilayered slabs as insulating materials in building – requirements, testing

DIN 1102 — Installation of DIN 1101 wood-wool slabs and sandwich composite panels

DIN 4108 pt 3 — Thermal insulation and energy economy in buildings – pt 3: protection against moisture subject to climate conditions; requirements and directions for design and construction

DIN 4108 pt 4 — Thermal insulation and energy economy in buildings – pt 4: characteristic values relating to thermal insulation and protection against moisture

DIN 4223 — Reinforced roofing slabs and ceiling tiles of steam-cured aerated and foamed concrete; guidelines for dimensioning, production, utilization and testing

DIN 18515 pt 1 — Cladding for external walls – pt 1: tiles fixed with mortar; principles of design and application

DIN 18516 pt 1 — Cladding for external walls, ventilated at rear – pt 1: requirements, principles of testing

DIN 18550 pt 1 — Plaster; terminology and requirements. Jan 1985

DIN 18550 pt 2 — Plaster; plasters made of mortars containing mineral binders; application. Jan 1985

DIN 18550 pt 3 — Rendering; rendering systems for thermal insulation purposes made of mortars consisting of mineral binders and expanded polystyrene (EPS) as aggregate. Mar 1991

DIN 18558 — Synthetic resin plasters; terminology, requirements, application. Jan 1985

DIN 68800 pt 2 — Protection of timber – pt 2: preventive constructional measures in buildings

DIN EN 12524 — Building materials and products – hygrothermal properties – tabulated design values

DIN EN ISO 12572 — Building materials – determination of water vapour transmission properties (ISO/DIS 12572: 1997)

DIN EN ISO 15148 — Building materials – determination of water absorption coefficient (ISO/DIS 15148: 1996)

Sound insulation

DIN 4109 — Sound insulation in buildings; requirements and testing. Nov 1989

DIN 4109 — Amendment 1: amendments to DIN 4109 (Nov 1989), DIN 4109 supp. 1 (Nov 1989) and DIN 4109 supp. 2 (Nov 1989). Aug 1992

DIN 4109 supp. 1 — Sound insulation in buildings; construction examples and calculation methods. Nov 1989

DIN 4109 supp. 2 — Sound insulation in buildings; guidelines for planning and execution; proposals for increased sound insulation; recommendations for sound insulation in personal living and working areas. Nov 1989

DIN 4109
supp. 3 — Sound insulation in buildings; calculation of R'$_{w,R}$ for assessing suitability as defined in DIN 4109 on the basis of the sound reduction index R$_w$ determined in laboratory tests. Jun 1996

DIN 4109/A1 (draft) — Sound insulation in buildings – requirements and verifications; amendment A1. Apr 1998

DIN 18005 pt 1 — Noise abatement in town planning; calculation methods

Fire protection

DIN 4102 — Fire behaviour of building materials and building components

DIN 4102 pt 1 — Building materials; concepts, requirements and tests

DIN 4102 pt 2 — Building components; definitions, requirements and tests

DIN 4102 pt 3 — Firewalls and non-loadbearing external walls; definitions, requirements and tests

DIN 4102 pt 4 — Synopsis and application of classified building materials, components and special components

Other standards

DIN 488 pt 1 — Reinforcing steels; grades, properties, marking. Sept 1984

DIN 4226 pt 1 — Aggregates for concrete; aggregates of dense structure (heavy aggregates); terminology, designation and requirements. Apr 1983

DIN 4226 pt 2 — Aggregates for concrete; aggregates of porous structure (lightweight aggregates); terminology, designation and requirements. Apr 1983

DIN 4108 pt 2 — Thermal protection and energy economy in buildings – pt 2: minimum requirements for thermal insulation

DIN 17440 — Stainless steels – technical delivery conditions for drawn wire. Sept 1996

DIN 18165 pt 2 — Fibre insulating building materials; impact sound insulating materials. Mar 1987

DIN 18165 pt 2 (draft) — Fibre insulating building materials – pt 2: impact sound insulating materials. May 1999

DIN 18195 pt 4 — Waterproofing of buildings and structures; damp-proofing against moisture from the ground; design and workmanship. Aug 1983

DIN 18195 pt 5 — Waterproofing of buildings and structures; waterproofing against water that exerts no hydrostatic pressure; design and workmanship. Feb 1984

DIN 18195 pt 6 — Waterproofing of buildings – pt 6: waterproofing against outside pressing water; design and execution. Sept 1998

DIN 18554 pt 1 — Testing of masonry; determination of compressive strength and elastic modulus. Dec 1985

DIN 18555 pt 3 — Testing of mortars containing mineral binders; hardened mortars; determination of flexural strength, compressive strength and bulk density. Sept 1982

DIN 51043 — Trass; requirements, tests. Aug 1978

DIN 52128 — Bituminous roof sheeting with felt core; definition, designation, requirements. Mar 1977

DIN EN 450 — Fly ash for concrete – definitions, requirements and quality control. Jan 1995

Bibliography and references

[1] Achtziger, J., Bruus-Jensen, T.: Einfluss der Mörtelart auf die Wärmeleitfähigkeit von Mauerwerk; das Mauerwerk, vol. 4, issue 2, April 2000

[2] Achtziger, J., Die Bestimmung des Wärmeschutzes von Außenwänden bewohnter Häuser; "boden, wand + decke" issue 3/1968

[3] Achtziger, J.: Bestimmung der Rechenwerte der Wärmeleitfähigkeit für Mauerwerk durch Messung und durch Berechnung; Mauerwerk Kalender, vol. 25

[4] Achtziger, J.: Praktische Untersuchung der Tauwasserbildung im Innern von Bauteilen mit Innendämmung; wksb special issue 1985

[5] Achtziger, J.: Tauwasserbildung im Innern von zweischaligem Mauerwerk mit Kerndämmung; Bauphysik 2/1984

[6] Achtziger, J.: Verfahren zur Beurteilung des Wärmeschutzes und der Wärmebrücken von mehrschaligen Außenwänden und Maßnahmen zur Verminderung der Transmissionswärmeverluste von Fassaden; dissertation, Berlin TU, Dept of Architecture

[7] Apitzsch, Ch.: Brandschutz mit Porenbeton; das Mauerwerk, issue 2, 1998

[8] Lightweight Concrete Study Group (ed.): Baustofflehre Leichtbeton. February 1997

[9] Exhibition catalogue: Les Architectes de la Liberté 1789–1799, École nationale supérieure des Beaux-arts, Paris, 1989

[10] Bachmann, H.: Hochbau für Ingenieure. 2nd, revised edition, Zürich: vdf. 1997

[11] Backstein, Die schönsten Ziegelbauten zwischen Elbe und Oder. Munich: Bucher Verlag, 2001

[12] Bandmann, Günter: Mittelalterliche Architektur als Bedeutungsträger, Berlin, 1994

[13] Construction Products Directive: Directive of the Council of 21 December 1988 (89/106/EEC)

[14] Behne, Adolf: Der moderne Zweckbau, Bauweltfundamente No. 10, Gütersloh/Berlin, 1964

[15] Belz, Walter: Zusammenhänge, Cologne, 1993

[16] Bender, W.: Lexikon der Ziegel. Wiesbaden: Bauverlag, 1992

[17] Berlage, Hendrik Petrus: Über Architektur und Stil, Basel, 1991

[18] Bertram, D.; González, A. C.; Kammerer, H.; Reeh, H.; Schulz, W.: Fertigbauteile aus Mauerwerk. Berlin: Ernst & Sohn. In: Mauerwerk-Kalender 25 (2000), pp. 281–289

[19] Bertrams-Vosskamp, U.: Betonwerkstein-Handbuch. 3rd edition. Düsseldorf: Beton-Verlag, 1994

[20] Bewag Aktiengesellschaft (ed.): Elektropolis Berlin, Historische Bauten der Stromverteilung, Berlin

[21] Binding, G.; Nussbaum, N.: Mittelalterlicher Baubetrieb nördlich der Alpen in zeitgenössischen Darstellungen, Darmstadt, 1978

[22] Boddenberg, R.: Brandverhalten von hinterlüfteten Außenwandbekleidungen, Stand der Diskussion; German Building Technology Institute Memos 5/1999

[23] Böhm, H.; Künzel, H.: Wie sind Putzrisse bei außenseitiger Wärmedämmung zu bewerten? Fraunhofer Institute for Building Physics, Memo 147

[24] Bossenmayer, H.: Eurocodes für den konstruktiven Ingenieurbau. Berlin: Ernst & Sohn. In: Mauerwerk-Kalender 25 (2000), pp. 685–692

[25] Brechner, H.: Kalksandstein. Planung, Konstruktion und Ausführung. 3rd edition. Düsseldorf: Beton-Verlag, 1994

[26] Federal Aerated Concrete Association (ed.): Porenbeton. Diagramme, Illustrationen und Bilder. Wiesbaden, November 1998

[27] Federal Autoclaved Aerated Concrete Association (ed.): Porenbeton – Technische Daten. Wiesbaden, 1997

[28] Burke, Kenneth: Perspectives by Incongruity, Bloomington, 1964

[29] Cammerer, J. S.: Der Wärme- und Kälteschutz in der Industrie, Berlin, Heidelberg, New York: Springer Verlag, 1980

[30] Conrads, Ulrich: Programme und Manifeste zur Architektur des 20. Jahrhunderts, Bauweltfundamente No.1, Gütersloh/Berlin, 1964

[31] Culler, Jonathan: Dekonstruktion, Reinbek, 1988

[32] Cziesielski, E. (ed.): Lehrbuch der Hochbaukonstruktionen. 3rd edition. Stuttgart: Teubner, 1997

[33] Derrida, Jaques: Mémoires, Vienna, 1988

[34] German Reinforced Concrete Committee (ed.): Richtlinien für die Bemessung und Ausführung von Flachstürzen. August 1977

[35] German Reinforced Concrete Committee (ed.): Richtlinien für die Bemessung und Ausführung von Flachstürzen. August 1977

[36] Dietrich, Conrad: Kirchenbau im Mittelalter, 2nd edition, Leipzig, 1997

[37] Dilly, Heinrich: Kunstgeschichte als Institution, Frankfurt/Main, 1979

[38] Droste, Thorsten; Budeit, Hans Joachim: Burgund, Munich 1998

[39] Dümmler, K.; Loeser, K.: Handbuch der Ziegelfabrikation. Halle a. S.: Knapp-Verlag, 1926

[40] Ebert, K.: Arbeitshilfen für die Bemessung von bewehrtem Mauerwerk nach DIN 1053-3 mit Beispielen. Berlin: Ernst & Sohn. In: Mauerwerk-Kalender 25 (2000), pp. 555–561

[41] Eichler, F.; Arndt, H.: Bautechnischer Wärme- und Feuchtigkeitsschutz, 2nd edition, Verlag für Bauwesen, Berlin, 1989

[42] Eligehausen, R.; Mallée, R.; Rehm, G.: Befestigungstechnik. Berlin: Ernst & Sohn. In: Beton-Kalender 86 (1997), pp. 609–754

[43] Eligehausen, R.; Pregartner, T.; Weber, S.: Befestigungen in Mauerwerk. Berlin: Ernst & Sohn. In: Mauerwerk-Kalender 25 (2000), pp. 361–385

[44] Erdmann, Wolfgang: Zisterzienser-Abtei Chorin, Königstein, 1994

[45] Erhorn, H.; Gertis, K.: Auswirkungen der Lage des Fensters im Baukörper auf den Wärmeschutz von Wänden; Fenster und Fassade 11 (1984) issue 2

[46] Erker, A., Heyder F.: Zum Einfluss der Querschnittsgestaltung von Hochlochziegeln auf Wärmeschutzanforderungen; Ziegelindustrie 2/96

[47] Ernst, M.: Untersuchungen zum Tragverhalten von bewehrtem Mauerwerk aus Hochlochziegeln. Research Reports; VDI series 4, No. 137. Düsseldorf: VDI Verlag, 1997

[48] Specialist Committee "Building" of the Employers' Liability Insurance Association Office for Safety and Health of the Umbrella Organization for the Commercial Employers' Liability Insurance Associations: Regeln für Sicherheit und Gesundheitsschutz beim Bauen mit Fertigbauteilen aus Mauerwerk. BGZ, St. Augustin

[49] fischerwerke Artur Fischer GmbH & Co. KG, D-72178 Waldachtal: catalogue of fixings "fischer Befestigungssysteme".

[50] Fitch, James M.: Vier Jahrhunderte Bauen in den USA, Bauweltfundamente Nr. 23, Gütersloh/Berlin, 1966

[51] Frank, Hartmut: Fritz Schumacher, Reformkultur und Moderne, Stuttgart, 1994

[52] Franke, L.: Zustandsbeurteilung und Instandsetzung von Sichtmauerwerk. Berlin: Ernst & Sohn. In: Mauerwerk-Kalender 20 (1995), pp. 661–685

[53] Fraunhofer Institute for Building Physics: Wärme- und Regenschutz bei zweischaligem Sichtmauerwerk mit Kerndämmung; Research Rep. B Ho 9/83

[54] Funk, P. (ed.): Mauerwerk: Kommentar zu DIN 1053 Teil 1 – Rezeptmauerwerk und DIN 1053 Teil 3 – Bewehrtes Mauerwerk, Ausgaben Februar 1990. Berlin: Ernst & Sohn, 1990

[55] Gadamer, Hans-Georg: Wahrheit und Methode, Tübingen, 1975

[56] Ganz, H.-R.: Vorgespanntes Mauerwerk. In: Schweizer Ingenieur und Architekt, issue 8 (1990), pp. 177–182

[57] Glitza H.: Zum Kriechen von Mauerwerk. In: Die Bautechnik (1985), No. 12, pp. 415–418

[58] Glitza, H.: Druckbeanspruchung parallel zur Lagerfuge. Berlin: Ernst & Sohn. In: Mauerwerk-Kalender 13 (1988), pp. 489–496

[59] Göbel, K.: Brücken zum umweltbewussten Bauen und Wohnen. Mainz: Verlagsanstalt Will & Rothe, January 1992

[60] González, A. C.; Schubert, P.; Krechting, A · Bewehrtes Mauerwerk. Berlin: Ernst & Sohn. In: Mauerwerk-Kalender 25 (2000), pp. 319–332

[61] Gösele, K.: Verschlechterung der Schalldämmung von Decken und Wänden durch anbetonierte Wärmedämmplatten; Gesundheitsingenieur, 1961

[62] Gösele/Schüle/Künzel: "Schall, Wärme, Feuchte"; Bauverlag, 1997

[63] Groetzberger, A.; Gertis, K. et al.: Transparente Wärmedämmung; Concluding Report of Federal Ministry of Research & Technology Project 03E-8411-A, Freiburg and Stuttgart (1987)

[64] Gropius, Walter: Architektur, Hamburg, 1955

[65] Gunkler, E.: Vorgespanntes Mauerwerk. Berlin: Ernst & Sohn. In: Mauerwerk-Kalender 25 (2000), pp. 333–359

[66] Gurlitt, Cornelius: Zur Befreiung der Baukunst, Bauweltfundamente No. 22, Gütersloh/Berlin, 1969

[67] Hahn, C.: Brandschutz im Mauerwerksbau mit Praxisbeispielen; Mauerwerk-Kalender 2000

[68] Hahn, C.: Brandschutz mit Mauerwerk, Teil 1: Anforderungen-Nachweise; das Mauerwerk, issue 2, 1998

[69] Hampe, E.; Schwarz, J.: Verhalten von Mauerwerksbauten unter seismischen Einwirkungen. Berlin: Ernst & Sohn. In: Mauerwerk-Kalender 15 (1990), pp. 603–668

[70] Hanimann, Joseph: Vom Schweren, Munich, 1999

[71] Harre, W.: Poroton-Handbuch. 6th edition. Mönchengladbach: Druckhaus B. Kühlen, 1996

[72] Häupl, P.; Stopp, H.; Strangfeld, P.: Softwarepaket COND zur Feuchteprofilbestimmung in Umfassungskonstruktionen; Bautenschutz + Bausanierung 12 (1989)

[73] Häupl, P.; Fechner, H.; Martin, R.; Neue, J.: Energetische Verbesserung der Bausubstanz mittels kapillaraktiver Innendämmung; Bauphysik 21, issue 4, 1999

[74] Hauser, G.: "Einfluss des Wärmedurchgangskoeffizienten und der Wärmespeicherfähigkeit von Bauteilen auf den Heizenergieverbrauch von Gebäuden, Literaturstudie"; Bauphysik 5, 1984

[75] Hebel (ed.): Handbuch Wohnbau. Technische Information für Planung und Bauausführung. 7th edition, 1998

[76] Heller, D.: Brandschutz mit Leichtbetonmauerwerk; das Mauerwerk, issue 2, 1998

[77] Hilsdorf, H. K.: Investigation into Failure Mechanism of Brick Masonry Loaded in Axial Compression. In: Designing, Engineering and Construction with Masonry Products. Gulf Publishing Company, Houston, Texas, 1967

[78] Hilti AG, 9494 Schaan, Liechtenstein: Handbuch der Befestigungstechnik.

[79] Hirsch, R.: Neu- und Weiterentwicklung im Mauerwerksbau mit allgemeiner bauaufsichtlicher Zulassung. Berlin: Ernst & Sohn. In: Mauerwerk-Kalender 25 (2000), pp. 23–173

[80] Hirsch, R.: Verzeichnis der allgemeinen bauaufsichtlichen Zulassungen im Mauerwerksbau. Berlin: Ernst & Sohn. In: Mauerwerk-Kalender (25, 2000), pp. 879–902

[81] Hirsch, R.; Irmschler, H.-J.: Zulassungsbedürftige Bauprodukte und Bauarten im Mauerwerksbau. Berlin: Ernst & Sohn. In: Mauerwerk-Kalender 23 (1998), p.163

[82] Hübsch, Heinrich: In welchem Style sollen wir bauen? Karlsruhe, 1828

[83] Hugues, Theodor; Greilich, Klaus; Peter, Christine: Bauen mit großformatigen Ziegeln

[84] Industrieverband Werktrockenmörtel e.V.; Arbeitsgemeinschaft Mauerziegel im Bundesverband der Deutschen Ziegelindustrie e.V.; Bundesverband der Deutschen Mörtelindustrie e.V.; German Stucco Federation (ed.) Außenputz auf Ziegelmauerwerk, 1998

[85] Building Research Institute, Aachen (ed.): Kriechverhalten von Mauerwerk. Research Report No. F 163, 1984

[86] Irmschler, H.-J.: Neue Baustoffe und Bauarten im Mauerwerksbau. Berlin: Ernst & Sohn. In: Mauerwerk-Kalender 19 (1994), p. 193ff

[87] Jaffé, H. L. C.: de Stijl 1917–1931, Bauweltfundamente No. 7, Gütersloh/Berlin, 1965

[88] Jäger, W.: Zum Stand der europäischen Bemessungsregeln im Mauerwerksbau – EN 1996-1-1. Berlin: Ernst & Sohn. In: Mauerwerk-Kalender 25 (2000), pp. 699–705

[89] Jäger, W.; Pohle, F.: Einsatz von hochfestem Natursteinmauerwerk beim Wiederaufbau der Frauenkirche Dresden. Berlin: Ernst & Sohn. In: Mauerwerk-Kalender 24 (1999), p. 729

[90] Jenisch, R.: Berechnung der Feuchtigkeitskondensation in Außenbauteilen und die Austrocknung abhängig vom Außenklima; Ges.-Ing. 92 (1971)

[91] Calcium silicate information (ed.): Kalksandstein: DIN 1053-1. Mauerwerk: Berechnung und Ausführung. Bau + Technik, 1997

[92] Kalksandstein, Planung, Konstruktion, Ausführung; 3rd edition; Kalksandstein Information GmbH + Co. KG

[93] Kieker, J.: Der Keller aus Mauerwerk. Berlin: Ernst & Sohn. In: Das Mauerwerk 4 (2000), H. 1, pp. 2–7

[94] Kießl, K.: Kapillarer und dampfförmiger Feuchtetransport in mehrschichtigen Bauteilen. Rechnerische Erfassung und bauphysikalische Anwendung. Dissertation, Essen University, 1983

[95] Kiessl, K.: Mineralfaserdämmung innen – auch ohne Dampfsperre?; Fraunhofer Institute for Building Physics, Memo 104

[96] Kinold, K.: 25 Jahre KS Neues. Munich: Callwey-Verlag, 1994

[97] Kirtschig, K.; Anstötz, W.: Zur Tragfähigkeit von nichttragenden inneren Trennwänden in Massivbauweise. Berlin: Ernst & Sohn. In: Mauerwerk-Kalender 11 (1986), pp. 697–734

[98] Kleinkott, Manfred: Die Backsteinbaukunst der Berliner Schule, Berlin, 1988

[99] Knöfel, D.; Schubert, P. (ed.): Manual "Mörtel und Steinergänzungsstoffe in der Denkmalpflege". Berlin: Ernst & Sohn, 1993

[100] Kokkelink, Günther; Lemke-Kokkelink, Monika: Baukunst in Norddeutschland, Hannover, 1998

[101] Kopacek, J.: Bearbeitungsstand der europäischen Normen für den Mauerwerksbau. Berlin: Ernst & Sohn. In: Mauerwerk-Kalender 25 (2000), pp. 669–683

[102] Krausse, Joachim mit Ropohl, Dieter und Scheiffele, Walter: Vom großen Refraktor zum Einsteinturm, Giessen, 1996

[103] Kruft, Hanno-Walter: Geschichte der Architekturtheorie, Munich, 1985

[104] Künzel, H.: Gasbeton, Wärme- und Feuchtigkeitsverhalten; Bauverlag, 1971

[105] Künzel, H.: Schäden an Fassadenputzen. Stuttgart: IRB-Verlag, 1994

[106] Künzel, H.: Schlagregenbeanspruchung von Gebäuden und Beurteilung des Schlagregenschutzes von Außenputzen; Fraunhofer Institute for Building Physics, Memo 69

[107] Lang, J.: Wirtschaftliche Erfüllung des normgemäßen Schallschutzes im Wohnungsbau; vol. I & II, Austrian Stone & Ceramic Industry Association, Vienna, 1985

[108] Lange, Karl-Ludwig: geformt, getrocknet, gebrannt, Velten, 1996

[109] Laternser, K.: Dübel mit allgemeiner bauaufsichtlicher Zulassung und europäischer technischer Zulassung. Berlin: Ernst & Sohn. In: Mauerwerk-Kalender 25 (2000), pp. 387–401

[110] Laternser, K.: Dübelverankerungen im Mauerwerk. Berlin: Ernst & Sohn. In: Mauerwerk-Kalender 24 (1999), pp. 667–706

[111] Lauber, Wolfgang: Architektur der Dogon, Munich, 1998

[112] Le Corbusier: Ausblick auf eine Architektur, Bauweltfundamente No. 2, Gütersloh/Berlin, 1969

[113] Ledoux, C. N.: L´architecture I und II, Nördlingen, 1987

[114] Loos, Adolf: Die Potemkinsche Stadt, Vienna, 1983

[115] Loos, Adolf: Ins Leere gesprochen, Vienna, 1981

[116] Loos, Adolf: Trotzdem 1900–1930, Vienna, 1982

[117] Luhman, Niclas: Zweckbegriff und Systemrationalität, Tübingen, 1968

[118] Lutz, P. et al.: Lehrbuch der Bauphysik, 3rd edition, B. G. Teubner, Stuttgart, 1989

[119] Manika/Paschen: Wärmebrückenkatalog; B. G. Teubner, Stuttgart, 1986

[120] Mann, W.: Entwicklung der europäischen und nationalen Mauerwerksnormen – Nationales Anwendungsdokument (NAD) zum Eurocode EC 6, vereinfachtes Berechnungsverfahren im EC 6, DIN 1053-100. Berlin: Ernst & Sohn. In: Mauerwerk-Kalender 23 (1998), pp. 1–5

[121] Mann, W.: Grundlagen der vereinfachten und der genaueren Bemessung von Mauerwerk nach DIN 1053-1, November 1996 Ausgabe. Berlin: Ernst & Sohn. In: Mauerwerk-Kalender 24 (1999), pp. 11–38

[122] Mann, W.: Zug- und Biegezugfestigkeit von Mauerwerk – theoretische Grundlagen und Vergleich mit Versuchsergebnissen. Berlin: Ernst & Sohn. In: Mauerwerk-Kalender 17 (1992), pp. 601–607

[123] Mann, W.: Zum Entwurf einer Neufassung der Mauerwerksnorm als DIN 1053-100. Berlin: Ernst & Sohn. In: Mauerwerk-Kalender 24 (1999), pp. 537–541

[124] Mann, W.; Bernhardt, G.: Rechnerischer Nachweis von ein- und zweiachsig gespannten, gemauerten Kellerwänden auf Erddruck. Berlin: Ernst & Sohn. In: Mauerwerk-Kalender 9 (1984), pp. 69–84

[125] Mann, W.; König, G.; Ötes, A.: Versuche zum Verhalten von Mauerwerk unter seismischer Beanspruchung. Berlin: Ernst & Sohn. In: Mauerwerk-Kalender 14 (1989), pp. 483–488

[126] Mann, W.; Müller; H.: Bruchkriterien für querkraftbeanspruchtes Mauerwerk und ihre Anwendungen auf gemauerte Windscheiben, parts 1-3, Chair of Structural Analysis in Buildings, Darmstadt Polytechnic, 1973

[127] Mann, W.; Müller; H.: Schubtragfähigkeit von gemauerten Wänden und Voraussetzung für das Entfallen des Windnachweises. Berlin: Ernst & Sohn. In: Mauerwerk-Kalender 10 (1985), pp. 95–114

[128] Mann, W.; Zahn, J.: Bewehrung von Mauerwerk zur Risssicherung und zur Lastabtragung. Berlin: Ernst & Sohn. In: Mauerwerk-Kalender 15 (1990), pp. 467–487

[129] Marquard, Odo: Abschied vom Prinzipiellen, Stuttgart, 1981

[130] Mayer, E.; Künzel H.: Notwendige Hinterlüftung an Außenwandbekleidungen aus großformatigen Bauteilen; Fraunhofer Institute for Building Physics, Memo 92

[131] Mayer, E.: Hinterlüftung von Fassadenbekleidungen aus kleinformatigen Elementen; Fraunhofer Institute for Building Physics, Memo 56

[132] Memo of the Building Employers' Liability Insurance Association (Bau-BG 4/91): Handhaben von Mauersteinen, April 1991 edition

[133] Metje, W.-R.: Zum Einfluss des Feuchtigkeitszustandes der Steine bei der Verarbeitung auf das Trag- und Verformungsverhalten von Mauerwerk. Berlin: Ernst & Sohn. In: Mauerwerk-Kalender 9 (1984), pp. 679–687

[134] Meyer, U.: Brandschutz mit Ziegelmauerwerk; das Mauerwerk, issue 2, 1998

[135] Meyer, U.: Rissbreitenbeschränkung durch Lagerfugenbewehrung in Mauerwerkbauteilen. Berlin: Ernst & Sohn. In: Mauerwerk-Kalender 21 (1996), pp. 653–663

[136] Müller, H.: Untersuchungen zum Tragverhalten von querkraftbeanspruchtem Mauerwerk, dissertation, Darmstadt Polytechnic, 1974

[137] Müller, Konrad Jörg: Ziegelarchitektur in Dörfern der Mark Brandenburg, Potsdam, 1998

[138] Müller-Wulckow, Walter: Architektur der zwanziger Jahre in Deutschland, Königstein, 1975

[139] Naumann, H.: Kosten- und flächensparendes Bauen: So sinken die Baukosten. Offprint from Baugewerbe 10/98

[140] Naumann, H.: Kostensparendes Bauen. Grundsätze optimierten Bauens. Offprint from Deutsches Ingenieurblatt, 12/96, 1–2/97, 3/97 & 4/97

[141] Neumann, D.; Weinbrenner, U.: Baukonstruktionslehre Teil 1. 31st edition. Teubner: Stuttgart, 1997

[142] Noack, W.: Ziegel-Lexikon. Ziegelforum München. 1998

[143] Offermann, K.: Bims als Baustoff. Stuttgart: IRB-Verlag, 1989

[144] Offermann, K.: Kalksandstein als Baustoff. Stuttgart: IRB-Verlag, 1988

[145] Ohler, A.: Quattro libri dell´architettura, English translation by Taverner, R. and Schofield, R.; Cambridge, Mass., 1997

[146] Palladio, A.: Die vier Bände zur Architektur, übersetzt von Andreas Beyer und Ulrich Schütte, Zürich/Munich, 1985

[147] Paulmann, K.: Neue Untersuchungen zur Luftschalldämmung von Wänden mit Wärmedämm-Verbundsystemen; Bauphysik 16, issue 4, 1994

[148] Pehnt, Wolfgang: Die Architektur des Expressionismus, Stuttgart, 1973

[149] Pevsner, Nikolaus: The Sources of Modern Architecture and Design, 1968

[150] Pevsner, Nikolaus: An Outline of European Architecture, 1967

[151] Pfefferkorn, W.: Dachdecken und Mauerwerk. Entwurf, Bemessen und Beurteilung von Tragkonstruktionen aus Dachdecken und Mauerwerk. Cologne-Braunsfeld: Verlagsgesellschaft Rudolf Müller, 1980

[152] Pfefferkorn, W.: Rissschäden an Mauerwerk. Ursachen erkennen, Rissschäden vermeiden. Stuttgart: IRB-Verlag. In: Schadensfreies Bauen, No. 7, 1994

[153] Plumridge, Andrew; Meulenkamp, Wim: Brickwork, 1993

[154] Pohl, R.: Standsicherheit gemauerter Ziegelkeller. Berlin: Ernst & Sohn. In: Das Mauerwerk 3 (1999), issue 4, pp. 168–172

[155] Popper, Karl: Logik der Forschung, Tübingen, 1976

[156] Posener, Julius: Anfänge des Funktionalismus, Bauweltfundamente No. 11, Gütersloh/Berlin, 1964

[157] Posener, Julius: Berlin auf dem Weg zu einer neuen Architektur, Das Zeitalter Wilhelms II., Munich/New York, 1995

[158] PREMUR/VSL – Vorgespanntes Mauerwerk. ZZ Zürcher Ziegeleien, 1989

[159] Reeh, H.: Aussteifung und Gesamtstabilität von Mauerwerksbauten. Berlin: Ernst & Sohn. In: Mauerwerk-Kalender 25 (2000), pp. 437–453

[160] Reichensperger, August: Die christlich-germanische Baukunst und ihr Verhältnis zur Gegenwart, Trier, 1845

[161] Reichert, H.: Konstruktiver Mauerwerksbau. Bildkommentar zur DIN 1053, February 1990 edition. 6th edition. Cologne: Müller, 1992

[162] Reichert, Huber: Konstruktiver Mauerwerksbau, Bildkommentar zur DIN 1053-1, 8th, revised edition. Cologne: Müller, 1999

[163] Directive "Bestimmung der wärmetechnischen Einflüsse von Wärmebrücken bei vorgehängten hinterlüfteten Fassaden". Fachverband Baustoffe und Bauteile für vorgehängte hinterlüftete Fassaden e.V., Berlin

[164] Riechers, H.-J.: Mauermörtel, Putzmörtel und Estrichmörtel. Berlin: Ernst & Sohn. In: Mauerwerk-Kalender 25 (2000), pp. 175–204

[165] Riechers, H.-J.: Werkmörtel für den Mauerwerksbau. Berlin: Ernst & Sohn. In: Mauerwerk-Kalender 24 (1999), pp. 547–568

[166] Rückward, W.: Einfluss von Wärmedämm-Verbundsystemen auf die Luftschalldämmung; Bauphysik 4, issue 2, 1982

[167] Sälzer, E.: Schallschutz mit Fassaden, Teil 1; Bauphysik, issue 5, 1993

[168] Schäfke, Werner: Mittelalterliche Backsteinarchitektur von Lübeck bis Marienburg, Cologne, 1995

[169] Schätz, M.; Schermer, D.: Normenentwicklung: Erdbeben in Mauerwerksbau. Düsseldorf: Springer VDI Verlag. In: Massivbau 2000 Research, Developments and Applications, 4th Munich Monolithic Construction Seminar 2000, Munich TU, March 2000

[170] Schinkel, Karl Friedrich: Das Architektonische Lehrbuch, Munich/Berlin, 1979

[171] Schmidt, Oliver H.; Feuerstake, Jürgen (ed.): Zisterzienserklöster in Brandenburg, Berlin, 1998

[172] Schmidt, S.: Memos of the German Masonry Association: Außenwandfugen bei Mauerwerksbauten. Berlin: Ernst & Sohn. In: Mauerwerk-Kalender 19 (1994), pp. 540–544

[173] Schmidt, S.: Memos of the German Masonry Association: Nichttragende innere Trennwände aus künstlichen Steinen und Wandplatten. Berlin: Ernst & Sohn. In: Mauerwerk-Kalender 19 (1994), pp. 517–525

[174] Schmitt, H.; Heene, A.: Hochbaukonstruktion: Die Bauteile und das Baugefüge. Grundlage des heutigen Bauens. Wiesbaden: Vieweg Verlag, 1993

[175] Schneider, K.-J.; Schubert, P.; Wormuth, R.: Mauerwerksbau. Gestaltung, Baustoffe, Konstruktion, Berechnung, Ausführung. 5th edition. Düsseldorf: Werner-Verlag, 1996

[176] Scholl, W.; Weber, L.: Einfluss der Lochung auf die Schalldämmung und Schall-Längsdämmung von Mauersteinen (Ergebnisse einer Literaturauswertung); Bauphysik 20, issue 2, 1998

[177] Schubert, P.: Bauschädenvermeidung. Düsseldorf: Werner. In: Mauerwerksbau aktuell. Jahrbuch für Architekten und Ingenieure (1997), pp. G.1–G.24

[178] Schubert, P.: E-Moduln von Mauerwerk aus Leichtbeton- und Porenbetonsteinen. Ehningen: Expert, 1993. In: Proceedings of the 3rd International Colloquium; part 2, pp. 1355-65.

[179] Schubert, P.: E-Moduln von Mauerwerk in Abhängigkeit von der Druckfestigkeit des Mauerwerks, der Mauersteine und des Mauermörtels. Berlin: Ernst & Sohn. In: Mauerwerk-Kalender 10 (1985), pp. 705–717

[180] Schubert, P.: Eigenschaftswerte von Mauerwerk, Mauersteinen und Mauermörtel. Berlin: Ernst & Sohn. In: Mauerwerk-Kalender 25 (2000), p. 5

[181] Schubert, P.: Eigenschaftswerte von Mauerwerk, Mauersteinen und Mauermörtel. Berlin: Ernst & Sohn. In: Mauerwerk-Kalender 25 (2000), pp. 5–22

[182] Schubert, P.: Formänderungen von Mauersteinen, Mauermörtel und Mauerwerk. Berlin: Ernst & Sohn. In: Mauerwerk-Kalender 17 (1992), pp. 623–637

[183] Schubert, P.: Putz auf Leichtmauerwerk, Eigenschaften von Putzmörteln. Berlin: Ernst & Sohn. In: Mauerwerk-Kalender 18 (1993), pp. 657–666

[184] Schubert, P.: Vermeiden von schädlichen Rissen in Mauerwerksbauteilen. Berlin: Ernst & Sohn. In: Mauerwerk-Kalender 21 (1996), pp. 621–651

[185] Schubert, P.: Zur Feuchtedehnung von Mauerwerk. Dissertation, RWTH Aachen, 1982

[186] Schubert, P.: Zur rissfreien Wandlänge von nichttragenden Mauerwerkwänden. Berlin: Ernst & Sohn. In: Mauerwerk-Kalender 13 (1988), pp. 473–488

[187] Schubert, P.: Zur Schubfestigkeit von Mauerwerk. Berlin: Ernst & Sohn. In: Mauerwerk-Kalender 23 (1998), pp. 733–747

[188] Schubert, P.; Dominik, A.; Meyer, U.; Fitzner, B.; Heuser, H.: Instandsetzung von Natursteinmauerwerk im Fassadenbereich. Berlin: Ernst & Sohn. In: Mauerwerk-Kalender 18 (1993), pp. 635–655

[189] Schubert, P.; Friede, H.: Spaltzugfestigkeit von Mauersteinen. In: Die Bautechnik (1980), No. 4., pp. 117–122

[190] Schubert, P.; Hoffmann, G.: Druckfestigkeit von Mauerwerk parallel zu den Lagerfugen. Berlin: Ernst & Sohn. In: Mauerwerk-Kal. 19 (1994), p. 715

[191] Schubert, P.; Metzemacher, H.: Biegezugfestigkeit von Mauerwerk senkrecht und parallel zur Lagerfuge. Building Research Institute, Aachen; Research Report No. F 275, 1987

[192] Schubert, P.; Meyer, U.: Druckfestigkeit von Mauerwerk mit Leichthochlochziegeln. In: Das Mauerwerk 3 (1999), issue 1

[193] Schubert, P.; Meyer, U.: Druckfestigkeit von Porenbeton- und Leichtbetonmauerwerk. Berlin: Ernst & Sohn. In: Mauerwerk-Kalender 18 (1993), pp. 627–634

[194] Schubert, P.: Formänderungen von Mauersteinen, Mauermörtel und Mauerwerk. Berlin: Ernst & Sohn. In: Mauerwerk-Kalender 17 (1992), p. 623

[195] Schüle; Giesecke; Reichardt: Untersuchungen über die Wärmeleitfähigkeit von Leichtbeton ohne und mit Quarzsandzusatz, Gesundheitsingenieur 97 (1976), pp. 314–318

[196] Schumacher, Fritz: Das Wesem des Neuzeitlichen Backsteinbaus, Munich, 1920, reprinted 1985

[197] Schumacher, Fritz; Thiersch, August: Architektonische Komposition, Leipzig, 1926

[198] Schwarz, B.: Solarenergienutzung durch Bauteile aus Beton "Gesundes Wohnen – ein Kompendium"; Düsseldorf: Beton-Verlag, 1986

[199] Schwarz, Felix; Gloor, Frank: "Die Form" Stimme des Deutschen Werkbundes, Bauweltfundamente No. 24, Gütersloh/Berlin, 1969

[200] Sedelmayer, Hans: Johann Bernhard Fischer von Erlach, Vienna, 1976

[201] Semper, Gottfried: Die vier Elemente der Baukunst, ein Beitrag zur vergleichenden Baukunde, Braunschweig, 1851

[202] Sherman, Paul: Louis H. Sullivan, ein amerikanischer Architekt und Denker, Bauweltfundamente No. 5, Gütersloh/Berlin, 1963

[203] Delmenhorst Local History Museum (ed.) in collaboration with Deutscher Wekbund Nord e.V. and Peter Struck: Fritz Höger 1877–1949, Oldenburg, 1999

[204] Stauder, D.: Transparentes Wärmedämm-Verbundsystem (TWDVS); B + B 3/96

[205] Tanner, Chr.: Hinterlüftete Fassaden, Federal Materials Testing and Research Institute R&D Report No. 127378

[206] Taut, Bruno: Frühlicht 1920–1922, Bauweltfundamente No. 8, Gütersloh/Berlin, 1963

[207] unipor-Ziegel-Gruppe: Planen und Bauen

[208] Viollet-le-Duc, Eugène Emanuel: Dictionnaire raisonné de l`architecture francaise du XIe au XVIe siècle, Paris, 1967

[209] Waltermann, G.: Brandschutz mit Kalksandsteinmauerwerk; das Mauerwerk, issue 2, 1998

[210] Warnecke, P.; Rostasy, F. S.; Budelmann, H.: Tragverhalten und Konsolidierung von Wänden und Stützen aus historischem Mauerwerk. In: Mauerwerk-Kalender 20 (1995), pp. 623–660

[211] Weber, H.; Hullmann, H.: Porenbeton Handbuch. Planen und Bauen mit System. 4th edition, Wiesbaden: Bauverlag, 1999

[212] Weber, Helmut: Walter Gropius und das Faguswerk, Munich, 1961

[213] Werner, H.: "Auswirkung der Strahlungsabsorption von Außenwandoberflächen und Nachtabsenkung der Raumlufttemperaturen auf den Transmissionswärmeverlust und den Heizenergieverbrauch"; Report EB-8, 1985

[214] Wessig, J.: Kalksandstein-Maurerfibel. 6th edition. Düsseldorf: Verlag Bau + Technik, 1998

[215] Wickop, Walter: Landbaufibel, Hannover, 1951

[216] Clay Brick Industry Association (ed.): Ziegel-Bau-Taschenbuch. Mainz: Krausskopf-Verlag, 1951–1964

[217] Wittkower, Rudolf: Grundlagen der Architektur im Zeitalter des Humanismus, Munich, 1969

[218] WTA Memo 2-2-91: Sanierungsputzsysteme: Wissenschaftlich-Technische Arbeitsgemeinschaft für Bauwerkserhaltung und Denkmalpflege e.V.

[219] WUFI: computer program for analysis of coupled heat and moisture transport in building components; Fraunhofer Institute for Building Physics, Stuttgart/Holzkirchen/Berlin

[220] Zilch, K.: Bemessung von Bauwerken gegen Erdbebenbelastungen. In: Die Bautechnik. issue 5 (1974), pp. 3–12

Index of names

Picture credits

Part 1 · Masonry in architecture
Archiv für Kunst und Geschichte Berlin:1.1.10, 1.1.25
Atelier Kinold; Munich: 1.1.44
Bildarchiv Foto Marburg: 1.1.21
Bildarchiv Monheim; Meerbusch: 1.1.12, 1.1.13, 1.1.20, 1.1.24, 1.1.73
Blaser, Werner; Basel: 1.1.32, 1.1.37, 1.1.78, 1.1.108
Budeit, Hans Joachim; Dortmund: 1.1.17–19, 1.1.22, 1.1.87, 1.1.106
Bürkle, Christoph; Sulgen, Switzerland: 1.1.88
Casals, Lluís; Barcelona: 1.1.118
Citterio, Antonio: 1.1.116
Conrad, Dietrich; Dresden: 1.1.16
Derwig, Jan; Amsterdam: 1.1.40
German Archaeological Institute, Athens: 1.1.9
Enders, Ulrike; Hannover: 1.1.3, 1.1.4, 1.1.46, 1.1.47
Fondation Le Corbusier/ © VG Bild-Kunst; Bonn: 1.1.89
Frahm, Klaus/artur; Cologne: 1.1.35
Funk, Susanne; Munich: 1.1.56
Gabriel, Andreas; Munich: 1.1.1, 1.1.84
Helle, Jochen/artur; Cologne: 1.1.112
Hirmer Fotoarchiv München: 1.1.5, 1.1.6
Hannover Municipal Building Authority: 1.1.34
Kahlfeldt Architekten; Berlin: 1.1.101
Kaltenbach, Frank; Munich: 1.1.8
Kleiner, S.: Wiener Ansichten, part III, pl. 18: 1.1.27
Müller, Bernd; Hannover: 1.1.64
Berlin State Archives: 1.1.30
Lessing, Erich/Archiv für Kunst u. Geschichte Berlin: 1.1.10
Oudsten, Frank den; Amsterdam: 1.1.36
Pehnt, Wolfgang; Cologne: 1.1.31
Petersen, Knud; Berlin: 1.1.86
Plunger, Max; S-Saltsjö Durnas: 1.1.43
Ramcke, Rolf; Hannover: 1.1.23, 1.1.26, 1.1.54, 1.1.57, 1.1.65, 1.1.66, 1.1.72, 1.1.74–77, 1.1.79, 1.1.80–1.1.83, 1.1.85, 1.1.90–95, 1.1.97–100, 1.1.102–105, 1.1.107, 1.1.109–111, 1.1.113-115
Schittich, Christian; Munich: 1.1.2, 1.1.14, 1.1.42
Schumacher, Fritz; Hamburg: 1.1.96
Seewald, Heike; Hemmingen: 1.1.55, 1.1.117

Berlin State Museums, Prussian Culture / Egyptology
     Museum & Papyrus Collection: 1.1.45
Berlin State Museums, Prussian Culture / Near East
     Museum / J. Liepe: 1.1.7
Hannover Public Libraries: 1.1.33
Berlin Technical University, Collection of Drawings: 1.1.39
Werner, Heike; Munich: 1.1.41

Part 2 · Fundamentals
Foto Kalksandstein-Information; Hannover: p. 146
Ziegel Klimaton; Brunnthal: p. 158, 159 left
Preton; Switzerland: p. 159 right

Part 4 · Built examples in detail
Binet, Hélène; London: pp. 328–330
Blonk, Arthur/arcasa; Wanneperveen, NL: pp. 272–275
Büttner, Dominic; Zürich: pp. 278, 280, 281, 283
Cook, Peter/View; London: pp. 365, 367, 368
Ferreira Alves, Luís Seixas; Porto: pp. 369–373
Frederiksen, Jens; Copenhagen: pp. 258–261
Gabriel, Andreas; Munich: p. 288
Gahl, Christian; Berlin: pp. 276, 277
Giovanelli, Francesca; Weiningen, Switzerland: pp. 267–271
Gisel, Georg; Zürich: pp. 304, 306
Halbe, Roland; Stuttgart: pp. 242, 245,
Halbe, Roland/artur; Cologne: pp. 298–303, 322, 323, 325
Henz, Hannes; Zürich: p. 305
Hueber, Eduard/archphoto; New York: pp. 347–351
Job, Roman; Munich: pp. 238, 239
Kaltenbach, Frank; Munich: p. 362
Kandzia, Christian; Esslingen: p. 244
Kinold, Klaus; Munich: pp. 262-266, 284–286, 289, 292–297, 311–313, 315–317
Kramer, Luuk; Amsterdam: pp. 334, 335, 337
Kubitza, Manuel; Cologne: pp. 308–310
Lindhe, Jens; Copenhagen: pp. 338–341
Lürman, Wolfgang; Munich: p. 291
Müller, Stefan; Berlin: pp. 319–321
von Quast, Siegfried; Murnau: pp. 247, 249
Richter, Ralph/architekturphoto; Düsseldorf: pp. 324, 326-327
Roth, Lukas; Cologne: pp. 243, 378-383
Schlötzer, Gerhard; Bamberg: p. 241
Schmitz, Arjen; Maastricht: pp. 352–356
Schuster, Oliver; Stuttgart: pp. 360, 361, 363
Seewald, Heike; Hemmingen: pp. 246, 248
Simonetti, Filippo; Brunate, Italy: pp. 357–359
Sorgedrager, Bart; Amsterdam: pp. 374–376
Suzuki, Hisao; Premià de Dalt, Barcelona: pp. 342–345
Willebrand, Jens; Cologne: pp. 331–333
Willig, Hajo; Hamburg: pp. 256, 257
Zimmermann, Reinhard; Zürich: pp. 250, 252, 253

Full page plates
Page 7   Ornamental masonry on the Samanide Mauso-
           leum in Buchara, Usbekistan, 10th century
           Photo: Christian Schittlich, Munich
Page 53   Northlight roofs to the Aymerich Wool Weaving
           Works, "Amati i Jover", in Terrassa, Spain, 1907.
           Photo: Manfred Hamm, Berlin
Page 203   Kühnen House, Kevelaer;
           architect: Heinz Bienefeld, 1988.
           Photo: Klaus Kinold, Munich
Page 235   Housing complex in Amsterdam;
           architects: Zeinstra, van der Pol, Amsterdam,
           1988. Photo: Luuk Kramer, Amsterdam

Acknowledgements

The publishers would like to express their gratitude to the
following persons for their suggestions and advice during
the production of this book:

     Prof. Dr.-Ing. Walter Haas, Munich
     Dipl.-Ing. Edgar Haupt, Odental
     Dipl.-Ing. Christine Peter, Munich
     Dipl.-Ing. Christian Peter, Munich
     Prof. Dr.-Ing. Jürgen J. Rasch, Karlsruhe
     Prof. Eberhard Schunck, Munich